John Squair, William Henry Fraser

The high school French grammar with exercises, vocabularies, and index

John Squair, William Henry Fraser

The high school French grammar with exercises, vocabularies, and index

ISBN/EAN: 9783337157227

Printed in Europe, USA, Canada, Australia, Japan

Cover: Foto ©Paul-Georg Meister /pixelio.de

More available books at **www.hansebooks.com**

THE HIGH SCHOOL
FRENCH GRAMMAR

With Exercises, Vocabularies, and Index.

BY

W. H. FRASER, B.A.,
Lecturer on Italian and Spanish, University of Toronto,

AND

J. SQUAIR, B.A.,
Lecturer on French, University College, Toronto.

Toronto :
ROSE PUBLISHING COMPANY, (LTD.).
1891.

PREFACE.

The High School French Grammar is intended to meet the requirements of both elementary and advanced classes. As will be seen from the table of contents, it is divided into four parts.

In Part I. the sounds of the language and their alphabetical representation are discussed. The results of the most recent investigations in phonetics have been utilized in so far as this could be done without the excessive use of technicalities. A system of phonetic transcription has been employed, under the conviction that in no other way can distinctions in sounds be intelligibly explained. Numerous examples have been given for exercise in pronunciation, as the fact is recognized that no amount of theory will in itself ensure correct pronunciation of a foreign language without long and careful practice in the utterance of its sounds. While it is not intended that the details of this part should be mastered by beginners, it is hoped that the full treatment here given to the important matter of pronunciation will prove useful, not only to advanced pupils, but to such teachers as have not enjoyed exceptional advantages.

Part II. consists of an exercise-book accompanied by a concise statement of the more important principles of grammar, and embraces a systematic presentation of the verb paradigms and other grammatical forms. This part, comprising somewhat more than a hundred pages, it is thought should afford material for about one year's work in elementary classes. The conjugation of the regular and auxiliary verbs is completed in seventeen lessons, the intention being to enable the pupil to begin as soon as possible the reading of easy French texts. The phonetic transcription of all words used, as well as of paradigms and grammatical forms, is given for the purpose of aiding the pupil at the outset to acquire a correct pronunciation under the direction of the teacher.

Part III. is a systematic grammar, in which the various parts of speech are taken up in order and fully discussed in detail. It is entirely independent of Part II., and numerous exercises of an advanced character are given in illustration of the theoretical matter. It will be noted that the illogical and inconvenient division into etymology and syntax has been discarded. In this connection it is believed that the full treatment of each part of speech continuously will contribute greatly to the convenience of both teacher and pupil. In its scope this part is intended to serve as a complete grammar of literary French of the present day. The older stages of the language and its derivation from Latin have been purposely left out of consideration. This has been done in the belief that the proper foundation for the study of French is a thorough knowledge of the language as it is now spoken and written.

Part IV. contains a series of progressive exercises on the translation of continuous English prose into French. Difficulties are explained by numerous references to the various sections in Part III. It is thought that Parts III. and IV. together will afford sufficient material for the work of the more advanced classes during one and a half or two years.

The Vocabularies at the end of the book contain all words needed for the translation of the exercises and extracts.

The addition of a very copious index will, it is hoped, render the grammar useful as a book of reference.

A list of the principal works consulted in the preparation of this volume is given below, both as an acknowledgment of the indebtedness of the authors and as a means of indicating to teachers and students some of the more important books for further study.

UNIVERSITY OF TORONTO,
    Toronto, September, 1891.

PRINCIPAL WORKS CONSULTED.

I. PHONETICAL WORKS:

Benecke, A., Die Französische Aussprache, zweite Auflage, Potsdam, 1880.

Beyer, Franz, Französische Phonetik, Cöthen, 1888.

Franke, Felix, Phrases de tous les jours, deuxième éd., Heilbronn, 1888; Ergänzungsheft zu Phrases de tous les jours, zweite Auflage, Heilbronn, 1889.

Lesaint, M.-A., Traité complet de la prononciation française, deuxième éd., Hambourg, 1871.

Passy, Paul, Les sons du fransais, Paris, 1887; Le français parlé, deuxième éd., Heilbronn, 1889.

Phonetische Studien (edited by Wilhelm Vietor), Marburg, 1887–90.

Plœtz, K., Systematische Darstellung der französischen Aussprache, elfte Auflage, Berlin, 1884.

Trautmann, M., Die Sprachlaute im Allgemeinen und Die Laute des Englischen, Französischen und Deutschen im Besondern, Leipzig, 1884–86.

Vietor, W., Elemente der Phonetik und Orthoepie des Deutschen, Englischen und Französischen, mit Rücksicht auf Die Bedürfnisse der Lehrpraxis, zweite Auflage, Heilbronn, 1887.

II. GRAMMARS:

Ayer, C., Grammaire comparée de la langue française, quatrième éd., Bâle, 1885.

Chassang, A., Nouvelle grammaire française, cours supérieur, dixième éd., Paris, 1884.

Clédat, L., Nouvelle grammaire historique du français, Paris, 1889.

Edgren, A. H., A Compendious French Grammar, Boston, 1890.

Fasnacht, G. E., A Synthetic French Grammar, London 1883; Progressive French Course, III. Year, London, 1882.

Lücking, G., Französische Grammatik, zweite Ausgabe, Berlin, 1883.

Mätzner, E., Französische Grammatik mit besonderer Berücksichtigung des Lateinischen, dritte Auflage, Berlin, 1885.

Pellissier, E., Accidence and Essentials of Syntax, London, 1888; French Syntax, London, 1887.

Plattner, Ph., Französische Schulgrammatik, zweite Auflage, Karlsruhe, 1887.

Plœtz, K., Kurzgefasste systematische Grammatik der französischen Sprache, dritte Auflage, Berlin, 1886.

Whitney, W. D., A Practical Grammar of French, Boston, 1886.

Williams, A., The Syntax of the Subjunctive Mood in French, Boston, 1885.

III. DICTIONARIES:

l'Académie française, Dictionnaire de, septième éd., Paris, 1878.

Bellows, J., Dictionary for the Pocket, French-English and English-French, 2nd ed., London, 1883.

Littré, É., Dictionnaire de la langue française, Hachette et Cie, Paris, 1873.

CONTENTS.

PART I.

	PAGE.
Orthographic Signs.	1
Sounds.	2
Pronunciation of the Alphabet.	10
Syllabication.	24
Stress.	24
Quantity of Vowel Sounds.	25
Liaison and Elision.	26
Punctuation.	27
Use of Capitals.	27
Table of Alphabetical Equivalents.	27
Examples of Phonetic Transcription.	29

PART II.

LESSON.

I. Present Indicative of **avoir**.—The Indefinite Article.—Gender, Number, Case. — 30

II. Present Indicative of **être**.—The Definite Article.—Plural of Nouns and Adjectives. — 31

III. Present Indicative of **avoir**, **être**, interrogatively.—Remarks on Interrogation.—Use of **oui**, **non**. — 34

IV. The Possessive Adjective.—The Pronoun **le**, **la**, **les**.—Use of **voici** and **voilà**.—**Il est** and **c'est**. — 36

V. Negative Conjugation.—Remarks on Negation.—Negative Conjugation interrogatively.—**Si**.—Position of the Adverb. — 39

VI. The regular Conjugations.—Remarks on Conjugation.—Present Indicative of **donner**, **finir**, **rompre**.—Use of the Present Indicative.—**N'est-ce pas?**. — 42

VII. The Genitive and Dative Relation.—Contraction of **de** and **à** with **le** and **les**.—The Dative Personal Pronoun 3rd Person. — 45

VIII. The Partitive Noun.—The General Noun.—Geographical Names.—Adjectival Phrases with **de**.—The Definite Article for Possession. — 48

CONTENTS.

LESSON.	PAGE.
IX. Past Participles.—Compound Tenses.—The Past Indefinite.—Word Order.—Agreement of Past Participle.—Use of Past Indefinite.—Frequent Idioms.	51
X. Imperfect Indicative of donner, finir, rompre.—Imperfect Indicative of avoir, être.—Use of Imperfect.—Place ' where,' ' whither'.	54
XI. Feminine of Adjectives.—Irregularities.—Position of Adjectives.—The Demonstrative Adjective.	58
XII. Past Definite of donner, finir, rompre.—Past Definite of avoir, être.—Use of Past Definite.—Personal Pronoun Objects.—Interrogative and Indefinite Adjectives.	62
XIII. Future Indicative of donner, finir, rompre.—Future of avoir, être.—Use of Future.—Comparison of Adjectives and Adverbs.	65
XIV. Conditional of donner, finir, rompre.—Conditional of avoir, être.—Conditional Sentences.	69
XV. Imperative of donner, finir, rompre.—Imperative of avoir, être.—Negative Imperative.—Position of Objects.—Pronominal Adverbs.—Position and use of y, en.—Y avoir.	72
XVI. Present Subjunctive of donner, finir, rompre.—Present Subjunctive of avoir, être.—Use of Subjunctive.—Tense Sequence.—Disjunctive Personal Pronouns.	76
XVII. Imperfect Subjunctive of donner, finir, rompre.—Imperfect Subjunctive of avoir, être.—Tense Sequence.	80
XVIII. Present Participle of donner, finir, rompre, avoir, être.—Use and Agreement of Present Participle.—Auxiliaries of Tense.—Agreement of Past Participle.—Use of Compound Tenses.	82
XIX. Use of Infinitive.—Formation of Tenses.	86
XX. Reflexive Verbs.—Se flatter.—Agreement of Past Participle.—Use of the Reflexive.—The Passive Voice.—Agent after the Passive.—Use of Passive.	89
XXI. Impersonal Verb.—Construction of Impersonal il est.—Conjugation of faire.	93
XXII. The Possessive Pronouns.—Conjugation of aller and envoyer.	97
XXIII. The Demonstrative Pronouns.—Ce and il (elle, etc.).—Conjugation of vouloir.	100
XXIV. Interrogative Pronouns.—Conjugation of pouvoir.	104

LESSON.	PAGE.
XXV. Relative Pronouns.—Agreement and Use of Relatives.—Conjugation of **connaître, savoir**.	107
XXVI. The Indefinite Pronouns.—Indefinite Adjectives and Pronouns.—Orthographical Irregularities of **manger, nettoyer, mener, céder, appeler**, etc.	111
XXVII. Cardinal Numerals.—Multiplicatives.—Idiomatic Expressions of Age.—Conjugation of **vendre, recevoir, devoir**.	116
XXVIII. Ordinal Numerals.—Fractions.—The Time of Day.—Dates, Titles, etc.—Date Idioms.—Names of Months and Days.—Conjugation of **partir**.	120
XXIX. Formation of Adverbs.—Comparison of Adverbs.—Position of Adverbs.—Conjugation of **croire, dire**.	123
XXX. Prepositions.—Prepositional Locutions.—Conjugation of **tenir, voir**.	127
XXXI. Conjunctions.—Conjugation of **mettre, prendre**.	131

PART III.

The Verb.	135
The Noun.	241
The Article.	254
The Adjective.	268
The Pronoun.	284
The Adverb.	326
The Numeral.	339
The Preposition.	345
The Conjunction.	354
The Interjection.	358
Abbreviations.	359

PART IV.

Exercises in Translation.	361
VOCABULARIES:	
French–English.	372
English–French.	379
INDEX.	398

NOTE.—In using the High School French Grammar, the following plan of work is recommended:

1. Learn the table of 'symbols and key-words' contained in §5.

2. Do the exercises of Part II., learning as much of the theory as is necessary for this purpose. To this should be added daily systematic exercises in pronunciation, particularly of the more difficult sounds.

3. Review the exercises of Part II., learning the whole of the theory. Continue the phonetic exercises.

4. At this stage, or earlier, the reading of simple texts, such as the High School French Reader, may be begun, the student using the theory contained in Part III. to explain difficult grammatical points.

5. Do the exercises of Part III., learning as much of the theory as is necessary for this purpose. Continue the phonetic exercises. The reading of texts may be continued, the student using Part III. as a book of reference.

6. Do the exercises of Part IV. Continue the phonetic exercises. Continue reading texts, using part III. for reference.

7. Learn systematically the theory of Part III., and complete the study of Part I., with exercises in phonetic transcription.

FRENCH GRAMMAR.
PART I.

ORTHOGRAPHIC SIGNS.

1. The alphabet. The letters of the alphabet, with their French names, are as follows:—

Letter.	Name.	Letter.	Name.	Letter.	Name.
A a	a	J j	ji	S s	esse
B b	bé	K k	ka	T t	té
C c	cé	L l	elle	U u	u
D d	dé	M m	emme	V v	vé
E e	é	N n	enne	W w	double vé
F f	effe	O o	o	X x	iks
G g	gé	P p	pé	Y y	i grec
H h	ache	Q q	ku	Z z	zède
I i	i	R r	erre		

NOTES.—1. The French alphabet corresponds with that of English, but k and w are hardly used except in foreign words of late introduction.

2. Words are commonly spelt by naming their letters, as above, together with the name of the accent (if any). A newer method, employed sometimes in teaching reading, is to name e by its 'sourd' sound (§ 17, 3), the other vowels as above, and the consonants by their actual sound in the word + the sound of e 'sourd.'

3. The *names* of the letters in the newer method are all masc.: Un n, un f (= un a, un fe), etc.

The *older names* are all masc., except for f, h, l, m, n, r, s: Un b, une s (= un bé, une esse), etc.

2. Other orthographic signs are as follows:—

1. The *acute accent* ´ (Fr. 'accent aigu'), used only over e (§17, 1): L'été, l'Écosse.

2. The *grave accent* ` (Fr. 'accent grave'), used over e (§ 17, 2), and also over a, u, but without affecting their sound. It sometimes distinguishes homonyms: à='to', a='has'; dès='since', des='of the'; où='where', ou='or'.

3. The *circumflex accent* ^ (Fr. 'accent circonflexe'), used over any vowel except y. It generally denotes etymological contraction, especially the loss of an earlier s : âne, tête, île, hôte, flûte.

Observe : None of the above *accent-marks* serve to denote *stress* (§ 66).

4. The *cedilla* ¸ (Fr. 'cédille'), used under c before a, o, u (§ 41, 2) : Façade, leçon, reçu.

5. The *diæresis* ¨ (Fr. 'tréma') shows that the vowel bearing it is divided in pronunciation from the preceding vowel : Noël, naïf, Moïse.

6. The *apostrophe* ' (Fr. 'apostrophe') shows the omission of a final vowel before a word beginning with a vowel sound : L'amie (=la amie), l'ami (=le ami), s'il (=si il).

7. The *hyphen* - (Fr. 'trait d'union') serves to connect words and syllables : Avez-vous?, tête-à-tête.

SOUNDS.

3. The pronunciation will be explained, as far as possible, by comparison with English sounds. It must never be forgotten, however, that the sounds of two languages *do not correspond exactly.* Important general distinctions, to be referred to later, are :—

1. French sounds (consonants as well as vowels) are almost all *narrow*, *i.e.*, uttered with *tenseness* of the organs directly concerned in their articulation. English sounds are commonly *wide*, *i.e.*, uttered with *laxness* of the organs.

NOTE.—To understand the distinction, compare the *narrow* vowel sound in 'fall' with the *wide* sound in 'not'.

2. *Lip-rounding* (as in sounding 'who,' 'no,' 'law') is much more energetic in French, and is more exclusively confined to the lips. Such sounds are said to be *rounded.*

3. Vowel sounds are in general more *resonant* in French, and *voiced* consonants more thoroughly *voiced.*

NOTE.—The sound produced by vibration of the vocal chords, as heard in all vowels and in many consonants, is called *voice*. The distinction between *voiceless* and *voiced* consonants may be observed by uttering in succession 'tome,' 'dome' or 'pet,' 'bet,' in which t, p are voiceless and d, b voiced.

4. English long vowel sounds, as in 'feel,' 'cold,' 'save,' etc., are all more or less *diphthongal.* French vowel sounds, whether long or short, are *uniform throughout their utterance.*

NOTE.—*Diphthongization* is still more noticeable in English as pronounced in England than in Canadian English.

4. The French language has *thirty-seven* sounds, without noting minor distinctions. To denote these sounds there are but *twenty-six* letters (§1, note 1), to which may be added two accent-marks (´ `) and the cedilla. Hence has resulted much confusion. Thus, in 'silence,' 'assaut,' 'science,' 'celui,' 'ça,' 'portion,' the heavy letters indicate the same sound in each word. So also in 'sot,' 'beau,' 'autre.'

[N.B. In explaining the pronunciation, these thirty-seven *sounds* will be first described, and, to avoid confusion, the sounds will be denoted by *symbols* (one for each sound), corresponding as far as possible with the letters of the alphabet and printed everywhere in italics. The pronunciation of the alphabet will then be dealt with (§§ 16...63).]

5. Reference-Table of Symbols and Key-Words.

[Opposite each symbol is a key-word, or example, in which the sound occurs.]

Symb.	Key-wd.	Symb.	Key-wd.	Symb.	Key-wd.	Symb.	Key-wd.
1. *à*	lâche	11. *g*	gare	21. *ò*	mort	31. *u*	sou
2. *á*	madame	12. *h*	habile	22. *ō*	bon	32. *ŭ*	oui
3. *ã*	plan	13. *i*	fini	23. *ŏ*	peu	33. *ü*	une
4. *b*	base	14. *ĭ*	viande	24. *œ*	leur	34. *ü̃*	suite
5. *d*	dit	15. *k*	car	25. *œ̃*	un	35. *v*	vite
6. *e*	le	16. *l*	lard	26. *p*	pas	36. *z*	zone
7. *é*	été	17. *m*	mal	27. *r*	rare	37. *ž*	jour
8. *è*	père	18. *n*	nid	28. *s*	sel	38. .	sign of length.
9. *ẽ*	fin	19. *ñ*	vigne	29. *š*	chat		
10. *f*	fini	20. *ó*	zone	30. *t*	terre		

6. Victor's diagram of the mouth (as adapted by Franke), showing *position of the tongue* in articulating each vowel sound:—

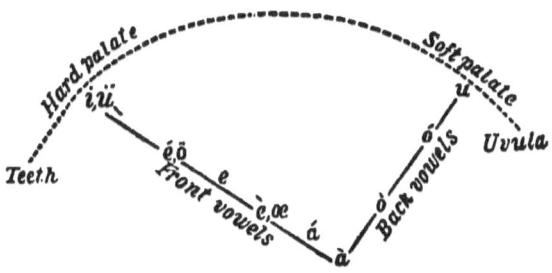

7. Diagram of the lips (after Passy), showing the various degrees of *rounding* :—

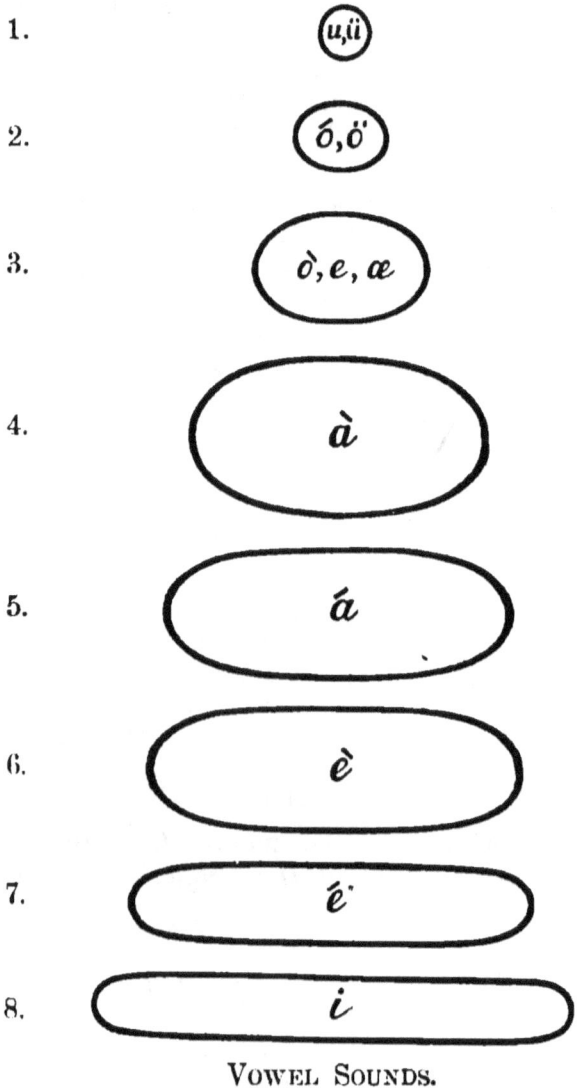

VOWEL SOUNDS.

8. à, á.

[N.B. The word 'like,' in comparing French and English sounds, means, of course, only 'resembling' or 'approximately like' (§ 3).]

1. *à.*—Like a in 'ah!', 'father,' inclining towards aw in 'saw.' Avoid the *rounding* (§3, 2) characteristic of the aw sound. Avoid *diphthongization* (§ 3, 4).

Ex.: Lâche, âme, grâce, tâche, pas, gras, las, helas!, je passe, Jacques.

[ARTICULATION.—Mouth well open, tongue lying flat (§ 6), *no rounding* (§§ 3, 2 and 7, 4).]

2. *á.*—Like a in 'father,' inclining slightly towards a in 'hat.' Avoid *diphthongization.*

Ex.: Ami, Canada, patte, rare, canne, arabe, aura, portal, dame, cap, face.

[ARTIC.—Mouth somewhat less open, tongue lying somewhat less flat (§6) than for *à* above. Lips tense, corners of mouth drawn back (§ 7, 5). *Narrow* (§ 3, 1).]

9. *i, ü.*

1. *i.*—Like ee in 'see.' Avoid the sound of i in 'bit.' Avoid *diphthongization.*

Ex.: Fini, lime, abîme, riche, livre, visibilité.

[ARTIC.—Tongue close to the palate (§ 6), the tip resting against the lower teeth. Lips tense, corners of the mouth drawn back, with lips forming an elongated narrow slit (§ 7, 8). *Narrow.*]

2. *ü.*—Has no English counterpart. To obtain the *ü* sound, utter a prolonged *i*, as above, and, during its continuance, round the lips tightly, with protrusion as for whistling. The resulting sound will terminate in *ü.*

Ex.: Une, nature, lune, dû, fûmes, sucre, turc, rue, du, ruse.

[ARTIC.—Tongue (practically) as for the *i* sound above (§ 6), lips as for *u* (§ 7, 1), closely rounded and protruded. *Narrow.*]

10. *é, ö, e, è, œ.*

1. *é.*—Like a in 'date,' 'area.' Avoid *prolonging* the sound. Avoid *diphthongization.*

Ex.: Général, dégénéré, créé, donné, été, vérité.

[ARTIC.—Mouth slightly more open than for the *i* sound (§ 9, 1, above), tongue drawn slightly backward (§ 6), though still touching the teeth, lips tense and drawn backwards (§ 7, 7). *Narrow.*]

2. **ö.**—Has no English counterpart. To obtain the *ö* sound, utter a prolonged *é*, as above, and, during its continuance, round the lips firmly, with protrusion as for whistling. The resulting sound will terminate in *ö*.

Ex.: Peu, bleue, monsieur, jeudi, Europe, feu, eux.

[ARTIC.—Tongue as for *é* above (§ 6), lips *rounded* (§ 7, 2) and advanced. *Narrow.*]

3. **e.**—Like English e in 'the book,' or a in 'Louisa,' but *rounded*.

Ex.: Le, me, te, se, ce, de, ne, que, cheval, ceci, celui.

[ARTIC.—Tongue slightly drawn back from the position of *é* above (§ 6), lips rounded (§ 11, 3) and slightly advanced.]

4. **è.**—Like the first part of the diphthong e in 'there,' when long; when short, like e in 'men.' Avoid *diphthongization*, when long.

Ex.: Père, thème, collège; progrès, tu es, il est, forêt, chef.

[ARTIC.—Tongue slightly drawn back from the position for *é* above (§6), mouth slightly more open, and lips less drawn backward (§ 7, 6) than for *é*. *Narrow.*]

5. **œ.**—Has no English counterpart. To obtain the sound, utter a prolonged *è* sound as above, and, during its continuance, round and advance the lips. The resulting sound will terminate in *œ*.

Ex.: Leur, peur, fleuve, peuple, seul, neuf.

[ARTIC.—Tongue as for *è* above (§ 6), lips rounded about as for *ö* (§ 11, 3) and advanced. *Narrow.*]

11. *u, ó, ò.*

1. **u.**—Like oo in 'too,' 'school.' Avoid *diphthongization*. Avoid the sound of oo in 'foot.'

Ex.: Coup, loup, goût, croûte, jour, douze, Louvre, amour.

[ARTIC.—Tongue drawn back as far as possible (§ 6), lips tightly rounded (§ 7, 1) and protruded as if for whistling. *Narrow.*]

2. **ó.**—Like o in 'so,' 'note,' 'omen.' Avoid *diphthongization*.

Ex.: Mot, zone, hôte, fosse, tome, gros.

[ARTIC.—Mouth more open than for *u* above, tongue slightly less drawn back (§ 6), lips less tightly rounded (§ 7, 2). *Narrow.*]

3. *ò*.—Intermediate between **u** in 'hum' and **o** in 'sot.' Best obtained by uttering *ó* above with mouth slightly more open and tongue slightly less drawn backward.

Ex.: Mort, sotte, encore, robe, Rome, porte, homme, école.

[ARTIC.—Mouth slightly more open than for *ó*, tongue less drawn back (§ 6), and less *rounding* (§ 7, 3). *Narrow.*]

NASAL VOWEL SOUNDS.

12. Principles of Formation. 1. In ordinary breathing, the soft palate (terminated by the uvula) hangs loosely down and the breath passes freely through nose or mouth, or through both. 2. In uttering ordinary vowels (as a, o, etc.), the soft palate presses backwards and upwards, closing the nose passage entirely. 3. If, however, a vowel is uttered with the soft palate hanging loosely, as in ordinary breathing, the breath escapes through both nose and mouth at once. The resonance of the air in the nose passages gives a new value to the vowel, which is said to be *nasalized* and is called a *nasal* vowel.

NOTE.—The process of nasalization may be well observed before a mirror while uttering the vowel *à* (§8, 1), which, if repeated with the soft palate hanging loosely, gives the corresponding nasal, as in 'blanc,' 'blanche.' The nasalization may be made more conspicuous by stopping the nostrils.

13.   *ã, ẽ, œ̃, õ.*

1. *ã*.—Is the nasal corresponding to *à* (pas, §8, 1).
Ex.: Plan, plante, enfant, danse, an.

2. *ẽ*.—Is the nasal corresponding to *è* (père, §10, 4).
Ex.: Fin, prince, pin, lapin, jardin.

3. *œ̃*.—Is the nasal corresponding to *œ* (leur, §10, 5).
Ex.: Un, brun, lundi, tribun, commun.

4. *õ*.—Is the nasal corresponding to *ò* (mort, §11, 3).
Ex.: On, monde, non, bonté, front.

N.B.—Avoid carefully the final sound of words like English 'sang,' 'long.'

[ARTIC.—Position of tongue, etc., etc., as for *à* (§8, 1), *è* (§10, 4), *œ* (§10, 5), *ò* (§11, 3), respectively. *Soft palate hanging loosely.*]

Semi-Vowel Sounds.

14. *ĭ, ŭ̈, ŭ.*—When the sounds *i* (§9, 1), *ü* (§9, 2), *u* (11, 1) are followed by a vowel in the same syllable, the stress of voice falls on that vowel; *i, ü, u* are then more rapidly and forcibly pronounced, and assume a consonantal value. This is shown by the ˘ placed over them.

1. *ĭ.*—Like very brief and *narrow* English **y** in 'yes.'
Ex.: Viande, nièce, pitié, vieux.

2. *ŭ̈.*—No counterpart in English (§9, 2). Avoid the sound of 'wall,' 'ruin.'
Ex.: Lui, celui, je suis, duel, écuelle.

3. *ŭ.*—Like very brief and *narrow* **w** in 'west,' 'we.'
Ex.: Oui, ouest.

[ARTIC.—Practically the same as for these sounds as ordinary vowels.]

Consonant Sounds.

15. *b, d, f, g, h, k, l, m, n, ñ, p, r, s, š, t, v, z, ž.*
1. *b.*—Like **b** in 'barb.'
Ex.: Barbare, beau.
[ARTIC.—*Narrow* (§3, 1), and fully *voiced* (§3, 3) throughout its continuance.]

2. *d.*—Like **d** in 'died.'
Ex.: Dame, de, ardeur.
[ARTIC.—The tongue further advanced towards the teeth than for the English sound. *Narrow*, and fully *voiced* throughout.]

3. *f.*—Like **f** in 'fat.'
Ex.: Facile, vif.
[ARTIC.—*Narrow*.]

4. *g.*—Like **g** in 'go.'
Ex.: Gant, aigu, augmenter.
[ARTIC.—*Narrow*, and fully *voiced* throughout.]

5. *h.*—Is silent.
Ex.: Homme, héros, héroïne, hasard.

6. *k.*—Like k in 'take.' Avoid the slight aspiration which generally follows the English sound.

Ex. : Car, lac, Canada.

[Artic.—*Narrow.*]

7. *l.*—Like l in 'law.'

Ex. : Le, là, lilas, sel.

[Artic.—*Narrow*, and fully *voiced* throughout.]

8. *m.*—Like m in 'man,' 'dumb.'

Ex. : Mal, blâmer, dame.

[Artic.—*Narrow*, and fully *voiced* throughout.]

9. *n.*—Like n in 'not,' 'man.'

Ex. : Ananas, cabane, nature.

[Artic.—The tongue is further advanced towards the teeth than for the English sound. *Narrow*, and fully *voiced* throughout.]

10. *ñ.*—Somewhat like ny in 'banyan' or ni in 'union.'

Ex.: Agneau, digne, montagne.

[Artic.—End of the tongue pressed against the lower teeth, body of the tongue at the same time closely pressed against the whole surface of the hard palate. *Narrow*, and fully *voiced* throughout.]

11. *p.*—Like p in 'pan,' 'top.' Avoid the slight aspiration which generally follows the English sound.

Ex. : Pas, papier, père, cap, captif.

[Artic.—*Narrow.*]

12. *r.*—Has no English counterpart. The sound is formed by resting the point of the tongue against the lower teeth and gums, raising at the same time the root of the tongue towards the soft palate, thus producing a trilling vibration of the uvula.

Ex.: Rare, rose, barbare, auteur, parole, libre.

[Artic.—*Narrow*, and fully *voiced* throughout.]

Note.—The above r sound (called in French r 'uvulaire,' or r 'gutturale'), is the one now most commonly heard. Another r sound (French r 'linguale,' or 'alvéolaire,') formerly universal, but at the present day heard in singing, on the stage (more or less), in country districts, or as an individual peculiarity, is formed by trilling the tip of the tongue against the roof of the mouth immediately behind the teeth, as in Scotch or Irish r.

13. *s.*—Like s in 'sing,' 'books.'

Ex.: Son, danser.

[ARTIC.—The tongue further advanced towards the teeth than for the English sound. *Narrow.*]

14. *š.*—Like sh in 'shall,' 'ash.'

Ex.: Chat, chercher.

[ARTIC.—The tongue further advanced towards the teeth than for the English sound. *Narrow.*]

15. *t.*—Like t in 'ton,' 'not.' Avoid the slight aspiration which generally follows the English sound.

Ex.: Table, amitié.

[ARTIC.—The tongue further advanced towards the teeth than for the English sound. *Narrow.*]

16. *v.*—Like v in 'van,' 'nave.'

Ex.: Vite, vous, vivre.

[ARTIC.—*Narrow*, and fully *voiced* throughout.]

17. *z.*—Like z in 'zone.'

Ex.: Zone, Balzac.

[ARTIC.—*Narrow*, and fully *voiced* throughout.]

18. *ž.*—Like z in 'azure,' or s in 'pleasure.'

Ex.: Jour, jadis, majesté.

[ARTIC.—*Narrow*, and fully *voiced* throughout. More lip protrusion than in English.]

PRONUNCIATION OF THE ALPHABET.

THE VOWELS.

[N.B.—Pronounce consonant sounds within words in one syllable with the *following* vowel (§64, 2).]

16. **Aa.**—Has *two* sounds:—

1. *Usually* that of *á* (madame, §8, 2). Thus, regularly at the *beginning* and *end* of words, or when coming before *two or more consonants*, and generally in *unstressed* (§67, 1) syllables.

Ex.: Adorer *(ádóré)*, Canada, sofà, déjà, **ma, ta, là**, patte, barbe, macadamisé.

So also in words like the following: Portal, par, cigale, dame, cabane, arabe, salade, vague, cap, attrape, délicate, lac, chaque, face, tache, carafe, paragraphe.

2. *Less frequently* that of *à* (lâche, §8, 1). Thus, â in a *stress-bearing syllable* (§67, 1), a before final s, a in -aille, -ail.

Ex.: Lâche *(làš)*, grâce, pas, cas, gras, hélas !, bataille *(bátàž)*, travail *(trávàž)*.

So also, in combinations like the following: Ah !, un a, basse, passe, passer, condamner, fâcher, écraser, proclamer, accabler, gagner, cadre, diable, cadavre, oracle, miracle, sabre, baron, Jeanne, Jacques, and in words ending in -asion, -assion, -ation, *e.g.*, occasion, compassion, nation, etc.

NOTE.—Some orthoepists distinguish three sounds of a, and there are many words of disputed pronunciation.

[EXCEPTIONS.—a is *silent* in août (*u*), curaçao (*-só*), taon (*tō*), Saône (*són*).]

17. Ee (é è ê).—Is varied in sound according to its *position* and *accent-mark*:—

1. Like *é* (été, §10, 1). Thus é regularly.

Ex.: Général (*žénérál*), l'été, pitié, parlé, né, vérité, dégénéré.

So also, e (without accent-mark) in *infinitives* in -er, in *nouns* and *adjs.* in -er (with silent r), -ez, -ied, and in clef, et, *e.g.*, donner (*dòné*), parler, février (*févrié*), étranger, premier, dernier, nez (*né*), chez, parlez, pied (*pié*), clef (*clé*), et (*é*).

[Exc.—Évènement (*évènmā*), and in older books all words in -ége, *e.g.*, collége (*còlèž*), now printed -ège; according to the decision of the Académie Française in 1877.]

2. Like *è* (père, §10, 4). Thus, è and ê.

Ex.: Père (*pèr*), mère, succès (*sükse̊*), règle, thème, collège, espèce; fête (*fèt*), même, forêt, être.

So also, e (without accent-mark) before **r (rr)**, before *two* (or more) *consonants*, or before l *mouillée* (§51), and in the endings -et, -ect, -ef, -el, -en, -em (n and m sounded): Fer, terre, lettre, richesse, vieillir (*vièžir*), soleil (*sòlèž*), cabinet, respect, chef, sel, Jérusalem, and in tu es, il est, les, des, mes, etc.

[Exc.—Moelle (*müál*) and derivatives.]

NOTE.—The *è* sound of e (variously denoted by è, ê, or e+*double consonant*) is required in a *stressed syllable* (§67, 1), *e.g.*, je mène, tête, chère, j'appelle, ancienne. This principle is important in the irregularities of certain verbs and adjectives.

3. Like *e* (le, §10, 3). Thus, e in *monosyllables*, and in *initial syllable before a single consonant*.

Ex.: Le, je, me, te, se, que, brebis, cheval, demoiselle (*dĕmŭăzĕl*), repas, second (*segō*), tenir, seras, ceci, celui.

So also, *before* ss in dessus, dessous and many words in ress-, *e.g.*, ressentir, etc., and generally *between three consonants, e.g.*, aigrement, appartement, mercredi, Angleterre.

Note.—An e with this sound is called in French e 'sourd.' It is *never found in a stressed syllable*.

Observe: The above rules for the pronunciation of e 'sourd' apply especially to deliberate or elevated diction and to words uttered singly. In ordinary conversation, and when consecutive syllables have e, it is slighted or wholly silent (Fr. e 'muet') where resulting combinations of consonants can be pronounced: Je ne sais pas = *že n sĕ pă;* je le dis = *že l di;* je te le prêterai = *ž te l prĕtré;* je ne le crois pas = *že n l krŭă pă;* un bon cheval = *ŏ̃ bō̃ švál*. The beginner should give the letter everywhere its full sound.

4. e is *silent when final* (except in monosyllables, see above), in the *verbal endings* -es, -ent, and also *within words after a vowel sound* and elsewhere *where difficult consonant combinations do not arise from its silence*. (See *Obs.* above.)

Ex.: Rue. (*rŭ*), donnée, rare, place, ai-je (*ĕ ž*), parlai-je (*párlĕ ž*), table, sabre, prendre, tu parles, ils parlent, gaieté, louerai (*luré*), lieutenant, ennemi, médecin, samedi.

Note.—Silent e is called in French e 'muet.'

[Exc.—e *silent* also in the following: Cerise, serein, and others as exceptions to 3, above; Jean (*zã*), Jeanne, Caen (*kã*), seoir (and cognates), and when used to soften g (§45, 2, note 2), *e.g.*, mangeant (*mãžã*), geôle, Georges, etc.]

Observe: The endings -le and -re with silent e are specially difficult. The beginner should sound the e, as in 3 above, and afterwards gradually drop the e sound: Table (*tă ble*), arbre (*ăr bre*), etc.

5. Like *á* (madame, §8, 2). Thus, in femme, in adverbs in -emment, *e.g.*, prudemment (*prŭdámã*), etc., in solennel (*sŏlánèl*) (and derivatives), in nenni (*náni*), and a few rarer words.

THE VOWELS.

18. Ii.—Has *two* sounds :—

1. Like *i* (fini, §9, 1). Thus i or î *everywhere, when forming a syllable of itself.*

Ex.: Fini, vie (*vi*), lime, abîme, île, finir, fils (*fis*), habile, visibilité, habiller (*ábilé*), famille.

2. Like *ĭ* (viande, §14, 1). Thus, when sounded *in one syllable with a following vowel.*

Ex.: Viande (*viăd*), nièce, siècle, bien (*biĕ*), pitié, aïeul (*ăĭul*).

19. Oo.—Has *two* sounds :—

1. Like *ó* (zone, §11, 2). Thus, as *final vowel sound* or when it has the *circumflex in the stressed syllable* (§67).

Ex.: Numéro (*nŭmĕró*), dos, mot, sirop, drôle (*drŏl*), hôte, vôtre.

So also, in combinations represented by: Zone, arrosent, idiome, tome, fosse, grosse.

[Exc.—Trop (*tró*, rather more general than *trŏ*).]

2. Like *ò* (mort, §11, 3). Thus, *generally.*

Ex.: Mort (*mòr*), corps, poste, étoffe, somme, robe, fol, école, Europe, dot (*dòt*), votre, octobre.

[Exc.—Silent in the following : Paon (*pă*), faon (*fă*).]

20. Uu.—Has *two* sounds :—

1. Like *ü* (une, §9, 2). Thus, everywhere *when forming a syllable of itself.*

Ex.: Une (*ŭn*), sur, pur, fut, fûmes (*fŭm*), du, due, vue, dur, turc (*tŭrk*), utile, juge, sucre, étude.

2. Like *ŭ* (lui, §14, 2 and §9, 2). Thus, regularly *when united into one syllable with a following vowel.*

Ex.: Lui (*lŭi*), celui, nuit, puits, je suis, pluie, écuelle (*ĕkŭĕl*), ruine.

3. It is generally *silent* in gu, qu (§45, 2, note 1 and §55).

Ex.: Guêpe (*yèp*), guerre, chaque (*šăk*), quel.

21. Yy.—Has everywhere the same sound as i (§18, 1, 2) similarly situated, except in certain combinations (§§23 and 30) :—

1. Like *i* (fini, §9, 1). Thus, everywhere *when forming a syllable of itself.*

Ex.: Il y a (*il i á*), martyre (*mártir*), lyre, analyse, hydre, système, tyran, Libye.

2. Like ĭ (viande, §14, 1). Thus, *when in one syllable with a following vowel.*

Ex.: Yacht (*iăk*), yole, yeux (*iŏ*), hyène.

THE VOWEL COMBINATIONS.

22. Ai (aĭ).—1. Like *é* (été, §10, 1). Thus, as a *verbal ending.*

Ex.: J'ai (*ž é*), donnai (*dŏné*), finirai.

So also, in the following: Gai, geai (*žé*), quai (*ké*), je sais (*sé*), il sait.

2. Elsewhere like *è* (père, §10, 4).

Ex.: Que j'aie (*ke z è*), je parlais, il vendait, ils lisaient, paix, chaise, clair, aurai-je, sais-je (*sè ž*), caisse, balai, lait, aigle, maître.

[Exc.—Like *e* (le, §10, 3) is -ais- everywhere in the conjugation of the verb faire, *e.g.,* faisant (*fezã*), nous faisons (*nu fezõ*).]

23. Ay.—1. Like *è* (père, §10, 4), unless followed by a vowel.

Ex.: Cambray (*kãbrè*).

2. Like *è* + *ĭ* (père, §10, 4, viande, §14, 1), *when followed by a vowel.*

Ex.: Payer (*pèĭé*), ayons (*èĭõ*).

[Exc.—Pays (*péi* or *pèi*), its compounds paysan (*péizã*), paysage, etc., abbaye (*ábéĭ*), Bayard (*báĭár*), Bayonne (*báĭŏn*), and rarer words.]

24. Au (eau).—Like *ó* (zone, §11, 2).

Ex.: Faute (*fót*), maux, fausse, eau (*ó*), rideau, beauté, beau.

[Exc.—au = *ò* (mort, §11, 3), in the following: Paul (*pòl*), Laure, and according to many in the fut. and condl. of the verb avoir, *e.g.,* aurait (*òrè*), etc., and in autel (*òtèl*), mauvais (*mòvè*), restaurant (*rèstòrã*).]

25. Ei.—Like *è* (père, §10, 4).

Ex.: Veine (*vèn*), reine, Seine, neige.

26.—Eu (eû, œu).—Has *two* sounds :—

1. Like *ŏ* (peu, §10, 2). Thus, as *final vowel sound* or *as initial vowel sound.*

Ex.: Feu (*fŏ*), je meus, il veut, bleue, lieue, monsieur (*mesiŏ*); bœufs (*bŏ*), œufs (*ŏ*), vœu (*vŏ*).

VOWEL COMBINATIONS.

2. Like œ (leur, §10, 5). Thus, *before* r (sounded), generally *before a final consonant* (sounded), before l mouillée, *before two consonants.*

Ex.: Fleur (*flœr*), beurre, neuf (*nœf*), seul, fauteuil, (*fōtœĭ*), feuille, peuple (*pœpl*), œuvre (*œvr*), bœuf (*bœf*), œuf (*œf*), mœurs (*mœrs*).

[Exc.—1. Eu = ü (une, §9, 2), wherever it occurs *in the conjugation of* avoir, *e.g.*, eu (*ü*), j'eus (*ž ü*), il eût (*il ü*), nous eussions, etc. 2. Eu = ŏ (peu, §10, 2), before a final z, l, or t sound, *e.g.*, creuse (*krŏz*), meule, émeute, and in jeûne (*žŏn*).]

27. Ey.—Precisely like ay (§23 above).

Ex.: Ney, bey (*bè*), grasseyer (*grásèĭé*), asseyez-vous (*asèĭé vu*).

28. Oi (oî oê).—Like ŭ + á (oui, §14, 3, and madame, §8, 2). Thus, *generally*, unless preceded by r in the same syllable.

Ex.: Moi (*mŭá*), toi, soi, loi, poil, chinois, étoile, soif, paroisse, gloire, boîte (*bŭát*), poêle (*pŭál*).

2. Like ŭ + à (oui, §14, 3, lâche, §8, 1), when preceded by r in the same syllable.

Ex.: Froid (*frŭà*), je crois, croire, droit, droite, trois, refroidi, roi, effroi, croise. So also, mois (*mŭà*), je bois, and some similar ones.

[Exc.—Oignon (*òñŏ*).]

29. Ou (oû, où).—Has *two* sounds :—

1. Like u (sou, §11, 1), everywhere *when forming a syllable of itself.*

Ex.: Coup (*ku*), doux, goût, jour, amour, rouge, Louvre, route.

2. Like ŭ (oui, §14, 3), when *forming one syllable with a following vowel.*

Ex.: Oui (*ŭi*), ouate, ouest, souhait (*sŭè*), tintouin (*tĕtŭĕ*).

30. Oy.—Like ŭ + á (oui, §14, 3, and madame, §8, 2), when final.

Ex.: Leroy (*lerŭà*).

2. Like ŭ + á + ĭ (viande, §14, 1), when *followed by a vowel.*

Ex.: Envoyer (*ăvŭáĭé*), royal, joyeux, voyage (*vŭáĭăž*).

31. Ue.—Like œ (leur, §10, 5), in the following :

Ex.: Accueil *(ákœĭ)*, recueil, cueillir *(kœĭir)*, orgueil (and their derivatives), cercueil *(serkœĭ)*, écueil.

32. Uy.—1. Like ü+i (lui, §14, 2, and fini, §9, 1), when final.

Ex.: Puy *(püi)*.

2. Like ü+i+ĭ (viande, §14, 1), when followed by a vowel.

Ex.: Ennuyeux *(ãnüiĭŏ)*, essuyer *(èsüiĭé)*.

The Nasal Vowels.

33.—1. The *sign of nasality* is a single n or m in the same syllable (§65) with the vowel sound.

Ex.: Man-ger *(mãžé)*, faim *(fẽ)*.

2. But if m or n is *followed by a vowel*, or is *doubled*, or *if mn occurs*, there is *no nasality*.

Ex.: Ananas *(ánáná)*, inutile *(inütil)*, innocent, nommer *(nòmé)*, automne *(óton)*.

34. Am, an, em, en.—All like ã (plãn, §13, 1).

Ex.: Plan *(plã)*, plante, tante, manger, parlant, viande, champ *(šã)*, camp, lampe, chambre, Adam, tempérance *(tãpérãs)*, membre, dent *(dã)*, tente, évidence, patient, patience.

[Exc.—1. As exceptions to §33, 2, above, observe the following: Enivrer *(ãnivré)*, enorgueillir, ennoblir, ennui and cognates, with ã). So also, emmener *(ãmené)* and most words in emm-. 2. Final -am, -em, -en is not nasal in most foreign proper names: Priam *(priám)*, Jérusalem. So also, hymen *(imèn)* and others. 3. -en=ẽ (fin, §13, 2), in -een, -ien, or -ien-: Européen *(öröpéẽ)*, bien, viendrai *(viẽdré)*. So also, examen *(égzámẽ)*.]

35. Aim, ain, eim, ein, im, in, ym, yn.—All like ẽ (fin, §13, 2).

Ex.: Faim *(fẽ)*, sainte *(sẽt)*, Reims *(rẽs)*, plein *(plẽ)*, feinte, peindre, grimper *(grẽpé)*, simple, limpide, fin *(fẽ)*, prince, princesse, symbole *(sẽbòl)*, nymphe, syntax *(sẽtáks)*.

36. Om, on.—Like õ (bõn, §13, 4).

Ex.: Nom *(nõ)*, tomber, comte, compter *(cõté)*, monde *(mõd)*, on, long, profond, annoncer.

[Exc.—on=e (le, §10, 3) in monsieur *(mesiŏ)*.]

THE CONSONANTS.

37. Um, un, eun.—All like œ̃ (un, §13, 3).

Ex.: Parfum *(parfœ̃)*, humble, un, brun *(brœ̃)*, lundi, emprunter, à jeun *(žœ̃)*.

[Exc.—Exceptions to -um and -un are: Le punch *(pŏnš)*, Humbert *(ŏbèr)*, album *(álbôm)*, and many such.]

38. Oin, ouin.—Both like ŭ+ẽ (oui, §14, 3, and fin, §13, 2).

Ex.: Loin *(lŭẽ)*, joindre, besoin, baragouin *(báráguẽ)*.

THE CONSONANTS.

39. General Rules:—1. *Final consonants* are usually *silent*.

Ex.: Chaud *(šó)*, long *(lŏ)*, loup, petit, vent, gros, trois, voix, nez, je mets, ils parlent.

2. *Final* **c, f, l, r** are more usually *sounded* than silent.
Ex.: Avec *(ávèk)*, sac, vif, actif, bal, seul, fer, amer.

3. A *doubled consonant* has usually *one sound*, not two.
Ex.: Aller *(álé)*, appeler, donner, terre.

[Exc.—A few important exceptions (mostly *learned* words) are noted under some of the consonants below. For details see dictionary.]

NOTE.—The so-called *double consonant* sound is more strictly a prolongation of the sound with a renewed effort of utterance, as in 'room-mate' when carefully pronounced. For convenience, these sounds will be denoted by the doubled symbol. Such sounds are, in any case, chiefly characteristic of careful or elevated diction.

40. Bb.—Like *b* (bas, §15, 1).

Ex.: Bas *(bá)*, barbare, beau, syllabe, plomber *(plŏbé)*, abbé, sabbat.
[Exc.—1. b *silent* in: Doubs, Lefebvre, and some others. 2. b *final* (§39, 2) is *sounded* in a few words (mostly foreign): Club *(klüb)*, nabab, Job, etc.; *but* Christophe Colomb *(còlŏ)*, after nasal.]

41. Cc.—Has *two* sounds:—
1. Like *k* (car, §15, 6). Thus, *before* **a, o, u** or *a consonant*, and when *final*.

Ex.: Car *(kár)*, Canada, cou, curé, clou *(klu)*, caractère, craie, lac *(lák)*, grec, public, duc, parc.

[Exc.—1. c *final* (§39, 2) is generally *silent* after a nasal: Banc *(bã)*, franc *(frã)*, *but* zinc *(zēk)* and donc *(dŏk)*, sometimes so before a vowel, when final, or before a pause), and in croc *(kró)*, échecs *(ěšè)*, estomac, tabac, and others rarer. 2. For words in -ct, see dictionary. 3. c=*g* (gare, §15, 4) in second *(seyõ)* and derivatives. 4. cc=$k+k$ in : Acclamation, its cognates, and some other learned words.]

2. Like *s* (sel, §15, 13). Thus, *before* e, i, y and with *cedilla before* a, o, u.

Ex. : Ciel *(siĕl)*, ceci, cela, ici, cygne *(siñ)*, place, ça *(sá)*, plaçant, reçois, reçu.

So also, the second c of cc (the first=k) before e, i : Accès *(aksè)*, accident.

NOTE.—In conjugation the *s* sound of c when required before a, o, u, is denoted by ç : Placer, plaçant ; recevoir, reçu, etc.

42. Ch.—Has *two* sounds :—
1. Like *š* (chat, §15, 14). Thus, *generally*.

Ex. : Chat *(šá)*, chaud, chose, chercher, machine, riche, chute.

2. Like *k* (car, §15, 6). Thus, in most *words from Greek*, and in *foreign words*.

Ex. : Chaos *(káó)*, chœur, choléra, chrétien, écho, yacht *(iák)*, Énoch, Michel-Ange *(mikèl āž)*, Munich.

[EXC.—1. Like *š* in : Achille *(ášil)*, Michel, archiduc, archevêque, chimère, monarchie, chérubin, punch *(põš)*, and others. 2. ch is *silent* in almanach.]

43. Dd.—Like *d* (dit, §15, 2).

Ex. : Dit *(di)*, dame, de, dé, dire, dorer, dur, salade, mode *(mòd)*, coude, perdre.

[EXC.—*Final* d (§39, 1) is *sounded* in sud *(süd)*, and in most foreign names, *e.g.*, Alfred, le Cid, David, etc., but note : Madrid *(-dri)*, Oxford *(-fòr)*, St. Bernard *(-ár)*.]

44. Ff.—Like *f* (fini, §15, 3).

Ex. : Fini *(fini)*, facile, fête, fumer, café, fleur, froid, bœuf *(bœf)*, bref, œuf, chef.

[EXC.—*Final* f (§39, 2) is *silent* in : Clef *(klé)*, chef-d'œuvre *(šĕ d œvr)*, œufs *(ö)*, bœufs, nerfs, and in neuf='nine' before consonant or h aspirate of a word multiplied by it, *e.g.*, neuf milles *(nö mil)*, *but* le neuf *(nœf)* mars.]

45. Gg.—Has *two* sounds :—
1. Like *g* (gare, §15, 4). Thus, before a, o, u or *a consonant*.

Ex. : Gare *(gár)*, gant, gorge, aigu *(èyü)*, gloire, grand, suggérer *(sügžéré)*, Bagdad.

2. Like ž (jour, §15, 18). Thus, before e, i, y.

Ex.: Génie *(žéni)*, âge, âgé, geindre, agir, gymnase *(žimnáz)*.
So also, the *second* g of gg before e, *e.g.*, suggérer *(sügzéré)*.

NOTE 1.—The *g* sound (gare, §15, 4) before e, i, is denoted by gu (u is silent), or gh : Gué *(gé)*, guerre *(ger)*, guide, guise, languir, Enghien.

NOTE 2.—The ž sound (jour, §15, 18) when required before a, o, u (generally in conjugation), is denoted by ge (e silent) : Mangeant *(mãžã)*, mangeons, geai *(žé)*, geôle, Georges, gageure *(gážür)*.

[EXC.—1. u is *sounded* in : Aiguille *(ègüïï)*, aiguiser, lingual *(lēgüál)*, linguiste *(lēgüïst)*, le Guide, Guise, their derivatives, and a few other words. 2. In aiguë, e takes *tréma* to show that u is sounded. 3. Final g (§39, 1), is *generally sounded* in foreign words : Grog, humbug, pouding, whig, Lessing.]

46. Gn.—Like ñ (vigne, §15, 10). Thus, *generally*.

Ex.: Vigne *(viñ)*, agneau, gagner, signal, magnifique, l'Allemagne.
[EXC.—1. In a number of learned words gn=g+n : Cognition *(kògnistō)*, diagnostique, stagnant, etc. 2. The g is *silent* in signet *(sinè)*, and in some proper names, *e.g.*, Regnard, etc.]

47. Hh.—Always *silent* (§15, 5).

Ex.: L'homme *(l òm)*, le héros *(le éró)*, le hasard, trahir, trahison, bonheur *(bònær)*.
As initial letter h is either h *mute*, treated as a vowel, or h *aspirate*, treated as a consonant and preventing *elision* (§73) and *liaison* (§70) : L'homme *(l òm)*, cet homme *(sèt òm)*, les hommes *(lèz òm)* ; le héros les hasards *(lè ázár)*.

[*Reference List* of the commoner words with h aspirate.]

hache	halle	harangue	harnais	héros	honte
haie	halte	harasser	harpe	hibou	hors
haïr	hamac	hardes	hasard	hideux	houille
haillon	hanche	hardi	hâte	hiérarchie	huit
haineux	hangar	haricot	haut	hocher	hutte

Generally also their compounds and derivatives, except those of héros.

48. Jj.—*Always* like ž (jour, §15, 18).

Ex.: Jour, jamais *(zámè)*, Japon, je, joli, jeune, majesté, Jean *(žã)*, j'ai *(ž é)*, Juge, Djinn *(džē)*.

49. Kk (ck).—*Always* like *k* (car, §15, 6).

Ex.: Kilo, kan *(kã)*, kaléïdoscope, moka, képi, coke *(kòk)*, Tokay, Cook ; arack *(árák)*, biftèck *(biftèk)*, Necker.

50. Ll.—Like *l* (lard, §15, 7). Thus, *always*, except l *mouillée* (§51, below).

Ex.: Le, la, les, livre, loup *(lu)*, lune, lilas, cheval, ciel, il, mil, Noël.

[Exc.—1. Final l (§39, 2) is *silent* in : Fusil *(füzi)*, chenil *(šeni)*, cul-de-sac, sourcil, outil, soûl, and some others. 2. l is *silent* in : Fils *(fis)*, La Rochefoucauld *(-kó)*, Perrault *(-ó)*, and similar proper names. 3. ll=*l*+*l* in words in ill-, like illégal *(illégál)*, and in some with -ll-, *e.g.*, allusion, etc.]

51. -(i)ll-, -il.—1. Like *ĭ* (viande, §14, 1). Thus, -ll- *preceded by* i *within a word*.

Ex.: Fille *(fĭ)*, famille *(fámĭĭ)*, briller *(brĭĭé)*, billet, tilleul, habiller, juillet *(žŭĭĭè)*.

2. So also -ill- and -il *preceded by a vowel*.

Ex.: Bataille *(bátăĭ)*, vieillard *(vĭĕĭár)*, feuille *(fwĭ)*, cueillir *(kœĭir)*, l'œillet *(lœĭè)*, mouillé *(mŭĭé)*; travail *(trăwĭĭ)*, soleil *(sŏlĕĭ)*, fauteuil *(fŏtœĭ)*, orgueil *(lorgœĭ)*, œil *(œĭ)*, fenouil *(fenŭĭ)*.

So also, -l in grésil *(grézĭĭ)*, mil *(mĭĭ)*='millet.'

Observe: Remember that initial ill- is not l *mouillée*.

[Exc.—1. -ll-=*l* (not *ĭ*) in billion *(bilĭŏ̃)*, codicille *(-sil)*, distiller *(distilé)* instiller, mille *(mil)*, milliard *(milĭar)*, millier *(milĭé)*, millimètre, myrtille *(mirtil)*, osciller *(òsillé)*, pupille, pusillanime *(-ll-)*, scintiller *(-ll-)*, titiller *(-ll-)*, tranquille *(trăkil)*, villa, village *(vilăž)*, ville *(vil)*, their compounds and derivatives. So also, in Achille, Lille and a few others. 2. Many words in -il, *e.g.*, avril, etc., are doubtful, see dictionary ; gentil=žătĭ in the sing. before a vowel or h mute, or when fem., otherwise žăti.]

NOTE.—The sound of l *mouillée* has been much disputed. As heard often in South France, Alsace, Switzerland, it resembles ly in 'steelyard' or lli in 'billiards' (so also, Littré) but custom and authority now alike demand the *ĭ* sound.

52. Mm.—Like *m* (mal, §15, 8).

Ex.: Mal *(mál)*, me, même, mot, blâmer, mémoire, homme *(òm)*. nommer *(nòmé)*.

[Exc.—1. m is *silent* when it is the *sign of a nasal vowel* (§33, 1): Nom *(nō)*. *Silent* also in : Damner *(dăné)*, condamner and derivatives, and in automne *(òtòn)*. 2. mm=*m*+*m* in some words with imm-, like immense *(immăs)*, etc., and in many learned and foreign words, *e.g.*, mammifère, Emma, etc.]

53. Nn.—Like *n* (nid, §15, 9).

Ex.: Nid *(nî)*, ananas, nature, cabane, le cap Horn *(òrn)*, bonne *(bòn)*, donner *(dòné)*.

[Exc.—1. n is *silent* when it is the *sign of a nasal vowel* (§33, 1) · Non *(nõ)*. 2. nn=*n*+*n* in such words as annales *(ànnál)*, innovation, and others in inn- (but not so in innocent, innocence, etc.); Anna *(ànná)*, Cinna, Annibal.]

54. Pp.—Like *p* (pas, §15, 11).

Ex.: Pas *(pà)*, papier, père, captif, pour, abrupt, psaume *(psóm)*, Ptolémée *(ptòlémé)*, appeler *(áplé)*, application *(áplikàsîõ)*.

[Exc.—Final p (§39, 1) is *sounded* in : Cap *(cáp)*, croup, sloop and a few others. 2. p is *silent* in : Baptême *(bátèm)*, baptiser, compte, dompter, sculpter, prompte, and their cognates ; *silent* in sept *(sèt)*, septième (all others with sept sound p). 3. ph=*f* (fîni, §15, 3): Philosophie *(fîlòzòfii)*, etc.]

55. Qq (qu).—Like *k* (car, §15, 6).

Ex.: Cinq *(sèk)*, qualité *(kálité)*, quantité, quatre, que, quel, quoi *(kñá)*, question, qui, bouquet, éloquent, Charles-Quint.

[Exc.—1. Final q (rare) is regularly *sounded:* Cinq, coq, etc , but is *silent* in cinq before consonant or h aspirate of a word multiplied by it e.g., cinq jours *(sè žur)* ; *but* le cinq *(sèk)* mars *(márs)*. 2. The n of qu (regularly silent)=*ñ* (§14, 3) before a in : Aquatic *(ákñátik)*, équateur, quadrupède, loquace, in their cognates and in some rarer words. 3. Similarly *ü* of qu=*ü̈* (§14, 2) before e, i in équestre *(ékü̈èstr)*, equilateral, quintuple, le Quirinal and some rarer words.]

NOTE.—When the *k* sound is required before e or i in inflection, it is denoted by qu : Vaincre, vainquez ; public, publique.

56. Rr.—Like *r* (rare, §15, 12).

Ex.: Rare *(rare)*, rose, riche, barbare, drap, gris, père, dormir, amour, arroser *(àrózé)*, torrent *(tòrã)*.

[Exc.—1. *Final* r (§39, 2) is *silent* in infinitives in -er, e.g., donner *(dòné)*, *silent* in most *nouns* and *adjs.* in -er (-ier) of *two or more* syllables, e.g., boucher *(bušé)*, danger, entier, léger, and in monsieur *(mesü)* ; but is *sounded* in *monosyllables*, e.g., fer *(fèr)*, fier, hier, etc., in : Amer *(ámèr)*, cuiller *(cü̈ièr)*, enfer, hiver, and in foreign proper names, e.g., Jupiter, etc. 2. rr=*r*+*r* in the *future* and *condl.* of acquérir, courir, mourir, quérir and their compounds, e.g., je courrai *(kurré)*, etc. 3. So also, in words in irr-, e.g., irrégulier and many such, and in some words like errata *(èrrátá)*, corroder, interrègne, etc.]

57. Ss.—Has *two* sounds:—

1. Like *s* (sel, §15, 13). Thus, when *initial* (or initial in part of a compound), and generally *before or after a consonant within a word*.

Ex.: Sel *(sĕl)*, sa, sur, silence, splendide, station, vraisemblamble *(vrĕsãmblábl)*, parasol, espérer, absurde *(ábsürd)*, bourse, danser.

So also, **ss** *always*: Casser *(cásé)*, tasse, la Suisse.

2. Like z (zone, §15, 17). Thus, when *between vowels*.

Ex.: Chose *(šöz)*, rose, poison *(pŭázō)*, ruse, hasard, visite, maison *(mĕzō)*, plaisir, désagréable.

[Exc.—*Final* **s** (§39, 1) is *sounded* in: Atlas *(átlás)*, bis, jadis, fils *(fĭs)*, mars *(márs)*, hélas, omnibus, ours, and some rarer words. So also in most proper names, *e.g.*, Gil Blas *(blás)*, Mars, etc. 2. Within words **s** is *silent* in many proper names, *e.g.*, Dufresne *(düfrĕn)*, Vosges *(vŏž)*, etc.; *silent* in words with des-, les-, etc., *e.g.*, Descartes *(děcárt)*, lesquels, mesdames; but *sounded* in Xavier de Maistre *(mĕstr)*, Malesherbes, Montesquieu, Robespierre, and rarer words. 3. **s** in trans- before a vowel=z: Transaction, etc.; *but* transir *(tr͞ánsir)*. 4. Gésir *(žĕzir)*, but in conjugation: Ils gisent *(žis)*, etc. 5. Note the following: Fils *(fĭs*, almost universal), gens *(g͞a*, occasionally and familiarly *g͞as)*, lis *(li* in fleur-de-lis, elsewhere *lis)*, mœrs *(mœrs*, rarely mœr), os (sing. *ŏs* or *ó*, plur. generally *ó)*, tous *(tu*, as adj., elsewhere generally *tus)*. For sens see dictionary.]

58. Sc.—Like *s* (sel, §15, 13) before e, i, y, and like *s + k* (car, §15, 6) before a, o, u.

Ex.: Scène *(sĕn)*, scie, Scylla; scandale *(sk͞ádál)*, discours, Escurial.

59. Sch.—Generally like *š* (chat, §15, 14).

Ex.: Schisme *(šism)*, Schah, Schiller.

[Exc.—Like *s + k* in schéma *(skémá)*, and a few others.

60. Tt.—Has *two* sounds:—

1. Like *t* (terre, §15, 15). Thus, *generally*.

Ex.: Terre *(tĕr)*, table, vertu, tête, votre, amitie *(ámĭtĭĕ)*, question, mixte, chrétien, nous portions *(pòrtĭõ)*, assiette *(asĭĕt)*, attraper *(atrápĕ)*.

2. Like *s* (sel, §15, 13). Thus, in words with -ti- whose English equivalents have the sh or cy sound, as in 'nation,' 'prophecy.'

THE CONSONANTS.

Ex.: Portion *(pòrsĭŏ)*, ambitieux *(ăbisĭŏ)*, essentiel, partiel, plénipotentiaire, inertie, patience, initial, initier, aristocratie *(ăristòkrási)*, prophétie, l'Égyptien.

So also: Satiété *(sasĭété)*, Miltiade, balbutier *(bălbüsĭé)*, and rarer words.

[Exc.—1. Final t (§39, 1) is *sounded* in: Net *(nèt)*, dot, fat, est = 'east,' ouest, Christ (*but* Jésus-Christ=*žézü kri*). So also in: Déficit, prétérit and some other borrowed words, and in many proper names, *e.g.*, Brest, etc., and generally in words in -ct, *e.g.*, abject *(ăbžèkt)*, strict, etc. 2. Note: But (*bü* or *büt*, the latter more common, especially as final word or before a pause), fait, n. m., *(fèt*, pl. *fè)*, sot *(só*, sometimes *sòt)*. For several words in -pect, -ct, see dictionary. 3. tt=*t+t* in a very few words: Guttural *(güttürál)*, Gambetta, etc. 4. th is *silent* in asthme *(ăsm)*, isthme, Goth.]

61. Vv, Ww.—1. Like *v* (vite, §15, 16).

Ex.: Vite *(vit)*, vanité, venu, vin, vous, vivre, savoir; wagon *(vágŏ)*, warrant *(várā)*, writ, Weimar.

2. *w = ü* (oui, §14, 3) in some words from English.

Ex.: Railway *(rèlüé)*, whig *(üig)*, William *(üillám)*.

62. Xx.—Has *two* sounds:—
1. Like *k + s* (car, §15, 6, and sel, §15, 13). Thus, generally *within a word*.

Ex.: Anxiété *(ăksiété)*, maxime, excuser, expérience, luxe, Alexandre.

2. Like *g + z* (gare, §15, 4, and zone, §15, 17). Thus in ex- or hex- *before a vowel* or h.

Ex.: Examen *(ègzámè)*, exécution *(ègzékūsĭŏ)*, exil, exorbitant, inexorable, hexamètre.

So also generally as initial, unless followed by t, y: Xavier *(gzávié)*, Xénéphon *(gz-)*, *but* xylographie *(ksi-)*, etc.

[Exc.—1. Final x (§39, 1) is *sounded* as *k+s* in: Index *(èdèks)*, phénix, etc., and in most proper names, *e.g.*, Halifax, etc. 2. x=*k* before an *s* sound: Excellent *(èksèlā)*. 3. Like *s* in: Six *(sis)*, dix *(dis)*, soixante *(süásāt)*, soixantième, and in some proper names, *e.g.*, Aix *(ès)*, Bruxelles *(brüsèl* or *brüksèl)*, etc. 4. Like *z* in deuxième *(dözĭèm)*, sixième, dixième, dix-huit and their derivatives.]

63. Zz.—Like *z* (zone, §15, 17).

Ex.: Zone *(zóne)*, zouave *(zŭáv)*, lézard, Zaïre, Balzac *(bălzák)*.

[EXC.—*Final z*, (§39,1) is *sounded* in : Gaz, in the endings -az, -oz, -uz of proper names, *e.g.*, Achaz, Buloz, Santa-Cruz, and like *s* in proper names in -ez : Cortez *(còrtès)*, Suez, and a few rarer ones. 2. Note : Coblentz *(kòblās)*, Metz *(mès)*, Retz *(rès)*.]

SYLLABICATION.

64. The most important general principles of syllabication are :—

1. A word has as many syllables as it contains simple vowel sounds.

Ex. : Beau-té, li-er, pè-re, Mo-ï-se.

2. A *consonant* between vowels, or a group of such consonants as *may be pronounced together, begins* a syllable.

Ex. : Ca-na-da, fi-nir, é-co-le, a-che-ter, é-cri-re, in-strui-re, ju-sti-ce, e-sca-lier.

Observe: A consonant in English between vowels frequently *ends* a syllable. Compare English 'in-di-vis-i-bil-i-ty' with French 'in-di-vi-si-bi-li-té.'

65. The ordinary rules for dividing consonants in *printing* and *writing* agree in general with the above principles. They are here given for reference :—

1. A *single consonant* (except x) goes with the following vowel : A-mi, é-co-le, a-ni-mal, ex-il.

2. *Doubled consonants* and *two unlike consonants* are *divided*, but the digraphs (**ch, ph, th, gn**) and most combinations of *consonant(s)* +l or r (**bl, br, cl, cr, dr, fl, fr, gl, gr, pl, pr, str**) are *undivided*, and are treated as single consonants : Al-ler ; a-che-ter, di-gra-phe, ma-thé-ma-ti-ques, vi-gne; o-bli-ger, dé-cla-rer, ré-gler, qua-tre, ou-vra-ge, é-cri-re, in-strui-re, com-bler, per-dre.

3. Of *three* consonants *one only* usually goes with the following vowel, exceptions being the undivided **sph** and the undivided l and r combinations above : Sanc-tu-aire, fonc-tion, atmo-sphè-re, com-bler, per-dre.

4. *Compounds* are usually divided into their parts : Dés-a-gré-a-ble, sub-or-don-ner, in-é-gal, bon-heur.

STRESS.

66. *Stress* is the force with which a syllable is uttered as compared with other syllables, as in '**pen**-cil,' 'con-**fus**-ing.'

67. 1. The stress in a French word regularly falls on the *last syllable*, unless the last syllable has e *mute*, in which case it falls on the *last but one*.

Ex.: Che-val, pè-re, par-ler, par-lent, cré-di-bi-li-té, é-ner-gi-e.

2. As compared with English, stress in French is very *weak*, the syllables being uttered with *almost equal force*. Compare English 'cred-i-bil-it-y' and French 'cré-di-bi-li-té.'

Observe: 1. In pronouncing French the *distinct utterance of every vowel sound* cannot be too carefully insisted on. 2. The *accent-marks have nothing to do with stress*.

NOTE.—As in words, so in a group of words (phrase), the stress tends to fall fully on the last syllable, being proportionately weakened in the individual words: Vous avez acheté un chapeau.

QUANTITY OF VOWEL SOUNDS.

68. *Three* degrees of length, *long, half-long* and *short*, are commonly distinguished as follows (final silent e being disregarded):—

1. A *final vowel sound* (including *nasals*) is *short*.

Ex.: Fini, vie, loue, parlé, rideau, sot, mais, fracas, Canada, donner, enfant, parlerons.

[Exc.—Dix, six, huit before a consonant or h aspirate, and a few exclamations, *e.g.*, ah !, oh !, etc.]

2. Final vowels *when sounded with following consonant(s)* are:

(a) Before an *r, z, ž, v, ĭ* sound, *all* vowels *long*: Genre *(žā.r)*, rouge *(ru.ž)*, chanvre *(šā.vr)*, rare *(rá.r)*, guerre *(gè.r)*, base *(bà.z)*, ruse, Meuse, collège *(còlè.ž)*, ai-je *(è.ž)*, parlerai-je, portai-je, cave *(ká.v)*, étuve, bataille *(bátà.ĭ)*, soleil.

(b) Before other consonant sounds, *nasals* are *long* (always); *à, ô, ö* are *long* (nearly always); *è long* or *short*; *other vowels* regularly *short*: Vendre *(vā.dr)*, prince *(prē.s)*, avalanche *(àválā.š)*, sainte *(sē.t)*, monde *(mō.d)*; je passe *(pà.s)*, faute *(fó.t)*, autre *(ó.tr)*, zone *(zó.n)*, fosse *(fó.s)*, meule *(mö.l)*; reine *(rè.n)*, renne *(rèn)*; cap *(káp)*, cape, glace, atroce, salade, poche, marine.

[Exc.—The letters â, ê, î, ô, û, eû as final vowel sounds are *generally long*, even when not before an *r, z, ž, v, ĭ* sound: Grâce *(grà.s)*, âne *(à.n)*, portâtes *(pòrtà.t)*, fête *(fè.t)*, île *(i.l)*, épître *(épi.tr)*, drôle *(dró.l)*, flûte *(flü.t)*, jeûne *(žö.n)*.]

3. As appears from these rules, *long vowel sounds* are *found only in the stress-bearing syllable.* The vowel sounds of *non-stress-bearing syllables* are regularly either *half-long* or *short* (practically short).

Ex.: Gracieuse, hôtel, français, goûter, maisonette, impassibilité.

LIAISON AND ELISION.

69. French, when uttered, really consists, not of *words*, as in the printed page, but of *syllable groups:* Qu'avez-vous dit? (= ká vé vu di).

70. *Within a syllable group*, but not elsewhere, a final consonant (whether usually sounded or not) is sounded in one syllable with the initial vowel sound of the next word. This is called in French 'liaison'='linking,' 'joining.'

71. A few of the consonants change their sound in *liaison*. Thus, final s or x = z, d = t, g = k, f = v, while the n of a nasal is carried on and the nasal vowel loses part of its nasality.

NOTE.—In the *liaison* of nasals, usage varies from almost full nasality to almost total absence of it.

72. The division of a sentence into syllable groups depends chiefly on the closeness of connection in sense and construction. The principal groups are :—

1. Subject, Predicate, Completion : C'est un bon ami *(sèt ã bōn ámi).* Nous avons acheté de beaux habits *(nuz ávōz ãštè de bóz ábi).*

2. The Verb with the Pronouns, Negatives, etc., grouped about it : Il ne vous en a pas acheté *(il ne vuz ãn á pàz ãštè).* Leur en avez-vous jamais acheté? *(lœ̃.r ãn ávé vu žámèz ãštè).*

3. Preposition, Article, Adjective, Substantive : Sans eux *(sãz ö);* les hommes *(lèz òm);* mes amis *(mèz ámi);* deux heures *(döz œ̃.r);* de bons amis *(bōz ámi);* un sang impur *(œ̃ sãk êpü.r);* neuf heures *(nœv œ.r).*

4. Adverb, Adjective : Très habile *(trèz ábil).*

Observe: A *pause always prevents liaison*, and t of et='and' is *always silent.*

NOTE.—*Liaison* depends considerably on the nature of the discourse, being more strictly observed in elevated diction.

73. On the same principle of syllable grouping depends *elision* of the final e in monosyllables (and in a few compounds of -que), of the final a in la before a vowel or h mute, and of the i of si before il(s) :

Ex.: L'arbre (=le arbre), qu'a-t-il? (=que a-t-il?), j'ai (=je ai), jusqu'à (=jusque à), s'il (=si il).

74. PUNCTUATION.

1. The same punctuation marks are used in French as in English. Their French names are :—

. point.	- trait d'union.	[ ] crochets.
, virgule.	— tiret, or tiret	{ accolade.
; point et virgule.	de séparation.	
: deux points.	... points suspensifs.	* astérisque.
? point d'interrogation.	" " guillemets.	† croix de renvoi.
! point d'exclamation.	( ) parenthèse.	

2. They are used as in English, but the *tiret* commonly serves to denote a *change of interlocutor.*

Ex.: " Qui est là ? dis-je.—Personne.—Quoi ! personne !—Personne, dit-il."

USE OF CAPITALS.

75. Capital letters (Fr. 'lettres majuscules,' 'capitales') are generally used as in English, with the following exceptions :—

1. A proper adjective has a capital *only when used as a noun denoting a person*: Un livre canadien, 'A Canadian book,' but Un Canadien, 'A Canadian.' Il comprend le français, 'He understands French.'

2. Names of days of the week and months are generally without a capital: Toronto, lundi, le 3 janvier, 'Toronto, Monday, the 3rd January.'

3. The word je='I,' within a sentence, *never has a capital*: Je lui ai dit ce que je pensais, 'I told him what I thought.'

TABLE OF ALPHABETICAL EQUIVALENTS.

76. The following examples show the various *alphabetical equivalents* of French sounds :—

1. *à.*—Lâche *(lă.š)*, pas *(pà)*, roi *(rŭà).*

2. *á.*—Madame *(mádám)*, là *(lá)*, femme *(fám)*, poêle *(pŭál)*, moi *(mŭá)*, boîte *(bŭát).*

3. *ã.*—Plan *(plã)*, lampe *(lã.p)*, dent *(dã)*, membre *(mã.br).* paon *(pã).*

4. *b.*—Base *(bà.s)*, abbé *(ábé)*.
5. *d.*—Dit *(di)*, addition *(ádisïõ)*.
6. *e.*—Le *(le)*, monsieur *(meslö)*, faisant *(fezã)*.
7. *é.*—Donné *(dòné)* parler *(párlé)*, je donnai *(že dòné)*, veto *(véto)*.
8. *è.*—Père *(pè.r)*, fête *(fè.t)*, terre *(tè.r)*, je parlais *(že párlè)*, Cambray *(kãbrè)*, reine *(rè.n)*, Ney *(nè)*, payer *(pèié)*.
9. *ẽ.*—Fin *(fẽ)*, faim *(fẽ)*, sainte *(sẽ.t)*, Reims *(rẽs)*, plein *(plẽ)*, simple *(sẽ.pl)*, symbole *(sẽbòl)*, syntaxe *(sẽtáks)*, je viendrai *(že vïẽdré)*, soin *(sũẽ)*, baragouin *(bárágũẽ)*.
10. *f.*—Fini *(fini)*, difficile *(difisil)*.
11. *g.*—Gare *(gá.r)*, guerre *(gè.r)*, second *(segõ)*, Enghien *(ãyïẽ)*.
12. *h.*—L'homme *(l òm)*.
13. *i.*—Fini *(fini)*, île *(i.l)*, lyre *(li.r)*.
14. *ï.*—Viande *(vïã.d)*, aïeul *(áïœl)*, yeux *(ïö)*, fille *(fïï)*, travailler *(trávàïé)*, travail *(trávà.ï)*, grésil *(gréziï)*.
15. *k.*—Car *(ká.r)*, accorder *(ákòrdé)*, chrétien *(krétïẽ)*, cinq *(sẽ.k)*, bouquet *(bukè)*, acquérir *(ákéri.r)*, kilo *(kiló)*, maxime *(máksim)*, sang impur *(sãk èpü.r)*.
16. *l.*—Lard *(lá.r)*, aller *(álé)*.
17. *m.*—Mal *(mál)*, homme *(òm)*.
18. *n.*—Nid *(ni)*, donner *(dòné)*.
19. *ñ.*—Vigne *(viñ)*.
20. *ó.*—Zone *(zó.n)*, côté *(kóté)*, faute *(fó.t)*, beauté *(bóté)*.
21. *ò.*—Mort *(mò.r)*, Paul *(pòl)*, album *(álbòm)*.
22. *õ.*—Bon *(bõ)*, comte *(cõ.t)*.
23. *ö.*—Peu *(pö)*, les bœufs *(lè bö)*, jeûne *(jö.n)*.
24. *œ.*—Leur *(lœ.r)*, cœur *(kœ.r)*, orgueil *(òrgœ.ï)*, œil *(œ.ï)*.
25. *œ̃.*—Un *(œ̃)*, parfum *(párfœ̃)*, à jeun *(á žœ̃)*.
26. *p.*—Pas *(pà)*, application *(áplikàsïõ)*, absolument *(ápsòlümã)*.
27. *r.*—Rare *(rá.r)*, torrent *(tòrã)*.
28. *s.*—Sel *(sèl)*, casser *(kàsé)*, scène *(sèn)*, place *(plás)*, façade *(fásàd)*, la portion *(lá pòrsïõ)*, soixante *(süásã.t)*.
29. *š.*—Chat *(šá)*, schisme *(šism)*.
30. *t.*—Terre *(tè.r)*, attention *(átãsïõ)*.
31. *u.*—Sou *(su)*, où *(u)*, goût *(gu)*, nou *(u)*.
32. *ü.*—Oui *(üi)*, moi *(müá)*, tramway *(trámüé)*.
33. *ü.*—Une *(ü.n)*, qu'il fût *(k il fü)*, il eut *(il ü)*, nous eûmes *(nuz ü.m)*.
34. *ü̃.*—Suite *(sü̃it)*.
35. *v.*—Vite *(vit)*, wagon *(vágõ)*, neuf heures *(nœv œ.r)*.

36. z.—Zone (zó.n), rose (ró.z), deux heures (döz œ.r), exact (ėgzákt).

37. ž.—Jour (žu.r), âgé (ážé), mangeant (mãžã).

Examples of Phonetic Transcription.

77. 1. Un jour au commencement d'une bataille, Henri
   ã žu.r ó kòmãsmã d ü.n bátà.ĭ ãri
Quatre ne dit à ses soldats que ces mots : "Je suis votre
kátr ne di á sè sòldá ke sè mó že süi vòtr
roi, vous êtes Français, voilà l'ennemi."
rŭà vuz è.t frãsè vŭálá l ènmi.

2. Un chien traversait une rivière sur un pont avec un
 ã̃ šĭã trávèrsèt ü.n rivìè.r sü.r ã̃ põ árèk ã̃
morceau de viande dans sa gueule. Il aperçut dans l'eau
mòrsó de vĭã.d dã sá gö.l il ápèrsü dã l ó
son ombre, et s'imagina que c'était un autre chien qui
sõn õ.br é s imážiná ke s étèt ã̃n ó.tr šĭã ki
portait aussi de la viande. Aussitôt, voulant la lui
pòrtèt ósi de lá vĭã.d ósitó vulã lá lüi
arracher, il lâcha le morceau qu'il tenait et se jeta dans
árášé il lášá le mòrsó k il tenè é se žtá dã
l'eau. Mais il n'attrapa ni la viande, ni l'image et il eut
l ó mèz il n átrápá ni lá vĭã.d ni l imá.ž é il ü
toutes les peines du monde à regagner le bord.
tut lè pè.n dü mõ.d á regãñé le bó.r.

  3. Du pain sec et du fromage
   dü pã̃ sèk é dü fròmá.ž
  C'est bien peu pour déjeuner.
   s è bĭã̃ pö pu.r dèžöné
  On me donnera, je gage
   õ me dònrá že gá.ž
  Autre chose à mon dîner :
   ó.tr šó.z á mõ diné
  Car Didon dîna, dit-on,
   ká.r didõ diná dit õ
  Du dos d'un dodu dindon.
   dü dó d ã̃ dodü dã̃dõ.

PART II.

LESSON I.

78. **Present Indicative of** *avoir*, 'to have.'

Sing.	Plur.
j'ai, *I have.*	nous avons, *we have.*
tu as, *thou hast (you have).*	vous avez, *you have.*
il a, *he (it) has.*	ils ont, *they have.*
elle a, *she (it) has.*	elles ont, *they (f.) have.*

[PRONUNCIATION.—ž é, tü à, il á, èl á, nuz ávõ, vuz ávé, ilz õ, el: õ.]

Observe: **Tu** = 'you' (sing.) in *familiar* or *affectionate* address. Elsewhere 'you' = *vous*.

79. **The Indefinite Article.**

Masc.	Fem.
un, *a (an).*	une, *a (an).*

[PRON.—œ̃, ü.n.]

80. The indefinite article is *repeated* before each noun to which it refers:

Une maison et un jardin. A house and garden.

81. Gender, Number, Case. 1. French nouns are either *masculine* or *feminine:* Père (*m.*), *father;* jardin (*m.*), *garden;* mère (*f.*), *mother;* beauté (*f.*), *beauty.*

NOTE.—Names of *male beings* are regularly *masculine*, names of *female beings feminine*. The gender of other nouns must be learned by observation. Pupils studying Latin should note that words from Latin *masculines* and *feminines* are usually *unchanged* in gender, but that Latin *neuters* have usually become *masculine* in French.

2. French has, like most languages, the following agreements: *(a) Verb* and *subject*, in number and person, *(b) adjective* and *noun*, in gender and number, *(c) pronoun* and *antecedent*, in gender and number. All these agreements are usually expressed by *change of form.*

3. Nouns have no case endings in French, the direct object *(acc.)* being expressed by *verb + noun*, the indirect obj. *(dat.)* by à + *noun*, and the possessive *(gen.)* by de + *noun*.

EXERCISE I.

Un ami *(ámi)*, friend.
Une amie *(ámi)*, friend.
Aussi *(ŏsi)*, also, too.
Un cheval *(ševál)*, horse.
Et *(é)*, and.
Un frère *(frè.r)*, brother.
Un jardin *(žárdẽ)*, garden.
Jean *(žã)*, John.

Un livre *(li.vr)*, book.
Mais *(mè)*, but.
Une maison *(mèzõ)*, house.
Marie *(mári)*, Mary.
Une poire *(pŭá.r)*, pear.
Une pomme *(pŏm)*, apple.
Une sœur *(sœ.r)*, sister.
Une voiture *(vŭátü.r)*, carriage.

A. 1. Nous avons, ils ont, tu as. 2. Vous avez, elles ont, il a. 3. J'ai, tu as, elle a. 4. Il a, vous avez, nous avons.

B. 1. You have, she has, they (f.) have. 2. I have, he has, thou hast. 3. We have, they (m.) have, you have. 4. She has, we have, you have.

C. 1. Nous avons une pomme, et vous avez une poire. 2. Jean a un cheval et une voiture aussi. 3. Marie a une sœur et une amie. 4. J'ai une poire, mais Jean a une pomme. 5. Ils ont un jardin et une maison. 6. Nous avons un ami et un frère, et elles ont une amie et une sœur. 7. Tu as un livre, et elle a une pomme et une poire. 8. Ils ont une maison et aussi un jardin. 9. Marie a un frère, et elle a aussi une sœur. 10. Jean et Marie ont une sœur.

D. 1. She has a brother and a sister too. 2. John has a horse, and he has also a carriage. 3. We have a house, and you have a garden. 4. Mary has a sister and a friend (f.). 5. They (m.) have a horse and carriage. 6. You (2nd sing.) have a brother and sister. 7. Mary has an apple; John has a pear. 8. We have a book; you have a pear. 9. I have a brother, and you (2nd sing.) have a friend (m.). 10. John has a horse and carriage, and I have a house and garden.

LESSON II.

82. Present Indicative of *être*, 'to be.'

SING.	PLUR.
je suis, *I am.*	nous sommes, *we are.*
tu es, *thou art (you are).*	vous êtes, *you are.*
il est, *he (it) is.*	ils sont, *they are.*
(elle est, *she (it) is.*)	(elles sont, *they (f.) are.*)

[PRON.—*že sŭi, tü è; il è, èl è, nu sŏm, vuz ê.t, il sõ, èl sõ.*]

83. **The Definite Article.**

	Sing.	Plur.
M.	le (l') } *the.*	les, *the.*
F.	la (l') }	

[Pron.—*le, lá, lè.*]
Observe: For the form l' see §73.

84. The definite article is *repeated* before each noun to which it refers :

La maison et le jardin.	The house and garden.
L'oncle et la tante.	The uncle and aunt.
Les frères et les sœurs.	The brothers and sisters.

85. Plural of Nouns and Adjectives. The plural of a noun or adjective is regularly formed by adding s to the singular :

| Le bon roi, la bonne reine. | The good king, the good queen. |
| Les bons rois, les bonnes reines. | The good kings, the good queens. |

The principal *exceptions* are :—

1. *Nouns* in -s, -x, -z and *masc. adjs.* in -s, -x remain *unchanged* in the plural :

Le bras, la voix, le nez.	The arm, the voice, the nose.
Les bras, les voix, les nez.	The arms, the voices, the noses.
Le mur est bas et vieux.	The wall is low and old.
Les murs sont bas et vieux.	The walls are low and old.

2. *Nouns* and *adjectives* in -au, *nouns* in -eu and *seven nouns* in -ou add x instead of s :

Le noyau, le château, le jeu, le vœu. — The kernel, the castle, the game, the vow.
Les noyaux, les châteaux, les jeux, les vœux. — The kernels, castles, games, vows.
Le beau livre. Les beaux livres. — The fine book. The fine books.

The seven nouns are : Bijou(x), *jewel,* caillou(x), *pebble,* chou(x), *cabbage,* genou(x), *knee,* hibou(x), *owl,* joujou(x), *toy,* pou(x), *louse.* But Clou(s), *nail,* sou(s), *half-penny,* etc., are regular.

3. *Nouns* (and the commoner *adjectives*) in -al change -al to -au and add x, as above.

| Un général rival. | A rival general. |
| Deux généraux rivaux. | Two rival generals. |

But *not :* Bal(s), *ball,* carnaval(s), *carnival,* and a few rarer nouns.

4. Note : Œil, pl. yeux, *eye;* travail, pl. travaux, *work;* ciel, pl. cieux, *heaven, sky.*

EXERCISE II.

L'arbre, m., *(á.rbr)*, tree.
L'argent, m., *(ár̃ã)*, money.
Avec *(ávèk)*, with.
La boîte *(bŭát)*, box.
Le chat *(šá)*, cat.
Le chien *(šĭe)*, dog.
La dame *(dám)*, lady.
Dans *(dã)*, in.
L'enfant, m. or f., *(ãfã)*, child.
La mère *(mè.r)*, mother.
Le monsieur *(mesĭõ)*, gentleman.
La montre *(mõ.tr)*, watch.
Ou *(u)*, or.
Le père *(pè.r)*, father.
Sous *(su)*, under.
Sur *(sü.r)*, on.
La table, f., *(tábl)*, table.

A. 1. Il est, il a, je suis. 2. Tu es, tu as, elle est. 3. Nous sommes, vous avez, elles sont. 4. Vous êtes, nous avons, ils ont. 5. Ils sont, j'ai, elle a.

B. 1. We are, thou art, you have. 2. We have, thou hast, he has. 3. I am, she is, they (f.) are. 4. They (m.) are, he is, you are. 5. They (f.) have, I have, he is.

C. 1. Les enfants sont avec le père et la mère. 2. Le frère ou la sœur est dans la maison. 3. La montre est avec l'argent dans la boîte. 4. Le chat et le chien sont dans le jardin. 5. Le monsieur et la dame sont dans la voiture. 6. La dame est avec les enfants sous l'arbre dans le jardin. 7. Les chevaux et la voiture sont sous l'arbre. 8. Je suis dans le jardin avec Marie et Jean. 9. La dame dans la voiture est la mère. 10. Le livre est sur la table dans la maison. 11. Jean et Marie ont le chien dans le jardin. 12. Vous êtes le père et la mère. 13. Le chat est dans la maison, mais le chien est dans le jardin. 14. Marie a les poires, mais Jean a les pommes. 15. Les frères et les sœurs sont dans la maison.

D. 1. The horses and carriages are under the trees. 2. John and Mary have the dog and cat in the garden. 3. The children are in the garden. 4. They (f.) have the money in a box. 5. The gentleman in the house has a watch. 6. The father or mother is in the house. 7. You (2nd sing.) have a dog and cat. 8. The gentleman has the horses. 9. The lady in the house is the mother. 10. The watch is in a box on the table. 11. The cat is under the table. 12. The children have the dog and cat under the tree. 13. The father and mother are in the garden with the children. 14. You have the apples, and we have the pears. 15. We are with the ladies and children in the carriage.

LESSON III.

86. Present Indicative of *avoir*, *être*, interrogatively.

Sing.	Plur.	Sing.	Plur.
[*Have I?*, etc.]	[*Have we?*, etc.]	[*Am I?*, etc.]	[*Are we?*, etc.]
ai-je ?	avons-nous ?	suis-je ?	sommes-nous ?
as-tu ?	avez-vous ?	es-tu ?	êtes-vous ?
a-t-il ?	ont-ils ?	est-il ?	sont-ils ?
(a-t-elle ?)	(ont-elles ?)	(est-elle ?)	(sont-elles ?)

[Pron.—1. ĕ.ž, á tü, á t il, á t ĕl, ávō nu, ávé vu, ō t il, ō t ĕl. 2. süi.ž, ĕ tü, ĕ t il, ĕ t ĕl, sŏm nu, ĕ.t vu, sō t il, sō t ĕl.]

Obs.: 1. The pronoun following the verb is joined to it by a hyphen. 2. Whenever the 3 sing. of a verb ends in a vowel, -t- is inserted between it and the following pronoun, as in a-t-il?, a-t-elle?.

87. Remarks on Interrogation. 1. In an interrogative sentence, the *personal pronoun subject* (so also ce = 'it,' etc., and on = 'one', etc.) *follows* the verb. See paradigm above.

2. But when the subject is a *noun*, the word order is Noun-Verb-Pronoun :

L'homme est-il là ?	Is the man there ?
Jean a-t-il mon chapeau ?	Has John my hat ?

3. Questions are also asked by *interrogative words*, as in English :

Qui est là ?	Qu'a-t-il ?	Who is there ?	What has he ?
Où est votre chapeau ?		Where is your hat ?	

4. The two above methods may, in certain cases, be combined :

Votre chapeau où est-il ?	Where is your hat ?
Où votre père a-t-il son argent ?	Where has your father his money ?

5. By *prefixing* the words **est-ce que ?**, lit., 'is it (the case) that ?,' any statement may be turned into a question :

Vous avez mon chapeau.	You have my hat.
Est-ce que vous avez mon chapeau ?	Have you my hat ?

88. Use of *oui, non*. 1. In answer to a question, **oui** = 'yes,' **non** = 'no,' are followed, for politeness, by **monsieur** (madame, etc.), or by a *complete phrase* or *sentence:*

Avez-vous mon chapeau?—Non, monsieur, *or* Oui, je l'ai, *or* Oui, madame, j'ai votre chapeau.

Have you my hat? No, (sir), *or*, Yes, (I have it), *or*, Yes, (madam, I have your hat).

EXERCISE III.

Le chapeau *(šapó)*, hat.
L'école, f., *(ékòl)*, school.
L'église, f., *(égli.z)*, church.
L'habit, m., *(ábi)*, coat.
Ici *(isi)*, here.
Là *(lá)*, there.
Madame *(mádám)*, madam.
Maman *(mámã)*, mamma.
Monsieur *(mesiö)*, sir.

Non *(nõ)*, no.
Où? *(u)*, where?
Oui *(üi)*, yes.
Que? *(ke)*, what?
Que, conj., *(ke)*, that.
Qui? *(ki)*, who?
La rue *(rü)*, street.
Le village *(vilá.ž)*, village.

A. 1. As-tu? Est-il? Est-ce qu'il est? 2. Est-ce qu'il a? A-t-il? Ont-ils? 3. Est-ce que je suis? Est-ce que vous avez? Sommes-nous? 4. Est-ce qu'ils ont? Sont-elles? Est-ce que tu as? 5. Avons-nous? Est-ce qu'elles sont? Est-ce que j'ai? 6. Es-tu? Est-ce que tu es? Est-ce que nous sommes? 7. Avez-vous? Êtes-vous? Suis-je?

B. 1. Am I? Art thou? Thou art. 2. Is he? Are they (m.)? Are we? 3. Are you? Have you? Have they (f.)? 4. They (m.) are. Have I? I have. 5. Hast thou? Has he? Have we? 6. We have. Have you? Have they (m.)?

C. 1. Jean où est-il? 2. Il est dans la rue. 3. Où est le chapeau? 4. Il est sur la table dans la maison. 5. Qu'avez-vous dans la boîte, monsieur? 6. J'ai l'argent et la montre. 7. Où sommes-nous, maman? 8. L'église où est-elle, madame? 9. Elle est dans le village. 10. Avez-vous une école ici? 11. Oui, madame, nous avons une école dans le village. 12. Qui est là avec le monsieur et la dame? 13. Qui a le livre? 14. Marie a le livre. 15. Où sont les poires? 16. Elles sont dans la boîte. 17. Marie a-t-elle une sœur? 18. Non, madame, mais elle a un frère. 19. Jean, est-ce que tu es là ? 20. Oui, maman, je suis ici dans le jardin. 21. Les messieurs et les dames où sont-ils ? 22. Ils sont dans la maison.

D. 1. Where are the children? 2. They are under the trees in the garden. 3. What have they (m.) in the box? 4. They have a hat in the box. 5. Where are the lady and gentleman? 6. They are in the house. 7. Is the church in the village? 8. Yes, the church is in the village, and the school too. 9. Are the horses under the trees. 10. No, sir, they are in the street. 12. Where are you (2nd sing.) Mary? 13. I am here, mamma, under the tree. 14. Is the dog there under the table? 15. No, madam, he is in the street. 16. Have you the hats and coats? 17. John and Mary, are you there? 18. Yes, mamma, we are here. 19. Have the gentlemen the horses and dogs? 20. Who has the hats? 21. They are there on the table.

LESSON IV.

89.   **The Possessive Adjective.**

Masc.	Fem.	Plur.	Masc.	Fem.	Plur.
mon	ma (mon)	mes, *my.*	notre	notre	nos, *our.*
ton	ta (ton)	tes, *thy.*	votre	votre	vos, *your.*
son	sa (son)	ses, *his, her, its.*	leur	leur	leurs, *their.*

[Pron.—1. mō, má, mè. 2. tō, tá, tè. 3. sō, sá, sè.
1. nôtr, nôtr, nó. 2. vôtr, vôtr, vó. 3. lœ.r, lœ.r, lœ.r.]

Obs.: 1. The forms **mon, ton, son** in parenthesis are used instead of **ma, ta, sa**, *before a vowel or h mute:* **Mon** amie, *my friend* (f.), **ton** histoire (f.), *your story*, **son** aimable tante, *his amiable aunt.* 2. Since **son** (**sa, ses**) means equally 'his,' 'her,' 'its,' it can only be known from the context which is meant.

90. Agreement. A possessive adjective *agrees* with the noun denoting the *object possessed*, and is *repeated* before each noun to which it refers :

J'ai ma plume. Elle a son livre.	I have my pen. She has her book.
Il a sa plume. Nous avons notre argent.	He has his pen. We have our money.
Ils ont leurs livres et leurs plumes.	They have their books and pens.

91. In speaking to a person of his (or her) relatives, the title **monsieur** (pl. *messieurs*), **madame** (pl. *mesdames*),

mademoiselle (pl. *mes*demoiselles) is often politely prefixed, but *never* in speaking to others of one's own relatives:

Madame votre mère est-elle malade ?	Is your mother ill?
Ma mère n'est pas malade.	My mother is not ill?

92. The Pronoun *le, la, les*. The personal pronoun, direct object, of the third person is:—

Masc.	Fem.	Plur.
le (l'), *him, it*.	la (l'), *her, it*.	les, *them*.

[Pron.—*le, lá, lè*.]

Obs.: 1. The forms are exactly like those of the definite article, but stand, not before nouns, but *instead* of nouns. 2. For the forms in parenthesis, see §73.

93. Position and Agreement. *Personal pronoun objects* in French are (with one important exception, §153) *placed immediately before the verb*, not after it like their English equivalents. For agreement, see §81:

Où est la règle ?—Marie l'a.	Where is the ruler ? Mary has it.
Avez-vous le papier et les plumes ?	Have you the paper and pens.
—Je les ai.	I have them.

94. Use of *voici* and *voilà*. 1. **Voici** *(vũási)* = 'here is' or 'here are,' and **voilà** *(vũálá)* = 'there is' or 'there are,' are *preceded* (like verbs) by the *pronouns* and *followed* by the *nouns* they govern.

2. **Voici** and **voilà** must be distinguished from **est** and **sont** + **ici** and **là**:

La dame est ici. Voici la dame.	The lady is here. Here is the lady.
Elles sont là. Les voilà.	They are there. There they are.

Note.—Voici and voilà are made up of voi(s)='see'+ci = 'here' and là = 'there' (lit., 'see here,' 'see there').

95. *Il est* and *c'est*. 1. Translate 'he,' 'she,' 'it,' 'they' by il(s), elle(s) with être + *an adj.*, or + *a predicate noun with adj. force*:

Elle est jeune. Il est âgé.	She is young. He is old.
Cette fleur est jolie ; elle est jolie.	This flower is pretty ; it is pretty.
Il est médecin. Elles sont marchandes.	He is a doctor. They are tradeswomen.
Elle est Allemande.	She is (a) German.

2. But translate 'he,' 'she,' 'it,' 'they' by ce with **être** + *a determinate noun*.

C'est un bon médecin.	He is a good doctor.
Est-ce un Français ?	Is he a Frenchman ?
Ce sont des hommes célèbres.	They are celebrated men.
Sont-ce vos amis ?	Are they your friends ?
C'est une jolie dame.	She is a pretty lady.

NOTE.—A noun with an *article*, a *possessive adjective*, etc., or in the *partitive* construction is said to be *determinate*.

EXERCISE IV.

La chambre *(šā.br)*, room.	Le fils *(fis)*, son.
Le champ *(šã)*, field.	Là-bas *(lá bà)*, yonder.
Le crayon *(krèlõ)*, pencil.	La malle *(mál)*, trunk.
Derrière *(dèriè.r)*, behind.	Le papier *(pápié)*, paper.
Devant *(devã)*, before, in front of.	La plume *(plüm)*, pen.
L'écurie, f., *(ékūri)*, stable.	La porte *(pò.rt)*, door.
L'encre, f., *(ã.kr)*, ink.	À présent *(prézã)*, now.
La fille *(fi.ĭ)*, daughter.	

A. 1. Où est-ce que tu as tes plumes, ma fille ? 2. Je les ai dans ma boîte, maman. 3. Ton papier et ton encre où sont-ils, mon fils ? 4. Les voilà, mon père, sur la table derrière la porte. 5. Vos chevaux, où sont-ils à présent, monsieur ? 6. Ils sont dans l'écurie. 7. Qui a mes livres ? 8. Voici vos livres. 9. Vos chapeaux sont dans la malle dans votre chambre. 10. Jean a sa plume, et Marie a son papier. 11. Où sont vos enfants, madame ? 12. Les voilà, là-bas, dans le champ. 13. Est-ce que vous avez vos plumes et vos crayons ? 14. Oui, monsieur, nous les avons. 15. Où est le chien ? 16. Le voilà devant la porte. 17. Voilà les chiens avec les enfants sous les arbres là-bas. 18. Les messieurs et les dames sont avec mon père et ma mère dans le village. 19. Qui est la dame devant la porte ? 20. C'est ma mère, monsieur. 21. Qui sont les messieurs sous les arbres devant l'école ? 22. Ce sont mon père et mon frère.

B. 1. Where are your brothers and sisters ? 2. They are in the field under the trees. 3. Who has the pen and paper ? 4. I have them. 5. There is our house yonder; who is the gentleman before the door ? 6. It is my father. 7. Their hats and coats are on the table behind the door. 8. Are the horses in the field now? 9. No, sir, they are in the stable. 10. Have you (2nd sing.) your ink and paper, my daughter? 11. No, mamma, they are on the table. 12. Are our pencils in the box? 13. No, here they are. 14. Where is our dog? 15. There he is with the children in the field. 16. Has Mary her pen and pencil? 17. No, sir, John has them. 18. Where is the church in your village? 19. There it is behind the trees. 20. John has his pen, and Mary has her pencil. 21. Who are the ladies in the carriage? 22. They are my sisters.

LESSON V.

96.   Negative Conjugation.

[*I have* not, *etc.*]   [*I am* not, *etc.*]
SING. je n'ai pas.   SING. je ne suis pas.
tu n'as pas.   tu n'es pas.
il n'a pas.   il n'est pas.
PLUR. nous n'avons pas.   PLUR. nous ne sommes pas.
vous n'avez pas.   vous n'êtes pas.
ils n'ont pas.   ils ne sont pas.

[PRON.—1. že né pà, tü n à pà, il n à pà, nu n ávõ pà, vu n ávé pà, il n õ pà. 2. že ne sẗï pà, tü n è pà, il n è pà, nu ne sòm pà, vu n è.t pà, il ne sõ pà.]

Observe: For elision of e in ne, see §73.

97. Remarks on Negation. 1. The negative, *along with a verb*, consists regularly of *two parts*, ne *preceding* the verb, and some other word or words (commonly pas) *following* the verb :

Je ne suis pas son ami.   I am not his friend.
Il n'est point habile.   He is not (at all) clever.
Je ne suis jamais en retard.   I am never late.
Il n'est plus ici.   He is no longer here (or he is not here now).
Ils n'ont que dix francs.   They have only ten francs.

Exc.—Both ne and pas generally *precede* the simple infin. : Donner ou ne pas donner, 'to give or not to give.'

2. If the verb is *omitted* (but *understood*), the **ne** is *omitted*:

Est-il là?—Pas encore (= il n'est pas encore là).   Is he there? Not yet (= he is not yet there).

3. Nothing but the *personal pronoun object(s)* may come between **ne** and the verb:

A-t-il la plume?—Il ne l'a pas.   Has he the pen? He has not (it).

98. Negative Conjugation interrogatively.

[*Have I not?, etc.*]

SING. n'ai-je pas?
n'as-tu pas?
n'a-t-il pas?

PLUR. n'avons-nous pas?
n'avez-vous pas?
n'ont-ils pas?

[*Am I not?, etc.*]

SING. ne suis-je pas?
n'es-tu pas?
n'est-il pas?

PLUR. ne sommes-nous pas?
n'êtes-vous pas?
ne sont-ils pas?

[PRON.—1. *n è.ž pà, n à tü pà, n à t il pà, n árõ nu pà, n àvé vu pà, n õt il pà.* 2. *ne sữi.ž pà, n è tü pà, n èt il pà, ne sòm nu pà, n è.t vu pà, ne sõt il pà.*]

99. Si. 'Yes,' in *correction* or *contradiction* of a *negative,* is more usually **si** (or **pardon**, etc.), *not* **oui**:

Je ne l'ai pas.—Si, monsieur, vous l'avez, *or* Mais si, monsieur, vous l'avez, *or* Pardon, monsieur, vous l'avez.   I haven't it.—Yes, (sir,) you have (it), *or* Excuse me, (sir,) you have (it).

Vous n'avez pas la lettre?—Si, je l'ai.   You have not the letter? Yes, I have (it).

100. Position of the Adverb. An adverb is regularly placed *after the verb* (rarely between subject and verb):

Charles porte souvent ma canne.   Charles often carries my cane.

EXERCISE V.

Aujourd'hui *(ôžurdǘi)*, to-day.
L'autre, m. or f., *(ô.tr)*, other.
Chez *(šé)*, at the house, shop, etc., of.
Le cousin *(kuzẽ)*, cousin.
La cousine *(kuzin)*, cousin.

Parce que *(pàrs ke)*, because.
La poche *(pòš)*, pocket.
Pourquoi? *(purkñá)*, why?
Quatre *(kàtr)*, four.
Quelquefois *(kèlkefǘá)*, sometimes.

Encore *(ăkò.r)*, still, yet.
La fille *(fi.ĭ)*, girl.
La forêt *(fòrè)*, forest.
Le franc *(frã)*, franc (about 20 cts.).
Le garçon *(gársō)*, boy.
En retard *(ã retá.r)*, late.
La robe *(ròb)*, dress.
Toujours *(tužu.r)*, always, still.
Trois *(trŭà)*.

Il est chez mon père. He is at my father's.

A. 1. Pourquoi n'êtes-vous pas chez votre cousin aujourd'hui? Parce que mon cousin est ici. 3. Vous n'avez pas mes crayons, monsieur? 4. Si, monsieur, les voici. 5. Votre cousine qu'a-t-elle dans sa malle? 6. Elle a ses robes et ses chapeaux dans sa malle. 7. Les garçons et les filles, pourquoi sont-ils en retard aujourd'hui? 8. Pardon, ils ne sont pas en retard. 9. Jean, est-il encore chez son père? 10. Non, monsieur, il n'est plus là. 11. Votre fils est-il chez son cousin à présent? 12. Non, monsieur, il est toujours chez notre ami. 13. Est-ce que nous ne sommes pas encore dans le village? 14. Pas encore. 15. N'as-tu que trois francs, mon fils? 16. J'ai trois francs ici dans ma poche et quatre francs dans la maison. 17. N'es-tu plus mon ami, mon garçon? 18. Oh si, monsieur, je suis toujours votre ami. 19. N'avez-vous pas votre livre? 20. Si, monsieur, nous l'avons. 21. Avez-vous encore ma plume? 22. Je ne l'ai plus; votre cousine l'a. 23. Pourquoi n'avez-vous qu'un cheval? 24. Parce que mon père a l'autre.

B. 1. Are you not at my father's now? 2. No, I am no longer there, I am at my cousin's. 3. Have you only one horse? 4. I have four horses and a carriage. 5. You have not your hat. 6. Oh yes, here it is. 7. Why is your cousin (f.) late to-day. 8. She is not late; she is never late. 9. Are your sisters not yet here? 10. Not yet, they are still at our cousin's (m.) 11. Have you not sometimes our pens and paper? 12. Yes, sometimes, but your brother has them now. 13. Are your sisters at your cousin's (f.) in the village. 14. No, they are no longer there. 15. Why have you only three books to-day? 16. Because my brother has the others. 17. Our books and paper are always on the table in the room. 18. I have only one franc in my pocket, but I have three francs in a box in my room. 19. Are you never late? ~~20.~~ Yes, sometimes, but I am not late to-day. 21. Where has your sister her hats and dresses? 22. She has them in her trunk in her room. 23. Haven't you your books to-day? 24. Yes, sir, we always have them.

LESSON VI.

101. The Regular Conjugations. French verbs are conveniently divided, according to the infinitive endings -er, -ir, -re, into three conjugations:—

I.	II.	III.
Donner, *to give.*	Finir, *to finish.*	Rompre, *to break.*

Like these respectively are conjugated all regular verbs with corresponding infinitive ending.

102. Remarks on Conjugation. 1. The distinctions of *voice, mood, tense,* etc., are in general as in English.

2. The distinction between *stem* (generally *invariable* in a given tense) and *ending* (*variable* for mood, tense, etc.) is of great importance.

3. English *periphrastic forms must not be literally translated* into French:

Je donne = { I give, *or* I am giving, *or* I do give. }   Donnez-vous? = { (Give you?), *or* Are you giving?, *or* Do you give? }

103. Present Indicative of *donner, finir, rompre.*

[*I give, am giving, etc.*] [*I finish, am finishing, etc.*] [*I break, am breaking, etc.*]

je donn e.	je fini s.	je romp s.
tu donn es.	tu fini s.	tu romp s.
il donn e.	il fini t.	il romp t.
nous donn ons.	nous finiss ons.	nous romp ons.
vous donn ez.	vous finiss ez.	vous romp ez.
ils donn ent.	ils finiss ent.	ils romp ent.

[Pron.—1. že pá:rl, tü pá.rl, il pá.rl, nn pärlõ, vn pärlé, il pá.rl.
2. že fini, tü fini, il fini, nn finisõ, vn finisé, il finis.
3. že rõ, tü rõ, il rõ, nn rõpõ, vn rõpé, il rõ.p.]

Note.—The letters i and iss of the enlarged stem of **finir** had their origin in *isc* of the Latin inchoative verb.

[103-105.] PRESENT INDICATIVE. 43

Conjugate also, *interrogatively* and *negatively*, according to rules already given (§§ 86, 87, 96, 97, 98):

[*Do I speak?, am I speaking?, etc.*] [*I do not finish, am not finishing, etc.*]
parlé-je, *or* est-ce que je parle?   je ne finis pas.
parles-tu, *or* est-ce que tu parles?   tu ne finis pas.
parle-t-il, *or* est-ce qu'il parle?   il ne finit pas.
parlons-nous, *or* est-ce que nous parlons?   nous ne finissons pas.
     etc.   etc.   etc.

[*Do I not break?, am I not breaking?, etc.*]
est-ce que je ne romps pas?
ne romps-tu pas?, *or* est-ce que tu ne romps pas?, etc.
ne rompons-nous pas?, *or* est-ce que nous ne rompons pas?, etc.

Obs.: 1. The form parlé-je? *(párlè.ž)* is commonly avoided by est-ce que? 2. When the 1 sing. pres. indic. is a *monosyllable* est-ce que? is *alone permissible* (est-ce que je romps?, etc.). But ai-je?, suis-je?, and some others are allowed.

104. The use of the Present Indicative is in general like that of English, but observe its idiomatic use to denote *what has been and still continues to be:*

Depuis (= 'since') quand (= 'when')   How long have you been here?
     êtes-vous ici?
Je suis ici depuis trois jours.   I have been here for three days
     (*or* for three days past, *or* for the
     last three days).

105. N'est-ce pas? (= lit., 'Is it not?') is equivalent to English 'Do I not?,' 'Is he not?,' 'Had they not?,' etc., etc.:

Il a rompu ma canne, n'est-ce pas? He broke my cane, did he not?

EXERCISE VI.

À *(á)*, to.
Avant *(avã)*, before (of time).
La branche *(brã.š)*, branch.
La canne *(kán)*, cane, walking-stick.
Depuis *(depǜi)*, since.
Le(la)domestique *(dòmèstik)*, servant.
Fatigué *(fátigé)*, tired.
Grand *(grã)*, great, large.
Méchant *(méšã)*, naughty.
Midi *(midi)*, noon.
De bonne heure. Early.

L'oncle *(õ.kl)*, uncle.
L'ouvrage, m., *(uvrá.ž)*, work.
Parler *(párlé)*, speak.
Petit *(peti)*, little.
Le professeur *(pròfèsœ.r)*, teacher.
La tante *(tã.t)*, aunt.
Quand *(kã)*, when.
La semaine *(semèn)*, week.
Le thème *(tè.m)*, exercise.
Le vent *(vã)*, wind.

A. 1. Jean que donne-t-il à sa mère ? 2. Il donne sa plume et son crayon. 3. Nous donnons nos livres et nos thèmes à notre professeur. 4. Pourquoi ne les donnez-vous pas à votre père ? 5. Finissez-vous votre ouvrage, mes enfants ? 6. Oui, monsieur, nous le finissons. 7. Les enfants donnent leur argent à leur père. 8. Je parle à ma mère et à ma sœur. 9. Mon père et ma mère parlent à mon oncle. 10. Le vent rompt les grands arbres. 11. Les petits garçons rompent les branches. 12. Les domestiques finissent leur ouvrage de bonne heure, n'est-ce pas ? 13. Oui, monsieur, ils le finissent toujours avant midi. 14. Vous rompez votre canne, n'est-ce pas ? 15. Non, madame, je ne la romps pas. 18. Pourquoi ne finissez-vous pas vos thèmes ? 19. Parce que nous sommes fatigués. 20. Pourquoi ne parles-tu pas à ton frère ? 21. Parce qu'il est méchant. 22. Finissez-vous vos thèmes ? 23. Non, monsieur, nous ne les finissons pas aujourd'hui. 24. Les enfants ne finissent-ils pas leurs thèmes ? 25. Oui, monsieur, ils les finissent. 26. Marie finit-elle son ouvrage ? 27. Oui, madame, elle le finit. 28. Donnes-tu ton argent à ton père ? 29. Non, monsieur, je ne le donne pas à mon père, je le donne à mon oncle. 30. Depuis quand les enfants sont-ils ici ? 31. Ils sont ici depuis une semaine.

B. 1. Do you finish your work early ? 2. I finish always before noon. 3. Why do you not give your exercise to your teacher, my boy *(enfant)?* 4. I do give it to my teacher. 5. Why is John breaking the box ? 6. He is breaking it because he is naughty ? 7. Does the wind not break the great branches ? 8. Yes, it breaks the branches and the trees too. 9. Are you giving your pens and pencils to your mother, my children ? 10. The servants are finishing their work, are they not ? 11. No, they are not finishing it to-day ; they are tired. 12. Why does that boy not speak to his sister ? 13. Because he is naughty. 14. We are giving our friend a horse and carriage. 15. You give your brother a book. 16. John does not speak to his brother. 17. Mary does not finish her exercise. 18. You are breaking the cane, are you not ? 19. No, sir, I am not breaking it. 20. Mary never speaks to her cousin (f.). 21. Why does Mary not give her cousin (f.) the book ?

23. Because she hasn't it. 24. Why do they (m.) not give their mother their money? 25. They give it to their father. 26. You do not finish your work? 27. Oh yes *(mais si)*, I do finish it. 28. The fathers are speaking to their sons. 29. The little boy does not finish his work. 30. The mother and her daughter are finishing their work. 31. How long have the ladies been there? 32. They have been there for a week.

LESSON VII.

106. The Genitive and Dative Relation. 1. A frequent use of **de** (= 'of,' etc.) + *a substantive* is to indicate the *possessive* or *genitive* relation :

La mère de Marie.	Mary's mother (*or* the mother of Mary)
Le père de mon père.	My father's father.
La branche d'un arbre.	The branch of a tree.

2. A frequent use of **à** (= 'to,' 'for,' etc.) + *a substantive* is to indicate the *indirect object* or *dative* relation:

Il parle à son père.	He is speaking to his father.
Je prête mon couteau à Jean.	I lend John my knife (*or* my knife to J.)

Obs.: The prep. in this construction must never be omitted before nouns as it often is in English.

3. Many verbs, such as those of *obeying, asking, depriving*, govern a *dative* in French, though not in English:

L'enfant obéit à son père.	The child obeys his father.
Le père ôte le couteau à son enfant.	The father takes away the knife from his child.
Il demande deux francs à son père.	He asks his father for two francs.

4. The verb **être** + **à** is often used to denote *simple ownership:*

Le livre à qui est-il?	To whom does the book belong? (*or* Whose is the book ?).
Le livre est à Jean.	The book is John's (*or* belongs to John).

5. **De** and **à** must be *repeated* before each noun they govern :

Je parle à mon frère et à ma sœur.	I speak to my brother and sister.

107. Contraction of *de* and *à* with *le* and *les*. De and *à* before the article le, les are *always contracted* as follows:—

du (=de le).   au (=à le).
de l'   à l'
de la   à la
des (=de les).   aux (=à les).

Obs.: *No contraction* with the pronoun le, la, les: Je parle de le donner, ' I speak of giving it.'

108. The Dative Personal Pronoun 3rd Person.

SING.   PLUR.
lui, *(to, for)* him, or *(to, for)* her.   leur, *(to, for)* them.

[PRON.—*lü̈i, læ.r.*]

109. Lui and **leur** *precede* the *verb* (§93), but *follow* le, la, les:

Nous lui parlons.   We are speaking to him (*or* to her).
Je donne une rose à Marie.   I am giving Mary a rose.
Je la lui donne.   I give her it (*or* it to her).
Je prête mes livres aux enfants. I lend the children my books.
Je les leur prête.   I lend them (to) them.

EXERCISE VII.

À *(á)*, to, at.   Demander *(demãdé)*, ask, ask for.
Aimer *(èmé)*, like, love.   La gare *(gá.r)*, (railway-)station.
Bien *(biẽ)*, well.   Obéir à *(òbéi.r)*, obey.
Le charpentier *(šarpãtié)*, carpenter.   La planche *(plã.š)*, board, plank.
Chercher *(šèršé)*, look for.   Prêter *(prètè)*, lend.
Le couteau *(kutó)*, knife.   Le sou *(su)*, cent, half-penny.
Déjà *(déžá)*, already.   Le voisin *(vüázẽ)*, neighbour.

A. 1. Le petit garçon que donne-t-il à son père? 2. Il lui donne le chapeau de sa sœur, n'est-ce pas? 3. Qui est là-bas dans le jardin de ton père? 4. C'est le charpentier; il cherche une planche. 5. La fille du monsieur, pourquoi n'obéit-elle pas à son professeur? 6. Elle ne lui obéit pas, parce qu'elle ne l'aime pas. 7. Jean demande un sou à son père. 8. À qui est le livre sur la table? 9. Il est à la dame. 10. Les chevaux des messieurs ne sont plus dans l'écurie. 11. Les malles des dames sont déjà à la gare. 12. Pourquoi ne prêtez-vous pas votre couteau à l'enfant ? 13. Il ne demande pas mon couteau. 14. Les enfants de nos amis ne leur obéissent pas toujours. 15. Que demandez-vous à votre mère ? 16. Je lui demande un couteau. 17. Les enfants de notre cousin donnent les pommes aux enfants du voisin. 18. Nous prêtons nos plumes aux enfants du professeur. 19. Voilà les chiens des messieurs dans le jardin de votre oncle. 20. Marie demande une pomme à sa mère, et une poire à sa sœur. 21. Où sont les planches du charpentier ? 22. Les voilà derrière l'écurie. 23. Jean, que cherches-tu dans la boîte de ta sœur ? 24. Je cherche les plumes de mon père. 25. Est-ce que vous obéissez à votre père et à votre mère ? 26. Oui, monsieur, nous leur obéissons toujours. 27. Que cherchez-vous dans le jardin ? 28. Nous cherchons le chapeau de l'enfant. 29. Tu ne demandes pas ton couteau à ta mère ? 30. Si, monsieur, je le lui demande.

B. 1. He gives his father his books, does he not ? 2. Yes, sir, he gives him them. 3. Does John obey his father and mother ? 4. Yes, he obeys them always. 5. Has your father's servant a dog ? 6. No, sir, the dog belongs to our neighbour. 7. The watch on the table is my father's. 9. Are the gentleman's horses still in the stable ? 10. No, sir, they are in the field. 11. Mary gives her book to the teacher. 12. Do the trunks belong to the ladies ? 13. Yes, sir, and the hats too. 14. The lady's children do not obey their teacher, because they do not like him. 15. Why do you (2nd sing.) not speak to the gentleman ? 16. Because I do not like him. 17. Where are the carpenter's boards ? 18. They are in the stable. 19. Why do you not give them to him ? 20. Because he does not ask for them. 21. Who has the apples ? 22. Our neighbour's children have them. 23. Why do you not obey your teacher ? 24. We obey him always. 25. Are you asking your father for the apples ? 26. Yes, sir, we ask him for them. 27. What are you looking for ? 28. I am looking for my father's hat. 29. Whose is the horse in the field ? 30. He is my uncle's. 31. Are the ladies' trunks at the station ? 32. Yes, sir, they are there. 33. I am speaking to the carpenter's son. 34. Why does our friend's daughter not obey her father ? 35. She obeys him always.

LESSON VIII.

110. The Partitive Noun. 'Some' (or 'any'), whether *expressed* or *implied* before a noun in English, is regularly *expressed* in French by **de** + *the definite article:*

J'ai de l'argent.	I have (some) money (lit., **of the** money).
A-t-il de l'argent ?	Has he (any) money ?
Avec des amis.	With (some) friends.

NOTE.—A noun in this construction is said to be used in a *partitive* sense or *partitively*, because a *part only* of the whole (money, friends, etc.), is denoted.

111. The definite article is *omitted* before a partitive noun, and **de** *alone* is used :—

1. When an adjective *precedes* the **noun** *(not when it follows):*

Nous avons de jolies fleurs.	We have (some) pretty flowers.
Avez-vous de bon fromage ?	Have you (any) good cheese ?
J'ai de votre argent.	I have some of your money.
But: **Des** soldats français.	(Some) French soldiers.

So also, when the *noun after an adj. is understood:*

De bonnes plumes et de mauvaises.	Good pens and bad (ones).

2. After a *negative:*

Il n'a pas de livres.	He has no (=not any) books.
Il n'a jamais d'argent.	He never has any money.

112. Both **de** and the *definite article* are *omitted :*—
1. After **de** in expressions of *quantity* or *number:*

Beaucoup de thé.		Much (*or* a great deal of) tea.	
Une livre de viande.	Assez de viande.	A pound of meat.	Enough (of) meat.
Un morceau de pain.	Trop de pain.	A piece of bread.	Too much bread.

2. After **ne ... ni ... ni** = ' neither ... nor,' and generally after **sans** = ' without ' :

Je n'ai ni plumes ni encre.	I have neither pens nor ink.
Sans amis et sans argent.	Without friends and without money.

113. The General Noun. 1. A noun used in a *general* sense takes the definite article in French, though not commonly in English :

L'homme est mortel.	Man is mortal.
Le fer est très utile.	Iron is very useful.
Le cheval est un animal utile.	The horse is a useful animal.
J'aime le thé et le café.	I like tea and coffee.
La nécessité est la mère de l'invention.	Necessity is the mother of invention.
J'étudie la musique et le français.	I study music and French.

2. This *general* sense is to be carefully distinguished from the *partitive* sense (§110):

Les hommes sont des animaux.	Men are animals.
Les arbres ont des branches.	Trees have branches.

114. Names of *continents, countries, provinces, large islands* as *subject* or *object* of a verb regularly take the *def. art.*:

La France est un beau pays.	France is a beautiful country.
Nous aimons le Canada.	We love Canada.

So also, after a *preposition* (except en = 'in,' 'to,' and de in certain constructions):

Nous demeurons au Canada.	We live in Canada.
But: Mon père est en Angleterre.	My father is in England.

115. After de the *definite article* is regularly *omitted before any noun* (whether the noun be *partitive, general, geographical,* or otherwise) in *adjectival* and *adverbial* phrases:

Une robe de soie.	A silk dress.
Il est digne de confiance.	He is worthy of confidence.
Un roi de France.	A French king.
L'arbre est couvert de feuilles.	The tree is covered with leaves.

116. *Possession* is expressed by the *definite article* (or by the *def. art. + a dat. pron.*) if there is *no ambiguity* as to the possessor:

Je vous donne la main.	I give you my hand.
Ils ôtent le chapeau.	They take off their hats.
Il leur coupe les cheveux.	He is cutting their hair.

EXERCISE VIII.

Animal, m., *(ánimál)*, animal.	L'or, m., *(ô.r)*, gold.
Assez de *(ásé)*, enough (of).	Le pain *(pè)*, bread.

Beau *(bó)*, beautiful.
Beaucoup de *(bóku)*, much, many.
Bon *(bŏ)*, good.
La capitale *(kápitál)*, capital.
Demeurer *(demŏré)*, live, dwell.
En *(ă)*, in.
L'épicier *(épislé)*, grocer.
Le fer *(fĕ.r)*, iron.
Le fromage *(frŏmá.ž)*, cheese.
L'homme *(ŏm)*, man.
Ici-bas *(isi bà)*, here below.
Le morceau *(mŏrsó)*, piece.

Le pays *(péi)*, country.
Penser *(pãsé)*, think.
Peu de *(pŏ)*, little.
Pour *(pu.r)*, for.
Riche *(riš)*, rich.
La soie *(sŭá)*, silk.
Travailler *(travăié)*, work.
Très *(trè)*, very.
Trop de *(trŏ)*, too much, too many.
Utile *(ŭtil)*, useful.
La vertu *(vèrtŭ)*, virtue.

Avez-vous encore de l'argent ?   Have you any more money ?
Je n'ai plus d'argent.   I have no more money.
Je n'ai guère d'argent.   I have but little money.
Je n'ai que peu d'amis.   I have but few friends.
Nous les aimons beaucoup.   We like them very much.

A. 1. La mère donne des pommes et des poires à sa fille. 2. Pourquoi ne demandes-tu pas un sou à ton père ? 3. Parce qu'il n'a pas d'argent. 4. L'épicier a de bon fromage. 5. Avez-vous encore du pain? 6. Je n'ai plus de pain. 7. Le monsieur est-il riche ? 8. Non, madame, il a très peu d'argent. 9. Les hommes aiment la vertu. 10. Le fer est très utile. 11. Le Canada est un beau pays. 12. Nos amis demeurent en France, mais nous demeurons au Canada. 13. Paris est la capitale de la France. 14. L'homme pense et travaille ici-bas. 15. Les chiens sont quelquefois très utiles. 16. Avez-vous des plumes ou des crayons? 17. Je n'ai ni plumes ni crayons. 18. Que donnez-vous à la sœur du professeur ? 19. Je lui donne des pommes. 20. Avez-vous beaucoup de pommes? 21. Nous n'avons que peu de pommes. 22. Que demandez-vous au monsieur ? 23. Je lui demande un morceau de pain. 24. Le cheval travaille pour l'homme. 25. La dame a une robe de soie. 26. Le monsieur a une montre d'or. 27. Nous avons trop de pain, mais pas assez de pommes. 28. Les enfants de nos amis ont de beaux chiens. 29. Nous n'avons plus de pommes, mais nous avons encore des poires. 30. Les hommes aiment beaucoup l'argent.

B. 1. Do you like pears? 2. Yes, we like them very much. 3. Horses are animals, and men are animals also. 4. Have you any good bread? 5. Yes, madam, we have good bread and good cheese also. 6. France is a beautiful country. 7. Ottawa is the capital of Canada. 8. Has the carpenter any money? 9. No, sir, he has no money. 10. Have we any ink and paper? 12. No, sir, we have neither ink nor paper. 13. Here below men work and think. 14. What are you asking my father for? 15. I am asking him for some paper. 16. The lady has a silk dress and a gold watch. 17. The grocer has good bread and cheese. 18. Have the children silk dresses? 19. No, madam, they have no silk dresses. 20. Have you much money? 21. We have but little money. 22. We have too many apples, but not enough pears. 23. We are not rich, we have neither gold watches nor silk dresses. 24. Have you many pens? 25. We have but few pens. 26. Have you any more paper? 27. I have no more paper, but I have still some ink. 28. I like apples and pears. 29. We have no more bread. 30. Paris and Ottawa are capitals. 31. Our friends are in France. 32. Horses are useful. 33. Children love their friends. 34. We have but few friends here. 35. I have but little money.

LESSON IX.

117. **Past Participles.**

[*Given.*]   [*Finished.*]   [*Broken.*]   [*Had.*]   [*Been.*]
donné.   fini.   rompu.   eu.   été.

[PRON.—*dòné, fini, rõpü, ü, été.*]

118. The Compound Tenses of a verb are formed from its *past participle* along with an auxiliary (usually avoir, sometimes être), as in the following section.

119.   **The Past Indefinite.**

[*I have given*, or   [*I have finished*, or   [*I have broken*, or
 I gave, etc.]   *I finished, etc.*]   *I broke, etc.*]
j'ai donné.   j'ai fini.   j'ai rompu.
tu as donné, etc.   tu as fini, etc.   tu as rompu, etc.

[*I have had*, or *I had*, etc.]	[*I have been*, or *I was*, etc.]
j'ai eu. nous avons eu.	j'ai été. nous avons été.
tu as eu. vous avez eu.	tu as été. vous avez été.
il a eu. ils ont eu.	il a été. ils ont été.

[PRON.—1. *zé ü, tü áz ü, il á ü, nuz avōz ü, vuz avéz ü, ilz ōt ü.* 2. *zé été, tü áz été, il á été, nuz avōz été, vuz avéz été, ilz ōt été.*]

120. Word Order. *The auxiliary is the verb in a compound tense*, and all rules of word order apply to it:

Le leur a-t-il donné?	Has he given it to them?
Nous ne l'avons pas fini.	We have not finished it.
N'a-t-elle jamais été ici?	Has she never been here?

121. Agreement of the Past Participle. 1. In a compound tense the *past participle agrees* in gender and number with a *direct object* which *precedes*:

| J'ai fini mes leçons; je les ai finies. | I have finished my lessons; I have finished them. |
| Quels livres leur a-t-il donnés? | What books did he give them? |

2. When *used as an adjective*, the past participle *agrees like an adjective*:

| Une canne rompue. | A broken cane. |

122. The Past Indefinite denotes not only what *has happened* or *has been happening*, but also what *happened* (= Eng. *past*):

J'ai fini mon ouvrage.	I (have) finished my work.
Il a été ici hier soir.	He was here yesterday evening.
Elle a chanté toute la matinée.	She has been singing all morning.
Je les ai visités en 1885.	I visited them in 1885.
J'ai quitté Paris l'hiver passé.	I left Paris last winter.
Dieu a créé le monde en six jours.	God created the world in six days.

N.B.—The Past Indefinite is the *ordinary past tense* of French. For the past tense of narrative in the literary style see §136.

123. Observe the following idiomatic expressions of frequent use, formed from **avoir** + *an undetermined noun*:

Avoir besoin de, *be in need of*, *need*.
Avoir chaud, *be warm*, ⎫ (of living
Avoir froid, *be cold*, ⎭ beings).
Avoir envie de, *wish to*, *desire to*, *etc*.
Avoir faim, *be hungry*.
Avoir honte de, *be ashamed of*.
Avoir mal à, *have...ache (a sore...)*.
Avoir peur de, *be afraid of*.
Avoir raison de, *be right to*.
Avoir soif, *be thirsty*.
Avoir sommeil, *be sleepy*.
Avoir tort de, *be wrong to*.

EXERCISE IX.

Allumer *(álümé)*, kindle, light.
Bien *(biè)*, very.
Le bois *(bŭá)*, wood.
Déchirer *(déširé)*, tear.
L'eau, f., *(ó)*, water.
La fenêtre *(fenè.tr)*, window.
Fermer *(fèrmé)*, close.
Le feu *(fŭ)*, fire.
Hier *(iè.r)*, yesterday.
Jouer *(žué)*, play.
La leçon *(lesõ)*, lesson.
Le mendiant *(mãdiã)*, beggar.
Pauvre *(pó.vr)*, poor.
Porter *(pòrté)*, wear.
Rester *(rèsté)*, stay.
Tomber *(tõbé)*, fall.

A. 1. Avez-vous fini vos leçons, mes enfants ? 2. Nous ne les avons pas encore finies. 3. Avez-vous donné l'argent au petit garçon ? 4. Je ne le lui ai pas donné. 5. Voilà le chapeau de votre père ; pourquoi ne le lui avez-vous pas donné ? 6. Je ne le lui ai pas donné, parce qu'il ne l'a pas demandé. 7. L'enfant a-t-il rompu les morceaux de bois ? 8. Non, monsieur, il ne les a pas rompus. 9. Marie pourquoi ne porte-t-elle pas sa robe de soie. 10. Parce qu'elle l'a déchirée. 11. Les dames ont froid ; pourquoi ne fermez-vous pas les fenêtres ? 12. Je ne les ai pas fermées, parce que j'ai chaud. 13. Marie ne porte pas sa robe de soie parce qu'elle a peur de la déchirer. 14. Vous avez tort de rester toujours ici. 15. Est-ce que j'ai tort, maman, de jouer avec Jean ? 16. Non, mon fils, tu as raison de jouer avec le petit garçon. 17. Jean a soif ; il demande de l'eau à sa mère. 18. Le pauvre mendiant a froid et faim ; il demande du pain. 19. Nous avons allumé le feu, parce que les dames et les messieurs ont froid. 20. Est-ce que vous avez eu froid hier ? 21. Oui, monsieur, nous avons eu bien froid. 22. Le petit garçon a peur de jouer avec les autres, il a peur de tomber. 23. Que demande-t-il ? 24. Il demande de l'argent ; il a besoin de plumes et de crayons. 27. N'as-tu pas honte de déchirer ta robe ? 28. Je ne l'ai pas déchirée, maman. 29. Que demandes-tu, mon enfant ? 30. Je demande du pain ; j'ai faim. 31. Pourquoi n'allumez-vous pas le feu ? 32. Parce que nous n'avons pas besoin de feu ; nous avons assez chaud. 33. Où est le chapeau de soie de votre père ? 34. Le voilà sur la table.

B. 1. Why have you not kindled the fire? 2. We are not cold; we are warm enough. 3. Why have you not closed the windows? 4. We have closed them. 5. Why did you not give your uncle the apples? 6. Because he has no need of apples. 6. There is your sister's silk dress; why did you not give it to her? 8. I did not give it to her, because she did not ask for it. 9. Were you not cold yesterday? 10. Yes, sir, we were very cold, but we are warm enough to-day. 11. Did the little boy break the pieces of wood? 12. Yes, he broke them. 13. Why does the lady not wear her silk dress to-day? 14. She does not wear it because she is afraid of tearing it. 15. Have you finished your exercises, *(mes)* children? 16. Yes, sir, we have finished them. 17. The poor little boy is hungry and cold; he has need of bread. 18. What is the beggar asking for? 19. He is asking for bread and water. 20. There is the gentleman's silk hat; why did you not give it to him? 21. I did not give it to him, because he did not ask for it. 22. Are you asking for water? 23. No, sir, I am asking for bread; I am hungry. 24. We are cold, why did you not close the windows? 25. We did not close them because we are warm enough. 26. There is a poor beggar; why do you not give him bread? 27. We have already given him bread and water. 28. Why does Mary no longer wear her silk dress? 29. Because she is afraid of tearing it. 32. Am I wrong in playing with the others? 33. No, my boy, you are right. 34. We gave the little boy bread, because he was hungry. 35. Are we right in giving him money? 36. No, sir, you are wrong; he does not need money.

LESSON X.

124. Imperfect Indicative of *donner, finir, rompre.*

[*I was giving, I used to give, etc.*]	[*I was finishing, I used to finish, etc.*]	[*I was breaking, I used to break, etc.*]
je donn **ais**.	je fin*iss* **ais**.	je romp **ais**.
tu donn **ais**.	tu fin*iss* **ais**.	tu romp **ais**.
il donn **ais**.	il fin*iss* **ait**.	il romp **ait**.
nous donn **ions**.	nous fin*iss* **ions**.	nous romp **ions**.
vous donn **iez**.	vous fin*iss* **iez**.	vous romp **iez**.
ils donn **aient**.	ils fin*iss* **aient**.	ils romp **aient**.

[PRON.—1. že dòně, tü dòně, il dòně, nu dònĭõ, vu dònĭé, il dòně. 2. že finisè, tü finisè, il finisè, nu finisĭõ, vu finisĭé, il finisè. 3. že rōpè, tü rōpè, il rōpè, nu rōpĭõ, vu rōpĭé, il rōpè.]

Obs.: The stem of **finir** shows the enlargement *iss* (§103, note).

125. Imperfect Indicative of *avoir*, *être*.

[*I had, used to have, etc.*]   [*I was, used to be, etc.*]

j'av ais.   nous av ions.   j'ét ais.   nous ét ions.
tu av ais.   vous av iez.   tu ét ais.   vous ét iez.
il av ait.   ils av aient.   il ét ait.   ils ét aient.

[PRON.—1. ž ávè, tü ávè, il ávè, nuz ávĭõ, vuz ávĭé, ilz ávè. 2. ž été, tü été, il été, nuz étĭõ, vuz étĭé, ilz été.]

126. The Imperfect denotes:—1. What *used to* happen or *continued to happen*:

Nous parlions souvent de la guerre.   We often used to speak (*or* spoke) of the war.
Mon oncle était négociant.   My uncle was a merchant.
Il marchait souvent à Paris.   He would often walk to Paris.
Les Romains brûlaient leurs morts.   The Romans were accustomed to burn their dead.

2. What *was happening*, when something else *happened* or *was happening*:

L'enfant pleurait, quand je l'ai trouvé.   The child was weeping, when I found him.
Il parlait, pendant que nous chantions.   He was speaking, while we sang (*or* were singing).

3. What *had been* and *still continued to be*, with **depuis**, etc. (cf. §104):

J'attendais depuis midi.   I had been waiting since noon.
Depuis quand étiez-vous là?   How long had you been there?

127. Place 'where', or 'whither', is denoted by à, en, dans, as follows:— 1. Place *at which, in which, to which*, usually à with *common nouns*:

Au jardin, à la poste.   In the garden, at the post-office.
Il est (marche) à la ville.   He is in (walks to) the city.
À la campagne.   In the country, to the country.
À l'église.   At church, to church.
À l'école.   At school, to school.

So also with names of *cities, towns, villages* and most *countries masc.:*

Il est (marche) à Paris.	He is in (walks to) Paris.
Nous demeurons au Canada.	We live in Canada.

2. Feminine names of *continents, countries, provinces, large islands* take **en**, always *without* the *definite article* (§114):

Il est (va) en France.	He is in (goes to) France.

3. **Dans** denotes *place within which* or *into which*, and is more specific than à or en:

L'argent est au magasin dans le tiroir.	The money is at the shop in the drawer.
Il entre dans la maison.	He goes into the house.

EXERCISE X.

Aller *(ále)*, go.
L'année, f., *(áné)*, year.
Apprendre *(áprã.dr)*, learn.
La dent *(dã)*, tooth.
Donner *(dòné)*, give away.
Dormir *(dòrmi.r)*, sleep.
L'école, f., *(ecòl)*, school.
Ensemble *(ãsã.bl)*, together.
La famille *(fámi.ĭ)*, family.
Jamais *(žámè)*, ever.
Londres, m., *(lõ.dr)*, London.
Lorsque *(lòrske)*, when (never interrog.).
Madame, Mme *(mádám)*, Mrs.
Mademoiselle, Mlle *(mádmñázèl)*, Miss.
Monsieur, M., *(mesiö)*, Mr.
La philosophie *(filòzòfi)*, philosophy.
Pleurer *(plöré)*, weep, cry.
Quand *(kã)*, when.
Rencontrer *(rãkõtré)*, meet.
Souvent *(surã)*, often.
La tête *(tè.t)*, head.
Triste *(trist)*, sad.
Trouver *(truvé)*, find.
La ville *(vil)*, town, city.

Qu'avez-vous, monsieur?	What is the matter with you, sir?
Je n'ai rien.	Nothing (is the matter with me).
L'année passée.	Last year.

A. 1. Avez-vous jamais été à Paris? 2. Non, monsieur, je n'ai jamais été à Paris, mais j'ai été à Londres. 3. Nous parlions souvent à monsieur votre père, lorsque il demeurait à Londres. 4. Les garçons de nos familles jouaient souvent ensemble, quand nous demeurions à la campagne. 5. Avez-vous été à l'église hier? 6. Oui, monsieur, nous avons été à l'église ensemble. 7. Quand avez-vous été à

Paris? 8. J'ai été à Paris l'année passée. 9. J'avais une montre d'or et un chapeau de soie, quand j'étais à la ville. 10. Vous avez rencontré M. Béjart, n'est-ce pas? 11. Oui, je l'ai rencontré, quand il demeurait à notre village. 12. M. Chopin est triste aujourd'hui, qu'a-t-il? 13. Il a mal aux dents. 14. Le petit garçon a sommeil; il a besoin de dormir. 17. Vous étiez triste hier; qu'aviez-vous, madame? 18. Je n'avais rien. 19. Depuis quand étiez-vous là, lorsqu'il a trouvé son argent? 20. Depuis une semaine; il l'a trouvé derrière la maison. 21. Il le cherchait depuis trois semaines, lorsqu'il l'a trouvé. 22. Les enfants où ont-ils été? 23. Ils ont été à l'école. 24. Avez-vous envie d'aller à la ville? 25. Non, monsieur, pas aujourd'hui. 26. Mlle Béjart a envie de porter sa robe de soie. 27. M. Jourdain avait envie d'apprendre la philosophie. 28. Lorsque j'étais à l'église hier, j'ai trouvé de l'argent. 29. Mlles Jourdain et Béjart étaient à l'église ensemble. 30. Le monsieur avait mal aux dents, et je ne lui ai pas parlé. 31. J'ai rencontré M. Chopin, quand il demeurait à la campagne. 32. Il avait souvent mal à la tête, quand il demeurait chez sa sœur. 33. Le monsieur n'avait pas peur de donner de l'argent à son vieux domestique.

B. 1. I often used to speak to him, when we lived in the city. 2. The children were at school, when we were at their father's. 3. When we were living in the village, we would often give money to the poor (pl.). 4. Why did you not speak to him? 5. Because he was tired. 6. Did you have the toothache yesterday? 7. No, sir, but I had the headache. 8. Mme Jourdain had no desire to learn philosophy. 9. M. Jourdain is sad to-day; what is the matter with him? 10. He is sad because he has given away his money to M. Dorante. 11. I found some money, when I was at church yesterday. 13. The father does not wish to give his son money. 14. I met him yesterday, when I was in the village. 15. His sister used to give him ink and pens, when they were at school. 16. What is the matter with you, my boy? 17. I am tired, and have need of sleep. 18. How long had you been in the country, when I gave your father the money? 19. Where were you, when the children were playing under the trees? 20. We were working in the field. 21. When I was at my father's, my brother had a desire to go to the city. 22. When did you give your brother your gold watch? 23. I gave it to him last year, when I was at my sister's. 24. You are sad to-day; what is the matter with you? 25. I have toothache and headache. 26. Why do you not look for a doctor? 27. Because we have no doctor in our village. 28. We were finishing our exercises, when you were at school. 29. We finished our lessons yesterday. 30. You have been crying, my son; what was the matter with you? 31. I was hungry, when I was at school, mamma. 32. How long had you been there, when I gave him the books? 33. I had been there a week.

LESSON XI.

128. The Feminine of an Adjective is regularly formed by adding **e** to the *masc. sing.*, but adjectives ending in **e** remain *unchanged:*

M. Grand,	*F.* grande,	*tall.*	*M.* Facile,	*F.* facile,	*easy.*
Joli,	jolie,	*pretty.*	Jeune,	jeune,	*young.*
Aîné,	aînée,	*elder.*	Sincère,	sincère,	*sincere.*

129. Irregularities consist chiefly in *changes of the stem* on adding the feminine sign **e**. Thus, when **e** is added:—

1. Final **f = v, x = s, r** (of nouns in -eur as adjs.) **= s, c = ch** or **qu, g = gu**:

M. Actif,	*F.* active,	*active.*	*M.* Blanc,	*F.* blanche,	*white.*
Bref,	brève (§17, 2),	*brief.*	Franc,	franche,	*frank.*
Heureux,	heureuse,	*happy.*	Sec,	sèche (§17, 2),	*dry.*
Précieux,	précieuse,	*precious.*	Public,	publique,	*public.*
Flatteur,	flatteuse,	*flattering.*	Long,	longue,	*long.*

[EXC.—For **x**: Doux, douce, *sweet;* faux, fausse, *false;* roux, rousse, *red* (of hair, etc.), retain the *s sound* (§15, 13) in the fem.]

2. Final -el, -eil, -ien, -on and frequently -s, -t *double the final consonant:*

M. Cruel,	F. cruelle, *cruel.*	M. Bas,	F. basse, *low.*
Pareil,	pareille, *like.*	Gras,	grasse, *fat.*
Ancien,	ancienne, *ancient.*	Gros,	grosse, *big.*
Bon,	bonne, *good.*	Muet,	muette, *dumb.*

So also, gentil, gentille, *nice;* nul, nulle, *null.*
But: Ras, rase, *flat;* prêt, prête, *ready,* and a few others.

3. The following have *two masc. forms,* one of which *doubles* l for the feminine:

M. Beau *or* bel,	F. belle, *fine.*	M. Nouveau *or* nouvel,	F. nouvelle, *new.*
Fou *or* fol,	folle, *mad.*	Vieux *or* vieil,	vieille, *old.*
Mou *or* mol,	molle, *soft.*		

Obs.: The form in -l is used only *before a vowel* or h *mute:* Le bel arbre; Le bel homme. But: L'arbre est **beau**; Le **beau** pays; Les **beaux** arbres; Les arbres sont **beaux**.

4. An o *before a final consonant* becomes è unless the consonant be doubled (§17, 2, note):

M. Cher,	F. chère, *dear.*	M. Sec,	F. sèche, *dry.*
Léger,	légère, *light.*	Complet,	complète, *complete.*
Bref,	brève, *brief.*	Secret,	secrète, *secret.*

130. Position. 1. An *attributive* adjective more usually *follows* its noun:

Un homme riche. Une pomme mûre. A rich man. A ripe apple.

2. Adjs. from *proper nouns,* adjs. of *physical quality, participles as adjs.,* almost always *follow:*

La langue anglaise.   The English language.
Du café chaud. Une lampe cassée. Hot coffee. A broken lamp.

3. The following, of very common occurrence, nearly always *precede:*

Bon, *good,* Beau, *handsome.* Jeune, *young.* Grand, *tall.* Long, *long.*
Mauvais, *bad.* Joli, *pretty.* Vieux, *old.* Gros, *big.* Court, *short.*
          Vilain, *ugly.*   Petit, *small.*

131. The Demonstrative Adjective.

Sing.	Plur.
M. ce (cet) }, this *or* that. F. cette	ces, these *or* those.

[PRON.—*se (sèt), sèt, sè.*]
Obs.: The form **cet** is used before a *vowel* or h *mute.*

132. To distinguish 'this' from 'that,' or for *emphasis*, **ci** (= ici) and **là** are respectively added to the noun by a hyphen:

Ce livre, cet amie, cet homme.	This (*or* that) book, friend, man.
Cette plume, cette amie.	This (*or* that) pen, friend.
Cet habile homme, ce bon oncle.	This (*or* that) clever man, good uncle.
Ces hommes, ces femmes.	These (*or* those) men, women.
Cet homme-ci et cette femme-là.	This man and that woman.

133. The demonstrative adjective is *repeated* before each noun to which it refers:

Cette maison et ce jardin.	This house and garden.

EXERCISE XI.

Aîné *(èné)*, elder, eldest.
Ancien *(ãsiē)*, former, old.
Beau *(bó)*, fine, fine-looking, handsome.
Blanc *(blã)*, white.
Complet *(kõplè)*, complete.
Deux *(dö)*, two.
Difficile *(difisil)*, difficult.
Étudier *(étüdié)*, study.
La femme *(fãm)*, woman.
Français *(frãsè)*, French.
Gentil *(zãti)*, nice.
La gouvernante *(guvèrnã.t)*, governess.
Grand *(grã)*, large.
Gros *(gró)*, large, big.
Joli *(zòli)*, pretty.
Le jour *(žu.r)*, day.
La langue *(lã.g)*, language.
Long *(lõ)*, long.
Maintenant *(mètenã)*, now.
Noir *(nùá.r)*, black.
Les œuvres, f., *(œ.vr)*, works.
Le panier *(pánié)*, basket.
Petit *(peti)*, small.
Le pommier *(pòmié)*, apple-tree.
Le poirier *(puárié)*, pear-tree.
Porter *(pòrté)*, wear.
Si *(si)*, so.
Vieux *(viö)*, old, aged.

A. 1. Les belles pommes ne sont pas toujours bonnes. 2. Ce garçon et cette fille sont les enfants de mon cousin. 3. Qui est ce bel homme là-bas? 4. C'est le frère de notre voisin. 5. J'ai trouvé de grosses poires dans le panier, mais elles ne sont ni jolies ni bonnes. 6. J'aime beaucoup cette petite fille, elle est si gentille. 7. J'ai rencontré l'autre jour votre ancienne gouvernante; elle est maintenant chez M. Ribot. 8. Qui est cette jolie petite fille sous l'arbre au jardin? 9. C'est la fille de notre ancien voisin. 10. Avez-vous étudié la langue française? 11. Un peu, et je l'aime beaucoup. 12. Les chevaux sont des animaux très utiles. 13. Avez-vous jamais eu les œuvres complètes de Molière ? 14. Oui, monsieur, mais je ne les ai plus. 15. Voilà un bel arbre ; c'est un pommier, n'est-ce pas ? 16. Non, monsieur, c'est un poirier. 17. L'autre jour, lorsque j'étais chez mon voisin, je lui ai donné un livre français. 18. À qui est ce grand chapeau ? 19. Il est à mon père. 20. Notre petite sœur portait hier une robe blanche. 21. Nous avions l'année passée un grand cheval blanc. 22. Qu'avez-vous, monsieur ? 23. J'ai soif, je cherche de l'eau. 24. Voilà de bonne eau, sur la table. 25. N'avez-vous pas encore fini vos leçons ? 26. Nous ne les avons pas finies ; elles sont trop longues. 27. Cette vieille femme où demeurait-elle l'année passée ? 28. Elle demeurait chez son fils aîné. 29. Ces petites filles pourquoi est-ce qu'elles pleuraient ? 30. Elles pleuraient parce qu'elles avaient froid. 31. Votre oncle porte-t-il un grand chapeau, ou un petit ? 31. Il porte un grand chapeau.

B. 1. The other day I met your old neighbour. 2. There is a fine horse ; whose is it ? 3. It is my brother's. 4. Whose are those beautiful children under the apple-tree in the garden ? 5. They are my brother's children. 6. Have you ever had Scott's complete works ? 7. Yes, I used to have them ; but I haven't them now. 8. Was not your sister wearing a white dress yesterday ? 9. No, sir, she was wearing a black dress. 10. Where does your old governess live now ? 11. She lives at my sister's, but last year she was living at my eldest brother's. 12. What was the matter with that little child ? 13. He was thirsty, and I gave him some water. 14. That old lady was living last year with her son ; where is she living now ? 15. She is living with her eldest daughter. 16. There are two fine trees ; they are pear-trees, are they not ? 17. No, sir, they are old apple-trees. 18. Did you meet the old gentleman in the village yesterday ? 19. Yes, sir, I met him and the old lady also. 20. I found some large apples in that little basket, but they are not good. 21. Who is that pretty little boy in the garden ? 22. He is my cousin's child. 23. The other day, when I was at my brother's, I gave his little girl a French book. 24 Your exercises are not long ; why have you not finished them ?

25. What language are you studying now? 26. I am studying the French language. 27. Do you find it difficult? 28. A little, but I like it very much. 29. That little boy was crying, was he not? 30. Yes, he had the toothache. 31. Had your father a large horse or a small one. 32. He had a large horse and a small one too. 33. What was that old gentleman looking for? 34. He was looking for his son's house. 35. In what house does his son live? 36. He lives in that large, white house behind the church.

LESSON XII.

134. The Past Definite of *donner, finir, rompre*

[*I gave, etc.*]	[*I finished, etc.*]	[*I broke, etc.*]
je donn **ai**.	je fin **is**.	je romp **is**.
tu donn **as**.	tu fin **is**.	tu romp **is**.
il donn **a**.	il fin **it**.	il romp **it**.
nous donn **âmes**.	nous fin **îmes**.	nous romp **îmes**.
vous donn **âtes**.	vous fin **îtes**.	vous romp **îtes**.
ils donn **èrent**.	ils fin **irent**.	ils romp **irent**.

[PRON.—1. *že dòné, tü dòná, il dòná, nu dòná.m, vu dòná.t, il dònè.r.* 2. *že fini, tü fini, il fini, nu fini.m, vu fini.t, il fini.r.* 3. *že rōpi, tü rōpi, il rōpi, nu rōpi.m, vu rōpi.t, il rōpi.r.*]

135. Past Definite of *avoir, être*.

[*I had, etc.*]		[*I was, etc.*]	
j'eus.	nous eûmes.	je fus.	nous fûmes.
tu eus.	vous eûtes.	tu fus.	vous fûtes.
il eut.	ils eurent.	il fut.	ils furent.

[PRON.—1. *ž ü, tü ü, il ü, nuz ü.m, vuz ü.t, ilz ü.r.* 2. *že fü, tü fü, il fü, nu fü.m, vu fü.t, il fü.r.*]

136. Use of the Past Definite.
The past definite is used in the *literary narrative style* to denote *what happened* (completed past action), or *what happened next* (successive events):

| Les Romains **brûlèrent** Carthage. | The Romans **burnt** Carthage. |
| Dieu **accepta** les présents d'Abel, qui *était* plus pieux que son frère ; mais il **détourna** les yeux de ceux | God **accepted** the gifts of Abel, who *was* more righteous than his brother ; but he **turned away** his |

[136-140.] INDEFINITE ADJECTIVES. 63

de Caïn, parce que son cœur n'*était* pas pur.... Un jour Caïn et Abel étaient seuls dans un champ, et Caïn se **jeta** sur Abel, et le tua.

eyes from those of Cain, because his heart *was* not pure..... One day Cain and Abel *were* alone in a field, and Cain **fell** upon Abel, and slew him.

Obs.: The past def. *never denotes* like the impf. (§126) what *was happening* or *used to happen* or *continued to happen.*

137. Personal Pronoun Objects. Some objective forms have been given in §§92, 109. The remaining ones are :—

DAT. or ACC.	DAT. or ACC.
me, *me, to (for) me.*	nous, *us, to (for) us.*
te, *thee, to (for) thee.*	vous, *you, to (for) you.*
se, *himself, herself, itself, one's self; to (for) himself,* etc.	se, *themselves, to (for) themselves.*

138. Position. They *precede* the verb (§93), and also *precede* le, la, les, if present :

Il me prête la plume.	He lends me the pen.
Il me la prête.	He lends it to me (me it).
Elle se flatte.	She flatters herself.
Elles se les empruntent.	They borrow them for themselves.

139. The Interrogative Adjective.

	SING.	PLUR.	
M.	quel ?	quels ?	} *which ?, what ?, what (a) !.*
F.	quelle ?	quelles ?	

Quel livre ? Quelle plume ?   Which (what) book ? Which (what) pen ?

Quelle belle scène ! Quels héros !   What a beautiful scene ! What heroes !

140. Indefinite Adjectives. Some of the commoner indefinites are :—

ADJS. : Quelque, *some ;* chaque, *each.*
ADJ. OR PRON. : Autre, *other ;* tout, toute, tous, toutes, *all, every.*

EXERCISE XII.

Anglais *(ăglè)*, English, Englishman.
L'arrivée, f., *(árivé)*, arrival.
Arriver *(árivé)*, arrive, come.
Le bois or les bois *(búá)*, woods, forest.
Chanter *(šăté)*, sing.
L'exemplaire, m., *(eqzăplè.r)*, copy.
L'heure, f., *(œ.r)*, hour.
Jeune *(žŏ.n)*, young.
Le matin *(máté)*, morning.
L'oiseau, m., *(ŭázó)*, bird.

La chanson *(šãsõ)*, song.
Le chasseur *(šásœ.r)*, hunter.
Le chêne *(šè.n)*, oak.
Le coquin *(kòkẽ)*, scoundrel.
Le défaut *(dèfó)*, fault.
Descendre *(dèsã.dr)*, alight.
Le dos *(dó)*, back.
Entrer *(ãtré)*, enter, go in.
L'espèce, f., *(èspè.s)*, sort, kind.

Partir *(párti.r)*, leave, go away.
La perdrix *(pèrdri)*, partridge.
Punir *(püni.r)*, punish.
Quitter *(kité)*, leave (tran.).
Se réunir *(réüni.r)*, assemble, meet.
Le soir *(sũá.r)*, evening.
Tout *(tu)*, all.
Tuer *(tüé)*, kill.

Hier soir.   Last evening.
À quatre heures.   At four o'clock.

A. 1. Mon père me donna un exemplaire des œuvres complètes de Shakespeare, quand j'étais jeune. 2. Caïn tua son frère Abel, et Dieu le punit. 3. Nos amis chantèrent hier soir de belles chansons chez mon père. 4. Quelle chanson chantait votre sœur hier soir, lorsque j'arrivai? 5. Elle chantait une belle chanson de Burns. 6. Ce jeune Anglais finit son ouvrage chez mon père hier soir, et il cherche maintenant encore de l'ouvrage. 7. Les chasseurs tuèrent hier beaucoup de perdrix dans le bois de mon père. 8. Quelle chanson avez-vous chantée? 9. Nous avons chanté une des belles chansons de Heine. 10. Où trouvâtes-vous vos amis? 11. Nous les trouvâmes chez notre cousin. 12. Nous rompîmes notre canne sur le dos de ce coquin. 13. Ces coquins se réunirent hier soir dans le bois derrière le village. 14. Nous finîmes notre ouvrage ce matin. 15. Nous avions l'argent, lorsqu'il arriva. 16. Qui vous donna ces belles pommes? 17. Notre cousin nous les donna, et il nous donna de belles poires aussi. 18. Notre ami rompit sa canne, lorsqu'il était à la ville. 19. Tous les hommes et toutes les femmes sont là-bas au champ. 20. Tous les enfants quittèrent l'école hier soir à quatre heures. 21. Les oiseaux se réunissent ce matin dans les arbres; ils ont envie de partir pour un pays chaud. 22. À quatre heures nous arrivâmes chez nos amis, nous descendîmes de la voiture, et nous entrâmes dans la maison. 23. Monsieur votre père vous donna-t-il cette montre? 24. Oui, madame, il me la donna. 25. Quel bel arbre! De quelle espèce est-il? 26. C'est un chêne anglais.

27. Tous les hommes ici-bas ont leurs petits défauts.
28. Quelle belle femme ! Qui est-ce *(è s)* ? 29. C'est la femme de notre ancien voisin.

B. 1. All those scoundrels arrived last evening. 2. Why do you not lend me your pen and ink ? 3. Because I lent them to your brother. 4. What song was your sister singing, when we arrived ? 5. She was singing one of Moore's beautiful songs. 6. Our friends broke their canes on that little scoundrel's back. 7. At four o'clock our friends arrived at our cousin's, alighted from their carriage, and went into the house. 8. All men have their faults. 9. Who gave you those books and pencils ? 10. Our teacher gave us them. 11. That young Frenchman finished his work this morning. 12. All the children are yonder in the woods. 13. The birds assemble in the trees; they are cold, and they have a desire to leave this cold country. 14. Of what sort is that tree yonder? 15. It is a French apple-tree. 16. What sort of hat was he wearing, when you met him ? 17. He was wearing a silk hat. 18. Did you meet those four large black horses yesterday ? 19. Yes, sir, we met them in front of the school. 20. All the children finished their work and left the school at four o'clock last evening. 21. Who gave you that fine copy of Shakespeare's works ? 22. My father gave it to me, when I was young. 23. Cain and Abel were brothers, but Cain did not love Abel, and he killed him. 24. The hunters went into my father's woods, and killed partridges and other birds. 25. All the boys and girls are at school to-day. 26. Have the children found their hats ? 27. Yes, they found them in the other room.

LESSON XIII.

141. Future Indicative of *donner, finir, rompre.*

[*I shall give, etc.*]	[*I shall finish, etc.*]	[*I shall break, etc.*]
je donner ai.	je finir ai.	je rompr ai.
tu donner as.	tu finir as.	tu rompr as.
il donner a.	il finir a.	il rompr a.
nous donner ons.	nous finir ons.	nous rompr ons.
vous donner ez.	vous finir ez.	vous rompr ez.
ils donner ont.	ils finir ont.	ils rompr ont.

[PRON.—1. že dònré, tü dònrà, il dònrá, nu dònrō, vu dònré, il dònrō. 2. že finiré, tü finirà, il finirá, nu finirō, vu finiré, il finirō. 3. že rōpré, tü rōprà, il rōprá, nu rōprō, vu rōpré, il rōprō.]

142. Future Indicative of *avoir, être*.

[*I shall have, etc.*]   [*I shall be, etc.*]
j'aur ai.   nous aur ons.   je ser ai.   nous ser ons.
tu aur as. vous aur ez.   tu ser as.   vous ser ez.
il aur a.   ils aur ont.   il ser a.   ils ser ont.

[PRON.—1. ž óré, tü órà, il órá, nuz órō, vuz óré, ilz órō. 2. že seré, tü serà, il será, nu serō, vu seré, il serō.]

143. The Future is used in general as in English, but observe its use in a subordinate sentence, when *futurity* is *implied:*

Je le lui donnerai, quand il arrivera.   I shall give it to him, when he comes.
Donnez-lui ce qu'il demandera.   Give him what he asks.

144. Comparison of Adjectives. 1. The *comparative* of an adjective is expressed by placing **plus** = 'more,' **moins** = 'less,' **aussi** = 'as,' before the adjective. 'Than' *or* 'as' = **que**:

Il est plus grand que Jean.   He is taller than John.
Il est moins grand que Jean. He is less tall than (not so tall as) John.
Il est aussi grand que Jean. He is as tall as John.

2. **Aussi** *negatively* may be replaced by **si**:

Il n'est pas aussi (*or* si) grand que Jean.   He is not so tall as John.

3. The *superlative* is expressed by **plus** or **moins** *preceded by* the *def. art.* or a *poss. adj.:*

Jean est le plus jeune des frères.   John is the youngest of the brothers.
Mes plus chers amis.   My dearest friends.

4. If the superlative *follows* the noun, the *def. art. is not omitted:*

Mes amis les plus fidèles.   My most faithful friends.
C'est la dame la plus instruite.   She is the most learned lady.

5. After a superlative, 'in' = **de** (not *à, dans,* etc.):

L'homme le plus riche de la ville.   The richest man in the city.

145. Irregular Comparison. Bon, mauvais, petit have a special comparative form:—

Pos.	Comp.	Superl.	Pos.	Comp.	Superl.
bon,	meilleur,	le meilleur.			
mauvais,	pire,	le pire.	*or* mauvais,	plus m.	le plus m.
petit,	moindre,	le moindre.	*or* petit,	plus p.	le plus p.

146. Adverbs are compared in general *like adjectives* (by plus and moins, *preceded* by invariable le in the superlat.), but note the following irregular forms:—

Pos.	Comp.	Superl.
bien, *well*.	mieux, *better*.	le mieux, *(the) best*.
mal, *badly*.	pis, *worse*.	le pis, *(the) worst*.
peu, *little*.	moins, *less*.	le moins, *(the) least*.

EXERCISE XIII.

Aimable *(èmábl)*, pleasant.
Après *(áprè)*, after.
Aussitôt que *(ósitó ke)*, as soon as.
L'avoine, f., *(ávŭán)*, oats.
Le bâton *(bátõ)*, stick.
Bientôt *(bĭětó)*, soon.
Le blé *(blé)*, wheat.
Canadien *(kánádĭè)*, Canadian.
Cher, -ère *(šè.r)*, dear.
Demain *(demè)*, to-morrow.
Le foin *(fŭè)*, hay.
Le fruit *(frŭi)*, fruit.
Grand *(grã)*, tall.
Méchant *(méšã)*, cross.
Moins, adv. and subst. *(mŭè)*, less.
Le monde *(mõ.d)*, world.
Plus, adv. and subst. *(plü)*, more.
Prochain *(próšè)*, next.
Le produit *(pródŭi)*, product.
Rouge *(ru.ž)*, red.

Tout de suite. Immediately.
L'année prochaine. Next year.
Après demain. The day after to-morrow.
Avoir (l')intention de. To intend to.

A. 1. Nous aurons une meilleure maison, quand nous serons assez riches. 2. Jean est le plus petit de la famille. 3. Nous donnerons de l'argent à ce pauvre mendiant. 4. Ce mendiant aura beaucoup d'argent. 5. Avez-vous donné le foin aux chevaux? 6. Non, monsieur, mais nous le leur donnerons tout de suite. 7. Mon père est plus grand que mon oncle. 8. Nos amis se réuniront à la ville après demain. 9. Nos cousins chanteront de leurs plus belles chansons, lorsqu'ils arriveront là-bas. 10. Ce cheval-ci est aussi bon que l'autre. 11. Les chasseurs rompront des bâtons et allumeront le feu, aussitôt qu'ils arriveront dans le bois. 12. Jean n'est pas si grand que sa sœur Marie. 13. Vous quitterez Toronto demain à quatre heures, n'est ce pas? 14. Non, monsieur, nous avons intention de partir après demain à quatre heures. 15. Notre chien est plus méchant que le chien de notre voisin. 16. L'avoine est moins chère que le blé. 17. Le chêne blanc est un meilleur bois que le chêne rouge. 18. La petite fille portait hier une robe blanche ; elle portera demain une robe rouge. 19. Nous avons moins chaud aujourd'hui qu'hier. 20. Nous aurons plus de pommes que de poires l'année prochaine. 21. Notre voisin a eu cette année moins de blé que d'avoine. 22. Le petit garçon a été méchant, et son père le punira. 23. Le foin sera moins cher l'année prochaine que cette année-ci. 24. Les pommes canadiennes sont les meilleures du monde. 25. Qu' étudierez-vous demain ? 26. Demain nous étudierons *l'Avare* de Molière. 27. Qui est cette belle dame ? 28. C'est la dame la plus aimable de toute la ville. 29. La pomme est le fruit le plus utile de notre pays.

B. 1. We shall leave this city, as soon as our friends arrive (fut.). 2. My sister is taller than my mother. 3. My uncle is not as tall as my father. 4. These apples are better than the others. 5. Apples are not so dear as pears (see No. 16 of *A*). 6. Why do you not close the windows ? 7. We shall close them immediately ; we are not so warm to-day as yesterday. 8. We shall have more wheat than oats next year. 9. Your father will punish you to-morrow, because you have been naughty. 10. Canadian apples are better than English apples ; they will be dear next year. 11. What kind of dress was your mother wearing yesterday? 12. Yesterday she wore a white dress ; to-morrow she will wear a black dress. 13. This dog is not so cross as the other [one]. 14. Our neighbours will assemble at the church to-morrow. 15. I am cold ; why have you not kindled the fire ? 16. I shall kindle it immediately. 17. Have you given the horses the hay ? 18. No, sir, but we shall give it to them immediately. 19. Who is that handsome man? 20. He is the most pleasant gentleman in the town. 21. Wheat is the most useful product of our country? 22. Red oak is not so good as white oak. 23 Our dog is not so cross as our neighbour's dog. 24. I am very cold; why do you not kindle the fire? 25. I shall kindle it immediately, and then you will be warmer. 26. The red house is larger than the white [one]. 27. He will break his cane over the back of that scoundrel. 28. When I am in the town, I shall give you some apples. 29. To-morrow we shall study Molière's *L'Avare*, and the day after to-morrow his *Misanthrope*. 30. Good fathers punish their children, when they are naughty. 31. We shall finish our lessons at four o'clock this evening. 32. John will soon be as tall as his father. 33. Mary will never be as tall as her mother. 34. Our neighbours will have a better house, as soon as they are rich enough. 35. The hunters will be in my father's woods to-day, and they will kill some partridges.

LESSON XIV.

147. Conditional of *donner, finir, rompre*.

[*I should give, etc.*]	[*I should finish, etc.*]	[*I should break, etc.*]
je donner ais.	je finir ais.	je rompr ais.
tu donner ais.	tu finir ais.	tu rompr ais.
il donner ait.	il finir ait.	il rompr ait.
nous donner ions.	nous finir ions.	nous rompr ions.
vous donner iez.	vous finir iez.	vous rompr iez.
ils donner aient.	ils finir aient.	ils rompr aient.

[PRON.—1. že dònrè, tü dònrè, il dònrè, nu dònriõ, vu dònrié, il dònrè. 2. že finirè, tü finirè, il finirè, nu finiriõ, vu finirié, il finirè. 3. že rõprè, tü rõprè, il rõprè, nu rõpriõ, vu rõprié, il rõprè.]

148. Conditional of *avoir, être*.

[*I should have, etc.*]		[*I should be, etc.*]	
j'aur ais.	nous aur ions.	je ser ais.	nous ser ions.
tu aur ais.	vous aur iez.	tu ser ais.	vous ser iez.
il aur ait.	ils aur aient.	il ser ait.	ils ser aient.

[PRON. -1. ž òrè, tü òrè, il òrè, nuz òriõ, vuz òrié, ilz òrè. 2. že serè, tü serè, il serè, nu seriõ, vu serié, il serè.]

149. Conditional Sentences. 1. The *conditional* is used to express what *would happen* (result) in case something else *were to happen* (condition):

(Condition) Si je récitais ma leçon sans fautes, *(Result)* le maître serait content.	If I said (*or* if I were to say, *or* were I to say, *or* should I say) my lesson without mistakes, the master would be pleased.

N.B.—Remember that a *result clause* in the *conditional* regularly has the *if clause* in the *imperfect indic.*, whatever be the corresponding Eng. form.

2. Similarly, a *result clause* in the *future* requires the *if clause* in the *present indic.*, whatever be the Eng. form:

(Condition) S'il est ici demain, *(Result)* je lui donnerai l'argent.	If he is (*or* be, *or* will be, *or* should be) here to-morrow, I shall give him the money.

Obs.: For elision of 1 in si, see §73.

3. After **si** = 'whether,' the *fut.* and *condl.* may be used, but never after **si** = 'if':

Je lui demande (demandais) s'il sera (serait) ici demain.	I ask (was asking) him whether he will be (would be) here to-morrow.

EXERCISE XIV.

Bâtir *(báti.r)*, build.
Car *(ká.r)*, for (conj.).
Chaud *(šó)*, warm, hot.
Content *(kōtā̃)*, pleased.
Fort *(fò.r)*, hard (adv.).
Froid *(frŭá)*, cold.
Gâter *(gáté)*, spoil.
Généreux *(žénérö̈)*, generous, liberal.
Heureux *(örö̈)*, happy.
L'hirondelle, f., *(irōdèl)*, swallow.
L'hiver *(ivè.r)*, winter.
Mauvais *(móvè)*, bad.
Neuf *(nœf)*, new.
L'ouvrier *(urrĭe)*, workman.
La pensée *(pā̃sé)*, thought.
Perdu *(pèrdü̆)*, lost.
Réciter *(résité)*, recite.
Sans *(sā̃)*, without.
Si *(si)*, if, whether.
Le temps *(tā̃)*, time.

Dans ce temps-là.	At that time.
Sans doute.	No doubt.

A. 1. Si les enfants des voisins sont à l'école, nous leur donnerons des pommes. 2. Si ma mère est encore ici, je lui réciterai ma leçon. 3. Si j'avais un livre, je vous le prêterais. 4. Je demanderai à mon père s'il a de l'argent. 5. S'il n'a pas d'argent, je le demanderai à ma mère. 6. Si vous aviez un enfant, vous le gâteriez, si vous ne le punissiez pas quelquefois. 7. Je ne le punirais pas, s'il n'était pas méchant. 8. Nos voisins bâtiraient une maison neuve, s'ils étaient assez riches. 9. Jean et Marie n'avaient pas un sou, ou ils l'auraient donné au pauvre mendiant. 10. Si les enfants ont rompu ces bâtons, nous les punirons. 11. Nous serons très contents, si nos amis sont à la ville. 12. Les petites filles seraient très contentes, si leurs amies étaient ici. 13. Les livres sont les meilleurs amis, s'ils sont bons. 14. Si un garçon aime les mauvais livres, il est perdu. 15. Nous aurions moins de mauvaises pensées, si nous les aimions moins. 16. Si un garçon aime les bons livres et les bonnes pensées, il sera bon et grand. 17. Si nos amis avaient moins d'argent, ils seraient plus heureux. 18. Nous n'étions pas très riches dans ce temps-là, ou nous aurions été plus généreux. 19. Les plus riches ne sont pas toujours les plus généreux. 20. Si les ouvriers n'avaient pas si froid, ils travailleraient plus fort. 21. Les hirondelles pourquoi nous ont-elles quittés ? 22. Si elles n'avaient pas si froid ici, elles resteraient tout l'hiver. 23. Si nous bâtissions une maison neuve, aurions-nous assez d'argent ? 24. Nous aurons assez d'argent l'année prochaine, et nous la bâtirons. 25. Les hirondelles nous quittent ; elles aiment mieux les pays chauds que les pays froids. 26. Lui auriez-vous donné vos plumes, s'il les avait demandées ? 27. Oui, et je lui aurais donné mon livre aussi.

B. 1. If you do not punish your children, you will spoil them. 2. If I had a knife, I should lend it to you. 3. If we had more money, should we be more happy ? 4. Rich men are not always the happiest. 5. We shall give our neighbour's children some apples, if they are there. 6. If we should give our uncle this money, would he be pleased ? 7. He would be pleased, if we were good children. 8. If I be there, I shall give you your books. 9. If he should be there, I shall ask him whether he has your books. 10. If that beggar should ask you for money, would you give it to him ? 11. Yes, I should give it to him, for he is cold and hungry. 12. The little birds are leaving us ; would they not stay, if they were not so cold ? 13. Yes, no doubt ; they do not like cold countries. 14. If a boy likes bad books, he will have bad thoughts. 15. Should you be glad, if we were to build a new house? 16. We had not a cent, or we should have given it to that poor man. 17. John will ask his father whether he has any money. 18. If his father has no money, he will ask his mother for it. 19. If those boys have broken those canes, the gentlemen will punish them. 20. If that lady were richer, she would be more generous. 21. If boys love great books and great thoughts, they will be great. 22. The swallows would stay here all winter, if they did not like warm countries better. 23. The workmen are not working to-day; they were too cold this morning. 24. At that time we were not rich, or we should have given more money to the poor. 25. If that boy's mother does not punish him, she will spoil him. 26. We do not punish children, if they are good. 27. A boy is lost, if he loves bad books. 28. If that young man had less money, he would be happier. 29. If you stay here, we shall be much *(bien)* pleased. 30. If you were to work hard, you would be happier. 31. The workmen would be cold, if they did not work. 32. He was very rich at that time, and used to give much money to the poor. 33. I should have given the beggar my money, if he had asked for it. 34. If you *(tu)* should recite your lesson well, your teacher would be much pleased. 35. Books are the worst friends, if they are bad.

LESSON XV.

150. Imperative of *donner, finir, rompre.*

[*Give, etc.*]	[*Finish, etc.*]	[*Break, etc.*]
donn e.	fini s.	romp s.
(qu'il donn e.)	(qu'il finiss e.)	(qu'il romp e.)
donn ons.	finiss ons.	romp ons.
donn ez.	finiss ez.	romp ez.
(qu'ils donn ent.)	(qu'ils finiss ent.)	(qu'ils romp ent.)

Obs.: The forms in parenthesis are subjunctive forms (§158) used as imperatives.

[PRON.—1. dòn, k il dòn, dònō, dòné, k il dòn. 2. fini, k il finis, finisō, finisé, k il finis. 3. rō, k il rō.p, rōpō, rōpé, k il rō.p.]

151. Imperative of *avoir, être*.

[Have, etc.]		[Be, etc.]	
	ay ons.		soy ons.
aie.	ay ez.	sois.	soy ez.
(qu'il ait.)	(qu'ils aient.)	(qu'il soit.)	(qu'ils soient.)

[Pron.—1. è, k il è, ètŏ, èté, k ilz è. 2. sŭá, k il sŭá, sŭátŏ, sŭáte, k il sŭá.]

152. The Negative Imperative.

[Do not give, etc.]	[Do not have, etc.]
ne donne pas.	n'aie pas.
(qu'il ne donne pas.)	(qu'il n'ait pas.)
ne donnons pas.	n'ayons pas.
ne donnez pas.	n'ayez pas.
(qu'ils ne donnent pas.)	(qu'ils n'aient pas.)

153. Position of Objects. 1. Personal pronoun objects *follow the imperative* (but *not* the subjunctive as imperat.), and are joined to it and to one another by *hyphens:*

Prêtez-lui la plume.	Lend him the pen.
Prêtez-la-lui.	Lend it to him.
Qu'il me la prête.	Let him lend it to me.

Obs.: **Moi** and **toi** are used *after an imperative* instead of me, te: Prêtez-moi la plume.

2. But if the imperative be *negative*, the general rule holds good (§93):

Ne la lui prêtez pas.   Do not lend it to him.

3. When a verb governs *two* objects, the *acc.* (le, la, les) stands *next the verb*, except when along with **lui** or **leur** *before* the verb (§§93, 109):

	Dat.	Acc.	Verb.	Acc.	Dat.
	Vous	nous les	donnez.	Donnez -les	-nous.
But:		Acc.	Dat.	Verb.	
	Vous	le	lui	donnez.	
	Vous	les	leur	donnez.	

154. The Pronominal Adverbs are:—

y, *to (at, on, in, into, etc.) it* or *them ; there, thither.*

en, *of (from, etc.) it* or *them ; some of it, some of them ; some, any ; thence, from there.*

155. Position of *y* and *en*. They follow the *same rules as pers. pron. objects*, and when along with pers. prons. always *stand last*, en *following* y.

156. Use of *y* and *en*. 1. They are equivalent to a *prep. + a pron.* standing for *things* (more rarely for persons). Thus y = à (**dans, sur,** etc.) + *pron.*, and en = de + *pron.*:

Pensez à mes paroles.—J'y pense.   Think of my words.—I think of them.
Donnez-moi le livre; j'en ai besoin.   Give me the book; I have need of it.

2. Used *partitively*, en = 'some' or 'any' may not be omitted, as often in Eng.:

Avez-vous de l'argent?—J'en ai.   Have you (any) money?—I have (some).
A-t-il une plume?—Il en a une.   Has he a pen?—He has one.
Il en a de bonnes.   He has (some) good ones.

3. *Place where, already mentioned* (or implied), is y or en:

Est-il au jardin?—Il y est.   Is he in the garden? He is in it (=there).
J'en arrive dans ce moment.   I come from it this moment.

157. Y avoir. Y + *the 3 sing. of avoir* forms a much used impersonal verb:—

il y a, *there is (or are)*.   il y aura, *there will be*.
il y avait, *there was (or were)*.   il y aurait, *there would be*.
il y eut, *there was (or were)*.   etc.

EXERCISE XV.

Le bonheur *(bónœ.r)*, happiness.
Commencer *(cômãsé)*, begin.
Le courage *(kurá.ž)*, courage.
Désirer *(dézíré)*, wish.
Le lait *(lè)*, milk.
La mariée *(márié)*, bride.
La prospérité *(pròspérité)*, prosperity.

Eh bien!   Very well!
Je n'en ai pas.   I have none.
Je n'en ai plus.   I have no more, I have none left, I have none now.
S'il vous plaît.   If you please.
Comme ils sont heureux!   How happy they are!

A. 1. Donnez-moi de ces poires, s'il vous plaît. 2. Non, monsieur, nous ne vous en donnerons pas, nous n'en avons pas assez. 3. Votre enfant demande des pommes ; lui en donnerai-je ? 4. Non, mademoiselle, ne lui en donnez pas. 5. Monsieur votre père désire du papier. 6. Donnez-lui-en. 7. Si j'avais de l'argent, je vous en donnerais. 8. Prêtez-moi votre plume. 9. Non, monsieur, je ne vous la prêterai pas. 10. Le cheval est-il à l'écurie ? 11. Oui, monsieur, il y est. 12. Est-ce qu'il y a des plumes dans la petite boîte ? 13. Non, monsieur, il n'y en a pas. 14. S'il y avait des pommes dans le panier, je vous en donnerais. 15. Vous avez de l'argent, n'est ce pas ? 16. Eh bien ! prêtez-en à mon père. 17. Voilà la mariée ; qu'elle soit heureuse ! 18. Ne pleure plus mon enfant ; aie du courage. 19. Finissez vos leçons, mes enfants, et n'en commencez plus ce soir. 20. Voilà des pommes, donnons-en aux enfants. 21. Non, monsieur, ne leur en donnons pas, ils n'en ont pas besoin. 22. Voilà les petits enfants ! Comme ils sont heureux ! 23. Qu'ils aient toujours du bonheur ! 24. Quelle belle mariée ! Comme elle est heureuse ! Qu'elle ait toujours de la prospérité ! 25. Avez-vous des chevaux, monsieur ? 26. Oui, monsieur, nous en avons un. 27. Qu'y a-t-il dans la boîte ? 28. Il y a des plumes. 29. La fille de notre voisin a-t-elle encore des poires ? 30. Elle n'en a guère. 31. Y a-t-il des chevaux dans ce champ ? 32. Oui, monsieur, en voilà sous cet arbre.

B. 1. Don't cry any more, my boy ; be happy. 2. Give us some bread, if you please. 3. We have none ; we gave it away to the beggar's children. 4. Are there any horses in the field ? 5. No, sir, there are none. 6. Lend me your horse and carriage, sir, if you please. 7. No, sir, I shall not lend them to you. 8. Have you any more money ? 9. I have but little. 10. Have you finished your lessons, my children. 11. Not yet, papa. 12. Very well, finish them, and don't begin any more this evening. 13. If there were any paper here, I would lend you some. 14. How happy the bride is ! May she always have prosperity ! 15. Give me some of those pencils, if you please. 16. What does your brother wish ? 17. He wishes some pens and paper. 18. Very well, give him some. 19. The beggar is asking for money. 20. Don't give him any; give him some bread and milk. 21. Let us give the beggar's child some money. 22. No, do not give him any, let us give him an apple. 23. Give us some more apples. 24. We have no more. 25. What a beautiful child! May he always be good and happy! 26. The little boy is asking for milk. 27. Very well, give him some. 28. Have you a cane, sir? 29. Yes, sir, I have two. 30. Have you any milk in the house? 31. Yes, madam, there is some on the table. 32. Let us have courage, and we shall be happy. 33. The children are asking for apples. 34. Don't give them any; they do not need them.

LESSON XVI.

158. Present Subjunctive of *donner, finir, rompre*.

[*I (may) give, etc.*]	[*I (may) finish, etc.*]	[*I (may) break, etc.*]
(que) je donn e.	(que) je finiss e.	(que) je romp e.
(que) tu donn es.	(que) tu finiss es.	(que) tu romp es.
(qu') il donn e.	(qu') il finiss e.	(qu') il romp e.
(que) nous donn ions.	(que) nous finiss ions.	(que) nous romp ions.
(que) vous donn iez.	(que) vous finiss iez.	(que) vous romp iez.
(qu') ils donn ent.	(qu') ils finiss ent.	(qu') ils romp ent.

[PRON.—1. *(ke) že dòn, (ke) tü dòn, (k) il dòn, (ke) nu dònĭṓ, (ke) vu dònĭé, (k) il dòn.* 2. *(ke) že finis, (ke) tü finis, (k) il finis, (ke) nu finisĭṓ, (ke) vu finisĭé, (k) il finis.* 3. *(ke) že rṓ.p, (ke) tü rṓ.p, (k) il rṓ.p, (ke) nu rṓpĭṓ, (ke) vu rṓpĭé, (k) il rṓ.p.*]

Obs.: 1. The conj. **que**='that,' in parentheses, is commonly learned with the subj. paradigm, but remember that **que** does *not* in itself *determine the mood*. 2. The paradigm meanings (' I may give,' etc.) are only *approximate*, as will be seen from the examples below.

159. Present Subjunctive of *avoir, être*.

[*I (may) have, etc.*]		[*I (may) be, etc.*]	
(que) j'aie.	(que) nous ayons.	(que) je sois.	(que) nous soyons.
(que) tu aies.	(que) vous ayez.	(que) tu sois.	(que) vous soyez.
(qu') il ait.	(qu') ils aient.	(qu') il soit.	(qu') ils soient.

[PRON.—1. *(ke) že, (ke) tü è, (k) il è, (ke) nuz èĭṓ, (ke) vuz èĭé, (k) ilz è.* 2. *(ke) že sŭá, (ke) tü sŭá, (k) il sŭá, (ke) nu sŭaĭṓ, (ke) vu sŭáĭé, (k) il sŭá.*]

160. Use of the Subjunctive. Some of the commoner uses of the subj. are:—

1. In a *subordinate clause* introduced by **que** = 'that':

a. After verbs such as **vouloir** = 'to will,' **désirer** = 'to desire,' **souhaiter** = 'to wish,' to denote what is *willed* or *desired* in the governing clause:

Nous désirons que vous restiez.	We desire you to remain (= that you (may) remain *or* should remain).
Je souhaite qu'il réussisse.	I wish that he may succeed.

b. After expressions of *joy, sorrow*, etc., in the governing clause, such as **être content** = 'to be glad,' **regretter** = 'to regret,' **être fâché** = 'to be sorry':

Je suis content qu'il soit absent.	I am glad (that) he is absent.
Nous regrettons qu'il n'ait pas réussi.	We regret that he has not succeeded.

c. After *impersonal verbs*, such as **il faut** = 'it is necessary,' **il semble** = 'it seems,' etc.:

Il faut que nous restions.	We must remain (= It is necessary that we (should) remain).

Obs.: **Que** is never omitted, as 'that' often is in English.

2. After certain *conjunctions* formed with **que**, such as **quoique** or **bien que** = 'although,' **afin que** = 'in order that,' **avant que** = 'before':

Quoiqu'il soit pauvre, il est heureux.   Although he is poor, he is happy.

161. Tense Sequence. A *present* or a *future* tense in the governing clause regularly requires the *present subjunctive* in the governed clause. So also for *compound* subj. tenses, the *auxiliary* being considered as the verb:

Pres. Il faut } que vous parliez. { You must speak.
Fut. Il faudra }   { You will have to speak.

162. Disjunctive Personal Pronouns. All the pers. pron. forms already given are used *along with the verb* (as *subject* or *object*), and hence are called *conjunctive*. The forms *not* immediately connected with a verb are called *disjunctive*. They are:—

SING.	PLUR.
moi, *I, me.*	nous, *we, us.*
toi, *thou, thee.*	vous, *you.*
lui, *he, him.*	eux, *they* (m.), *them* (m.).
elle, *she, her.*	elles, *they* (f.), *them* (f.).

[PRON.—*mŭá, tŭá, lŭi, ĕl, nu, vu, ö, ĕl.*]

163. Some Uses of the Disjunctive Pers. Pron. are :—

1. *Absolutely* (a *verb* being *implied*, but not expressed):
   Qui est là?—Moi (eux, elles).   Who is there? I (they).

2. After a *preposition:*
   Pour elle. Avec moi. Sans eux.   For her. With me. Without them.

3. As predicate after ce + être :
   C'est **moi,** c'est **toi,** c'est **lui,** c'est **elle.**   It is **I, thou, he, she.**
   C'est **nous,** c'est **vous,** ce sont **eux (elles).**   It is **we, you, they.**

EXERCISE XVI.

Abîmer *(ábimé)*, spoil.
Absent *(ábsã)*, absent.
Afin que *(áfĕ ke)*, in order that, so that.
L'argent, m., *(áržã)*, silver.
Avant que *(ávã ke)*, before.
Bien que *(bĭĕ ke)*, although.
Content *(kōtã)*, glad.
Le dé *(dé)*, thimble.
Désirer *(déziré)*, wish, want.
Fâché *(fàšé)*, sorry.
Il faut *(fó)*, it is necessary, must.
Frapper *(frápé)*, knock.
Intelligent *(ĕtĕližã)*, intelligent.
Nécessaire *(nésèsè.r)*, necessary.
Le parent *(párã)*, relative, parent.
Le pasteur *(pástœ.r)*, pastor.
Perdre *(pè.rdr)*, lose.
Pour que *(pu.r ke)*, in order that, so that.
Quoique *(kŭáke)*, although.
Regretter *(regrèté)*, regret.
Souhaiter *(sŭèté)*, wish.

Chez nous, chez moi, etc.   At our house, with us, at my house, etc.
J'en suis fâché.   I am sorry for it.
J'en suis content.   I am glad of it.

A. 1. Il faut que nous finissions notre ouvrage avant quatre heures. 2. Il faut que le fils du médecin soit chez nous ce soir. 3. Êtes-vous content que mon frère ait rompu sa canne sur le dos de ce coquin-là? 4. J'en suis bien content. 7. Nous sommes bien contents que vous ayez trouvé votre argent. 8. Je suis fâché que tu aies perdu le dé d'argent de ta mère. 9. Nous ne bâtirons pas une maison, avant que nous soyons assez riches. 10. Le professeur désire que vous finissiez vos thèmes. 11. Nous regrettons beaucoup que le pasteur soit absent. 12. Marie est très contente qu'elle soit aussi grande que moi. 13. Quoique Jean soit plus grand que Marie, il est moins intelligent qu'elle. 14. Je demande de l'argent à mon père, afin que j'en aie assez. 15. Ma mère désire que nous fermions les fenêtres, afin que nous ayons plus chaud. 16. Nos amis désirent que nous restions chez eux. 17. Bien que vous lui donniez beaucoup d'argent, il n'en aura jamais assez. 18. Les mères aiment toujours leurs enfants, quoique les enfants soient quelquefois méchants. 19. Le père n'est pas content que vous ayez donné de l'argent à son fils. 20. Si nous finissions notre ouvrage, vous en seriez content, n'est-ce pas? 21. Qui frappe? 22. C'est moi, le petit Jean? 23. Que désires-tu, mon enfant? 24. Je désire, madame, que votre petit garçon joue avec moi. 25. Il faut que nous allumions le feu, parce que nous avons froid. 26. Où demeurez-vous à présent? 27. Je demeure à la ville; j'ai quitté la maison de mon père. 28. Je souhaite que vous ayez beaucoup de bonheur. 29. Ce livre-là est à moi; je désire que vous me le donniez. 30. Pourquoi la petite fille désire-t-elle que je lui donne ce livre? 31. Parce qu'il est à elle. 32. Il faut que le domestique rompe ces morceaux de bois, et qu'il allume le feu, car nous avons froid.

B. 1. I desire you to finish your exercise. 2. Though children are sometimes naughty, their mothers always love them. 3. What do you want, my little girl? 4. I want your little girl to play with me. 5. You must close the windows, for we are cold. 6. I am very glad that you are here. 7. Are you not sorry that your sister is not with us? 8. Yes, I am very sorry for it. 9. Are you not glad that we have a good fire in our room? 10. Yes, I am very glad of it. 11. Though John is older than Mary, she is more intelligent than he. 12. Who is knocking? 13. It is we, your neighbor's children. 14. What do you want? 15. We want your little boys to play with us. 16. Does your mother wish us to live with *(chez)* you? 17. No, she wishes you to live with her. 18. We shall not have a carriage, before we are rich enough. 19. I am sorry that I have lost my mother's silver thimble. 20. My father is sorry that you spoiled his silk hat. 21. You have left your father's house; I wish you may have much happiness. 22. I wish you to live with us. 23. If you were to live with us, we should be happy. 24. Children must obey their parents. 25. Our friends desire us to live with them. 26. I want you to close the windows, so that we shall not be cold. 27. I am glad the beggar is no longer hungry. 28. I want you to break your cane on that scoundrel's back. 29. My mother's silver thimble is lost; she wishes us to find it. 30. That little boy is very much pleased that he is as tall as his brother. 31. You must give some bread to that poor child, for he is very hungry. 32. You have spoiled my brother's silk hat; are you not sorry for it? 33. Yes, I am sorry that I have been naughty.

LESSON XVII.

164. Imperfect Subjunctive of *donner, finir, rompre.*

[*(That) I gave, might give, etc.*]	[*(That) I finished, might finish, etc.*]	[*(That) I broke, might break, etc.*]
(que) je donn asse.	(que) je fin isse.	(que) je romp isse.
(que) tu donn asses.	(que) tu fin isses.	(que) tu romp isses.
(qu') il donn ât.	(qu') il fin ît.	(qu') il romp ît.
(que) nous donn assions.	(que) nous fin issions.	(que) nous romp issions.
(que) vous donn assiez.	(que) vous fin issiez.	(que) vous romp issiez.
(qu') ils donn assent.	(qu') ils fin issent.	(qu') ils romp issent.

[PRON.—1. *(ke) že dònàs, (ke) tü dònàs, (k) il dònà, (ke) nu dònàsiõ, (ke) vu dònàsié, (k) il dònàs.* 2. *(ke) že finis, (ke) tü finis, (k) il fini, (ke) nu finisiõ, (ke) vu finisié, (k) il finis.* 3. *(ke) že rõpis, (ke) tü rõpis, (k) il rõpi, (ke) nu rõpisiõ, (ke) vu rõpisié, (k) il rõpis.*]

165. Imperfect Subjunctive of *avoir, être.*

[*(That) I had, might have, etc.*]	[*(That) I was, were, might be, etc.*]
(que) j'eusse. (que) nous eussions.	(que) je fusse. (que) nous fussions.
(que) tu eusses. (que) vous eussiez.	(que) tu fusses. (que) vous fussiez.
(qu') il eût. (qu') ils eussent.	(qu') il fût. (qu') ils fussent.

[PRON.—1. *(ke) ž üs, (ke) tü üs, (k) il ü, (ke) nuz üsiõ, (ke) vuz üsié, (k) ilz üs.* 2. *(ke) že füs, (ke) tü füs, (k) il fü, (ke) nu füsiõ, (ke) vu füsié, (k) il füs.*]

166. Tense Sequence. *Any other tense than the present* or *future* (§161) in the governing clause regularly requires the *imperfect subjunctive* in the governed clause. So also for *compound subj.* tenses, the *auxiliary* being considered as the *verb:*

IMPF. Je désirais		I was desiring him to remain.
PAST. DEF. Je désirai	qu'il restât.	I desired him to remain.
CONDL. Je désirerais		I should desire him to remain.

EXERCISE XVII.

Il fallait que j' y fusse. { It was necessary for me to be there. / I had (was obliged) to be there.

Je désirerais que vous y fussiez. I should like you to be there.

A. 1. Nous désirions que vous y fussiez avant notre arrivée. 2. Je lui ai donné de l'argent, afin qu'il en donnât au mendiant. 3. Nous étions contents que vous ne fussiez plus pauvre. 4. Le père était fâché que son fils eût donné de l'argent à ce coquin. 5. Il fallait que j'eusse de l'argent, afin que j'en donnasse aux pauvres. 6. Notre père désirait que nous y fussions, avant que les autres arrivassent. 7. Bien que nos voisins fussent riches, ils n'étaient pas heureux. 8. Nos amis désiraient que nous demeurassions chez eux. 9. Je désirerais que vous rompissiez ces morceaux de bois, et que vous allumassiez le feu. 10. Nous désirerions qu'il fût là, parce que son père le demande. 11. Le professeur désirerait que vous finissiez votre thème tout de suite. 12. Si vous rompiez ces bâtons, nous aurions bientôt un bon feu. 13. J'étais très content que vous fussiez content. 14. Pourquoi avez-vous rompu ces bâtons? 15. Parce que notre père désirait que nous les rompissions. 16. J'ai fermé les fenêtres, pour que vous n'eussiez pas froid. 17. Le fils de cette vieille femme désirait qu'elle demeurât chez lui. 18. Nous désirions que nos amis demeurassent chez nous. 19. Quoique Marie fût plus jeune que Jean, elle était plus intelligente que lui. 20. Nous regrettions que le pauvre mendiant eût froid. 21. Bien qu'ils eussent froid, ils ne désiraient pas que nous fermassions les fenêtres. 22. Les pauvres petits oiseaux étaient bien contents que les enfants leur donnassent des morceaux de pain. 23. Désireriez-vous que je vous donnasse de l'argent? 24. Oui, monsieur, car j'en ai grand besoin. 27. Mon père ne désirait pas que le petit garçon abîmât son chapeau. 26. Nos cousins n'avaient plus de pommes, ou notre oncle aurait désiré qu'ils vous en eussent donné.

B. 1. We should like you to give us some paper and pens. 2. The teacher would like you to finish your lessons at once. 3. We gave the poor little birds bread, so that they might not be hungry and cold. 4. You would soon have a good fire, if you would break those pieces of wood. 5. We wanted you to give us some bread. 6. Although our friends were poor, they were always happy. 7. We regretted that our friends had no more money. 8. We were wishing that you were here. 9. We gave money to the beggar, before we gave our children any. 10. Our cousins were wishing that their father would live with them. 11. The children closed the windows, so that we should not be cold. 12. We were there, before the others arrived. 13. The carpenter would like you to give him some boards. 14. I should like you to be there. 15. It was necessary for me to close the windows. 16. I should not like the servant to spoil my gold watch. 17. Your father was sorry that you had given money to that beggar. 18. I was very glad that you were happy. 19. Our children had no more money, or we should have liked them to give you some. 20. I had to be there, before the others came. 21. Although John was older than Mary, he was not so intelligent as she. 22. I should like my father to be happy, when he is *(sera)* old. 23. That little boy was glad that I had given him some apples. 24. Our parents loved us, although we were often naughty. 25. Did he not wish us to come?

LESSON XVIII.

167. Present Participle of *donner, finir, rompre, avoir, être.*

[*Giving.*] [*Finishing.*] [*Breaking.*] [*Having.*] [*Being.*]
donn ant.   finiss ant.   romp ant.   ay ant.   ét ant.

[PRON.—1. *dònā.* 2. *finisā.* 3. *rōpā.* 4. *èiā.* 5. *étā.*]

168. Use and Agreement. The pres. part. has the force of an *adjective* or of a *verb.* As an *adjective,* it *agrees*; otherwise it is *invariable:*

Une scène frappante. Les mourants.	A striking scene. The dying.
Elles sont charmantes.	They are charming.
Pleurant, elle continua son récit.	Weeping, she continued her story.
Il tombait souvent en marchant.	He often fell while walking.

N. B.—En is the only prep. followed by a pres. part.—all others take the *infin*: Le crime de voler, 'The crime of stealing'; Sans y penser, 'Without thinking of it.'

169. Use of Auxiliaries of Tense. Avoir + *the past part.* forms the compound tenses of *all transitive* and of *most intransitive* verbs (§170):

Perf. Infin. avoir donné, *to have given*. Perf. Part. ayant donné, *having given*. Past Indef. j'ai donné, *I have given, gave*, etc. Plupf. Indic. j'avais donné, *I had given*, etc. Past Anterior. j'eus donné, *I had given*, etc. Fut. Anterior. j'aurai donné, *I shall have given*, etc. Condl. Ant. j'aurais donné, *I should have given*, etc. Perf. Subj. (que) j'aie donné, *(that) I may have given*, etc. Plupf. Subj. (que) j'eusse donné, *(that) I might have given*, etc.

170. Être + *the past part.* forms the compound tenses of *all reflexive* verbs (§175) and of a *few intransitives*, of which the following are the most important:

venir, *to come.*	naître, *to be born.*
arriver, *to arrive, come.*	mourir, *to die.*
aller, *to go.*	décéder, *to die.*

So also, most of the *intransitive compounds* of venir (devenir, *become*; revenir, *come back*, etc.).

Note.—The use of avoir is *rare* with entrer, *enter*, retourner, *go back*, tomber, *fall*.

Thus: [*I have arrived*, etc.]

je suis ⎫
tu es ⎬ arrivé(e).
il (elle) est ⎭

nous sommes ⎫
vous êtes ⎬ arrivé(e)s.
ils (elles) sont ⎭

171. Agreement of Past Participle. The past part. of a verb conjugated with être *always agrees with the subject* (unless the verb be reflexive, §177):

Marie et Georges étaient arrivés.	Mary and George had arrived.
Quand êtes-vous arrivé(e) ?, *or* arrivé(e)s ?	When did you arrive?
Elle parle d'être arrivée.	She speaks of having arrived.

172. Use of Compound Tenses. 1. The *pluperfect* is of commoner occurrence than the *past anterior*, and is regularly used after **si** = 'if,' or when *custom, continuance,* etc., is implied :

Si j'avais eu l'argent, je l'aurais donné.	If I had had the money, I should have given it.
J'avais souvent fini avant son arrivée.	I often had finished before his arrival.

2. The *past anterior* is rarely used except after conjunctions of time, such as **lorsque, quand** = 'when,' **après que** = 'after,' **aussitôt que, dès que** = 'as soon as,' etc. :

Aussitôt qu'il eut fini, il partit.	As soon as he had finished, he went away.

3. Observe the use of the *future perfect* in a subordinate clause in which *futurity is implied* :

Je lui parlerai, quand il aura fini.	I shall speak to him, when he has finished.

4. The rules for *conditional* sentences (§149) and *tense sequence* with the subjunctive (§§161, 166) apply to the *auxiliary* of comp. tenses :

Si j'avais bien récité, le maître aurait été content.	If I had recited well, the master would have been pleased.
Je suis content que vous ayez réussi.	I am glad that you have succeeded.

EXERCISE XVIII.

Acheter *(ăšté)*, buy.
L'affaire, f., *(áfè.r)*, affair.
Amuser *(ămüzé)*, amuse.
L'Angleterre, f., *(ăgletè.r)*, England.
Le bonheur *(bŏnœ.r)*, good fortune.
Le chant *(šā)*, singing, song.
Charmer *(šărmé)*, charm.
Le fat *(fát)*, fop.
La femme *(făm)*, wife.
Le malheur *(măloe.r)*, misfortune.

Toute la journée. All day (long), the whole day.
Presque toujours. Almost always.
Aux États-Unis. To (*or* in) the United States.

A. 1. Si elle était arrivée plus tôt, nous lui aurions donné de l'argent. 2. Si le petit garçon était allé à l'école, sa mère aurait été contente. 3. Il ne serait pas allé en Angleterre, s'il avait été plus heureux au Canada.

4. Ayant froid, nous avons fermé les fenêtres. 5. Ces petites filles sont charmantes. 6. Étant en France, il a acheté des robes de soie pour sa femme. 7. Chantant dans les arbres, les petits oiseaux nous amusent toute la journée. 8. Voilà une canne rompue. 9. Oui, ce petit fat l'a rompue en marchant. 10. Le chant de ces oiseaux nous a charmés toute la journée. 11. À quelle heure monsieur votre frère est-il arrivé? 12. Il est arrivé à midi. 13. Je désirerais que ma sœur fût arrivée. 14. Je désirerais que mes sœurs ne fussent pas allées à l'église aujourd'hui. 15. Avez-vous fermé les fenêtres? 16. Oui, monsieur, nous les avons fermées. 17. Je donnerai des pommes au petit garçon, quand il sera arrivé. 18. Ma sœur était très contente que je fusse arrivé. 19. Vous êtes contente, n'est-ce pas mademoiselle, que ce petit fat ait rompu sa canne? 20. Oui, monsieur, j'en suis très contente. 21. Si nous étions arrivés de bonne heure, les professeurs en auraient été contents. 22. Depuis quand êtes-vous dans ce pays-ci? 23. Nous sommes arrivés l'année passée. 24. Avez-vous jamais parlé à mon père de cette affaire? 25. Oui, je lui en ai souvent parlé. 26. Je suis toujours content du bonheur des autres.

B. 1. If we had arrived sooner, my father would have been pleased at it. 2. Little girls are almost always charming. 3. Being in England, my mother bought a silk hat for my father. 4. If I had given the beggar money, he would have been glad of it. 5. If the little girls had gone to school to-day, I should have been sorry for it. 6. If our neighbors had been happier in Canada, they would not have gone to the United States. 7. If that little fop had broken his cane while walking, would you have been glad of it? 8. No, sir, I am never glad at the misfortunes of others. 9. Having had many misfortunes in this country, they have gone to the United States. 10. How long have you been in this city? 11. We arrived last week. 12. Having given money to the beggar, I have none left. 13. If you had come sooner, I should not have gone to church to-day. 14. I should very much like that my daughters had come. 15. Would you not like very much that the boys had not gone to school to-day? 16. Yes, I am sorry that they have gone to school. 17. Singing and playing, the little children have amused their mothers all day long. 18. We had gone to church before you had arrived. 19. That bird's song has charmed us all day long. 20. Did you close the doors and windows? 21. Yes, sir, we closed them. 22. If the children had come sooner, we should have given them some apples. 23. I shall give the little boy some money, when he has finished his work. 24. When did you speak to your mother of that affair? 25. I have never spoken to her about it. 26. Having given away my apples to the children, I have none left. 27. If my brother were here, I should be very glad of it. 28. If I had bought a silk hat, I should have no money left. 29. I am glad that he has gone. 30. I should like him to have come.

LESSON XIX.

173. Use of the Infinitive. Some of the commoner uses of the infinitive are:—

1. *Without any preposition:*

a. After such verbs as **vouloir** = 'will,' **désirer** = 'wish,' 'like to,' **pouvoir** = 'can,' 'may,' **savoir** = 'know how to,' 'can,' **devoir** = 'ought,' **oser** = 'dare,' **falloir** = 'be necessary,' etc., and after many *verbs of motion:*

Pouvez-vous rompre ce bâton ?	Can you **break** this stick ?
Il vous faut **travailler** davantage.	You must **work** more.
Allez **chercher** du papier.	Go and **get** some paper.

b. After verbs of *perceiving*, such as **voir** = 'see,' **écouter** = 'listen to,' **regarder** = 'look at,' etc. So also, after **faire** = 'make,' 'cause to,' and **laisser** = 'let,' 'allow':

Je vois **venir** le train ; je le vois venir.	I see the train **coming**; I see it coming.

Obs.: In construction (*b.*) governed *nouns* regularly *follow* the *infinitive*, but the *pers. pron. obj. accompanies the finite verb.*

2. *Preceded by* **de**, after **être** as *impers. verb + adj.*, after many verbs like **regretter** = 'regret,' **être fâché** = 'be sorry,' **prier** = 'beg,' 'request,' **ordonner** = 'order,' etc., after nouns to form an *attributive phrase*, and after *most adjectives:*

Il est facile de faire cela.	It is easy to do that.
Je vous prie de m'aider.	I beg you to help me.
Le crime de voler.	The crime of stealing.
Vous êtes libre de retourner.	You are free to go back.

3. *Preceded by* à, after verbs like **réussir** = 'succeed,' **persister** = 'persist,' **aimer** = 'like,' 'love,' **enseigner** = 'teach,' **aider** = 'help,' etc., after *some adjectives*, and after *nouns* to denote *destination, purpose*, etc.:

Il a persisté à nous interrompre.	He persisted in interrupting us.
Cela est facile à faire.	That is easy to do.
Une maison à vendre.	A house for sale (=to be sold).

174. Formation of Tenses. By the following rules, the various tenses of *all regular verbs* and of *most irregular verbs* may be known from five forms of the verb, called *principal parts* or *primary tenses:*

1. Pres. Infin.	2. Pres. Part.	3. Past Part.	4. Pres. Indic.	5. Past Def.
Gives the Fut. Indic. by adding: -ai, -as, -a, -ons, -ez, -ont.	Gives the Impf. Indic. by changing -ant into: -ais, -ais, -ait, -ions, -iez, -aient.	Gives the Comp. Tenses with the aux. avoir or être (§169, 170).	Gives the Imperat. by *dropping* the *pron. subject* of the 2nd sing. and 1 and 2 plur.	Gives the Impf. Subj. by changing the final letter (-i or -s) into: -sse, -sses, -t, -ssions, -ssiez, -ssent, and putting a *circumflex* over the *last vowel of the 3 sing.*
Condl. by adding: -ais, -ais, -ait, -ions, -iez, -aient. *Drop* in both tenses the *final* e of the 3rd conjugation.	Pres. Subj. by changing -ant into: -e, -es, -e, -ions, -iez, -ent.	The Passive with the aux. être (§179).	N.B.—The s of the 1st conj. 2nd sing. is also dropped, except before y and en (§154).	

Obs.: The tenses (except the *future* and *conditional*) are not derived from the principal parts. The method is merely an aid to memory.

Exercise.—Write out the principal parts of donner, finir, rompre, and form their various tenses according to the above scheme.

EXERCISE XIX.

Aimer mieux *(èmé miŭ)*, prefer.
Cela *(selá)*, that.
Dire *(di.r)*, say, tell.
Faire *(fè.r)*, do.
Laisser *(lèsé)*, let.
Offenser *(òfãsé)*, offend.
Oser *(ôzé)*, dare.
Les parents *(párã)*, relatives.

La permission *(pèrmisĩõ)*, permission.
Le plaisir *(plèzi.r)*, pleasure.
Prier *(prié)*, ask, beg.
Réussir *(réüsi.r)*, succeed.
Vendre *(vã.dr)*, sell.
Visiter *(vizité)*, visit.
Voir *(vŭá.r)*, see.

Chez moi (toi, etc.). At home.

A. 1. Aimez-vous à visiter vos cousins de Londres? 2. J'aime mieux visiter mes parents de Paris. 3. Pourquoi n'osez-vous pas parler au professeur? 4. Parce que j'ai peur de l'offenser. 5. Avez-vous peur de dire cela à votre père? 6. Je n'ai pas peur de le lui dire, parce qu'il m'aime bien. 7. J'ai prié mon père de me laisser aller à l'école. 8. Cet homme-là ne laisse jamais son petit garçon aller à l'école. 9. Je suis fâché de vous dire que vous avez tort. 10. J'ai demandé à mon père la permission d'aller à la ville. 11. Avez-vous besoin de travailler? 12. Oui, monsieur, j'en ai grand besoin. 13. Voilà une maison à vendre! À qui est-elle? 14. Elle est à notre voisin, M. Blanc. 15. Je regrette beaucoup de ne pas avoir été ici, quand vous m'avez visité. 16. Si vous réussissez à faire cela, nous en serons contents. 17. J'ai le grand plaisir de vous dire que vous avez raison. 18. Mon petit frère n'aime pas à travailler; il aime mieux jouer avec les autres garçons. 19. Nous aurons le grand plaisir de visiter nos parents, quand nous serons à Londres. 20. Pourquoi ne laissez-vous pas entrer ce chien? 21. Je n'ose pas le laisser entrer. J'en ai peur. 22. Que désirez-vous, monsieur? 23. Je désire parler à M. Blanc. 24. Je ne désire pas aller à l'église ce matin; j'aime mieux rester chez moi. 25. Voilà de jolies pommes; je désirerais en avoir. 26. Je vous prie, monsieur, de me donner de l'argent. 27. J'aurais grand plaisir de vous en donner, si j'en avais. 28. Je regrette de ne pas avoir demandé de l'argent à mon père. 29. Il n'aurait pas réussi à bâtir cette maison, si je ne lui avais pas prêté de l'argent. 30. Votre petit garçon pourquoi n'est-il pas à l'école ? 31. J'ai peur de l'y laisser aller.

B. 1. Does your brother like to work? 2. Yes, he likes to work, but he prefers to play. 3. I am sorry to say that I was wrong. 4. He asked his father to let him go to school. 5. His father does not wish to let him go to school. 6. Why does he not dare to speak to his father? 7. He is afraid of offending him. 8. I am glad to have the permission of speaking to you about it *(en)*. 9. We shall have the great pleasure of visiting our friends, when we are in Toronto. 10. Your friends and relatives will have the pleasure of speaking to you, when you are in Toronto. 11. I am afraid to speak of it to my father; I prefer to speak of it to my mother. 12. There is a very fine silk hat; I should like to have it. 13. Do you need to work? 14. Yes, sir, I have great need of working. 15. I don't like to go to church to-day; I prefer to stay at home. 16. I asked our neighbor to let me have some apples, but he has no more. 17. He is sorry to say that he has none. 18. Why is that little girl not at school? 19. Her mother is afraid to let her go to school. 20. There is a nice little house for sale. 21. I should like to buy it, but I have not money enough. 22. Shall I not have the pleasure of seeing you, when you are here? 23. Oh, yes, sir, with great pleasure. 24. He will not succeed in building his house, if he does not have more money. 25. I should not have succeeded in seeing him, if my brother had not been with me. 26. I am glad to say to you that you are right. 27. If we succeed in do-doing that, we shall be much pleased (at it). 28. I shall be glad to stay at home to-morrow. 29. Are you afraid of saying that to your mother? 30. No, sir, I am not afraid of saying it to her. 31. My brothers and sisters will be glad to see me.

LESSON XX.

175. Reflexive Verbs. The *subject* of a reflexive verb acts on itself as *reflexive object*. The *compound tenses* are *always* formed with être, as in the following section.

176. Conjugation of *se flatter* :—

PRES. INFIN. se flatter, *to flatter one's self.*
PERF. INFIN. s'être flatté(e)(s), *to have flattered one's self.*
PRES. PART. se flattant, *flattering one's self.*
PERF. PART. s'étant flatté(e)(s), *having flattered one's self.*

PRES. INDIC.
[*I flatter myself, etc.*]
je me flatte.
tu te flattes.
il (elle) se flatte.
nous nous flattons.
vous vous flattez.
ils (elles) se flattent.
etc.

PAST. INDEF.
[*I have flattered myself, etc.*]
je me suis ⎫
tu t'es   ⎬ flatté(e).
il (elle) s'est ⎭
nous nous sommes ⎫
vous vous êtes   ⎬ flatté(e)s.
ils (elles) se sont ⎭
etc.

177. The Past Participle agrees with the *reflexive object* (unless it be *indirect*) :

Ils se sont flattés. — They have flattered themselves.
Elle s'est réjouie. — She (has) rejoiced.
But : Elles se sont acheté des robes. — They have bought themselves dresses.

NOTE.—The aux. être is considered as replacing avoir, and the agreement is explained by the general principle (§121).

178. Use of the Reflexive. 1. The reflexive is very common in French, and is often expressed in English by the *passive* (especially of *unspecified agent*), or by a *non-reflexive* verb (generally *intransitive*). A *reflexive + a prep.* has often the value of an English *transitive :*

Ma montre s'est trouvée. — My watch has been found.
S'arrêter. Se porter. — To stop. To be (said of health).
Se hâter. Se tromper. — To hasten. To be mistaken.
Se douter de. Se fier à. — To suspect. To trust.

2. In the *plural*, reflexive verbs express either *reflexive* or *reciprocal* action :

Elles se flattent. — They flatter themselves (*or* one another).

179. The Passive Voice is formed from the various tenses of être + *the past participle*, which *agrees* with the *subject* :—

USE OF THE PASSIVE.

Pres. Indic.	Past Indef.
[*I am* (or *am being*) *praised, etc.*]	[*I have been* (or *was*, or *was being*) *praised, etc.*]
je suis ⎫	j'ai été ⎫
tu es ⎬ loué(e).	tu as été ⎬ loué(e).
il (elle) est ⎭	il (elle) a été ⎭
nous sommes ⎫	nous avons été ⎫
vous êtes ⎬ loué(e)s.	vous avez été ⎬ loué(e)s.
ils (elles) sont ⎭	ils (elles) ont été ⎭
etc.	etc.

Obs.: The past part. été is *always invariable*.

180. Agent after the Passive. 'By' is usually **par** when *specific intention* is implied, and **de** when the action is *habitual, usual,* or *indefinite:*

| L'Amérique fut découverte par Colomb. | America was discovered by Columbus. |
| Cette dame est estimée de tous. | This lady is esteemed by all. |

181. Use of the Passive. Unless the agent is specified, the passive is commonly *avoided* in French, either by using **on** = 'one,' etc., or by a *reflexive verb* (§178):

| On m'a trompé. | I have been deceived. |
| Cette histoire se raconte partout. | This story is told everywhere. |

EXERCISE XX.

L'absence, f., (*ábsã.s*), absence.
Alors (*álò.r*), then.
S'amuser (*ámüzé*), enjoy one's self.
S'arrêter (*árètè*), stop (intr.).
Le bal (*bál*), ball.
Le chemin (*šemẽ*), road.
La chose (*šó.z*), thing.
Comment? (*kòmã*), how?
Se douter de (*duté*), suspect.
Une fois (*fuá*), once.
Mal, (adv.) (*mál*), ill, badly.
Malade (*máládé*), ill, sick.
Mesdemoiselles (*mèdemüázèl*), young ladies (in address).
Se porter (*pòrté*), be (of health).
Quelque chose (*kèlke*), something.
La récompense (*rékõpã.s*), reward.
Se réjouir (*réžui.r*), rejoice.
Respecter (*respèkté*), respect.
Se tromper (*trõpé*), make a mistake, be mistaken.
Voler (*vòlé*), steal.

Comment vous portez-vous?	How are you?
Je me porte bien.	I am well.
Je me porte mal.	I am ill.
Je me suis trompé de porte.	I am (*or* was) at the wrong door.
Je m'en suis douté.	I suspected it.
Tout le monde.	Every body.

A. 1. La voiture de la dame s'est arrêtée devant notre porte. 2. J'ai honte de dire que je me suis trompé dans cette affaire. 3. Madame votre mère comment se porte-t-elle aujourd'hui ? 4. Elle se porte très bien, monsieur. 5. Qui frappe à notre porte ? 6. C'est M. Blanc ; il s'est trompé de porte. 7. Comment vous portez-vous, madame, depuis un an ? 8. Très mal, madame ; j'ai été malade toute l'année. 9. Où avez-vous intention d'aller, monsieur ? 10. J'ai intention d'aller au village. 11. Eh bien, alors, vous vous êtes trompé de chemin. 12. Si je ne m'étais pas trompé de chemin, j'aurais été déjà chez moi. 13. Que demande ce petit garçon ? 14. Il s'est trompé de porte ; il cherche la maison de M. Mercier. 15. Mademoiselle votre sœur comment s'est-elle portée depuis son absence ? 16. Elle n'a été malade qu'une fois. 17. Tu as été méchant, mon fils ? 18. Oui, maman. 19. Je m'en suis doutée. 20. Vous êtes-vous bien amusées au bal, mesdemoiselles ? 21. Nous nous y sommes bien amusées. 22. Réjouissez-vous, parce que votre récompense sera grande. 23. Amusez-vous, mes enfants ; vous ne serez pas toujours jeunes. 24. Cette dame est aimée de tout le monde. 25. Je me suis douté de quelque chose ; ce coquin a volé la montre d'or de notre voisin. 26. Vous avez tort, madame ; vous vous êtes trompée dans cette affaire. 27. Mais non, monsieur, je ne me suis pas trompée. 28. Comme les petits enfants s'amusent ! 30. Ce jeune homme est aimé et respecté de tous ses voisins. 31. N'êtes-vous pas fâché que je me sois trompé ? 32. Je suis content que vous vous soyez trompé.

B. 1. How are you this morning, sir ? 2. I am very well, madam. 3. Have you been well the whole year ? 4. I have been ill only once. 5. Our neighbor's horses stopped in front of our gate. 6. I am sorry to say that you are mistaken. 7. Where do you desire to go, young ladies ? 8. We desire to go to church, sir. 9. Well then, you have taken the wrong road. 10. Rejoice, for you will have a great reward. 11. How did you enjoy yourselves at the ball, last evening, young ladies ? 12. Those young ladies are loved and respected by everybody. 13. The book was found by my brother. 14. Our neighbor's watch was stolen by that little rascal. 15. Who is at our door? 16. It is M. Mercier. 17. What is he asking for? 18. He is at the wrong door; he is looking for M. Blanc's house. 19. Enjoy yourselves *(mes)* boys; you will work better for it *(en)*. 20. If those gentlemen had not taken the wrong road, they would have been at home now. 21. I suspected something; that rascal has stolen my watch. 22. I have lost my watch and money. 23. I suspected it. 24. If I am not mistaken, I shall soon be at home. 25. That gentleman is wrong; he is mistaken in that affair. 26. Are you not ashamed to say that I am mistaken? 27. That young man is loved by everybody. 28. My father is not well; he has been ill for a year. 29. How those dogs enjoy themselves! 30. Did you enjoy yourself in Paris? 31. I am sorry that I was mistaken. 32. We are very glad that he was not mistaken. 33. Everybody is mistaken sometimes. 34. Why do you not stop? 35. Let us stop; we have taken the wrong road. 36. Do not stop; you have not taken the wrong road. 37. Our neighbors have but few friends. 38. You are wrong; they have many friends and relatives in the country.

LESSON XXI.

182. Impersonal Verbs are conjugated, in the 3rd sing. only, with the subject **il** (= 'it,' 'there,' used *indefinitely* and *absolutely*). Such are :—

1. Verbs describing *natural phenomena*, as also in English:

Pleut-il?—Non, monsieur, il neige. Is it raining? No, it is snowing.
Il a dégelé. Il pleuvra bientôt. It thawed. It will rain soon.

a. So also, **faire** = 'to do,' 'make,' used impersonally :

Quel temps fait-il?—Il fait beau (temps). What kind of weather is it? It is fine (weather).
Il a fait froid. Il faisait obscur. It was cold. It was dark.
Il fait trop chaud dans cette chambre. It is too hot in this room (*or* this room is too hot).

Obs.: Distinguish the above from constructions with a *personal* subject: Le temps est beau, 'The weather is fine.' L'eau est froide, 'The water is cold.'

2. The irreg. verb **falloir** = 'to be necessary,' 'must,' 'be obliged to,' 'have to,' etc. :—

Infin.	*Pres. Part.*	*Past Part.*	*Pres. Indic.*	*Past Def.*
falloir.	——	fallu.	il faut.	il fallut.
Fut.	*Impf.*			*Impf. Subj.*
il faudra.	il fallait.			il fallût.
Condl.	*Pres. Subj.*			
il faudrait.	(qu)'il faille.			

Il faut que je parte. ⎫
Il me faut partir. ⎭ I must go.

Il lui faudra rester. ⎫
Il faudra qu'il reste. ⎭ He will have to (be obliged to, etc.) stay.

Il ne faut pas voler.   We must not steal.

a. Followed by a noun, **falloir** = 'need' (also expressed by **avoir besoin de**), and takes the *dative of the person needing*:

Il faut un chapeau à Jean. ⎫
Jean a besoin d'un chapeau. ⎭ John needs a hat.

3. **Avoir** *preceded by* y *and used impersonally:*

Il y a.   Il y a eu.   There is (*or* are).   There has (*or* have) been.
Il y avait. Il y avait eu. There was (*or* were).   There had been.
         etc., like **avoir**.

a. Distinguish **voilà** = 'there *(emphatic)* is *or* are' from **il y a** = 'there *(unemphatic)* is *or* are,' and observe the use of **il y a** in expressing *time* (reckoned *backwards*):

Voilà un bel arbre !	There is a fine tree !
Il y a un bel arbre dans la cour.	There is a fine tree in the yard.
Nous sommes arrivés il y a trois jours. ⎫ Il y a trois jours que nous sommes arrivés. ⎭	We came three days ago.
Il y a trois jours que nous sommes ici.	We have been here for three days (past).

183. **Il est** (il était, etc.) *impersonally* always requires **de** before a following *infinitive:*

Il est facile de faire cela.   It is easy to do that.

IMPERSONAL VERBS.

184. Conjugation of *faire*, 'to do,' 'make,' 'cause to,' etc. :—

Pres. Infin.	Pres. Part.	Past Part.	Pres. Indic.	Past Def.
faire.	faisant.	fait.	fais. faisons.	fis.
Fut.	*Impf.*		fais. faites.	*Impf. Subj.*
ferai.	faisais.		fait. font.	fisse.
Condl.	*Pres. Subj.*	[*Impve.* fais, faisons, faites.]		
ferais.	fasse, (-es, -e), fassions, (-iez, -ent).			

EXERCISE XXI.

Agréable *(ágréábl)*, agreeable.
La carafe *(káráf)*, decanter, water-bottle.
Le clou *(klu)*, nail.
Comme *(kòm)*, like.
Continuer *(kòtinüé)*, continue.
Faire *(fè.r)*, make.
Frais, fraîche *(frè, frè.š)*, fresh, cool.

Le lac *(lák)*, lake.
La livre *(li.vr)*, pound.
Longtemps *(lõtã)*, long, a long time.
Le temps *(tã)*, weather.
Trouver *(truvé)*, find, think.
La viande *(vlã.d)*, meat.

Je fais venir du pain. — I send for bread.
Je me fais faire un habit. — I am having (getting) a coat made.
Je me suis fait faire un habit. — I (have) had a coat made.
Bon jour. — Good morning. Good day. Good afternoon.
Bon soir. — Good evening. Good night.
Vous trouvez? — Do you think so?

A. 1. Bon jour, monsieur, comment vous portez-vous ce matin? 2. Je ne me porte pas bien, il fait trop chaud. 3. Vous trouvez? Moi j'aime le temps chaud. 4. Trouvez-vous que ce temps est trop froid? 5. Non, madame, je l'aime comme cela. 6. Il fait chaud aujourd'hui, mais il fera plus chaud demain. 7. Je ferai bâtir une maison, quand je serai assez riche. 8. Il faudra que je sois chez moi ce soir. 9. Il y a de belles pommes dans ce panier. 10. Voilà de belles pommes dans ce panier! 11. Y a-t-il longtemps que vous êtes ici? 12. Il y a quatre ans que nous sommes ici. 13. Que faut-il à Marie? 14. Il lui faut une robe neuve. 15. Je désire que vous me fassiez faire une table. 16. Je désire qu'il fasse chaud demain. 17. Bon soir, madame; il fait beau, n'est ce pas? 18. Ce monsieur s'est fait faire un habit. 19. Je m'en suis fait faire un aussi. 20. Il fait bien chaud, mais l'eau du lac est encore froide. 21. Comment trouvez-vous le temps au Canada? 22. Je le trouve presque toujours bien agréable. 23. Est-ce qu'il y a de l'eau fraîche dans la maison? 24. Oui, monsieur, en voilà dans la carafe sur la table. 25. Que vous faut-il ce matin, monsieur? 26. Il me faut une livre de viande et quatre livres de pain. 27. Il faut que nous fassions venir du village de la viande et du pain. 28. L'eau du lac sera plus chaude, s'il continue à faire chaud. 29. Le fils du charpentier a fait venir du village des planches et des clous. 30. Il faudra que nous arrivions avant midi. 31. Que ce pauvre chien a chaud! 32. Il faut des planches au charpentier. 33. Qu'en fera-t-il? 34. Il en fera une table. 35. Que faites-vous, madame? 36. Je fais une robe pour ma petite fille, et j'en fais venir une autre de la ville.

B. 1. What does Mary need. 2. She needs books and paper. 3. We must send for bread and meat. 4. We wish that you would get a carriage made for us. 5. It is very warm to-day. 6. Do you think so? I found it very agreeable. 7. I have had a coat made. 8. Where is it? 9. There it is on the table. 10. I do not like warm weather. 11. How warm that poor horse is! 12. I am getting a table made. 13. We had a house built last year. 14. Are there any fine pears in the house? 15. Yes, there are some in that basket. 16. That gentleman's son sends to the village for meat and bread. 17. Has not the carpenter's son sent to the village for boards and nails? 18. Yes, sir, and there they are behind the stable. 19. We must have a house built next year. 20. Have you been long here? 21. I have been here for four hours. 22. Good morning, sir; it is very fine, is it not? 23. Yes, sir, but it will be warmer. 24. If it continues to be warm, the lake water will be warmer. 25. There is good fresh water in the decanter. 26. What does the carpenter need? 27. He needs nails and boards. 28. What will he do with them? 29. He will make a table with them. 30. I wish it would be fine to-morrow. 31. It will not be cold to-day. 32. I shall have a coat made next week. 33. And I shall have one made too. 34. Will the gentleman send to the village for a silk hat? 35. No, there are none in the village. 36. I had a coat made, and I shall have another one made. 37. I need four pounds of bread and one pound of meat. 38. Give me some water; I am not well to-day, it is too warm.

LESSON XXII.

185. The Possessive Pronouns.

Singular.		Plural.		
M.	*F.*	*M.*	*F.*	
le mien	la mienne	les miens	les miennes,	*mine.*
le nôtre	la nôtre	les nôtres,		*ours.*
le tien	la tienne	les tiens	les tiennes,	*thine, yours.*
le vôtre	la vôtre	les vôtres,		*yours.*
le sien	la sienne	les siens	les siennes,	*his, hers, its, one's.*
le leur	la leur	les leurs,		*theirs, one's.*

[Pron.—1. *le miĕ, lá mièn, lè miĕ, lè mièn.* 2. *le nô.tr, la nô.tr, lè nô.tr.* 3. *le tiĕ, lá tièn, lè tiĕ, lè tièn.* 4. *le vô.tr, lá vô.tr, lè vô.tr.* 5. *le siĕ, lá sièn, lè siĕ, lè sièn.* 6. *le lœ.r, lá lœ.r, lè lœ.r.*]

Obs.: 1. The fem. (except for **leur**) is formed as in adjs. of like ending (§§128, 129, 2). 2. De and à+le mien, etc., contract as usual (§107); du mien (=de+le mien), aux miennes (=à+les miennes), etc. 3. Note the accent mark in nôtre, vôtre, absent in the poss. adj. notre, votre (§89). 4. Since le sien (la sienne, etc.)='his,' 'her,' 'its,' 'one's,' the context determines which sense is intended.

186. Agreement. Possessive pronouns agree in *gender* and *number* with the name of the *object possessed*, and in *person* with the *possessor:*

J'ai mes livres et elle a { le sien. I have my books, and she has hers.
                          { les siens.

187. Use of Possessive Pronouns. 1. After être, mere *ownership* is regularly expressed by à + *a pers. pron.* (disj.), while the use of a *poss. pron.* implies *distinction of ownership:*

Cette montre est à moi.   This watch is mine (*or* belongs to me, *i.e.*, I am the owner of it).

Cette montre est la mienne.   This watch is mine (as distinguished from one or more others *not* mine).

G

2. The *emphatic* 'my own,' etc., is generally translated by the *pron. simply:*

Cherchez mon thème et le vôtre. Look for my exercise and your own.

3. The idiom 'a friend of mine' = **un de mes amis**:

Cette dame-là est une de mes tantes.   That lady is an aunt of mine.

Il a amené de ses amis.   He brought some friends of his.

Obs.: Remember that **mon, ton,** etc. (§89) are always *adjectives*, and stand *before* nouns, while **le mien, le tien,** etc., are always *pronouns*, and stand *instead* of nouns.

188. Conjugation of *aller*, 'to go':—

Pres. Infin.	*Pres. Part.*	*Past Part.*	*Pres. Indic.*		*Past Def.*
aller.	allant.	allé.	vais.	allons.	allai.
Fut.	*Impf.*		vas.	allez.	*Impf. Subj.*
irai.	allais.		va.	vont.	allasse.
Condl.	*Pres. Subj.*	[*Impve.* va, allons, allez.]			
irais.	aille, (-es, -e), allions, (-iez), aillent.				

189. Conjugation of *envoyer*, 'to send':—

Pres Infin.	*Pres. Part.*	*Past Part.*	*Pres. Indic.*		*Past Def.*
envoyer.	envoyant.	envoyé.	envoie.	envoyons.	envoyai.
Fut.	*Impf.*		envoies.	envoyez.	*Imp. Subj.*
enverrai.	envoyais.		envoie.	envoient.	envoyasse.
Condl.	*Pres. Subj.*	[*Impve.* envoie, envoyons, envoyez.]			
enverrais.	envoie, (-es, -e), envoyions, (-iez), envoient.				

EXERCISE XXII.

Couper *(kupé)*, cut.   Le marchand *(máršã)*, merchant.
L'étoffe, f., *(étòf)*, cloth.   Le retour *(retu.r)*, return.
Le laitier *(lètié)*, milkman.

Va chercher du bois.   Go and get some wood.
Il ira en chercher.   He will go for some.
Je l'enverrai chercher du lait.   I shall send him (*or* her) for (some) milk.
J'enverrai chercher du lait.   I shall send for (some) milk.
J'irai trouver mon père.   I shall go to (for) my father.
Je vais faire cela.   I am going to do that.
À votre retour.   On your return.

USE OF POSSESSIVE PRONOUNS.

A. 1. Si vous allez chercher du lait, je vous en donnerai à votre retour. 2. Où vas-tu, mon garçon? 3. Je vais trouver mon père. 4. Je vais chercher du lait chez le laitier. 5. Je vais trouver ma mère et la vôtre. 6. Je désire que vous alliez trouver votre cousin et le mien. 7. Le charpentier va chercher mes planches et les siennes. 8. Où êtes-vous allé hier? 9. Je suis allé trouver ma tante et ma cousine. 10. Qu'avez-vous envoyé chercher? 11. J'ai envoyé chercher des planches et des clous. 12. Nos voisins et les leurs sont allés chercher du bois. 13. Nos voisins sont allés chercher leurs chevaux et les nôtres, mais ils ne les ont pas trouvés. 14. Je désire envoyer chercher de l'étoffe chez le marchand. 15. Donnez-moi de vos pommes, je n'en ai pas moi-même. 16. Le fils du charpentier va couper des planches. 17. Nos cousins vont arriver demain? 18. Nous arriverons après-demain. 19. Qu'allez-vous faire maintenant? 20. Je vais me faire faire un habit. 21. Il va faire chaud demain. 22. Nous allons avoir chaud ici, si vous fermez les fenêtres. 23. Vous n'avez pas de pain; nous irons en chercher, si vous en désirez. 24. Jean, va chercher mon chapeau. 25. J'y vais tout de suite. 26. Nous désirons que nos fils aillent à l'école. 27. Si mon père envoie chercher des planches, j'en ferai une table. 28. Si mon fils était ici, je l'enverrais chercher des pommes. 29. Il faut que ce petit garçon aille trouver sa mère. 30. S'il ne faisait pas si chaud j'irais faire mon ouvrage.

B. 1. Where are you going, sir, this morning? 2. I am going to my uncle. 3. Go and get some milk. 4. I do not wish any, I have some. 5. I shall send for some bread, if you wish any. 6. I am going for my horses and yours. 7. Have you not my watch and your own? 8. No, sir, there is yours on the table. 9. The carpenter's son is going for my boards and his own. 10. What did you send for, sir? 11. I sent for apples and pears. 12. I am going for apples, and I am going to give you some on your return. 13. Our cousins and yours have gone for water. 14. I wish to send to the merchant's for cloth. 15. Give me some of your money, I have none. 16. You are going to cut wood, are you not? 17. No, I am not going to cut any. 18. The carpenter and his son are going to cut our wood and their own. 19. It is going to be warm to-day. 20. We shall not be too warm, if you close the window. 21. My son must go to school. 22. I wish my daughter to go to school. 23. What are you going to do now? 24. I am going to have a table made. 25. If the carpenter sends for boards, he will give me some. 26. If John were here, we should send him for water. 27. This little boy must go and get some bread. 28. If it were not so cold, I should go to church. 29. When are you going to do your work? 30. I am going to do it to-morrow; it is too warm to-day.

LESSON XXIII.

190. The Demonstrative Pronouns.

1. ce, invar., *this (these), that (those), he (she, it, they).*
2. ceci, invar., *this.*
3. cela, invar., *that.*
4. celui, m. s., ⎫ *that (one), the one,*   ceux, m. pl., ⎫ *those (ones), the*
   celle, f. s., ⎭ *he, (she).*   celles, f. pl., ⎭ *ones, they.*
5. celui-ci, m. s., ⎫ *this (one), the*   ceux-ci, m. pl., ⎫ *these (ones), the*
   celle-ci, f. s., ⎭ *latter.*   celles-ci, f. pl., ⎭ *latter.*
6. celui-là, m. s., ⎫ *that (one), the*   ceux-là, m. pl., ⎫ *those (ones), the*
   celle-là, f. s., ⎭ *former.*   celles-là, f. pl., ⎭ *former.*

[PRON.—1. *se*. 2. *sesi*. 3. *selá*. 4. *selẅi, sel, sö, sél*. 5. *selẅi si, sel si, sö si, sel si*. 6. *selẅi lá, sel lá, sö lá, sel lá*.]

191. Use of ce.
It is used most commonly with être, and must be carefully distinguished both from il (elle, etc.) and from il *impersonal*. Thus,

1. **Ce** and the *personal* **il** (elle, etc.):

C'est Jean. C'est mon ami.	It is John. It (he) is my friend.
C'est une Allemande. C'est elle.	She is a German. It is she.
C'est moi. C'est vous. Ce sont eux.	It is I. It is you. It is they.
Ce sera bien peu. C'était assez.	That will be very little. It was enough.
Voilà des fleurs; elles sont jolies.	There are flowers; they are pretty.
Je connais cet homme; il est médecin.	I know that man; he is a doctor.
Il est Français.	He is a Frenchman.

2. Ce and the *impersonal* il :

C'est facile. Ce sera facile à faire.	That is easy. That will be easy to do.
C'est clair, vous avez tort.	It is clear, you are wrong.
Il est facile de faire cela.	It is easy to do that.
Il est clair que vous avez tort.	It is clear that you are wrong.

192. Ceci = 'this' (the *nearer*) and cela = 'that' (the *farther away*) denote something *pointed out* or *indicated*, but *not yet named:*

Cela est joli, mais je préfère ceci.	That is pretty, but I prefer this.

NOTE.—Cela is often contracted to ça in familiar language: ça ne fait rien, 'That doesn't matter.'

193. Celui = 'that (one)', 'the one,' 'he,' is used of persons or things, and is regularly followed by a *relative clause* or a de *clause:*

Celui dont vous parliez est arrivé.	He of whom you spoke has come.
Ceux qui étudient apprennent.	Those who study learn.
Mes plumes et celles de mon frère.	My pens and my brother's.
Celles que vous avez apportées.	The ones (pens) you brought.

Obs.: 'This' and 'that' as adjectives are ce (cet), cette, ces (§131).

194. 1. Celui-ci = 'this,' 'this one,' 'he,' and celui-là = 'that,' 'that one,' are used of persons or things *already mentioned*, to contrast the *nearer* and the *more remote:*

Voici les deux chaines; gardez celle-ci et donnez-moi celle-là.	Here are the two chains; keep this (one) and give me that (one).

2. 'The latter' = celui-ci, and 'the former' = celui-là :

Cicéron et Virgile étaient tous deux célèbres; celui-ci était poète et celui-là orateur.	Cicero and Virgil were both celebrated; the former was an orator and the latter a poet.

Obs.: The Fr. idiom is, lit., 'the *latter* and the *former*.'

195. Conjugation of *vouloir*, 'to will' 'wish,' etc. :—

Infin.	*Pres. Part.*	*Past Part.*	*Pres. Indic.*	*Past Def.*
vouloir.	voulant.	voulu.	veux. voulons.	voulus.
Fut.	*Impf.*		veux. voulez.	*Impf. Subj.*
voudrai.	voulais.		veut. veulent.	voulusse.
Condl.	*Pres. Subj.*	[*Impve.* ——, ——, veuillez.]		
voudrais.	veuille, (-es, -e), voulions, (-iez), veuillent.			

EXERCISE XXIII.

Le beurre *(bœ.r)*, butter.
Le conseil *(kōsè.l̆)*, advice.
Cueillir *(kœĭi.r)*, gather.
Entrer *(ătré)*, come in.
Facile *(făsil)*, easy.
La fièvre *(jĭè.vr)*, fever.
Le général *(zénérăl)*, general.

Les habits, m., *(ăbi)*, clothes.
Merci *(mèrsi)*, I thank you, thanks.
Le poète *(pŏ̀ète)*, poet.
La prune *(prŭne)*, plum.
Savoir *(săvŭă.r)*, know.
Mon vieux *(vĭŏ)*, old boy, old fellow.

Comment allez-vous?
Comment ça va-t-il? } (familiar). How are you? How goes it?
Comment ça va?
Et vous? — And how are you?
Cela ne fait rien. — That makes no difference
Qu'est-ce que cela lui fait? — What is that to him?
Cela ne lui fait rien. — That is nothing to him.
Nous voudrions bien en avoir. — We should like to have some.
Voulez-vous bien m'en donner? — Will you have the kindness to give me some?

A. 1. Qui frappe? C'est moi. 2. Voulez-vous entrer? Oui, monsieur, avec grand plaisir. 3. Voulez-vous me donner mon habit et celui de mon frère? 4. Nous allons chercher nos chevaux et ceux de nos voisins. 5. Vous voudriez aller chercher des pommes, n'est-ce pas? 6. Oui, monsieur, et nous voudrions aller chercher des prunes et des poires. 7. Voulez-vous bien envoyer chercher du pain et du beurre? 8. Oui, madame, j'en enverrai chercher. 9. Comment ça va, mon vieux? 10. Ça ne va pas très bien, j'ai eu la fièvre. 11. Mais vous allez mieux à présent, n'est-ce pas? 12. Vous avez perdu de l'argent, n'est-ce pas? 13. Oh oui, mais ça ne me fait rien; j'en ai assez. 14. Nous voudrions bien finir notre ouvrage avant midi. 15. Cet habit-là est à mon frère, et celui-ci est à moi. 16. Qui est celui-là? 17. C'est mon frère. 18. Que va-t-il faire? 19. Il va cueillir des pommes. 20. À qui sont ces chapeaux? 21. Celui-ci est à moi, et celui-là est à mon père. 22. J'ai ma montre et celle de ma sœur. 23. Voulez-vous bien nous donner un conseil? 24. Avec plaisir; que voudriez-vous savoir? 25. Je n'ai plus d'argent, mais cela ne fait rien. 26. Napoléon et Wellington étaient deux grands généraux ; celui-ci était Anglais et celui-là Français. 27. Voulez-vous bien envoyer chercher de l'encre et du papier ? 28. Oui, madame, je vais en envoyer chercher tout de suite. 29. Bon jour, mon vieux ; comment ça va ? 30. Ça va très bien, merci ; et vous ? 31. Cette montre-là est à mon frère, et celle-ci est à ma sœur. 32. Où sont nos habits, et ceux de nos enfants ? 33. Les voilà sur la table. 34. Ce sont mon frère et ma sœur là-bas, n'est-ce pas ? 35. Oui, monsieur, ce sont eux. 36. Mon père m'a donné ces prunes-ci, et il a donné celles-là à ma sœur. 37. Voilà nos clous, ceux du charpentier et les vôtres. 38. Je voudrais bien savoir où sont mes habits et ceux de mon frère. 39. Je voudrais bien avoir de cette belle étoffe. 40. Voulez-vous demander à votre mère du pain pour ces pauvres enfants ? 41. Oui, monsieur, si vous le voulez.

B. 1. How are you this morning, old boy ? 2. I am very well, thanks ; and how are you ? 3. I am not very well, it is too warm. 4. Will you have the kindness to send for my books and my brother's ? 5. I shall send for them immediately. 6. He has lost some money, but what is that to him ? 7. He has no more money, but that is nothing to him. 8. Napoleon and Victor Hugo were two great men ; the former was [a] general, and the latter [a] poet. 9. These apples are mine, and those are my brother's. 10. I should like to have my watch and my sister's. 11. We are going after our books and our sister's. 12. I should like to go for some ink and paper. 13. Oh no, sir, I shall send for some. 14. Will you have the kindness to lend me some money ? 15. I should like to lend you some, but I have no more. 16. Good morning, my friend, how are you ? 17. Not very well ; I have been ill. 18. What was the matter with you ? 19. I had the fever. 20. I should like to know where the carpenter's boards are and our own. 21. I should like to have [some] of those beautiful apples. 22. I have lost my book, but that makes no diference. 23. How do you like *(trouver)* Victor Hugo's works *(œuvres)* ? 24. I prefer Shakespeare's. 25. Will you ask your father for some money ? 26. He will not give you any, but that makes no difference; here is some. 27. These are our horses and our neighbor's. 28. Will you have the kindness to give me my ink and my brother's. 29. We have no more money, but that is nothing to us; we shall soon have some. 30. We should like to know where our carriage is and our brother's. 31. That garden is mine, and this one is yours. 32. My table is in this room, and my brother's is in that one. 33. This is easy to do; that is difficult. 34. These boys are good, but those boys are naughty. 35. My uncle's children are naughty, but our neighbor's are good. 36. I am going to send for some money, if you wish some. 37. I should like to have some, if you would have the kindness to send for some. 38. We should like to finish our book before (the) evening. 39. We have lost some of our money, but that makes no difference. 40. Will you have the kindness to give me my book and my brother's.

LESSON XXIV.

196. The Interrogative Pronouns.

1. qui?, *who?, whom?*
2. que?, *what?*
3. quoi?, *what?*
4. lequel?, m. s., lesquels?, m. pl. ⎫ *which?, which one(s)?, what*
   laquelle?, f. s., lesquelles?, f. pl. ⎭ *one(s)?.*

[Pron.—1. *ki.* 2. *ke.* 3. *kŭá.* 4. *lekèl, làkèl, lèkèl, lèkèl.*]

Obs.: Both parts of **lequel** (**le** and **quel**) are inflected (§§83, 129, 2), and the usual contractions with **de** and **à** (**duquel**, etc., §107) take place.

197. Use of Interrogatives.
1. **Qui?** = 'who?', 'whom?' is used of *persons:*

Qui sonne?	Who is ringing?
Dites-moi qui sonne.	Tell me who is ringing.
Qui sont-elles?	Who are they?
De qui parlez-vous?	Of whom do you speak?
Qui a-t-il frappé?	Whom did he strike?

2. 'Whose?' denoting *ownership simply* = à qui (§106, 4), otherwise generally de qui? (but *never* dont, §201, 2):

À qui est ce livre?	Whose book is this?
De qui êtes-vous fils?	Whose son are you?

CONJUGATION OF *pouvoir*.

3. **Que?** = 'what?' stands *always with a verb*:

Qu'est-ce? Que vous a-t-il dit?   What is it? What did he tell you?

4. 'What?,' as *subject*, is usually **qu'est-ce qui?** and, 'what?' in *indirect question* is usually **ce qui** (ce que, etc. §201, 1):

Qu'est-ce qui vous a frappé?   What struck you?
Je ne sais pas ce qui m'a frappé.   I do not know what struck me.
Dites-moi ce que vous désirez.   Tell me what you want.

5. **Quoi?** = 'what?' stands regularly *after a preposition* or *absolutely* (verb understood):

À quoi pensez-vous?   What are you thinking of?
Je cherche quelque chose.—Quoi?   I am looking for something.—What?

6. **Lequel** (laquelle, etc.) = 'which?', 'which *or* what one?,' agrees in *gender* with the *noun* referred to:

Laquelle des dames est là?   Which of the ladies is there?
Auxquels des messieurs parliez-vous?   To which of the gentlemen were you speaking?

Obs.: Eng. 'which?' and 'what?' as adj.=some form of **quel?** (§139).

198. Conjugation of *pouvoir*, 'to be able,' 'can,' 'may,' etc. :—

Infin.	*Pres. Part.*	*Past Part.*	*Pres. Indic.*		*Past Def.*
pouvoir.	pouvant.	pu.	puis (peux).	pouvons.	pus.
Fut.	*Impf.*		peux.	pouvez.	*Impf. Subj.*
pourrai.	pouvais.		peut.	peuvent.	pusse.
Condl.	*Pres. Subj.*				
pourrais.	puisse, (-es, -e), puissions, (-iez, -ent).				

EXERCISE XXIV.

Amusant *(ámüzā)*, amusing.
Le beau-frère *(bófrè.r)*, brother-in-law.
La belle-sœur *(bèl sœ.r)*, sister-in-law.
Le bout *(bu)*, end.
Comme *(kòm)*, as.

Frapper *(fräpé)*, strike.
L'histoire, f., *(istúá.r)*, story.
Négligent *(néglizā)*, careless.
Le porte-monnaie *(pòrt mònè)*, purse.
Raconter *(rákōté)*, tell, relate.
Le seau *(só)*, pail.
Le sucre *(sükr)*, sugar.

Vous pouvez le faire, si vous voulez.   You may do it, if you wish.
Vous pouvez le faire, quand vous voudrez.   You may do it, when you wish.

Je voudrais bien le faire.	I should like to do it.
Comme vous voudrez.	As you like.
Qu'a-t-il pu lui donner ?	What can he have given him?
Cela se peut bien.	That may well be (may be so).

A. 1. Qui avez-vous trouvé chez votre cousin ? 2. J'y ai trouvé son beau-frère et sa belle-sœur. 3. À qui avez-vous donné votre couteau ? 4. Je l'ai donné à mon petit frère. 5. Si je puis savoir qui lui a donné ce couteau, j'en serai content. 6. Vous pouvez le faire comme vous voudrez. 7. Votre ami que vous a-t-il donné ? 8. Il m'a donné de l'argent. 9. J'ai voulu voir mes amis, mais je n'ai pas pu. 10. Si nous avions pu le faire, nous en aurions été contents. 11. Qui va chercher de l'eau ? 12. Moi j'irai en chercher, si je puis trouver un seau. 13. Auquel de ces garçons avez-vous parlé ? 14. J'ai parlé au fils du marchand. 15. Lequel de ces messieurs est votre oncle ? 16. Mon oncle est celui au bout de la table. 17. De quoi avez-vous besoin ? 18. J'ai besoin d'une livre de sucre. 19. Ce monsieur a rompu ma canne ; à quoi pensait-il ? 20. Qui cherchiez-vous ? 21. Je cherchais le frère de notre voisin et celui de notre ami. 22. Lesquels de ces chevaux sont à vous ? 23. Le blanc est à nous, et le noir est à mon oncle. 24. J'enverrai chercher de l'étoffe pour ma robe, si je puis trouver mon porte-monnaie. 25. Auxquels des chevaux avez-vous donné du foin ? 26. J'en ai donné au vôtre et à celui du voisin. 27. Quand pourrai-je faire mon ouvrage ? 28. Vous pouvez le faire, quand vous voudrez. 29. Pourrons-nous partir demain pour la ville ? 30. Vous pouvez partir aujourd'hui, si vous le voulez. 31. Nous voudrions bien envoyer chercher le médecin. 32. Comme vous voudrez. 33. Votre ami que vous a-t-il pu dire ? 34. Il nous a raconté une histoire amusante. 35. Chez qui demeurez-vous, depuis que vous êtes ici ? 36. Je demeure chez ma sœur. 37. Ce petit garçon a frappé sa sœur. 38. Cela se peut bien ; c'est un méchant petit garçon.

B. To whom did you give the money ? 2. I gave it to the merchant's son. 3. Who has stolen your purse ? 4. The beggar has stolen it. 5. With whom have you been living, since you have been in Toronto ? 6. I have been living at my brother's. 7. What are you thinking of? 8. Whom are you thinking of? 9. I am thinking of my mother. 10. Which of those gentlemen are your cousins? 11. My cousins are those under the tree. 12. If our friends had been able to do it, we should have been glad of it. 13. To which of those ladies did you give your purse? 14. I gave it to the one who is in the carriage. 15. Your sister has lost her purse. 16. That may well be, for she is very careless. 17. I should like to go and get some cloth for my dress. 18. You may go and get some, whenever you wish. 19. To which of the horses did you give water? 20. We gave some to ours and to our friend's. 21. Whom did you find at your neighbor's? 22. We found (there) your brother-in-law and sister-in-law. 23. The little boy asks who is here. 24. That little girl would like to finish her lesson. 25. She may finish it, whenever she wishes. 26. You may speak to the beggar, if you wish. 27. I should like to go to church to-day. 28. As you wish. 29. I should like to see my friends, but I have not been able. 30. What can you have done to M. Mercier? 31. Who will go and get some bread? 32. I shall go and get some, if I can find my purse. 33. The servant will get some water, if he can find the pail. 34. What were you speaking of to my father? 35. I was speaking to him of my brother and our neighbor's. 36. For whom were you looking this morning? 37. I was looking for our cousins, but I was not able to find them. 38. May I go now? 39. You may do as you wish.

LESSON XXV.

199. **The Relative Pronouns.**

1. qui, *who, which, that, whom (after a prep.)*.
2. que, *whom, which, that*.
3. dont, *whose, of whom, of which*.
4. où, *in which, into which, at which, to which, etc.*
5. lequel, m. s., lesquels, m. pl. }
   laquelle, f. s., lesquelles, f. pl. } *who, whom, which, that*.
6. quoi, *what, which*.

[PRON.—1. *ki*. 2. *ke*. 3. *dõ*. 4. *u*. 5. *lekèl, lákèl, lèkèl, lèkèl*. 6. *kuá*.]

Obs.: For the contraction of de and à with lequel see §107 above.

200. Agreement. A relative pronoun (whether *variable* or *invar.* in form) is of the *gender*, *number* and *person* of its *antecedent*:

Moi qui étais (vous qui étiez) là. I who was (you who were) there.
Les lettres que j'ai apportées. The letters which I have brought.

Obs.: Hence the past part. agrees as above with a *preceding relative object* (§121).

201. Use of the Relative. 1. The relative pronoun of most common use is **qui** as *subject*, and **que** as *direct object* of a verb. **Qui** = 'whom' (of *persons only*) is also used after a *prep.*:

La dame **qui** chante. The lady who sings.
Les livres **qui** sont à moi. The books which are mine.
Les tableaux **que** j'ai achetés. The pictures that I have bought.
L'oncle chez **qui** je demeurais. The uncle with whom I lived.

2. The force of **de** + *a relative* is generally expressed by **dont** = 'whose,' 'of whom,' 'of which,' etc.:

Les amis **dont** nous parlions. The friends of whom we were speaking.
La table **dont** le pied était cassé. The table of which the leg was broken.

a. Observe the order of words in:

L'écolier **dont** j'ai l'ardoise. The pupil whose slate I have.

3. **Où** (most usually *adverb*) sometimes has the force of **dans** (etc.) + *a relative:*

La maison **où** (=dans laquelle) je demeure. The house in which I live.

4. **Lequel** (laquelle, etc.) = 'who,' 'whom,' 'which,' 'that' *must* be used of *animals* and *things after a prep.*, and *may* be so used of *persons:*

Les chevaux **auxquels** je donne le foin. The horses to which I give the hay.
Le monsieur **auquel** je parle. The gentleman to whom I speak.

a. **Lequel** is also used instead of **qui** (que, etc.) *to avoid ambiguity:*

Les sœurs de nos amis, **lesquelles** sont chez nous à présent. The sisters of our friends, who (the sisters) are with us now.

5. **Quoi** stands *after a preposition* (rarely otherwise):

Voilà de **quoi** je parlais. That is what I was speaking of.

6. The absolute 'what,' 'which,' 'that which' as *subject* is **ce qui**, and as *object* or *predicate* **ce que**; 'of what,' 'that of which' is **ce dont**:

Je vois ce qui vous amuse.	I see what amuses you.
Je sais ce que je sais.	I know what I know.
Vous savez ce que je suis.	You know what I am.
Il est sourd, ce qui est dommage.	He is deaf, which is a pity.
Ce dont j'ai besoin.	What I have need of.

7. 'He (*or* she) who,' 'the one(s) who,' 'the one(s) which,' 'those who,' etc. = **celui + qui** (que, etc.):

Nous admirons ceux que nous aimons.	We admire those whom we love.
Ma bague est plus jolie que celles que vous avez.	My ring is prettier than the ones you have.

202. The relative pronoun, often omitted in English, *is never omitted in French:*

Le tableau que j'ai vu hier.   The picture I saw yesterday.

203. Conjugation of *connaître*, 'to know,' 'be acquainted with,' etc. :—

Infin.	*Pres. Part.*	*Past Part.*	*Pres. Indic.*		*Past Def.*
connaître.	connaissant.	connu.	connais.	connaissons.	connus.
Fut.	*Impf.*		connais.	connaissez.	*Impf. Subj.*
connaîtrai.	connaissais.		connaît.	connaissent.	connusse.
Cond.	*Pres. Subj.*	[*Impve.* connais, connaissons, connaissez.]			
connaîtrais.	connaisse, (-es, -e), connaissions, (-iez, -ent).				

204. Conjugation of *savoir*, 'to know,' 'know' (by mental effort), 'know how to,' etc. :—

Infin.	*Pres. Part.*	*Past Part.*	*Pres. Indic.*		*Past Def.*
savoir.	sachant.	su.	sais.	savons.	sus.
Fut.	*Impf.*		sais.	savez.	*Impf. Subj.*
saurai.	savais.		sait.	savent.	susse.
Cond.	*Pres. Subj.*	[*Impve.* sache, sachons, sachez.]			
saurais.	sache, (-es, -e), sachions, (-iez, -ent).				

EXERCISE XXV.

Auparavant *(ópárávã)*, before, formerly.	La poste *(pòst)*, post-office.
Juste *(žüst)*, just.	La propriété *(pròpriété)*, property.
La justice *(žüstis)*, justice.	Rendre *(rã.dr)*, give back.
La personne *(pèrsòn)*, person.	Se respecter *(respèkté)*, respect one's self.
Porter *(pòrté)*, carry, take.	Se trouver *(truvé)*, be.

A. 1. Je connais le monsieur qui est avec monsieur votre père. 2. Savez-vous ce que je vais faire ? 3. Oui, monsieur, vous allez faire ce que j'ai fait. 4. Je fais toujours ce qui est juste. 5. Nous n'aimons pas ceux qui ne font pas ce qui est juste. 6. Qui sont ces deux messieurs ? 7. Celui à qui je parlais est mon oncle, et l'autre est mon cousin. 8. La maison où nous demeurons est la propriété de M. Ribot. 9. Les dames dont nous parlions sont ici. 10. Qui avez-vous rencontré à la ville ? 11. J'ai rencontré beaucoup de personnes dont je ne connaissais que peu auparavant. 12. Le monsieur dont vous avez trouvé la montre est arrivé. 13. Les maisons que nous avons achetées sont dans votre rue. 14. La lettre que ma fille a portée à la poste est pour mon frère. 15. La dame qui était malade se porte mieux à présent. 16. Le monsieur chez qui je demeurais n'est plus ici. 17. C'est nous qui avons fait cela. 18. C'est moi qui ai fait bâtir cette maison. 19. La dame qui a perdu le porte-monnaie que vous avez trouvé vous prie de le lui rendre. 20. Qui est celui-là ? 21. C'est le fils du monsieur qui était ici. 22. La table que le charpentier a faite n'est pas assez grande. 23. La table qui se trouve dans votre chambre est à moi. 24. Le monsieur que nous connaissions ne demeure plus ici. 25. Je sais bien ce que vous savez. 26. Nous connaissons la petite fille que vous avez rencontrée dans la rue. 27. Savez-vous que j'ai fait bâtir une maison ? 28. Non, monsieur, je ne le savais pas. 29. Savez-vous qui est chez nous ? 30. Je vous ai donné ce que vous avez demandé. 31. Je vous ai donné ce dont vous avez besoin. 32. Ce qui est juste réussira. 33. Ce dont vous avez besoin n'est pas ici. 34. Le monsieur dont nous avons acheté la maison est M. Mercier. 35. Savez-vous où est la maison de M. David ? 36. Connaissez-vous la maison de M. David ? 37. Celui qui ne fera pas cela sera puni.

B. 1. I know what you have done. 2. Do you know what I am going to do ? 3. No, sir, I do not know what you are going to do. 4. Do you know the lady who was with my mother ? 5. No, sir, I do not know her. 6. We always do what is just. 7. I love those who do what is just. 8. He who does not what is just will be punished.

9. Who are those boys? 10. The one to whom I was speaking is the carpenter's son, and the other is the merchant's. 11. The children of whom we were speaking have come. 12. The house in which we live is in your street. 13. The white house where our cousins live is the property of M. David. 14. The letters we carried to the post-office were for our uncle. 15. The lady who lost her purse is my mother. 16. We do not know the gentleman whose purse you have found. 17. My cousin who was ill is better now. 18. The box which is in your room is my sister's. 19. Do you know where my pencil is? 20. I do not know. 21. Do you know M. David's house? 22. I do not know it. 23. I shall give you back what you have given me. 24. The little girl (whom) we met in the street is my cousin. 25. The little boy whose pencil we found has come, and asks for it. 26. The horse which is yonder in the field is mine. 27. I gave her what she asked for. 28. Whom did you meet at your uncle's? 29. We met many persons whom we did not know before. 30. What are you asking for? 31. I am asking for what I need. 32. I give you what you need. 33. I don't give you what you ask for; I give you what you need. 34. The gentleman with whom I used to live is not here now. 35. The lady whose house we bought is Mme Ribot. 36. He who does not love justice will not succeed. 37. She who does not respect herself will not be respected. 38. If everybody did what is just, we should all be happy. 39. Will you carry to the post-office the letters which I have given you? 40. Excuse me, sir, you have not given me any letters. 41. You are right; there they are on the table. 42. Give them to me now, and I shall go at once. 43. Thank you; you are very kind *(bon)*.

LESSON XXVI.

205. The Indefinite Pronouns of most frequent occurrence:—

1. **On** = 'one,' 'some one,' 'we,' 'you,' 'they,' 'people,' etc., makes a statement *without specifying any particular person,* and often corresponds to an Eng. *passive* (especially when the *agent* is *not specified*):

On dit que la reine est malade.	They say (it is said) the queen is ill.
On ne peut pas faire cela.	You cannot do that.
On sonne.	Some one is ringing.
On vous demande.	You are wanted.
On a attrapé le larron.	The thief has been caught.

Obs.: 1. The verb with **on** is always *3rd sing*. 2. **On** often becomes **l'on** after a vowel sound (especially after **et, ou, on, qui, que, quoi, si**) to avoid hiatus, but not usually when the *following word begins with* l.

2. **Quelqu'un** (f. **quelqu'une**) = 'somebody,' 'some one,' 'any one,' with its plur. **quelques-uns** (f. **quelques-unes**) = 'some,' 'some people,' 'any,' 'a few,' is the *pron.* corresponding to the *adj.* **quelque** (§140).

Il y a quelqu'un à la porte.	There is somebody at the door.
J'ai vu quelques-unes de vos amies.	I have seen some (a few) of your friends.
Avez-vous des cerises?	Have you any cherries?
J'en ai quelques-unes.	I have a few.

3. **Quelque chose** = 'something,' 'anything,' is *masculine*, though formed from the fem. noun **chose**:

Quelque chose est tombé.	Something has fallen.
Avez-vous quelque chose?	Is there anything the matter with you?
Quelque chose de bon?	Something good.

4. Along with **ne** + *a verb* or when *alone* (a verb being understood) **personne** = 'nobody,' 'not anybody,' 'no one,' and **rien** = 'nothing,' 'not anything':

Je n'ai parlé à personne.	I spoke to nobody (did not speak to anybody).
Vous n'avez rien apporté.	You have brought nothing (not brought anything).
Qu'a-t-il dit?—Rien.	What did he say? Nothing.
Il n'a rien dit de mauvais.	He said nothing bad.
Personne ici!	No one here!

206. Certain forms serve both as *adjectives* and as *pronouns*. Such are:—

1. **Autre** = 'other' (**un autre** = 'another,' **l'autre** = 'the other'):

Une autre fois. D'autres causes.	Another time. Other causes.
Les autres le diront aussi.	(The) others will say so too.

a. Distinguish: 'Donnez moi une autre (*i. e., a different*) plume' and 'Donnez-moi encore une ('another,' *i. e., an additional*) plume.'

2. From **autre** are formed various locutions:

Il donne beaucoup aux autres.	He gives much to others.
L'une et l'autre occasion.	Both occasions.
Les uns et les autres sont arrivés.	Both (all) have come.
Donnez ceci à l'un ou à l'autre.	Give this to either.
Ce n'est ni pour les uns ni pour les autres.	It is for neither (none of them).
Elles se flattent les unes les autres.	They flatter each other.
Ils ont peur les u .: des autres.	They are afraid of one another.

3. When used with **ne** + *a verb* or when *alone* (verb understood) **aucun, nul, pas un** as adjs. = 'no,' 'not one,' 'not any,' as *prons.* = 'none,' 'no one,' 'not one':

Aucun écrivain ne constate cela.	No writer states that.
A-t-on de l'espoir?—Aucun.	Have they any hope? None.

4. **Tel** as *adj.* = 'such,' **un tel** = 'such a.' 'Such' *as an adv.* is expressed by **si** or **tellement** (not **tel**):

Tels sont mes malheurs.	Such are my misfortunes.
Ne croyez pas une telle histoire.	Do not believe such a story.
Une si belle étoile.	Such a beautiful star.
Un homme tellement cruel.	Such a cruel man.

5. **Même** *before a noun* or *as a pronoun* = 'same.' **Même** *following* the *noun* or *pron.* qualified = 'self,' 'very,' 'even,' and agrees, but has *no article*. As *adverb*, **même** (invar.) = 'even':

La même chose. Ce sont les mêmes.	The same thing. They are the same.
Dieu est la bonté même.	God is goodness itself.
Les enfants mêmes furent tués.	The very children were killed.
Nous-mêmes. Elles-mêmes.	We ourselves. They themselves.
Ils nous ont même insultés.	They even insulted us.

207. Orthographical Irregularities of *manger, commencer, nettoyer, céder, appeler,* etc.:—

1. In conjugating verbs in -ger, *e.g.*, manger, 'to eat,' g becomes ge whenever the ending begins with a or o (§45,2). Similarly, c of verbs in -cer, *e.g.* commencer, 'to commence,' becomes ç (§41,2):

Pres. Part.	Pres. Indic.	Impf.	Past Def.	Impf. Subj.
mangeant.	mangeons.	mangeais.	mangeai.	mangeasse.
commençant.	commençons.	commençais.	commençai.	commençasse.

H

2. Verbs in -oyer, *e.g.*, nettoyer, 'to clean,' change **y** to **i** whenever it comes before **e** in conjugation:

| *Pres Indic.* | *Pres. Subj.* | *Fut.* | *Condl.* |
| nettoie. | nettoie. | nettoierai. | nettoierais. |

3. In most verbs with stem-vowel e, *e.g.*, mener, 'to lead,' e becomes è when the ending has e *mute*, and also in the *fut.* and *condl.* (§17,2). So also, verbs with stem-vowel é + *a cons.*, *e.g.*, céder, 'to yield,' but *not* in *fut.* and *condl.*:

Pres. Indic.	*Pres. Subj.*	*Fut.*	*Condl.*
mène.	mène.	mènerai.	mènerais.
cède.	cède.	céderai.	céderais.

4. But most verbs in -eler, -eter, *e.g.*, appeler, 'to call,' jeter, 'to throw,' double **l** or **t** before e *mute* and also in the *fut.* and *condl.* (§17, 2):

Pres. Indic.	*Pres. Subj.*	*Fut.*	*Condl.*
appelle.	appelle.	appellerai.	appellerais.
jette.	jette.	jetterai.	jetterais.

EXERCISE XXVI.

Amener *(ámné)*, lead, bring.
Apporter *(ápòrté)*, carry, bring.
L'après-midi, f., *(áprè-midi)*, afternoon.
Attraper *(átrápé)*, catch.
Commencer, *(kòmãsé)*, begin (to, à).
À côté *(kòté)*, next door.
Le déjeuner *(déžöné)*, breakfast.
Le dîner *(diné)*, dinner.
Manger *(mãžé)* eat.
La pâtisserie *(pátisri)*, pastry.
Le poisson *(püásõ)*, fish.
Se promener *(pròmné)*, take a walk.

Ainsi de suite. So forth.
Tous les jours. Every day.
Le matin. In the morning.

A. 1. Que mangeâtes-vous au grand dîner hier? 2. Nous mangeâmes bien des choses, du poisson, de la viande, de la pâtisserie, et ainsi de suite. 3. À quelle heure commencez-vous à faire cela? 4. Nous commençons à midi. 5. Qui amènerez-vous cette après-midi? 6. J'amènerai mon fils et ma fille. 7. Qu'avez-vous apporté? 8. J'ai apporté mes livres. 9. Avez-vous amené quelqu'un? 10. Non, monsieur, je n'ai amené personne. 11. Vous n'avez rien apporté. 12. Oh si, nous avons apporté quelque chose de bon. 13. À quelle heure vous promenez-vous? 14. Je me promène tous les jours à quatre heures. 15. Nous nous promènerons demain à quatre heures. 16. Avez-vous quelque chose de bon pour nous? 17. Nous n'avons rien de bon pour vous. 18. À quelle heure se promène-t-on ici? 19. On se promène le matin et le soir. 20. Est-ce que quelqu'un vous a apporté de la viande? 21. Personne ne m'a rien apporté. 22. Est-ce qu'il y a quelqu'un à la porte? 23. Personne n'est à la porte. 24. Qu'est-ce qu'on fait là-bas? 25. On bâtit une maison. 26. Les enfants qu'est-ce qu'ils ont fait? 27. Ils n'ont rien fait de bon; ils ont coupé le pommier. 28. On amène les chevaux. 29. On vous demande, monsieur. 30. Qui est-ce qui me demande? 31. C'est le monsieur qui demeure à côté. 32. Qu'est-ce qu'on vous a apporté? 33. On ne m'a rien apporté.

B. 1. What did you eat at the breakfast? 2. We ate bread, fish and fruit. 3. When (at what hour) did you begin to work? 4. We began to work at noon. 5. Does your son take a walk in the morning? 6. Yes sir, he takes a walk in the morning and in the evening. 7. What have your cousins brought you? 8. They have not brought me anything. 9. Has anyone brought anything good for the children? 10. No one has brought anything good. 11. Whom are you bringing? 12. I am not bringing any one. 13. Our cousins will take a walk at four o'clock this afternoon. 14. Whom will he bring this afternoon? 15. He will not bring any one. 16. What will they (*on*) bring to-morrow? 17. They (*on*) will not bring anything. 18. He did not bring anything. 19. Oh yes, he brought his books and paper. 20. When do you begin to play? 21. We begin at four o'clock. 22. What has been brought to you? 23. Nothing has been brought to me. 24. You are wanted, madam. 25. Who is it? 26. It is the lady who lives next door. 27. What have those men been doing? 28. They have been doing nothing good. 29. When (at what hour) will you take a walk to-morrow? 30. We always take a walk at four o'clock. 31. To whom have you spoken about (*de*) that? 32. I have not spoken of it to anyone. 33. That scoundrel has been caught. 34. You (*tu*) are crying, my child; what is the matter with you? 35. I have lost my book.

LESSON XXVII.

208.   **Cardinal Numerals.**

1. un, une, *f.*, *(ŏẽ, ü.n)*.
2. deux *(dŏ)*.
3. trois *(trŭá)*.
4. quatre *(kátr)*.
5. cinq *(sẽk)*.
6. six *(sis)*.
7. sept *(sèt)*.
8. huit *(ŭit)*.
9. neuf *(nœf)*.
10. dix *(dis)*.
11. onze *(õ.z)*.
12. douze *(du.z)*.
13. treize *(trè.z)*.
14. quatorze *(kátð.rz)*.
15. quinze *(kẽ.z)*.
16. seize *(sè.z)*.
17. dix-sept *(di sèt)*.
18. dix-huit *(diz ŭit)*.
19. dix-neuf *(diz nœf)*.
20. vingt *(vẽ)*.

21. vingt et un *(vêt é ẽ)*.
22. vingt-deux *(vêt dŏ)*.
30. trente *(trã.t)*.
31. trente et un *(trã.t é ẽ)*.
40. quarante *(kárã.t)*.
50. cinquante *(sẽkã.t)*.
60. soixante *(sŭásã.t)*.
70. soixante-dix *(sŭásã.t dis)*.
71. soixante-onze *(sŭásã.t õ.z)*.
80. quatre-vingt(s) *(kátr vẽ)*.
81. quatre-vingt-un *(kátr vẽ ẽ)*.
90. quatre-vingt-dix *(-vẽ dis)*.
91. quatre-vingt-onze *(-vẽ õ.z)*.
100. cent *(sã)*.
101. cent un *(sã ẽ)*.
200. deux cent(s) *(dŏ sã)*.
201. deux cent un *(dŏ sã ẽ)*.
1000. mille *(mil)*.
1001. mille un *(mil ẽ)*.
2000. deux mille *(dŏ mil)*.

Nouns of number: 1,000,000 = un million *(miliõ)*; 2,000,000 = deux millions; 1,000,000,000 = un milliard *(miliá.r)*.

Obs.: 1. The *hyphen* unites together compound numerals under 100, except where *et* occurs. 2. **Et** stands regularly in 21 31, 41, 51, 61, is *optional* in 70, 71, *omitted* in 81 and elsewhere. 3. '**A** (*or* one) **hundred**'= cent (no un). '**A** (*or* one) **thousand**'= mille.

[PRON.—1. The *final consonant* of 5, 6, 7, 8, 9, 10, is *silent before initial consonant* (or h asp.) *of a word multiplied by them*, not elsewhere: Cinq livres *(sẽ li.vr)*, but le cinq mai *(le sẽk mè)*. 2. *No elision* or *liaison* occurs *before* **huit**, **onze**: Le onze *(le õ.z)*; les onze francs *(lè õ.z frã)*; le huit *(le hŭit)*; les huit livres *(lè ŭi li.vr)*. 3. t is *sounded* in **vingt** from 21 to 29, is *silent* from 80 to 99, is *silent* in cent un. deux cent un, etc.]

209. Quatre-vingt and the *multiples of* **cent** take -s only when *immediately preceding a noun*, or when they themselves are *used as nouns of number:*

Quatre-vingts francs.	Eighty francs.
Trois cents francs.	Three hundred francs.
Les cinq cents. Les quatre vingts.	The five hundreds. The four twenties.

But: Trois cent un francs. Quatre-vingt-un francs, etc.

Obs.: They are *not nouns of number* in *dates* or when used *as ordinals* (§218).

210. Multiplicatives. 'Once' = **une fois**, 'twice = **deux fois**, 'three times' = **trois fois**, etc.:

Dix fois dix font cent.   Ten times ten make 100.

211. Idiomatic Expressions of Age. Observe the following :—

Quel âge avez-vous?	How old are you?
J'ai vingt ans.	I am twenty (years old).
Une fille âgée de six ans.	A girl six years old (*or* of age).
À l'âge de vingt-cinq ans.	At the age of twenty-five (years).
Je suis majeur. Elle est mineure.	I am of age. She is not of age.

212. Conjugation of *vendre*, 'to sell ':—

Infin.	*Pres. Part.*	*Past Part.*	*Pres. Indic.*	*Past Def.*
vendre.	vendant.	vendu.	vends. vendons.	vendis.
Fut.	*Impf.*		vends. vendez.	*Impf. Subj.*
vendrai.	vendais.		vend. vendent.	vendisse.
Condl.	*Pres. Subj.*	[*Impve.* vends, vendons, vendez.]		
vendrais.	vende (-es, -e), vendions (-iez, -ent).			

Obs.: The only irregularity of **vendre** is the omission of the **t** in the 3 sing. pres. indic. Elsewhere it is like **rompre.**

213. Conjugation of *recevoir*, 'to receive ':—

Infin.	*Past Part.*	*Past Part.*	*Pres. Indic.*	*Past Def.*
recevoir.	recevant.	reçu.	reçois. recevons.	reçus.
Fut.	*Impf.*		reçois. recevez.	*Impf. Subj.*
recevrai.	recevais.		reçoit. reçoivent.	reçusse.
Condl.	*Pres Subj.*	[*Impve.* reçois, recevons, recevez.]		
recevrais.	reçoive, (-es, -e), recevions, (-iez), reçoivent.			

Obs.:: See §41, 2, for the **ç** before **o** or **u**.

NOTE.—The few verbs in -**oir** form, in some grammars, a separate conjugation (the *3rd*, verbs in -**re** being the 4th).

214. Conjugation of *devoir*, 'to owe,' 'ought,' 'am to,' etc.:

Infin.	*Pres. Part.*	*Past Part.*	*Pres. Indic.*	*Past Def.*
devoir.	devant.	dû (f. due, pl. du(e)s).	dois. devons.	dus.
Fut.	*Impf.*		dois. devez.	*Impf. Subj.*
devrai.	devais.		doit. doivent.	dusse.
Condl.	*Pres. Subj.*	[*Impve.* dois, devons, devez.]		
devrais.	doive, (-es, -e), devions, (-iez), doivent.			

EXERCISE XXVII.

La colline *(kŏlin)*, hill.
Combien? *(kŏblɛ̃)*, how much? how many?
Coûter *(kuté)*, cost.
La cuisine *(küizin)*, kitchen.
Le jour *(zu.r)*, day.
Laisser *(lɛsé)*, let have.
Le mètre *(mè.tr)*, yard.

Combien de fois? — How often? How many times?
Huit jours. — A week.
Quinze jours. — A fortnight.
À combien la livre cette viande se vend-elle? — At how much a pound does that meat sell?
Je dois partir demain. — I am to go away to-morrow.
Il devrait le faire. — He ought to do it.
Il a dû le faire. — He must have done it.
Il aurait dû le faire. — He ought to have done it.

A. 1. Combien de personnes y a-t-il dans la maison? 2. Il y en a quinze. 3. Cette étoffe se vend cher; elle se vend vingt francs le mètre. 4. Je dois donner vingt francs au marchand; combien devez-vous lui en donner? 5. Je dois lui en donner vingt-cinq. 6. Le professeur a dû te voir hier, car il a parlé de toi à mon père. 7. Ce sucre-ci se vend moins cher que celui-là. 8. Ma mère doit partir pour les États-Unis demain soir. 9. J'aurais dû le donner à ma mère. 10. Le marchand aurait dû le vendre à dix-sept sous la livre. 11. Les enfants devraient obéir à leurs parents. 12. Il faut que vous me le vendiez neuf sous le mètre. 13. Je dois le vendre onze sous la livre. 14. Combien de fois avez-vous été à Londres? 15. J'y ai été trois fois. 16. Je n'ai été qu'une fois aux États-Unis. 17. Ce petit garçon quel âge a-t-il? 18. Il a sept ans, et sa petite sœur en a cinq. 19. À combien le mètre cette étoffe se vend-elle? 20. Elle se vend dix francs le mètre. 21. Vous devriez me laisser cette étoffe beaucoup moins cher. 22. Je ne puis pas vous la laisser moins cher, madame ; elle m'a coûté très cher. 23. Cette étoffe-ci m'a coûté trois fois plus cher que celle-là. 24. Combien en avez-vous encore ? 25. Je n'en ai plus. 26. Monsieur votre père est maláde ; vous devriez envoyer chercher le médecin. 27. Depuis quand votre petite fille est-elle malade ? 28. Elle est malade depuis huit jours. 29. Nos amis sont chez vous depuis quinze jours. 30. J'ai été cinq fois à Londres. 31. Vous devez aller à la ville demain, n'est-ce pas ?

B. 1. How often have you been in France? 2. I have been there three times. 3. At what price a yard does that cloth sell? 4. It sells at ten francs a yard. 5. That cloth is (costs) dear ; you ought to let me have it cheaper (less dear). 6. I cannot let you have it cheaper. 7. That coat cost me three times as dear as this one. 8. Your father must have seen you. 9. How many have you still? 10. I have no more. 11. At how much a pound does that sugar sell? 12. It sells at five cents a pound. 13. I am to sell it at fourteen cents a yard. 14. I am going to buy it at nineteen francs a pound. 15. You ought to have given the knife to your mother. 16. Your father is ill; you ought to send for the doctor. 17. He ought to have had his house built on the hill. 18. This sugar sells cheaper than that; it sells at four cents a pound. 19. I am to leave for France to-morrow. 20. How many francs have you still? 21. I have ten; how many have you? 22. I ought to go to church to-day. 23. Our neighbors are to have six horses next year ; how many are you to have? 24. This cloth ought to cost less than that. 25. That little boy ought to have gone to school to-day. 26. That little girl must have gone to school. 27. The merchant should have let us have it cheaper. 28. How often have you given that boy money? 29. I have given him some three times. 30. How old is your brother? 31. He is fifteen years old, and my sister is twelve. 32. I met two carriages ; they must have been our neighbor's. 33. How many horses are there in the stable? 34. There are nine. 35. How much sugar is there in the kitchen? 36. There are ten pounds (of it).

LESSON XXVIII.

215. Ordinal Numerals, from *3rd* up, are formed *by adding* -ième to the corresponding *cardinal*, final e being dropped. **Cinq** adds **u** and **neuf** changes **f** to **v** before -ième:

1st. premier *(premyé)*, f. première.
2nd. { second *(segõ)*, f. seconde.
{ deuxième *(dŏzyè.m)*.
3rd. troisième *(trŭazyè.m)*.
4th. quatrième *(kátryè.m)*.
5th. cinquième *(sĕkyè.m)*.
6th. sixième *(sizyè.m)*.
7th. septième *(sètyè.m)*.
8th. huitième *(hüityè.m)*.
9th. neuvième *(nŏvyè.m)*.
10th. dixième *(dizyè.m)*.
11th. onzième *(õzyè.m)*.
21st. vingt et unième *(vĕt é ünyè.m)*.
22nd. vingt deuxième *(vĕt dŏzyè.m)*.

216. Fractions. The *numerator* is expressed by a *cardinal*, the *denominator* by an *ordinal*, as in English. 'Half' = **moitié**, f. (as *noun*) and **demi** (as *adj.*) ; ¼ = **un quart** ; ⅓ = **un tiers** :

Un huitième. Les trois dixièmes.	One-eighth. The three-tenths.
La moitié de l'année.	(The) half (of) the year.
Une heure et demie.	An hour and a half.
Une demi-heure.	Half an hour.
Les trois quarts de cette somme.	Three-fourths of that sum.

Obs.: 1. *Before* its noun **demi** is *invar.* and joined by a *hyphen*, but agrees else-where. 2. Use **la moitié** (*not* **demi**) where 'the half of' is (or may be) used in English.

217. The Time of Day is indicated as follows :—

Quelle heure est-il ?	What o'clock is it ?
Il est deux heures.	It is two o'clock.
Trois heures et demie.	Half past three.
Trois heures (et) un quart.	A quarter past three.
Quatre heures moins un quart.	A quarter to four.
Trois heures dix (minutes).	Ten minutes past three.
Quatre heures moins cinq (minutes).	Five minutes to four.
Il est midi et demi.	It is half past twelve (noon).
Il est minuit.	It is twelve o'clock (night).
À sept heures du soir.	At seven o'clock in the evening.
À quelle heure ?	At what o'clock ?
À trois heures précises.	At three o'clock precisely.
Vers les trois heures.	About three o'clock.

Obs. : 1. 'It is '= il est (always *sing*.); 'it was '= il était, etc. 2. Heure(s) is *never omitted*. 3. Et is only *essential at the half hour*. 4. 'Demie' agrees with heure understood. 5. The word minutes is *often omitted*. 6. 'A quarter to,' *or* 'so many minutes to' is denoted by the following hour moins (= 'less' *or* 'minus') the specified time. 7. 'Twelve o'clock' is *never* douze heures.

218. Dates, Titles, etc. 1. Premier = 'first' is the *only ordinal* used to denote the *day of the month* or the *numerical title of a ruler :*

Le premier mai. Charles premier. The first of May. Charles the First.
Paris, le deux mai. Louis quatorze. Paris, the 2nd of May. Louis XIV.

2. *Other numerical titles* (of books, chaps., scenes, etc.) are as in Eng. :

Tome troisième (*or* trois). Volume third (*or* three).
La dixième scène du second acte. The tenth scene of the second act.

219. Date Idioms. Observe the following :—

Quel jour du mois { est-ce? { What day of the month is it?
                  { avons-nous ? { What date is it? (What is the date?).
C'est (*or* nous avons) le seize. It is the 16th.
Le six janvier. On the 6th of January.
Ils sont arrivés lundi. They came on Monday.
Nous allons le lundi et le jeudi. We go on Mondays and Thursdays.
Il va tous les dimanches. He goes every Sunday.
D'aujourd'hui en huit. A week from to-day (fut.).
Il y a quinze jours. A fortnight ago.
C'est aujourd'hui mercredi. To-day is (this is) Wednesday.
Ce sera demain jeudi. To-morrow will be Thursday.
Tous les jours. Tous les deux jours. Every day. Every other day.

220. Names of Months and Days (all masc.) are :—

Janvier *(žãvié)*, January. Juillet *(žũiìè)*, July.
Février *(févrié)*, February. Août *(u)*, August.
Mars *(márs)*, March. Septembre *(septã.br)*, September.
Avril *(avril)*, April. Octobre *(òktòbr)*, October.
Mai *(mè)*, May. Novembre *(nòvã.br)*, November.
Juin *(žũè)*, June. Décembre *(désã.br)*, December.

Dimanche *(dimã.š)*, Sunday. Mercredi *(mérkredi)*, Wednesday.
Lundi *(lõdi)*, Monday. Jeudi *(žödi)*, Thursday.
Mardi *(márdi)*, Tuesday. Vendredi *(vãdrdi)*, Friday.
Samedi *(sámdi)*, Saturday.

221. Conjugation of *partir,* 'to set out,' 'go,' and *sortir,* 'to go out':—

Infin.	Pres. Part.	Past Part.	Pres. Indic.	Past Def.
partir.	partant.	parti.	pars. partons.	partis.
Fut.	Impf.		pars. partez.	Impf. Subj.
partirai.	partais.		part. partent.	partisse.
Condl.	Pres. Subj.	[Impve. pars, partons, partez.]		
partirais.	parte, (-es, -e), partions, (-iez, -ent).			

So also **sortir** : Je sors, tu sors, il sort, nous sortons, etc., etc.

EXERCISE XXVIII.

Assassiner *(ăsăsiné)*, assassinate, murder.
La belle-mère *(bèl mè.r)*, mother-in-law.
Le chapitre *(šápitr)*, chapter.
Se coucher *(kušé)*, lie down, go to bed.
La fête *(fê.t)*, festivity, birth-day.
Se lever *(levé)*, rise.
Le minuit *(minŭi)*, midnight.
Le mois *(mŭa)*, month.
Rentrer *(rātré)*, return home.
Le tome *(tó.m)*, volume.
Le train *(trĕ)*, train.
Le volume *(vŏlŭm)*, volume.

A. 1. Monsieur votre père quand part-il pour la France? 2. Il part le dix août. 3. Nous allons à la ville le jeudi et le samedi. 4. Le premier juin est ma fête. 5. Le dix-neuf juillet est la fête de ma sœur. 6. Vous trouverez cela dans le deuxième volume des œuvres de Molière. 7. Quel jour du mois avons-nous? 8. C'est aujourd'hui le vingt. 9. Nous sommes partis de notre pays le quinze février, et nous sommes arrivés en Angleterre le premier mars. 10. À quelle heure mademoiselle votre sœur est-elle sortie? 11. Elle est sortie à dix heures moins quinze. 12. Quelle heure est-il? 13. Il est midi et demi. 14. À quelle heure du matin vous levez-vous? 15. Je me lève à six heures et demie. 16. Mon frère sort tous les jours à huit heures et quart pour aller à l'école. 17. Je vais vous donner la moitié de ma pomme. 18. Voilà un bon jeune homme; il va tous les dimanches à l'église. 19. Henri quatre fut assassiné. 20. J'ai trouvé cela dans ce livre, tome trois, chapitre quatre. 21. Cela se trouve dans le cinquième chapitre du sixième volume des œuvres de Voltaire. 22. Je voudrais qu'il sortît à onze heures précises. 23. Quel jour est-ce? 24. C'est lundi. 25. Nos amis vont arriver vers les quatre heures. 26. Il va partir pour les États-Unis le onze du mois prochain. 27. Le douze mars il a fait bien froid. 28. Le matin nous sortons à neuf heures et un quart, et le soir nous rentrons à cinq heures. 29. Madame votre belle-mère est sortie à midi un quart. 30. Elle va rentrer à trois heures. 31. Nous nous couchons toujours avant minuit. 32. Ce monsieur déjeunera aujourd'hui à midi précis.

B. 1. When did your mother go out? 2. She went out at a quarter past twelve. 3. What o'clock is it? 4. It is half-past two. 5. When do you rise [in] the morning? 6. I rise always at a quarter past six. 7. He will leave on the fifteenth of March for England. 8. The children will return home about five o'clock. 9. I go to church every Sunday. 10. Our little boy goes to school every morning at half-past eight. 11. There is a good little boy; he rises every morning at six o'clock. 12. The fifth of July is my brother's birthday. 13. Those children go to bed every evening at half-past eight. 14. That is found in the first chapter of the fifth volume of Bacon's works. 15. We find that in Voltaire's works, volume two, chapter four. 16. We shall go out at half-past three. 17. We shall return home at a quarter to five. 18. At half-past twelve o'clock we shall breakfast. 19. The train will arrive at five minutes to four. 20. At what o'clock in the morning do you leave for the city? 21. I leave every morning at a quarter to ten. 22. What day is it? 23. It is Tuesday. 24. What day of the month is it? 25. It is the tenth. 26. My uncle and aunt will leave for France on the twentieth of June. 27. We shall go out at three o'clock precisely. 28. We shall return about five. 29. We go to the city Fridays and Saturdays. 30. Henry the Eighth had six wives. 31. At what o'clock shall you go to bed? 32. I shall go to bed at twelve o'clock precisely.

LESSON XXIX.

222. Formation of Adverbs. 1. Adverbs may be formed from most adjectives by adding -**ment** to the *feminine* of the adjective:

M.	F.	Adv.	M.	F.	Adv.
Pur,	pure,	purement.	Heureux,	heureuse,	heureusement.
Mortel,	mortelle,	mortellement.	Facile,	facile,	facilement.
Premier,	première,	premièrement.	Autre,	autre,	autrement.

2. The fem. sign **e** *after a vowel* is *dropped* when adding -ment:

Poli, polie, poliment.   Absolu, absolue, absolument.

3. Observe the following correlative adjectives and adverbs:

Adj.	Adv.
Bon = 'good.'	Bien = 'well.'
Mauvais = 'bad.'	Mal = 'badly.'

223. Comparison of Adverbs. 1. Adverbs are compared *like adjectives* (§144) by **plus** (... que), **moins** (... que), **aussi** (... que), but **le** in the superlative is *invariable*:

Souvent, plus souvent, le plus souvent.   Often, oftener, oftenest.
Plus vite que vous.   More quickly than you.
Aussi vite que moi.   As quickly as I.

2. 'More than,' 'less than,' as *adverbs of quantity before a numeral* = **plus de**, **moins de**, respectively:

Nous avons plus de vingt francs.   We have more than twenty francs.
En moins d'une demi-heure.   In less than half an hour.

224. Adverbs Irregularly Compared are:—

Pos.	Comp.	Sup.	Pos.	Comp.	Sup.
Bien,	mieux,	le mieux.	Beaucoup,	plus,	le plus.
Mal,	pis,	le pis.	Peu,	moins,	le moins.

Obs.: Beaucoup = 'much,' or 'very much,' and is *never modified* by another adv.

225. 'As much' = **autant**; 'so much' = **tant**; 'worse' (of health) = **plus mal**.

Obs.: Never use 'aussi beaucoup' *or* 'si beaucoup.'

226. Position of the Adverb. See §100. Note that **aujourd'hui** = 'to-day,' **hier** = 'yesterday,' **demain** = 'to-morrow,' **ici** = 'here,' **là** = 'there,' **tôt** = 'early,' and **tard** = 'late,' *never come between the auxiliary and the participle:*

Nous sommes arrivés hier.   We came yesterday.

227. Conjugation of *croire*, 'to believe,' 'think':—

Infin.	Pres. Part.	Past Part.	Pres. Indic.		Past Def.
croire	croyant.	cru.	crois.	croyons.	crus.
Fut.	*Impf.*		crois.	croyez.	*Impf. Subj.*
croirai.	croyais.		croit.	croient.	crusse.
Condl.	*Pres. Subj.*	[*Impve.* crois, croyons, croyez.]			
croirais.	croie, (-es, -e), croyions, (-iez), croient.				

228. Conjugation of *dire*, 'to say,' 'tell':—

Infin.	Pres. Part.	Past Part.	Pres. Indic.		Past Def.
dire.	disant.	dit.	dis.	disons.	dis.
Fut.	*Impf.*		dis.	dites.	*Impf. Subj.*
dirai.	disais.		dit.	disent.	disse.
Condl.	*Pres. Subj.*	[*Impve.* dis, disons, dites.]			
dirais.	dise, (-es, -e), disions, (-iez, -ent).				

EXERCISE XXIX.

Absolument *(ápsòlümã)*, absolutely.
Avant hier *(ávãt iè.r)*, day before yesterday.
Le bateau *(bátó)*, boat.
Le cordonnier *(kòrdònié)*, shoemaker.
Élevé *(élvé)*, raised, bred.
Facilement *(fásilmã)*, easily.
Fou *(fu)*, mad, insane.

Honnête *(ònè.t)*, honest, true.
Marcher *(màrśé)*, go, walk.
Le navire *(návi.r)*, ship.
Poliment *(pòlimã)*, politely.
Le soulier *(sulié)*, shoe.
Tant *(tã)*, so much, so many.
La vapeur *(vápœ.r)*, steam.

Bateau à vapeur. — Steam-boat.
Qu'y a-t-il de nouveau ?
Que dit-on de nouveau ? — What is the news?
Croyez-vous que cela soit vrai ? — Do you think that is true?
Je ne crois pas que cela soit vrai ? — I do not think that is true.
Je crois que cela est vrai. — I think that is true.
Je le crois. — I think so.
On croit. — It is believed (people believe, it is thought).
On dit. — It is said (people say).
Il le dit. — He says so.

A. 1. Que dit-on de nouveau? 2. On ne dit rien de nouveau. 3. Qu'avez-vous dit à mon père? 4. Je lui ai dit que vous étiez ici. 5. Voilà une maison qui est bien bâtie ; je voudrais qu'elle fût la mienne. 6. Mes souliers sont mal faits; mon cordonnier n'est pas un honnête homme. 7. Ce petit garçon est bien élevé; il parle très poliment. 8. Le train va plus vite que le bateau à vapeur. 9. Cet homme-là ne sait pas ce qu'il dit; il est absolument fou. 10. Cela se fait très facilement. 11. Ce monsieur se porte mieux, depuis qu'il est ici. 12. Quand avez-vous parlé à M. Robert de cette affaire? 13. Je lui en ai parlé hier. 14. Croyez-vous que cela se fasse facilement? 15. Non, monsieur, je ne le crois pas. 16. Je ne crois pas que notre cheval soit meilleur que celui de mon oncle. 17. À qui avez-vous donné tout cet argent? 18. Je ne l'ai donné à personne. 19. Ce bateau à vapeur-ci marche plus vite que celui-là. 20. Je l'aurai fait demain avant votre arrivée. 21. Qu'avez-vous apporté? 22. J'ai apporté des livres. 23. Qui avez-vous amené? 24. J'ai amené ma petite sœur. 25. Combien d'argent avez-vous? 26. J'ai plus de trente francs. 27. De quoi avez-vous besoin? 28. Je n'ai besoin de rien. 29. Hier j'ai rencontré le monsieur dont on a tant parlé. 30. Je n'ai rien dit à ce monsieur. 31. Je n'ai rencontré personne hier. 32. Cet homme parle beaucoup, mais il ne dit rien. 33. Pourquoi n'avez-vous pas dit à votre père que j'étais parti? 34. J'avais peur de le lui dire.

B. 1. What was that gentleman saying to you? 2. He was telling me that he had had a house built. 3. My hat is badly made. 4. How is your mother to-day? 5. She is not well; she has been ill for two weeks. 6. The steamboat does not go so fast as the train. 7. Steam-boats go faster than horses. 8. What is the news to-day? 9. There is nothing new. 10. It is said that he will not be there to-morrow. 11. It is believed that the ship will arrive to-day. 12. Why did you not tell your mother that you had lost your money? 13. I was afraid to tell her (it). 14. There is the gentleman you have spoken so much about. 15. That man speaks too much; he does not know what he says. 16. I do not believe that that is true. 17. My uncle has very many apples this year. 18. I met the lady yesterday of whom our cousins spoke so much. 19. This horse goes faster than that one. 20. I wish that horse were mine. 21. That man is very well-bred. 22. My house is badly built; the carpenter was not an honest man. 23. Your house is better built than your brother's. 24. That man is absolutely mad; he does not know what he is saying. 25. How much money have you? 26. I have less than twenty francs. 27. Do you think they will be here to-morrow? 28. Yes, I think so. 29. Do you say that you met him yesterday? 30. No, I do not say so; I met him the day before yesterday. 31. My mother is better since she has been here. 32. What did you say to that gentleman? 33. I told him that I was going to leave to-morrow.

LESSON XXX.

229. Prepositions. The commoner English prepositions, with some of their French equivalents, are :—

1. 'About' = **environ, vers, sur** :

Environ dix francs.	About ten francs.
Vers les dix heures.	About ten o'clock.
Avez-vous de l'argent sur vous?	Have you any money about you?

2. 'Above' = **au-dessus de** :

La cuisine est au-dessus de la cave.	The kitchen is above the cellar.

3. 'After' (of *time, rank, order*) = **après** :

Après le bal.	After the ball.
Le premier après le roi.	Next after the king.
Mettez l'adjectif après le nom.	Place the adjective after the noun.

4. 'Among,' 'in the midst of' = **parmi** ; 'among' (*distributively*) = **entre** :

Une brebis parmi les loups.	A sheep among wolves.
Partagez l'or entre les hommes.	Divide the gold among the men.

5. 'As far as' = **jusque, jusqu'à** :

Allez jusqu'au bout de la rue.	Go as far as the end of the street.

6. 'At' = **à, chez** :

À l'école. À Berlin. À cinq heures.	At school. At Berlin. At 5 o'clock.
À la maison (chez moi, etc.).	At home.
Chez M. Scott.	At Mr. Scott's.

7. 'Before,' 'in front of' = **devant** ; 'before' (of *time, rank, order*) = **avant** :

La charrue devant les bœufs (prov.).	The cart before the horse.
Avant midi. La vérité avant tout.	Before noon. Truth before all.

8. 'Behind' = **derrière** :

Le jardin est derrière la maison.   The garden is behind the house.

9. 'Below,' 'under' = **au-dessous de** :

Rouen est au-dessous de Paris.   Rouen is below Paris.

10. 'By' (agent of the *passive*) = **par** or **de** ; 'by' *(means)* = **par** ; 'by' *(measure)* = **de** :

Tué par une balle. Aimé de tous.   Killed by a bullet. Loved by all.
Par la poste. Par le chemin de fer.   By post. By railway.
Plus grand d'un pouce. De beaucoup.   Taller by an inch. By far.

11. 'For' = **pour** ; 'for' (of *future time*) = **pour**, or is unexpressed. Time *not future* is *never* pour :

Il mourut pour la patrie.   He died for his country.
Je resterai (pour) huit jours.   I shall stay for a week.
Il était quinze jours absent.   He was absent for a fortnight.
Voilà une heure que vous lisez. ⎫
Vous lisez depuis une heure.   ⎬ You have been reading for an hour.
Il y a une heure que vous lisez. ⎭

12. 'In' = **dans** (§127), **en** (§127) ; 'in' (time *within which*) = **en** ; 'in' (time *at end of which*) = **dans** :

Je partirai dans quinze jours.   I shall go in a fortnight.
On peut aller à Londres en dix jours.   One can go to London in ten days.

13. 'To' = **à** (§106) ; 'to' (of *motion*) = **à**, **en** (§127), **chez** ; 'to' *(sentiment towards)*, **pour**, **envers** :

Donnez la pomme à l'enfant.   Give the apple to the child.
Nous allons en France, à Paris.   We are going to France, to Paris.
Nous allons chez M. Scott.   We are going to Mr. Scott's.
Il est bon pour moi.   He is kind to me.
Aimable envers tous.   Friendly to all.

14. 'Towards' = **vers** ; 'towards' (of *conduct* or *disposition*) = **envers** :

Vers midi. Poli envers moi.   **Towards** noon. Polite towards me.

15. 'With,' 'along with,' 'in company with' = **avec** ; 'with,' 'at the house, etc., of' = **chez** ; 'with' (of *instrument, manner*, etc.) = **avec** :

Dînez avec moi à l'hôtel.   Dine with me at the hotel.
Notre neveu demeure chez nous.   Our nephew lives with us.
Attacher avec une corde.   To tie with a rope.
Avec énergie.   With energy.

230. Prepositional Locutions, like au-dessus de, jusqu'à, etc., are used precisely like simple prepositions:

Il passa à travers le bois.	He passed through the wood.
Au delà de la rivière.	Beyond the stream.

231. A *verb form* governed by a preposition must be in the *infinitive*, except after en:

Sans penser. En disant.	Without thinking. While saying.
Après avoir pensé.	After having thought.

232. Conjugation of *tenir*, 'to hold' and *venir*, 'to come':—

Infin.	*Pres. Part.*	*Past Part.*	*Pres. Indic.*	*Past Def.*
tenir	tenant.	tenu.	tiens. tenons.	tins.
Fut.	*Impf.*		tiens. tenez.	*Impf. Subj.*
tiendrai.	tenais.		tient. tiennent.	tinsse.
Condl.	*Pres. Subj.*	[*Impve.* tiens, tenons, tenez.]		
tiendrais.	tienne, (-es, -e), tenions, (-iez), tiennent.			

So also, **venir**: Je viens, tu viens, il vient, etc., etc.

233. Conjugation of *voir*, 'to see':—

Infin.	*Pres. Part.*	*Past Part.*	*Pres. Indic.*	*Past Def.*
voir.	voyant.	vu.	vois. voyons.	vis.
Fut.	*Impf.*		vois. voyez.	*Impf. Subj.*
verrai.	voyais.		voit. voient.	visse.
Condl.	*Pres. Subj.*	[*Impve.* vois, voyons, voyez.]		
verrais.	voie, (-es, -e), voyions, (-iez), voient.			

EXERCISE XXX.

Accompagner *(ăkōpáñé)*, accompany.
L'assemblée, f., *(ăsăblé)*, meeting, gathering.
Bon pour *(bō pu.r)*, kind to.
Le chemin de fer *(šemē de fe.r)*, railway.
Dernièrement *(dèrnièrmā)*, lately.
Dîner *(diné)*, dine.
La lieue *(liŭ)*, league.
Le paysan *(péizā)*, peasant.

Pendre *(pā.dr)*, hang.
Le printemps *(prētā)*, spring.
Rappeler *(ráplé)*, recall.
Regarder *(regárdé)*, look at.
Le restaurant *(rèstórā)*, restaurant.
Le souvenir *(suvni.r)*, remembrance, recollection.
Sur *(sü.r)*, on, about.
Le tableau *(tăbló)*, picture.

De temps à autre.	Now and then.
Il est venu me voir.	He came to see me.

Venez me voir.	Come and see me.
Il vient de me voir.	He has just seen me.
Il a passé chez nous.	He called on us.
Il a passé devant chez nous.	He passed our house.
Rappelez-moi au bon souvenir de nos amis.	Remember me to our friends.

A. 1. Il viendra nous voir après cinq heures. 2. Il nous a accompagnés jusque chez nous. 3. Nous verrons nos amis ce soir à l'assemblée. 4. Avez-vous vu mon père dernièrement? 5. Oui, monsieur, je viens de parler avec lui. 6. Dites à votre ami de passer chez nous ce soir. 7. Quand avez-vous vu ce monsieur-là? 8. Il vient de passer devant la maison. 9. Nos amis viendront avant l'hiver. 10. Il y a un grand pommier devant la porte de la maison du paysan. 11. Il a passé chez nous en allant à l'église. 12. Pendez ce tableau-ci au-dessus de celui-là. 13. Combien d'argent avez-vous sur vous? 14. J'ai environ vingt-cinq francs. 15. Il demeure à environ dix lieues d'ici. 16. Cette dame sera ici vers les onze heures. 17. Avez-vous jamais demeuré en Angleterre? 18. Oui, madame; j'y ai demeuré pendant environ trois ans. 19. Ce monsieur est bien aimable, n'est-ce pas? 20. Oui, monsieur, il est toujours très bon pour moi. 21. Venez nous voir de temps à autre. 22. Cette petite fille est aimée de tout le monde. 23. Mon père est arrivé par le chemin de fer. 24. Voulez-vous bien dîner avec moi au restaurant? 25. Non, monsieur, j'aimerais mieux que vous veniez dîner chez moi. 26. La dame m'a dit qu'elle viendrait avec les enfants. 27. Je demeure au Canada depuis environ huit ans. 28. Regardez ce petit tableau qui pend au-dessous du grand. 29. Nous allons voir nos amis dans une semaine. 30. Eh bien, rappelez-moi à leur bon souvenir.

B. 1. My father has just departed for France. 2. When will you come to dine with us? 3. We shall come and dine with you next Thursday. 4. Last evening, as he was going to church, he called on us. 5. When did you see our friend? 6. I have just been speaking with him about that affair. 7. Tell your friend to come and see me tomorrow evening. 8. Have you any money about you? 9. Not much, I think; about ten francs. 10. The gentleman told me that he would come about five o'clock. 11. The children will come before noon. 12. I lived in France for *(pendant)* four years. 13. I have lived in Toronto for about ten years. 14. That gentleman is very pleasant, is he not? 15. Yes, he has always been very kind to me. 16. That lady lives about twenty leagues from here. 17. Do you see that small picture which hangs under the large one? 18. You will come and see me this evening, will you not? 19. Yes, I shall be there at a quarter to eight. 20. There is an apple-tree before the door of his house. 21. He passed our house at half-past nine. 22. How long have you lived in Canada? 23. I have lived here for about three years. 24. Did you come by the railway? 25. No sir, I came by the steam-boat. 26. When shall you see your father and mother? 27. I shall see them in two weeks. 28. Well, remember me to them, when you see (fut.) them. 29. Come and see us now and then. 30. You shall see your friends at the gathering this evening, shall you not? 31. We believe so; if we see them, we shall tell them that you are here. 32. Your friends will come before (the) spring.

LESSON XXXI.

234. Conjunctions. 1. 'And' after a *verb of motion* is *unexpressed :*

Allez leur parler.   Go and speak to them.

2. In sentences of *negative* force, **et** and **ou** become **ni**:

Il est sans argent ni amis.   He is without money or friends.

3. **Lorsque** and **quand** are equivalents, but **quand** (*not* **lorsque**) serves also as an *interrogative:*

Quand est-il arrivé?   When did he come?

4. The following conjunctions require the *subjunctive* in the subordinate clause

Afin que, *in order that.*
Avant que, *before.*
Bien que, *although.*
Au cas que, *in case that.*
En cas que, *in case that.*
De crainte que, *for fear that.*

Non (pas) que, *not that.*
De peur que, *for fear that.*
Pour que, *in order that.*
Pourvu que, *provided (that).*
Quoique, *although.*
Supposé que, *suppose that.*

5. **De sorte que** = 'so that,' 'so as to,' takes the *indicative* to denote *result*, and the *subjunctive* to denote *purpose:*

Il a joué de sorte qu'il a gagné sans peine. — He played in such a way that he won without difficulty.

Épargnez votre argent de sorte que vous en ayez pour la vieillesse. — Save your money so as to have some for old age.

6. **Jusqu'à ce que** = 'until' may *always* take the subjunctive, but the indic. is often used when referring to *completed past action:*

Il marcha jusqu'à ce qu'il nous rencontra (rencontrât). — He walked until he met us.

7. **Si** = 'if' *regularly* takes the *indicative* and *exceptionally* the *subjunctive* (as a substitute for the plupf. indic.):

Si j'avais (or j'eusse) su cela. — If I had known that.

8. **Que** = 'that' takes indicative *or* subjunctive according to the context. It is *never omitted*, as often in English:

Je dis que vous avez raison. — I say that you are right.
Je suis fâché que vous ayez raison. — I am sorry (that) you are right.

235. Conjugation of *mettre*, 'to place,' 'put':—

Infin.	*Pres. Part.*	*Past Part.*	*Pres. Indic.*		*Past Def.*
mettre.	mettant.	mis.	mets.	mettons.	mis.
Fut.	*Impf.*		mets.	mettez.	*Impf. Subj.*
mettrai.	mettais.		met.	mettent.	misse.
Condl.	*Pres. Subj.*	[*Impve.* mets, mettons, mettez.]			
mettrais.	mette, (-es, -e), mettions, (-iez, -ent).				

236. Conjugation of *prendre*, 'to take':—

Infin.	*Pres. Part.*	*Past Part.*	*Pres. Indic.*		*Past Def.*
prendre.	prenant.	pris.	prends.	prenons.	pris.
Fut.	*Impf.*		prends.	prenez.	*Impf. Subj.*
prendrai.	prenais.		prend.	prennent.	prisse.
Condl.	*Pres. Subj.*	[*Impve.* prends, prenons, prenez.]			
prendrais.	prenne, (-es, -e), prenions, (-iez), prennent.				

EXERCISE XXXI.

Après que *(ápre̤ ke)*, after (that).
Attendre *(átã.dr)*, wait, wait for.
Aussitôt que *(ósitó ke)*, as soon as.
Le libraire *(libre̤.r)*, bookseller.
L'oie, f., *(ñá)*, goose.
Ôter *(óté)*, take off.

Le coin *(kŭã)*, corner.	La pierre *(piè.r)*, stone.
Courir, run, *(kuri.r)*.	Prendre *(prã.dr)*, take, get.
Dès que *(dè ke)*, as soon as, when.	Prendre garde *(gãrd)*, take care.
Écrire *(ékri.r)*, write.	pay attention, look out.
Emporter *(ãpòrté)*, take away.	Le surtout *(sürtu)*, overcoat.
Ennuyer *(ãnŭilé)*, annoy.	Tant que *(tã ke)*, as long as.
L'injure, f., *(ẽžü.r)*, insult.	

À la bonne heure!	All right!
Il m'a dit des injures.	He insulted me.
Il fait glissant.	It is slippery.
Je l'ai mis à la porte.	I kicked (turned) him out of doors.
Il met son habit.	He puts on his coat.
Il se met bien.	He dresses well.
Elle est bien mise.	She is well dressed.
Ils se mettent à table.	They sit down to dinner, etc.
Il se met à travailler.	He begins to work.
Prends garde au chien.	Beware of the dog.
Prends garde de tomber.	Beware of falling (take care not to fall).
Où avez-vous pris ce livre?	Where did you get this book?

A. 1. Après qu'il sera arrivé, il vous dira ce qu'il veut. 2. Après avoir mis son habit il est sorti. 3. Cet homme-là m'a dit des injures, et je l'ai mis à la porte. 4. Mettez cet homme à la porte; tant qu'il sera ici il nous ennuiera. 5. Aussitôt que vous arriverez là-bas, dites à nos amis de nous écrire. 6. Attendez-nous ici, jusqu'à ce qu'il vienne. 7. Nous nous mettons à table à six heures précises. 8. Je me suis mis à travailler avant qu'il arrivât. 9. Mes enfants, prenez garde aux oies en passant devant chez M. Simon. 10. Il fait glissant ce matin; prenez garde de tomber. 11. Il ne sait pas s'il viendra. 12. Ce monsieur se mettait toujours bien, avant qu'il eût ce grand malheur. 13. Cette jeune dame est toujours bien mise. 14. S'il avait pris garde, il ne serait pas tombé. 15. Voilà un méchant cheval; prenez garde à lui. 16. Où avez-vous pris ce beau chapeau? 17. Je l'ai acheté chez M. Simon au coin de la rue. 18. Ôtez votre surtout, monsieur, et dînez avec nous. 19. Prenez garde! cela va tomber. 20. Prenez garde à cet enfant. 21. On le trompera, s'il ne prends pas garde. 22. Prenez garde de perdre votre porte-monnaie. 23. Ce pauvre mendiant est sans parents ni amis. 24. Notre chien a apporté cela, sans qu'on le lui ait dit. 25. Dès que mon chien m'a vu, il s'est mis à courir vers moi. 26. Prenez la lettre qui est sur la table, et emportez-la à la poste. 27. Restez avec nous ; nous allons nous mettre à table. 28. Il m'a fallu le mettre à la porte. 29. Les enfants ne feront pas leur ouvrage, sans qu'on le leur dise. 30. Mettons nos chapeaux, et allons nous promener. 31. À la bonne heure ! allons-y.

B. 1. Take off your overcoat and hat; we are going to sit down to dinner. 2. Take care not to fall; it is very slippery. 3. I had to turn him out of doors; he insulted me. 4. Take care! That child will fall. 5. That is a cross dog; beware of him. 6. As soon as we arrive there, we shall tell our friends what you said. 7. After they have arrived, they will do what you wish. 8. Our friends sit down to dinner at seven o'clock precisely. 9. (My) children, take care of the dog, as you pass Mr. Robinson's. 10. Kick that dog out; as long as he is here, he will be annoying us. 11. He will be deceived, if he does not look out. 12. Look out! That stone will fall. 13. That is a fine book ; where did you get it? 14. I bought it at the bookseller's at the corner of the street. 15. We begin to study at seven o'clock in the morning. 16. Take that letter to the post-office. 17. Take that hat which is on the table. 18. Take that child to school. 19. Will you take a walk this morning? 20. No, I think it is too slippery ; I am afraid of falling. 21. That young gentleman is always well dressed. 22. That lady dresses well, but that gentleman dresses badly. 23. If you had taken care, you would not have fallen. 24. Wait for them, until we come. 25. Tell your friends to write to us, as soon as you get there. 26. That dog brought that without being told. 27. We began to work, before our friends came. 28. Will you wait for us until we come? 29. Why are you putting on your overcoat? 30. I am going for a walk, if it is not too cold and *(ni trop)* slippery. 31. That poor man is without bread or fire. 32. We shall do that without being told. 33. Put on your hat and overcoat, and let us go for a walk. 34. All right! Let us go.

PART III.

THE VERB.

REGULAR VERBS.

237. Regular verbs are conveniently divided into *three* classes or conjugations, according as the present infinitive ends in **-er, -ir, -re**, and are inflected in their simple tenses as follows :—

I.	II.	III.

Infinitive Mood.

PRESENT.	PRESENT.	PRESENT.
donn er, *to give.*	fin ir, *to finish.*	romp re, *to break.*

Participles.

PRESENT.	PRESENT.	PRESENT.
donn ant, *giving.*	fin *iss* ant, *finishing.*	romp ant, *breaking.*
PAST.	PAST.	PAST.
donn é, *given.*	fin i, *finished.*	romp u, *broken.*

Indicative Mood.

PRESENT.	PRESENT.	PRESENT.
[*I give, am giving, etc.*]	[*I finish, am finishing, etc.*]	[*I break, am breaking, etc.*]
je donn e.	je fin *i* s.	je romp s.
tu donn es.	tu fin *i* s.	tu romp s.
il donn e.	il fin *i* t.	il romp t.
nous donn ons.	nous fin *iss* ons.	nous romp ons.
vous donn ez.	vous fin *iss* ez.	vous romp ez.
ils donn ent.	ils fin *iss* ent.	ils romp ent.

IMPERFECT.	IMPERFECT.	IMPERFECT.
[*I was giving, used to give, etc.*]	[*I was finishing, used to finish, etc.*]	[*I was breaking, used to break, etc.*]
je donn ais.	je fin iss ais.	je romp ais.
tu donn ais.	tu fin iss ais.	tu romp ais.
il donn ait.	il fin iss ait.	il romp ait.
nous donn ions.	nous fin iss ions.	nous romp ions.
vous donn iez.	vous fin iss iez.	vous romp iez.
ils donn aient.	ils fin iss aient.	ils romp aient.

PAST DEFINITE.	PAST DEFINITE.	PAST DEFINITE.
[*I gave, etc.*]	[*I finished, etc.*]	[*I broke, etc.*]
je donn ai.	je fin is.	je romp is.
tu donn as.	tu fin is.	tu romp is.
il donn a.	il fin it.	il romp it.
nous donn âmes.	nous fin îmes.	nous romp îmes.
vous donn âtes.	vous fin îtes.	vous romp îtes.
ils donn èrent.	ils fin irent.	ils romp irent.

FUTURE.	FUTURE.	FUTURE.
[*I shall give, etc.*]	[*I shall finish, etc.*]	[*I shall break, etc.*]
je donner ai.	je finir ai.	je rompr ai.
tu donner as.	tu finir as.	tu rompr as.
il donner a.	il finir a.	il rompr a.
nous donner ons.	nous finir ons.	nous rompr ons.
vous donner ez.	vous finir ez.	vous rompr ez.
ils donner ont.	ils finir ont.	ils rompr ont.

CONDITIONAL.	CONDITIONAL.	CONDITIONAL.
[*I should give, etc.*]	[*I should finish, etc.*]	[*I should break, etc.*]
je donner ais.	je finir ais.	je rompr ais.
tu donner ais.	tu finir ais.	tu rompr ais.
il donner ait.	il finir ait.	il rompr ait.
nous donner ions.	nous finir ions.	nous rompr ions.
vous donner iez.	vous finir iez.	vous rompr iez.
ils donner aient.	ils finir aient.	ils rompr aient.

Imperative Mood.

PRESENT.	PRESENT.	PRESENT.
[*Give, etc.*]	[*Finish, etc.*]	[*Break, etc.*]
2. donn e.	2. fin *i* s.	2. romp s.
3. (qu'il donn e.)	3. (qu'il fin *iss* e.)	3. (qu'il romp e.)
1. donn ons.	1. fin *iss* ons.	1. romp ons.
2. donn ez.	2. fin *iss* ez.	2. romp ez.
3. (qu'ils donn ent)	3. (qu'ils fin *iss* ent.)	3. (qu'ils romp ent.)

Subjunctive Mood.

PRESENT.	PRESENT.	PRESENT.
[*(That) I (may) give, etc.*]	[*(That) I (may) finish, etc.*]	[*(That) I (may) break, etc.*]
(que) je donn e.	(que) je fin *iss* e.	(que) je romp e.
(que) tu donn es.	(que) tu fin *iss* es.	(que) tu romp es.
(qu') il donn e.	(qu') il fin *iss* e.	(qu') il romp e.
(que) nous donn ions.	(que) nous fin *iss* ions.	(que) nous romp ions.
(que) vous donn iez.	(que) vous fin *iss* iez.	(que) vous romp iez.
(qu') ils donn ent.	(qu') ils fin *iss* ent.	(qu') ils romp ent.

AUXILIARY VERBS—SIMPLE TENSES.

238. The auxiliary verbs **avoir**, *to have* and **être**, *to be*, are conjugated in their simple tenses as follows:—

Infinitive.

PRES. avoir, *to have.* PRES. être, *to be.*

Participles.

PRES. ayant, *having.* PRES. étant, *being.*
PAST. eu, *had.* PAST. été, *been.*

Indicative.

PRESENT.	PRESENT.
[*I have, am having, etc.*]	[*I am, am being, etc.*]
j'ai. nous avons.	je suis. nous sommes.
tu as. vous avez.	tu es. vous êtes.
il a. ils ont.	il est. ils sont.

IMPERFECT.

[*I had, was having, etc.*]
j'avais.   nous avions.
tu avais.   vous aviez.
il avait.   ils avaient.

PAST DEFINITE.

[*I had, etc.*]
j'eus.   nous eûmes.
tu eus.   vous eûtes.
il eut.   ils eurent.

FUTURE.

[*I shall have, etc.*]
j'aurai.   nous aurons.
tu auras.   vous aurez.
il aura.   ils auront.

CONDITIONAL.

[*I should have, etc.*]
j'aurais.   nous aurions.
tu aurais.   vous auriez.
il aurait.   ils auraient.

IMPERFECT.

[*I was, was being, etc.*]
j'étais.   nous étions.
tu étais.   vous étiez.
il était.   ils étaient.

PAST DEFINITE.

[*I was, etc.*]
je fus.   nous fûmes.
tu fus.   vous fûtes.
il fut.   ils furent.

FUTURE.

[*I shall be, etc.*]
je serai.   nous serons.
tu seras.   vous serez.
ils sera.   ils seront.

CONDITIONAL.

[*I should be, etc.*]
je serais.   nous serions.
tu serais.   vous seriez.
il serait.   ils seraient.

Imperative.

PRESENT.

[*Have, etc.*]
         1. ayons.
2. aie.   2. ayez.
3. (qu'il ait.)   3. (qu'ils aient.)

PRESENT.

[*Be, etc.*]
         1. soyons.
2. sois.   2. soyez.
3. (qu'il soit.)   3. (qu'ils soient.)

Subjunctive.

PRESENT.

[*(That) I (may) have, etc.*]
(que) j'aie.   (que) nous ayons.
(que) tu aies.   (que) vous ayez.
(qu') il ait.   (qu') ils aient.

IMPERFECT.

[*(That) I (might) have, etc.*]
(que) j'eusse.   (que) nous eussions.
(que) tu eusses.   (que) vous eussiez.
(qu') il eût.   (qu') ils eussent.

PRESENT.

[*(That) I (may) be, etc.*]
(que) je sois.   (que) nous soyons.
(que) tu sois.   (que) vous soyez.
(qu') il soit.   (qu') ils soient.

IMPERFECT.

[*(That) I (might) be, etc.*]
(que) je fusse.   (que) nous fussions.
(que) tu fusses.   (que) vous fussiez.
(qu') il fût.   (qu') ils fussent.

NOTE.—From **avoir** (or **être**)+*a past participle* are formed the *compound tenses* and from **être**+*a past participle* the *passive voice*. Such formations are, in reality, "verb phrases," of which the auxiliary is the verb. They are closely analogous to corresponding English constructions. **Avoir** and **être** are also used as independent verbs.

IRREGULAR VERBS IN -er.

239. Verbs in -*cer* and -*ger*. 1. Verbs in -cer, *e.g.*, avancer *(ávãsé)*, 'advance,' require the *s* sound of c (§15, 13) throughout their conjugation, and hence c becomes ç before a or o of an ending (§41, 2, note), but not elsewhere:

Pres. Part.	*Pres. Indic.*	*Impf. Indic.*	*Past Def.*	*Impf. Subj.*
avançant.	avance.	avançais.	avançai.	avançasse.
	avances.	avançais.	avanças.	avançasses.
	avance.	avançait.	avança.	avançât.
	avançons.	avancions.	avançâmes.	avançassions.
	avancez.	avanciez.	avançâtes.	avançassiez.
	avancent.	avançaient.	avancèrent.	avançassent.

2. Verbs in -ger, *e.g.*, manger *(mãžé)*, 'eat,' require the *ž* sound of g (§15, 18) throughout, and hence g becomes ge before a or o (§45, 2, note), but not elsewhere:

Pres. Part.	*Pres. Indic.*	*Impf. Indic.*	*Past Def.*	*Impf. Subj.*
mangeant.	mange.	mangeais.	mangeai.	mangeasse.
	manges.	mangeais.	mangeas.	mangeasses.
	mange.	mangeait.	mangea.	mangeât.
	mangeons.	mangions.	mangeâmes.	mangeassions.
	mangez.	mangiez.	mangeâtes.	mangeassiez.
	mangent.	mangeaient.	mangèrent.	mangeassent.

240. Verbs in -*yer*. Verbs in -oyer and -uyer *change* y to i whenever it comes *before* e in conjugation, but not elsewhere. Verbs in -ayer and -eyer may either *retain* y throughout or *change* it to i before e:

Pres. Indic.	*Fut.*	*Condl.*	*Pres. Subj.*
nettoie, etc.	nettoierai, etc.	nettoierais, etc.	nettoie, etc.
paye, paie, } etc.	payerai, paierai, } etc.	payerais, paierais, } etc.	paye, paie, } etc.

241. Stem-Vowel e(*é*). Verbs with stem-vowel e require the *è* sound of e (§10, 4) whenever the ending has e *mute* (-e, -es, -e, -ent) and in the *fut.* and *condl.* So also, stem-vowel é, but *not* for the *fut.* and *condl.* This is shown orthographically as follows :—

1. By changing e or é to è (§17, 2, note), *e.g.*, mener, 'lead,' céder, 'yield':

Pres. Indic.	Pres. Subj.	Fut.	Condl.
mène.	mène.	mènerai.	mènerais.
mènes.	mènes.	mèneras.	mènerais.
mène.	mène.	mènera.	mènerait.
menons.	menions.	mènerons.	mènerions.
menez.	meniez.	mènerez.	mèneriez.
mènent.	mènent.	mèneront.	mèneraient.

But céder:

| cède, etc. | cède, etc. | céderai, etc. | céderais, etc. |

Obs.: In mené-je?, e of the ending is not mute, and hence *no accent* on the stem-vowel.

Like mener: Verbs with stem-vowel e (for exceptions in -eler and -eter, see below).

Like céder: Verbs with stem-vowel é + *consonant*, *e.g.*, régner, 'reign,' etc.

Note.—Verbs like créer, 'create,' are regular: Je crée, etc.

2. *Most verbs* in -eler, -eter, however, indicate the è sound of e by *doubling* l or t (§17, 2, note), *e.g.*, appeler, 'call,' jeter, 'throw':

Pres. Indic.	Pres. Subj.	Fut.	Condl.
appelle.	appelle.	appellerai.	appellerais.
appelles.	appelles.	appelleras.	appellerais.
appelle.	appelle.	appellera.	appellerait.
appelons.	appelions.	appellerons.	appellerions.
appelez.	appeliez.	appellerez.	appelleriez.
appellent.	appellent.	appelleront.	appelleraient.

So also, jeter:

| jette, etc. | jette, etc. | jetterai, etc. | jetterais, etc. |

A *few verbs* in -eler, -eter take the *grave accent* precisely like mener, *e.g.*, acheter, 'buy':

| achète, etc. | achète, etc. | achèterai, etc. | achèterais, etc. |

Exceptions like acheter :

agneler, *lamb*.	*épousseter, *dust*.	modeler, *model*.
becqueter, *peck*.	étiqueter, *label*.	peler, *peel*.
bourreler, *goad*.	geler, *freeze*.	rapiéceter, *piece*.
démanteler, *dismantle*.	harceler, *harass*.	trompeter, *trumpet*.
écarteler, *quarter*.	marteler, *hammer*.	

*Fut. épousseteral according to the *Dictionnaire de l'Académie*.

Exceptions like appeler *or* acheter :

botteler, *bale* (*hay, etc.*).	caqueter, *cackle*.	crocheter, *pick* (*a lock*).
canneler, *groove*.	ciseler, *chisel*.	

242. Aller, *to go* :—

Infin.	Pres. Part.	Past Part.	Pres. Indic.		Past Def.
aller.	allant.	allé.	vais.	allons.	allai.
Fut.	Impf. Indic.		vas.	allez.	Impf. Subj.
irai.	allais.		va.	vont.	allasse.
Condl.	Pres. Subj.	[*Impve.* va, allons, allez.]			
irais.	aille, (-es, -e), allions, (-iez), aillent.				

Like aller :
s'en aller, *go away*.

243. Envoyer, *to send* :—

Infin.	Pres. Part.	Past Part.	Pres. Indic.		Past Def.
envoyer.	envoyant.	envoyé.	envoie.	envoyons.	envoyai.
Fut.	Impf. Ind.		envoies.	envoyez.	Impf. Subj.
enverrai.	envoyais.		envoie.	envoient.	envoyasse.
Condl.	Pres. Subj.	[*Impve.* envoie, envoyons, envoyez.]			
enverrais.	envoie, (-es, -e), envoyions, (-iez), envoient.				

Like envoyer :
renvoyer, *send away, dismiss*.

Irregular Verbs in -ir.

244. Acquérir, *to acquire* :—

Infin.	Pres. Part.	Past Part.	Pres. Indic.		Past. Def.
acquérir.	acquérant.	acquis.	acquiers.	acquérons.	acquis.
Fut.	Impf. Ind.		acquiers.	acquérez.	Impf. Subj.
acquerrai.	acquérais.		acquiert.	acquièrent.	acquisse.
Condl.	Pres. Subj.	[*Impve.* acquiers, acquérons, acquérez.]			
acquerrais.	acquière, (-es, -e), acquérions, (-iez), acquièrent.				

Like acquérir :

conquérir, *conquer*.	†querir *or* quérir, *seek*.	requérir, *require, claim*.
s'enquérir, *inquire*.	reconquérir, *reconquer*.	

†Has only the *infinitive*.

245. Bénir, *to bless :—*

Is *regular*, but has also an *irreg. past part.* bénit, used only as *adj. :*
De l'eau bénite. Du pain bénit.   Holy water. Consecrated bread.

246. Courir, *to run :—*

Infin.	*Pres. Part.*	*Past Part.*	*Pres. Indic.*		*Past Def.*
courir.	courant.	couru.	cours.	courons.	courus.
Fut.	*Impf. Ind.*		cours.	courez.	*Impf. Subj.*
courrai.	courais.		court.	courent.	courusse.
Condl.	*Pres. Subj.*	[*Impve.* cours, courons, courez.]			
courrais.	coure, (-es, -e), courions (-iez, -ent).				

Like **courir** are its *compounds :*

accourir, *run up, hasten.* discourir, *discourse.* recourir, *run again, apply.*
concourir, *co-operate, con-* encourir, *incur.* secourir, *succor, help.*
  cur, compete. parcourir, *run over.*

NOTE.—**Courre**, *chase* (a hunting term) sometimes replaces **courir** in the infin.

247. Cueillir, *to gather, pick :—*

Infin.	*Pres. Part*	*Past Part.*	*Pres. Indic.*		*Past. Def.*
cueillir.	cueillant.	cueilli.	cueille.	cueillons.	cueillis.
Fut.	*Impf. Ind.*		cueilles.	cueillez.	*Impf. Subj.*
cueillerai.	cueillais.		cueille.	cueillent.	cueillisse.
Condl.	*Pres. Subj.*	[*Impve.* cueille, cueillons, cueillez.]			
cueillerais.	cueille, (-es, -e), cueillions, (-iez, -ent).				

Obs. : The *pres. indic., fut.* and *condl.* are like those of **donner**.

Like **cueillir :**

accueillir, *welcome.* *assaillir, *assail.* tressaillir, *start.*
recueillir, *gather, collect.* †saillir, *jut out.*

*Regular in *fut.* and *condl. :* **Assaillirai**, etc.
†**Saillir**, *gush out, rush forth*, is regular like **finir**.

248. Dormir, *to sleep:—*

Infin.	*Pres. Part.*	*Past Part.*	*Pres. Indic.*		*Past Def.*
dormir.	dormant.	dormi.	dors.	dormons.	dormis.
Fut.	*Impf. Ind.*		dors.	dormez.	*Impf. Subj.*
dormirai.	dormais.		dort.	dorment.	dormisse.
Condl.	*Pres. Subj.*	[*Impve.* dors, dormons, dormez.]			
dormirais.	dorme, (-es, -e), dormions, (-iez, -ent).				

IRREGULAR VERBS.

Like dormir :
endormir, *put to sleep.*
s'endormir, *fall asleep.*
redormir, *sleep again.*
rendormir, *put to sleep again.*
se rendormir, *go to sleep again.*
bouillir, *boil.*
ébouillir, *boil away.*

rebouillir, *boil again.*
mentir, *lie.*
démentir, *contradict, belie.*
partir, *set out.*
départir, *distribute.*
se départir, *desist.*
repartir, *set out again, reply.*
se repentir, *repent.*
sentir, *feel.*

consentir, *consent.*
pressentir, *forebode.*
ressentir, *resent.*
servir, *serve.*
se servir, *make use.*
desservir, *clear the table.*
sortir, *go out.*
ressortir, *go out again.*

NOTE.—Asservir, *enslave*, assortir, *sort, match*, ressortir, *depend* (on, à), répartir, *distribute*, are like finir.

249. Faillir, *to fail* :—

Infin.	*Pres. Part*	*Past Part.*	*Pres. Indic.*	*Past Def.*
faillir.	faillant.	failli.	faux. faillons.	faillis.
Fut.	*Impf. Ind.*		faux. faillez.	*Impf. Subj.*
faudrai.	faillais.		faut. faillent.	faillisse.
Condl.	*Pres. Subj.*	[*Impve.* ——, ——, ——]		
faudrais.	faille, (-es, -e), faillions, (-iez, -ent).			

Like faillir :
Détaillir, *faint, fail* (but *pres. indic.* usually défaus, défaus, défaut).
NOTE —Faillir, *fail in business*, is usually like finir.

250. Férir, *to strike* :—

Used only in 'Sans coup férir,' ' Without striking a blow,' and in the *past part.* féru, *wounded* (a veterinary term).

251. Fleurir, *to flourish, be prosperous* :—

Pres. Part. florissant, *Impf. Ind.* florissais when used of *persons* or a collection of persons, (*or* fleurissais when used of *things*) ; otherwise like finir.

NOTE.—Fleurir, *blossom, bloom* (lit.) is like finir.

252. Fuir, *to flee, fly* :—

Infin.	*Pres. Part.*	*Past Part.*	*Pres. Indic.*	*Past Def.*
fuir.	fuyant.	fui.	fuis. fuyons.	fuis.
Fut.	*Impf. Ind.*		fuis. fuyez.	*Impf. Subj.*
fuirai.	fuyais.		fuit. fuient.	fuisse.
Condl.	*Pres. Subj.*	[*Impve.* fuis, fuyons, fuyez.]		
fuirais.	fuie, (-es, -e), fuyions, (-iez), fuient.			

Like fuir :
S'enfuir, *flee, escape.*

253. Gésir, *to lie, lie buried* :—

Infin.	Past Part.	Past Part.	Pres. Indic.	Past Def.
gésir.	gisant.	——	—— gisons.	——
Fut.	*Impf. Ind.*		—— gisez.	*Impf. Subj.*
——	gisais.		gît. gisent.	——
Condl.	*Pres Subj.*	[*Impve.* ——, ——, ——]		

Note.—Its most frequent use is in *epitaphs* : **Ci-gît**, 'Here lies,' **Ci-gisent**, 'Here lie.'

254. Haïr, *to hate* :—

Infin.	Pres. Part.	Past Part.	Pres. Indic.	Past Def.
haïr.	haïssant.	haï.	hais. haïssons.	haïs.
Fut.	*Impf. Ind.*		hais. haïssez.	*Impf. Subj.*
haïrai.	haïssais.		hait. haïssent.	haïsse.
Condl.	*Pres. Subj.*	[*Impve.* hais, haïssons, haïssez.]		
haïrais.	haïsse, (-es, -e), haïssions, (-iez, -ent).			

Obs. : **Haïr** loses its *diæresis* in the *pres. indic. sing* and *imperat. sing.* and takes no *circumflex* accent; otherwise like **finir**.

255. Issir, *to spring* (from, de), *be descended* :—

Used only in the *past part.* **issu** : Je suis issu, etc.

256. Mourir, *to die* :—

Infin.	Pres. Part.	Past Part.	Pres. Indic.	Past Def.
mourir.	mourant.	mort.	meurs. mourons.	mourus.
Fut.	*Impf. Ind.*		meurs. mourez.	*Impf. Subj.*
mourrai.	mourais.		meurt. meurent.	mourusse.
Condl.	*Pres. Subj.*	[*Impve.* meurs, mourons, mourez.]		
mourrais.	meure, (-es, -e), mourions, (-iez), meurent.			

Obs. : The *stem-vowel* **ou** becomes **eu** wherever it bears the *stress*.

Like **mourir** :

se mourir, *be dying* (used only in *infin., pres.* and *impf. indic.*).

257. Ouïr, *to hear* :—

Is hardly used beyond the *infin.* and *past part.* : 'J'ai ouï dire,' 'I have heard said,' etc.

258. Ouvrir, *to open* :—

Infin.	Pres. Part.	Past Part.	Pres. Indic.	Past Def.
ouvrir.	ouvrant.	ouvert.	ouvre. ouvrons.	ouvris.
Fut.	*Impf. Ind.*		ouvres. ouvrez.	*Impf. Subj.*
ouvrirai.	ouvrais.		ouvre. ouvrent.	ouvrisse.
Condl.	*Pres. Subj.*	[*Impve.* ouvre, ouvrons, ouvrez.]		
ouvrirais.	ouvre, (-es, -e), ouvrions, (-iez, -ent).			

Obs. : The *pres. indic.* is like that of **donner**.

Like ouvrir:

entr'ouvrir, *open slightly.* découvrir, *discover.* offrir, *offer.*
rouvrir, *open again.* recouvrir, *cover again.* souffrir, *suffer.*
couvrir, *cover.*

259. Tenir, *to hold:—*

Infin.	Pres. Part.	Past Part.	Pres. Indic.		Past Def.
tenir.	tenant.	tenu.	tiens.	tenons.	tins.
Fut.	Impf. Ind.		tiens.	tenez.	Impf. Subj.
tiendrai.	tenais.		tient.	tiennent.	tinsse.
Condl.	Pres. Subj.	[*Impve.* tiens, tenons, tenez.]			
tiendrais.	tienne, (-es, -e), tenions, (-iez), tiennent.				

Obs.: The *stem-vowel* e becomes ie wherever it bears the *stress.*

Like tenir are its *compounds* and also venir and its *compounds:*

s'abstenir, *abstain.* venir, *come.* parvenir, *attain.*
appartenir, *belong.* avenir, *happen.* prévenir, *prevent.*
contenir, *contain* advenir, *happen.* provenir, *proceed*(from, de).
détenir, *detain.* convenir, *agree, suit.* revenir, *come back.*
entretenir, *entertain.* controvenir, *violate.* redevenir, *become again.*
maintenir, *maintain.* circonvenir, *circumvent.* se souvenir, *recollect.*
obtenir, *obtain.* devenir, *become.* subvenir, *aid.*
retenir, *retain.* disconvenir, *be discordant.* survenir, *occur.*
soutenir, *sustain.* intervenir, *intervene.* se ressouvenir *recollect.*

260. Vêtir, *to clothe:—*

Infin.	Pres. Part.	Past Part.	Pres. Indic.		Past Def.
vêtir.	vêtant.	vêtu.	vêts.	vêtons.	vêtis.
Fut.	Impf. Ind.		vêts.	vêtez.	Impf. Subj.
vêtirai.	vêtais.		vêt.	vêtent.	vêtisse.
Condl.	Pres. Subj.	[*Impve.* vêts, vêtons, vêtez.]			
vêtirais.	vête, (-es, -e), vêtions, (-iez, -ent).				

Like vêtir:

dévêtir, *divest.* revêtir, *clothe, invest.*
se dévêtir, *take off clothing.* se revêtir, *put on clothing.*

IRREGULAR VERBS IN -re.

261. Battre, *to beat:—*

Loses one t in *pres. indic. sing.:* Bats, bats, bat; otherwise like rompre.

Like battre:

abattre, *fell.* débattre, *debate.* rabattre, *diminish the price.*
combattre, *fight, oppose.* se débattre, *struggle.*

J

262. Boire, *to drink* :—

Infin.	Pres. Part.	Past Part.	Pres. Indic.	Past Def.
boire.	buvant.	bu.	bois. buvons.	bus.
Fut.	*Impf. Ind.*		bois. buvez.	*Impf. Subj.*
boirai.	buvais.		boit. boivent.	busse.
Condl.	*Pres. Subj.*	[*Impve.* bois, buvons, buvez.]		
boirais.	boive, (-es, -e), buvions, (-iez), boivent.			

Like boire :
emboire, *coat* (in painting).   imboire, *imbibe, imbue.*
*s'emboire, *become dull.*   reboire, *drink again.*

*Used in 3rd pers.

263. Bruire, *to murmur, rustle* :—

Infin.	Pres. Part.	Past Part.	Pres. Indic.	Past Def.
bruire.	bruyant.	bruit.	bruis. ——	——
Fut.	*Impf. Ind.*		bruis. ——	*Impf. Subj.*
bruirai.	bruyais.		bruit. ——	——
Condl.	*Pres. Subj.*	[*Impve.* ——, ——, ——]		
bruirais.	——			

NOTES.—1. The *pres. part.* **bruyant**, 'noisy,' is used as *adj.* only. 2. The forms **bruissant, bruissais**, etc., **bruisse**, etc., are also in use.

264. Clore, *to close, enclose* :—

Infin.	Pres. Part.	Past Part.	Pres. Ind.	Past Def.
clore.	——	clos.	clos. ——	——
Fut.	*Impf. Ind.*		clos. ——	*Impf. Subj.*
clorai.	——.		clôt. ——	
Condl.	*Pres. Subj.*			
clorais.	close, (-es, -e), closions, (-iez, -ent).			

Like clore :
déclore, *throw open.*   *enclore, *inclose.*
*éclore, *hatch, open* (of flowers).   †forclore, *foreclose, debar.*

*Has also *pres. plur.*, **éclosons**, etc., *impf. indic.*, **éclosais**, etc. Its *fut.* and *condl.* have *circumflex*, **éclôrai**, etc.
†Hardly used beyond the *infin., past part.,* and *comp. tenses.*

265. Conclure, *to conclude* :—

Infin.	Pres. Part.	Past Part.	Pres. Indic.	Past Def.
conclure.	concluant.	conclu.	conclus. concluons.	conclus.
Fut.	*Impf. Ind.*		conclus. concluez.	*Impf. Subj.*
conclurai.	concluais.		conclut. concluent.	conclusse.
Condl.	*Pres. Subj.*	[*Impve.* conclus, concluons, concluez.]		
conclurais.	conclue, (-es, -e), concluions, (-iez, -ent).			

Like conclure:
exclure, *exclude.* *inclure, *inclose.* †reclure, *shut up.*
Past. part.* is **inclus.
†Used only in *infin., past part.,* and *comp. tenses. Past part.* **reclus.**

266. Conduire, *to conduct, drive, lead:*—

Infin.	*Pres. Part.*	*Past Part.*	*Pres. Indic.*		*Past Def.*
conduire.	conduisant.	conduit.	conduis.	conduisons.	conduisis.
Fut.	*Impf. Ind.*		conduis.	conduisez.	*Impf. Subj.*
conduirai.	conduisais.		conduit.	conduisent.	conduisisse.
Condl.	*Pres. Subj.*	[*Impve.* conduis, conduisons, conduisez.]			
conduirais.	conduise, (-es, -e), conduisions, (-iez, -ent).				

Like Conduire:
se conduire, *conduct one's self.*
éconduire, *show out, dismiss.*
reconduire, *lead back.*
*duire, *please, suit.*
déduire, *deduct.*
enduire, *coat (with plaster).*
induire, *induce.*
introduire, *introduce.*
produire, *produce.*
réduire, *reduce.*
reproduire, *reproduce.*
séduire, *seduce.*
traduire, *translate.*
construire, *construct.*
déconstruire, *take apart.*
instruire, *instruct.*
reconstruire, *reconstruct.*
détruire, *destroy.*
cuire, *cook.*
recuire, *cook again.*
†luire, *shine.*
†reluire, *glisten.*
‡nuire, *injure.*

*Only in *3rd sing.* and *plur. pres. indic.* and *3rd sing. impf.* Obsolescent.
†*Past part.* **lui** and **relui** respectively. No *past def.* or *impf. subj.*
‡*Past part.* **nui.**

267. Être, *to be:*—
See §238 for the full conjugation.

268. Confire, *to preserve, pickle:*—

Pres. Infin.	*Pres. Part.*	*Past Part.*	*Pres. Indic.*		*Past Def.*
confire	confisant.	confit.	confis.	confisons.	confis.
Fut.	*Impf. Ind.*		confis.	confisez.	*Impf. Subj.*
confirai.	confisais.		confit.	confisent.	confisse.
Condl.	*Pres. Subj.*	[*Impve.* confis, confisons, confisez.]			
confirais.	confise, (-es, -e), confisions, (-iez, -ent).				

Like confire:
déconfire, *discomfit.* circoncire (p. p. -cis), *circumcise.* suffire (p. p. suffi), *suffice.*

269. Connaître, *to know, be acquainted with:*—

Infin.	*Pres. Part.*	*Past Part.*	*Pres. Indic.*		*Past Def.*
connaître.	connaissant.	connu.	connais.	connaissons.	connus.
Fut.	*Impf. Ind.*		connais.	connaissez.	*Impf. Subj.*
connaîtrai.	connaissais.		connait.	connaissent.	connusse.
Condl.	*Pres. Subj.*	[*Impve.* connais, connaissons, connaissez.]			
connaitrais.	connaisse, (-es, -e), connaissions, (-iez, -ent).				

Obs.: Stem-vowel **i** has *circumflex* (**î**) everywhere *before* **t.**

Like connaître:

méconnaître, *not to know.*
reconnaître, *recognize.*
paraître, *appear.*
apparaître, *appear.*
comparaître, *appear* (law term).
disparaître, *disappear.*
reparaître, *re-appear.*
*paître, *graze.*
repaître, *feed, feast.*
se repaître, *feed, feast.*

*Lacks the *past part.*, *past def.*, and *impf. subj.*

NOTE.—**Apparoir** (also used in 3rd sing. **il appert**, 'it appears') and **comparoir**, are infin. archaic variants of **apparaître** and **comparaître**.

270. Coudre, *to sew:*—

Infin.	*Pres. Part.*	*Past Part.*	*Pres. Indic.*	*Past Def.*
coudre.	cousant.	cousu.	couds. cousons.	cousis.
Fut.	*Impf. Ind.*		couds. cousez.	*Impf. Subj*
coudrai.	cousais.		coud. cousent.	cousisse.
Condl.	*Pres. Subj.*	[*Impve.* couds, cousons, cousez.]		
coudrais.	couse, (-es, -e), cousions, (-iez, -ent).			

Like coudre :
découdre, *rip, unsew.*   recoudre, *sew again.*

271. Craindre, *to fear:*—

Infin.	*Pres. Part.*	*Past Part.*	*Pres. Indic.*	*Past Def.*
craindre.	craignant.	craint.	crains. craignons.	craignis.
Fut.	*Impf. Ind.*		crains. craignez.	*Impf. Subj.*
craindrai.	craignais.		craint. craignent.	craignisse.
Condl.	*Pres. Subj.*	[*Impve.* crains, craignons, craignez.]		
craindrais.	craigne, (-es, -e), craignions, (-iez, -ent).			

Like craindre :

in **-aindre** :
contraindre, *constrain.*
plaindre, *pity.*
se plaindre, *complain.*
in **-eindre** :
astreindre, *abstract.*
atteindre, *attain.*
ceindre, *enclose, gird.*
dépeindre, *depict.*
empreindre, *imprint.*
enceindre, *gird.*
enfreindre, *infringe.*

épreindre, *squeeze out.*
éteindre, *extinguish.*
étreindre, *draw tight.*
feindre, *feign.*
geindre, *groan.*
peindre, *paint.*
rattendre, *overtake.*
repeindre, *paint again.*
restreindre, *restrain.*
teindre, *dye.*
déteindre, *fade.*
reteindre, *dye again.*

in-**oindre** :
joindre, *join.*
adjoindre, *adjoin.*
conjoindre, *conjoin.*
déjoindre, *disjoin.*
disjoindre, *disjoin.*
enjoindre, *enjoin.*
rejoindre, *rejoin.*
oindre, *anoint.*
*poindre, *dawn.*

*Hardly used beyond the *infin.* and *fut.*

272. Croire, *to believe* :—

Infin.	Pres. Part.	Past Part.	Pres. Indic.	Past Def.
croire.	croyant.	cru.	crois. croyons.	crus.
Fut.	*Impf. Ind.*		crois. croyez.	*Impf. Subj.*
croirai.	croyais.		croit. croient.	crusse.
Condl.	*Pres. Subj.*	[*Impve.* crois, croyons, croyez.]		
croirais.	croie, (-es, -e), croyions, (-iez), croient.			

Like croire :

*accroire, *believe (an untruth).*   †décroire, *disbelieve.*

*Found only in faire accroire, 'to cause to believe (an untruth).'
†Used only in 'je ne crois ni ne décrois,' 'I neither believe nor disbelieve.'

273. Croître, *to grow* :—

Infin.	Pres. Part.	Part Part.	Pres. Indic.	Past Def.
croître.	croissant.	crû (f. crue).	croîs croissons.	crûs.
Fut.	*Impf. Ind.*		croîs. croissez.	*Impf. Subj.*
croîtrai.	croissais.		croît. croissent.	crûsse.
Condl.	*Pres. Subj.*	[*Impve.* croîs, croissons, croissez.]		
croîtrais.	croisse, (-es, -e), croissions, (-iez, -ent).			

Obs.: The *circumflex* distinguishes otherwise like forms of croître and croire, but is *optional* in the *impf. subj.* (except the 3rd sing.).

Like croître :

*accroître, *increase.*   *recroître, *grow again.*   *surcroître, *overgrow.*
décroître, *decrease.*

*No *circumflex* in *past part., past def. 3rd sing.* and *3rd plur.*

274. Dire, *to say, tell* :—

Infin.	Pres. Part.	Past Part.	Pres. Indic.	Past Def.
dire.	disant.	dit.	dis. disons.	dis.
Fut.	*Impf. Ind.*		dis. dites.	*Impf. Subj.*
dirai.	disais.		dit. disent.	disse.
Condl.	*Pres. Subj.*	[*Impve.* dis, disons, dites.]		
dirais.	dise, (-es, -e), disions, (-iez, -ent).			

Like dire :

*contredire, *contradict.*   *interdire, *interdict.*   *prédire, *predict.*
*dédire, *retract, deny.*   *médire (de), *slander.*   redire, *say again.*

*The *2nd plur. impve.* is : Contredisez, dédisez, interdisez, etc.

NOTE—Maudire is like dire only in *infin., past part.* (maudit), *fut.* and *condl.* ; otherwise like finir.

275. Écrire, *to write* :—

Infin.	Pres. Part.	Past Part.	Pres. Indic.		Past Def.
écrire.	écrivant.	écrit.	écris.	écrivons.	écrivis.
Fut.	*Impf. Ind.*		écris.	écrivez.	*Impf. Subj.*
écrirai.	écrivais.		écrit.	écrivent.	écrivisse.
Condl.	*Pres. Subj.*	[*Impve.* écris, écrivons, écrivez.]			
écrirais.	écrive, (-es, -e), écrivions, (-iez, -ent).				

Like **écrire** are all verbs in -(s)crire :
circonscrire, *circumscribe*. prescrire, *prescribe*. souscrire, *subscribe*.
décrire, *describe*. proscrire, *proscribe*. transcrire, *transcribe*.
inscrire, *inscribe*. récrire, *rewrite*.

276. Faire, *to do, make* :—

Infin.	Pres. Part.	Past Part.	Pres. Indic.		Past Def.
faire.	faisant.	fait.	fais.	faisons.	fis.
Fut.	*Impf. Subj.*		fais.	faites.	*Impf. Subj.*
ferai.	faisais.		fait.	font.	fisse.
Condl.	*Pres. Subj.*	[*Impve.* fais, faisons, faites.]			
ferais.	fasse, (-es, -e), fassions, (-iez, -ent).				

Obs. : See §22, 2, Exc., for *pronunciation* of **faisant**, etc.

Like **faire** :
contrefaire, *imitate*. méfaire, *harm*. refaire, *do again*.
défaire, *undo*. parfaire, *complete*. satisfaire, *satisfy*.
forfaire, *forfeit*. redéfaire, *undo again*. surfaire, *overcharge*.
*malfaire, *do ill*.
*Used in *infin.* only.

277. Frire, *to fry* (intr.) :—

Infin.	Pres. Part.	Past Part.	Pres. Indic.		Past Def.
frire.	—	frit.	fris.	—	—
Fut.	*Impf. Ind.*		fris.	—	*Impf. Subj.*
frirai.	—		frit.	—	—
Condl.	*Pres. Subj.*	[*Impve.* fris, —, —]			
frirais.	—				

278. Lire, *to read* :—

Infin.	Pres. Part.	Past Part.	Pres. Indic.		Past Def.
lire.	lisant.	lu.	lis.	lisons.	lus.
Fut.	*Impf. Ind.*		lis.	lisez.	*Impf. Subj.*
lirai.	lisais.		lit.	lisent.	lusse.
Condl.	*Pres. Subj.*	[*Impve.* lis, lisons, lisez.]			
lirais.	lise, (-es, -e), lisions, (-iez, -ent).				

Like **lire** :
élire, *elect*. réélire, *re-elect*. relire, *read again*.

279. Mettre, *to place, put* :—

Infin.	Pres. Part.	Past Part.	Pres. Indic.		Past Def.
mettre.	mettant.	mis.	mets.	mettons.	mis.
Fut.	*Impf. Ind.*		mets.	mettez.	*Impf. Subj.*
mettrai.	mettais.		met.	mettent.	misse.
Condl.	*Pres. Subj.*	[*Impve.* mets, mettons, mettez.]			
mettrais.	mette, (-es, -e), mettions, (-iez, -ent.)				

Like **mettre** :
se mettre, *begin*.   démettre, *dismiss*.   promettre, *promise*.
admettre, *admit*.   émettre, *emit*.   remettre, *put back, hand to*.
commettre, *commit*.   s'entremettre, *interpose*. repromettre, *promise again*.
compromettre, *compro-*   omettre, *omit*.   soumettre, *submit*.
mise.   permettre, *permit*.   transmettre, *transmit*.

280. Moudre, *to grind* :—

Infin.	Pres. Part.	Past Part.	Pres. Indic.		Past Def.
moudre.	moulant.	moulu.	mouds.	moulons.	moulus.
Fut.	*Impf. Ind.*		mouds.	moulez.	*Impf. Subj.*
moudrai.	moulais.		moud.	moulent.	moulusse.
Condl.	*Pres. Subj.*	[*Impve.* mouds, moulons, moulez.]			
moudrais.	moule, (-es, -e), moulions, (-iez, -ent).				

Like **moudre** :
émoudre, *whet*.   remoudre, *grind again*.   rémoudre, *sharpen*.

281. Naître, *to be born, arise, spring up* :—

Infin.	Pres. Part.	Past Part.	Pres. Indic.		Past Def.
naître.	naissant.	né.	nais.	naissons.	nacquis.
Fut.	*Impf. Ind.*		nais.	naissez.	*Impf. Subj.*
naîtrai.	naissais.		naît.	naissent.	nacquisse.
Condl.	*Pres. Subj.*	[*Impve.* nais, naissons, naissez.]			
naîtrais.	naisse, (-es, -e), naissions, (-iez, -ent).				

Obs.: Stem-vowel **i** has the *circumflex* (î) everywhere *before* **t**.

Like **naître**
renaître, *revive*.

282. Plaire, *to please* :—

Infin.	Pres. Part.	Past Part.	Pres. Indic.		Past Def.
plaire.	plaisant.	plu.	plais.	plaisons.	plus.
Fut.	*Impf. Ind.*		plais.	plaisez.	*Impf. Subj.*
plairai.	plaisais.		plaît.	plaisent.	plusse.
Condl.	*Pres. Subj.*	[*Impve.* plais, plaisons, plaisez.]			
plairais.	plaise, (-es, -e), plaisions, (-iez, -ent).				

Like **plaire** :
complaire, *humour*.   déplaire, *displease*.   *taire, *say nothing about*.
*Il tait has *no circumflex*.

283. Prendre, *to take* :—

Infin.	Pres. Part.	Past Part	Pres. Indic.		Past Def.
prendre.	prenant.	pris.	prends.	prenons.	pris.
Fut.	*Impf. Ind.*		prends.	prenez.	*Impf. Subj.*
prendrai.	prenais.		prend.	prennent.	prisse.
Condl.	*Pres. Subj.*	[*Impve.* prends, prenons, prenez.]			
prendrais.	prenne, (-es, -e), prenions, (-iez), prennent.				

Like **prendre** are its *compounds :*
apprendre, *learn.*   entreprendre, *undertake.*   rapprendre, *learn again.*
déprendre, *part.*   s'éprendre, *be taken (with).*   reprendre, *take back.*
désapprendre, *unlearn.*   se méprendre, *be mistaken.*   surprendre, *surprise.*
comprendre, *understand.*

284. Résoudre, *to resolve* :—

Infin.	Pres. Part.	Past Part.	Pres. Indic.		Past Def.
résoudre.	résolvant.	résolu.	résous.	résolvons.	résolus.
Fut.	*Impf. Ind.*	résous (no f.).	résous.	résolvez.	*Impf. Subj.*
résoudrai.	résolvais.		résout.	résolvent.	résolusse.
Condl.	*Pres. Subj.*	[*Impve.* résous, résolvons, résolvez.]			
résoudrais.	résolve, (-es, -e), résolvions, (-iez, -ent).				

Like **résoudre** :
*absoudre, *absolve.*   *dissoudre, *dissolve.*
**Past part.* absous (f. absoute), dissous (f. dissoute) respectively; lack *past def.* and *impf. subj.*

285. Rire, *to laugh* :—

Infin.	Pres. Part.	Past Part.	Pres. Indic.		Past Def.
rire.	riant.	ri.	ris.	rions.	ris.
Fut.	*Impf. Ind.*		ris.	riez.	*Impf. Subj.*
rirai.	riais.		rit.	rient.	risse.
Condl.	*Pres. Subj.*	[*Impve.* ris, rions, riez.]			
rirais.	rie, (-es, -e), riions, (-iez), rient.				

Like **rire** :
se rire, *make sport* (of, de).   sourire, *smile.*

286. Sourdre, *to rise, spring up* :—

Infin.	Pres. Part.	Past Part.	Pres. Indic.		Past Def.
sourdre.	sourdant.	——	——	——	il sourdit.
Fut.	*Impf. Ind.*		——	——	*Impf. Subj.*
il sourdra.	il sourdait.		sourd.	sourdent.	il sourdît.
Condl.	*Pres. Subj.*	[*Impve.* ——, ——, ——]			
il sourdrait.	il sourde.				

NOTE.—Little used beyond the *infin.* and *3rd sing. pres. indic.*

287. Suivre, *to follow*:—

Infin.	Pres. Part.	Past Part.	Pres. Indic.		Past Def.
suivre.	suivant.	suivi.	suis.	suivons.	suivis.
Fut.	Impf. Ind.		suis.	suivez.	Impf. Subj.
suivrai.	suivais.		suit.	suivent.	suivisse.
Condl.	Pres. Subj.	[Impve. suis, suivons, suivez.]			
suivrais.	suive, (-es, -e), suivions, (-iez, -ent).				

Like suivre:
s'ensuivre (impers.), *it follows*. poursuivre, *pursue*.

288. Tistre, *to weave*:—

Used only in the *past part.* tissu and *comp. tenses.*

289. Traire, *to milk*:—

Infin.	Pres. Part.	Past Part.	Pres. Indic.		Past Def.
traire.	trayant.	trait.	trais.	trayons.	—
Fut.	Impf. Ind.		trais.	trayez.	Impf. Subj.
trairai.	trayais.		trait.	traient.	—
Condl.	Pres. Subj.	[Impve. trais, trayons, trayez.]			
trairais.	traie, (-es, -e), trayions, (-iez), traient.				

Like traire:
abstraire, *abstract.*   extraire, *extract.*   soustraire, *subtract.*
attraire, *attract.*   rentraire, *darn.*   *braire, *bray.*
distraire, *distract.*   retraire, *redeem* (legal).

*Commonly used only in the *infin.* and the *3rd pers. pres. indic. fut.* and *condl.*

290. Vaincre, *to conquer, vanquish*:—

Infin.	Pres. Part.	Past Part.	Pres. Indic.		Past Def.
vaincre.	vainquant.	vaincu.	vaincs.	vainquons.	vainquis.
Fut.	Impf. Ind.		vaincs.	vainquez.	Impf. Subj.
vaincrai.	vainquais.		vainc.	vainquent.	vainquisse.
Condl.	Pres. Subj.	[Impve. vaincs, vainquons, vainquez.]			
vaincrais.	vainque, (-es, -e), vainquions, (-iez, -ent).				

Obs.: Stem c (=k) becomes qu (§55, note) before any vowel except u.

Like vaincre:
convaincre, *convict.*

291. Vendre, *to sell*:—

Irregular only in *3rd sing. pres. indic.*: Il vend (t omitted).

Like vendre:
All verbs in -andre, -endre (except prendre), -erdre, -ondre, -ordre.

292. Vivre, *to live* :—

Infin.	Pres. Part.	Past Part.	Pres. Indic.		Past Def.
vivre.	vivant.	vécu.	vis.	vivons.	vécus.
Fut.	Impf. Ind.		vis.	vivez.	Impf. Subj.
vivrai.	vivais.		vit.	vivent.	vécusse.
Condl.	Pres. Subj.	[*Impve.* vis, vivons, vivez.]			
vivrais.	vive, (-es, -e), vivions, (-iez, -ent).				

Like **vivre** :
revivre, *revive*. survivre, *survive*.

Irregular Verbs in -oir.

293. Avoir, *to have* :—
See §238 for the full conjugation of this verb.

Like **avoir** :
ravoir, *have again* (used only in *infin.*).

294. Recevoir, *to receive* :—

Infin.	Pres. Part.	Past Part.	Pres. Indic.		Past Def.
recevoir.	recevant.	reçu.	reçois.	recevons.	reçus.
Fut.	Impf. Ind.		reçois.	recevez.	Impf. Subj.
recevrai.	recevais.		reçoit.	reçoivent.	reçusse.
Condl.	Pres. Subj.	[*Impve.* reçois, recevons, recevez.]			
recevrais.	reçoive, (-es, -e), recevions, (-iez), reçoivent.				

Note.—The few verbs in **-oir** (all irregular) form, in some grammars, a separate conjugation (the *3rd*, verbs in -re being the *4th*).

Like **recevoir** are all verbs in **-evoir** :
apercevoir, *perceive*. décevoir, *deceive*. percevoir, *collect (taxes)*.
concevoir, *conceive*. *devoir, *owe*. *redevoir, *still owe*.

*The *past parts.* are dû (f. due, pl. du(e)s) and redû (f. redue, pl. redu(e)s) respectively.

295. Asseoir, *to seat* :—

Infin.	Pres. Part.	Past Part.	Pres. Indic.		Past Def.
asseoir.	{ asseyant. { assoyant.	assis.	{ assieds. { assois.	{ asseyons. { assoyons.	assis.
Fut.	Impf.		{ assieds. { assois.	{ asseyez. { assoyez.	Impf. Subj.
{ assiérai. { asseyerai. { assoirai.	{ asseyais. { assoyais.		{ assied. { assoit.	{ asseyent. { assoient.	assisse.
Condl.	Pres. Subj.	[*Impve.* { assieds, asseyons, asseyez.] { assois, assoyons, assoyez.]			
{ assiérais. { asseyerais. { assoirais.	{ asseye, (-es, -e), asseyions, (-iez, -ent). { assoie, (-es, -e), assoyions, (-iez), assoient.				

Like asseoir :
s'asseoir, *sit down.*   se rasseoir, *sit down again.*   *messeoir, *fit badly.*
rasseoir, *reseat, calm.*   *seoir, *be becoming.*   †surseoir, *suspend, reprieve.*

*Used in 3rd pers. of the following: *Pres. indic.* sied, siéent (messied, messiéent); *impf. indic.* seyait, seyaient (messeyait, messeyaient); *pres. subj.* siée, siéent (messiée, messiéent); *fut.* siéra, siéront (messiéra, messiéront); *condl.* siérait, siéraient (messiérait, messiéraient).

†Like the forms in oi(oy) of asseoir, but *fut.* and *condl.* surseoirai(s).

296. Déchoir, *to decline, decay:—*

Infin.	Pres. Part.	Past Part.	Pres. Indic.		Past Def.
échoir.	——	déchu.	déchois.	déchoyons.	déchus.
Fut.	Impf. Ind.		déchois.	déchoyez.	Impf. Subj.
décherrai.	——		déchoit.	déchoient.	déchusse.

Condl.	Pres. Subj.	[Impve. déchois, déchoyons, déchoyez.]
décherrais.	déchoie, (-es, -e), déchoyions, (-iez), déchoient.	

Like déchoir :
*choir, *fall.*   *rechoir, *fall again.*
*Hardly used beyond the *infin.* and *comp. tenses.*

297. Échoir, *to devolve, expire, fall due:—*

Infin.	Pres. Part.	Past Part.	Pres. Indic.		Past Def.
échoir.	échéant.	échu.	——	——	il échut.
Fut.	Impf.		——	——	ils échurent.
*il écherra.	il échoyait.		{ échoit.	{ échoient.	Impf. Subj.
Condl.	Pres. Subj.		{ échet.	{ échéent.	il échût.
*il écherrait.	il échoie.	[Impve. ——, ——, ——]			

*Or regular : il échoira(it).

298. Falloir (impers.), *to be necessary, must, etc.:—*

Infin.	Pres. Part.	Past Part.	Pres. Indic.	Past Def.
falloir.	——	fallu.	il faut.	il fallut.
Fut.	Impf. Ind.			Impf. Subj.
il faudra.	il fallait.			il fallût.
Condl.	Pres. Subj.	[Impve. ——, ——, ——]		
il faudrait.	il faille.			

299. Mouvoir, *to move:—*

Infin.	Pres. Part.	Past Part.	Pres. Indic.		Past Def.
mouvoir.	mouvant.	mû (f. mue,	meus.	mouvons.	mus.
Fut.	Impf. Ind.	pl. mu(e)s).	meus.	mouvez.	Impf. Subj.
mouvrai.	mouvais.		meut.	meuvent.	musse.
Condl.	Pres. Subj.	[Impve. meus, mouvons, mouvez.]			
mouvrais.	meuve, (-es, -e), mouvions, (-iez), meuvent.				

Obs.: Stem-vowel ou becomes eu wherever it is *stressed.*

Like mouvoir:
*émouvoir, *arouse*.   *promouvoir, *promote*.
Past part. has no circumflex.

300. Pleuvoir (impers.), *to rain*:—

Infin.	Pres. Part.	Past Part.	Pres. Indic.	Past Def.
pleuvoir.	pleuvant.	plu.	il pleut.	il plut.
Fut.	*Impf. Ind.*			*Impf. Subj.*
il pleuvra.	il pleuvait.			il plût.
Condl.	*Pres. Subj.*	[*Impve.* ——, ——, ——]		
il pleuvrait.	il pleuve.			

301. Pouvoir, *to be able, can, may, etc.*:—

Infin.	Pres. Part.	Past Part.	Pres. Indic.	Past Def.
pouvoir.	pouvant.	pu.	puis *or* peux. pouvons.	pus.
Fut.	*Impf. Ind.*		peux. pouvez.	*Impf. Subj.*
pourrai.	pouvais.		peut. peuvent.	pusse.
Condl.	*Pres. Subj.*	[*Impve.* ——, ——, ——]		
pourrais.	puisse, (-es, -e), puissions, (-iez, -ent).			

Obs.: The *1st sing. pres. indic.* in *negation* is usually 'je ne peux pas,' *or* 'je ne puis'; in *questions* only 'puis-je?'; otherwise 'puis' *or* 'peux.'

302. Savoir, *to know, know how to, etc.*:—

Infin.	Pres. Part.	Past Part.	Pres. Indic.	Past Def.
savoir.	sachant.	su.	sais. savons.	sus.
Fut.	*Impf. Ind.*		sais. savez.	*Impf. Subj.*
saurai.	savais.		sait. savent.	susse.
Condl.	*Pres. Subj.*	[*Impve.* sais, sachons, sachez.]		
saurais.	sache, (-es, -e), sachions, (-iez, -ent).			

303. Valoir, *to be worth*:—

Infin.	Pres. Part.	Past Part.	Pres. Indic.	Past Def.
valoir.	valant.	valu.	vaux. valons.	valus.
Fut.	*Impf. Ind.*		vaux. valez.	*Impf. Subj.*
vaudrai.	valais.		vaut. valent.	valusse.
Condl.	*Pres. Subj.*	[*Impve.* vaux, valons, valez.]		
vaudrais.	vaille, (-es, -e), valions, (-iez), vaillent.			

Like valoir:

équivaloir, *be equivalent*.   *prévaloir, *prevail*.   chaloir (hardly used beyond: 'Il ne me chaut de,' 'I care not for).
revaloir, *pay back, return like for like*

Pres. subj. prévale, etc.

304–306.]   LIST OF IRREGULAR VERBS.   157

304. Voir, *to see :—*

Infin.	Pres. Part.	Past Part.	Pres. Indic.	Past Def.
voir.	voyant.	vu.	vois. voyons.	vis.
Fut.	Impf. Ind.		vois. voyez.	Impf. Subj.
verrai.	voyais.		voit. voient.	visse.
Condl.	Pres. Subj.	[Impve. vois, voyons, voyez.]		
verrais.	voie, (-es, -e), voyions, (-iez), voient.			

Obs.: Stem-vowel **i** becomes **y** before *any other vowel than* **o**.

Like voir:
entrevoir, *catch sight of.*   *pourvoir, *provide.*   †prévoir, *foresee.*
revoir, *see again.*   *dépourvoir, *strip, leave destitute.*

*Past def. -vus, etc.; impf. subj. -vusse, etc.; fut. and condl. regular (-voirai(s), etc.).

†Fut. and *condl. regular* (-voirai(s), etc.).

305. Vouloir, *to will, wish, desire, etc. :—*

Infin.	Pres. Part.	Past. Part.	Pres. Indic.	Past Def.
vouloir.	voulant.	voulu.	veux. voulons.	voulus.
Fut.	Impf. Ind.		veux. voulez.	Impf. Subj.
voudrai.	voulais.		veut. veulent.	voulusse.
Condl.	Pres. Subj.	[Impve. veux, voulons, voulez.]		
voudrais.	veuille, (-es, -e), voulions, (-iez), veuillent.			

Obs.: Stem-vowel **ou** becomes **eu** wherever it is *stressed.*

NOTE.—The regular *impve.* veux, voulons, voulez is *rare*; veuillez= 'have the kindness to' generally serves as *2nd plur. impve.*

306. Reference List of Irregular Verbs.

[Each verb in the list is referred to the § in which its irregularity is explained. For verbs in -cer, -ger, see §239; for verbs in -yer, §240; for verbs with *stem-vowel* e or é, §241; for verbs in -andre, -endre, -erdre, -ondre, -ordre, §291.]

A.
abattre........ §261
absoudre........ 284
abstenir........ 259
abstraire....... 289
accourir........ 246
accroire......... 272
accroître........ 273
accueillir....... 247
acquérir........ 244
adjoindre....... 271
admettre....... 279

advenir........ §259
aller........... 242
apercevoir... . 294
apparaître...... 269
apparoir........ 269
appartenir...... 259
apprendre.... . 283
assaillir........ 247
asseoir......... 295
astreindre 271
atteindre........ 271
attraire........ 289

avenir.......... §259
avoir........... 238
B.
battre.......... 261
bénir........... 245
boire 262
bouillir 248
braire.......... 289
bruire.......... 263
C.
ceindre....... .. 271
chaloir......... 303

choir............§296	déchoir..........§296	éclore............§264
circoncire....... 268	déclore.......... 264	éconduire......... 266
circonscrire..... 275	déconfire........ 268	écrire............ 275
circonvenir...... 259	déconstruire..... 266	élire............. 278
clore............ 264	découdre......... 270	emboire.......... 262
combattre........ 261	découvrir........ 258	émettre.......... 279
commettre........ 279	décrire.......... 275	émoudre.......... 280
comparaître...... 269	décroire......... 272	émouvoir......... 299
comparoir........ 269	décroître........ 273	empreindre....... 271
complaire........ 282	dédire........... 274	enceindre........ 271
comprendre....... 283	déduire.......... 266	enclore.......... 264
compromettre.... 279	défaillir........ 249	encourir......... 246
concevoir........ 294	défaire.......... 276	endormir......... 248
conclure......... 265	déjoindre........ 271	enduire.......... 266
concourir........ 246	démentir......... 248	enfreindre....... 271
conduire......... 266	démettre......... 279	enfuir........... 252
confire.......... 268	départir......... 248	enjoindre........ 271
conjoindre....... 271	dépeindre........ 271	enquérir......... 244
connaître........ 269	déplaire......... 282	ensuivre......... 287
conquérir........ 244	dépourvoir....... 304	entremettre...... 279
consentir........ 248	déprendre........ 283	entreprendre..... 283
construire....... 266	désapprendre.... 283	entretenir....... 259
contenir......... 259	desservir........ 248	entrevoir........ 304
contraindre...... 271	déteindre........ 271	entr'ouvrir...... 258
contredire....... 274	détenir.......... 259	envoyer.......... 243
contrefaire...... 276	détruire......... 266	épreindre........ 271
contrevenir...... 259	devenir.......... 259	éprendre......... 283
convaincre....... 290	dévêtir.......... 260	équivaloir....... 303
convenir......... 259	devoir........... 294	éteindre......... 271
coudre........... 270	dire............. 274	être............. 238
courir........... 246	disconvenir...... 259	étreindre........ 271
courre........... 246	discourir........ 246	exclure.......... 265
couvrir.......... 258	disjoindre....... 271	extraire......... 289
craindre......... 271	disparaître...... 269	**F.**
croire........... 272	dissoudre........ 284	faillir.......... 249
croître.......... 273	distraire........ 289	faire............ 276
cueillir......... 247	dormir........... 248	falloir.......... 298
cuire............ 266	duire............ 266	feindre.......... 271
D.	**E.**	férir............ 250
débattre......... 261	ébouillir........ 248	fleurir.......... 251
décevoir......... 294	échoir........... 297	forclore......... 264

F	**O**	**R**
forfaire ....§276	obtenir.........§259	rabattre..........§261
frire............ 277	offrir............ 258	rapprendre 283
fuir 252	oindre.......... 271	rasseoir 295
G	omettre......... 279	ratteindre 271
geindre......... 271	ouïr............. 257	ravoir............ 293
gésir............ 253	ouvrir........... 258	reboire........... 262
H	**P**	rebouillir......... 248
haïr............. 254	paître........... 269	recevoir.......... 294
I	paraître 269	rechoir.......... 296
imboire......... 262	parcourir........ 246	reclure 265
inclure.......... 265	parfaire......... 276	reconduire....... 266
induire.......... 266	partir............ 248	reconnaître....... 269
inscrire.......... 275	parvenir......... 259	reconquérir....... 244
instruire........ 266	peindre 271	reconstruire 266
interdire......... 274	percevoir 294	recoudre 270
intervenir....... 259	permettre 279	recourir 246
introduire 266	plaindre......... 271	recouvrir 258
issir............. 235	plaire 282	récrire........... 275
J	pleuvoir......... 300	recroître......... 273
joindre.......... 271	poindre 271	recueillir 247
L	poursuivre....... 287	recuire 266
lire 278	pourvoir......... 304	redéfaire......... 276
luire............. 266	pouvoir.......... 301	redevenir........ 259
M	prédire.......... 274	redevoir.......... 294
maintenir....... 259	prendre 283	redire 274
malfaire......... 276	prescrire 275	redormir......... 248
maudire......... 274	pressentir 248	réduire........... 266
méconnaître..... 269	prévaloir 303	réélire............ 278
médire.......... 274	prévenir......... 259	refaire........... 276
méfaire.......... 276	prévoir........... 304	rejoindre 271
mentir 248	produire 266	relire............ 278
méprendre...... 283	promettre 279	reluire........... 266
messeoir........ 295	promouvoir..... 299	remettre......... 279
mettre 279	proscrire 275	remoudre........ 280
moudre 280	provenir......... 259	rémoudre........ 280
mourir 256	**Q**	renaître 281
mouvoir 299	querir ⎫........ 244	rendormir 248
N	quérir ⎭	rentraire 289
naître........... 281		renvoyer......... 243
nuire 266		

repaître ....§269	**S.**	surseoir.............§295
reparaître........ 269	saillir...........§247	survenir........... 259
repartir.......... 248	satisfaire........ 276	survivre 292
repeindre........ 271	savoir............ 302	**T.**
repentir......... 248	secourir.......... 246	taire............. 282
reprendre........ 283	séduire........... 266	teindre........... 271
reproduire....... 266	sentir............ 248	tenir............. 259
repromettre..... 279	seoir............. 295	tistre............ 288
requérir......... 244	servir............ 248	traduire.......... 266
résoudre......... 284	sortir............ 248	traire............ 289
ressentir........ 248	souffrir.......... 258	transcrire........ 275
ressortir........ 248	soumettre........ 279	transmettre....... 279
ressouvenir...... 259	sourdre 286	tressaillir....... 247
restreindre...... 271	sourire........... 285	**V.**
reteindre........ 271	souscrire......... 275	vaincre........... 290
retenir........... 259	soustraire........ 289	valoir............ 303
retraire......... 289	soutenir.......... 259	vendre............ 291
revaloir.......... 303	souvenir.......... 259	venir 259
revenir........... 259	subvenir......... 259	vêtir............. 260
revêtir........... 260	suffire........... 268	vivre 292
revivre........... 292	suivre............ 287	voir.............. 304
revoir............ 304	surcroître 273	vouloir........... 305
rire.............. 285	surfaire.......... 276	
rouvrir........... 258	surprendre....... 283	

EXERCISE XXXII.
(Irregular verbs in -er.)

1. What are you eating? 2. We are eating apples. 3. It was necessary that they should eat. 4. Who is calling? 5. We are calling. 6. The general leads his army. 7. We shall lead the horses. 8. Who is throwing stones? 9. It will freeze. 10. He is buying a coat. 11. We never yield. 12. They will never yield. 13. The servant is peeling apples. 14. When will he pay? 15. They never pay. 16. The servant is cleaning the kitchen. 17. We shall clean our gun. 18. The little girl wipes the dishes. 19. The farmer sows the seed. 20. It is freezing. 21. We are going to school. 22. We went home. 23. They used to go to market on Saturdays. 24. He will send it. 25. The servant is bringing the horses. 26. I send him there. 27. I shall go to school. 28. Let them go to the city. 29. It was necessary that you should go. 30. They will buy a box. 31. Let us bring the children. 32. Bring the children. 33. Let him not throw stones. 34. We

have led the horses to the stable. 35. Let us trace a line. 36. We are advancing. 37. They were eating. 38. We ate. 39. They will eat. 40. Let us advance. 41. Let us never yield. 42. Let us call the children. 43. Let us not go there. 44. The Queen has been reigning a long time. 45. The children were throwing stones. 46. He led the horse to the stable. 47. He paid the money. 48. The servant wiped the dishes. 49. The child traced a line.

EXERCISE XXXIII.

(Irregular verbs in -ir.)

1. He is running. 2. Shall we run? 3. Run fast, my little boy. 4. He is acquiring a fortune. 5. If was necessary that we should run. 6. They will conquer their enemy. 7. The general has acquired glory. 8. He gives him consecrated bread. 9. They acquire knowledge. 10. We shall acquire property. 11. There is holy water. 12. Let us not run. 13. Let them acquire it. 14. We are gathering apples. 15. It was necessary that they should gather flowers. 16. He welcomed me. 17. We shall gather them. 18. Let us not start with (de) fear. 19. He assails his enemy. 20. He will assail his enemy. 21. He is sleeping. 22. Let us not sleep. 23. He must sleep. 24. We shall soon sleep. 25. They fall asleep. 26. He is leaving for France. 27. He left yesterday. 28. If he were asleep, I should call him. 29. He will go out. 30. Let him not go out. 31. The water boils. 32. The water was boiling. 33. When he speaks, he lies. 34. He makes use of it. 35. He will feel it. 36. If he were here, we should not sleep. 37. The water will soon boil. 38. He has run. 39. It was necessary that we should sleep. 40. I have not slept. 41. He never lies. 42. The horses would run, if they were not tired. 43. They ran. 44. We acquired it. 45. The horses run over the field. 46. He does not consent to it. 47. He will never consent to it. 48. Let him not make use of it. 49. We were running. 50. We fell asleep.

EXERCISE XXXIV.

(Irregular verbs in -ir—*Continued.*)

1. He failed on *(en)* that occasion. 2. It is a prosperous country. 3. He flees. 4. Let us not flee. 5. They fled. 6. He will not flee. 7. It was necessary that I should flee. 8. Here lies a hero. 9. Here lie the remains of the great Napoleon. 10. I hate evil. 11. Men hate their enemies. 12. Let us not hate our enemies. 13. He hates his father. 14. Let him not hate his father. 15. It was not necessary that he should hate his father. 16. She dies. 17. They will die. 18. Let

K

us not die. 19. It was necessary that he should die. 20. He died. 21. She will die. 22. Let him not die. 23. If they died, we should be sorry for it. 24. That tree is dying away. 25. Open the door. 26. We have opened the box. 27. He offers me his book. 28. She used to suffer a great deal. 29. If we had any, we should offer you some. 30. Columbus discovered America. 31. We held it. 32. Let him not hold it. 33. I hold it. 34. Let us hold it. 35. We are coming. 36. We shall come. 37. We should come, if you would come. 38. If I should come, I should find it. 39. They are coming back. 40. It is necessary that he come. 41. It was necessary that he should come. 42. Hold it. 43. He has held it. 44. The purse contains money. 45. If he comes, we shall be glad (of it). 46. They will come back. 47. He is ill clad. 48. He clothes himself well. 49. He will clothe his child. 50. It is necessary that he clothe his child.

EXERCISE XXXV.
(Irregular verbs in -re.)

1. We beat the horse. 2. He fells the tree. 3. It is necessary that he fight the enemy. 4. We drink water. 5. They drink milk. 6. They were drinking wine. 7. We shall drink water. 8. Let him drink milk. 9. He has drunk the wine. 10. It was necessary that we should drink wine. 11. We shall not drink wine. 12. The wind rustles in the trees. 13. He encloses his garden. 14. He will close the bargain. 15. Those flowers will soon open. 16. He is concluding his argument. 17. Let us conclude the bargain. 18. We concluded the affair. 19. If he were there, he would conclude the affair. 20. It was necessary that he should conclude the bargain. 21. He drives the cows to the field. 22. They destroyed their books. 23. They will construct houses. 24. Let us translate this phrase. 25. It was necessary that we should translate that book. 26. He led his horse to the stable. 27. We were translating our exercise. 28. We constructed a house. 29. Let him translate his lesson. 30. I have translated a book. 31. I translated a book. 32. She was preserving plums. 33. We are preserving cherries. 34. That suffices. 35. That will be sufficient. 36. Let that suffice. 37. Five francs a day are sufficient for him. 38. I know that gentleman. 39. It is necessary that we should know him. 40. Let him appear. 41. The cows eat the grass. 42. It was necessary that we should know him. 43. It was necessary that he should appear. 44. He will not disappear. 45. We used to know him. 46. When he appears, we shall conclude the affair.

47. Let him recognize him. 48. You know him ; do you not? 49. You will know him. 50. He reappeared.

EXERCISE XXXVI.
(Irregular verbs in -re—*Continued.*)

1. The little girl is sewing. 2. We were sewing. 3. They will sew. 4. She sewed. 5. They had sewed. 6. Let us sew. 7. Let her not sew. 8. Let us not fear. 9. They fear. 10. Let him not be afraid. 11. We shall not fear. 12. Men fear death. 13. They pity us. 14. He was painting a picture. 15. Put out the fire. 16. Let him put out the lamp. 17. It was necessary that we should rejoin our friends. 18. The general girds on his sword. 19. I feared the rain. 20. I believe you. 21. We shall not believe it. 22. Let us believe it. 23. I used to believe it. 24. It is necessary that he should believe it. 25. He did not believe it. 26. It was necessary that he should believe it. 27. We did not believe it. 28. Do not believe it. 29. The flowers are growing. 30. The tree grows. 31. That tree will grow fast. 32. We grew. 33. It was necessary that we should grow. 34. The trees were growing fast. 35. Let it grow. 36. He has believed. 37. The tree has grown. 38. Do not say so (*le*). 39. We say so. 40. We should not say so, if we did not believe it. 41. It is not necessary that he should say so. 42. They used to say so. 43. Let him not say so. 44. It was not necessary that we should say so. 45. Do not say so again. 46. Do not slander. 47. They do not say so. 48. Cain was cursed by (*de*) God. 49. We do not curse our enemies. 50. If I should say so, would you believe me ?

EXERCISE XXXVII.
(Irregular verbs in -re – *Continued.*)

1. I was writing, when he came. 2. Let us write our exercise. 3. We wrote a letter. 4. Write your lesson. 5. Let him write. 6. We shall write our letter. 7. It was necessary that you should write. 8. He has described his travels. 9. They are writing. 10. Would you write, if I should write? 11. Do what I say. 12. He did not do it. 13. He has not done his work. 14. Let us do our work. 15. Let him do what I said. 16. It was necessary that you should do so. 17. I shall do so, when you come. 18. If you do so, we shall do so. 19. If you should say so, we should do it. 20. I was doing my work, when he came. 21. It is necessary that we do that. 22. If I do this, will you do that? 23. I was reading, when he came. 24. He will never read that book. 25. Read that letter. 26. They are reading their book.

27. Did we not read the newspaper? 28. If I should read this book, would you read that one? 29. Is he reading the newspaper? 30. It was necessary that I should read the letter. 31. May he not read that book? 32. Did they not read this book? 33. I placed the book on the table. 34. Do not commit that crime. 35. It is necessary that he put on his coat. 36. We shall put on our clothes. 37. They have placed their books on the table. 38. We shall not permit it. 39. Does he permit it? 40. It was necessary that he should not permit it. 41. What would you say, if we should permit it? 42. The miller grinds the wheat. 43. We are grinding wheat. 44. We ground the wheat. 45. Let him grind the wheat. 46. The prophet said that a child would be born. 47. We are born weak. 48. We were born [on] the same day. 49. Let a young nation arise! 50. It was necessary that hatred should arise between them.

EXERCISE XXXVIII.

(Irregular verbs in -re—*Continued*.)

1. That does not please him *(lui)*. 2. You please me. 3. Come when it pleases you. 4. Do so if you please. 5. May it please you. 6. Take your places. 7. He takes his hat from *(sur)* the table. 8. If I should take it, what would you do? 9. Let him take his book. 10. It was necessary that he should take the medicine. 11. We took our places. 12. Have you learnt your lesson? 13. He will not undertake that. 14. Fire resolves wood into *(en)* smoke. 15. We have resolved to *(de)* do it. 16. He solved the difficulty. 17. He will solve the difficulty. 18. Let us not laugh at *(de)* him. 19. Why is he laughing? 20. If I should laugh, what would you say? 21. It was not necessary that he should laugh. 22. We laugh at them. 23. Water springs from the earth. 24. Follow me. 25. The dog follows his master. 26. Let him follow us. 27. It is not necessary that we should follow you. 28. We followed him. 29. If I should follow him, it would please him. 30. We shall never follow him. 31. Is he not milking the cow? 32. If I should do that, he would not milk the cows. 33. When we were in the country, we used to milk the cows. 34. Let him milk the cow. 35. That distracts him from his work. 36. The general conquers his enemies. 37. We conquer our passions. 38. If you were to conquer your passions, you would be happy. 39. Our army will conquer. 40. We have conquered our enemies. 41. Let him conquer his passions. 42. He is not selling his house. 43. He will never sell it. 44. Horses live on *(de)* hay. 45. He lives only for him-

self. 46. Let us live in *(en)* peace. 47. He will live yet [a] long time. 48. Louis XIV. lived in the 17th century. 49. Long live the Queen! 50. Hurrah for Canada!

EXERCISE XXXIX.

(Irregular verbs in -oir.)

1. We receive our friends. 2. He has received the letter. 3. Let us not receive the money. 4. If they should receive us, we should be glad. 5. We owe him *(lui)* money. 6. We shall owe him something. 7. If they receive it, we shall tell (it to) you. 8. Let him not receive it. 9. We received the money. 10. Sit down. 11. He sits down. 12. They will sit down. 13. Let us sit down. 14. It was necessary that we should sit down. 15. If we should sit down, would you tell *(raconter)* us a story? 16. Let them not sit down. 17. That does not become him *(lui)*. 18. That will not become us. 19. We sit down. 20 The payment falls due. 21. His influence has declined. 22. It will be necessary to do it. 23. It is necessary to be there. 24. Passion moves men. 25. Steam and water drive *(mouvoir)* machines. 26. His story moved *(émouvoir)* the audience. 27. Such a story must move men. 28. We shall go, if it does not rain. 29. It was raining, when we came. 30. It will rain. 31. I did not think it would rain. 32. It has rained. 33. I shall come, if I can. 34. I shall come when I can. 35. They cannot go away. 36. I would do so, if I could. 37. I wish that he may not be able to do so. 38. I could do that, if I were rich. 39. You may do so, if you desire. 40. Could *(condl.)* you not give me some? 41. We know our lesson. 42. Do you know how to do that? 43. That child cannot write; he is too young. 44. I cannot write; I have a sore finger. 45. Do you know that gentleman? 46. I used to know how to swim. 47. Your father must not know that. 48. We knew it. 49. We shall know it to-morrow.

EXERCISE XL.

(Irregular verbs in -oir—*Continued*.)

1. That horse is worth one hundred dollars. 2. Virtue is worth more *(mieux)* than riches. 3. Those houses are worth more *(plus)* than these 4. That was worth more last year. 5. That will be worth more next year. 6. If that were worth more, I should take it. 7. He has nothing (which is) of value *(subj.)*. 8. We shall never see him again. 9. Do you see him? 10. I saw him. 11. We saw him. 12. If we should see him, we should tell (it to) him. 13. When we see him, we shall speak to to him about it. 14 We must see our parents. 15. It was necessary

that we should see our children. 16. I have seen him. 17. If we wished to do it, we could do it. 18. You may come, when you wish. 19. He will wish to do that, when he can. 20. Be so good as to sit down. 21. If you will sell your house, I shall buy it. 22. Will you be so kind as to give me some? 23. We do not wish to do that. 24. Would you like to see him? 25. I should like to see him, if I could. 26. I could do this, if I wished. 27. If it rains, we cannot go. 28. If they were willing, they could do it. 29. If they are not willing to tell (it to) you, you will not know how to do it.

Use of Auxiliary Verbs.

307. Avoir + *the past participle* forms the compound tenses of *all transitive* and of *most intransitive* verbs, as follows:—

Infinitive.

PERFECT. avoir donné (fini, rompu, eu, été), *to have given (finished, etc.).*

Participle.

PERFECT. ayant donné (fini, etc.), *having given (finished, etc.).*

Indicative.

PAST INDEFINITE. j'ai donné, tu as donné, il a donné, nous avons donné, vous avez donné, ils ont donné (j'ai fini, etc., etc.), *I have given, I gave, etc. (I have finished, etc., etc.).*

PLUPERFECT. j'avais donné, etc., etc., *I had given, etc., etc.*

PAST ANTERIOR. j'eus donné, etc., etc., *I had given, etc., etc.*

FUTURE ANT. j'aurai donné, etc., etc., *I shall have given, etc., etc.*

CONDL. ANT. j'aurais donné, etc., etc., *I should have given, etc., etc.*

Subjunctive.

PERFECT. (que) j'aie donné, etc., etc., *(that) I (may) have given, etc., etc.*

PLUPERFECT. (que) j'eusse donné, etc., etc., *(that) I (might) have given, etc., etc.*

308. Être + *the past participle* forms the compound tenses of *all reflexive verbs* (§322) and of the following *intransitives* denoting *motion* or *change of condition*:—

aller, *go.*
arriver, *arrive.*
choir, *fall.*
décéder, *die.*
échoir, *fall due.*
éclore, *hatch out.*
entrer, *enter, go (come) in.*
mourir, *die.*
naître, *be born.*
venir, *come.*

AUXILIARY VERBS.

So also, the following *compounds* of **venir**:

devenir, *become.* parvenir, *attain.* survenir, *supervene.*
redevenir, *become again.* provenir, *proceed.*
intervenir, *intervene.* revenir, *come back.*

[*To have gone.*] [*Having died.*]
être allé(e) or allé(e)s. étant mort(e) or mort(e)s.

[*I (have) arrived, etc.*]

je suis arrivé(e).	nous sommes arrivé(e)s.
tu es "	vous êtes "
il (elle) est "	ils (elles) sont "

309. 1. **Avoir** *or* **être** + *the past participle* forms the compound tenses of a number of *intransitives* (see list below), the general distinction being that **avoir**, when so used, denotes *action*, while **être** denotes *state* or *condition* resulting from action:

La pluie a passé par la fenêtre. The rain came through the window.
La pluie est passée. The rain is past.
Elle a grandi bien vite. She grew up very fast.
Elle est grandie. She is grown up.

2. *Reference-list* of verbs with **avoir** *or* **être**:

aborder, *land.*   *descendre, *descend.*   redescendre, *come down again.*
accourir, *run to.*   disparaître, *disappear.*   remonter, *go up again.*
accroître, *increase.*   échapper, *escape.*   *rentrer, *go in again.*
apparaître, *appear.*   échouer, *be stranded, fail.*   repasser, *pass again.*
baisser, *fall, decline.*   embellir, *grow handsomer.*   *ressortir, *go out again.*
cesser, *cease.*   émigrer, *emigrate.*   ressusciter, *revive.*
changer, *change.*   empirer, *grow worse.*   rester, *remain.*
croître, *grow.*   expirer, *expire.*   *retomber, *fall again.*
déborder, *overflow.*   grandir, *grow up.*   *retourner, *go back.*
déchoir, *decay.*   *monter, *go up.*   sonner, *strike, toll.*
décroître, *decrease.*   *partir, *set out.*   *sortir, *go out.*
dégénérer, *degenerate.*   passer, *pass.*   *tomber, *fall.*
demeurer, *remain.*   réchapper, *escape again.*   vieillir, *grow old.*

*Very generally with **être**, and placed by some grammarians among verbs taking **être**.

a. Any verb in the list, used *transitively*, must, of course, take **avoir** (§307).

Il m'a passé la plume. He handed me the pen.
Avez-vous rentré votre blé? Have you hauled in your wheat?
Ils ont descendu le tableau. They have taken down the picture.

b. The *meaning* also determines the auxiliary in a few other cases:

Avoir.	Être.
convenir, *suit, become.*	convenir, *agree.*
disconvenir, *not to suit, be discordant.*	disconvenir, *deny.*
repartir, *reply*	repartir, *go away again.*

Nous sommes convenus du prix. — We agreed on the price.
Le prix ne m'a pas convenu. — The price did not suit me.

EXERCISE XLI.

Qu'est devenu son frère?	What has become of his brother?
Je sais ce qu'il est devenu.	I know what has become of him.
Elle est née.	She was born.
Elle est morte.	She died.
Elle est montée.	She has gone up (*or* upstairs).

NOTE.—In this exercise, verbs having the asterisk in the list §309, 2, are to be conjugated with être when intransitive.

1. Your mother has come, has she not? 2. No, she has not yet come; she will come to-morrow. 3. Our friends have gone to church; let us go (there) too. 4. The old gentleman who lived in that house died last night. 5. (The) Queen Victoria was born on the twenty-fourth of May. 6. My little sister was born on the tenth of March. 7. How old is your father? 8. He is seventy; he was born before the death of Napoleon. 9. What has become of your brother? 10. He has gone to (*partir pour*) France. 11. When did he go? 12. He went yesterday morning. 13. Is your father out? 14. No sir, he is in. 15. When did your father return? 16. He has not yet returned; he will return next week. 17. The servant has brought down the trunk. 18. Where is your sister? 19. She has gone down for breakfast. 20. Where are the children? 21. They have gone upstairs. 22. Why did they not come down when I was there? 23. What is the matter, my child? 24. It was slippery, and I fell. 25. My father has gone into the house. 26. Although he was born rich, he is now poor. 27. He died poor, although he was once rich. 28. I have not seen him to-day; what has become of him? 29. I don't know what has become of him. 30. Have you taken up the gentleman's trunks? 31. Not yet, but I shall take them up immediately. 32. At what o'clock did your sister go out this morning? 33. She went out at half-past nine. 34. Where is my sister? 35. She has gone upstairs; she has gone to get her books.

310. Other Verb Phrases. Several verbs, when followed by an *infinitive*, have a sort of auxiliary function somewhat analagous to that of **avoir (être)** + *a past part.*, and serve to form verb phrases of various values (*modal, temporal*, etc.) :—

1. **Vouloir** = 'will,' 'wish to,' 'want to,' 'desire to,' etc. :

Je ne veux pas rester.	I will not remain.
Il voudrait (bien) le savoir.	He would like to know it.
Elle n'a pas voulu m'écouter.	She would not listen to me.
Il aurait voulu le faire.	He would have liked to do so.
Veuillez le faire.	Be so good as to do so.

a. Distinguish from 'will' of *simple futurity* :

Elle vous écoutera.   She will listen to you.

2. **Devoir** = 'ought,' 'should,' 'must,' 'be to,' 'have to,' 'be obliged to,' 'intend to,' etc., varies in force in different tenses·

Pres.	Impf.	Fut.
[*I am to (have to, intend to, must) remain,* etc.]	[*I was to (had to, intended to) speak,* etc.]	[*I shall have to (be obliged to) come back,* etc.]
je dois rester.	je devais parler.	je devrai revenir.
tu dois rester, etc.	tu devais parler, etc.	tu devras revenir, etc.

Condl.	Past. Indef.	Condl. Ant.
[*I ought to (should) write,* etc.]	[*I have had to (have been obliged to) stop, must have stopped,* etc.]	[*I ought to have (should have) known,* etc.]
je devrais écrire.	j'ai dû m'arrêter.	j'aurais dû savoir.
tu devrais écrire, etc.	tu as dû t'arrrêter, etc.	tu aurais dû savoir, etc.

3. **Pouvoir** = 'can,' 'be able to,' 'be permitted to,' 'may,' etc. :

Il ne pouvait pas porter le sac.	He could not carry the sack.
Puis-je aller?	May I go?
Ils auraient pu le faire.	They could (might) have done it.
Je pourrais le faire, si je voulais.	I could do it, if I would.
Pourraient-ils en trouver ?	Could they find any ?
Pourrais-je vous demander ?	Might I ask you ?

4. **Savoir** = 'know how to,' 'can,' etc. :

Elle sait chanter et danser.   She can sing and dance.

a. *Distinguish* savoir in this sense from pouvoir:

Elle est enrouée et ne peut pas chanter ce soir.	She is hoarse and cannot sing this evening.

b. The *condl. with* ne has peculiar idiomatic force:

Je ne saurais le croire.	I cannot believe it.

5. Oser = 'dare':

Je n'ose pas le lui dire.	I dare not tell him so.

NOTE.—The above five verbs are sometimes called *modal auxiliaries*.

6. Faire = 'make,' 'cause to,' 'cause to be,' 'have,' 'order,' 'order to be,' etc.:

J'ai fait étudier les enfants.	I have made the children study.
Il les fera écouter.	He will make them listen.
Il s'est fait faire un habit.	He had a coat made for himself.
Faites chercher un médecin.	Send for a doctor.

a. A *governed subst. follows* the *infin.*, but a governed *conj. pers. pron.* (not reflex.) goes with faire:

Faites venir le domestique.	Have the servant come.
Faites-le venir.	Have him come.

b. If the *infin.* with faire have a *dir. obj.* (not reflex.), the *personal obj.* of faire must be *indirect*; otherwise nearly always *direct*:

Je fis écrire mon fils.	I had my son write.
Je fis écrire un thème à mon fils.	I made my son write an exercise.
Faites-le-lui écrire.	Make him write it.
Je le leur fis voir.	I showed them it.

c. Possible *ambiguity* is sometimes *avoided* by par:

Il fit porter le sac par le guide.	He had the sack carried by the guide.

d. A *reflexive infin.* (not reciprocal) usually *omits* its *pron.*:

Faites-les asseoir.	Have them sit down.
But: Faites-les s'accuser.	Make them accuse one another.

e. Note the *passive force* of a *transitive* infin. after faire:

Je ferai écrire une lettre.	I shall have a letter written.

7. Laisser = 'let,' has usually the same constructions as faire:

Laissez écrire les enfants.	Let the children write.
Laissez-leur (*or* -les) écrire un thème.	Let them write an exercise.

8. The *pres.* and *impf.* of aller + *infin.* give a kind of *immediate future*, as also in Eng. :

Il va l'acheter.	He is going to (is about to) buy it.
Nous allions nous arrêter.	We were about to stop.
Il allait se noyer.	He was on the point of drowning.

9. Similarly the *pres.* and *impf.* of venir de + *infin.* give a kind of *immediate past:*

Je viens de le voir.	I have just seen him.
Il venait de l'entendre.	He had just heard it.

EXERCISE XLII.

Si vous vouliez bien me le dire.	If you would kindly tell me.
Faites-les entrer.	Show them in.

1. We do not wish to leave this country; we should like to remain here, but if we cannot, we shall go. 2. You ought to go home (my) children; it is late. 3. We cannot go home; it is dark, and our father told us to *(de)* wait for him. 4. We cannot go away before six o'clock; we are to wait here till our friends come. 5. We could have written the letter, if we had known that you desired it. 6. That beggar could have had work, if he had wanted it, but he was too lazy; he would not work, and now he must beg. 7. Those children cannot read yet; they are too young. 8. If they had been able to read, they would not have believed all that was said to them. 9. You ought to let them go away, for their father told them that they were to leave before (the) night. 10. You might have seen them, if you had been willing to come with me. 11. Our teacher told us that we were to write this exercise. 12. We are to have a house built next year. 13. Their teacher made them write their exercise. 14. We should like to have a house built, if we were rich enough. 15. We said to the innkeeper, will you be so kind as to have our horses saddled? We are going to start. 16. Opium makes [us] sleep. 17. It is very warm; if this great heat continues, it will kill the crops.

EXERCISE XLIII.

1. Those children make a great deal of noise; they talk too much; make them be silent. 2. That girl could write, if she wished (it). 3. If you would kindly tell me where the doctor lives, I should send for him. 4. Do you know Daudet's *La Belle-Nivernaise?* 5. Oh yes, it is a charming book; I liked it so well that I had my pupils read it. 6. That is a beautiful picture. 7. Yes, I have just been showing it to

your mother and sister. 8. When did you see my father? 9. I had just been speaking with him, when you came. 10. What are you going to do to-morrow? 11. To-morrow we are to go to see the *Invalides* and the *Arc de Triomphe*, and the day after to-morrow we are to see *Notre Dame* and the *Louvre* (m.) 12. We ought to have visited the *Louvre* when you were with us; you could have shown us the fine pictures. 13. May I go with you, when you visit the *Louvre* next time? I should like to have explained to me some of the beauties of the finest pictures. 14. That gentleman must have been in Paris, for he speaks French like a Parisian. 15. Why did you not make those ladies sit down, when they were here? 16. They said they would not stay, because you were out. 17. There are ladies at the door. 18. Very well, show them in. 19. Your son ought to write his exercises. 20. Very well, make him write them. 21. If I had made him study his lessons when he was at school, he would have become a better man.

Agreement of Verb and Subject.

311. General Rule. The verb agrees with its subject in *number* and *person:*

Les hommes sont mortels.	Men are mortal.
Tout le monde est ici.	Everybody is here.
Toi et moi (nous) ne faisons qu'un.	You and I are but one.

312. Simple Subject. Special rules for the agreement of a verb with *one* subject are:—

1. A *collective subj. sing.*, when *not followed by* **de**, or when *followed by* **de** + *the sing.*, has a *sing.* verb:

Le peuple français est brave.	The French people are brave.
Le sénat l'a décidé.	The senate has (*or* have) decided it.
La plupart du monde le croit.	Most people believe it.

2. A *collective subj. sing.* + **de** and a *plur.* takes a *plur.* verb, unless the sense of the collective be dominant:

Une nuée de sauvages l'attaquèrent.	A cloud of savages attacked him.
Une nuée de traits l'obscurcit.	A cloud of arrows hid him.
Une partie des soldats restent.	A part of the soldiers remain.
Une partie des bourgeois protesta.	A part of the citizens protested.
Cette sorte de poires est chère.	This sort of pears is dear.

a. When so used, *adverbs of quantity, e.g.* beaucoup, peu, etc., the *nouns* nombre, quantité (without art.) and la plupart are regularly *plur.* in sense; so also, force (de being understood):

Beaucoup de gens pensent ainsi.	Many people think so.
Peu de gens le savent.	Few people know it.
Que d'ennemis m'attaquent !	How many enemies attack me !
Nombre d'Athéniens avaient fui.	A number of Athenians had fled.
La plupart des soldats périrent.	Most of the soldiers perished.
Force sots le tenteront.	Many a fool will try it.

b. Beaucoup, peu, combien, used *absolutely*, are *sing.* or *plur.* according to the sense of the de clause *implied*; la plupart when so used is always *plur.*:

Beaucoup (*sc.* de gens) le croient.	Many (*sc.* people) believe it.
Peu (*sc.* de ceci) me suffira.	Little (*sc.* of this) will suffice me.
La plupart votèrent contre.	The majority voted nay.

c. Plus d'un is *sing.* (unless reciprocal or repeated) and moins de deux is *plur.*:

Plus d'un témoin a déposé.	More than one witness has sworn.
Moins de deux ne valent rien.	Less than two is no use.
Plus d'un fripon se dupent (l'un l'autre).	More rogues than one cheat each other.
Plus d'un officier, plus d'un général furent tués.	More than one officer, more than one general was killed.

3. Ce (sing.) requires a *plur.* verb only when the predicate is a *plur. noun*, a *plur. pron. 3rd pers.*, or when ce refers to a *preceding plur.*:

Sont-ce vos amis ?—Ce sont eux.	Is it your friends? It is they.
Ce doivent être les siens.	Those must be his.
Ce sont nos semblables.	They are our fellow-creatures.
Ses désirs, ce sont sa loi.	His desires are his law.

But: C'est moi; c'est toi; c'est lui; c'est nous; c'est vous.

a. The *3rd sing.* is often used *for the 3rd plur.* in this construction, more especially in familiar language or to avoid harsh locutions:

Est-ce les Anglais que je crains ?	Is it the English that I fear?
C'est eux qui l'ont fait.	It is they who did it.
C'est des bêtises.	That is stupidity.
Ne fût-ce que quelques lignes.	If it were only a few lines.

b. The verb with ce is *sing.* when the predicate is a *numeral* + a noun of *collective* force:

C'est dix heures qu'il sonne.	It is ten o'clock that is striking.

e. **Si ce n'est** is always *sing.*:

Qui, si ce n'est nos parents? — Who, if it is not our parents?

4. **Il** (impers.) always has a *sing.* verb, whatever be the logical subject:

Il est arrivé bien des choses. — Many things have happened.
Il en reste trois livres. — Three pounds of it remain.

a. **Importer** is construed *personally* or *impersonally:*

Qu'importe (importent) les dépens? — What matters the cost?

313. Composite Subject. A verb common to *two or more subjects* is regularly *plur.*; when the subjects *differ in pers.* the verb agrees with the *1st pers.* (if any), otherwise with the *2nd:*

Sa sœur et lui sont là. — His sister and he are there.
Quels sont vos amis? — Who are your friends?
Toi et moi ne faisons qu'un. — You and I are but one.
Qui êtes-vous? — Who are you?

a. With subjects of different pers., *pleonastic* nous, vous, is *generally* used:

Vous et lui (vous) l'avez vu. — You and he have seen it.

b. With **ou** = 'or,' **ni...ni** = 'neither...nor,' the verb is *sing.*, if the sense is clearly *alternative* (*i.e.*, the one subj. excluding the other), otherwise generally *plur.*; **l'un ou l'autre** is *always sing.:*

Sa vie ou sa mort en dépend. — His life or death depends on it.
Ni lui ni votre frère n'aura ce poste. — Neither he nor your brother will have that post.
Ni l'un ni l'autre ne sont bons. — Neither are good.
L'une ou l'autre viendra. — The one or the other will come.
L'un ou l'autre jour me convient. — Either day suits me.

c. If the subjects (generally without **et**) are *synonymous* (or nearly so), or form a *climax*, the verb *may be sing.:*

Sa **dignité**, sa **noblesse frappa** tout le monde. — His **dignity**, his **nobility struck** everybody.
L'heure, le lieu, le bras se choisit aujourd'hui. — The hour, the place, the arm are chosen to-day.
Une excuse, un mot le **désarme**. — An excuse, a word **disarms** him.

d. When the subjects are *recapitulated* by a word in the *sing.*, e.g., tout, rien, etc., the verb is *sing.* agreeing with it:

Remords, crainte, périls, rien ne m'a retenue.	Remorse, fear, dangers, nothing deterred me.

e. With an *intervening clause*, e.g. ainsi que, plus que, etc., the subject is usually only *apparently composite:*

La vertu, plus que le savoir, élève l'homme.	Virtue, more than knowledge, elevates man.

f. Even with et the sense is occasionally *sing.* or *distributive* or *alternative*, and a *sing.* verb is required:

Le bien et le mal est en ta main.	Good and ill are in thy hand.
L'un et l'autre peut se dire.	Both may be said.
L'été est revenu et le soleil.	Summer has returned and the sun.
Tombe Argos et ses murs.	Down falls Argos and its walls.

314. Relative Subject. The verb agrees with the *rel. pron. subj.*, which is itself of the *num.* and *pers.* of the *antecedent* (see also Relat. Pron.):

C'est nous qui l'avons fait.	It is we who have done it.
Dieux (vous) qui m'exaucez!	(Ye) Gods who hear me!

EXERCISE XLIV.

1. The French people are brave and gay; they *(il)* have their *(ses)* defects, but also their good qualities. 2. Few people believe that the earth is not round. 3. Most people believe that the earth will be destroyed. 4. The greater part of his friends abandoned him. 5. Many think that our friends will not succeed. 6. A great number of men were killed. 7. The Canadian people are brave, they *(il)* will always be free. 8. More than one house was burnt. 9. Less than two will not be enough. 10. Is it your friends who live in the house on the hill? 11. Yes, it is they; they have lived there for two years. 12. You and he were there, were you not? 13. Yes, he and I were there, and your brother too. 14. Will you and your brother come and see us, when you are in Toronto? 15. We shall be very happy to *(de)* visit you. 16. Do you see those two children? Both were born [on] the same day. 17. You or I shall speak. 18. There happen many misfortunes here below. 19. There arose a great quarrel between them. 20. Who went for the doctor? 21. It was (pres.) I who went for him. 22. Do you see those two gentlemen? Both have had houses built this year. 23. Religion, truth, honour, all was abandoned. 24. Many think that you will never be able to

build your house. 25. The majority are not always right. 26. If there happened such misfortunes to me, I should leave the country. 27. Were it only a few lines, I should like you to write to me. 28. If you and I were young, fine things would be done (reflex. impers.). 29. Who can have done that, if not our friends? 30. Neither he nor his brother can go away; both must stay.

Position of Subject.

315. The subject usually *precedes* the verb. Exceptions to this rule are noted in the following sections.

316. Interrogative Word Order. *Direct interrogation* is expressed as follows:—

1. A *personal pronoun subject* (also **ce** *or* **on**) *follows the verb* and is joined to it by a *hyphen:*

Parlez-vous français? Est-ce lui? Do you speak French? Is it he?

a. The letter -t- is inserted after a *3rd sing. with final vowel* before a pron. with *initial vowel:*

Parla-t-elle? Parle-t-on? Did she speak? Do they speak?

b. A final e of the *1st sing.* takes *acute accent:*

Donné-je? (*dònè že*). Do I give?

2. A *noun subject precedes* the verb and is *repeated* after it by a *pleonastic pronoun;* so also, poss., demonstr. and indef. prons.:

Cet homme parle-t-il anglais? Does that man speak English?
Cela est-il vrai? Is that true?
Les miens ne sont-ils pas bons? Are mine not good?

3. Questions are also asked by *interrogative words* (adj. pron. adv.):

Quel poète a écrit cela? What poet wrote that?
À quelle heure partira son ami? At what o'clock will his friend go?
Qui est là? Qu'y a-t-il? Who is there? What is the matter?
Lequel des deux est parti? Which of the two has gone?
Combien coûte cela? }
Combien cela coûte-t-il? } How much does that cost?

a. The word order of *either* of the last two examples is commonly permissible for *noun subject* under this rule.

b. The word order of the *last example* is *obligatory* when the verb has a *direct object* (not reflexive) or a prepositional *complement*, or when *am-*

biguity might arise; this arrangement is *preferable* after pourquoi? or a *compound tense*:

Où le roi tient-il sa cour?	Where does the king hold his court?
De quoi le roi parle-t-il?	Of what is the king speaking?
Quel prix le roi paya-t-il?	What price did the king pay?
Jean qui aime-t-il?	Whom does John love?
Pourquoi mon ami part-il?	Why does my friend go?
Quand ce roi fut-il décapité?	When was this king beheaded?

4. By prefixing **est-ce que?** a statement becomes a question without change in its word order:

Est-ce que vous partez?	Are you going away?
Quand est-ce que vous partez?	When are you going away?

a. The use of est-ce que? is *permissible* with *all forms of* the verb, but is *obligatory* with a *monosyllabic 1st sing.* (except ai-je?, suis-je?, dis-je?, dois-je?, fais-je?, puis-je?, sais-je?, vais-je?, vois-je?), and is *preferable* to avoid forms like donné-je?:

Est-ce que je sers, moi?	Do I serve?
Est-ce que je parle de lui?	Do I speak of him?

5. Interrogation is also expressed by mere *inflection of voice*, without change in word order:

Vous partez déjà?	You are going already?

317. Rhetorical Inversions. Owing to rhetorical considerations the *noun subject* not uncommonly *follows* the verb, or the sentence assumes *interrogative form*, though not interrogative, as follows:—

1. In *interjected remarks* explanatory of direct quotation, as in English:

Fais comme tu voudras, dit-il. Do as you please, said he.
Que veux-tu? demanda la mère. What do you wish? asked the mother.

2. In *optative clauses* when **que** is *omitted*, and also after the rare omission of **si**, *if:*

Vive le roi! Périsse le tyran!	(Long) live the king! Perish the tyrant!
Voulait-il de l'argent, son père lui en donnait toujours.	If he wished money, his father always gave him some.
Ne fût-ce que pour cela.	If it were only for that.

K

3. Very commonly after *certain adverbs:*

Du moins devrait-il attendre.	He should at least wait.
A peine le jour fut-il arrivé.	Hardly had the day arrived.

Such adverbs are:

à peine, *hardly.*	*peut-être, *perhaps.*	toutefois, *although.*
aussi, *hence.*	encore, *besides.*	en vain, *in vain.*
aussi bien, *moreover.*	toujours, *however.*	rarement, *rarely.*
au moins, *at least.*	tout au plus, *at most.*	probablement, *probably.*
du moins, *at least.*	d'autant plus, *the more.*	etc.

*Peut-être que does not cause inversion: 'Peut-être qu'il le fera,' 'Perhaps he will do so.'

4. Sometimes in *exclamatory* sentences:

Avons-nous crié!	How we shouted!

5. When a *predicate adjective heads the phrase:*

Telle fut la fin de Carthage.	Such was the end of Carthage.
Quelque riche que soit cet homme.	However rich that man is.

*6. Very commonly in a *relative clause* (especially when a second relative clause qualifies its subject):

Il fera ce que peut faire un homme qui se respecte.	He will do what a man can who respects himself.
Dites-moi ce qu'a fait votre ami.	Tell me what your friend did.
Dis-moi où est ton ami.	Tell me where your friend is.

NOTE.—The relative is *unstressed* (proclitic) and naturally stands next the verb which governs it.

*7. Commonly after c'est que and in the *second member of a comparative sentence:*

C'est en vous qu'espèrent tous.	It is in you that all hope.
J'en ai plus que n'en a mon ami.	I have more of it than my friend has.

*8. Commonly when an *adverb, e.g.,* ainsi, ici, là, etc. or an *adverbial phrase* heads the sentence:

Ainsi va le monde.	So goes the world.
Bientôt viendra le printemps.	Spring will soon come.
À la tête de l'armée fut porté l'étendard sacré.	At the head of the army was carried the sacred standard.

*10. Quite *exceptionally,* when the *verb* comes *first:*

Viendra un autre.	(Along) will come another.
Étant données les conditions.	Granted the conditions.

*Holds good only for *noun subject,* except very rarely, *e.g.,* ainsi dit-il.

NOTE.—*No inversion* of *noun subject* usually occurs if the verb has a *direct object* or a prepositional *complement.*

318. *Indirect interrogation* has no special rules of word order apart from those of the clause in which it occurs:

Dis-moi ce qu'il a dit.   Tell me what he said.

EXERCISE XLV.

1. Is that book yours or your brother's? 2. How much did these books cost? 3. I do not know how much they cost. 4. Does that merchant provide you cheap with what you need? 5. What is the matter with that boy this morning? 6. I do not know what is the matter with him. 7. Do I say, or can I say, the half of what he has done? 8. Whatever men may do, they cannot escape death. 9. What books did your father buy, when he was in the city? 10. Your father told me what your brother had done. 11. Your brother told me what he had done. 12. Will you tell me where those men were, when you saw them? 13. I cannot tell you where they were. 14. We have more books than that gentleman has. 15. We have more books than you have. 16. Virtue is a beautiful thing, hence we love it. 17. My father is here; perhaps he will come to see you. 18. However good men may be, they are sometimes poor. 19. Such are my reasons for doing so. 20. You have told me that my friend has gone; I did not know (impf.) it, but perhaps you are right. 21. I wish you were here, were it only to encourage us. 22. That man does not respect himself, hence he cannot be good. 23. Come and see us, said he, as soon as you can (fut.). 24. If I do this, thought he, I shall be punished, hence I shall not do it. 25. When was your little brother born? 26. I do not know where that man died. 27. To whom did your friend give his gold watch? 28. I do not know; perhaps he gave it to his sister. 29. I cannot do *(de)* such things; am I not [an] Englishman? 30. Do I not tell you that I shall be there, and that I shall see you?

THE PASSIVE VOICE.

319. Formation. The passive voice of a transitive verb is formed from the auxiliary être + *the past participle*, which *agrees* with the *subject* of the verb in *gender* and *number*:

PRES. INFIN.   être loué(e) *or* loué(e)s, *to be praised.*
PERF. INFIN.   avoir été loué(e) *or* loué(e)s, *to have been praised.*
PRES. PART.   étant loué(e) *or* loué(e)s, *being praised.*
PERF. PART.   ayant été loué(e) *or* loué(e)s, *having been praised.*

Pres. Indic.	Past Indef. Indic.
[*I am (I am being) praised, etc.*]	[*I have been (I was) praised, etc.*]

je suis \
tu es   } loué(e). \
il (elle) est /

nous sommes \
vous êtes   } loué(e)s. \
ils (elles) sont /

j'ai été \
tu as été } loué(e). \
il (elle) a été /

nous avons été \
vous avez été   } loué(e)s. \
ils (elles) ont été /

etc., etc., throughout.

Obs.: 1. The past participle été is *always invariable*. 2. The past participle after **vous** *agrees with the sense:* 'Madame, vous serez méprisée de tous,' 'Madam, you will be despised by all.'

320. The Agent. The person *by whom* the action is done is usually denoted by **par**, when a *specific intention* or *definite volition* is implied, and by **de** when the action is *habitual, usual,* or *indefinite:*

Elle fut saisie par le voleur.	She was seized by the thief.
Ils sont aimés de tous.	They are loved by everybody.
La reine fut suivie de ses dames.	The queen was followed by her ladies.
Le général fut suivi de près par l'ennemi.	The general was closely followed by the enemy.

321. Remarks. 1. *Transitives only* regularly have the passive voice, but the *intransitives* **obéir, désobéir, pardonner** may also be made passive:

Vous êtes pardonnés tous.	You are all pardoned.
Elle est toujours obéie.	She is always obeyed.

2. The passive is *much less used* than in English, especially if the agent be not specified, or if the corresponding French verb is intransitive, or if an indir. obj. be present. *Substitutes are:*

a. A *verb with* the indefinite **on**:

On m'a trompé.	I have been deceived.
On se doute de moi.	I am suspected.
On a répondu à ma question.	My question has been answered.
On lui a rendu l'argent.	The money has been given back to him.

b. A *reflexive construction:*

Ce livre se publie à Paris.	This book is published in Paris.
La guerre se continua.	The war was continued.
Voilà ce qui se dit.	This is what is being said.

3. A *transitive infinitive* has *passive force* after **faire, laisser, voir**, etc., and also when à + *infinitive* is used *adjectivally:*

Le ferez-vous vendre?	Will you have it sold?
Je la vis battre.	I saw her beaten.
Une faute à éviter.	A mistake to be avoided.

EXERCISE XLVI.

On lui obéit. } Il est obéi. }	He is obeyed.
On me l'a pardonné.	I have been pardoned (for) it.

1. America was discovered by Christopher Columbus. 2. The first steam-boat was built by Fulton. 3. We have been deceived by that scoundrel. 4. We have been deceived. 5. That gentleman has been mistaken in that affair. 6. Where is that said? 7. Oh, that is said everywhere. 8. Who committed that crime? 9. It was our neighbor's brother. 10. Will he not be punished? 11. No, he has been pardoned for it. 12. I have often seen it done. 13. I have been told that you had it done. 14. Is that not done everywhere? 15. Oh, no, that is never done amongst respectable people. 16. How unfortunate he is! He is a good fellow, but he is deceived and suspected everywhere. 17. How little it is! It can hardly be seen. 18. That man is not a good teacher; he is not obeyed by his pupils. 19. There is a house to be sold. 20. There is an exercise to be done. 21. That beggar was given bread and milk. 22. We were made read our lesson. 23. That is a man to be feared. 24. They were told that you were not here. 25. Why should we not have been told that our friends had gone away?

THE REFLEXIVE VERB.

322. 1. A *reflexive* verb (or a verb used reflexively) represents the *subject as acting on itself* as reflexive object.

2. Etre + *the past participle* forms the compound tenses of *all* reflexive verbs, as follows:—

PRES. INFIN. se flatter, *to flatter one's self.*
PERF. INFIN. s'être flatté(e) *or* flatté(e)s, *to have flattered one's self.*
PRES. PART. se flattant, *flattering one's self.*
PERF. PART. s'étant flatté(e) *or* flatté(e)s, *having flattered one's self.*

Indicative.

PRESENT.
[*I flatter myself, etc.*]
je me flatte.
tu te flattes.
il (elle) se flatte.
nous nous flattons.
vous vous flattez.
ils (elles) se flattent.

PAST INDEF.
[*I* (have) *flattered myself, etc.*]
je me suis ⎫
tu t'es ⎬ flatté(e).
il (elle) s'est ⎭
nous nous sommes ⎫
vous vous êtes ⎬ flatté(e)s.
ils (elles) se sont ⎭

etc., etc.

Imperative.

[*Flatter thyself, etc.*]
flattons-nous.
flatte-toi. flattez-vous.
(qu'il se flatte.) (qu'ils se flattent.)

[*Do not flatter thyself, etc.*]
ne nous flattons pas.
ne te flatte pas. ne vous flattez pas.
(qu'il ne se flatte pas.) (qu'ils ne se flattent pas.)

NOTES.—1. **Se flatter, se flattant**, etc., are the infinitive and participial forms found in dictionaries, but **se** must be replaced by **me, te**, etc., according to the sense.

2. Except in the use of **être** as aux., reflexive verbs have *no peculiarities of conjugation* on account of being reflexive.

323. Reflexive or Reciprocal. A reflexive verb often has *reciprocal* force, *especially in* the *plural*. Ambiguity is generally avoided by some modifying expression:

Elles se flattent. ⎧ They flatter themselves.
⎨ They flatter each other.

Elles se flattent l'une l'autre. They flatter one another.
On se dupe mutuellement. They cheat each other.

324. Agreement of Past Participle. 1. In compound tenses, the past participle of a reflexive *agrees* in gender and number with the *reflexive object, unless that object be indirect:*

Elle s'est écriée. She cried out.
Elle s'est dit à elle-même. She said to herself.
Ils se sont écrit. They wrote to each other.
Elles se sont acheté des robes. They bought themselves dresses.

2. Besides the reflexive object, a *direct object* may precede the verb, and with this object the participle *agrees:*

Les plumes qu'ils se sont achetées. The pens they bought themselves.

NOTES.—1. The auxiliary être is considered as replacing **avoir**, and the above agreements are explained by the general principle (§121).

2. The agreement with **vous** is according to the sense : ' Vous **vous** êtes trompée, madame,' ' You were mistaken, madam.'

325. Omission of Reflexive Object. 1. It is always omitted with the *past participle as attributive adjective:*

Le temps écoulé. The time past by.

2. So also, usually the *reflex. infin. after* **faire** (and often after **laisser, sentir, voir**), but with frequent exceptions; so with *reciprocal* force is *not omitted*

Je les ferai taire (= se taire).	I shall make them keep silent.
Je les vois assembler.	I see them assemble.
But: Laissez-les s'accuser.	Let them accuse each other.
" Un cri le fit se dresser.	A cry made him jump up.
" Cette seule différence eût fait se récrier Jansénius.	This difference alone would have made Jansenius protest.

326. Remarks. The reflexive construction is much *commoner than in English:*

1. It often translates the English *passive*, especially when the *agent* is *not specified:*

La bourse s'est trouvée. The purse has been found.

Cela se raconte partout. That is being told everywhere.

2. Or it is expressed by an English *non-reflexive* (generally *intransitive):*

S'arrêter; s'écrier; se porter.	Stop; exclaim; be (of health).
S'asseoir; se hâter; se tromper, etc.	Sit down; hasten; be mistaken.

3. Or the French *reflexive + a preposition* has the value of an English *transitive:*

S'approcher de; se douter de.	Approach; suspect.
S'attendre à; se fier à.	Expect; trust.
Se passer de; se souvenir de, etc.	Do without; recollect.

327. S'en Aller. The conjugation of s'en aller = ' to go away' presents special difficulty:—

PRES. INDIC.	PAST INDEF. INDIC.
[*I go away, etc.*]	[*I have gone (I went) away, etc.*]
je m'en vais.	je m'en suis ⎫
tu t'en vas.	tu t'en es ⎬ allé(e).
il s'en va.	il (elle) s'en est ⎭
nous nous en allons.	nous nous en sommes ⎫
vous vous en allez.	vous vous en êtes ⎬ allé(e)s.
ils s'en vont.	ils (elles) s'en sont ⎭
IMPVE.	IMPVE. (neg.).
[*Go away, etc.*]	[*Do not go away, etc.*]
allons-nous-en.	ne nous en allons pas.
va-t'en. allez-vous-en.	ne t'en va pas. ne vous en allez pas.
(qu'il s'en aille.) (qu'ils s'en aillent.)	(qu'il ne s'en aille pas.) (qu'ils ne s'en aillent pas.)

Est-ce que je m'en vais ?   Ils ne s'en sont pas allés.
Vous en allez-vous ?   Ne nous en sommes-nous pas al-
S'en sont-elles allées ?   lé(e)s ?

EXERCISE XLVII.

*Elle s'est rappelé ce que j'ai dit. ⎫
*Elle s'est souvenue de ce que j'ai dit. ⎬ She remembered what I said.

Je me le rappelle. ⎫
Je m'en souviens. ⎬ I remember it.

Je me le rappelle. ⎫
Je me souviens de lui. ⎬ I remember him.

Ils se souviennent de moi.   They remember me.
Je m'en sers.   I use it (I make use of it).
Il s'en passe.   He does without it.
Elle s'est fait mal à la main. She (has) hurt her hand.
Elle s'est cassé le bras.   She has broken her arm.
Elle s'est tue.   She became silent.

*In *se rappeler*, *se* is indirect, in *se souvenir*, *se* is direct.

1. They have not yet gone away; they will remain here till to-morrow. 2. When you are in front of Mr. Jackson's, be good enough to stop. 3. How have you been during these years? 4. I have been very well. 5. How has your mother been, since she has been living in Toronto? 6. How unfortunate I am, she exclaimed, my friends remember me no longer. 7. When the door opens, we can go in. 8. Where is my book? I cannot do without it. 9. Why do you not make use of that pen? 10. It is not a good pen; I cannot use it. 11. There are

some ladies in the parlour; very well, have them sit down, and ask them to wait a little. 12. Why are you crying, my little girl? 13. I have fallen and hurt myself. 14. Where did you hurt yourself? 15. I hurt my hand. 16. Why did those ladies not sit down? 17. They would not sit down, because they could not stay. 18. If you wish to use this ink and paper, I shall give you some. 19. It was very slippery this morning, and my mother in going down the street, fell and broke her arm. 20. If you cannot do without this book, I shall lend it to you. 21. I can do without it now, but I shall need it next week. 22. Do you remember what was told you last evening? 23. No, I do not remember it. 24. Did that little girl hurt herself badly, when she fell? 25. Yes, she hurt herself very badly; she broke her arm. 26. Have those young ladies written letters to each other? 27. They have written many; they have been writing to each other for two years. 28. I am not well this morning; I hurt my head. 29. Are you using your pen now? 30. No, I am not using it; you may have it, if you need it. 31. Do you remember the gentleman who lived in that large house on the hill? 32. Yes, I remember him very well. 33. One cannot do without money; it is useful everywhere. 34. I remembered what he had said, as soon as I saw him. 35. Be silent, (my) children, you are speaking too loud. 36. As soon as I came, he became silent.

EXERCISE XLVIII.

Comment vous appelez-vous?	What are you called? / What is your name?
Je m'appelle Jean.	I am called John (My name is John).
Se promener à pied (à cheval).	To take a walk (a ride).
Se promener en voiture (en bateau).	To take a drive (a row *or* sail).
Elle s'est couchée à dix heures.	She went to bed at ten.
Elle s'est levée à six heures.	She rose at six.
Attendez-moi.	Wait for me.
Elle ne s'y est pas attendue.	She did not expect it.
Le prêtre les a mariés.	The priest (has) married them.
Elle s'est mariée à (*or* avec) mon cousin.	She (has) married my cousin.
Elle s'est mariée hier.	She was married yesterday.
Il est allé se promener en bateau.	He has gone for a row (*or* sail).
Allons nous promener.	Let us go for a walk.
Elle s'est endormie.	She fell asleep.
Se connaît-il en tableaux?	Is he a good judge of pictures?
Il s'y connaît assez bien.	He is a pretty good judge of them.
Vous ennuyez-vous ici?	Are you tired of being here?

1. What is that little boy's name? 2. His name is Henry. 3. What are you going to do to-day? 4. We are going to go for a drive. 5. We are not going for a drive; we prefer to go for a walk. 6. Let us go to bed now, and then we shall get up early. 7. Is your brother out? 8. Yes, he has gone for a drive. 9. While we were out for a drive, we met your brother on horseback. 10. While they were out for a ride, they met us on foot. 11. Let us go for a walk in that beautiful forest. 12. Has he gone for a ride or a walk? 13. He has gone for a sail. 14. The children went to bed at eight o'clock, and they will get up at six. 15. We shall wait for him here; he has gone for a walk. 16. That does not surprise me; I was expecting it. 17. I was not expecting to see him there. 18. Mr. Jackson has married his eldest daughter to a very rich man. 19. Who married them? 20. It was the priest who lives in the little village. 21. My cousin was married yesterday. 22. To whom was she married? 23. She was married to the gentleman who lived here last year. 24. When are you going to get married? 25. I shall never get married. 26. What is the name of the gentleman who married your cousin? 27. If the children had not gone early to bed last night, they would not be able to rise early this morning. 28. That surprises my mother; she was not expecting it. 29. We went to bed, and (we) fell asleep immediately. 30. Are you not a pretty good judge of books? 31. Yes, I am a pretty good judge of them. 32. Is your mother not tired of being here? 33. I think so; I shall ask her to go for a walk with us. 34. Do you ever get tired of being in the country? 35. No, I never tire of being there; I love the fields and trees.

IMPERSONAL VERBS.

328. An impersonal verb (or a verb used as such) is one conjugated, in the *3rd sing. only*, with the subject il(= 'it,' 'there') used *indefinitely* and *absolutely, e.g.,* **tonner** = 'thunder.'

Indicative.

PRES. il tonne, *it thunders.*   PAST INDF. il a tonné, *it has thundered.*
IMPF. il tonnait, *it thundered.*   PLUPF. il avait tonné, *it had thundered.*
PAST DEF. il tonna, *it thundered.* PAST ANT. il eut tonné, *it had thundered.*

etc., etc., like 3 sing. of donner.

NOTE.—Apart from being limited to the 3rd sing., their conjugation does not differ from that of ordinary verbs. Some are regular, others irregular.

329. 1. Verbs denoting *natural phenomena* and *time* are impersonal, as in English:

Il tonne ; il a plu ; il pleuvra.	It thunders ; it rained ; it will rain.
Il a gelé hier ; il dégèle.	It froze yesterday ; it is thawing.
Il est une heure ; il est tard.	It is one o'clock ; it is late.

Such verbs are :

pleuvoir, *rain*.	grêler, *hail*.	geler, *freeze*.
neiger, *snow*.	éclairer, *lighten*.	dégeler, *thaw*.

2. **Faire** = 'make,' is also much used impersonally to describe *weather, temperature*, etc. :

Quel temps fait-il ?	What kind of weather is it ?
Il fait beau (temps) ce matin.	It is fine (weather) this morning.
Il a fait bien froid hier.	It was very cold yesterday.
Est-ce qu'il fera obscur ce soir !	Will it be dark this evening ?
Il faisait (tombait) de la pluie.	It was raining.
Il faisait du vent aussi.	It was windy too.

Obs. : Distinguish from constructions with a *personal subject* : 'Le temps est beau,' 'The weather is fine' ; 'L'eau est froide,' 'The water is cold.'

330. Y avoir. 1. The verb **avoir**, *preceded by* **y**, used impersonally = 'there is,' 'there are' (was, were), etc. :

Il y a. Il y a eu. Y a-t-il ?	There is. There has been. Is there ?
Il n'y a pas. Il n'y a pas eu.	There is not. There has not been.
Y a-t-il eu ? N'y a-t-il pas eu ?	Has there been ? Has there not been ?
Y aura-t-il ? Il peut y avoir.	Will there be ? There may be.

2. **Il est** (était, etc.) is sometimes used for **il y a** in this sense :

Il est des hommes qui le croient.	There are men who think so.

3. **Il y a** = 'there is,' 'there are,' ('there' *unstressed*) is distinguished from **voilà** = 'there is,' 'there are,' ('there' *stressed*)—the one *indefinite* and *general*, the other *specific* and *local* :

Il y a des plumes sur la table.	There are pens on the table.
Voilà les plumes, sur la table !	There are the pens, on the table.

4. **Y avoir** also forms idiomatic expressions of *time* (reckoned backwards) and *distance* :

Ils sont arrivés il y a trois jours.	They came three days ago.
Il y avait trois jours que j'étais là.	I had been there three days.
Combien y a-t-il à la ville ?	How far is it to the city ?
Il y a dix milles d'ici à la ville.	It is ten miles from here to the city.

331. Falloir = 'be necessary,' expresses the various meanings of 'must,' 'be obliged to,' 'have to,' 'need,' as follows:

1. 'Must' + *infinitive* = **falloir** + **que** *and subjunctive:*

Il faut que je parte. — I must go.
Il faudra que vous restiez. — You will have to (be obliged to) stay.

2. Or the *subject* of 'must,' etc., if a *personal pronoun*, becomes *indirect object* of **falloir** + infinitive:

Il me faudrait rester. — I should be obliged to remain.
Il leur faut faire cela. — They must do that.
Il lui a fallu parler. — He was forced (obliged) to speak.

3. The *infinitive* construction *without indirect object* is used in *general* or *indefinite* statement:

Il faut faire son devoir. — One must do one's duty.
Il ne faut pas voler. — We must not steal.

4. **Falloir** + *indirect object* and a *substantive* signifies *lack, need:*

Il faut une ardoise à Jean. — John needs a slate.
Il leur faudra cent francs. — They will need a hundred francs.

5. **S'en falloir** = 'lack':

Il s'en faut de beaucoup que l'un vaille l'autre. — The one is not nearly so good as the other.

332. Other Impersonals. 1. Besides **faire** and **avoir**, already noted, many other verbs take a special meaning as impersonals:

De quoi s'agit-il ? — What is the matter ?
Il est souvent arrivé que, etc. — It has often happened that, etc.
Il vaudra mieux ne rien dire. — It will be better to say nothing.
Il y va de ses jours. — His life is at stake.
Il se peut que je me trompe. — It may be that I am mistaken.

Obs.: Compare the literal meanings: **Agir**, *act*, **arriver**, *arrive*, **valoir**, *be worth*, **aller**, *go*, **pouvoir**, *be able*.

2. Many verbs may stand in the 3rd sing. with impersonal **il** *representing a logical subject* (sing. or plur.) following the verb:

Il viendra un meilleur temps. — There will come a happier time.
Il en reste trois livres. — There remain three pounds of it.
Il est arrivé des messagers. — Messengers have arrived.

333. Omission of *il*. Il is *understood* in certain phrases, such as:

Reste à savoir.	It remains to be seen.
N'importe.	No matter (it matters not).
Mieux vaut tard que jamais.	Better late than never.

LESSON XLIX.

Il fait obscur. } Il fait noir.	It is dark.
Il se fait tard.	It is getting late.
Il fait jour.	It is day (daylight).
Il fait du soleil.	The sun is shining.
Il fait du brouillard.	It is foggy.
Il fait bon.	It is comfortable (pleasant).
Il tombe de la neige.	It is snowing.
Il fait doux.	It is mild.

1. If the weather is fine, we shall go for a row this afternoon. 2. It was raining this morning, but now the sun is shining. 3. It is not comfortable here; let us go out for a walk. 4. It is getting late; let us go home. 5. It was raining last evening, then it froze, and now it is slippery. 6. It is not comfortable in those countries where it is very *(faire beaucoup de)* foggy. 7. It is too windy; we shall not go for a row. 8. It is getting late; the children will have to go to bed. 9. What time is it? 10. I do not know, but it is already daylight. 11. Is it? Well then, we shall have to get up immediately. 12. It had been snowing for two days, and we couldn't go for a drive. 13. It has been raining since yesterday morning, and it will be better to remain here. 14. My sister is very ill; her life is at stake. 15. We cannot go away; it is raining. 16. No matter; I do not fear the rain. 17. How did you enjoy yourself yesterday? 18. We did not enjoy ourselves at all; it was raining all day. 19. If it is very dark this evening, we shall not go to see our friends. 20. Yes, it will be better to stay at home; we can easily amuse ourselves. 21. How long have you been in this city? 22. I came here three years ago. 23. What sort of weather will it be to-morrow? 24. I do not know; I am not a good judge of such things. 25. It has been raining for two days; we are tired of being here. 26. In winter it is generally mild in Italy, but it is often cold in Canada. 27. Those two men are disputing; what is the matter? 28. It is about *(s'agir de)* the price of a horse which one sold to the other. 29. It was very warm yesterday, but it rained in the night, and now it is very

comfortable. 30. I think (that) it will rain, but it may be that I am mistaken. 31. We need another house; this one is too small. 32. Their number is far from being complete. 33. Letters have come which tell us that there has been a great storm in the United States. 34. How far is it from Toronto to Montreal? 35. By the railroad it is three hundred and thirty-three miles.

The Indicative Mood.

334. The indicative is the mood of *assertion* (direct or indirect) and of *interrogation* (direct or indirect). It stands both in *principal* and in *subordinate* clauses (affirmative or negative):

Dieu créa le monde.	God created the world.
Moïse dit que Dieu créa le monde.	Moses says that God created the world.
Où allez-vous?	Where are you going?
Dites-moi où vous allez.	Tell me where you are going.
Je le ferais, si je pouvais.	I should do so, if I could.

NOTES.—1. It should be noted especially that the *indic.* is regularly the mood of *indirect discourse* and of '*if*' *clauses*. 2. When the verb of a subordinate clause is subjunctive, the mood is determined by the context and not simply by the fact that the clause is subordinate.

Tenses of the Indicative.

335. Periphrastic Forms. Such forms, so common in English, are not used in French:

Je parle.	I speak (am speaking, do speak).
Il a écrit.	He has written (has been writing).
Il disait.	He was saying (used to say, etc.).

336. Elliptical Forms. Ellipsis of part of a verb form is common in English; in French the form is either *fully given* or *entirely avoided*:

J'irai.—Moi, je n'irai pas.	I shall go.—I shall not (go).
Il a promis de venir, mais il n'est pas venu.	He promised to come, but he did not (come).
Il est venu.—Vraiment!	He has come.—Has he! (Indeed!).
Vous viendrez, n'est-ce pas?	You will come, will you not?
Il était sorti, n'est-ce pas?	He had gone out, had he not?

337. Present. The present tense is used :—

1. To denote what *is happening* (including the *habitual* and the *universally true*):

Je crois qu'il pleut. — I think that it is raining.
Il se lève toujours de bon matin. — He always rises early.
L'homme propose et Dieu dispose. — Man proposes and God disposes.

2. To denote what *has happened* and *still continues*, after **il y a... que, voici (voilà)... que, depuis, depuis quand?, depuis... que**:

Depuis quand attendez-vous ? — How long have you been waiting?
Il y a (*or* voici, voilà) trois jours que j'attends, *or* j'attends depuis trois jours. — I have waited (have been waiting) for three days.

Obs.: This idiom is always expressed in English by 'have,' 'have been,' etc.

3. Instead of a *past* tense in animated narrative :

La nuit approche, l'instant arrive, César se présente, etc. — Night draws on, the moment comes, Cæsar appears, etc.

a. This use is much commoner than in English, especially side by side with past tenses.

b. C'est... que + *a past tense* = 'was... that':

C'est là que je l'ai vu. — It was there that I saw him.

4. Instead of a *future* in familiar style :

Nous partons demain matin. — We go to-morrow morning.

5. As a *virtual future* after **si** = 'if':

Je serai content, si vous venez. — I shall be glad, if you (will) come.

338. Imperfect. The action (or state) denoted by the imperfect is in general viewed as being *in progress* (*i.e.*, as *contemporaneous, customary, continued,* etc.). It is used:—

1. To denote what *was happening*, when something else happened or was happening :

Il était nuit, quand je sortis. — It was night, when I went out.
Il parlait, pendant que je chantais. — He was talking, while I sang.

2. To denote what *used to happen* :

Il se levait de bon matin. — He used to rise early.
Je parlais souvent de cela. — I often spoke (used to speak, would speak) of that.
Les Romains brûlaient leurs morts. — The Romans were accustomed to burn their dead.

3. To denote what *continued to happen*:

Son père était négociant et demeurait dans cette rue.	His father was a merchant and lived in this street.

4. To denote what *had happened* and *still continued*, after **il y a... que, voici (voilà)... que, depuis, depuis quand?, depuis... que** (cf. §337, 2):

Je le disais depuis longtemps.	I had long been saying so.
Voilà un an que je le disais.	I had been saying so for a year.

5. In *indirect discourse*, after a past tense, *instead of* the *present*:

Je croyais qu'il revenait.	I thought he was coming back.
Je demandai où il était.	I asked where he was.
But: " Où est-il ? ", demandai-je.	" Where is he ? ", I asked.

6. Regularly in an 'if' *clause* when the 'result' *clause* is *conditional*:

S'il venait, je serais content.	If he came, I should be glad.

7. Occasionally, instead of the *plupf.* and the *condl. ant.* in conditional sentences:

Si je ne l'arrêtais pas (=avais pas arrêté), il tombait (=serait tombé) du wagon.	Had I not stopped him he would have fallen from the train.

8. Sometimes instead of the *past def.* (§340):

La lecture finie, le père Alphée se dressait, marchait à grands pas, voilà s'écriait-il, etc.	The reading concluded, father Alpheus rose, walked about with great strides, there cried he, etc.

a. This use renders the narrative especially graphic and vivid.

339. Past Indefinite. The past indefinite is used:—

1. To denote what *has happened* or *has been happening* (= English tense with 'have,' reference to the present being implied):

J'ai fini mon ouvrage.	I have finished my work.
L'avez-vous vu dernièrement ?	Have you seen him lately ?
Je l'ai souvent rencontré.	I have often met him.
J'ai chanté toute la matinée.	I have been singing all morning.

2. To denote what *happened* (= English *past tense*, no reference to the present being implied):

Ils sont arrivés ce soir.	They arrived this evening.
Je l'ai vu il y a dix ans.	I saw him ten years ago.
De quoi est-il mort ?	What did he die of ?

a. This is the ordinary past tense of *conversation* (including narrative in conversation), *correspondence*, etc. It is also a very common past tense of *newspaper narrative style*, interchangeably with the past def. (§341, 3).

b. A historical statement of *detached fact*, of which the time is *unspecified*, is very commonly in the *past indef.* :

Morse a inventé le télégraphe.	The telegraph was invented by Morse.
Troie a été détruite par les Grecs.	Troy was destroyed by the Greeks.

3. Occasionally instead of a *future anterior :*

Attendez, j'ai bientôt fini.	Wait, I shall have finished soon.

340. Past Definite. The past definite is used in the *literary narrative style* to denote a *past event* or *a succession of such past events as mark the progress of the narrative*; it answers the question 'what happened?', or 'what happened next?' :

Dieu créa le monde.	God created the world.
La guerre dura sept ans.	The war lasted seven years.
On força le palais, les scélérats n'osèrent pas résister longtemps et ne songèrent qu'à fuir. Astarbé voulut se sauver dans la foule, mais un soldat la reconnut ; elle fut prise.	They broke into the palace, the villains did not dare to resist long, and only thought of fleeing. Astarbé tried to escape in the crowd, but a soldier recognized her ; she was captured.

a. Some verbs have a special force in the past def. :

Avoir ; j'eus.	To have ; I received.
Savoir ; je sus.	To know ; I found out (learned).
Connaître ; je connus.	To know ; I realized.

341. Examples of Narrative. The following examples illustrate the principal uses of the *past def., impf., past indef.*, and *historical present*, in narration:

1. Les Turcs, qui cependant entouraient cette maison tout embrasée, voyaient avec une admiration mêlée d'épouvante que les Suédois n'en sortaient point ; mais leur étonnement fut encore plus grand lorsqu'ils virent ouvrir les portes, et le roi et les siens fondre sur eux en désespérés. Charles et ses principaux officiers étaient armés d'épées et de pistolets :

chacun **tira** deux coups à la fois à l'instant que la porte **s'ouvrit**; et dans le même clin d'œil, jetant leurs pistolets et s'armant de leurs épées, ils **firent** reculer les Turcs plus de cinquante pas; mais le moment d'après cette petite troupe **fut** entourée: le roi, qui était en bottes selon sa coutume, **s'embarrassa** dans ses éperons, et **tomba**; vingt et un janissaires **se jettent** aussitôt sur lui : il **jette** en l'air son épée pour s'épargner la douleur de la rendre ; les Turcs l'**emmènent** au quartier du bacha.—*Voltaire.*

2. Stanislas se **déroba** un jour à dix heures du soir de l'armée suédoise, qu'il **commandait** en Poméranie, et **partit** avec le baron Sparre, qui a été depuis ambassadeur en Angleterre et en France, et avec un autre colonel : il **prend** le nom d'un Français, nommé Haran, alors major au service de Suède, et qui est mort depuis commandant de Dantzick.—*Voltaire.*

3. LONDRES, 5 août.—Hier soir, à onze heures et demie, un incendie a **éclaté** dans l'atelier de composition de la *National Press Agency.*

Plusieurs pompes à vapeur **arrivèrent** immédiatement sur le lieu du sinistre, et l'incendie **s'étendit** avec une telle rapidité, que toute la maison a été complètement détruite.

Il n'y a pas eu d'accidents de personnes.—*Le Matin.*

342. Pluperfect and Past Anterior. 1. Both denote what *had happened*, like the Eng. plupf. :

Lorsque je l'**avais** (**eus**) fini.   When I had finished it.

2. The *plupf.* is of much *commoner occurrence* than the past ant., and can alone be used after **si** = 'if,' or when *custom, continuance,* etc., is implied (cf. §338):

Si je l'**avais** vu, je l'aurais dit.   Had I seen it, I should have said so.
J'**avais** toujours **fini** avant midi.   I always had finished before noon.

3. The *past anterior* denotes what *had happened immediately before another event.* It is rarely used except after conjunctions of time, such as **lorsque, quand, après que, aussitôt que, ne ... pas plus tôt ... que,** etc. :

Après qu'il **eut dîné**, il partit.   After he had dined, he set out.

343. Future. The *future* is used :—
1. To denote what *will happen :*

Ils **viendront** demain.   They will come to-morrow.
Je les **verrai** bientôt.   I shall see them soon.
Je ne sais pas s'il **viendra**.   I know not whether he will come.

a. Distinguish Eng. 'will' of *futurity* from 'will' of *volition* and from 'will' of *habitual* action:

Il ne restera pas.	He will not stay.
Il ne veut pas rester.	He will not stay.
Ce chasseur reste souvent au bois pendant des mois entiers.	That hunter will often remain whole months in the woods.

b. Observe the following commonly occurring forms:

Ne voulez-vous pas rester?	Will you not stay?
Je ne resterai pas.	I shall not stay.

2. Regularly in a subordinate clause of *implied futurity:*

Payez-le, quand il viendra.	Pay him, when he comes.
Faites comme vous voudrez.	Do as you please.
Tant que je vivrai.	As long as I live.

3. To denote *probability, supposition,* etc.:

Il sera malade.	I suppose (no doubt) he is ill.

4. Sometimes with *imperative* force:

Tu ne tueras point.	Thou shalt not kill.
Vous voudrez m'écouter.	Be good enough to hear me.

a. This use is common in *official* style (edicts, etc.).

344. Future Anterior. The *future anterior* is used:—

1. To denote what *will have happened:*

Il aura bientôt fini.	He will soon have done.

2. To denote *implied futurity* (cf. §343, 2) and *probability,* etc. (cf. §343, 3):

Quand vous serez rentré, je sortirai.	When you have come home, I shall go out.
Je me serai trompé.	I must have made a mistake.

345. Conditional. 1. The main use of the *conditional* is to denote *result dependent on condition, i.e.,* what *would happen* in case something else *were to happen:*

Je serais content, s'il venait.	I should be glad, if he came.

a. The condition on which the result would depend is often merely *implied,* but not formally stated:

Hésiter serait une faiblesse.	To hesitate would be weakness.

b. Distinguish Eng. 'should' of *duty*, etc., 'would' of *volition*, and 'would' of *past habit* from condl. 'should' and 'would.'

Je devrais partir.	I should (ought to) set out.
Il ne voulait pas écouter.	He would not listen.
J'allais souvent le voir.	I would often go to see him.

2. It corresponds to an Eng. *past* in a subordinate clause of *implied futurity* (cf.§343, 2):

Je prendrais ce qui resterait.	I should take what remained.

3. It stands for the *fut.* in *indirect discourse:*

Je croyais qu'il pleuvrait.	I thought it would rain.
A-t-il dit s'il le ferait ?	Did he say whether he would do so ?
But: 'Je le ferai,' dit-il.	'I shall do so,' said he.

4. It is used in statement or request expressed with *deference* or *reserve:*

Je le croirais au moins.	I should think so at least.
Auriez-vous la bonté d'aller ?	Would you have the kindness to go ?
Cela ne serait jamais vrai.	That never could (can) be true.
Je ne saurais vous le dire.	I cannot tell you.

5. It sometimes denotes *probability, supposition,* etc., in exclamations and questions (cf.§343, 3):

Serait-il vrai qu'il l'a dit ?	Can it be true that he said so ?
Serait-il possible ?	Can (could) it be possible ?

6. It sometimes denotes *concession* after **quand, quand même,** or with **que**:

Quand (même) il me tuerait, etc.	Even if he should kill me, etc.
Vous me le jureriez que je ne vous croirais pas.	Even if you swore it to me, I should not believe you.

7. It is used to give the substance of *hearsay information:*

À ce qu'on dit, le roi serait malade.	By what they say, the king is ill.

346. Conditional Anterior. Its uses are precisely parallel with those of the conditional (§345); it denotes what *would have happened*, etc., etc.:

Je serais sorti, s'il était venu.	I should have gone out, had he come.
Je reviendrais dès que je l'aurais vu.	I should return when I had seen him.
Selon les journaux, la guerre se serait déclarée hier soir.	According to the newspapers, war was declared last evening.

347. Imperative Mood. It is used in general as in English:—

Lisez-le. Ne le lisez pas.	Read it. Do not read it.
Allons-nous-en à présent.	Let us go away now.
Veuillez m'écouter.	Be good enough to hear me.

a. The *1st plur.* sometimes serves *instead* of the lacking *1st sing.*:

Soyons digne de ma naissance.	Let me be worthy of my birth.
Pensons un moment.	Let me think a moment.

b. The imperatives **va, allons, allez, voyons** often have special idiomatic force:

Allons donc! Allons, du courage!	Nonsense! Come, courage!
J'en suis content, allez!	I am glad of it, I can assure you!
Voyons, que pensez-vous?	Come now, what do you think?

c. An *imperat. perfect* is *rare:*

Ayez fini votre tâche ce soir.	Have your task done to-night.

EXERCISE L.

C'est à peine s'il sort à présent.	He hardly ever goes out now.
À peine le soleil fut-il (était-il) levé, qu'on aperçut 'ennemi.	Hardly was the sun up, when the enemy was seen.
Il fait bon marcher.	{ The walking is good. { It is good walking.

1. When that man is working, he will often stop to *(pour)* speak with his companions. 2. How long have you been reading? 3. I have been reading for an hour. 4. It was at your house that we met those gentlemen. 5. We shall be glad, if you are there. 6. We shall be glad, when you are there. 7. We often used to go for a walk, when we lived at your house, but here it is not good walking, so we hardly ever go out now. 8. When we were young, our mother would often tell us fairy stories which interested us very much. 9. We remember them yet, and we hope (that) we shall never forget them. 10. I had been there ten days, when he came. 11. He had been reading an hour, before his sister rose. 12. He asked me where I came from, and where I was going. 13. I answered him that I came from Montreal, and (that I) was going to Hamilton. 14. He wrote me a letter saying that he wished to see me. 15. He said in his letter that he had been ill, but that he was better now. 16. When he lived with us, we would often go out for a walk before breakfast. 17. The eldest of the miller's sons received the mill, but the youngest received only the cat. 18. As soon as he learned that I was to go out for a walk, he wished to go also. 19. If he had

seen it, he would have told me (it). 20. When I had finished my lessons, I would always go out for a walk. 21. When he had finished his dinner to-day, he went out. 22. Hardly had he finished his work, when his friend came. 23. We do not know whether our friends will come. 24. Our father did not know whether he would come. 25. Why is that work not done? 26. I told my brother to *(de)* do it, but he will not do it. 27. Will you buy my horse? 28. No, I shall not buy him; I do not need him. 29. Good morning, gentlemen, will you walk in? 30. No thank you, we shall not go in. 31. As long as we live, we shall not forget your kindness. 32. As soon as he comes, I shall tell him. 33. We shall do as we please. 34. You may start when you will. 35. He may come when he likes.

EXERCISE LI.

1. We shall soon have finished our work. 2. When you have finished your lesson, you may go out for a walk. 3. Everybody should learn the ten commandments. 4. They tell us: Thou shalt not *(point)* have any other gods. 5. Thou shalt not take the name of thy God in vain. 6. Thou shalt not steal *(dérober)*. 7. That poor child is very weak; it can hardly walk; it must have been ill. 8. My brother told me that you were not well. 9. You must have made a mistake, for I am very well; I never was better in *(de)* my life. 10. We should be sorry, if you should do so. 11. You should be virtuous, if you wish to be happy. 12. I told him (that) he ought to obey his teacher, but he would not listen to me. 13. Men should love their enemies, but generally they do not. 14. The little boy must have broken that stick; I saw him there. 15. I often used to go to see him, when he lived in our city. 16. He says (that) it will rain. 17. He said (that) it would rain. 18. Can it be possible that my father's watch is stolen (use: *on*)? 19. I could do that, if I wished. 20. I could do that, when I was young. 21. Could you tell me where *le Boulevard des Italiens* is? 22. I could not tell you (it): I have not been long in Paris. 23. Can it be true that he has done that? 24. One would think that you were [a] Parisian, you speak French so well. 25. Even if that were true, I should not go. 26. Even if it should not rain, I shall not go for a drive. 27. According to the newspapers, a great quantity of money was stolen (use: *on*). 28. By what he says, his neighbors are poor. 29. When I was in Europe, I saw a horse as big as an elephant. 30. Nonsense! You are joking. 31. Come! Come! (my) children, you are making too much noise. 32. Let us go away. 33. Go away. 34. I did not think he would know it. 35. If you will not do it, we shall not do it.

EXERCISE LII.

(On the Imperfect and Past Definite.)

The two kings *met* (each other) on the 13th of July in a vast plain between Warsaw *(Varsovie)* and Cracow *(Cracovie)*. Augustus *had* nearly twenty-four thousand men; Charles *had* only ten thousand. At the first volley, the Duke of Holstein, who *commanded* the Swedish cavalry, *received* a cannon-shot in the back. The king *asked* if he *was* dead: he *was told* (use: on) that he was *(que oui)*: he *made* no reply; (some) tears *fell* from his eyes; he *(se) hid* his *(le)* face [for] a moment with his *(les)* hands; then he *rushed* into the midst of the enemy at the head of his guards.

The king of Poland *did* all that one *should* expect from a prince who *was fighting* for his crown; he himself *brought back* his troops three times to the charge; but he *fought* with his Saxons only; the Poles, who *formed* his right wing, *fled* at the beginning of the battle. Charles *won* a complete victory. He *did* not *stay* on the field of battle, but *(et) marched* direct to Cracow, pursuing the king of Poland, who *kept fleeing* before him.

THE SUBJUNCTIVE MOOD.

348. The subjunctive denotes, in general, what is viewed as being *desirable* or *undesirable, uncertain, contingent*, etc., and usually stands in a subordinate clause.

349. Subjunctive in Noun Clause. The subjunctive is used in a clause introduced by **que** and serving as *logical subject* or as *object* of a verb:—

1. After expressions of *desiring* (including willing, wishing, preferring) and *avoiding:*

Je désire (veux) qu'il parte.	I desire (wish) him to go.
Je souhaite qu'il ait du succès.	I wish that he may have success.
Il préfère que vous restiez.	He prefers that you should stay.
Évitez qu'il ne vous voie.	Avoid his seeing you.

Such are:

aimer, *like.*	éviter, *avoid.*	il me tarde, *I long.*
aimer mieux, *prefer.*	préférer, *prefer.*	vouloir, *will, wish.*
avoir envie, *be desirous.*	prendre garde, *take care (lest).*	etc.
désirer, *desire, wish.*	souhaiter, *wish.*	

a. **Prendre garde** requires **ne** in the subj. clause; so also, **éviter** generally.

Prends garde que cela ne se fasse.   Take care lest that happen.

2. After expressions of *commanding* (including requesting, exhorting), *forbidding, consenting:*

Vous **ordonnez** que j'aille.	You order me to go.
Je **demande** que vous me payiez.	I ask that you should pay me.
Dis-leur qu'ils soient prêts.	Tell them to be ready.
Le médecin **défend** que je sorte.	The doctor forbids me to go out.
Je **consens** que cela se fasse.	I consent that that be done.

Such are:

admettre, *admit*.	demander, *ask*.	permettre, *permit*.
agréer, *permit*.	empêcher, *hinder*.	prier, *beg, ask*.
avoir soin, *take care*.	exhorter, *exhort*.	souffrir, *suffer*.
conjurer, *implore*.	exiger, *exact*.	supplier, *beg, pray*.
consentir, *consent*.	laisser, *allow*.	trouver naturel, *find natural*.
convenir, *agree*.	s'opposer, *oppose*.	veiller, *take care*
défendre, *forbid*.	ordonner, *order*.	etc.

So also, **dire**, *tell*, **écrire**, *write*, **entendre**, *mean*, **prétendre**, *intend*, when denoting *command*.

a. The *fut.* or *condl.* often stands after **commander, ordonner, convenir**:

La cour **ordonne** qu'il payera.   The court orders him to pay.

b. The *indic.* regularly stands after verbs of *decision* or *decree* (**décider**, *decide*, **arrêter**, **décréter**, *decree*, **régler**, *ordain*, etc.):

Le roi **décrète** qu'il sera pendu. The king decrees that he shall be hanged.

c. The subjunctive after **empêcher** usually has **ne**:

Empêchez qu'il ne sorte.   Prevent his going out.

3. After expressions of *judgment* or *opinion* involving *approval* or *disapproval:*

J'**approuve** qu'il revienne.	I approve of his coming back.
Il **mérite** qu'on le craigne.	He deserves to be feared.
Il **vaut mieux** que vous **restiez**.	It is better for you to stay.
Il **faudra** qu'il **parte** demain.	He will have to go to-morrow.

Such are:

approuver, *approve*.	être indigne, *be unworthy*.	trouver mauvais, *disapprove*.
avoir intérêt, *be interested*.	juger à propos, *think fit*.	trouver juste, *think just*.
blâmer, *blame*.	louer, *praise*.	trouver injuste, *think unjust*.
désapprouver, *disapprove*.	mériter, *deserve*.	valoir, *be worthy*.
être d'avis, *be of opinion*.	tenir (à ce que), *insist*.	etc.
être digne, *be worthy*.	trouver bon, *approve*.	

So also, a large number of *impersonals* of like force:

THE SUBJUNCTIVE MOOD.

il convient, *it is fitting*.
c'est assez, *it is enough*.
il est, *it is*....
+à propos, *proper*.
+bien, *well*.
+bon, *good*.
+convenable, *fitting*.
+essentiel, *essential*.
+à désirer, *to be desired*.
+facile, *easy*.
+important, *important*.
+indispensable, *indispensable*.
+juste, *just*.
+naturel, *natural*.
+nécessaire, *necessary*.
+à souhaiter, *to be wished*.
+(tout) simple, *(quite) simple*.
+temps, *time*.
il faut, *it is necessary, must*.
il importe, *it is important*.
il peut se faire, *it may be*.
il suffit, *it suffices*.
il vaut mieux, *it is better*.
etc., and their opposites.

4. After expressions of *emotion* or *sentiment*, such as *joy, sorrow, anger, shame, wonder, fear*:

Êtes-vous content qu'il soit ici?	Are you glad he is here?
Je regrette qu'il soit parti.	I regret that he has gone.
Il est fâché que vous le blâmiez.	He is angry that you blame him.
Il a honte que vous le sachiez.	He is ashamed that you know it.
Je m'étonne qu'il n'ait pas honte.	I wonder he is not ashamed.
J'ai peur qu'il n'ait trop dit.	I fear he has said too much.

Such are:

admirer, *be astonished*.
s'affliger, *grieve*.
avoir honte, *be ashamed*.
avoir crainte, *fear*.
avoir peur, *fear*.
craindre, *fear*.
déplorer, *deplore*.
c'est, *it is*...
+un bonheur, *fortunate*.
+dommage, *a pity*.
+une honte, *a shame*.
+honteux, *a shame*.
+pitié, *a pity*.
il est, *it is*...
+curieux, *strange*.
+étonnant, *astonishing*.
+fâcheux, *annoying*.
+heureux, *fortunate*.
enrager, *be enraged*.
s'étonner, *be astonished*.
être, *be*...
+affligé, *grieved*.
+bien aise, *very glad*.
+charmé, *delighted*.
+content, *glad*.
+désolé, *very sorry*.
+étonné, *astonished*.
+fâché, *sorry, angry*.
+heureux, *happy*.
+indigné, *indignant*.
+joyeux, *glad*.
+mécontent, *displeased*.
+satisfait, *satisfied*.
+surpris, *surprised*.
+triste, *sad*.
se fâcher, *be sorry, angry*.
se plaindre, *complain*.
redouter, *fear*.
regretter, *regret*.
se réjouir, *rejoice*.
se repentir, *repent*.
rougir, *blush*.
soupirer, *sigh*.
trembler, *tremble*.
etc.

a. When it is *feared* something *will happen* the subj. has ne; when it is feared something *will not happen* the subj. has ne... pas; when the expression of fearing is *neg., interrog., condl.*, ne is usually *omitted*; with *double negation* ne... pas stands in both:

Je crains qu'il ne vienne.	I fear he will come.
Je crains qu'il ne vienne pas.	I fear he will not come.
Je ne crains pas qu'il vienne.	I do not fear he will come.
Craignez-vous qu'il vienne?	Do you fear he will come?
Ne craignez-vous pas qu'il ne vienne.	Do you not fear he will come?
Si je craignais qu'il vînt.	If I feared he would come.
Je ne crains pas qu'il ne vienne pas.	I do not fear he will not come.

b. After expressions of *emotion* or *sentiment* (except *fear*), which admit de after them, **de ce que** + *indic.* may be used :

J'ai honte de ce qu'il a échoué. I am ashamed that he failed.

5. After expressions of *doubt, denial, despair, ignorance* or very *slight probability:*

Il doute que je sois loyal. He doubts that (whether) I am honest.
Je nie que cela soit vrai. I deny that that is true.
Il est rare que vous ayez tort. You are rarely in the wrong.

Such are :

contester, *dispute.*	+faux, *false.*	de (à) quoi sert-il ?, *of what use is it ?*
désespérer, *despair.*	+impossible, *impossible.*	il ne sert de (à) rien, *it is of no use.*
disconvenir, *deny.*	+possible, *possible.*	
dissimuler, *not confess.*	+rare, *rare.*	
se dissimuler, *be hidden.*	il s'en faut, *there is wanting.*	il se peut, *it may be.*
douter, *doubt.*	ignorer, *not know.*	il ne se peut pas, *it cannot be.*
il est, *it is* . . .	nier, *deny.*	il semble, *it seems.*
+douteux, *doubtful.*		etc.

a. **Il semble** regularly has the *subj.*, since it indicates *slight probability* as distinguished from **Il paraît** = 'it appears,' 'is evident,' and **Il me semble** = 'it appears to me' (personal conviction) :

Il semble que vous me craigniez. It seems that you fear me.
Il me semble (il paraît) que vous me craignez. It seems to me (it appears) that you fear me.

b. Verbs of *doubt* and *denial* used *negatively* or *interrogatively* regularly require ne in the subj. clause :

Je ne nie pas que je ne le sois. I do not deny that I am such.

c. **Ignorer** + *negative* = 'know well,' and hence takes *indic.* :

Je n'ignore pas qu'il a menti. I know well he has lied.

NOTE.—**Peut-être que,** *perhaps,* and **sans doute que,** *doubtless,* require the *indic.*

6. After expressions of *perceiving, thinking, knowing, declaring, resulting,* but *only* when *uncertainty* or *doubt* is implied by *negation, interrogation,* or *condition ;* otherwise the *indic.* :

Verra-t-on que j'aie pleuré ? Will they see that I have wept ?
Je ne crois pas que ce soit lui. I do not think that that is he.
Espérez-vous qu'il réussisse ? Do you hope he will succeed ?
Je ne suis pas sûr qu'il vienne. I am not sure he will come.
Si je prétendais qu'il eût tort. If I claimed that he was wrong.
But : Je crois que c'est lui. I think it is he.
   J'espère qu'il réussira. I hope he will succeed.

Such are:

affirmer, *affirm.*	espérer, *hope.*	prévoir, *foresee.*
s'apercevoir, *perceive.*	être certain, *be certain.*	promettre, *promise.*
apprendre, *learn, hear.*	être persuadé, *be persuaded.*	se rappeler, *recollect.*
assurer, *assure.*	être sûr, *be sure.*	reconnaître, *acknowledge.*
s'attendre, *expect.*	se figurer, *imagine.*	remarquer, *remark.*
avertir, *warn.*	se flatter, *flatter one's self.*	répéter, *repeat.*
avouer, *declare.*	imaginer, *imagine.*	répondre, *answer.*
conclure, *conclude.*	s'imaginer, *imagine.*	savoir, *know.*
connaître, *recognize.*	juger, *judge, think.*	sentir, *feel, notice.*
croire, *believe, think.*	jurer, *declare.*	soutenir, *maintain.*
déclarer, *declare.*	oublier, *forget.*	se souvenir, *recollect.*
deviner, *guess.*	penser, *think.*	supposer, *suppose.*
dire, *say, tell.*	persuader, *persuade.*	trouver, *find, think.*
se douter, *suspect.*	pressentir, *forebode.*	voir, *see.*
écrire, *write.*	prétendre, *assert, claim.*	etc.
entendre dire, *hear said.*	prévenir, *forewarn.*	

So also, a number of *impersonals* of like force :

il s'ensuit, *it follows.*	+évident, *evident.*	+sûr, *sure.*
il est avéré, *it is stated.*	+démontré, *demonstrated.*	+vraisemblable, *probable.*
il est, *it is* . . .	+incontestable, *indisputable.*	il résulte, *it follows.*
+certain, *certain.*	+probable, *probable.*	il me semble, *it seems to me.*
+clair, *clear.*		

a. Negative question usually implies *affirmation*; hence the *indic.*:

Ne trouves-tu pas qu'il est beau? Don't you think he is handsome?

b. When what the speaker regards as *fact* follows the negative or conditional clause, or when a person is questioned as to his *knowledge of* what is regarded as *fact*, the *indic.* stands :

Il ne croit pas qu'il y a un Dieu. He does not believe there is a God.
S'il savait que tu es ici. If he knew you were here.
Savez-vous qu'il est arrivé? Do you know that he has come?

c. Il me semble + *negation* has *subj.*; with *interrogation* + *negation* the *indic.*:

Il ne me semble pas qu'il soit fou. It does not seem to me he is mad.
Ne vous semble-t-il pas qu'il est fou? Does it not seem to you he is mad?

d. A *preceding dependent clause* with this class of verbs always has the *subj.*:

Qu'il ait échoué, je le sais. That he has failed, I know.

NOTE.—For the choice between que clause and infin. see §302.

350. Subjunctive in Adjectival Clause. The subjunctive is used as follows in clauses introduced by a *relative pronoun* :—

1. When *purpose* or *unattained result* is expressed:

Montrez-moi un chemin qui conduise à la science. — Show me a way which leads to knowledge.

a. The *indic.*, however, is used to express what is regarded as *fact* or *certain result*:

Montrez-moi le chemin qui conduit à la ville. — Show me the road which leads to the town.

J'irai où je serai libre. — I shall go where I shall be free.

2. When the principal clause contains *general negation, interrogation implying negative answer,* or *condition* (all of which imply *non-existence* of the antecedent):

Il n'a pas de raison qui vaille. — He has no reason worth anything.
As-tu un seul ami qui soit fidèle? — Have you one friend who is true?
Si j'ai un ami qui soit fidèle c'est lui. — If I have one friend who is true, it is he.

a. General negation is sometimes merely *implied*:

Il y a peu de gens qui le sachent. — There are few people who know it.

b. When the negation is *not general* or when the *interrog.* does *not imply negative answer,* the *indic.* stands:

Ce n'est pas vous que je crains. — It is not you that I fear.
N'est-ce point un songe que je vois! — Is it not a dream that I see!

c. In a *negative relat.* clause ne (*not* 'ne … pas') is used when the principal clause is *negative* or implies negation:

Est-il un seul qui ne tremble? — Is there one who does not tremble?

3. After an *expression of opinion* containing a *superlative* or **seul, unique, premier, dernier** (all with superlative force):

C'est le meilleur ami que j'aie. — He is the best friend that I have.
C'est le seul ami que j'aie. — He is the only friend I have.

a. What is stated *unreservedly* as *fact* requires the *indic.*:

C'est la seule chose qu'il a dite. — It is the only thing he said.

4. With *concessive* force in *compound relat.* and *indefinite* clauses (= 'whoever,' 'whatever,' etc.):

Quoi que vous fassiez. — Whatever you do.
Qui qu'on y puisse élire. — Whomsoever may be elected to it.
Qui que tu sois, parle. — Whoever you are, speak?
Quelles que soient vos raisons. — Whatever be your reasons.

THE SUBJUNCTIVE MOOD.

351. Subjunctive in Adverbial Clause. The subjunctive is used in clauses of adverbial force, as follows:—

1. After conjunctions of *time before which* or *up to which* (avant que, en attendant que, jusqu'à ce que):

Dis-le-lui, avant qu'il parte.	Tell it to him, before he goes.
Asseyez-vous, en attendant qu'il revienne.	Sit down until he comes back.
J'attendis jusqu'à ce qu'il revînt.	I waited till he returned.

a. Jusqu'à ce que may have the *indic.*, when referring to *completed past event:*

Il resta jusqu'à ce que j'y étais.	He waited till I was there.

2. After conjunctions of *purpose* or *result* (afin que, pour que, de crainte que, de peur que):

J'écris ceci afin que (pour que) vous sachiez la vérité.	I write this in order that you may know the truth.
Je le tins de crainte qu'il ne tombât.	I held him for fear he would fall.

a. So also, de sorte que, en sorte que, de telle sorte que, de façon que, de manière que, tel ... que, tellement ... que, when denoting *purpose* (but *not* result):

Agis de sorte que tu réussisses.	Act in such a way as to succeed.
But: J'agis de sorte que j'ai réussi.	I acted so that I succeeded.

3. After conjunctions of *condition* (en cas que, au cas que, à moins que ... ne, pourvu que, supposé que, en supposant que):

Je viendrai au cas que je sois libre demain, ou à moins que je ne sois retenu.	I shall come in case I am free tomorrow, or unless I am detained.

a. After si = 'if,' the *plupf. subj.* stands *exceptionally* (§355, *b*).

b. À (la) condition que takes *indic. or subj.*:

Je lui donne l'argent à (la) condition qu'il partira (*or* parte).	I give him the money on condition that he will go.

NOTE.—Dans le cas où, au cas où usually have *condl.*: 'Au cas où cela serait vrai,' 'In case that should be true.'

4. After conjunctions of *concession* (quoique, bien que, encore que, nonobstant que, soit que ... soit que *or*

ou que, pour (si) peu que, si tant est que, malgré que):—

Bien qu'il soit malade, il ira.	Although he is ill, he will go.
Pour peu qu'il fût malade, il se croyait mourant.	If he were ever so little ill, he thought himself dying.

a. The use of a *subj.* after adverbial quelque (tout, si, etc.)+que= 'however' depends on the same principle :

Quelque grand que vous soyez.	However great you may be.
Si brave qu'il se croie.	However brave he thinks himself.

b. **Quand** (même) *concessively* sometimes takes *plupf. subj.* for *condl. ant.* (cf. §345, 6):

Quand (même) il m'eût dit cela.   Even if he had told me that.

5. After conjunctions of *negative* force (**non que, non pas que, loin que, sans que**) :

Il partit sans que je le susse.   He went away without my knowing it.

6. After **que** *replacing* any *conjunction requiring* the *subj.*, and also after **que** *replacing* **si** = 'if' :

Venez que (=afin que, pour que) je vous voie.	Come, that I may see you.
Si je vais et que je le voie.	If I go, and if I see him.

352. Subjunctive in Principal Clause. The subjunctive is sometimes used in principal clauses, as follows :—

1. Either with or without **que** to denote what is *desired*, etc. :

Ainsi soit-il ! Vive le roi !	So be it ! (Long) live the king !
Plût à Dieu qu'il en fût ainsi !	Would to God it were so !
Qu'il parte tout de suite.	Let him go at once.
Je meure, si je mens !	May I die, if I am lying !
Le croie qui voudra !	Let him believe it who will !

a. **Que**+*3rd pers. pres. subj.* regularly serves as *impve.* ; so also, sometimes the *1st sing.* :

Qu'il parte.	Let him go.
Que je vous entende.	Let me hear you.

NOTE.—This construction, as also those without **que**, may be explained by ellipsis of some expression of *desire, command,* etc. (§349, 1, 2).

2. The *pres. subj. 1st sing.* of **savoir**, and sometimes of **se souvenir**, to denote *modified assertion:*

Je ne sache rien de plus beau.	I know nothing finer.
Il n'est pas là, que je sache.	He is not there, as far as I know.

Note.—**Sache** so used, and **vive** in **qui vive?** = 'who goes there?', are regarded by many as irreg. indic. forms.

3. The *plupf. subj.* stands exceptionally for *condl. ant.* in a 'result' *clause* and for the *plupf. indic.* in an 'if' *clause* (§355, *b*); also, sometimes after **quand même** in a *concessive* clause (cf. §351, 4, *b*).

a. The *pres. subj.* also sometimes expresses *condition* or *concession:*

Vienne l'ennemi, il s'enfuit.	If the enemy comes, he flees.
Qu'il perde ou gagne, il partira.	Though he lose or win, he will go.

353. Tense Sequence. The tense of the subjunctive is usually determined by the tense of the finite verb in the governing clause, as follows:—

1. A *present* (including *pres. subj.* and *impve.*) or a *future* in the governing clause requires the *pres. subj.* in the governed clause:

Je doute	⎫	I doubt that (whether) he will come.
Quoique je doute	⎪ qu'il vienne.	Though I doubt that he will come.
Doutez	⎬	Doubt that he will come.
Je douterai	⎭	I shall doubt that he will come.

2. Any other tense than the above (*i.e.*, an *impf., past def., condl.*, etc.) requires the *impf. subj.:*

Je doutais	⎫	I doubted that (whether) he would come.
Quoique je doutasse	⎪ qu'il vînt.	Though I doubted that he would come.
Je doutai	⎬	I doubted that he would come.
Je douterais	⎭	I should doubt that he would come.

3. Compound tenses follow the same rules, the *auxiliary being reckoned as the verb:*

Je doute (j'ai douté, quoique je doute, quoique j'aie douté, je douterai, j'aurai douté) qu'il vienne *or* soit venu.	I doubt (I have doubted, though I doubt, though I have doubted, I shall doubt, I shall have doubted) that he will come *or* has come.
Je doutais (j'avais douté, quoique je doutasse, je doutai, j'eus	I doubted (I had doubted, though I doubted, I doubted, I had doubted,

douté, quoique j'eusse douté, je | though I had doubted, I should
douterais, j'aurais douté) qu'il | doubt, I should have doubted) that
vînt *or* fût venu. | he would come *or* had come.

Obs.: As appears from the above, the subjunctive *simple* tenses express *uncompleted* event, and the *compound* tenses *completed* event, with reference to the time of the governing verb.

4. The following *exceptional cases* depend mainly on the sense of the context:

a. The sequence after the *past indef.* depends upon its value as a *past* or as a *present past* (§339, 1, 2):

J'ai douté qu'il vienne (soit v.). I have doubted that he will (has) c.
J'ai douté qu'il vînt (fût venu). I doubted that he would (had) come.

b. After verbs of *saying*, etc. (§349, 6), the *impf. subj.* may stand for the *perf.*:

Je ne dis pas qu'il fût à blâmer. I do not say he was to blame.

c. In a *relat. clause* a *perf.* may stand for a *plupf.*:

Il portait cet habit la seule fois | He was wearing that coat the only
que je l'aie vu. | time that I saw him.

d. The *condl.* of *modified assertion* (§345, 4), being virtually a *pres.*, is commonly followed by the *pres.* or *perf. subj.*:

Je désirerais que vous veniez. I should like you to come.
Il faudrait qu'il aille. He would have to go.

e. The *impf.* or *plupf.* subj. with the force of an Eng. *condl.* may follow *any tense:*

Il n'y a pas de rang qu'elle ne pût tenir. There is no rank she could not hold.
Je doute qu'il jouât (eût joué), | I doubt that he would play (would
s'il avait (avait eu) de l'argent. | have played), if he had (had had) money.

EXERCISE LIII.

Je tiens à ce que vous appreniez le latin. | I am (most) anxious that you shall learn Latin.
Nous n'aimerions pas qu'on se moquât de nous. | We should not like to be made sport of.
Il me tarde que cela soit fait. | I am longing for that to be done.
Je voudrais bien que vous le fassiez. | { I wish you would do it. / I should like you to do it.

1. Our teacher said that he wished us to write our exercise. 2. If you wish to go to the city, you may (*pouvoir*) go (there), but if you wish

us to go (there), we tell you plainly that we cannot. 3. I wish you to do your work before (the) breakfast. 4. Our friends wish us to stay with them this week. 5. My father is most anxious that I should learn French, but I don't like it. 6. Would you prefer that I should go to church this morning? 7. We should not like our friends to be made sport of. 8. You say that you are going into business with that man; take care lest he deceive you. 9. I am longing for my house to be finished. 10. I am anxious that he should come to see us, when he visits Toronto. 11. My teacher told me that I should write my exercise. 12. My father told me that he had seen you. 13. The law forbids that to be done. 14. These children must stay in; their parents have forbidden them to go out. 15. I shall give orders not to admit them (use: *on*). 16. I did not ask that I should be answered (use: *on*) before the others. 17. I shall avoid her speaking to me about it. 18. The doctor ordered that he should be given no wine. 19. We do not ask that you should pay the money. 20. The rain hinders people (*on*) from going out to-day. 21. I wish you to know that he is my friend. 22. You approve of my coming back, do you not? 23. Yes, I wish you had never gone away. 24. It is better for the children to go to school. 25. What shall I say to that man? He has insulted me. 26. That makes no difference, he is not worthy of being answered (use: *on*). 27. The doctor gave orders that my father should go out for a drive every day. 28. He has torn his book; he deserves to be punished (use: *on*). 29. I should like you to go for a walk with me. 30. Weakness often hinders good intentions from being fulfilled. 31. I long for his return. 32. There is no more bread; I should like you to go and get some. 33. That man is most anxious that his children should go to school, but he is too poor to (*pour*) buy them books. 34. Take care that the dog does not bite you; he is very cross. 35. That young man is not very amiable; we should not like him to treat us as he has treated his father.

EXERCISE LIV.

1. It is fitting that children should obey their parents. 2. It is good that men should sometimes undergo misfortunes. 3. It may be that he has returned, but I have not seen him. 4. It is natural that we should hate our enemies. 5. It is getting late; it is time that we should go home. 6. He had to learn French, for he lived in France. 7. We are very glad that you have come. 8. We are very sorry that you did not come. 9. I am surprised that he said so, because he told me that he would not say so. 10. It is a pity we cannot always be happy. 11. It is a shame for those young men to be so ignorant. 12. It is sad

that a man like him should be so poor. 13. I fear he will commit some crime, 14. I am glad you are so well, 15. I am afraid my father is not well enough to (*pour*) go with us. 16. I wonder he did not come last night. 17. I know why he did not come,; he was afraid it would rain. 18. He was not afraid it would rain; he was afraid a certain person would be there whom he did not wish to see. 19. I do not fear he will not go. 20. Are you not afraid he will be able to prevent your intentions from being fulfilled? 21. I doubt whether he will be able to come. 22. I do not deny that I am glad of your ill-fortune. 23. Do you doubt that he is an honest man? 24. Not at all; I know that he is an honest man; I have known him for twenty years. 25. I do not doubt that you will be able to fulfil all your intentions. 26. It seems he has not received [any] of my letters. 27. It cannot be that you are ignorant of his intentions. 28. How is your father? 29. He is very well; he is rarely ill. 30. It seems to me it will be dangerous if we do not follow his advice. 31. That child is afraid you will hurt him. 32. I am glad you did not hurt yourself, when you fell. 33. We regret very much that we did not see you, when you were in Paris. 34. Are you not afraid that you will tire of being in the country? 35. I am not afraid that I shall tire of being in the country.

EXERCISE LV.

1. Our neighbour is an honest man; I hope he will succeed. 2. I do not think he will succeed; he has not much ability. 3. We thought he would come to-day. 4. You told me that you did not think he would go away, did you not? 5. Do you think we must believe what he says? 6. It is probable that we shall go away to-morrow. 7. It is not certain that our friends will come to-morrow. 8. Is it probable that you will go away to-day? 9. We are sure that we saw them yesterday. 10. Are you not sure that you saw them yesterday? 11. Do you think your father will go to France this summer? 12. It is probable he will go there. 13. It is certain that all men will die. 14. Is it certain that our friends will be there this evening? 15. Is it not certain that your neighbour will buy your house? 16. Does he imagine we shall do that, merely to *(pour)* please him? 17. We are not sure that will please him. 18. Do you think you will go for a walk this evening? 19. Yes, I think I shall go out with my brother. 20. Give me the book which contains that beautiful story of which you were speaking. 21. Give me a book which contains some beautiful stories. 22. I should like to buy a house which would suit me better than this one. 23. I am looking for a grammar in which I can find better exercises.

24. I have a grammar which has better exercises. 25. Send me some clothes which I can wear in the house. 26. Has he a single friend who is true to him? 27. He has not a single friend who is true to him. 28. There is nobody here who can speak French. 29. I have nothing which is of value. 30. There are no houses here which are as large as those in the city. 31. There are few people here who have learned French. 32. It is the finest thing one can see. 33. That is the largest ship I have ever seen. 34. Whatever you do, you will not be able to persuade me that you are right. 35. Whoever you are, you will have to obey the laws, as long as you are in this country.

EXERCISE LVI.

Que veut-il dire?	What does he mean?
On se fie à lui.	{ Men trust him. { He is trusted.
Faites-moi savoir.	Send me word (let me know).
Je ne reçois plus de ses nouvelles.	I never hear from him now.
Il est très occupé.	He is very busy.
Il s'occupe de cela.	He takes an interest in that.

1. I have told him nothing which could influence him. 2. I know no book which pleases me better. 3. I want a house which will suit me better. 4. Mr. Jackson is the richest man I know. 5. However good men may be, they do not escape misfortune. 6. Let us go out for a walk before your father returns. 7. We rose this morning before the sun rose. 8. Will you not stay here until the weather is warm? 9. Oh, no; we must leave before it begins to be warm. 10. We are going to work until we go to bed. 11. You must always act so that men may respect you. 12. Tell the truth always, so that men may trust you. 13. He insulted me so that I put him out doors. 14. That gentleman made a speech, but he spoke in such a way that one could not tell what he meant. 15. I did not trust him, for fear that he might deceive me. 16. He passed our house, before we had finished our breakfast. 17. I explained it to him, for fear he might not know what you meant. 18. I cannot trust you, unless you explain to me what you mean. 19. In case you cannot come, will you be kind enough to send me word. 20. We shall send you our horses and carriage, in case you need them. 21. In case what he says is true, we shall send you word. 22. Although the children have gone to bed, they have not yet gone to sleep. 23. However little you may like that man, you must confess that he is an honest man. 24. Although we used to be good friends, I never hear from him now. 25. Not that he has forgotten me, but

he is so much occupied with his business. 26. Far from his saying that he hates you, I assure you that he will say he loves you. 27. He gave her the money without my knowing it. 28. Even if he had told me that he liked me, I should not have believed it. 29. Though Canada be less interesting than England, we love it better. 30. I cannot go out, without my dog following me. 31. If we are there and see him, we shall tell him what you say. 32. Although he is far away, I hear from him occasionally. 33. Not that we take no interest in your enterprise, but we are so busy with our own work that we can't think of anything else. 34. We are at the wrong door; would you be kind enough to tell us where we are, so that we can find where our friends live? 35. We shall rise early to-morrow morning, so as to be at the station before our friends start.

EXERCISE LVII.

1. Would to God he were here! 2. Let him be silent, if he cannot say what he means. 3. The Frenchmen shout "Hurrah for France!" 4. He doubted whether there is a God. 5. I should like you to write me a letter, when you are absent. 6. If his father should say so, he would have to do it. 7. I was most anxious that he should succeed in his enterprise. 8. We were not willing that you should go away without our seeing you. 9. His father gave orders that he should be taken to school, even though he might not be willing to go. 10. The doctor forbade that the patient should go for a walk. 11. I was longing for that to be done. 12. He would not permit it to be done. 13. The rain hindered us all day from going out. 14. It was necessary that we should go away before the others came. 15. It was better that we should be here without their knowing it. 16. I was afraid that he had said too much. 17. I doubted whether he would be able to pay that price. 18. I was very sorry that we had not been able to go for a walk together; I am sure we should have enjoyed ourselves. 19. Our friends were glad that you had visited them, before they left for France. 20. He told me he would go away, unless he succeeded better. 21. We did not say you should write the letter; you may do as you wish. 22. Did you fear he would go away without coming to see you? 23. My father thought you would come, but my mother thought you would not come. 24. It was impossible that he should not be mistaken; he trusts those who are not worthy of confidence. 25. We are not sure they would come. 26. We waited until they came. 27. We have taken care that they should not see us. 28. No man has ever lived who could equal him in prudence. 29. He was the noblest man I have ever known.

30. I left Russia when I was a boy; I sought a country where I might be free. 31. Did he ever have a friend who was faithful to him? 32. Show me a house which will suit me better than this one. 33. I have never seen anything which suited me better. 34. Why did your father come? 35. He came in case I should be ill. 36. Although he was very ill, he would not go home.

CONDITIONAL SENTENCES.

354. A conditional sentence consists regularly of two parts—the *condition* (introduced by *si* = 'if') and the *result:*

(Condition) Si j'avais le temps,	If I had time, I should go.
(Result) j'irais.	

a. The condition may, of course, *precede* or *follow* the result:

Irez-vous, s'il pleut?	Will you go, if it rains?
S'il ne fait pas beau, je n'irai pas.	If it is not fine, I shall not go.

b. The condition is often *disguised* or *implied*, or the result *understood:*

Hésiter serait une faiblesse.	To hesitate would be weakness.
Je n'irais pas (si j'étais de lui).	I should not go (if I were he).
Ah! si j'étais à sa place.	Ah, if I were in his place!

355. Mood and Tense. A 'result' clause in the *pres. indic., impve.,* or *fut.*, regularly requires the 'if' clause in the *pres. indic.;* a 'result' clause in the *condl.* regularly requires the 'if' clause in the *impf. indic.:*

S'il a le temps, il va.	If he has time, he goes.
S'il a le temps, dites-lui d'aller.	If he has (have, will have, should have) time, tell him to go.
S'il a le temps, il ira.	If he has (have, will have, should have) time, he will go.
S'il avait le temps, il irait.	If he had (had he, were he to have, if he should have, should he have) time, he would go.

Obs.: The *condition* is regularly expressed by the *indicative* (pres. or impf.), whatever be the corresponding English form.

a. The above rules hold good for *compound tenses*, the *auxiliary being considered as the verb:*

S'il l'a dit, il le fera.	If he has said it, he will do it.
S'il est venu, faites-moi savoir	If he has come, let me know.

S'il a eu le temps, il sera venu.	If he has had time, he will have come.
Si j'avais eu le temps, je serais allé.	If I had had time, I should have gone.
S'il était brave, il aurait fait cela.	If he were brave, he would have done that.

b. Sometimes the *plupf. subj.* stands in the 'if' *clause* or the 'result' *clause*, or in *both:*

S'il eût (*or* avait) su cela, il ne l'eût (*or* aurait) pas dit.	Had he known that, he would not have said so.

c. Occasionally the *impf. indic.* stands in the 'if' *clause* instead of the *plupf.*, and in the 'result' *clause* instead of the *condl. ant.:*

Si Stanislas demeurait (avait demeuré), il était (aurait été) perdu.	If Stanislas had remained, he would have been lost.

d. Quite rarely the condition is expressed by *inversion* (without si):

N'était-ce la crainte de cela.	If it were not for fear of that.
Eût-il été moins riche.	If he had been poorer.

e. A *virtual condition* (concession) is sometimes expressed by various locutions:

Quiconque le fera.	Whoever (if any one) does it.
Il le dirait, le ferait-il?	Even if he said it, would he do it?
Quand même il ne l'aurait pas dit.	Even though he had not said so.
Il le dirait que je ne le croirais pas.	Even if he said it, I should not believe it.

f. The *past def.* is found in the 'if' *clause* only in the expression s'il en fut:

Riche, s'il en fut (jamais), mais corrompu.	Rich, if any one ever was, but corrupt.

g. Si = 'whether' may take the *fut.* or *condl.*, but *never* si = 'if':

Dis-moi si tu iras (irais).	Tell me whether (if) you will (would) go.

EXERCISE LVIII.

Je lui ai dit son fait.	I (have) told him what I thought of him.
Nous nous plaisons à la ville.	We like it (like to be) in the city.
Il se plaît à la campagne.	He likes it (likes to be) in the country.
Qu'il fasse beau, ou qu'il pleuve. S'il fait beau, ou qu'il pleuve.	Whether it is fine, or whether it rains.

CONDITIONAL SENTENCES.

Quand même ce serait vrai. { Even if it were true.
{ Even were it true.
Il s'en plaint. He complains of it.

1. If it does not rain, will you go for a walk to-morrow morning? 2. No, even if it should not rain; I must go down town to-morrow morning on business. 3. If it were to rain to-day, we should not go down town. 4. If I had known that you were in town, I should have gone to see you. 5. Had it not been so warm to-day, I should have gone away. 6. If the Germans had not taken Alsace, the French would not hate them so much to-day. 7. If I come here next year, I shall bring my brother with me. 8. If I were you, I should tell him what I think of him. 9. If I be present, when he arrives, I shall tell him what I told you. 10. If it is cold in winter, we go to Florida; if it is mild, we remain in Canada. 11. If my father likes it in the country, he will stay there till (the) autumn. 12. If I should like it in the city, I shall stay there always. 13. I can never trust that boy; if he should tell me anything, I should not believe him. 14. Whether it rains or is fine, we shall come. 15. He is a good (*brave*) man, if there ever was one. 16. If that man were as rich as Crœsus, he would not be satisfied. 17. See what that man has done to me! He is a scoundrel, if there ever was one. 18. If I should go to sleep before you come, be good enough to wake me. 19. Will you not go down town with me? 20. I cannot go, I am not well; if I were better, I should go willingly. 21. If he had risen at six o'clock, he would not have been late for the train. 22. Yes, he would *(si! si!)*. He would have been late, even if he had risen at half-past five, for the train left at a quarter past five. 23. I have been told that your friend has insulted you; is it true? 24. No, but even if it were true, I should pardon (it to) him. 25. Did our friend tell you last evening whether he was coming to-morrow? 26. Yes, he told me that he would come. 27. That man told me that he had a thousand dollars. 28. Were he to swear it, I should not believe it. 29. If you meet him, and he should ask you where I am, do not tell (it to) him. 30. Whether he comes, or not, (that) makes no difference to me. 31. If I were he, I should tell that scoundrel what I thought of him. 32. If we liked it in the country, we should stay there. 33. If he had insulted me like that, I should have kicked him out. 34. Even were you to hate me, I should not complain (of it). 35. I should have liked it in the country, if it had not rained without ceasing.

The Infinitive Mood.

355. The infinitive is a *verbal noun*. As a verb it *governs*; as a noun it serves as *subject, object*, etc.

Voir c'est croire.	Seeing is believing.
Vous devriez lui parler.	You ought to speak to him.
Il lit sans comprendre.	He reads without understanding.

356. The chief difficulty in the use of the infin. is to determine, (1) when it should stand *without prep.*, (2) when it should have **à**, (3) when it should have **de**.

357. Infinitive without Preposition. The infin. without any preposition is used:—

1. As *subject*, or in *apposition:*

Mentir est honteux.	To lie (lying) is base.
À quoi sert parler?	Of what use is it to talk?
Vivre c'est souffrir.	To live is to suffer.

2. As *predicate* after a few verbs (see list below):

Vous semblez hésiter.	You seem to hesitate.
Il est censé l'avoir fait.	He is supposed to have done it.

3. As *logical subject* after a few *impersonals* (see list below):

Il vaudrait mieux se taire.	It would be better to keep quiet.
Il fait cher vivre à Paris.	Living is dear in Paris.

4. As object or complement after the so-called *modal auxiliaries* (§310, 1-5), after most verbs of *motion* (and causation of motion), after verbs of *desiring* and *preferring*, after verbs of *perceiving*, after verbs of *thinking* and *intending*, after verbs of *saying* and *declaring*, and after certain verbs of *lacking* and *failing* (see list below):

Faites-lui apprendre sa leçon.	Make him learn his lesson.
Voulez-vous dîner chez nous?	Will you dine with us?
Envoyez chercher le médecin.	Send for the doctor.
Je désirerais lui parler.	I should like to speak to him.
Je les vois venir.	I see them come (coming).
Quand comptez-vous revenir?	When do you expect to come back?
Il prétend avoir raison.	He claims to be in the right.
J'avais beau crier.	It was in vain that I shouted.

5. Sometimes in elliptical expressions as *imperative, interrogative* (dir. or indir.), or *absolutely:*

Voir les affiches.	See the posters.
Que faire ? Où me cacher ?	What (am I) to do ? Where hide ?
Je ne sais que faire.	I know not what to do.
Penser qu'il a dit cela !	To think that he said that !

6. *Reference-list* of verbs requiring *direct infinitive:*

accourir, *hasten.*	envoyer, *send.*	préférer 1, *prefer.*
affirmer, *affirm.*	espérer 1, *hope.*	prétendre 3, *assert.*
aimer (condl.), 3 *should like.*	être, *be.*	se rappeler 1, *recollect.*
aimer autant, *like as well.*	être censé, *be supposed.*	reconnaître, *acknowledge.*
aimer mieux, *prefer.*	faillir 2, *be on point of.*	regarder, *look at.*
aller, *go.*	faire, *make, cause.*	rentrer, *go in again.*
apercevoir, *perceive.*	il fait (impers.), *it is.*	retourner, *go back.*
assurer, *assure.*	falloir, *be necessary.*	revenir, *come back.*
avoir beau, *be in vain.*	se figurer, *imagine.*	savoir, *know how to, can.*
avouer, *avow.*	s'imaginer, *fancy.*	sembler, *seem.*
compter 1, *intend.*	juger, *consider.*	sentir, *hear, feel.*
confesser, *confess.*	jurer 4, *swear, attest by oath.*	souhaiter 1, *wish.*
courir, *run.*	justifier, *justify.*	soutenir, *maintain.*
croire, *think.*	laisser 3, 4, *let, allow.*	supposer, *suppose.*
daigner, *deign.*	mener, *lead, bring.*	être supposé, *be supposed.*
déclarer, *declare.*	mettre, *set, put at.*	témoigner, *testify.*
déposer, *testify.*	monter, *go up.*	se trouver, *be.*
descendre 3, *come (go) down.*	nier 1, *deny.*	valoir autant, *be as good.*
désirer 1, *desire, wish.*	oser, *dare.*	valoir mieux, *be better.*
devoir, *ought, to be, etc.*	ouïr, *hear.*	venir 3, 4, *come.*
dire 4, *say.*	paraître, *appear.*	voir, *see.*
écouter, *listen to.*	penser 3, *intend, be near.*	voler, *fly.*
entendre, *hear, intend.*	pouvoir, *can, may.*	vouloir, *will, wish.*

1 Sometimes takes **de**.
2 Sometimes takes **à** or **de**.
3 See also list of verbs requiring **à** (§358, 7).
4 See also list of verbs requiring **de** (§359, 6).

a. **Devoir** = 'owe,' 'be indebted' with indir. obj. takes de :

Je lui dois d'être encore en vie.	I owe to him that I am still alive.

b. **Faire** takes de in ne faire que de :

Il ne fait que de s'amuser.	He does nothing but amuse himself.

c. **Ne pas laisser** = 'not to cease,' etc., takes de :

Il ne laisse pas de le dire.	He is always saying so (says so for all that).

358. Infinitive with à. The infinitive preceded by **à** = 'to,' 'in,' 'at,' 'by,' etc., is used :—

1. As *direct object* of a few *transitives* (see list below):

J'aime à chanter.	I like to sing.
Continuez à lire.	Continue to read.
Il m'enseigne à chanter.	He teaches me to sing (singing).
J'ai à étudier demain.	I have to study to-morrow.
Il n'y a pas à se plaindre.	There is nothing to complain of.

2. As *complement* after many verbs to denote the *object to which the action tends* (answering the question 'to do what?') or *the object in, at, on, about which the action takes place* (answering the question 'in doing what?' 'at doing what?' etc.):

Il aspire à devenir riche.	He aspires to become rich.
Poussez-les à agir.	Urge them to act.
Je les ai invités à venir.	I have invited them to come.
Aidez-moi à porter cette malle.	Help me to carry this trunk.
Il réussit à me trouver.	He succeeded in finding me.
Je suis à écrire une lettre.	I am (busy) writing a letter.
Il s'amuse à me taquiner.	He amuses himself teasing me.
J'ai gagné à vendre ma maison.	I gained by selling my house.
Il joue à faire le malade.	He plays at being sick.

3. As the *complement* of certain *adjectives* (see the Adj.) and *nouns* denoting *fitness, tendency, purpose*, etc.:

Ceci est bon à manger.	This is good to eat.
Je suis prêt à vous écouter.	I am ready to hear you.
Quelque chose d'utile à savoir.	Something useful to know.
Cela est facile à faire.	That is easy to do.
La tendance à se croire grand.	The tendency to think one's self great.
Une bonne à tout faire.	A maid of all work.

a. So also, le premier, le dernier, le seul:

Il n'est pas le seul à le dire.	He is not the only one to say so.

4. To form *adjectival phrases* denoting *use, fitness, quality*, etc.:

Une salle à manger.	A dining-room.
Une chose à voir.	A thing worth seeing.
Des contes à dormir debout.	Very tiresome stories.
Un spectacle à faire peur.	A terrible sight.
De manière à réussir.	In such a way as to succeed.
Vous êtes à plaindre.	You are to be pitied.
C'est à en mourir.	It is enough to kill one.

5. To form *adverbial phrases*:

Elle chante à ravir.	She sings **charmingly**.
Elle pleurait à faire pitié.	She wept **pitifully**.
À vrai dire, je le plains.	**To tell the truth**, I pity him.
Il passe le temps à lire.	He passes his time **reading**.
Elle est laide à faire peur.	She is **frightfully** ugly.

7. *Reference-list* of verbs requiring *infinitive with* à:

s'abaisser, *stoop.*
abandonner (s'-), *give up.*
aboutir, *end (in), tend.*
s'abuser, *be mistaken (in).*
s'accorder[2], *agree (in).*
être d'accord, *agree (in).*
accoutumer (s'-)[2], *accustom.*
s'acharner, *be bent (on).*
admettre, *admit.*
s'adonner, *addict o. s.*
aguerrir (s'-), *inure.*
aider, *help.*
aimer[2,4], *like.*
amener, *lead.*
amuser (s'-), *amuse (in, by).*
animer (s'-), *excite.*
appeler, *call.*
appliquer (s'-), *apply.*
apprendre, *learn, teach.*
apprêter (s'-), *get ready.*
s'arrêter, *stop.*
aspirer, *aspire.*
assujettir (s'-), *subject.*
astreindre, *compel.*
s'astreindre, *bind o. s.*
attacher, *attach.*
s'attacher, *be intent (on).*
attendre (s'-), *expect.*
autoriser, *authorize.*
s'avilir, *stoop.*
avoir, *have, must.*
avoir (de la) peine, *have difficulty (in).*
balancer, *hesitate.*
se borner, *limit o. s.*
chercher, *seek, try.*
commencer[2], *begin.*
se complaire, *take pleasure (in).*

concourir, *co-operate (in).*
condamner (se-), *condemn.*
condescendre, *condescend.*
conduire, *lead.*
consacrer (se-), *devote.*
consentir[2], *consent.*
consister, *consist (in).*
conspirer, *conspire.*
consumer (se-), *consume (in).*
continuer[1], *continue.*
contraindre[1], *constrain.*
contribuer, *contribute.*
convier[2], *invite.*
coûter, *cost.*
décider[3], *induce.*
se décider, *resolve.*
défier[3], *challenge, incite.*
demander[1], *ask.*
demeurer, *remain.*
dépenser, *spend (in).*
désapprendre, *forget.*
descendre[4], *stoop, abase, o.s.*
destiner, *destine.*
déterminer[3], *induce.*
se déterminer, *resolve.*
dévouer (se-), *devote.*
différer[2], *delay.*
disposer (se-), *dispose.*
divertir (se-), *amuse.*
donner, *give*
dresser, *train.*
s'efforcer[1], *try.*
s'égayer, *divert o.s. (by).*
employer (s'-), *employ (in).*
s'empresser[1,3], *be eager.*
encourager, *encourage.*
engager (s'-)[2], *engage, advise.*
enhardir[2], *embolden.*
s'enhardir[2], *venture.*

s'ennuyer[2,3], *tire o. s. (in).*
enseigner, *teach.*
s'entendre, *know well how.*
entraîner, *allure.*
essayer[1], *try.*
s'essayer, *try o. s. (in).*
être[3], *be occupied (in, at).*
être à[3], *be one's turn.*
s'étudier, *apply o. s.*
s'évertuer, *exert o. s., try.*
exceller, *excel (in)*
exciter (s'-), *excite.*
exercer (s'-), *exercise (in).*
exhorter, *exhort.*
exposer (s'-), *expose.*
se fatiguer[3], *tire o.s. (in, at).*
finir (neg.)[3], *have done.*
forcer[1], *force.*
gagner, *gain (by).*
habituer[2], *accustom.*
s'habituer, *accustom o. s.*
haïr, *hate.*
se hasarder[2], *venture.*
hésiter[2], *hesitate.*
inciter, *incite.*
incliner, *incline.*
induire, *induce.*
instruire, *instruct.*
intéresser (s'-), *interest (in).*
inviter, *invite.*
jouer, *play (at).*
laisser[3,4], *leave.*
se lasser[3], *tire o. s. (in).*
manquer[3], *be remiss (in).*
mettre, *put, set.*
se mettre, *set about.*
montrer, *show how.*
obliger[1,3], *oblige, force.*
s'obliger[2], *bind o. s.*

s'obstiner, *persist (in)*.
occuper (s'-)3, *employ (in)*
s'offrir2, *offer*.
s'opiniâtrer, *persist (in)*.
parvenir, *succeed (in)*.
passer, *spend (in)*.
pencher, *incline*.
penser4, *think (of)*.
perdre, *lose (in, by)*.
persévérer, *persevere (in)*.
persister, *persist (in)*.
se plaire, *delight (in)*.
se plier, *submit*.
porter, *induce*.
pousser, *urge, incite*.
prendre garde3, *take care*.
prendre plaisir, *delight (in)*.

se prendre, *begin*.
préparer (se-), *prepare*.
prétendre4, *aspire*.
prier3, *invite (formally)*.
procéder, *proceed*.
provoquer, *incite*.
recommencer1, *begin again*.
réduire, *reduce*.
se réduire, *confine o. s.*
refuser3, *refuse to give*.
se refuser, *refuse*.
renoncer, *renounce*.
répugner, *be reluctant*.
se résigner, *resign o. s.*
résoudre3, *induce*.
se résoudre, *resolve*.

rester, *remain*.
réussir, *succeed (in)*.
servir, *serve*.
songer, *think (of)*.
souffrir1, *suffer*.
suffire, *suffice*.
surprendre, *discover*.
tarder, *be long, delay (in)*.
tendre, *tend*.
tenir, *be anxious*.
travailler, *work*.
trembler3, *tremble (at, on)*.
trouver, *find*.
venir3,4, *happen*.
viser, *aim*.
vouer (se-), *devote*.

1 Or **de**.
2 Sometimes takes **de**.
3 See also list of verbs requiring **de** (§359, 6).
4 See also list of verbs requiring direct infinitive (§357, 6).

a. **Suffire** sometimes takes **pour**:

Cela suffira pour l'amuser.   That will suffice to amuse him.

b. The infin. after être à often has passive force:

Cet ouvrage est à refaire.   That work is to be done again.

c. **Haïr** may take **de** when *negative:*

Il ne hait pas à (d') être endetté.   He does not dislike being in debt.

359. Infinitive with *de*. The infinitive preceded by **de** = 'to,' 'of,' 'from,' 'for,' 'at,' etc., is used:—

1. As *logical subject* of an *impersonal verb* (for rare exceptions see §357, 3):

Il est facile de faire cela.   It is easy to do that.
Il importe d'arriver à temps.   It is important to arrive in time.
Bien vous sied de vous taire.   It well becomes you to be silent.
C'est pitié de le voir.   It is pitiful to see him.

a. Similarly as *subject* in inverted sentences:

C'est une folie (que) d'aller là.   It is madness to go there.

2. As *complement* of most *adjectives* and *nouns:*

Le désir de partir.   The desire of going.
La nécessité de rester.   The necessity of remaining.
Il n'est pas digne de vivre.   He is not worthy to live.
J'ai envie de pleurer.   I feel like crying.

a. So also, many expressions, like the last example, made from *verb* +*noun*, *e.g.*, **avoir besoin** (**honte, peur, raison, soin, tort**, etc.), **faire envie** (**plaisir, semblant**, etc.), **courir risque**, etc., etc.

3. After verbs as *object* or *complement*, usually to denote the *source* or *occasion* of action (answering 'whence?', 'concerning what?') or to denote *separation* or *cessation* from (answering 'from what?'). See list below:

Je me réjouis de le voir.	I rejoice to see it.
Elle se pique d'être la première.	She prides herself on being first.
Prenez garde de tomber.	Take care not to fall.
Il s'excuse d'aller.	He excuses himself from going.
Promettez de ne pas le dire.	Promise not to tell it.

4 As *historical infinitive* (= a past def.):

Et l'ennemi de s'enfuir. And the enemy fled.

a. This construction is generally to be explained by ellipsis of commencer, se hâter, etc.

5 After **que** in the second member of a comparison, unless the sentence be very short:

Il vaudra mieux rester que de partir si tard.	It will be better to stay than to go so late.
But. Mieux vaut savoir qu'avoir.	Better wisdom than wealth.

6. *Reference-list* of verbs requiring *infinitive with* **de**:

s absenter, *absent o. s. (from)*.
s absoudre, *absolve o. s (from)*
s abstenir, *abstain (from)*
accorder, *grant*.
avoir accoutume, *be accustomed*.
accuser (s -), *accuse (of)*
achever, *finish*.
admirer, *wonder (at)*.
affecter, *affect*.
s'affliger, *grieve (at, over)*.
ambitionner, *aspire*.
s'apercevoir, *perceive*.
s'applaudir, *congratulate o. s. (on)*.
appréhender, *fear*.
arrêter, *prevent (from)*, determine.
s'attrister, *become sad (at)*
avertir, *notify, warn*.

aviser, *think (of)*.
blâmer, *blame (for)*.
brûler *long*.
censurer, *censure (for)*.
cesser, *cease*.
se chagriner, *grieve (at, over)*.
charger, *charge*.
se charger, *undertake*.
choisir, *choose*.
commander, *command*.
commencer 1, *begin*
conjurer, *beseech*.
conseiller, *advise*.
consoler, *console (for)*
se contenter, *be satisfied*.
continuer 1, *continue*.
contraindre 1, *constrain*.
convaincre, *convict (of)*
convenir, *agree*
craindre, *fear*.

crier, *cry*.
décider 3, *decide, resolve*.
décourager (se-), *discourage (from)*.
dédaigner, *disdain*.
défendre, *forbid*.
se défendre, *forbear, excuse o. s*.
défier 3, *defy*.
se défier, *distrust*.
dégoûter, *disgust (with)*.
délibérer, *deliberate (about)*.
demander 1, *ask*.
se dépêcher, *make haste*
désaccoutumer (se-), *disaccustom (from)*.
désespérer, *despair (of)*.
déshabituer (se-), *disaccustom (from)*
déterminer 3, *resolve*.

détester, *detest.*
détourner, *dissuade (from).*
dire 4, *bid.*
discontinuer, *cease.*
disconvenir, *deny.*
se disculper, *excuse o. s. (for).*
dispenser, *dispense (from).*
dissuader, *dissuade (from).*
douter, *hesitate.*
se douter, *suspect.*
écrire, *write.*
s'efforcer 1, *try.*
s'effrayer, *be afraid.*
empêcher, *prevent.*
s'empêcher, *abstain (from).*
s'empresser 3, *hasten.*
s'empresser 1, *be eager.*
enjoindre, *enjoin*
s'ennuyer 2, 3, *be tired (of).*
s'enorgueillir, *be proud.*
enrager, *be enraged (at).*
entreprendre, *undertake.*
épargner, *spare.*
essayer 1, *try*
s'étonner, *be astonished.*
être à 2, 3, *be duty (or office) (of).*
éviter, *avoid.*
excuser (s'-), *excuse (from).*
exempter, *exempt (from).*
faire bien, *do well.*
se fatiguer 3, *be tired (of).*
feindre, *feign.*
féliciter (se-), *congratulate (on).*
finir 3, *finish.*
se flatter, *flatter o. s.*
forcer 1, *force.*
frémir, *shudder.*
gager, *wager.*
garder (se-), *forbear.*
gémir, *groan.*
gêner, *incommode.*
se glorifier, *boast (of).*
gronder, *scold (for).*

hasarder, *venture.*
se hâter, *hasten.*
imaginer, *imagine.*
s'impatienter, *be impatient.*
imputer, *impute.*
s'indigner, *be indignant.*
s'ingérer, *meddle (with).*
inspirer, *inspire.*
interdire, *interdict (from).*
jouir, *enjoy.*
juger bon, *think fit.*
jurer 4, *promise (on oath).*
ne pas laisser 3, 4, *not to cease.*
se lasser 3, *be weary (of).*
louer, *praise (for).*
mander, *bid.*
manquer 3, *fail, be on point of.*
méditer, *meditate.*
se mêler, *meddle (with).*
menacer, *threaten.*
mériter, *deserve.*
se moquer, *make sport (of).*
mourir, *die, long.*
négliger, *neglect.*
notifier, *notify.*
obliger 1, *oblige, force.*
obliger 3, *do favour.*
obtenir, *obtain.*
s'occuper 3, *be intent (on).*
offrir, *offer.*
omettre, *omit.*
ordonner, *order.*
oublier 2, *forget.*
pardonner, *forgive.*
parier, *bet.*
parler, *speak.*
se passer, *do without.*
permettre (se-), *permit*
persuader, *persuade.*
se piquer, *pride o. s. (on).*
plaindre, *pity*
se plaindre, *complain (of).*
prendre garde 3, *take care not, beware (of).*

prendre soin, *take care.*
prescrire, *prescribe.*
presser, *urge.*
se presser, *hasten.*
présumer, *presume.*
prier 3, *beg, pray.*
priver (se-), *deprive (of).*
projeter, *intend.*
promettre (se-), *promise.*
proposer, *propose.*
se proposer, *intend.*
protester, *protest.*
punir, *punish (for)*
recommander, *recommend*
recommencer 1, *begin again*
refuser 3, *refuse.*
regretter, *regret.*
se réjouir, *rejoice.*
remercier, *thank (for).*
se repentir, *repent (of).*
reprendre, *reprove (for)*
réprimander, *reprimand (for).*
reprocher (se-), *reproach (with).*
résoudre 3, *resolve*
se ressouvenir, *remember.*
rire (se-), *laugh.*
risquer, *risk.*
rougir, *blush.*
sommer, *summon.*
se soucier, *care.*
souffrir 1, *suffer.*
soupçonner, *suspect.*
sourire, *smile.*
se souvenir, *recollect.*
suggérer, *suggest*
supplier, *beseech.*
tâcher 2, *try.*
tenter 2, *attempt.*
trembler 3, *tremble, fear.*
trouver bon, *think fit*
se vanter, *boast (of).*
venir 3, 4, *have just.*

1 Or à.
2 Sometimes à.
3 See also list of verbs requiring à (§358, 7)
4 See also list of verbs requiring direct infinitive (§357, 6).

360. Distinctions. As appears from the list, the same verb sometimes requires à, de, or the direct infin. The following are examples of the principal cases in which the sense varies with the construction:—

1. Aimer:

J'aimerais bien le connaître.	I should like to know him.
J'aime mieux vous dire tout.	I prefer to tell you all.
Aimez-vous à demeurer ici?	Do you like to live here?

2. Décider:

Il m'a décidé à entrer.	He induced me to go in.
Nous décidâmes de partir.	We decided to set out.

3. Défier:

On le défia à boire.	They challenged him to drink.
Je vous défie de prouver cela.	I defy you to prove that.

4. Descendre:

Descends chercher ton chapeau.	Go down and get your hat.
Il a descendu même à voler.	He even descended to theft.

5. Déterminer:

Je l'ai déterminé à rester.	I induced him to stay.
Il avait déterminé d'aller.	He had determined to go.

6. Dire:

Il dit l'avoir vu.	He says he saw it.
Je lui ai dit de venir.	I told him to come.

7. S'empresser:

Il s'empressait à lui plaire.	He was eager to please her.
Il s'empressa de répondre.	He hastened to reply.

8. Être:

Je suis à écrire des lettres.	I am (busy) writing letters.
C'est à vous de parler.	It is your place to speak.
C'est à vous à parler.	It is your turn to speak.

9. Se fatiguer:

Il se fatigua à jouer au billard.	He fatigued himself playing billiards.
Il est fatigué de jouer.	He is tired playing.

10. Finir:

Il ne finit pas à me le dire.	He was never done telling me so.
J'ai fini de travailler.	I have finished working.

11. **Jurer:**
Je jure l'avoir vu. — I swear I saw it.
Je jure de le faire. — I swear I will do it.

12. **Laisser:**
Je l'ai laissé dire. — I let him talk.
Je vous laisse à penser. — I leave you to think.
Il ne laissa pas de parler — He did not stop talking.

13. **Se lasser:**
Il s'est lassé à courir. — He tired himself out (by) running.
Il se lasse de courir. — He is tired of running.

14. **Manquer:**
Je manquai de tomber. — I was on the point of falling.
Il a manqué à faire son devoir. — He has failed to do his duty.

15. **Obliger:**
Je l'ai obligé à (de) le faire. — I obliged him to do it.
Obligez-moi de le faire. — Oblige me by doing it.

16. **S'occuper:**
Il s'occupe à rien faire. — He is busy doing nothing.
Il s'occupe de tout voir. — He is intent on seeing everything.

17. **Penser:**
Que pensez-vous faire? — What do you intend to do?
Je pensai tomber. — I thought I should fall.
Je pense à répliquer à cela. — I think of replying to that.

18. **Prendre garde:**
Prenez garde à le faire. — Take care to do it.
Prenez garde à ne pas le faire. — Take care not to do it.
Prenez garde de le faire. — Take care not to do it.

19. **Prétendre:**
Il prétend vous connaître. — He asserts that he knows you.
Il prétend à devenir savant. — He aspires to become learned.

20. **Prier:**
Il m'a prié à dîner. — He invited me to dine.
Je vous prie de m'aider. — I pray (ask) you to help me.

21. **Refuser:**
Me refusez-vous à manger? — Do you refuse to give me food?
Je refuserai d'aller. — I shall refuse to go.

THE INFINITIVE MOOD.

22. Résoudre:
Il m'a résolu à l'acheter. — He induced me to buy it.
Je suis résolu de l'acheter. — I am determined to buy it.

23. Trembler:
Il tremble à me voir. — He trembles when he sees me.
Il tremble de me rencontrer. — He fears to meet me.

24. Venir:
Venez nous voir. — Come to see us.
Si vous venez à le voir. — If you happen to see him.
Je viens de le voir. — I have just seen him.

361. Infinitive with other Prepositions. The infin. stands also after **par, pour, sans, après, entre,** and after locutions ending in **de** or **à** (**afin de, afin que de, jusqu'à,** etc.):—

1. **Par** = 'by,' usually only after **commencer** and **finir**:
Il finit par m'insulter. — He ended by insulting me (*or* He finally insulted me).

2. **Pour** usually translates 'in order to,' 'for the purpose of;' sometimes also 'for,' 'from,' 'because,' 'though,' etc., and 'to' after **assez, trop,** etc.:

Il faut manger pour vivre. — We must eat (in order) to live.
Il est mort pour avoir trop bu. — He died from over-drinking.
Il fut puni pour avoir ri. — He was punished for laughing.
Pour être pauvre, il n'est pas larron. — Though poor, he is no thief.
Il est trop franc pour se taire. — He is too frank to keep quiet.

a. **Pour** after a verb of motion (§357, 4) emphasizes the *purpose*:
J'irai pour le voir. — I shall go to see him.

3. **Sans** = 'without':
N'allez pas sans manger. — Do not go without eating.

4. **Après** = 'after' requires the *perf. infin.*:
Après avoir dîné, je partis. — After having dined, I set out.

362. Infinitive for Subordinate Clause. 1. An infinitive construction usually replaces a **que** clause of which the subject is the same with that of the subject or object (dir. or indir.) of the principal clause:

Il croit vous avoir vu. — He thinks that he has seen you.
Dites-leur de s'en aller. — Tell them to be gone.

2. Similarly **afin de, à moins de, après, avant de, de crainte de, de peur de, de façon à, de manière à, pour, sans,** etc. +*the infin.* stand for **afin que,** etc. +*the subjunctive*, but only when the *subject* of both verbs is the same:

Il partit sans me voir.   He went without seeing me.
But : Il partit sans que je le visse.   He went without me seeing him.

363. Infinitive with Passive Force. A *transitive* infin. has passive force after verbs of *perceiving* (**voir,** etc.), after **faire, laisser,** and after **à** in certain cases:

J'ai vu bâtir cette maison.   I saw this house being built.
Je me fais faire un habit.   I am having a coat made.
Vous êtes à plaindre.   You are to be pitied.

NOTE.—This construction may be explained by supplying some such ellipsis as the following: 'J'ai vu bâtir une maison (**à** *or* **par quelqu'un**),' 'I have seen somebody building a house.'

364. Infinitive for English *-ing*. The infin. must be used to translate many such forms (see §366, 2, 3, 4).

EXERCISE LIX.

Je vais faire { une promenade. / un tour de promenade. } I am going for a walk.
Je voudrais le faire.   I should like to do it.
Je voudrais qu'il le fasse (fît).   I should like him to do it.
Il fait beau marcher (se promener). { The walking is good. / It is good walking.
Vous avez beau dire (parler). { It is vain (useless) for you to speak. / You may say what you like.
J'ai cru voir passer quelqu'un.   I thought I saw some one go by.
Je les ai écoutés chanter.   I listened to them sing(ing).
Il a pensé mourir.   He was near dying.
Je pense à le faire.   I am thinking about doing it.
Il ne fait que de venir (arriver).   He has just come.
Il veut faire à sa tête.   He will have his own way.
J'aimerais autant aller.   I would as soon go.
Faites-le monter.   Send (show) him up (stairs).

1. Let us go for a walk this morning; the walking is good, and it is cool. 2. Living is always dearer in the city than in the country. 3. Are the children coming? 4. Yes, I saw them coming,

when I was on the hill. 5. I should like to speak to the doctor, when he comes. 6. I should like you to speak to my father, when you see him. 7. When do you expect to be there? 8. I expect to be there in a fortnight. 9. He might say what he liked, nobody would believe him. 10. It was useless for us to speak, nobody would listen to us. 11. I like better to live in the country than in the city. 12. My friends have left me, and I know not what to do. 13. I think it is going to be warm to-day. 14. My father thought he heard some one go by, but I think he was mistaken. 15. My father was very ill last year; he was near dying. 16. His little boy fell into the water, and was near being drowned. 17. I was thinking about going to see you. 18. I hope I shall see you, when you come. 19. I hope he will come to see me, when he is here. 20. Did you see my sister at the ball? 21. I thought I saw her, but I am not sure (of it). 22. I am thinking about writing him a letter, but I do not like writing letters, and so I delay (it) from week to week. 23. I should like better to go than to stay. 24. It would be better to go than to stay. 25. Come and see us, whenever you wish. 26. My master has just come; after he has dined I shall tell him that you are here. 27. I hope I shall be able to go for a walk with you to-morrow. 28. I hope you will not go away, before I have seen you. 29. We ought to go and see your father, before he leaves. 30. It is useless for you to say anything; he will have his own way. 31. You may say what you like; young people will have their own way. 32. I would as soon go as stay. 33. I am not very well this morning; I am going to send for the doctor. 34. The doctor has just come; shall I send him up? 35. We thought we heard some one go by, but we must have been mistaken.

EXERCISE LX.

Il est à travailler.	He is busy working.
J'y suis accoutumé.	I am used to it.
Il finira mal.	He will come to a bad end.
Se plaire à mal faire.	To delight in evil- (wrong-) doing.
Il tarde à venir.	He is long in coming.
Tenez-vous (beaucoup) à y aller?	Are you (very) anxious to go there?
Je n'y tiens pas.	I am not anxious (for it).

1. Continue reading, until you are called. 2. We are busy writing our exercises. 3. I have my work to do. 4. Our teacher taught us to do that. 5. Will you help me to do my work? 6. I should like to help you, but I have work to do also. 7. I have difficulty in believing that he has done that. 8. How old is that child?

9. He is two years old; he is beginning to talk. 10. The servant is busy washing dishes in the kitchen. 11. We are occupied to-day in writing to our friends. 12. He spends his time in reading novels. 13. He is not lazy; he sets about writing his lesson as soon as his teacher tells (it to) him. 14. Do you not get tired (in) reading those difficult works? 15. A little; but I am rather used to it. 16. He lost a great deal in selling his house. 17. That boy persists in reading bad books; he will come to a bad end. 18. The wicked delight in evil-doing. 19. Our friends invited us to stay with them. 20. I should like to know where my mother is; she is long in coming. 21. I wish she would come; I long to see her. 22. Are you anxious to have it to-day? 23. Oh no, I am not anxious for that; but I must have it to-morrow. 24. Are those apples good to eat? 25. We are looking for a maid of all work. 26. That young lady sings and dances charmingly. 27. There are five bed-rooms in that house. 28. That poor little girl has hurt her hand; she is crying pitifully. 29. Our neighbour has died; his family is to be pitied. 30. That young man seems to delight in wrong-doing. 31. Are you not very anxious to see your friends? 32. Yes, I should like to see them; I have not seen them for a long time. 33. That is very difficult to do; I should like you to help me. 34. I am always ready to help you. 35. I am glad to know that you are not the only one to say so. 36. That scoundrel did not succeed in deceiving us.

EXERCISE LXI.

Il fait semblant de dormir.   He pretends to be asleep.
Bien faire, mal faire.   To do well, to do evil (wrong).

1. Our teacher tells us that it is easy to read that book. 2. I am ashamed to say that we are mistaken. 3. He pretends to be asleep. 4. She pretends to be reading. 5. It is difficult to say whether we are right or wrong. 6. He is wrong to believe that we are his enemies. 7. Will you permit me to go to bed? 8. Promise us not to go away without telling us (it). 9. I am very glad to say that I shall be able to come and see you at once. 10. We are sorry to tell you that we cannot come. 11. Cease to do evil; learn to do well. 12. Hasten to finish your work before leaving. 13. Let us hasten to leave, or we shall be late. 14. I am afraid to speak, although I know it is my place to tell them that they have done wrong. 15. He commenced by telling me that he was a rich man's son, and he finished by asking me to lend him five dollars. 16. Take care not to fall. 17. If you happen to see him, tell him that I shall not go away before seeing him. 18. I have just

seen him; and he told me to tell you that he was coming to-morrow. 19. We *(on)* should not live to eat. 20. It is too cold to go for a walk. 21. It is not cool enough to go for a walk. 22. I rose early this morning, in order to be able to do my work before going down town. 23. We learn French, in order to be able to read French books. 24. After writing our exercises we went for a walk. 25. That little boy was punished for having lied. 26. That young girl is much to be pitied; her father and mother are dead. 27. Before going we should like to see you. 28. We should like to see you before you go. 29. We saw those houses being built. 30. He did that without telling us (it). 31. We went away without his seeing us. 32. It was very windy, and we would not go out for a sail for fear of being drowned. 33. Although he made me many compliments at first, he finally insulted me. 34. Your father has just come; shall I tell him to wait here, or should you like to see him at once? 35. I have not time to see him now; I shall try to see him to-morrow. 36. We cannot hinder him from doing so.

The Present Participle.

365. The participial form in -ant serves as a *verbal adjective*, as a *present participle* (without en), and as a *gerund* (with en):—

1. As a *verbal adjective*, it denotes *quality* or *state*, and *agrees* like an adjective: *

Elle paraît bien portante.	She seems well.
Les enfants doivent être obéissants.	Children must be obedient.
Les vivants, et les mourants.	The living and the dying.
Des paroles consolantes.	Comforting words.

Obs.: The verbal adj., attributively, regularly *follows* the noun, as in the last example.

a. Some verbs have a *special form* for the verbal adjective:

ADJ.	PART.	ADJ.	PART.
différent, *different*.	différant.	négligent, *careless*.	négligeant.
convaincant, *convincing*.	convainquant.	savant, *learned*.	sachant.
fatigant, *fatiguing*.	fatiguant.	puissant, *powerful*.	pouvant.
etc.	etc.	etc.	etc.

2. As a *present participle*, it is used, in general, like the English present participle, to denote *simultaneous action, manner, cause, motive,* etc., and is *invariable*:

Pleurant, elle continua le récit.	Weeping, she continued the story.
Je le trouvai riant comme un fou.	I found him laughing like mad.
Elle ne sortit pas, étant malade.	She did not go out, being ill.

Ayant parlé ainsi, il sortit. Having thus spoken, he went out.
Il n'entrera pas, moi vivant. He shall not enter, while I live.

NOTES—1. It is often difficult to determine whether the form in -ant is participle (invar.) or adj. (var.). As a participle, the *action* (generally transitory) is prominent, but as an adjective, *quality* or else *continued action* (state) is denoted. It is nearly always a participle when it has a *complement* or a construction peculiar to the verb, such as *object, negative, adverb following*: 'Une femme mourante,' 'A dying woman'; 'Des gens mourant de faim,' 'People dying of hunger'; 'Les ennemis se retirèrent, brûlant les villes partout,' 'The enemies retired, burning the towns everywhere'; 'Une femme ne craignant rien,' 'A woman fearing nothing'; 'Des dames parlant doucement,' 'Ladies speaking softly'; 'De soi-disant amis,' 'So-called friends.' 2. In the last example, **soi-disant**, though adj. in force, remains invar. in view of the lit. meaning, 'calling themselves.' 3. **Ayant** and **étant** are also always *invariable*.

3. As a *gerund*, it denotes either *simultaneous action* or *means by which*, and is *invariable;* en = 'while,' 'in,' 'on,' 'when,' 'as,' 'by,' etc., or is untranslated:

En jouant, j'ai perdu ma montre. While playing, I lost my watch.
En rentrant, j'ai trouvé la lettre. On returning, I found the letter.
Vous perdrez, en agissant ainsi. You will lose, if you act thus.
En lisant on apprend à lire. By reading one learns to read.

a. Both participle and gerund denote simultaneous action, but the use of **en** (strengthened sometimes by **tout**) usually emphasizes the *continuity* of the action:

(En) disant ceci, il prit la lyre. (While) saying this, he took the harp.
Tout en pleurant, elle continua. Still weeping, she went on.

b. The gerund usually refers to the *subject:*

Je l'ai vu en allant à la poste. I saw him while going to the post.
But: L'appétit vient en mangeant. One's appetite comes while eating.

c. En is sometimes *omitted*, especially after aller:

Généralement parlant. Generally speaking.
Il s'en va (en) grondant. Off he goes grumbling.

d. The gerund denotes *progressive action* in a few expressions formed from aller:

Cela alla (en) diminuant. That kept growing less and less.

366. English Forms in -*ing*. These are variously translated into French; idiomatic differences are:—

1. Periphrastic tense forms are avoided in French:

Il a joué toute la matinée. He has been playing all morning.

2. English gerunds are translated by an -**ant** form only when the prep. **en** may be used; otherwise by an *infinitive*, a *noun*, or a *clause:*

En lisant on apprend à lire.	By reading one learns to read.
But: Il parle de partir.	He speaks of going away.
Il fut pendu pour avoir volé.	He was hanged for having stolen.
Elle partit sans dire adieu.	She went without saying good-bye.
Voir c'est croire.	Seeing is believing.
J'aime la chasse (*or* à chasser).	I like hunting.
Je suis étonné qu'il soit venu.	I am surprised at his coming.

3. After verbs of *perception* (**entendre, sentir, voir,** etc.), the *relative* or *infinitive* construction is much commoner than the participle:

Je les vois venir (qui viennent *or* venant)	I see them coming.
Les voilà qui passent!	See them passing!
Il a vu sortir mes frères.	He saw my brothers going out.
Les avez-vous entendus frapper (qui frappaient)?	Did you hear them knocking?
Je la vis frapper l'enfant.	I saw her striking the child.

4. Compound nouns with a first component in **-ing** are not literally translated:

Une machine à coudre.	A sewing-machine.

5. It is often more elegant to avoid a French form in **-ant**, even when permissible:

Pendant mon voyage.	While travelling.

EXERCISE LXII.

Cette femme me fait pitié.	I am sorry for that woman.
Il s'est fâché contre moi.	He got angry with me.

1. Knowing so many things, those gentlemen must be very learned. 2. The field of battle was covered with the dead and dying. 3. I am sorry for that poor woman; she is always ill. 4. In neglecting her duties, she shows herself careless. 5. Their misfortunes went on increasing from day to day. 6. Don't you see them coming? 7. Yes; there they come! 8. Man is the only speaking creature. 9. Canadians will say (pres.) that, generally speaking, Canadians are better than Englishmen. 10. How happy those peasants are! They are always sing-

ing their beautiful songs, as they work. 11. One's appetite comes while eating; but, said the Gascon, I have been eating two hours, and it has not come yet. 12. I like reading, but I prefer hunting and fishing. 13. Where are the children? 14. There they are, playing under the trees. 15. Our neighbour's son has made astonishing progress at (the) college. 16. The sewing-machine is an American invention, but there are many of them in Europe now. 17. Our friends were very much astonished at our coming; they thought we were in Europe. 18. As we were taking a walk this morning, we met the old gentleman who used to live next door. 19. Our neighbours are speaking of going away, but I do not think they will. 20. That young man went away without saying good-bye; he must have got angry with me. 21. That prince has powerful enemies. 22. That lady, being ill, has not come to-day. 23. Those children, having finished their work, have gone out. 24. Those so-called learned men, who really know nothing, are very tiresome. 25. Who is that man going past? 26. That is the would-be nobleman. 27. England has the most powerful fleet in the world. 28. That little girl, having been ill, cannot go to school. 29. Our friends, being tired, have gone to bed. 30. Seriously speaking, that young man is not worthy of being respected. 31. Those children appear to be well. 32. If the population of the towns goes on increasing, and that of the country diminishing, we shall probably have great misfortunes. 33. I saw him coming down the street, before I met you. 34. While travelling, I saw many astonishing things. 35. Did you not see my brothers going out?

The Past Participle.

367. The past participle is used, (1) without auxiliary, (2) with être, (3) with avoir (or être used as avoir).

368. Without Auxiliary. A past participle without any auxiliary has the force of an *adjective* (attributive, predicative, appositive), and *agrees* like an adj. in gender and number with the word qualified:

Des fêtes données par le roi.	Festivities given by the king.
Les battus ; les morts.	The beaten ; the dead.
Le passé n'est plus à nous.	The past is no longer ours.
Jean et Marie semblent fatigués.	John and Mary look tired.
Tenez les portes fermées.	Keep the doors closed.
Il me regardèrent étonnés.	They looked at me astonished.

a. Certain past participles have *prepositional* force when *preceding* the subst., and are *invariable*, but are *variable* when *following:*

Vu les difficultés.	In view of the difficulties.
Excepté eux ; eux exceptés.	Except them ; they excepted.

Such are: **Approuvé, attendu, certifié, collationné, y compris, non compris, entendu, excepté, ouï, payé, passé, supposé, vu,** etc.

b. **Ci-inclus** = 'enclosed' and **ci-joint** = 'herewith,' are invariable when beginning a sentence or when followed by a noun without article:

Vous recevez ci-joint copie, etc.	You receive herewith a copy, etc.
Ci-inclus la copie, etc.	Herewith the copy, etc.

But: J'envoie ci-jointe une (la) copie, etc.

369. With *être*. A past participle with **être** *agrees* with the *subject* (except in the compound tenses of reflexives, §324):

Ils sont (ont été) battus.	They are (have been) beaten.
Marie et Louise sont venues.	Mary and Louisa have come.
Ils sont sortis.	They have gone out.
Les dames étant arrivées.	The ladies having come.
Elle parla d'avoir été blessée.	She spoke of having been wounded.

a. Hence the past part. of an impers. verb with **être** is *invariable*, agreeing strictly with the grammatical subject **il**:

Il était venu des soldats.	Soldiers had come.

370. With *avoir*. 1. A past participle with **avoir** *agrees* with a *preceding direct object;* otherwise it is invariable:

La pièce que j'ai écrite, l'avez-vous lue?	Have you read the play I wrote?
Quels livres a-t-il apportés?	What books did he bring?
But: J'ai écrit la lettre.	I have written the letter.
Elles ont lu et écrit.	They have read and written.
Je lui ai donné la lettre.	I have given her the letter.

2. Similarly, the past participle of a reflexive verb (conjugated with **être** for **avoir**) always *agrees* with the *reflexive object*, unless that object be indirect:

Ils se sont réjouis.	They have rejoiced.
Elles s'étaient trompées.	They were mistaken.
Elle s'est blessée.	She wounded herself.
Elle s'est laissée tomber.	She has fallen (fell).

But : Ils se sont écrit. — They wrote to each other.
Elle s'est blessé la main. — She wounded her hand.
Ils se sont arrogé ce privilège — They assumed that privilege.
Ils se sont plu à Paris. — They enjoyed themselves in Paris.

a. Besides the indir. reflexive obj., a direct obj. may be present, with which the following past participle agrees :

Les robes qu'elle s'est achetées. — The dresses she bought herself.

371. Remarks. All cases of the agreement of the past part. depend upon the above general principles; special difficulties are :—

1. The past participle of an **impersonal verb** is *invariable:*

La belle journée qu'il a **fait** ! — What a fine day it was !
La disette qu'il y a **eu.** — The scarcity there was.

2. A noun denoting *distance, time, price, weight,* etc. with such verbs as **marcher, courir, vivre, coûter, peser, valoir,** etc., is *adverbial accusative* (*not* dir. obj.); hence no agreement :

Les dix milles que j'ai marché. — The ten miles I walked.
Les cent francs que cet ouvrage m'a valu. — The hundred francs that book cost me.

a. Such verbs *transitively* (or figuratively with transitive force) follow the general rule :

La malle que j'ai pesée. — The trunk which I weighed.
Les dangers qu'il a courus. — The dangers he incurred.
La peur que cela a coûtée. — The fear which that caused.

3. A past participle preceded by an expression of *number* or *quantity,* a *collective,* etc., is variable or invariable according to the sense (cf. §§311-314) :

Que de maux il a soufferts ! — What ills he endured !
C'est la moitié des meubles qu'on a saisie. — It is the half of the furniture that has been seized.
La moitié des meubles que j'ai vendue. — The half of the furniture which I sold.
Quelle joie, quel bonheur vous lui avez procuré ! — What joy, what happiness you have procured him !

a. **En** (partitive) is never direct object; agreement, however, takes place with **combien, plus, moins,** preceding **en,** if the sense be plural:

Combien Dieu en a-t-il exaucés!	How many of them God has heard!
Plus on vous a donné de livres, plus vous en avez lus.	The more books you were given, the more of them you read.

4. When an infinitive (with or without a prep.) follows, the past part. is *invariable* when the preceding dir. obj. is governed by the *infin.*, and *variable* if governed by the *past part. alone:*

La lettre que j'ai voulu écrire.	The letter I wished to write.
La lettre que j'ai oublié d'écrire.	The letter I forgot to write.
Il nous a priés d'aller.	He begged us to go.
On nous a dit de sortir.	They told us to go out.

a. **Entendu, vu, laissé** *agree* when the infin. has *active* force, but are *invariable,* it it has *passive* force (§363):

La dame que j'ai entendue chanter.	The lady I heard sing(ing).
Les enfants que j'ai vu battre.	The children I saw beaten.

b. After **dû, pu, voulu, osé,** with auxiliary force, a governing infin. is either expressed or implied; hence no agreement:

J'ai lu tous les livres que j'ai pu (lire).	I read all the books that I could (read).
But: Les livres que j'ai voulus.	The books I wished.

c. **Fait** + *infin.* is *invariable:*

Les médecins qu'il a fait venir.	The doctors he sent for.

d. The past part. of **avoir à** is *variable* or *invariable:*

Les lettres que j'ai eu (eues) à lire.	The letters I had to read.

5. The relative pron. **que** is sometimes direct object of a verb in a following **que** clause (either fully expressed or implied), and hence the past participle is *invariable:*

Des choses que j'ai cru qu'il ferait.	Things I thought he would do.
J'ai lu les livres qu'il a voulu (que je lusse).	I read the books which he wished (me to read).

EXERCISE LXIII.

Elle s'y est plu.	She liked it there.
Vous êtes-vous bien amusé?	Did you have a good time?
Elles se sont donné la main.	They have shaken hands.
Elles se sont brouillées.	They have fallen out.
Les grandes chaleurs qu'il a fait.	The great heat that there has been.

1. That is the old lady whom I saw fall in the street yesterday. 2. She fell in front of Mr. Simon's, and I helped her to get up. 3. Our friends have gone away, but they will come back to-morrow. 4. Your mother has been in the country; how did she like it there? 5. She enjoyed herself (there) very much; she intends to go back again soon. 6. Your sister and mother have come. 7. You will find enclosed [a] copy of the contract which we have signed. 8. The ten hours that he has slept have not been enough to rest him. 9. The children had a good time to-day at the picnic. 10. Where is the servant? 11. I have let her go to see her friends. 12. Those are the three miles that I ran to *(pour)* fetch the doctor. 13. Those are the dangers we have incurred to save our country! 14. She remembered the dangers I had incurred. 15. Did those two ladies shake hands? 16. No; they did not even look at each other. 17. Those ladies have written each other many letters. 18. There are the letters I wrote. 19. Those young ladies have fallen out, and have burnt the letters they wrote to each other. 20. They have said good-bye to each other. 21. They have lost what they have given each other. 22. The great heat that there has been has killed the crops. 23. The person I asked *(prier)* to sing will not sing. 24. What difficulty we have had to remember what you told us! 25. The crops are poor this year; the great heat has killed them. 26. That is the house which we had built. 27. How many houses they have built! 28. How many beautiful houses they have had built! 29. That is the lady we heard sing at the concert last evening. 30. Those are the children we saw playing this morning. 31. Those are the beautiful songs we heard sung at the concert. 32. Do you remember the houses we saw being built last year? 33. There is a letter which I forgot to put in the post. 34. He has read all the books he could. 35. There are the books we sent for. 36. We have told them to go out. 37. Those are the books which I thought he would read.

GOVERNMENT OF VERBS.

372. Transitives. 1. A transitive verb governs a *direct object*, as in English:

J'ai écrit la lettre (des lettres).   I wrote the letter (letters).

2. A transitive can have only *one* direct object; other substantives related to it must stand as indirect object or as prepositional complement:

Pardonnez-lui ses péchés.   Pardon him his sins.
Je donne le dé à la fille.   I give the girl the thimble.
Je lui donne le dé avec plaisir.   I give her the thimble with pleasure.
Je conseille à mon fils d'aller.   I advise my son to go.

a. By an extension of this principle, the verb **faire** = 'make,' 'cause to,' etc. + *infin.* requires an *indir.* personal object, when the infin. has a dir. obj.; otherwise not:

Je fais lire ce livre à mon fils.	I make my son read this book.
Je lui fais lire ce livre.	I make him read this book.
But: Je fais lire mon fils.	I make my son read.
Je le fais lire.	I make him read.

b. **Laisser, voir, entendre, ouïr**, may have, and frequently do have, the same construction:

Laissez-le (-lui) lire le livre.	Let him read the book.
Je l' (lui) ai vu jouer ce rôle.	I saw him play that part.
But: Laissez lire l'enfant.	Let the child read.

373. Intransitives. An intransitive verb can have no direct object, but may, of course, have an indir. obj. or a prepositional complement:

Il parle à ce soldat.	He is speaking to that soldier.
Il lui parle de la guerre.	He speaks to him of the war.

a. A very few intransitives govern a direct object anomalously:

Où avez-vous passé l'été?	Where did you pass the summer?
Il va tout droit son chemin.	He goes straight on his way.

NOTE.—Many verbs serve both as *transitives* and *intransitives:* 'Il est descendu (intr.),' 'He has gone down'; 'Il a descendu le tableau (tran.), 'He has taken down the picture.'.

374. Predicative Complement. Nouns are used predicatively after certain verbs, as follows:—

1. In *nominative* relation:

Ils sont Anglais (médecins).	They are Englishmen (doctors).
Elle est morte jeune fille.	She died a young girl.

Such verbs are:

demeurer, *remain.*	mourir, *die.*	rester, *remain.*
devenir, *become.*	naître, *be born.*	sembler, *seem.*
entrer, *enter.*	paraître, *appear.*	sortir, *go out.*
être, *be.*	passer, *pass.*	etc.
être censé, *be supposed.*		

2. In *accusative* relation:

On le fit roi.	They made him king.
Je le connais honnête homme.	I know him to be an honest man.

238 FRENCH GRAMMAR. [374, 375.

Such verbs are:

appeler, *call.*
couronner, *crown.*
croire, *believe.*
déclarer, *declare.*
élire, *elect.*

estimer, *esteem.*
faire, *make.*
se faire, *become.*
instituer, *institute.*
juger, *judge.*

se montrer, *show one's self.*
nommer, *name.*
proclamer, *proclaim.*
savoir, *know.*
etc.

375. Prepositional Complement. The use of de and à alone presents special difficulty, since other prepositions have, in general, their usual literal force :—

1. Some verbs with **de** have the force of an English *transitive*, de being untranslated:

Il médit de ses voisins.   He slanders his neighbours.
Il ne jouit de rien.   He enjoys nothing.

abuser de, *misuse.*
s'apercevoir de, *perceive.*
s'approcher de, *approach.*
avoir besoin de, *need.*
avoir peur de, *fear.*
avoir pitié de, *pity.*
convenir de, *admit.*
se défier de, *mistrust.*

se démettre de, *resign.*
disconvenir de, *deny.*
douter de, *suspect, doubt.*
se douter de, *suspect.*
gémir de, *bemoan.*
jouir de, *enjoy.*
manquer de, *lack.*
médire de, *slander.*

se méfier de, *mistrust.*
partir de, *leave.*
se passer de, *do without.*
se servir de, *use.*
se souvenir de, *recollect.*
se tromper de, *mistake.*
user de, *employ, use.*
etc.

2. Similarly, some verbs with **à** have the force of an English *transitive*, à being untranslated:

Il obéit à son père.   He obeys his father.
Je lui ai résisté.   I have resisted him.

Such verbs are:

aller à, *fit, suit.*
arriver à, *reach.*
attenter à, *attempt.*
compâtir à, *pity.*
convenir à, *suit.*
déplaire à, *displease.*
désobéir à, *disobey.*
se fier à, *trust.*
importer à, *concern.*

nuire à, *harm.*
obéir à, *obey.*
obvier à, *obviate.*
ordonner à, *order.*
pardonner à, *pardon.*
parvenir à, *attain.*
permettre à, *permit.*
persuader à, *persuade.*
plaire à, *please.*

promettre à, *promise.*
remédier à, *remedy.*
renoncer à, *renounce.*
répondre à, *answer.*
résister à, *resist.*
ressembler à, *resemble.*
succéder à, *succeed.*
survivre à, *survive.*
etc.

3. In some instances, on the contrary, a French *transitive* has the force of an Eng. *verb + a prep.*:

Payez-lui les livres.   Pay him for the books.
Je regarde cet arbre-là.   I am looking at that tree.

Such verbs are:

accepter, *accept of.*	demander, *ask for.*	payer, *pay for.*
admettre, *admit of.*	désirer, *wish for.*	regarder, *look at.*
approuver, *approve of.*	écouter, *listen to.*	rencontrer, *meet with.*
attendre, *wait for.*	envoyer chercher, *send for.*	souhaiter, *wish for.*
chercher, *look for.*	espérer, *hope for.*	etc.

4. **De** and **à** frequently have, as compared with English, a special idiomatic force with certain verbs:

Cela dépend de vous. — That depends on you.
Pensez à votre devoir. — Think of your duty.

Such verbs are:

s'affliger de, *grieve at.*	se désoler de, *grieve over.*	punir de, *punish for.*
approcher (s'-) de, *draw near to.*	diner de, *dine on.*	récompenser de, *reward for.*
	féliciter de, *congratulate on.*	se réjouir de, *rejoice at.*
blâmer de, *blame for.*	gémir de, *lament over.*	remercier de, *thank for.*
complimenter de, *compliment on.*	louer de, *praise for.*	rire de, *laugh at.*
	se mêler de, *meddle with.*	triompher de, *triumph over.*
consoler de, *console for.*	se nourrir de, *live on.*	vivre de, *live on.*
déjeuner de, *breakfast on.*	profiter de, *profit by.*	etc.
dépendre de, *depend on.*		

---

acheter qqch. à qqu., *buy something from (or for) some one*
arracher qqch. à qqu., *snatch from.*
cacher qqch. à qqu., *hide from.*
conférer qqch. à qqu., *confer on.*
demander qqch. à qqu., *ask for (of).*
dérober qqch. à qqu., *steal from.*
emprunter qqch. à qqu., *borrow from.*
infliger qqch. à qqu., *inflict on.*
inspirer qqch. à qqu., *inspire with.*
mêler qqch. à qqch., *mingle with.*
ôter qqch. à qqu., *take away from.*
pardonner qqch. à qqu., *pardon for.*
payer qqch. à qqu., *pay for.*
penser à qqch. or à qqu., *think of.*
prendre qqch. à qqu., *take from.*
pourvoir à qqch., *provide for.*
procurer qqch. à qqu., *procure for.*
prodiguer qqch. à qqu., *lavish on.*
reprocher qqch. à qqu., *reproach with.*
souhaiter qqch. à qqu., *wish.*
voler qqch. à qqu., *steal from.*

5. Many verbs have a *double* construction with varying meaning:

Ils jouent aux cartes. — They are playing cards.
Elle joue du piano. — She is playing the piano.

Such verbs are:

abuser qqu., *deceive.*
" de qqch., *misuse.*
assister qqu., *help.*
" à qqch., *be present at, witness.*
concourir à qqch., *contribute to.*
" pour qqch., *compete for.*
convenir à qqu., *suit.*
convenir de qqch., *agree about.*
croire, qqu. or qqch., *believe.*
" à, en, *believe in.*
demander qqu. or qqch., *ask after.*
" qqch. à qqu., *ask for (from, of).*
hériter de qqu., *be heir of.*
" de qqch., *inherit.*

jouer qqu., *deceive*.
" d'un instrument, *play on an instrument*.
" à un jeu, *play (at) a game*.
manquer qqu. or qqch., *miss*.
" de, *lack*.
" à, *fail in*.
penser à, *think of (about)*.
penser de, *have opinion of*.
prétendre qqch., *assert*.
" à, *aspire to*.
servir, *serve* (tr. and intr.).
" de, *serve as*.
" à, *be useful for*.
se servir de, *make use of*.

suppléer qqu., *take the place of*.
" à qqch., *complete*.
toucher qqu. or qqch., *touch*.
" de l'argent, *draw money*.
" à, *meddle with, be near to*.
" d'un instrument, *play an instrument* (keyed).
user qqch., *wear out*.
" de, *make use of*.
en user de, *deal, act*.
veiller qqu., *watch over, nurse*.
" à qqch., *attend to, watch over*.
" sur qqu., *watch over*.
etc.

376. Position. Objects and prepositional complements regularly *follow* the verb, the direct obj. (if any) being first; but if of unequal length, the longer usually last. For position of personal pronouns see the Pronoun.

377. Composite Complement. The various parts of a complement must be of the *same grammatical value, i.e.*, all nouns, all verbs, etc.:

Il apprend à lire est à chanter.	He learns to read and sing.
Il apprend la lecture et le chant.	He learns reading and singing.

378. Manifold Verb. Two or more verbs can govern the same complement only if alike in government:

Il aime et respecte son **oncle**.	He loves and respects his uncle.
Il aime son **oncle** et lui obéit.	He loves and obeys his uncle.

EXERCISE LXIV.

Il se croit honnête homme.	He thinks he is an honest man.
Il ne s'en est pas aperçu.	He did not notice it.
Ce chapeau ne lui va pas.	That hat does not fit him.
Il ne (nous) est pas permis de...	We are not permitted to...
Je le lui ai payé.	I paid him for it.
Je l'en ai remercié.	I thanked him for it.
Je pense à vous.	I am thinking of you.
Que pensez-vous de cela ?	What do you think of that ?

1. We shall make them do their work. 2. They *(on)* have made her suffer great ills. 3. Show them up-stairs, when they come. 4. I have seen the children play. 5. We have seen him play that part. 6. He

was born [a] poet. 7. He has become [a] soldier. 8. What will become of us! 9. I believe he is an honest man. 10. He thinks he is [a] scholar. 11. I know he is [a] scholar. 12. We should not slander our neighbours. 13. I perceived their dejection, as soon as I came in; did you? (see §336). 14. No, I did not notice it. 15. We cannot do without our books; we are going to use them to-morrow. 16. I remember the sorrows you made me undergo. 17. These gloves do not fit me. 18. That young lady's gloves do not fit her. 19. I shall look for a house which suits me better (see §350, 1). 20. That house does not suit our friends. 21. I cannot trust him; he often lies. 22. The son resembles his father. 23. We are not permitted to leave the city. 24. The law does not permit children to marry. 25. The king pardons him his crime. 26. Did you pay the tailor for your coat? 27. I have not paid him for it yet. 28. What are you looking at? 29. I am looking at those men working in the field. 30. Wait for me, till I come. 31. I think of my friends who have gone away. 32. Do you think of the money you have lost? 33. I do not. 34. Shall you be at the ball this evening? 35. I do not know; that depends on you. 36. Did you thank him for having lent you his book? 37. I did. 38. He stole that watch from his father; what do you think of that? 39. He is laughing at us. 40. Those men were playing cards. 41. Those young ladies play on the violin. 42. You believe me; do you not? 43. Yes, I believe you. 44. That old lady believes in ghosts. 45. He loves and obeys his parents. 46. He missed the train; did he not? 47. I am short of money this morning; I cannot pay you. 48. He fails in his duty, when he does not pay his debts. 49. Have you asked your father for money? 50. I have not asked him for any.

THE NOUN.

Gender of Nouns.

379. Nouns in French are either *masculine* or *feminine*. As an aid to memory, general rules for determining gender are given in the following sections.

380. Gender by Meaning. 1. Names of *male beings* are usually *masc.*, and names of *female beings fem.*:

Un homme; une femme.	A man; a woman.
Un bœuf; une vache.	An ox; a cow.

P

a. Most nouns denoting professions, *e.g.*, docteur, *doctor*, écrivain, *writer*, imprimeur, *printer*, etc., and a few nouns lacking a fem. form, *e.g.*, ange, *angel*, témoin, *witness*, etc., remain masc., when applied to females.

Elle est **un auteur** distingué.	She is a celebrated authoress.
Marie est **un ange**.	Mary is an angel.

b. Some names of lower animals are *masc. only*, *e.g.*, éléphant, *elephant*, hibou, *owl*; others are *fem. only*, *e.g.*, fourmi, *ant*, souris, *mouse*; ambiguity may be avoided by adding mâle or femelle:

Un éléphant mâle (femelle).	A he- (she-) elephant.

c. Some nouns are *fem. only*, whether applied to males or females:

caution, *surety*.	personne, *person*.	vedette, *scout*.
connaissance, *acquaintance*.	pratique, *customer*.	victime, *victim*.
dupe, *dupe*.	recrue, *recruit*.	vigie, *look-out man*.
ganache, *blockhead*.	sentinelle, *sentinel*.	etc.

2. The following are *masculine*:—

(1) Names of *cardinal points* and *winds*:

Le nord; le sud; le zéphyr.   The north; the south; the zephyr.

a. Feminine *exceptions* are:

bise, *north wind*.   mousson, *monsoon*.   tramontane, *north wind*.
brise, *breeze*.

(2) Names of *seasons, months, days* (of the week):

Le printemps; octobre; lundi.   Spring; October; Monday.

(3) Names of *countries* (not in -e):

Le Canada; le Dauphiné; le Chili.   Canada; Dauphiny; Chili.

(4) Most names of *mountains* (not in -es) and most names of *rivers*:

Le Hartz; le Jura; les Appenins. Harz mts.; mt. Jura; the Appenines.
Le Volga; le Rhône; le Rhin.   The Volga; the Rhone; the Rhine.
But fem. Les Alpes (Pyrénées, Vosges, etc.).

a. The rivers of France in -e are nearly all *feminine*:

La Seine (Loire, etc.).   The Seine (Loire, etc.).

(5) Names of *trees* and *shrubs*:

Le chêne (bouleau, érable, pommier). The oak (birch, maple, apple-tree).

a. Feminine *exceptions* are:

aubépine, *hawthorn*.	ébène, *ebony*.	ronce, *bramble*.
bourdaine, *buckthorn*.	épine, *thorn*.	vigne, *vine*.
bruyère, *heath*.	hièble, *dwarf-elder*.	viorne, *wild clematis*.

(6) Names of *weights* and *measures* (metrical system) :
Un mètre (gramme, litre, etc.). A metre (gramme, litre, etc.).

(7) Names of *metals* and *chemicals :*
Le fer (or, cuivre, argent, sulphate). Iron (gold, copper, silver, sulphate).

a. Feminine *exceptions* are :
fonte, *cast-iron*. tôle, *sheet-iron*.

(8) Words and phrases *not nouns* when *used as nouns :*
Le beau ; le blanc ; le français. The beautiful ; white ; French.
Un a ; un mais ; un ouï-dire. An 'a'; a 'but'; a rumour.
Le devant (derrière) de la main. The front (back) of the hand.

a. Adjs. referring to concrete objects have the gender of the noun understood ; for letters of the alphabet, see also §1, note 3 :
Une belle (*sc.* dame, femme, etc.). A beauty.
Une capitale (*sc.* ville, lettre). A capital.

3. The following are *feminine :—*
(1) Names of *countries* in -e :
La France (Asie, Normandie). France (Asia, Normandy).

a. Masculine *exceptions* are :
le Bengale, *Bengal*. le Mexique, *Mexico*. le Pélopon(n)èse, *Peloponnesus*.
le Hanovre, *Hanover*. le Maine, *Maine* (in Fr.). etc.

(2) Most names of *cities* and *towns* (especially in -e, -es) :
Rome ; Athènes ; Tyr ; Ilion. Rome ; Athens ; Tyre ; Ilium.

a. Masculine *exceptions* are :
le Caire, *Cairo*. Londres, *London*. Paris, *Paris*.
le Hâvre, *Havre*. Versailles, *Versailles*. etc.

NOTES.—1. Any name of a town or city is *masc.* as a *collective :* 'Tout Rome le sait,' 'All Rome knows it.' 2. In case of doubt as to the gender, the name may always be preceded by **la ville de** = 'the town (city) of.'

(3) Names of *holydays* (**fête de** being understood) :
La Saint-Martin ; la mi-juin. Martinmas ; mid-June.

a. Observe :
Noël (*or* la Noël, *or* la fête de Noël), *Christmas*.

(4) Names of *arts, sciences, trades :*
La peinture (chimie, librairie). Painting (chemistry, book-trade).

a. Principal *exception :*
le dessin, *drawing*.

381. Gender by Endings. 1. *Masculine* are most nouns ending as follows :—

(1) In a *vowel sound* (not -e mute):

Un opéra (côté, chapeau, cheveu.) An opera (side, hat, hair).
Un parti (zéro, caillou, tissu). A party (zero, pebble, tissue).

a. Feminine *exceptions* are :

guérilla, *guerilla*.	moitié, *half*.	bru, *daughter-in-law*.
gutta-percha, *gutta-percha*.	fourmi, *ant*.	glu, *bird-lime*.
polka, *polka*.	merci, *mercy*.	tribu, *tribe*.
razzia, *raid*.	foi, *faith*.	vertu, *virtue*.
tombola, *charity-lottery*.	loi, *law*.	eau, *water*.
véranda, *verandah*.	paroi, *wall*.	peau, *skin*.
cité, *city*.	virago, *virago*.	etc.

Further, abstracts in -té, -tié :

amitié, *friendship*.	liberté, *liberty*.	santé, *health*.
charité, *charity*.	pitié, *pity*.	etc.

(2) In a *consonant:*

Le sac (pied, joug, sol, nez, temps). The sack (foot, yoke, soil, nose, time).

a. Feminine *exceptions* are :

clef, *key*.	chair, *flesh*.	vis, *screw*.	croix, *cross*.
nef, *ship, nave*.	cour, *court*.	dent, *tooth*.	faux, *scythe*.
soif, *thirst*.	cuiller, *spoon*.	dot, *dower*.	noix, *walnut*.
faim, *hunger*.	mer, *sea*.	forêt, *forest*.	paix, *peace*.
façon, *fashion*.	tour, *tower*.	gent, *tribe*.	perdrix, *partridge*.
fin, *end*.	brebis, *sheep*.	mort, *death*.	poix, *pitch*.
leçon, *lesson*.	fois, *time*.	nuit, *night*.	toux, *cough*.
main, *hand*.	oasis, *oasis*.	part, *part, share*.	voix, *voice*.
rançon, *ransom*.	souris, *mouse*.	chaux, *lime*.	etc.

Further, nouns in -son, -ion and most *abstracts* in -eur (cf. §382, *a*) :

chanson, *song*.	nation, *nation*.	faveur, *favour*.
maison, *house*.	occasion, *occasion*.	fureur, *fury*.
raison, *reason*.	possession, *possession*.	peur, *fear*.
trahison, *treason*.	couleur, *colour*.	etc.

(3) In -acle, -age, -asme, -ège, -ème, -isme, -tère :

Le spectacle (voyage, sarcasme, The spectacle (journey, sarcasm, college, diadème, magnétisme, college, diadem, magnetism, mystère). tery).

a. For *exceptions*, see dictionary ; the following *fems.* in -age should be noted :

cage, *cage*.	nage, *swimming*.	plage, *beach*.
image, *image*.	page, *page (of a book)*.	rage, *rage*.

GENDER OF NOUNS.

2. *Feminine* are most nouns ending as follows :—
(1) In -e *preceded by a vowel or double consonant:*

Une année (vie, vue, raie, soie, roue, pluie, famille, flamme, couronne, tristesse, botte).

A year (life, sight, streak, silk, wheel, rain, family, flame, crown, sadness, boot).

a. For *exceptions*, see dictionary.

(2) In -ace, -ade, -ance, -ence, -euse, -ière, -oire, -ude, -ure :

La préface (salade, constance, présence, défense, lumière, histoire, habitude, culture).

The preface (salad, constancy, presence, defence, light, history, habit, culture).

a. For *exceptions*, see dictionary.

382. Gender by Derivation. 1. Nouns derived from Latin *mascs.* are regularly *masc. :*

Mur (L. *murum*) ; livre (L. *librum*) ; ordre (L. *ordinem*) ; poète (L. *poeta*).

Wall ; book ; order ; poet.

a. Exceptions are not uncommon (see dictionary) ; Latin *masc.* abstracts in -or (acc. -orem) have become *fem.* (except m. honneur, déshonneur, labeur, amour) :

candeur, f. (L. *candorem*), *candour.*
*couleur, f. (L. *colorem*), *colour.*
douleur, f. (L. *dolorem*), *pain.*
erreur, f. (L. *errorem*), *error.*
fureur, f. (L. *furorem*), *fury.*
etc.

*Masc. in such phrases as 'couleur de feu,' 'couleur de rose,' etc., *e.g.*, 'ce ruban est d'un beau couleur de rose.'

2. Nouns derived from Latin *fems.* are regularly *fem. :*

Justice (L. *justitiam*) ; charité (L. *caritatem*) ; main (L. *manum*) ; foi (L. *fidem*).

Justice ; charity ; hand ; faith.

a. Exceptions are not uncommon (see dictionary).

3. Nouns derived from Latin *neuters* are regularly *masc.:*

Corps (L. *corpus*); fer (L. *ferrum*); or (L. *aurum*); pré (L. *pratum*); siècle (L. *sæculum*); verbe (L. *verbum*).

Body ; iron ; gold ; meadow ; century ; verb.

a. More than a hundred *neuter plurs.* in -a have become *fem. sing.* in French, just as if derived from nouns in -a of the Lat. 1st declension :

arme (L. *arma*), *arm.*
date (L. *data*), *date.*
dette (L. *debita*), *debt.*
étude (L. *studia*), *study.*
feuille (L. *folia*), *leaf.*
graine (L. *grana*), *seed.*
huile (L. *olea*), *oil.*
joie (L. *gaudia*), *joy.*
lèvre (L. *labra*), *lip.*
œuvre (L. *opera*), *work.*
pomme (L. *poma*), *apple.*
etc.

383. Nouns of Double Gender. 1. Some nouns denoting persons (mostly in -e) and adjs. in -e, when so used, are either *masc.* or *fem.*:

Un (une) artiste; un (une) élève.   An artist; a pupil.
Un (une) malade; un (une) rebelle.   A patient; a rebel.

Such nouns are:

aide, *assistant*.	*enfant, *child*.	propriétaire, *owner*.
camarade, *comrade*.	esclave, *slave*.	pupille, *ward*.
compatriote, *compatriot*.	locataire, *tenant*.	etc.

*Always *masc.* in the plur.

2. The meaning of some nouns varies with the gender:

Un critique; une critique.   A critic; a criticism.
Le mode; la mode.   The mode, mood (gram.); the fashion.

Such nouns are:

	Masc.	Fem.		Masc.	Fem.
aide,	*assistant*,	*assistant, help*.	page,	*page*,	*page (of a book)*.
aune,	*alder*,	*ell*.	pendule,	*pendulum*,	*clock*.
crêpe,	*crape*,	*pancake*.	poêle,	*stove, pall*,	*frying-pan*.
critique,	*critic*,	*criticism*.	politique,	*politician*,	*politics*.
garde,	*guard* (mil.), *keeper*,	*keeper, body of troops, watch, hilt*.	poste, somme,	*position*, *sleep, nap*,	*post-office*. *sum*.
guide,	*guide*,	*rein*.	souris,	*smile*,	*mouse*.
livre,	*book*,	*pound*.	statuaire,	*sculptor*,	*sculpture*.
manche,	*handle*,	*sleeve*.	tour,	*turn, trick*,	*tower*.
mémoire,	*memorandum*,	*memory*.	trompette,	*trumpeter*,	*trumpet*.
merci,	*thanks*,	*mercy, pity*.	vapeur,	*steamer*,	*steam*.
mode,	*mode, mood*,	*fashion*.	vase,	*vase*,	*slime, mud*.
moule,	*mould*,	*mussel*.	voile,	*veil*,	*sail*.
mousse,	*cabin-boy*,	*moss*.	etc.		
office,	*service*,	*larder*.			

3. The following nouns are *masc.* or *fem.*, either with identical or closely related meaning:—

a. **Après-midi** = 'afternoon' and **automne** = 'autumn' are usually *masc.*, sometimes *fem.*

b. **Amour** (m.) = 'love,' 'loved object,' 'passion,' 'amour'; **amour** (f. s. poet.) = 'passion,' 'amour'; **amours** (f. pl.) = 'passion,' 'amours.'

c. **Délice** = 'delight' and **orgue** = 'organ' (mus.) are *masc.* in *sing.* and *fem.* in *plur.*

d. **Hymne** (m.) = 'hymn,' 'song of praise'; **hymne** (f.) = '(church) hymn' (more usually 'cantique,' m.).

e. **Couple** (m.) = 'couple,' 'pair' (joined by affection, sentiment, etc.); **couple** (f.) = 'couple,' 'two' (two like objects taken together):

Un couple d'amants.   A pair of lovers.
Une couple d'œufs.   Two (a couple of) eggs.
Note: Une **paire** de gants, etc.   A pair of gloves, etc.

f. **Pâque** or **pâques** (m. s.)='Easter'; **pâques fleuries** (f. pl.)= 'Palm Sunday' (so also in other phrases); **pâque** (f.)='passover.'

g. **Orge** (f.)='barley' is *masc.* in **orge mondé (perlé)**='pot-(pearl-) barley.'

h. **Foudre** (f.)='thunderbolt' is sometimes *masc.* in poetry or elevated prose; **foudre** (m.) in **le foudre de Jupiter**='Jove's thunderbolt' and in figurative expressions, *e.g.*, **un grand foudre de guerre**= 'a great warrior.'

i. **Œuvre** (f.)='work,' 'works,' is sometimes *masc.* in elevated style; **œuvre** (m. s.)='works' (collectively of an engraver or musician); **le grand œuvre**='the philosopher's stone'; **le gros œuvre**='heavy stone-work'; **de l'œuvre** (m.)='silver-lead.'

j. **Gens** (pl. m. or f.)='people,' 'persons,' etc. Attributive adjs. are *fem.* when *preceding* and *masc.* when *following* **gens**, but *predicatives* (before or after) are *masc.* 'All' is translated by **toutes** only when *attributive* and *separated* from **gens** by an *adj. variable for the fem.*; otherwise by **tous**:

De vieilles gens résolus.	Resolute old people.
Les petites gens et les grands.	The small people and the great.
Merci, bonnes gens, merci.	Thanks, good people, thanks.
Heureux les gens de bon cœur.	Happy (are) the good-hearted.
Toutes les vieilles gens.	All the old people.
But: Tous les habiles gens.	All the clever people.
Tous ces gens-ci.	All these people.
Tous sont de bonnes gens.	All are good people.
Les gens sont tous ici.	The people are all here.

NOTES.—1. A pron. to which **gens** is antecedent is *masc.*: 'Les gens **qui** sont venus,' 'The people who have come.' 2. **Gens** in expressions like **gens de robe**='lawyers' and in **jeunes gens**='young men' is always *masc.*

384. Formation of the Feminine. Most nouns denoting living beings distinguish the masc. and fem. as follows:—

1. Some by a *different word*:

M.	F.	M.	F.
bœuf, *ox*,	vache.	mari, *husband*.	femme.
bouc, *he-goat*.	chèvre.	oncle, *uncle*.	tante.
coq, *cock*.	poule.	parrain, *god-father*.	marraine.
frère, *brother*.	sœur.	porc, *pig*.	truie.
homme, *man*.	femme.	etc.	etc.

a. The fem. form is often obviously *cognate:*

M.	F.	M.	F.
ambassadeur, *ambassador.*	ambassadrice.	gouverneur, *tutor.*	gouvernante.
canard, *drake.*	cane.	loup, *wolf.*	louve.
*chanteur, *singer.*	cantatrice.	mulet, *mule.*	mule.
cochon, *hog.*	coche.	*procureur, *proxy.*	procuratrice.
compagnon, *companion.*	compagne.	serviteur, *servant.*	servante.
dindon, *turkey-cock.*	dinde.	vieillard, *old man.*	vieille.
empereur, *emperor.*	impératrice.	etc.	etc.

*Also in -euse, see §415, 2, (2), *a.*

2. Some by *adding* -esse to the last consonant:

M.	F.	M.	F.
abbé, *abbot.*	abbesse.	ogre, *ogre.*	ogresse.
âne, *ass.*	ânesse.	pair, *peer.*	pairesse.
chanoine, *canon.*	chanoinesse.	pauvre, *pauper.*	pauvresse.
comte, *count.*	comtesse.	prêtre, *priest.*	prêtresse.
diable, *devil.*	diablesse.	prince, *prince.*	princesse.
drôle, *rogue.*	drôlesse.	suisse, *Swiss.*	suissesse.
druide, *druid.*	druidesse.	tigre, *tiger.*	tigresse.
hôte, *host.*	hôtesse.	traître, *traitor.*	traitresse.
maître, *master.*	maîtresse.	etc.	etc.

a. So also the following, but with *changes in the stem:*

M.	F.	M.	F.
dieu, *god.*	déesse.	*chasseur, *huntsman.*	chasseresse.
doge, *doge.*	dogaresse.	défendeur, *defendant.*	défenderesse.
duc, *duke.*	duchesse.	*demandeur, *plaintiff.*	demanderesse.
larron, *thief.*	larronnesse.	enchanteur, *enchanter.*	enchanteresse.
nègre, *negro.*	négresse.	pécheur, *sinner.*	pécheresse.
patron, *patron.*	patronnesse.	*vendeur, *seller* (law).	venderesse.
prophète, *prophet.*	prophétesse.	vengeur, *avenger.*	vengeresse.
bailleur, *lessor.*	bailleresse.		

*Also in -euse, see §415, 2, (2), *a.*

3. A few nouns take -ine:

czar, *czar.*	czarine.	Philippe, *Philip.*	Philippine.
héros, *hero.*	héroïne.	etc.	etc.

4. Most other nouns follow the analogy of adjs. of like termination, and will be noted under the Adjective.

EXERCISE LXV.

1. Tell the servant to put the frying-pan on the stove. 2. That man is a regular dupe. 3. He is not a friend; he is a mere acquaintance.

4. He was received with all the honours. 5. That poet is always singing of his first love. 6. The errors of men are numerous. 7. The old man has *(faire)* a nap after dinner. 8. He paid me a large sum of money. 9. My memory is not good; give me a memorandum of that affair. 10. Steam makes the steamer go. 11. That man and his wife are a happy couple. 12. I have Hugo's works at home. 13. The works of the engraver Barye were exhibited in Paris in 1889. 14. Old people are generally less thoughtless than young people. 15. Those people are not all good. 16. All those people were present. 17. All good people are worthy of respect. 18. All the clever people in *(de)* the town were present at the ball. 19. Happy [are] the people who do not love vice. 20. All the young men of the village were present at the celebration.

NUMBER OF NOUNS.

385. General Rule. The plural of a noun is regularly formed by adding s to the sing :

Roi(s); reine(s); ville(s); jardin(s). King(s); queen(s); town(s); garden(s).

386. Principal Exceptions. The following are the principal exceptions to the above rule :—

1. Nouns in -s, -x, -z remain *unchanged* in the plur.; so also *invariable words* when used as nouns :

Le bras ; la voix ; le nez.	The arm ; the voice ; the nose.
Les bras ; les voix ; les nez.	The arms ; the voices; the noses.
Les oui et les non ; les on dit.	The ayes and noes; the rumours.
Plusieurs peu font un beaucoup.	Many littles make a 'muckle.'

2. Nouns in -au, -eu and *seven* in -ou take -x :

Noyau(x); château(x); jeu(x), Kernel(s); castle(s); game(s); vow(s).
vœu(x).

The seven nouns in -ou are :

bijou(x), *jewel.*	genou(x), *knee.*	joujou(x), *toy.*
caillou(x), *pebble.*	hibou(x), *owl.*	pou(x), *louse.*
chou(x), *cabbage.*		

But: Clou(s), *nail,* sou(s), *half-penny,* etc.

3. Most nouns in -al change -al to -au and add -x as above :

Général ; cheval ; journal.	General ; horse ; newspaper.
Généraux ; chevaux ; journaux.	Generals ; horses ; newspapers.

a. But the following, and a few rarer ones in -al, are *regular:*

aval(s), *endorsement.* cal(s), *callosity.* chacal(s), *jackal.*
bal(s), *ball (for dancing).* carnaval(s), *carnival.* régal(s), *treat.*

4. The following in -ail have the plural in -aux :

bail (-aux), *lease.* travail (-aux), *work.* vitrail (-aux), *stain-*
corail (-aux), *coral.* vantail (-aux), *folding-door.* *ed-glass window.*
soupirail (-aux), ventail (-aux), *ventail.*
air-hole.

But: détail(s), *detail;* éventail(s), *fan,* etc., are *regular.*

NOTE.—**Bestiaux** (pl.), *cattle* is often given as the plur. of **bétail**, *cattle;* it is from an obsolete form **bestiail**, parallel to **bétail**.

5. **Gent** = 'race,' 'tribe,' has the plural **gens** = 'people,' etc.

NOTE.—A similar omission of **t** in the plur. of nouns in -ant, -ent, now archaic, is maintained in the *Revue des deux Mondes, e.g., enfans* for *enfants.*

387. Double Plurals. The following have *two* plural forms, mostly with varying meaning :

aïeul (aïeux), *ancestor.* œil (yeux) *eye.*
" (aïeuls), *grandfather* " (œils-) in compounds, *e.g.*
ail (aulx), *garlic.* œils-de-bœuf, *oval windows.*
" (ails), " pal (paux), *pale, stake.*
ciel (cieux), *sky, heaven, climate.* " (pals), " "
" (ciels), *bed-tester, sky (in paint-* travail (travaux), *work.*
ing), roof (of a quarry). " (travails), *report (of a minis-*
ter, etc.), brake (for horse-shoeing).

Obs: The **x** plur. regularly has the *literal* meaning of the word.

388. Foreign Nouns. Nouns of foreign origin take -s usually only when fully naturalized, but usage varies greatly (see dictionary) :—

a. Partial list of *variable* foreign nouns :

accessit(s), *honourable men-* bill(s), *bill.* toast(s), *toast.*
tion. duo(s), *duo.* tramway(s), *street-railway.*
album(s), *album.* jury(s), *jury.* vivat(s), *hurrah.*
alibi(s), *alibi.* opéra(s), *opera.* etc.
bifteck(s), *beefsteak.* pensum(s), *task.*

b. Partial list of *invariable* foreign nouns :

amen. item. interim. post-scriptum. vade mecum
déficit. in-folio. magnificat. requiem. veto.
facsimile. in-octavo. nota bene. Te Deum. etc.

c. A few Italian nouns retain their plural in **i**:

dilletante(-i), *dilletante*. soprano(-i), *soprano*. quintetto(-i), *quintette*.
libretto(-i), *libretto*. lazzarone (-i), *beggar*. etc.

389. Compound Nouns. The only components which take a plur. sign are *nouns* and *adjectives*. The following are special rules:—

1. Compounds *without hyphen* are treated as one word and follow the *general rules:*

Portemanteau(x); grand'mère(s). Valise(s); grandmother(s).

a. Exceptions are:

bon(s)homme(s), *goodman, etc.* madame (mesdames), *madam, Mrs.*
gentil(s)homme(s), *nobleman*. mademoiselle (mesdemoiselles), *Miss.*
monsieur (messieurs), *Mr., sir, etc.* monseigneur (messeigneurs), *my lord.*

2. When placed in juxtaposition and connected by a hyphen *nouns* and *adjs.* are *variable:*

Chef(s)-lieu(x); chou(x)-fleur(s); County-town(s); cauliflower(s);
grand(s)-père(s). grandfather(s).

a. **Demi-** is *invariable* in compounds:

Des demi-heures. Half-hours.

b. Further *exceptions* are:

blanc-seing(s), *signature in blank*. terre-plein(s), *platform*.
chevau-léger(s), *light-horseman*. etc.

3. Of two nouns joined by preposition and hyphens the *first* only is *variable:*

Arc(s)-en-ciel; chef(s)-d'œuvre. Rainbow; masterpiece.

a. The preposition de is sometimes *understood*

bain(s)-marie, *water-bath*. timbre(s)-poste, *postage-stamp*.
hôtel(s)-dieu, *hospital*. etc.

b. The following are *invariable*, since the idea conveyed by their plur. does not properly belong to the first component simply:

coq-à-l'âne, *cock-and-bull story*. pot-au-feu, *beef and soup*.
pied-à-terre, *temporary lodging*. tête-à-tête, *private interview*.

4. A noun with preceding invariable component is usually *variable:*

Anglo-Saxon(s); Anglo-Saxon;
avant-garde(s); tire-bouchon(s); vanguard; corkscrew; viceroy;
vice-roi(s); bouche-trou(s); stop-gap.

a. But the final noun remains *invariable* when the plur. idea does not properly belong to it :

abat-jour, *lamp-shade.*	gagne-pain, *means of living.*	réveille-matin, *alarm-clock.*
coupe-gorge, *cut-throat place.*	perce-neige, *snow-drop.*	serre-tête, *head-band.*
crève-cœur, *heart-break.*	prie-dieu, *praying-stool.*	etc.
contre-poison, *antidote.*	boute-en-train, *jolly fellow.*	

b. On the other hand, a final noun of clearly plur. sense *retains* -s *in* the *sing :*

un (des) casse-noisettes, *nut-cracker.* un (des) porte-clefs, *turnkey.*
un (des) cure-dents, *tooth-pick.* etc.

5. *Invariable words* (verb, adv., prep., etc.) are *invariable* in compounds :

Des **on dit** ; des **passe-partout**. Rumours ; master-keys.

a. **Garde-** is usually *variable* in compounds denoting *persons*, and *invariable* in those denoting *things :*

des gardes-malades. sick-nurses.
But : des garde-robes. wardrobes.

390. Plural of Proper Nouns. 1. Names of *persons* or *families* are usually *invariable* in the plur.:

Les deux **Racine**.	The two Racines.
Les **Corneille** et les **Racine** de la scène.	The Corneilles and Raciues of the stage (*i. e.*, Corneille, Racine and others like them).
Les **Duval** sont arrivés.	(The) Duvals have come.

a. A few *Latin names* (originally plur. in form) and certain well-known *historical names* of families and dynasties take -s :

Les Bourbons.	Les Gracques.	Les Pharaons.	Les Tudors.
Les Césars.	Les Guises.	Les Scipions.	etc.
Les Condés.	Les Horaces.	Les Stuarts.	

b. Names of persons used as *common nouns* to denote 'persons like' or 'works by' those named are *often variable*, but usage is not fixed :

Les Corneilles sont rares. Corneilles are rare.
J'ai vu deux Raphaëls. I saw two Raphaels.
But : Les Hamlet ; les La Fontaine ; les Goethe ; les Washington, etc.

2. Names of *places* take -s when the *idea is plur. :*

Les Indes ; les Vosges.	The Indies ; the Vosges.
Les deux Romes.	The two Romes (*i.e.*, the old and new).

Case Relation and Agreement of Nouns.

391. Case Relations. The noun in French does not vary in form to denote case; it is used:—

1. With verbs, as *subject, object, predicate* (cf. §372-4):

Le père aime son fils. — The father loves his son.
Jean est devenu soldat. — John has become a soldier.

2. In *appositions* and with *adjectival force:*

Henri IV, roi de France. — Henry IV., King of France.
Un roi enfant. — A child king.

3. After *prepositions:*

J'ai parlé à son père. — I have spoken to his father.

4. *Absolutely,* generally with *adverbial* force:

Le dîner fini, il partit. — The dinner ended, he set out.
Il était là, le chapeau à la main. — He was there (with) his hat in his hand.
Je suis venu samedi. — I came on Saturday.
Il est resté trois heures. — He stayed three hours.
J'ai marché dix milles. — I walked ten miles.
Nous l'avons acheté dix francs. — We bought it for ten francs.

5. *Vocatively:*

Bonjour, mes amis. — Good morning, my friends.

392. Agreement. A predicate noun, or a noun used adjectivally, usually agrees like an adj. with the word referred to (see agreement of the Adjective):

Ils (elles) sont Allemand(e)s. — They are Germans.
La reine mère. — The queen mother.

EXERCISE LXVI.

Tomber à genoux. — To fall on one's knees.
Le petit bonhomme. — The brave little fellow.

1. That man has broken his two arms. 2. The 'ifs' and the 'buts' are often convenient words. 3. The criminal fell on his knees before the king. 4. 'That little boy likes to pick up pebbles. 5. The generals have good horses. 6. We read the newspapers before going down town [in] the morning. 7. Frenchmen like carnivals and balls. 8. Our neighbour has some beautiful corals at home. 9. The Minister of Public

Works has ordered a railway to be constructed. 10. His grandfathers are dead. 11. Our ancestors were great men who left [behind them] many noble works. 12. The poor boy had tears in his (*aux*) eyes when he was told that his bird was dead. 13. That painter makes beautiful skies. 14. Several Te Deums were sung this year in that church. 15. Give me two postage-stamps, if you please. 16. We had some delightful private interviews. 17. Those corkscrews are useless. 18. Those lamp-shades are very pretty. 19. Give me a tooth-pick, if you please. 20. Do not condemn me on rumours. 21. The two Corneilles were dramatic authors. 22. All the Ribots were present. 23. I have two Molières at home. 24. The Bourbons have been very unfortunate; I pity them. 25. I saw the school-boys marching yesterday; the brave little fellows were really fine-looking. 26. The noblemen of France have suffered much during this century. 27. There are two gentlemen and two ladies waiting for you. 28. Good morning, ladies; how do you do? 29. I have visited all the county-towns of that part of France. 30. Many of Molière's works are masterpieces.

THE ARTICLE.

393. The Indefinite Article.

Masc.	Fem.
un, a (*an*).	une, a (*an*).

394. The Definite Article.

Sing.	Plur.
M. le (l') *the.* *F.* la (l')	*M.* or *F.* les *the.*

Obs.: For the forms in parenthesis, see §73.

395. Contractions. The prepositions de, à + le, les, are always contracted as follows:

de + le = du.	à + le = au.
de + les = des.	à + les = aux.

Notes.—1. No contraction takes place with la, l'. 2. Formerly en + les was contracted to ès, a form still used in academical titles, *e. g.*, 'Maître ès arts,' 'Master o Arts.'

396. Agreement and Repetition. The article agrees in gender and number with its noun, and is regularly repeated (as also **de, à**) before each noun or adjective denoting a distinctive object.

Une maison et un jardin.	A house and garden.
Le flux et le reflux.	High and low tide.
Au bon et au mauvais côté.	On the good and bad side.
Les bons et les mauvais.	The good and the bad.
Des hommes ou des femmes.	Men or women.
La langue française ou l'anglaise.	The French language or the English.
But: Le bon et pieux prêtre.	The kind and pious priest.
Le delta ou basse Égypte.	The Delta or Lower Egypt.

a. The def. art. is *not repeated* when one adj. precedes nouns joined by et:

Les principales villes et provinces de la France. — The principal towns and provinces of France.

b. Sing. adjs. in apposition to a plur. noun *omit* the article:

Les langues française et anglaise. The French and English languages.
Or: La langue française et la langue anglaise.
La langue française et l'anglaise.

c. A few expressions of collective force, like the following, are *permissible*, but are either not obligatory or are confined to set expressions:

Les père et mère.	The parents.
Les lundi et mardi.	(On) Mondays and Tuesdays.
Les trois et quatre avril.	The third and fourth of April.
Les officiers et soldats.	The officers and soldiers.
École des ponts et chaussées.	School of bridges and roads.

d. For the repetition of superlative le, la, les, see Comparison of Adjs.

Use of the Article with Nouns.

397. French and English agree to a considerable extent in the use of the article; differences are noted below.

398. The Indefinite Article. 1. Its use corresponds in general with that of Eng. 'a,' 'an'; its plur. is the partitive **des** (§401):

Un homme; une femme; des gens.   A man; a woman; people.

2. Contrary to Eng. usage, the indef. art. also commonly stands before a noun denoting an *immaterial object*

(usually an abstract noun), when *qualified* by an adj. or clause :

Il montra un soin extrême. — He showed extreme care.
Il a une patience à toute épreuve. — He has patience equal to anything.
Elle jouit d'une bonne santé. — She enjoys good health.
C'est une nouvelle triste. — It is sad news.

a. The adjective may be understood in exclamations :

Voilà une patience ! — There is patience for you !

NOTE.—For several cases in which the Eng. indef. is replaced by the French def. or *vice versa*, or is omitted, see below.

399. The General Noun. A noun used in a *general* sense (*i. e.*, 'in general,' 'all,' 'every,' etc., being implied with it) regularly has the *def. art.* in French, though not usually in English :

La vie est courte. — Life is short.
Le fer et le cuivre sont utiles. — Iron and copper are useful.
J'étudie la musique. — I am studying music.
Les Français aiment la gloire. — The French love glory.
Le cheval est l'ami de l'homme. — The horse is the friend of man.
Le noir vous sied bien. — Black becomes you.
J'aime les pommes et les poires. — I like apples and pears.
Le beau et l'utile. — The beautiful and the useful.
Le boire et le manger. — Eating and drinking.

a. So also, *names of languages* (except after en); but not, however, with adverbial force after parler :

Sait-il le français? — Does he know French?
Il parle bien le français. — He speaks French well.
But : Dites cela en français. — Say that in French.
Parlez-vous français? — Do you speak French?

400. The Partitive Noun. A noun implying 'an undetermined quantity or number of' is said to be used *partitively* or in a partitive sense (cf. §110, note).

401. Partitive *de* + Def. Art. The partitive sense, expressed in Eng. by the noun simply, or else the noun preceded by 'some' or 'any', is regularly expressed in French by the *noun preceded by* de + *the def. art.* :

USE OF THE ARTICLE WITH NOUNS.

Du pain trempé dans du vin.	(Some) bread dipped in wine.
A-t-il des amis?	Has he (any) friends?
Des enfants poussaient des cris désespérés.	Some children were uttering terrible cries.
Il est des gens qui le croient.	There are people who believe it.
C'est du Carlyle pur.	That is pure Carlyleism.

NOTE.—This use of de.+*def. art.*, or even of de alone (see next §), is often called the *partitive article*; it is entirely identical in form with de+*art.* in other senses, *e.g.*, 'Je vends du blé', 'I sell wheat'; 'Quel est le prix du blé?', 'What is the price of the wheat?'

402. Partitive *de* without Art. The partitive sense is expressed by de *alone + the noun* as follows:—

1. When an adjective precedes the noun; so also, when a noun is understood after an adj.:

Avez-vous de bon papier?	Have you any good paper?
Donnez-moi de ces plumes-là.	Give me some of those pens.
J'ai de vos livres.	I have some of your books.
De bon vin et de mauvais (*sc.* vin).	Good wine and bad.
De gros livres et de petits (*sc.* livres).	Big books and little ones.
But: Des soldats français.	French soldiers.
J'ai du pain blanc.	I have white bread.

a. The art. is *not omitted* when the noun has a distinctive adjunct:

Du bon papier qu'il a acheté.	Some of the good paper he bought.

b. The art. is *not omitted* when adj. and noun are indivisible in sense (*i.e.*, when forming a real or a virtual compound):

Des grands-pères; des petits-fils.	Grandfathers; grandchildren.
Des petits pois; du bon sens.	Green peas; common sense.
Des jeunes gens; de la bonne foi.	Young men; honesty.

c. Familiarly, the art. is often used contrary to the rule:

Du bon vin; du vrai bonheur.	Good wine; true happiness.

2. After a general negation (implying non-existence of the object in question):

Il n'a pas de montre.	He has no (not any) watch.
Je n'ai point de livres.	I have no (not any) books.
Sans avoir d'argent.	Without having (any) money.
Il ne fit pas de remarques.	He made no remarks.
Pas d'argent et pas d'amis.	No money and no friends.

But the article is *not omitted* (the negation being no longer general):

a. When the noun has a distinctive adjunct:

Je n'ai plus du vin de cette année.	I have no more of this year's wine.
Je n'ai pas de l'argent pour le gaspiller.	I have no money to waste (=I have money, but not to waste).

b. In contrasts:

Pas du lait, mais du thé.	Not milk, but tea.

c. In negative interrogation implying affirmative answer:

N'avez-vous pas des amis, de la santé, de l'influence?	Have you not friends, health, influence?

403. Omission of the Partitive Sign. The partitive sense is expressed by the noun simply, when the prep. de forms an essential part of the governing expression. This is the case:—

1. In expressions of quantity or number, *e.g.*, **livre, morceau, douzaine, foule, beaucoup, peu, assez**, etc., etc.:

Une livre de **thé** (**noix**).	A pound of **tea** (**nuts**).
Un morceau de **papier**.	A piece of **paper**.
Une foule de **gens**.	A crowd of **people**.
Peu de **temps**; beaucoup d'**amis**.	Little **time**; many **friends**.
Assez de **livres**.	Enough **books** (*or* books enough).
Des milliers d'**étoiles**.	Thousands of **stars**.
Que de **gens** assemblés!	What a number of **people** assembled!

a. Analogous to the above are expressions like the following:

Trois jours de **marche**.	Three days' **march**.
Cent soldats de **tués**.	A hundred soldiers **killed**.
Quelque chose (rien) de **bon**.	Something (nothing) **good**.

b. **Bien**='beaucoup' regularly has **de** + *def. art.*:

Bien de l'argent; bien du monde.	Much money; many people.
Il a bien des bons livres.	He has many good books.
But: Bien d'autres.	Many others.

NOTE.—**Bien** in other senses does not take **de**: 'J'ai bien faim,' 'I am very hungry.'

c. **La plupart**='most,' 'the greater part,' etc., has **de** + *def. art.*:

La plupart des hommes.	Most men.
La plupart du temps.	Most of the time.

d. Expressions of quantity or number with a distinctive adjunct have de+*def. art.*; so also, beaucoup, peu, etc., absolutely:

Une livre du thé de ce marchand.	A pound of this tradesman's tea.
Beaucoup des gens ont peur.	Many of the people are afraid.

2. After a verb requiring de before its complement, and in phrases (adjectival or adverbial) formed from de + *noun*:

Il vit de pain (not 'de du pain').	He lives on bread.
Il manquait d'argent.	He lacked money.
Il était couvert de plaies.	He was covered with wounds.
Une robe de soie.	A silk dress.
Un homme de génie.	A man of genius.
Une bourse pleine d'or.	A purse full of gold.

NOTES.—1. In both cases (§403, 1, 2) the disappearance of the partitive de is caused by its coincidence with a governing de. 2. The negative construction (§402, 2) is really parallel, the particles pas, point, etc., being etymologically nouns.

404. General and Partitive Sense. The general sense of a noun (§399) is to be carefully distinguished from the partitive sense (§400):

Les oiseaux ont des ailes.	Birds have wings.
Les hommes sont des animaux.	Men are animals.

405. Article with Titles. A title of dignity or profession, preceding a proper name, regularly takes the def. art., except in direct address:

La reine Victoria est aimée.	Queen Victoria is beloved.
Le docteur Ribot est arrivé.	Doctor Ribot has come.
Qu'est-ce que le père Daru dit?	What does Father Daru say?
But: Bonjour, docteur Ribot.	Good morning, Doctor Ribot.

a. So also, when such title is preceded by a title of courtesy (monsieur, madame, etc.), whether in speaking to or in speaking of the person:

Bonjour, monsieur le docteur.	Good morning, doctor.
Monsieur le président l'a dit.	The president said so.

b. A preceding attributive adj. may have the force of a title:

La petite Claire; le gros Robert. Little Clara; big Robert.

406. Article for Possessive. The def. art. is commonly used with the force of a poss. adj., when no ambiguity arises from its use:

Donnez-moi la main. — Give me your hand.
Il a perdu la vie. — He has lost his life.
Elle a ôté les gants. — She took off her gloves.

a. The use of *indir. pron. obj.* + *def. art.* often avoids ambiguity:

Le courage lui manqua. — His courage failed (him).
Il s'est déchiré l'habit. — He tore his coat.
Il m'a déchiré l'habit. — He tore my coat.

b. Possessive force appears also in **avoir mal (froid, chaud,** etc.), à + *def. art.* + *a noun* denoting part of the person; similarly, in phrases of personal description made up of **avoir** + *def. art.* + *noun* + *adj.*:

J'ai mal à la tête. — I have a headache (my head aches).
Il a mal aux yeux. — He has sore eyes (his eyes, etc.).
Il a froid aux pieds. — He has cold feet (his feet, etc.).
Il a la tête grosse (*or* une grosse tête). — He has a large head.
Il a les bras longs (*or* de longs bras). — He has long arms.
Le chêne a l'écorce rude. — The oak has (a) rough bark

407. Article Distributively. 1. The def. art. with distributive force replaces Eng. 'a' of weight, measure, number, when indicating price:

Deux francs la livre (le mètre). — Two francs a pound (a metre).
Des œufs dix sous la douzaine. — Eggs at ten cents a dozen.
Des poires un sou la pièce. — Pears at a cent apiece.

a. Otherwise **par** is generally used with price:

Cinq francs par jour. — Five francs a (per) day.
Cent francs par tête. — A hundred francs a (per) head.
Trois francs par leçon. — Three francs a (per) lesson.

2. The def. art. is also used distributively with names of days:

Il vient le dimanche. — He comes (on) Sundays (=every S.).
Le bateau part les lundis. — The boat goes (on) Mondays (=every M.).

408. Omission of the Article. The article (whether def., indef., or partitive) is frequently omitted. This takes place:—

1. In a large number of expressions made up of *verb* + *noun*:

J'ai sommeil; il a honte. — I am sleepy; he is ashamed.
Je vous demande pardon. — I beg your pardon.

Further examples are:

avoir besoin, *need*.	donner avis, *notify*.	faire place, *make room*.
avoir faim, *be hungry*.	donner ordre, *give orders*.	prendre congé, *take leave*.
avoir bonne mine, *look well*.	faire attention, *pay attention*.	prendre garde, *take care*.
avoir peur, *be afraid*.		rendre visite, *pay a visit*.
avoir tort, *be (in the) wrong*.	faire cadeau, *make a present*.	trouver moyen, *find means*.
courir risque, *run the risk*.	faire faillite, *fail (in business)*.	etc., etc.
demander conseil, *ask advice*.		

2. In many adjectival and adverbial phrases made up of *prep. + noun*:

D'après nature ; devant témoins.   After nature ; before witnesses.
Sans cause ; à travers champs.   Without cause ; across the fields.

Further examples are:

à bord, *on board*.	chien de berger, *shepherd's dog*.	par chemin de fer, *by railway*.
à cheval, *on horseback*.		par exemple, *for example*.
à dessein, *intentionally*.	homme de cœur, *man of feeling*.	par expérience, *by experience*.
à genoux, *on one's knees*.		par terre, *by land*.
à pied, *on foot*.	homme de génie, *man of genius*.	sans crainte, *without fear*.
pot à fleurs, *flower-pot*.		sans raison, *without reason*.
moulin à vent, *wind-mill*.	en bateau, *in a boat*.	sous condition, *on condition*.
après dîner, *after dinner*.	en été, *in summer*.	sous presse, *in the press*.
avec intérêt, *with interest*.	en voiture, *in a carriage*.	sur papier, *on paper*.
avec plaisir, *with pleasure*.	par an, *by the year*.	etc., etc.
sortir de table, *leave the table*.		

3. Before a predicate noun which qualifies in a general way the personal subject (or object) of **être, devenir, paraître, sembler, rester, créer, faire, nommer,** etc., (§374):

Ils sont **Russes**.	They are **Russians**.
Elle est **modiste**.	She is a **milliner**.
Nous sommes **médecins**.	We are **doctors**.
Il paraît **honnête homme**.	He seems an **honest man**.
Son frère se fit **soldat**.	His brother became a **soldier**.
On l'a ordonné **prêtre**.	He was ordained a **priest**.
Soyons **amis**.	Let us be **friends**.

NOTE.—Nouns so used are usually those of *nationality, profession, title*, and their function is adjectival. Whenever a predicate noun denotes an *individual* or a *species*, it must have the art.: 'La rose est **une** fleur', 'The rose is **a** flower'; 'Les rois sont **des** hommes', 'Kings are men.'

b. The art. is *not omitted* when the predicate noun has a distinctive adjunct :

Son frère est un artiste de mérite. — His brother is an artist of merit.
Ils sont devenus des généraux distingués. — They became distinguished generals.

c. Observe the predicative force of a noun after **traiter+de, qualifier+de**:

Il m'a traité de sot. — He called me a fool.
Je qualifie cela de **fraude**. — I call that fraud.

d. After **c'est, ce sont**, the noun is logical subject (not pred.), and hence the art. or some other determinating word must be used with it:

C'est une Allemande. — She is (a) German.
Ce sont les (mes) gants. — Those are the (my) gloves.

4. Before such an appositive noun as serves merely the purpose of a parenthetical explanation:

L'Avare, **tragédie** de Molière. — L'Avare a tragedy by Molière.
Paris, **fils** de Priam, ravit Hélène, **femme** de Ménélas. — Paris, the (a) son of Priam, carried off Helena, (the) wife of Menelaus.

a. Thus is explained the omission of the art. in numerical titles:

Jacques premier (deux). — James the First (the Second).

b. An apposition which *distinguishes, contrasts, compares*, regularly has the art., as in English

Pierre le Grand. — Peter the Great.
Racine le fils et non R. le père. — Racine the son and not R. the father.
Montréal la plus grande ville du Canada. — Montreal the largest town in Canada.
M. Cook, un ami de mon père. — Mr. Cook, a friend of my father.

c. Colloquially, the art. is often *omitted* in contrasts:

Dumas père et Dumas fils. — Dumas the elder and D. the younger.

NOTE.—Pseudo-apposition (really ellipsis of **de** or of a **de** clause) is found in many cases like ' L'église (*sc.* de) Saint-Pierre', 'St. Peter's Church'; 'des meubles (*sc.* du temps de) Louis XV', 'Louis XV. furniture'; 'La rue (*sc.* de) Mirabeau', Mirabeau Street.'

5. In condensed sentences (such as titles of books, etc., addresses, advertisements, proverbs, antithetical expressions, etc.), and usually after **ni ... ni, sans ... ni, soit ... soit, tant ... que, jamais**:

Causes de la perte de Rome.	Causes of the fall of Rome.
Portrait de Napoléon III.	(A) portrait of Napoleon III.
Soldats, officiers, citoyens, tous accoururent.	Soldiers, officers, citizens, all hastened up.
Beauté, talent, esprit, tout s'use à la longue.	Beauty, talent, wit, everything wears out in the long run.
Il loge rue Richelieu.	He lives in Richelieu street.
Maison à vendre.	(A) house for sale.
Chapeaux pour hommes.	Mens' hats.
Corps et âme ; nuit et jour.	Body and soul ; night and day.
Soit peur, soit prudence, il évita le combat.	Whether from fear or prudence, he avoided the combat.
Il n'a ni père ni mère.	He has neither father nor mother.
Sans amis ni argent.	Without friends or money.
Tant hommes que femmes.	As well men as women.
Jamais père a tant aimé.	Never did a father love so much.

409. Unclassified Examples. The following examples show idiomatic distinctions in the use of the art. which cannot conveniently be brought under general rules :

Vous êtes le bienvenu.	You are welcome.
Demander (faire) l'aumône.	Ask (give) alms.
Avoir le temps.	To have time.
Aller à l'école (l'église).	To go to school (church).
Commander le respect.	Command respect.
Le feu s'est déclaré.	Fire broke out.
Faire la guerre.	Make war.
Jeter (lever) l'ancre.	Cast (weigh) anchor.
Garder le silence.	Keep silence.
Mettre le feu à.	To set fire to.
Sur (vers) les trois heures.	Towards three o'clock.
Au revoir !	Good-bye !
L'année dernière (prochaine).	Last (next) year.
La semaine (l'année) passée.	Last week (year).
Le vendredi saint.	Good Friday.
Le mercredi aux cendres.	Ash Wednesday.
Le printemps, l'été, etc.	Spring, summer, etc.
Au printemps, en été, etc.	In spring, in summer, etc.
La (sc. fête de) Saint-Michel.	Michaelmas.

La (*sc.* fête de) mi-juin.	Mid-June.
La moitié de l'année.	(The) half (of) the year.
Les deux tiers du temps.	Two-thirds of the time.
Tous (les) deux ; tous (les) trois.	Both ; all three.
Tous les mois.	Every month.
Le ministre de la guerre.	The minister of war.
Le meilleur des amis.	The best of friends.
Il cria à l'assassin.	He cried murder.
Je l'ai dit au hasard.	I said it at random.
Prendre le deuil de quelqu'un.	Go into mourning for somebody.
Sentir la fumée.	Smell of smoke.
Je vous souhaite la bonne année.	I wish you a happy new year.
Il n'a pas le sou.	He has not a cent.
Il est plus grand que vous de la tête.	He is taller than you by a head.
Un homme à la barbe noire.	A man with a black beard.
La belle question !	What a (fine) question !
À la (*sc.* mode) française.	In the French style.
S'en aller à l'anglaise.	To take French leave.
À la (*sc.* mode de) Henri IV.	In the style of Henry IV.
Cent (mille) ans.	A hundred (a thousand) years.
Les amis, où allez-vous ?	(My) friends, where are you going ?

THE ARTICLE WITH PROPER NAMES.

410. Names of Persons. 1. Names of persons usually take no article, as in English :

Corneille ; George Fox.	Corneille ; George Fox.

a. The def. art. is a constituent part of some surnames :

Les romans de Lesage.	The novels of Lesage.
Les fables de La Fontaine.	The fables of La Fontaine.

2. The def. art. is used according to Italian analogy in the French form of a few famous Italian surnames ; so also, in a very few non-Italian names :

Le Corrège ; le poème du Tasse.	Correggio ; the poem of Tasso.
Le Poussin ; le Camoëns.	Poussin ; Camoens.

3. The art. is used when the name has a distinctive adjunct, when it is plur., or when used as a common noun :

Le Christ.	Christ (= the 'Anointed').
Le Satan de Milton le grand Condé.	Milton's Satan; the Great Condé.
Les Corneille et les Racine.	A Corneille a Racine (= Corneille, Racine and others like them).
C'est un Alexandre.	He is an Alexander.
C'est du Cicéron tout pur.	It is pure Ciceronian.
J'ai lu le Télémaque.	I have read Télémaque.

4. Familiarly, (often in a depreciatory sense) the def. art. is not uncommon, especially with names of females:

Sans attendre la Barbette.	Without waiting for Barbara.
Le Duval me l'a dit.	Duval told me so.

411. Names of Countries. 1. Names of *continents, countries, provinces, large islands*, regularly take the *def. art.*; always so when standing as subject or object of a verb:

L'Asie est un grand continent.	Asia is a large continent.
Nous aimons le Canada.	We love Canada.
La Normandie; l'Angleterre.	Normandy; England.

a. A few countries named after cities have *no article:*

Naples; Parme; Bade.	Naples; Parma; Baden.

NOTE.—Names of less important islands are treated like names of cities, or are preceded by l'île de, or, if plur., les îles: 'Il va à (l'île de) Corfu'; 'il est aux Açores (aux îles Lipari).'

2. Before names of continents, European countries sing., and fem. countries sing. outside of Europe, **en** denotes 'where,' 'where to,' and the art. is *omitted;* so also, after **de** denoting 'point of departure from' and after **de** in most adjectival phrases:

Il est en (va en) Europe.	He is in (is going to) Europe.
Il voyage en France (Portugal).	He travels in France (Portugal).
Il vient d'Espagne (Danemarck).	He comes from Spain (Denmark).
Le roi de Portugal (Espagne).	The King of Portugal (Spain).
Le fer de Suède; les vins de France.	Swedish iron; French wines.

a. Exceptions are very rare, *e.g.* 'au Maine,' 'Le duc du Maine,' etc.

NOTE.—In an adj. phrase, **de** denoting *titular distinction, origin, description*, or mere *apposition (e.g.,* 'le pays de France') usually omits the art., while **de** denoting *possession*, etc., retains it.

3. But the def. art. is *not omitted* (in answer to 'where?' 'where to?', or after **de** as above) when the name is plur., or has a distinctive adjunct, or denotes a masc. country outside of Europe:

Il est **aux** Indes.	He is in India.
Il va **aux** États-Unis.	He goes to the United States.
Aux Pays-Bas.	In (to) the Netherlands.
L'impératrice **des** Indes.	The Empress of India.
Venir **des** Indes (**de** l'Inde).	To come from India.
Dans la France méridionale.	In Southern France.
Dans l'Amérique du Nord.	In North America.
La reine de la Grande-Bretagne.	The Queen of Great Britain.
Il revient **de** l'Afrique australe.	He returns from South Africa.
Au Canada (Japon).	In (to) Canada (Japan).
Chassé **de la** Chine.	Expelled from China.
Le consul **du** Pérou.	The consul of Peru.
Le fer **du** Canada.	Canadian iron.

Obs.: When the def. art. is used, 'where,' 'where to'= **à** (general) or **dans** (specific).

b. In a few names like 'Asie Mineure,' 'basse Bretagne', the adj. is no longer felt to be distinctive:

En Asie mineure.   In Asia Minor.

4. Omission of the art. in the predicate, in enumerations, titles, etc., sometimes occurs (cf. §408, 3, 4):

La Gaule est devenue **France**.	Gaul became France.
Espagne, Italie, Belgique, tout eût pris feu.	Spain, Italy, Belgium, all would have caught fire.

412. Names of Cities. Names of cities and towns usually have *no article*, unless used with a distinctive adjunct:

Londres, Paris, Québec.	London, Paris, Quebec.
À Toronto (Montréal).	To *or* in Toronto (Montreal).
But: **La** Rome de ce siècle.	(The) Rome of this century.
La Nouvelle-Orléans.	New Orleans.

a. The def. art. is an essential part of several names of cities:

Le Caire; le Hâvre; la Havane.   Cairo; Havre; Havana.

413. Names of Mountains and Rivers. Names of mountains always, and names of rivers regularly, have the *def. art.*:

Les Alpes; le Nil; le mont Blanc.   The Alps; the Nile; Mt. Blanc.

a. For rivers, the usage after en, de, is parallel with that described in §411, 2, 3 :

De l'eau de Seine. Seine water.
Un abordage a eu lieu en Seine. A collision occurred on the Seine.

EXERCISE LXVII.

1. He showed remarkable courage in struggling with his difficulties. 2. We used to enjoy good health, when we lived in France. 3. Do you not like music? 4. I do, when it is good. 5. Gold and silver are abundant in that country. 6. The rich have much gold and silver. 7. Does that young lady know Greek? 8. She does not, but she knows French and German well. 9. Does your mother speak French? 10. Yes, she speaks French and German well. 11. We have French and German books in our library. 12. Have you any good sugar for sale, sir? 13. Have you any of my books in your library? 14. Have you any of the good wine you bought last year? 15. We have no pens and no paper. 16. They have no more money, and so they must stay at home. 17. That is not wine; it is water. 18. It is not money I ask you for, but friendship. 19. Why do you complain; have you not friends? 20. I should like to buy a pound of tea; have you any of the good tea which you ordered from China? 21. I shall give you something good, if you come to see me. 22. He promised me something very beautiful, but he never gave it to me. 23. Many people believe that he will come to a bad end. 24. Many others believe that he will succeed well. 25. Most people are ignorant of their true interests. 26. We were absent most of the time. 27. Silk dresses and gold watches are not always necessary. 28. Horses are animals which are useful to men. 29. Queen Victoria has been reigning a long time. 30. The President of the French Republic has signed the treaty. 31. King Louis XIV. is often called the Great. 32. That old man has a long beard. 33. Give me your hand, and I shall help you to rise. 34. We shook hands before we parted. 35. She has not taken off her hat and gloves; she says she cannot stay. 36. I have tooth-ache and ear-ache, and so I cannot go out. 37. That little girl has blue eyes, and blond hair. 38. I had my hair cut before starting. 39. What is the matter with you, my little boy? 40. My hands and feet are cold.

EXERCISE LXVIII.

Combien les avez-vous payés? How much did you pay for them?
Je les ai payés dix francs la douzaine. I paid ten francs a dozen for them.
Il part pour la France. He is starting for France.
Au nord de la France. In the north of France.

1. You have some very fine pears; how much did you pay for them? 2. I paid two cents apiece for them. 3. That is not dear; I thought that pears would not sell so cheap this year. 4. Carpenters are earning ten francs a day at present. 5. We do not go to school on Saturday. 6. He will come on Saturday. 7. You were wrong to come on Wednesday, you should always come on Thursday. 8. Did I step on your toe? I ask your pardon. 9. Are you going on horseback or on foot? 10. How we love spring! 11. In spring nature awakes from its long repose. 12. In winter we have often much snow in Canada. 13. Those gentlemen are Frenchmen. 14. Our neighbour is a carpenter. 15. His son has become a distinguished physician. 16. Charles the First, King of England, was beheaded. 17. She was born in Marseilles, a city of southern France. 18. We were without friends and money. 19. Those children have neither father nor mother. 20. He will come home at Michaelmas. 21. Those ladies dress in French style. 22. Have you ever read Tasso's great poem? 23. Yes, and Ariosto's also. 24. We are to start for Europe to-morrow. 25. Normandy is a province of France. 26. Did you ever live in Paris? 27. Yes, I lived a long time in France, and in England too. 28. My brother has lived in China, but he is living now in Japan. 29. The United States is the most important country in North America. 30. Havre is an important seaport of the north of France. 31. New Orleans is a large city of the United States. 32. French wines are celebrated in all parts of the world. 33. That traveller comes from Africa, and is going to South America. 34. Ladies, you are welcome; we are always glad to receive you. 35. Our neighbour goes to the city every other day.

THE ADJECTIVE.

THE FEMININE OF ADJECTIVES.

414. General Rule. The feminine of an adjective is regularly formed by adding e to the masc. sing., but adjectives ending in -e remain unchanged:

M.	F.		M.	F.	
grand,	grande,	*tall.*	facile,	facile,	*easy.*
joli,	jolie,	*pretty.*	jeune,	jeune,	*young.*
rusé,	rusée,	*cunning.*	sincère,	sincère,	*sincere.*
blessé,	blessée,	*wounded.*	célèbre,	célèbre,	*celebrated.*
mort,	morte,	*dead.*	etc.	etc.	

414, 415.] THE FEMININE OF ADJECTIVES. 269

a. Similarly, *nouns* of like termination (but see §384, 2):

marquis, *marquis,*	marquise.		artiste, *artist,*	artiste.
ami, *friend,*	amie.		camarade, *comrade,*	camarade.
cousin, *cousin,*	cousine.		concierge, *porter,*	concierge.
lapin, *rabbit,*	lapine.		malade, *patient,*	malade.

b. Adjectives in -gu are regular, but require the *tréma* (cf. §45, Exc. 2), *e.g.,* aigu, *sharp,* aiguë.

c. The circumflex in dû (f. due) distinguishes it from du='of the,' and disappears in the fem. (§294); observe also mû (f. mue, §299).

d. Besides adjs. in -e, a very few others are invariable for the fem., *e.g.,* capot (in être capot='have come to grief'), grognon, *grumbling,* rococo, *rococo,* sterling, *sterling,* and rarer ones.

NOTE.—Here also properly belongs grand in grand'mère, etc. In O. F. grand was masc. or fem., but grammarians at a later date gave it the apostrophe to denote the supposed elision of e, after the general analogy.

415. Special Rules. 1. Irregularities consist chiefly of changes in the stem on adding the fem. sign e; thus, when e is added:—

(1) Final **f** = v, **x** = s, **c** = ch (in some) and **qu** (in others), **g** = gu:

actif, *active,* active. heureux, *happy,* heureuse. †public, *public,* publique.
bref, *brief,* brève. *blanc, *white,* blanche. long, *long,* longue.

*So also: Franc, *frank,* franche; sec, *dry,* sèche.
†So also: Ammoniac (-que), *ammoniac;* caduc (-que), *decrepit;* franc (-que), *Frankish;* turc (-que), *Turkish.*

a. Similarly, *nouns* of like termination:

veuf, *widower,* veuve. époux, *spouse,* épouse. turc, *Turk,* turque.

NOTE.—Here also belongs bailli, *bailiff* (O. F. baillif), baillive.

b. The adjs. doux, douce, *sweet;* faux, fausse, *false;* roux, rousse, *red* (of hair, etc.); retain the s sound (§15, 13) in the fem., denoted by c (§41, 2) and ss (§57, 1) respectively; grec, *Greek,* has fem. grecque (cf. cqu in acquérir (§76, 15); préfix *(préfiks),* *prefixed,* is regular.

(2) Final -el, -eil, -ien, -on, and usually -s, -t, double the final consonant:

cruel, *cruel,*	cruelle.		épais, *thick,*	épaisse.
pareil, *like,*	pareille.		exprès, *express,*	expresse.
ancien, *old,*	ancienne.		profès, *professed,*	professe.
bon, *good,*	bonne.		muet, *dumb,*	muette.
bas, *low,*	basse.		sot, *foolish,*	sotte.
gros, *big,*	grosse.		etc.	etc.

But: ras, rase, *flat*; gris, grise, *grey*; mat, mate, *dead, dull*; prêt, prête, *ready*; dévot, dévote, *devout*; bigot, bigote, *bigoted*; cagot, cagote, *hypocritical*; idiot, idiote, *idiotic*, and a few rarer ones.

a. Similarly, *nouns* of like termination (but see §384):

mortel, *mortal*, mortelle.	lion, *lion*, lionne.	poulet, *chicken*, poulette.
chien, *dog*, chienne.	chat, *cat*, chatte.	linot, *linnet*, linotte.

b. A very few adjs. and nouns of other endings follow this analogy:

paysan, *peasant*, paysanne.	gentil, *nice*, gentille.
rouan, *roan*, rouanne.	nul, *null*, nulle.

NOTE.—The doubling of the final consonant in -el, -ion, -et serves to denote the required è sound (§17, 2, n.); a few adjs. in -et (see (4), below) denote this è sound by the grave accent without doubling.

(3) The following have two masc. forms, one of which doubles l for the fem., like the above:

beau *or* bel, *fine*,	belle.	mou *or* mol, *soft*,	molle.
fou *or* fol, *mad*,	folle.	nouveau *or* nouvel, *new*,	nouvelle.
jumeau *or*(O.F. jumel),*twin*,jumelle.		vieux *or* vieil, *old*,	vieille.

Obs.: The -l form is regularly used only before a *vowel* or h *mute* (cf. §129, 3, Obs.); **vieux** before a vowel is *permissible*, *e.g.*, 'un **vieux** ami' (better: 'un **vieil** ami').

a. Analogous are a few nouns:
chameau, *camel*, chamelle. jouvenceau, *young fellow*, jouvencelle, etc.

(4) Before *final* r and in -et of a few adjs. e becomes è (cf. §17, 2, n.); so also in **bref** (brève), **sec** (sèche):

cher, *dear*, chère.	complet, *complete*, complète.
léger, *light*, légère.	etc. etc.

a. Similarly, *nouns* in -er:
berger, *shepherd*, bergère. étranger, *stranger*, étrangère, etc.

b. The complete list of adjs. in -et with fem. in -ète is:

(in)complet, (in)*complete*.	(in)discret, (in)*discreet*.	replet, *over-stout*
concret, *concrete*.	inquiet, *uneasy*.	secret, *secret*.

NOTE.—The grave accent denotes the required è sound (§17, 2, note).

(5) The following fem. stems show etymological elements which have disappeared in the masc.:

coi (L. *quietus*), *quiet*, coite.	frais(L.L.*frescus*),*cool*,fraîche.
bénin (L. *benignus*), *benign*, bénigne.	tiers (L. *tertius*), *third*, tierce.
favori(It.*favorito*),*favourite*,favorite.	

2. Adjectives in -eur form their fem. as follows:—
(1) **Majeur, mineur, meilleur** and those in **-érieur** are *regular:*

majeur, *major,*	majeure.	extérieur, *exterior,*	extérieure.
meilleur, *better,*	meilleure.	supérieur, *superior,*	supérieure.
mineur, *minor,*	mineure.	etc.	etc.

a. Similarly, *nouns* of like termination:

mineur, *minor,* mineure.   prieur, *prior,* prieure.   inférieur, *inferior,* inférieure.

(2) Those in -eur with a cognate present participle in -ant change -r to s and add e:

causeur, *talkative,*	causeuse.	rêveur, *dreamy,*	rêveuse.
flatteur, *flattering,*	flatteuse.	trompeur, *deceitful,*	trompeuse.
menteur, *lying,*	menteuse.	etc.	etc.

a. Similarly, *nouns* of like termination (but see also §384, 1, *a*, 2, *a*):

danseur, *dancer,*	danseuse.	buveur, *drinker,*	buveuse.
chanteur, *singer,*	chanteuse.	vendeur, *seller,*	vendeuse.
flatteur, *flatterer,*	flatteuse.	etc.	etc.

(3) Those in -teur (with no cognate pres. part. in -ant) have the fem. in -trice:

créateur, *creative,*	créatrice.	accusateur, *accusing,*	accusatrice.
directeur, *directive,*	directrice.	etc.	etc.

a. Similarly, *nouns* of like termination (but see §384, 1, *a*, 2, *a*):

accusateur, *accuser,*	accusatrice.	créateur, *creator,*	créatrice.
acteur, *actor,*	actrice.	etc.	etc.

THE PLURAL OF ADJECTIVES.

416. General Rule. Most masc. adjectives and *all* feminines form their plur. by adding s to the sing. (cf. §385):

grand(s),	grande(s).	jeune(s),	jeune(s).	(bas), basse(s).
joli(s),	jolie(s).	aigu(s),	aiguë(s).	(doux), douce(s).
rusé(s),	rusée(s).	complet(s),	complète(s).	etc. etc.

417. Special Rules. The following rules are parallel with those for the irreg. plur. of nouns (cf. §386):—

1. Masc. adjs. in -s, -x (none in -z) remain *unchanged.*

bas, bas,   frais, frais.   soumis, soumis.   faux, faux.   heureux, heureux.
épais, épais.   gris, gris.   doux, doux.   vieux, vieux.   etc.   etc.

2. Masc. adjs. in -eau (three only) and one in -eu take x:

beau(x), *fine.* nouveau(x), *new.* jumeau(x), *twin.* hébreu(x), *Hebrew.*
But: bleu(s), *blue;* feu(s), *late, deceased.*

3. Masc. adjs. in -al regularly have the plur. in -aux:

amical(-aux).   fiscal(-aux).   loyal(-aux).   spécial(-aux).
brutal(-aux).   général(-aux).   martial(-aux). trivial(-aux).
capital(-aux).   légal(-aux).   moral(-aux).   etc.
cardinal(-aux). libéral(-aux).   principal(-aux).
égal(-aux).   local(-aux).   rural(-aux).

a. **Fatal** makes 'fatals;' Littré gives also **final(s)**.

b. According to the *Dictionnaire de l'Académie* the following have *no* masc. plur.:

*automnal.   frugal.   *jovial.   naval.   †pascal.
*colossal.   glacial.   natal.   *partial.

*Littré gives a plur. in -aux.
†Littré admits a plur. in -aux, and quotes authority for a plur. in -s.

NOTES.—1. There are upwards of a hundred and fifty adjs. in -al. The *Dict. de l'Académie* is silent regarding the masc. plur. of some sixty of these, to nearly fifty of which, however, Littré gives a plur. in -aux. The following have not been pronounced upon by either authority: Brumal, déloyal, diagonal, instrumental, labial, médicinal, mental, monacal, paradoxal, quadragésimal, total, virginal. 2. Regular plurs. in -als were formerly much commoner, and usage is still unsettled for some words. When the plur. is wanting or doubtful it is often avoided, *e.g.*, 'Un repas frugal; des repas simples.' Plurs. commonly so avoided are: Fatal, final, frugal, glacial, initial, matinal, natal, naval, théâtral.

AGREEMENT OF ADJECTIVES.

418. General Rule. An adjective, whether attributive or predicative, regularly agrees in *gender* and *number* with its substantive:

Les saisons froides sont saines.   Cold seasons are healthful.
Elles sont contentes.   They are pleased.
Ils se disaient malades.   They said they were ill.
Je les crois sincèr(e)s.   I believe them sincere.

a. When the substantive has a *de* clause, the agreement is parallel with that explained for subject and verb (cf. §312, 2).

b. The agreement with **vous** is according to the sense:

Madame, vous êtes bien bonne.   Madam, you are very kind.

419. Manifold Substantive. 1. One adj. qualifying two or more substantives is made *plur.*, and agrees in

AGREEMENT OF ADJECTIVES.

gender with both, if of the same gender; if of different gender, the adj. is *masc.*:

De la viande et des pommes de terre froides.	Cold meat and potatoes.
Sa sœur et lui sont contents.	His sister and he are pleased.

a. When substantives are joined by **ou, ni . . . ni**, or are *synonomous*, or form a *climax*, etc., the principles stated for agreement of subject and verb apply (cf. §313).

b. When nouns differ in gender, the masc. one is usually placed nearest the adj., especially when the fem. form is distinct from the masc. :

La mer et le ciel bleus.	The blue sea and sky.

2. When the noun is followed by a *prep. + noun*, the agreement is, of course, according to the meaning:

Une table de bois dur.	A table of hard wood.
Une table de bois carrée.	A square wooden table.

420. Manifold Adjective. When two or more adjs. denoting different objects sing. refer to one noun, the noun is made plur., and the adjs. follow it in the sing., or the noun is made sing., and the art. repeated with each adj. :

Les nations grecque et romaine.	The Greek and Roman nations.
La nation grecque et la romaine.	The Greek nation and the Roman.
Or : La nation grecque et la nation romaine.	

a. The agreement for a *preceding ordinal* is parallel to this:

Le sixième et septième rangs.	The sixth and seventh ranks.
Le sixième rang et le septième.	The sixth rank and the seventh.
Le sixième et le septième rang.	The sixth and the seventh rank.

421. Special Cases. 1. Adjectives used as *adverbs* are regularly invariable:

Cette rose sent doux.	That rose smells sweet.
Les livres coûtent cher ici.	Books cost dear here.

a. **Possible**, replacing a clause, and **fort** in **se faire fort** = 'to pledge one's self,' are considered as adverbs:

J'ai fait le moins de fautes possible.	I have made as few mistakes as possible.
Elle se fait fort de le payer.	She pledges herself to pay it.

2. Compound adjectives (with or without hyphen) are treated as follows :—

(1) Both components are variable when co-ordinate, except first components in -o :

Des sourd(e)s-muet(te)s.	Deaf-mutes.
Des oranges aigres-douces.	Sourish oranges.
But : Les lettres gréco-romaines.	Græco-Roman literature.

(2) A subordinate component is usually invariable (being regarded as adverbial), but the principle is not fully carried out :

Des mots grecs-moderne.	Modern Greek words.
Des enfants court vêtus.	Short-coated children.
Une dame haut placée.	A lady of high rank.
Des enfants mort- (nouveau-) nés.	Still- (new-) born infants.

a. But the subordinated component is *variable* in **frais cueilli** = 'freshly gathered,' in **ivre mort** = 'dead drunk,' in **grand ouvert** = 'wide open,' and in **premier, dernier, nouveau** + *a past part.* (except **nouveau-né,** see above) :

Des fleurs fraîches cueillies.	Freshly gathered flowers.
La porte est grande ouverte.	The door is wide open.
Les nouveaux mariés.	The bridegroom and bride.

3. Nouns serving as adjs. of colour are regularly invariable :

Des robes lilas (citron).	Purple (lemon-coloured) dresses.

a. **Rose, cramoisi, pourpre,** are *exceptions,* and vary :

Des robes roses (cramoisies).	Pink (crimson) dresses.

b. Modified adjs. of colour are also usually *invariable* (the modifier being also invar. by rule, 2 (2), above) :

Des cheveux blond ardent.	Reddish blond hair.

NOTE.—These constructions are explained by supplying the ellipsis : ' Des robes (couleur de) lilas' ; ' Des cheveux (couleur de) blond ardent.'

4. A few adjs. are variable or invariable according to position or context :—

a. **Demi** = 'half,' **nu** = 'naked,' **plein** = 'full of,' are *invariable before* and *variable after* the noun ; so also, **excepté** and others (§368, *a, b*) ; **franc de port** = 'post-paid ' (also 'franco,' adv.) is *invariable before* and *usually variable after :*

Une demi-heure ; une heure et demie.	Half an hour ; an hour and a half.
Il a de l'or plein ses poches.	He has his pockets full of gold.
Il est nu-tête ; il a les bras nus.	He is bareheaded; his arms are bare.
Il a les yeux pleins de larmes.	His eyes are full of tears.
Recevoir franc de port une lettre.	To receive a letter post-paid.
Des lettres franches de port.	Post-paid letters.

Obs.: **Demi, nu**, when preceding, form a compound with hyphen.

b. **Feu**='late,' 'deceased,' is *invar.* when *preceding the def. art.* (or determinative) and *variable after* it:

Feu la reine (la feue reine).	The late queen.

c. After **avoir l'air**='have an air (appearance)' the adj. agrees with **air**; but agrees with the subject of the verb when='seem,' 'appear' (always so of things):

Cette dame a l'air hautain.	That lady has a haughty air.
Elle a l'air malheureuse.	She seems unhappy.
Cette soupe a l'air bonne.	This soup seems good.

5. A very few adjs. are always invariable:

Nous avons été capot.	We had come to grief.
Vingt livres sterling.	Twenty pounds sterling.

422. Nouns as Adjectives. By a sort of apposition, nouns are frequently used as adjs.; when so used, they usually agree like adjs.:

Une maîtresse cheminée.	A main chimney.
Des philosophes poètes.	Poet philosophers.

But: La race nègre ; un pied mère, etc.

a. **Témoin**='witness,' at the head of a phrase, is *adverbial* and *invariable:*

J'ai bien combattu, témoin les blessures que j'ai reçues.	I have fought well, witness the wounds I received.

b. For nouns as adjs. of colour, see §421, 3.

COMPARISON OF ADJECTIVES.

423. The Comparative. It is regularly denoted by placing **plus** = 'more,' **moins** = 'less' (for inequality), and **aussi** = 'as' (for equality) before each adjective compared; 'than' or 'as' = **que**:

Il est plus grand que Jean.	He is taller than John.
Il est moins grand que Jean.	He is less tall than (not so tall as) John.
Il est aussi grand que Jean.	He is as tall as John.
Il est plus diligent et plus attentif que Jean.	He is more diligent and (more) attentive than John.
Il est plus faible que malade.	He is more weak than ill.

a. Aussi, used *negatively*, may be replaced by si :

Il n'est pas aussi(si) grand que J.	He is not so tall as John.

b. When aussi or si is omitted, comme (*not* que) is used :

Un roi riche comme Crésus.	A king as rich as Crœsus.

c. After plus, moins, affirmatively, 'than'=que...ne before a *finite verb :*

Il est plus grand qu'il ne(le)paraît.	He is taller than he seems.

d. 'More and more (*or* -er and -er)'=de plus en plus ; 'less and less (*or* -er and -er)'=de moins en moins ; 'the more (less)...the more (less)'=plus (moins)...(et) plus (moins) ; 'the more (*or* -er)...'=d'autant plus... :

L'air devint de plus en plus froid.	The air became colder and colder.
Il devint de moins en moins actif.	He became less and less active.
Plus il devient riche (et) moins et est généreux.	The richer he becomes the less generous is he.
Il en sera d'autant plus riche.	He will be the richer for it.

424. Irregular Comparison. The adjectives bon, mauvais, petit, have a special comparative form :

Pos.	Comp.	Pos.	Comp.
bon, *good*,	meilleur.	*or* bon,	plus bon (rare).
mauvais, *bad*,	pire.	*or* mauvais,	plus mauvais.
petit, *small*,	moindre.	*or* petit,	plus petit.

a. Bon is hardly ever compared regularly :

À bon marché, à meilleur marché.	Cheap, cheaper.
Cela sent bon (meilleur).	That smells good (better).

But : Ce n'est ni plus bon ni plus mauvais.

NOTES.—1. In expressions like 'Ce vin est plus ou moins bon,' bon is not really comparative. 2. Some grammarians admit plus bon = 'more good-natured.'

b. Pire is, in general, stronger than plus mauvais, and may serve also as a comparative to méchant = 'bad,' 'evil,' 'wicked.'

Cet homme est méchant (pire).	That man is bad (worse).

[424–426.] COMPARISON OF ADJECTIVES. 277

c. In general, **moindre** = 'less,' 'lesser,' 'less (in importance)' and **plus petit** = 'smaller,' 'less (in size)':

Votre douleur en sera moindre.	Your sorrow will hence be less.
Une plus petite pomme.	A smaller apple.

425. The Superlative Relative. 1. It is denoted by placing the definite article (variable) or a possessive adjective (variable) before the comparative of inequality:

Elle est la moins aimable.	She is the least amiable.
Mes meilleurs amis.	My best friends.
La moindre difficulté.	The slightest difficulty.

a. When the superlative follows the noun, the *def. art.* is *not omitted*:

C'est l'enfant le plus diligent et le plus attentif de tous.	He is the most diligent and attentive boy of all.
Mes amis les plus fidèles.	My most faithful friends.

2. After a superlative, 'in' = **de** (not **à, dans,** etc.); 'among' = **entre** or **d'entre**:

L'homme le plus riche de la ville.	The richest man in the city.
Le meilleur écrivain du Canada.	The best writer in Canada.
Le plus brave (d')entre les Grecs.	The bravest among the Greeks.

426. The Superlative Absolute. It is expressed by **le** (invar.) + **plus** (**moins**) before the adj., or else by an adverb (**très, bien, fort, extrêmement,** etc.) or other modifying expression:

Elle est le plus heureuse (moins heureuse) quand elle est seule.	She is happiest (least happy) when she is alone.
Vous êtes très aimable.	You are very (most) kind.
C'est tout ce qu'il y a de plus beau.	It is most beautiful.
Un brave des braves.	One of the bravest.
Un homme des plus dignes.	A most worthy man.
Une dame on ne peut plus digne.	A most worthy woman.
Des tribus sauvages au possible.	Most savage tribes.

a. Occasionally it is denoted by *repetition* of the adj. (fam.), or by *-issime* (fam.):

Cet homme est rusé, rusé!	That man is very, very cunning!
Il est richissime.	He is very wealthy.

427. Remarks. 1. Comparative and superlative are undistinguishable in constructions requiring a def. art. before the comparative:

Le plus fort de mes deux frères. — The stronger of my two brothers.

2. **De** denotes 'by how much' after a comparative or superlative:

Plus âgé de trois ans. — Older by three years.
Il est le plus grand de beaucoup. — He is the tallest by far.
But: Il est beaucoup plus grand. — He is much taller.

3. Observe the following:

Les **basses** classes. — The **lower** classes.
J'ai fait mon **possible**. — I did my **utmost**.

POSITION OF ADJECTIVES.

428. Predicative Adjectives. They are placed, in general, as in English:

Elles sont **contentes**. — They are **pleased**.
Elle parut **fatiguée**. — She seemed **tired**.
Brave, savant, vertueux, il se fit aimer de tous. — Brave, learned, virtuous, he made himself beloved by all.

a. Observe the position after **assez**, after **plus** (**moins**) ... **plus** (**moins**) and in exclamations with **combien !, comme !, que !, tant !**:

Il est **assez** sot pour le croire. — He is **silly enough** to believe it.
Plus il devint **riche moins** il fut généreux. — The **richer** he became the **less** generous was he.
Que vous êtes aimable ! — How kind you are !

429. Attributive Adjectives. When used literally, to define, distinguish, specify, emphasize, etc., they usually *follow;* but when used figuratively, or as mere ornamental epithet, or denoting a quality viewed as essential to the object, or when forming, as it were, one idea with the noun, they usually *precede:*

Une rue **étroite**; une **étroite** amitié. — A narrow street; an intimate friendship.
Un roi **savant**; le **savant** auteur. — A learned king; the learned author.
Le **fameux** Pitt; un **rusé** coquin. — The famous Pitt; a cunning rogue.

a. The following, of very common use, generally *precede:*

beau.	grand.	joli.	meilleur.	pire.	vilain.
bon.	gros.	long.	moindre.	sot.	
court.	jeune.	mauvais.	petit.	vieux.	

430. Special Rules for Attributives. 1. Certain adjs. serve regularly to *define, distinguish*, etc., and hence regularly *follow;* such are :—

(1) Adjectives of physical quality :

Une table **carrée**; une pierre **dure**; de l'eau **froide** (**chaude**); de l'encre **noire**; une sauce **piquante**.	A **square** table; a **hard** stone; **cold** (**hot**) water; **black** ink; a **piquant** sauce.

a. By the general rule (§429) they sometimes *precede :*

De **noirs** chagrins; une **verte** vieillesse; le **bleu** ciel d'Italie.	**Dark** sorrows; a **green** old age; the **blue** sky of Italy.

(2) Adjectives of nationality, religion, profession, title, and those from proper names :

La loi **anglaise**; un prêtre **catholique**; une splendeur **royale**; le latin **cicéronien**.	The **English** law; a **Catholic** priest; **royal** splendour; **Ciceronian** Latin.

(3) Participles used as adjectives :

Une étoile **filante**; un homme **instruit**; une porte **ouverte**.	A **shooting** star; an **educated** man; an **open** door.

a. By the general rule (§429) they sometimes precede :

Une **éclatante** victoire.	A **signal** victory.

b. Past participial forms which have become real adjs. (*e.g.*, **prétendu, absolu, parfait, dissolu, feint, rusé**, etc.), very often precede (**prétendu** nearly always) :

Une **feinte** modestie.	**Feigned** modesty.
Le **prétendu** comte.	The **would-be** count.

2. Adjectives sometimes follow the noun on account of their adjuncts or their function ; thus :—

(1) When modified by an adverb (other than **aussi, si, très, bien, fort, plus, moins, assez**) :

Un discours extrêmement **long**.	An extremely **long** speech.
But : Un très **long** discours.	

(2) When modified by an adverbial phrase, or in comparisons :

Une contrée **riche** en vins.	A district **rich** in wines.
Un guerrier **brave** comme un lion.	A warrior as **brave** as a lion.

(3) Nouns used appositively as adjectives :
Une puissance amie. A friendly power.

3. Two or more adjs., with one noun, follow, in general, the rules stated, but if joined by a conjunction they all follow, in case one is such as must follow :

Une jolie petite fille. A pretty little girl.
Une belle maison blanche. A beautiful white house.
Un object blanc et étincelant. A white and dazzling object.
Une dame belle et savante. A beautiful and learned lady.

a. The more specific of two or more adjs. which follow comes last, contrary to English usage :

Des écrivains français habiles. Clever French writers.

4. A considerable number of adjs. differ more or less widely in meaning, according as they precede or follow :

Mon cher enfant ; une robe chère. My dear child ; a costly dress.
Une franche coquette ; une fem- A thorough coquette ; a plain-
  me franche.   spoken woman.

Such adjectives are :

ancien.	dernier.	fort.	honnête.	nouveau.	pur.
bon.	différent.	brave.	jeune.	parfait.	sage.
brave.	digne.	furieux.	maigre.	pauvre.	seul.
certain.	divers.	galant.	malhonnête.	petit.	simple.
cher.	fameux.	grand.	mauvais.	plaisant.	triste.
commun.	faux.	gros.	méchant.	premier.	véritable.
cruel.	fier.	haut.	mort.	propre.	vrai, etc.

NOTE.—Distinctions of this kind depend, in the main, upon the general principles laid down above, but they are too numerous and too subtle to be given in detail here. Observation, and the use of a good dictionary will, in time, make the learner familiar with the most important of them.

431. Determinatives. Such adjectives (including numerals, possessives, demonstratives, indefinites) *precede*:

PREPOSITIONAL COMPLEMENT OF ADJECTIVES.

432. An adjective is often followed by a complement connected with it by a preposition (à, de, en, envers, etc.). The prep. to be used is determined by the meaning of the adj., as explained in the following sections.

433. Adjective + *à*. The prep. à = 'to,' 'at,' 'for,' etc., is required after most adjs. denoting *tendency, fitness* (and opposites), *comparison*, etc. :

433-434.] COMPLEMENT OF ADJECTIVES.

Cet homme est adonné à la boisson.	That man is addicted to drink.
Il est favorable à mes projets.	He is favorable to my projects.
Il est bien habile aux affaires.	He is very clever in business.
Un homme supérieur à tous.	A man superior to all.
Ce n'est bon à rien.	That is good for nothing.

Such adjectives are:

accoutumé, *accustomed (to)*.	fidèle, *faithful (in)*.	pareil, *similar (to)*.
adroit, *clever (at)*.	fort, *clever (at)*.	porté, *inclined (to)*.
agréable, *pleasant (to)*.	hardi, *bold (in)*.	prêt, *ready (to)*.
antérieur, *anterior (to)*.	impropre, *unfit (for)*.	prompt, *prompt (in)*.
ardent, *ardent (in)*.	inférieur, *inferior (to)*.	propice, *propitious (to)*.
bon, *good, fit (for)*.	infidèle, *unfaithful (to)*.	propre, *fit (for)*.
cher, *dear (to)*.	inutile, *useless (to)*.	semblable, *similar (to)*.
convenable, *suitable (to)*.	lent, *slow (in)*.	utile, *useful (to)*.
égal, *equal (to)*.	nuisible, *hurtful (to)*.	etc.
exact, *exact (in)*.	opposé, *opposed (to)*.	

a. **Bon pour** = 'good for,' 'beneficial to,' 'kind to.'

434. Adjective + *de*. The prep. de = 'of,' 'from,' 'with,' etc., is required after most adjs. denoting *source* or *origin* (hence also, feeling, sentiment, abundance), *separation* (hence also, absence, distance, want, etc.), and after most past participles as adj. to denote the *agent* (cf. §320):

Êtes-vous natif de Paris?	Are you a native of Paris?
Ils sont contents de mon succès.	They are pleased at my success.
Elle est pleine de vanité.	She is full of vanity.
Je suis libre de douleur.	I am free from pain.
Il est inconnu de tous.	He is unknown to all.

Such adjectives are:

absent, *absent (from)*.	éloigné, *distant (from)*.	lourd, *heavy (with)*.
affligé, *grieved (at)*.	enchanté, *delighted (with)*.	malheureux, *unhappy (at)*.
aise, *glad (of)*.	ennuyé, *weary (of)*.	offensé, *offended (at)*.
alarmé, *alarmed (at)*.	étonné, *astonished (at)*.	pauvre, *poor (in)*.
ambitieux, *ambitious (of)*.	exempt, *free (from)*.	plein, *full (of)*.
avide, *greedy (of)*.	fâché, *sorry (for)*.	ravi, *delighted (with)*.
béni, *blessed (by)*.	fier, *proud (of)*.	satisfait, *satisfied (with)*.
capable, *capable (of)*.	glorieux, *proud (of)*.	soucieux, *anxious (about)*.
charmé, *delighted (with)*.	hérissé, *bristling (with)*.	souillé, *soiled (with)*.
chéri, *beloved (by)*.	heureux, *glad (of)*.	sûr, *sure (of)*.
confus, *confused (at)*.	honteux, *ashamed (of)*.	surpris, *surprised (at)*.
contrarié, *vexed (with)*.	ignorant, *ignorant (of)*.	triste, *sad (at)*.
dénué, *destitute (of)*.	indigne, *unworthy (of)*.	vain, *vain (of)*.
dépourvu, *devoid (of)*.	inquiet, *uneasy (about)*.	vexé, *vexed (at)*.
désireux, *desirous (of)*.	ivre, *intoxicated (with)*.	victorieux, *victorious (over)*.
différent, *different (from)*.	jaloux, *jealous (of)*.	vide, *empty (of)*.
digne, *worthy (of)*.	libre, *free (from)*.	etc.

a. **Fâché contre** = 'angry at *or* with (a person).'

435. Adjective + *en*.) En is required after a few adjs. denoting *abundance, skill*, etc. :

Le Canada est fertile en blé.	Canada is fertile in wheat.
Il est expert en chirurgie.	He is expert in surgery.

Such adjectives are :

abondant, *abounding* (in).   fort, *strong* (in), learned (in).   riche, *rich* (in).
fécond, *fruitful* (in).   ignorant, *ignorant* (in).   savant, *learned* (in).

a. Fort and ignorant sometimes have sur :

Il est fort sur l'histoire.	He is well versed (good) in history.
Ignorant sur ces matières-là.	Ignorant about those matters.

436. Adjective + *envers*. Envers is used after most adjs. denoting *disposition* or *feeling towards:*

Il est libéral envers tous.   He is liberal towards all.

Such adjectives are :

affable, *affable*.	honnête, *polite*.	poli, *polite*.
bon, *kind*.	indulgent, *indulgent*.	prodigue, *lavish*.
charitable, *charitable*.	ingrat, *ungrateful*.	reconnaissant, *grateful*.
civil, *civil*.	insolent, *insolent*.	respectueux, *respectful*.
cruel, *cruel*.	juste, *just*.	responsable, *responsible*.
dur, *hard, harsh*.	méchant, *malicious*.	rigoureux, *stern*.
généreux, *generous*.	miséricordieux, *merciful*.	sévère, *severe, stern*
grossier, *rude*.	officieux, *obliging*.	etc.

a. Bon, dur, very frequently take pour ; indulgent may take pour or à ; civil, sévère, may take à l'égard de :

Il est bon (dur) pour moi.	He is kind (harsh) to me.
Indulgent pour (à) ses enfants.	Indulgent to his children.
Civil (sévère) à l'égard de ses domestiques.	Civil (harsh) to his servants.

EXERCISE LXIX.

1. That little boy's grandmother has given him a knife. 2. That little girl is very foolish. 3. I know those old ladies well ; they are our old neighbours. 4. What a fine looking man ! Do you know him ? 5. There are some beautiful trees ! 6. The prince addressed him most flattering words. 7. That statesman is celebrated for his liberal principles. 8. There are, according to Catholic doctrine, seven capital sins. 9. The man and his wife were both old. 10. The French and Italian nations are often called Latin nations. 11. Those flowers smell sweet, do they not ? 12. That large building is the school for *(de)* deaf-mutes. 13. He left the door wide open, when he went out this morning.

14. The newly married couple had just left the church. 15. My mother had blue eyes and light auburn hair. 16. When I was young, I used to go barefoot to school. 17. That lady looks kind. 18. A pound sterling is worth twenty-five francs. 19. He is getting richer and richer. 20. He is richer than people *(on)* believe. 21. The older one is, the wiser one should be. 22. My brother is older than I by four years. 23. The richer one part of the population becomes, the poorer the rest often become. 24. Your house is small, but ours is smaller still. 25. That man is bad, but his brother is still worse. 26. The dearer those articles are, the less of them we shall be able to buy. 27. Our house is good, but yours is better. 28. His most intimate friends knew nothing of his good fortune. 29. Men are often the most unhappy, when they ought to be the most happy. 30. Is that not a splendid sight? 31. Yes, it is most beautiful! 32. The richest men in the world are not always the happiest. 33. She is shorter than I by three inches.

EXERCISE LXX.

1. You are all welcome, ladies; how kind you are to come to see me! 2. What a pretty little girl! What is her name? 3. There were black horses and white ones in the procession. 4. Will you give me some cold water to *(pour)* drink? 5. Whose is that broken cane? 6. Our neighbour is not an educated man. 7. Our friends live in a beautiful white house behind the town. 8. The English language is spoken in all parts of the world. 9. I have just seen that pretended nobleman go by. 10. We have just been at a political meeting, where we listened to a very long speech. 11. My dear child, you are too young to wear dear dresses! 12. I love that gentleman; he is so kind to children. 13. Are you not ready to start? You are very slow in dressing. 14. I am very glad to see you; when are you coming to visit me? 15. I am very sorry to say that I have no time to visit you before I go away. 16. We are charmed with the beautiful present you gave *(faire)* us. 17. You are not angry with me, are you? 18. I do not like that man; he is too severe with his children. 19. That is a nice little girl; she is so polite to everybody. 20. That little boy is very clever at history and arithmetic. 21. That army is weak in numbers. 22. We must be charitable to everybody. 23. Living languages are more useful than dead languages. 24. We must not confound the verbal adjectives with the present participles. 25. That young man is the living image of his father. 26. The more learned that man becomes, the less generous he becomes.

THE PRONOUN.

THE PERSONAL PRONOUN.

437. **Personal Pronouns.**

1. Conjunctive forms :—

	1ST PER.	2ND PER.	3RD PER. (m.).	3RD PER. (f.).	3RD REF. (m.f.).
(Sing.) N.	je, *I*.	tu, *thou*.	il, *he, it*	elle, *she, it*.	
D.	me, *(to) me*.	te, *(to) thee*.	lui, *(to) him*.	lui, *(to) her*.	se, *(to)-self*.
A.	me, *me*.	te, *thee*.	le, *him, it*.	la, *her, it*.	se, *-self*.
(Plur.) N.	nous, *we*.	vous, *you*.	ils, *they*.	elles, *they*.	
D	nous, *(to) us*.	vous, *(to) you*.	leur, *(to) them*.	leur, *(to) them*.	se, *(to)-selves*.
A.	nous, *us*.	vous, *you*.	les, *them*.	les, *them*.	se, *-selves*.

2. Disjunctive forms :—

	1ST PER.	2ND PER.	3RD PER. (m.).	3RD PER. (f.).	3RD REF. (m.f.).
(Sing.) N. A. P.	} moi, *I, me*.	toi, *thou, thee*.	lui, *he, him*.	elle, *she, her*.	soi, *one's self*, etc.
(Plur.) N. A. P.	} nous, *we, us*.	vous, *you*.	eux, *they, them*.	elles, *they, them*.	

[N.=nominative ; D.=dative ; A.=accusative ; P.=object of a prep.].

NOTE.—A more scientific terminology would be 'unstressed' and 'stressed' instead of 'conjunctive' and 'disjunctive,' as indicating the real distinction between the two sets of forms, *e.g.*, '**Je** (unstressed) parle'; 'Qui parle?—**Moi**' (stressed). As a matter of fact, the unstressed forms usually stand in immediate connection with the verb (as subject or object), hence the term 'conjunctive', while the stressed forms are usually employed otherwise, hence the term 'disjunctive.' The distinction of 'unstressed' and 'stressed' is common to most other kinds of pronouns as well.

438. **Pronominal Adverbs.**

y, *to* (*at, on, in, into*, etc.) *it* or *them* (pron.) ; *there, thither* (adv.)..
en, *of (from*, etc.) *it* or *them* (pron.) ; *some, any, some of it, some of them* (partitive pron.) ; *thence, from there* (adv.).

NOTE.—Y and en were originally adverbs (y from L. *ibi*='there,' and en from L. *inde*='thence'), but they are now usually pronominal in function, and are used precisely like the conjunctive forms.

439. Agreement. The personal pronoun regularly agrees with its antecedent in gender, number, and person :

Nous les avons frappé(e)s.   We have struck them.
Elle lit la lettre ; elle la lit.   She reads the letter ; she reads it.

a. The 1st pers. plur. for the 1st pers. sing. is used by sovereigns and authorities, and by writers, as in English :

Nous (le roi) avons ordonné et ordonnons ce qui suit.	We (the king) have ordained and ordain as follows.
Comme nous avons dit déjà.	As we have said already.

b. **Vous** = 'you' (sing. or plur.) has a plur. verb; its other agreements, as also those of **nous** above, are according to the sense:

Nous (la reine) sommes contente.	We (the queen) are satisfied.
Madame, vous êtes bien bonne.	Madam, you are very kind.

c. For impve. 1st plur. instead of 1st sing., see §347, *a*.

d. Il and le are used as invariable neutral forms, when the antecedent is one to which gender cannot be ascribed:

Y en a-t-il?—Je le crois.	Is there any (of it)? I think so.

440. Case Relations of Conjunctives. 1. The nominative forms stand as *subject* and the accusative forms as *direct object* to a verb; their use is obvious:

Il (subj.) nous (dir. obj.) a vus.	He saw us.

a. The conjunctive may not be used when there are two accusatives:

Je blâme lui et elle.	I blame him and her.

2. The dative forms denote the person or thing for whose 'advantage' or 'disadvantage' the action is done (denoted by à = 'to,' 'for,' 'from,' with nouns, cf. §81, 3):

Je leur prêterai les livres.	I shall lend them the books.
On lui a volé son argent.	His money has been stolen from him.

But the conjunctive form must not be used:—

(1) When two datives are joined by a conjunction, or when in emphasis a second dat. is implied:

Je parle à lui et à elle.	I speak to him and to her.
Je donne le livre à elle (pas à lui).	I give the book to her (not to him).

(2) When the conjunctive dir. obj. is any other pron. than **le, la, les**:

Je vous présente à elle.	I introduce you to her.
Il se présenta à moi.	He introduced himself to me.

But: Je le (la, les) leur présente, etc.

(3) After verbs of *motion* and some others, to denote the 'object towards which the action tends' (the relation, though expressed by à, not being really dative):

Je courus à lui.	I ran to him.
Cette maison est à moi.	That house belongs to me.
Il pense (songe, rêve) à eux.	He thinks (muses, dreams) of them.

Such verbs are:

accoutumer, *accustom*.	comparer, *compare*.	prendre intérêt, *take interest*.
aller, *go*.	courir, *run*.	prétendre, *aspire*.
appeler, *call*.	être (à), *belong (to)*.	recourir, *have recourse*.
en appeler, *appeal*.	faire attention, *pay attention*.	renoncer, *renounce*.
aspirer, *aspire*.	habituer, *accustom*.	revenir, *come back*.
attirer, *attract*.	marcher, *march*.	rêver, *dream*.
avoir affaire, *have to do*.	penser, *think*.	songer, *muse*.
avoir recours, *have recourse*.	prendre garde, *pay heed*.	venir, *come*.

a. Certain verbs of this class, when not literal, take the conjunctive dative:

Il lui vint une idée.	There occurred to him an idea.
Vous nous reviendrez.	You will come to see us again.

NOTE.—The *ethical* dative, denoting the person 'interested in' or 'affected by' an action (rare in Eng.), is common in French: 'Goutez-moi ce vin-là', 'Just taste that wine'; 'Ne me faites pas cela encore', 'Don't do that again (I tell you).'

441. Impersonal *il*. For il (invar.) as the subject of an impersonal verb, see §§328-33.

442. Predicative *le, la, les*. As predicate the acc. 3rd pers. is either *variable* (le, la, les) or *invariable* (le):—

1. Le (la, les) when referring to a *determinate noun* (cf. §95, 2, note), or to an adj. used as such, *agrees*:

Êtes-vous sa mère?—Je la suis.	Are you his mother?—I am.
Êtes-vous la mariée?—Je la suis.	Are you the bride?—I am.
Sont-ce là vos livres?—Ce les sont.	Are those your books?—They are.

2. Le (invar.) is used when referring to an *adjective*, or to a noun as adjective:

Êtes-vous fatiguée?—Je le suis.	Are you tired?—I am.
Êtes-vous mère?—Je le suis.	Are you a mother?—I am.
Sont-ils Anglais?—Ils le sont.	Are they English?—They are.

443. Pleonastic *le*. The neutral form le (§439, *d*) is often pleonastic, as compared with English usage:

Êtes-vous mère ?—Je le suis.	Are you a mother ?—I am.
Qu'ils soient venus, je le sais.	That they have come, I know.
Fais du bien, quand tu le peux.	Do good, when you can.
Ce qu'il voulait, il le veut encore.	What he wished, he still wishes.
Je suis prête, s'il le faut.	I am ready, if need be.
J'irai si vous le désirez.	I shall go, if you wish (it).
Ils sont comme je (le) désirerais.	They are as I should like.
Il est plus âgé que je ne (le) suis.	He is older than I am.

Obs. : This **le** is *optional* in comparative clauses.

a. **Le** is also used in a number of fixed expressions :

Il ne le cède à personne.	He yields to nobody.
Nous l'avons emporté.	We have carried the day.
Il l'a échappé belle.	He had a narrow escape.

b. **Le** may sometimes be translated by 'one' or 'so.'

Il est soldat ; je le suis aussi.	He is a soldier ; I am one too.
Sois brave, et je le serai aussi.	Be brave, and I shall be so too.

444. Reflexives. 1. A special conjunctive reflexive form (**se** for dat. or acc. of either gen. or num.) is required in the 3rd pers. only ; for the 1st and 2nd pers. the ordinary forms are used (cf. §322, 2) :

Il (elle) se loue.	He (she) praises him (her) -self.
Ils (elles) se le sont dit.	They said so to each other

But : Je me loue ; tu te loues ; nous nous louons ; vous vous louez.

2. The disjunctive **soi** is hardly used beyond the 3rd sing. in an indefinite or general sense :

Chacun travaille pour soi.	Every one works for himself.
On doit parler rarement de soi.	One should rarely speak of one's self.
De soi le vice est odieux.	In itself vice is hateful.

But: Elle est contente d'elle-même ; ils ne songent qu'à eux-mêmes, etc.

a. The use of **soi** is rarer for the fem. than for the masc. :

Un bienfait porte sa récompense avec soi (lui).	A good deed brings its reward with it.
La guerre entraîne après elle (soi) des maux sans nombre.	War brings after it countless evils.

NOTE.—**Soi** is no longer used of persons denoted by a general noun, *e.g.*, 'L'avare ne vit que pour **lui-même**' (*not* 'pour soi'), nor is it used, as formerly, of persons to avoid ambiguity, *e.g.*, 'Quoique son frère soit dans la misère, il ne pense qu'à **lui-même** (*not* 'à soi').

445. Uses of *en*. 1. En is in function an equivalent of **de** + *a pron.* (3rd pers. of either gender or number); it is used of things, and less commonly of persons:

Je parle des plumes; j'en parle.	I speak of the pens; I speak of them.
Donnez-les-moi; j'en ai besoin.	Give me them; I need them.
Il est mon ami; j'en réponds.	He is my friend; I answer for him.
Il aime ses fils, et il en est aimé.	He loves his sons, and is loved by them.
Vous voilà; j'en suis content.	There you are; I am glad of it.
Vient-il de Toronto?—Il en vient.	Does he come from T.? He does.

a. The antecedent is often understood or indefinite:

Voyons! où en étions nous?	Let me see, where were we?
Ils en sont venus aux mains.	They came to blows.
Il m'en veut.	He has a grudge against me.
Tant s'en faut.	Far from it.
C'en est fait de lui.	It is all up with him.
À vous en croire.	If one is to believe you.
Quoi qu'il en soit.	However it may be.
Je n'en puis plus.	I am done out.
Il y en a qui le croient.	There are some who think so.

2. Through a somewhat special application of the general principle, it is further used:—

(1) In a *partitive* sense:

Voici du papier; en voulez-vous?—Merci, j'en ai.	Here is some paper; do you wish any of it?—Thank you, I have some.
Avez-vous une plume?—J'en ai une (j'en ai plusieurs).	Have you a pen?—I have one (I have several).
Il me faut en acheter d'autres.	I must buy others.

(2) **En** = 'thereof' + *the def. art.* replaces a possessive adj. referring to a possessor in the preceding sentence, but only when the thing possessed is a dir. obj., a subject of **être**, or a predicate noun:

J'aime ce pays; j'en admire les institutions.	I like this country; I admire its institutions.
Blâmez les péchés de ces gens, mais n'en blâmez pas les malheurs.	Blame the sins of those people, but do not blame their misfortunes.
Cette affaire est délicate; le succès en est douteux.	That affair is delicate; its success is doubtful.
Ceci est la gloire du pays; cela en est la honte.	This is the country's glory; that is its disgrace.

But : Cette maison a **ses** défauts (—possessor not being in the previous sentence) ; J'aime ces vers ; **leur** harmonie me ravit (—the thing possessed being subject of another verb than être) ; J'admire ce pays ; il est fameux pour **ses** bonnes lois (—the thing possessed being governed by a prep.).

446. Use of *y*. **Y** is in function equivalent to à (en, dans, etc.) + *a pron.* (3rd pers. of either gender or number) ; it is used of things, and rarely of persons :

Je pense à mes péchés ; j'y pense.	I think of my sins ; I think of them.
Il est en Europe ; il y est, et moi j'y vais aussi.	He is in Europe ; he is there, and I am going there too.
Il se connaît en ces choses, mais moi je ne m'y connais pas.	He is an expert in those things, but I am not.
Il aspire à cela ; il y aspire.	He aspires to that ; he aspires to it.
Vous fiez-vous à lui ?—Je m'y fie.	Do you trust him ?—I trust him.

a. The antecedent is often understood or indefinite :

Il y va de votre vie.	Your life is at stake.
J'y suis ! Qu'y a-t-il ?	I have it ! What is the matter ?
Il s'y prend adroitement.	He goes about it cleverly.
Est-ce que Monsieur B. y est ?	Is Mr. B. at home ?
Y pensez-vous !	You don't mean it !

447. Position of Conjunctive Objects. 1. They stand immediately *before* their governing verb (except the impve. affirmative) :

Je leur en parlerai.	I shall speak to them of it.
Je l'y ai envoyé pour le leur dire.	I sent him there to tell them it.
Il lui faut parler ; il faut lui parler.	He must speak ; one must speak to him.

Obs. : Remember that the aux. is the verb in compound tenses.

a. With negative infin., the object *may* stand between **ne** and **pas** (point, rien, etc.) ; similarly *adv.* + *infin.* :

Je suis étonné de ne point le voir (*or* ne le point voir).	I am astonished not to see him.
Pour les bien considérer.	To consider them well.

b. The objects of an infin. governed by **faire, laisser** (cf. §310, 6, 7) or a verb of perceiving (**entendre, voir,** etc.), *accompany the finite verb:*

Je le lui ferai dire.	I shall make him say it.
Il se le voit refuser.	He sees himself refused it.
Faites-vous-la raconter.	Have it related to you.

S

c. A similar arrangement is *permissible* with aller, venir, envoyer, etc. +*infin.*:

J'enverrai le chercher *or* Je l'en- I shall send for him.
    verrai chercher.
Envoyez-le chercher. Send for it.

NOTE.—In the older language, objects of an infin. often stood *before modal auxiliaries*, *e.g.*, 'Je vous dois dire', but usage hardly permits this now, except for en, y, *e.g.*, 'Ce qu'on en doit attendre.'

2. Conjunctive objects stand immediately *after* an *imperative* affirmative:

Regardez-les; écoutez-nous. Look at them; listen to us.
Donnez-le-lui; allons-nous-en. Give it to him; let us go away.
But: Ne les regardez pas; ne nous écoutez point; ne le lui donnez pas, etc.

a. The rule does not apply to the subjunctive as impve. (§352, 1, *a*):

Qu'il les écoute. Let him listen to them.

NOTES.—1. Formerly, but rarely now, an impve. affirmative when joined to another by et (ou, mais) might have an object before it: 'Achetez-les et les payez,' etc. 2. **Voici** and **voilà**, which are imperatives by derivation, are always preceded by their conjunctive object: '**Les** voici; **en** voilà, etc.'

3. When a verb governs two (or more) objects, they are arranged with respect to each other as follows:—

(1) Of accusatives and datives, the *accusative* (le, la, les) stands *next to the verb*, except when along with lui or leur before the verb:

Il nous (dat.) les (acc.) donne. He gives them to us.
Donnez-les (acc.) -nous (dat). Give them to us.
But: Il les (acc.) lui (dat.) donne; il les (acc.) leur (dat.) donne.

a. After an impve., the dat. nous, vous, may precede the acc. in familiar language, *e.g.*, 'Conservez-vous-le'; 'Tenez-vous-le pour dit.'

b. When there are *two direct* or *two indirect* objects they become disjunctive and follow the verb, *e.g.*, 'J'ai vu lui et elle'; 'Je parle à lui et à elle.

(2) **Y**, **en** *follow all other forms*, y preceding en (if both be present):

Il m'en a donné; va-t'en. He gave me some; be gone.
Il nous y en a donné. He gave us some of it there.

(3) *Reference-table* showing possible combinations of two pronouns:

(Before the Verb.)					(After the Verb.)		
me le	te le	se le	le	lui	-le -moi	-le -toi	-le -lui
me la	te la	se la	la	lui	-la -moi	-la -toi	-la -lui
me les	te les	se les	les	lui	-les-moi	-les-toi	-les-lui
nous le	vous le	se le	le	leur	-le -nous	-le -vous	-le -leur
nous la	vous la	se la	la	leur	-la -nous	-la -vous	-la -leur
nous les	vous les	se les	les	leur	-les-nous	-les-vous	-les-leur
m' en	t' en	s' en	lui en		-m' en	-t' en	-lui-en
m' en	t' en	s' en	l' en		-m' en	-t' en	-l' en
nous en	vous en	s' en	leur en		-nous-en	-vous-en	-leur-en
nous en	vous en	s' en	les en		-nous-en	-vous-en	-les-en
m' y	t' y	s' y	[lui y]		[-m' y]	[-t' y]	[-lui-y]
m' y	t' y	s' y	l' y		[-m' y]	[-t' y]	-l'y
nous y	vous y	s' y	leur y		-nous-y	-vous-y	-leur-y
nous y	vous y	s' y	les y		-nous-y	-vous-y	-les -y
	y en					-y-en	

Obs.: 1. The disjunctive forms **moi, toi** are used instead of **me, te** after the verb, except before **en**. 2. After the verb, the forms are joined to it and to each other by hyphens, apostrophe instead of hyphen being used according to §73. 3. Combinations of *three* forms are rare, *e.g.*, 'Il **nous y en** a donné'; they are usually avoided, *e.g.*, 'Donnes-y-en à moi' for 'Donne-m'y-en.' 4. The forms in [ ] are almost always avoided, either by transposition or by some other form of expression, *e.g.*, 'Menes*-y-moi' or 'Mène-moi là' for 'Mène-m'y,' etc.

*See §174, 4, N.B.

448. For the position of personal pronoun subject see §§315, 316, 317.

449. Omission of Object. The object of the second of two verbs in a compound tense joined by **et** or **ou** may be omitted along with the auxiliary and the subject:

Il l'a pris et tué (*or* l'a tué *or* il l'a tué).   He caught and killed it.

But: Il l'a pris, l'a tué (—not joined by et or ou); il le prend, et (il) le tue (—tense not compound).

NOTE.—The verbs must be alike in government, must have the same aux., must both be affirmative or negative, otherwise no omission is allowed.

450. Disjunctives. When, for any reason, the pron. is *stressed* (§66), the disjunctive form is usually employed (see §437, note); thus, the disjunctives are used :—

1. Absolutely (a verb being implied, but not expressed) :

Qui est là ?—Moi (eux, elle).	Who is there ?—I (they, she).
Qui as-tu vu ?—Lui (eux).	Whom did you see ?—Him (them).
Toi absent (parti), que ferai-je ?	You absent (gone), what shall I do ?

a. So also, in comparisons, and analogously, after ne ... que :

Je suis plus grand que toi.	I am taller than you.
Faites comme eux.	Do as they do.
Je n'ai vu que lui.	I have seen him only.

2. In appositions (often emphatic) :

Moi, je l'ai vu (moi-même).	(Why) I saw it myself.
Toi qui l'as vu, tu me crois.	You who saw it (you) believe me.
Lui aussi (il) le sait.	He too knows it.
Cela vous est facile à vous.	That is easy for you.

a. With lui so used (and sometimes eux) the conjunctive subject may be omitted :

Lui seul (il) ne le voulait pas.	He alone did not wish it.
Lui travaillait ; eux jouaient.	He worked ; they played.

NOTE.—Je soussigné = 'I the undersigned' is a relic of the earlier language.

3. As logical subject after ce + être :

C'est moi (toi, vous) ; ce sont eux, etc.   It is I (thou, you) ; it is they.

4. With an infinitive :

Moi t'oublier ! jamais.	I forget thee ! Never.
Et eux de s'enfuir.	And they made off.

5. When the subject or object is composite, see also §440, 1, *a* and 2, (1) :

Son frère et lui sont venus.   His brother and he have come.

a. A composite subject or object is usually summed up by a pleonastic appositive conjunctive (especially when the components are unlike in pers.) :

Vous et lui (vous) l'avez vu.	You and he saw it.
Je vous envoie, toi et ton frère.	I send you and your brother.

6. After a preposition :

Je parle de toi et d'eux.	I speak of you and of them.
Ils sont chez eux.	They are at home.
Il se moque de nous.	He makes sport of us.

a. Observe the peculiar use of a *prep.* + *disj.* as a sort of emphatic appositive of possession.

J'ai une maison à moi.	I have a house of my own.
Mon idée à moi, c'est, etc.	My (own) idea is, etc.

NOTE.—A disjunctive for things after a prep. is usually avoided, either by means of **en**, **y**, or else by an adverb (**dedans**, **dehors**, **dessus**, **devant**, **derrière**, etc. : 'Je ne vois rien là-dedans (in it)'; 'Voyez sur la table, cherchez dessus (on it) et dessous (under it).'

7. For **moi** and **toi** after impve., see §447, 3, (3) obs.

451. Pronouns in Address. In addressing *one person* **vous** is, in general, the pronoun of formality and respect, whilst **tu** denotes familiarity, affection, solemnity, etc. Hence :—

1. **Tu** = 'you' (one person) is generally used between members of the same family (husband and wife, parents and children, brothers and sisters), between very intimate friends, between children, by grown persons to children and sometimes to servants, by everybody to animals and inanimate objects :

Où es-tu, mon cher père ?	Where are you, my dear father ?
Est-ce toi, mon enfant ?	Is that you my child ?
Pauvre chien, tu as faim.	Poor dog, you are hungry.

2. **Tu** = 'thou' is used in poetry and elevated prose, and by Protestants in addressing God (Roman Catholics use **vous**):

Nous te (vous) louons, ô Dieu !	We praise thee, O God !

3. **Vous**, with the above limitations, is used, both in the sing. and plur., as in English.

EXERCISE LXXI.

1. Are there any good pens in the box? 2. There are none. 3. Do you know that old man? 4. I know him and his brother. 5. Do you know that man and his wife? 6. We know both him and her. 7. We know him only. 8. Did you see my father and mother? 9. We saw her only. 10. Are you going to give them some money? 11. I have already given them some. 12. Will you give me some apples? 13. I shall give you and him some. 14. Have you spoken to my cousin of your plan? 15. I have spoken of it to her and her mother. 16. Will you have the goodness to introduce us to your mother? 17. 'I shall

have great pleasure in introducing you to her. 18. I was thinking of you, when you came in. 19. Do you think of me, when I am far away? 20. Yes, I always think of you. 21. Whose is that house? 22. It is mine. 23. As soon as the child saw his mother, he ran to her. 24. Are you that young man's sister? 25. I am. 26. Are you satisfied, madam? 27. I am. 28. Are you a Canadian, sir? 29. I am. 30. Are you the gentlemen we met yesterday? 31. We are. 32. I shall go for the doctor, if you wish. 33. I shall do the work, if it is necessary. 34. That man is richer than we are? 35. Why do you tell me to be brave; I am so already. 36. He carried the day over all his rivals. 37. Tell me where he lives, if you know. 38. He is a Canadian, and I am one too. 39. Do you know the Robinsons? 40. Yes, they are very fastidious people, and I do not like to have to do with them. 41. There is the box; put the pens into it. 42. Go there, my child; do not stay here. 43. Do not go there, my daughter; you will hurt yourself. 44. Give them some, my little boy. 45. He is a bad man; I cannot trust him. 46. The earth around those flowers is dry; throw some water there, my daughter. 47. Let us not go away; let them laugh at us if they will. 48. The children wish to go to the celebration; let us take them there. 49. That boy has apples and pears; let us ask him for some. 50. That boy has your knife; take it away from him.

EXERCISE LXXII.

1. My father did not hurt himself, but he had a narrow escape. 2. Every one for himself is too often the maxim of men. 3. One should not always be thinking of one's self. 4. The selfish live only for themselves. 5. Do you need money? 6. I do. 7. Do you come from London? 8. We do. 9. I cannot understand why he has a grudge against me. 10. However that may be, it is all over with him. 11. Have you any money? 12. I have, but I should like to have more. 13. How many apples have you? 14. I have six. 15. Here are some fine pears; do you wish any? 16. Yes, I should like some, for I have none. 17. Canada is my country; I love its blue sky and free institutions. 18. I planted this apple-tree; I hope I shall eat its fruit. 19. Do you ever think of your country, when you are in foreign countries? 20. When I am far away, I always think of it. 21. My brother has gone home, and I am going too. 22. I see a crowd of people in the street; what is the matter? 23. Were you ever in Europe? 24. I never was. 25. We shall make him do it, when we come. 26. The doctor is at home; shall I send for him? 27. There they are; go and get them. 28. There is some water; give us some, for we are thirsty.

29. Do not give them any; they do not need any. 30. Where are the children? 31. They are coming up the street. 32. Do not listen to them; they are making sport of you. 33. There is my hat; give it to me, if you please. 34. That is my hat; do not give it to him. 35. Let us go away; it is getting late. 36. If you have any money, give me some. 37. He gives himself some, but he will not give us any. 38. Take us there. 39. Give it to us; do not give it to them. 40. What are you doing, naughty dog? Go away. 41. I saw him, and gave him the money. 42. They are worthy people; I love and admire them. 43. Our duty to our parents is to love and obey them. 44. It is I who was there. 45. My father and I were not there. 46. What were you and he doing? 47. He was writing, and I was reading. 48. He has a house of his own. 49. You and he were there; were you not? 50. There is the box; I should like to know whether there is anything in it.

The Possessive Pronoun.

452. **Possessives.**

1. Adjectival forms:—

Sing.		Plur.	
m. mon	} mes, *my*.		
f. ma (mon)			
m. ton	} tes, *thy, your*.		
f. ta (ton)			
m. son	} ses, } *his, her,*		
f. sa (son)	*its, one's*.		
m. } notre	nos, *our*.		
f.			
m. } votre	vos, *your*.		
f.			
m. } leur	leurs, *their*.		
f.			

2. Pronominal forms:—

Sing.		Plur.	
m. le mien	les miens	} *mine*.	
f. la mienne	les miennes		
m. le tien	les tiens	} *thine, yours*.	
f. la tienne	les tiennes		
m. le sien	les siens	} *his, hers, its,*	
f. la sienne	les siennes	*one's own*.	
m. le nôtre	} les nôtres, *ours*.		
f. la nôtre			
m. le vôtre	} les vôtres, *yours*.		
f. la vôtre			
m. le leur	} les leurs, *theirs*.		
f. la leur			

Obs.: 1. The forms in parenthesis, mon, ton, son, are used instead of ma, ta, sa, *before a vowel or* h *mute*: 'Mon amie', 'my friend (f.)'; 'ton histoire (f.)', 'your story'; 'son aimable tante,' 'his amiable aunt.' 2. Since son (sa ses)='his', 'her' 'its', 'one's', the context determines which sense is intended.

Obs.: 1. The fem. (except for leur) is formed as for adjs. of like ending. 2. De, à+le, les, contract as usual; thus, du mien (=de+le mien), aux miennes (=à+les miennes), etc. 3. Note the accent mark in nôtre, vôtre, absent in notre, votre. 4. Since le sien (la sienne, etc.)='his', 'hers,' 'its'; 'one's', the context determines which sense is intended.

NOTE.—The regular fem. forms, ma, ta, sa, were at one time used before a vowel sound; a trace of this usage survives in ma mie (for m'amie), m'amour.

453. Agreement. The possessives agree in *gender* and *number* with the noun denoting the object possessed, and in *person* with the possessor :

Elle a son crayon et les miens.	She has her pencil and mine.
Il a sa plume et les vôtres.	He has his pen and yours.

a. The possessive adj. must be repeated precisely like the def. art. (cf. §396):

Mes parents et mes amis.	My relatives and friends.

b. When the possessor is *indefinite*, son (sa, etc.) and le sien (la sienne, etc.), are used:

On doit tenir sa parole.	One must keep one's word.
Se charger des affaires d'autrui et négliger les siennes.	To undertake the business of others and neglect one's own.

454. Use of Adjectival Forms. They are used, in general, like the corresponding English forms ; idiomatic distinctions and special rules are :—

1. The possessive adj. is commonly replaced by the *def. art.* (cf. §406), when no ambiguity arises from its use :

Donnez-moi la main.	Give me your hand.
Il m'a déchiré l'habit.	He has torn my coat.
But : Il a déchiré son habit.	He has torn his coat.

a. If the sense is *specific, emphatic,* or *distinctive,* the possessive is used :

Mon bras me fait mal.	My arm pains me.
Voilà ma migraine encore !	There is my sick-headache again !
Je l'ai vu de mes propres yeux.	I saw it with my own eyes.
Elle lui a donné sa main.	She has given him her hand (*sc.* in marriage).

2. En + *the def. art.* serves in certain cases as a substitute for **son, leur** (see §445, 2, (2)) :

a. This construction is more usual for things than for persons ; for things personified, for names of places, or to avoid ambiguity, son, leur are not uncommon :

La nécessité parle ; il faut suivre sa loi.	Necessity speaks ; we must follow her law.
Vous rappelez-vous cette ville ? Ses promenades sont très belles.	Do you remember that city ? Its promenades are very fine.

La source de toutes les passions est la sensibilité, l'imagination détermine leur pente.	Sensation is the source of all the passions, imagination determines their tendency.

3. The emphatic 'own' is denoted by **propre** or by an apposition with **à** :

Je l'ai écrit de ma propre main.	I wrote it with my own hand.
C'est mon opinion à moi.	That is my own opinion.
Cf. also : J'ai un cheval à moi.	I have a horse of my own.
C'est à moi à jouer.	It is my turn to play.

a. Along with son the à construction often avoids ambiguity :

Son père à lui.	His (*i.e., not* 'her') father.

4. **Mon (ma)** is commonly used, in direct address, before the name of a relative (*not* before **papa, maman**) or the title of a superior officer :

Bonjour mon père (mon colonel).	Good morning father (colonel).
But : Est-ce toi papa (maman) ?	Is that you papa (mamma) ?

NOTE.—This usage explains the origin of **monsieur** (=mon+sieur), **madame** (=ma+dame), etc.

5. In speaking to a person of his or her relatives **votre (vos)** is often preceded by **monsieur**, etc., for politeness (cf. §91) :

Madame votre mère y est-elle ?	Is your mother in ?

6. When there is plurality of possessor, the object possessed usually remains singular, if it is singular as regards the individual possessor :

Les hommes songent moins à leur âme qu'à leur corps.	Men think less of their souls than of their bodies.
Ils ont perdu la vie.	They lost their lives.

a. Sometimes the sense demands a plural :

Leurs têtes se ressemblent.	Their heads are alike.

455. Use of Pronominal Forms. They are used, in general, like the corresponding English forms ; idiomatic distinctions and special rules are :—

1. 'Mine,' etc., after être is regularly expressed by à + moi, etc., when denoting *ownership simply*, while le mien, etc., denotes a *distinction of ownership :*

Cette montre est à moi. } Cette montre est la mienne.	That watch is mine.

2. The pronominal form sometimes stands *without article* in the predicate after certain verbs:

Ces opinions sont vôtres.	Those opinions are yours.
Elle deviendra mienne.	She shall become mine.
Je les ai fait miens.	I made them mine.

Such verbs are:

être.   devenir.   dire.   faire.   regarder comme, etc.

3. The idiom 'a friend of mine,' etc., is not literally translated:

Un de mes amis.	A friend of mine.
Un médecin de mes amis.	{ One of my friends, (who) is a doctor. { A doctor, a friend of mine.
Un ami à moi.	A friend of mine.
Mon ami que voici.	This friend of mine.
Cf.: Un tour de sa façon.	One of his tricks.

a. The use of **mien (tien, sien)** attributively in this sense is *familiar*.

Un mien parent.	A relative of mine.
Une sienne cousine.	A cousin of his.

4. Emphatic 'own' is rendered by **propre**, or is, more usually, untranslated:

Son avis et le mien (propre).   His opinion and my own.

5. When used *absolutely* (*i.e.*, without antecedent) the singular denotes 'property,' 'what is mine,' etc., and the plural 'relatives,' 'friends,' 'allies,' etc.:

Je ne demande que le mien.	I ask only for what is mine.
Les nôtres se sont bien battus.	Our soldiers (etc.) fought well.

a. Familiarly, the feminine means 'pranks,' etc.:

Il fait encore des siennes.   He is at his pranks again.

NOTE.—Other absolute uses are not permissible, *e.g.*, 'Votre lettre (*not* 'la vôtre') de la semaine dernière.'

EXERCISE LXXIII.

Elle lui a fermé la porte au nez.	She shut the door in his face.
Cela lui a fait venir l'eau à la bouche.	That made his mouth water.
Cette nuit; de toute la nuit.	Last night; all night.

1. My father and yours will soon be here. 2. I have your books and my own. 3. Our friends are coming by the railway; yours are coming by the steamer. 4. My brother and sister have gone away; they will

not be back till Wednesday next. 5. One should not fail to pay one's debts. 6. I had my hair cut this morning; I am afraid I shall catch a cold. 7. The duke was presented to the queen, and he kissed her hand. 8. She has cut her finger. 9. I shall love him, as long as my heart beats. 10. It was so warm that I could not close my eyes all night. 11. Close your eyes, and open your mouth. 12. He shuts his eyes to the light. 13. He was walking [with] his eyes closed; he fell and broke his arm. 14. I have my hands full; I cannot help you. 15. I went to see him, but he shut the door in my face. 16. It is a very cold morning; will you not warm your hands? 17. Thank you; my hands are not cold. 18. That clumsy fellow stepped on my toe, and he hurt me very much. 19. My head aches this morning; I did not close my eyes last night. 20. The sight of those beautiful apples made my mouth water. 21. He stood there, [with] his arms folded, awaiting his fate like a brave soldier. 22. As long as my heart beats, I shall never forget you. 23. If they come here, we shall shut the door in their face. 24. Do you see those poor children; those beautiful pears made their mouths water. 25. Let us hope that the law has not lost its force in this country. 26. He has a watch of his own. 27. Whom do you mean; his father or her father? 28. I mean *her* father. 29. This house is his, not yours. 30. They lost their lives fighting for their *(la)* country. 31. Negroes have dark skins and large mouths. 32. One of my friends who is a doctor told me the following story. 33. I am going to take away these books of yours. 34. The difference between mine and thine is not always easy to determine. 35. I love very much these books of mine.

The Demonstrative Pronoun.

456. Demonstratives.

1. Adjectival forms:—

Sing.		Plur.
m. ce (cet)	} *this, that.*	ces.
f. cette		
m. ce(cet)....-ci	} *this.*	ces....-ci.
f. cette....-ci		
m. ce(cet)...-là	} *that.*	ces....-là.
f. cette...-là		

Obs.: The form cet is used before a vowel or h mute: Cet arbre; cet homme; cet autre dé; *but:* ce chêne; ce hêtre.

2. Pronominal forms:—

Sing.		Plur.
m. celui	} *that (one), etc.*	ceux
f. celle		celles
m. celui-ci	} *this (one), etc.*	ceux-ci
f. celle-ci		celles-ci
m. celui-là	} *that (one), etc.*	ceux-là
f. celle-là		celles-là

Invar. { ce, *this(these),that(those),he(she,it,they).*
ceci, *this.*
cela, *that.*

Obs.: The e of ce is elided before a vowel or h mute (§73); c' becomes ç' before a (§41, 2): 'ç'a été.'

457. Agreement. The adjectival form agrees in gender and number with the noun before which it stands; the pronominal form agrees in gender and number with the noun instead of which it stands:

Cette plume et celle de Jean.	This pen and that of John.
J'aime ces livres-ci, mais je n'aime pas ceux-là.	I like these books, but I do not like those.

a. The demonstr. adj. must be repeated like the def. art. (cf. §396.)

458. Use of Adjectival Forms. Ce (cette, etc.) = 'this' *or* 'that'; to distinguish 'this' from 'that' -ci and -là are respectively added to the noun:

Lis ce livre-ci; lis ce livre-là.	Read this book; read that book.
J'aime ces tableaux-là.	I like those pictures.

a. Ce (cette, etc.), referring to what has been already mentioned, sometimes has the force of 'that':

Le télégraphe, cette grande découverte de notre siècle.	The telegraph, that great discovery of our century.

b. The *def. art.* replaces the demonstr. adj. in a few idioms:

Ne parlez pas de la sorte.	Do not speak in that way.
J'irai à l'instant.	I shall go this (very) moment.

Use of Pronominal Forms :—

459. Celui. The pronoun celui (celle, etc,) = 'that,' 'that one,' 'the one,' 'he', is regularly used only along with a *relative clause* or a *de clause:*

Ceux qui rient pleureront.	Those who laugh will weep.
Celle dont je parle est venue.	She of whom I speak has come.
Le devoir d'aimer Dieu et celui d'aimer son prochain.	The duty of loving God and that of loving one's neighbour.
Cette robe et celle que j'ai vue.	This dress and the one I saw.
Mes plumes et celles de mon frère.	My pens and my brother's.

Obs.: Note the use of celui=Eng. possessive noun substantively.

a. The relative sentence is sometimes elliptically expressed by the past participle:

Les découvertes énumérées sont celles faites par Edison.	The discoveries enumerated are those made by Edison.

b. Celui-là replaces celui when the predicate comes before the relat.:

Celui-là est riche qui est toujours content.	He (that man) is rich who is always happy.

460. Celui-ci, celui-là. The pronouns celui-ci (celle-ci, etc.) = 'this,' 'this one,' 'he,' 'the latter' and celui-là (celle-là, etc.) = 'that,' 'that one,' 'the former,' are used to contrast the *nearer* with the *more remote:*

Voici les deux chaînes ; gardez celle-ci, et renvoyez celle-là.	Here are the two chains; keep this (one), and send back that (one).
Veut-il ceux-ci ou ceux-là ?	Does he wish these or those?
Cicéron et Virgile étaient Romains ; celui-ci était poète, et celui-là orateur.	Cicero and Virgil were Romans; the former was an orator, and the latter a poet.

Obs.: The idiom in the last example is lit. 'the *latter*..., the *former*.'

a. 'This' *or* 'that' for emphasis, not contrast, is celui-là :

C'est une bonne loi (que) celle-là.   This (that) is a good law.

461. Ce + être. Ce = 'this,' 'that,' 'these,' 'those,' 'he,' 'she,' 'it,' 'they,' according to the context, is used with être (or devoir, pouvoir, savoir + être), as follows :—

1. As representative subject, when the logical subject is :—

(1) A proper noun, or a determinate noun (including adjs. as such) :

C'est Marie et sa mère.	It is Mary and her mother.
Ce sera un beau spectacle.	That (it) will be a fine sight.
Ce sont nos plumes.	These (those) are our pens.
Était-ce le meilleur ?	Was it the best?
Ce sont des Allemands.	They (those) are Germans.
C'est mon ami(e).	He (she) is my friend.
Ce peut être Jean.	That may be John.

a. Before être + an indeterminate noun il (ils, elles) is the regular construction :

Il est temps d'aller.	It is time to go.
Ils sont amis (Allemands).	They are friends (Germans).
Elle est couturière.	She is a seamstress.

NOTE.—For a few expressions like c'est dommage, etc., in which c'est stands with an indeterminate noun, see 2, (1), note 3 below.

b. Il est is always used to indicate hours of the day :

Il est midi (trois heures).   It is noon (three o'clock).

But: Quelle heure est-ce qui vient de sonner ?—C'est cinq heures (—according to rule).

c. Observe the use of **ce** in the following date idioms:

C'est aujourd'hui lundi.	To-day is Monday.
Ce sera demain le quatre.	To-morrow will be the fourth.

(2) **A pronoun**:

Qui est-ce?—Ce sont eux.	Who is it?—It is they.
Ce sont les leurs.	Those are theirs.
C'est ceci; c'est cela.	It is this; it is that.
C'étaient les mêmes.	They (those) were the same.
Ce doivent être les miens.	Those must be mine.

(3) **An infinitive (or infin. with de)**:

Ce serait tout perdre.	That would be losing everything.
Voir c'est croire.	Seeing is believing.
Ce que je crains c'est de l'offenser.	What I fear is to offend him.

(4) **A noun sentence**:

Est-ce que vous n'irez pas?	Will you not go?
Où est-ce qu'il est?	Where is it that he is?
Ce n'est pas qu'il ait peur.	It is not that he is afraid.

a. The noun sentence may be understood:

Vous irez, n'est-ce pas? (=n'est-ce pas que vous irez?).   You will go, will you not?

(5) **An adverb of quantity**:

Combien est-ce?   Ç'a été trop.   How much is it?   It was too much.

NOTE.—For agreement of the verb, see §312, 3.

2. **Ce** stands as real subject, when the complement of **être** is:—

(1) An adj., an adj. + **à** + *infin.*, an infin. preceded by **à**, an adverb (in all cases without further syntactical connection, see *a*, below):

C'est facile (vrai, bien).	That (it) is easy (true, well).
Ce doit être (ne saurait être) vrai.	That must be (cannot be) true.
Il est parti, c'est clair.	He is gone, that is clear.
C'est clair, il est parti.	It is clear, he is gone.
C'est à désirer.	That (it) is to be desired.
Où sera-ce?	Where will it (that) be?
C'était bien mal à vous.	That was very wrong of you.

a. When followed by **de** +*infin.* or by a **que** *clause*, the regular construction for the above is impersonal **il** (*not* 'ce'); so also the parenthetical **il est vrai** and **n'est-il pas vrai?** (=**n'est-ce pas?**), though without syntactical connection:

Il est facile de dire cela.	It is easy to say that.
Il est triste de vous voir ainsi.	It is sad to see you thus.
Il est clair que j'ai raison.	It is clear that I am right.
Il est à désirer que la guerre finisse bientôt.	It is to be desired that the war will soon end.
On rit, il est vrai, mais attendez.	They laugh, to be sure, but wait.
Il est bien mal à vous de parler ainsi.	It is very wrong of you to speak so.

NOTES.—1. Colloquially, **c'est** is pretty freely used instead of **il est** before **de** +*infin.* or a **que** *clause:* 'C'est facile de faire cela'; 'C'est clair que j'ai raison,' etc. 2. This use of **ce** is permissible in the literary style only in expressions of *emotion, e.g.*, **C'est heureux (malheureux, beau, triste, étonnant,** etc.**), c'est à présumer (craindre, regretter,** etc.**):** 'C'est triste de vous voir'; 'C'est à craindre qu'il ne soit noyé.' 3. The **ce** construction is obligatory after a few noun phrases of like value, *e.g.*: **C'est dommage (pitié, plaisir, justice,** etc.**):** 'C'est pitié de l'entendre.'

(2) A prepositional clause, or a conjunction:

C'est pour vous.	It (that) is for you.
C'est pourquoi je suis venu.	That is why I came.
C'est comme vous (le) dites.	It is as you say.

462. *Ce* + a Relative. **Ce** (as antecedent) + *a relative* denotes 'that which,' 'what,' 'which,' etc.:

Ce qui m'amuse.	What (that which) amuses me.
Ce que je dis est vrai.	What I say is true.
Ce dont nous parlions.	What we were speaking of.
Ce à quoi je pense.	What I am thinking of.
Il est âgé, ce qui est dommage.	He is old, which is a pity.

a. **Ce**, so used, either immediately precedes the relative, or is, for emphasis, divided from it by **être** + *a predicate substantive:*

Ce qu'il veut est la gloire.	What he desires is glory.
C'est la gloire qu'il veut.	It is glory that he desires.

NOTE.—This type of construction is widely used to render a predicate substantive emphatic, *e.g.*, 'C'est ton frère **qui** le dit'; 'C'est à vous **que** (='à qui') je parle'; 'C'est mourir **que** de vivre ainsi'; 'C'est une belle ville **que** Paris.'

463. Other uses of ce. Apart from its use with être or with a relative, ce is found in a few phrases only, mostly archaic, familiar or jocular:

Ce devint un usage.	This (that) became a custom.
Tu crains, ce lui dit-il.	You fear, said he to him.
Sur ce, je vous quitte.	And now, I leave you.
De ce non content.	Not satisfied with this.

a. The parenthetical **ce semble** may be used only when unconnected (cf. §461, 2, (1), *a*), otherwise **il semble**:

C'est lui, ce me semble, au moins.   It's he, it seems to me, at least.
But: Il me semble que c'est lui.

464. Pleonastic *ce*. As compared with Eng., ce is often pleonastic; thus, it is used with être + *a logical subj.*:—

1. Regularly, after **celui qui** and **ce qui**:

Celle qui l'a dit c'est vous.	The one who said so is you.
Ce que je crains ce sont mes prétendus amis.	What I fear is my would-be friends.
Ce à quoi je pense c'est sa santé.	What I think of is his health.

2. Regularly, between infinitives (not negative):

Penser, c'est vivre.   To think is to live.
But: Végéter (ce) n'est pas vivre.

3. Regularly, in inversions with **que**:

C'est une belle ville que Paris.   { Paris is a beautiful city.
                                    { It is a fine city, (' is ') Paris.

4. Optionally, in other inversions for emphasis:

La guerre (ce) serait la ruine.   War would be ruin.

NOTE.—When the complement of être is an adj. or participle, pleonastic ce may not be used: 'Ce qui est utile n'est pas toujours juste.'

465. *Ceci* and *cela*. Ceci = 'this' (the nearer) and cela = 'that' (the more remote) are used to denote something indicated, but not yet named:

Gardez ceci et donnez-moi cela.   Keep this and give me that.

Obs.: If the object has been already named, or if the name is fully implied by the context, **celui-ci (-là)** must be used.

a. Ceci also refers to what is about to be said, and cela to what has been said:

Réfléchissez bien à ceci.	Think well on this.
Je ne dis pas davantage, cela suffit.	I say no more, that is enough.

b. **Ceci** (*not* 'cela') may have a predicate noun:

Ceci est un secret, *or* C'est ici un secret (rarer). — This is a secret.

But: C'est là un secret. } That is a secret.
Cela c'est un secret. }

NOTE.—**Cela** is not so divided before **même, seul**, and its division in negations is optional: 'Cela seul (même) en est la cause'; 'Cela n'est pas (*or* ce n'est pas là) une faute.'

c. **Cela** (*not* 'ceci') = 'this' before a **de** clause:

Paris a cela d'avantageux. — Paris has this advantage.

d. **Cela** may be replaced by **là** after **de** and **par**:

De là vient que, etc. — From that it comes that, etc.
Il faut commencer par là. — We must begin with that.

e. **Cela** is often contracted to **ça** colloquially:

Ça ne fait rien. — That doesn't matter.

f. **Ça** is sometimes used familiarly or contemptuously of *persons* instead of a personal pronoun:

Regardez comme ça mange. — Look how they (etc.) eat.
Ça veut faire à sa tête. — You (etc.) wish to do as you please.

NOTE.—Distinguish **ça** from **çà** (adv.) and **çà !** (interj.).

EXERCISE LXXIV.

1. I have never read that book, but I have read this one, and I like it very much. 2. These houses are not so fine as those. 3. You should not eat in that way. 4. Have patience, I shall be (pres.) there this moment. 5. Those who do wrong will be punished. 6. He of whom you were speaking yesterday has arrived. 7. Which of those horses do you like best? 8. I like the one you bought better than your brother's, but I like my own best. 9. This house and the one in which our neighbours live will be sold to-morrow. 10. Our house and our neighbour's are both brick houses. 11. These facts, and those discovered since that time, prove that, although he was a great scholar, he was wrong. 12. I saw the man *(celui)* last evening who wanted to buy my horse. 13. Who are those two gentlemen? 14. This is Mr. Robinson, and that is Mr. Jones. 15. You are looking for apples; very well, will you take these or those? 16. I will take these; those are too small. 17. How is butter selling to-day? 18. That sells at two francs a pound, and this, which is finer, at two francs fifty centimes. 19. Gambetta and Hugo were distinguished men; the former was an

orator, the latter a poet. 20. That is a fine horse! How much is he worth? 21. Why do these people not reply, when we speak to them? 22. They are Russians; they do not understand you. 23. Who did that? 24. It was John who did it. 25. What o'clock is it? 26. It is half-past ten. 27. What day of the month is it? 28. To-day is the tenth. 29. Is that the house of which you spoke to me? 30. No, it is the next one. 31. Who is that lady? 32. She is the lady who lives next door. 33. What I fear is that he will never come back. 34. It is not that he is losing his money, but he is destroying his health also. 35. It is time to go home.

EXERCISE LXXV.

C'est une belle chose que de protéger les faibles.	It is a fine thing to protect the weak.
Ce sont des qualités nécessaires pour régner que la douceur et la fermeté.	Mildness and firmness are necessary qualities for ruling.
Il a cela de bon.	He has this good thing about him.

1. It is they who have done it. 2. It was kind of you to help those poor people. 3. You can do it; it is easy. 4. That was not kind of you; you should have allowed me to do it. 5. You are rich; it is easy for you to say so. 6. It is a pity that we did not know it sooner. 7. It is unfortunate that he did not come yesterday. 8. My father told me you were here; that is why I came. 9. It is to be feared that the traveller has died of hunger. 10. It is to be desired that those misfortunes will never happen. 11. What we were speaking of has happened. 12. What I am thinking of is the way of preventing that misfortune. 13. What he says is true. 14. It's a fine thing, ('is') money! 15. It is not to you that I speak. 16. He has lost all his money, which is sad. 17. What a beautiful thing is virtue! 18. It is money that he wishes. 19. He is a fine young man, ('is') John! 20. It would be a good thing to go away. 21. It is a fine thing to love virtue. 22. Health and good sense are qualities necessary for succeeding in the world. 23. You are the one who did that. 24. Love is the strongest of all passions. 25. This does not belong to me, but that does. 26. Give me this; keep that for yourself. 27. He has this good thing about him, that he always tells the truth. 28. What a lazy beast; and yet he thinks that he works! 29. Did he give you back your pencil? 30. No, but that does not matter; I have another here. 31. It is difficult to translate the word 'that' into French. 32. I am sure that that 'that' that that man uses is superfluous.

The Interrogative Pronoun.

466. **Interrogatives.**

1. Adjectival forms :—

	SING.	PLUR.	
m.	quel?	quels?	} *which?,*
f.	quelle?	quelles?	*what?, etc.*

Obs.: For the fem. and plur. cf. §§415, 1, (2) and 416.

2. Pronominal forms :—

	SING.	PLUR.	
m.	lequel?	lesquels?	} *which?, which*
f.	laquelle?	lesquelles?	*or what one(s)?*

(Invar.) qui?, *who?, whom?*
quo?, *what?*
quoi?, *what?*

Obs.: 1. **Lequel = le + quel**, both parts being inflected (§§394, 466, 1); de, à contract with le, les (duquel, auquel, etc., cf. §395).
2. **Que = qu'** before a *vowel* or **h** mute (§73).

467. Agreement. The adjectival forms agree like ordinary adjectives; the variable pronominal forms agree in *gender* (not necessarily in number) with the nouns for which they stand; **qui?** assumes the *number* of the noun or pron. referred to:

Quels livres avez-vous?	Which (what) books have you?
Quelles sont vos raisons?	What are your reasons?
Laquelle des dames est venue?	Which of the ladies has come?
Qui sonne? Qui sont-elles?	Who rings? Who are they?

468. Quel?, Lequel?. The adj. **quel?** (**quelle?**, etc.) = 'which?', 'what?' and the pron. **lequel?** (**laquelle?**, etc.) = 'which (one)?', 'what (one)?' refer either to persons or things, and stand both in direct and indirect questions:

Quels livres avez-vous?	Which (what) books have you?
Dites-moi quel livre il a.	Tell me which (what) book he has.
Desquels avez-vous besoin?	Which (ones) do you need?
Dites-moi lesquels vous avez.	Tell me which (ones) you have.
Quelle dame est arrivée?	Which (what) lady has come?
Je ne sais pas laquelle.	I do not know which (one).
Quelles sont vos raisons?	What are your reasons?
Quel homme est-ce là?	What (what kind of) man is that?
Auquel des hommes parle-t-il?	To which of the men does he speak?

a. **Quel!** in exclamations sometimes = 'what a !', 'what !':

Quel héros! Quels héros!	What a hero! What heroes!
Quelle belle scène!	What a beautiful scene!

b. **Quel?** as predicative adj. often replaces **qui?** = 'who?':

Quels sont ces gens-là?	Who are those people? (*or* what kind of people are those?)
Sais-tu quelle est cette dame?	Do you know who that lady is?

NOTE.—A pleonastic **de** is commonly used before alternatives after **quel?**, **lequel?** and other interrogatives, probably caused by case attraction with **des deux**, often present in such expressions : 'Quel (des deux) est le plus habile, de cet homme-ci ou de celui-là?'; 'Laquelle est la plus illustre, d'Athènes ou de Rome?'

469 Qui?. 1. The pron. **qui?** = 'who?', 'whom?', is regularly used of *persons* only, and stands in both direct and indirect questions:

Qui frappe? Qui est là?	Who is knocking? Who is there?
De qui (à qui) parle-t-il?	Of whom (to whom) is he speaking?
Qui avez-vous vu?	Whom did you see?
Qui êtes-vous?	Who are you?
Dites-moi qui est venu.	Tell me who has come.

a. **Qui?** is sometimes used (though rarely and not necessarily) as subject to a transitive verb in the sense of 'what?':

Qui vous amène de si bonne heure?	What brings you so early?

b. **Qui?**, predicatively, is often replaced (especially when fem. or plur.) by **quel?**:

Quelle est cette dame?	Who is that lady? (What l. is that?).
Quels sont-ils?	Who are they?

2. 'Whose?', denoting *ownership simply*, = **à qui?**; otherwise generally **de qui?**, sometimes **quel?** (but *never* 'dont'):

À qui est cette maison-là?	Whose house is that?
De qui êtes vous fils?	Whose son are you?
Quelle maison a été brûlée?	Whose (what) house was burnt?

NOTE.—Compare with this the idiom **c'est à qui**: 'C'était à qui finirait le premier,' 'It was a strife as to who would finish first.'

470. Que?, Quoi?. The form **que?** = 'what?' is *conjunctive*, while **quoi?** = 'what?' is *disjunctive;* their uses in detail are :—

1. **Que?** stands regularly as *direct object* or as *predicate*, and in direct question only:

Que vous a-t-il dit?	What did he say to you?
Que cherchez-vous?	What are you looking for?
Que sont-ils devenus?	What has become of them?

a. **Que?** (alternatively with **quoi?**) may stand with an infin. in indirect question:

Je ne sais que (quoi) dire.	I know not what to say.

b. **Que?** (**que!**) sometimes has adverbial force:

Que ne m'avez-vous dit cela?	Why did you not tell me that?
Que vous êtes heureux!	How happy you are!
Que d'argent perdu!	What a quantity of money lost!

2. 'What?' as *subject* of a verb is regularly **qu'est-ce qui?**:

Qu'est-ce qui vous a frappé?	What struck you?

a. The form **que?** may stand as *subject* to a few intransitives (mostly such as may also be impers.), but never as subject to a transitive:

Que sert de pleurer?	What is the use of crying?
Que vous en semble?	What do you think of it?
Qu'est-ce?	What is it?

3. **Quoi?** is used *absolutely* (*i.e.*, with ellipsis of the verb), and after a prep.:

Il y a du nouveau.—Quoi?	There is news.—What?
Quoi de plus beau que cela?	What finer than that?
Quoi! vous l'admirez!	What! You admire him!
À quoi pensez-vous?	What are you thinking of?
En quoi puis-je vous servir?	In what can I help you?

a. In cases of special emphasis **quoi?** may be direct object:

Je reçois quoi?—Des lettres.	I receive what?—Letters.

b. With an infin., **que?** or (more emphatic) **quoi?** is used:

Que (quoi) faire?	What is one to do?
Je ne sais que (quoi) répondre.	I know not what to answer.

471. Interrogative Locutions. The use of interrogative phrases (formed with **est-ce**, etc.) instead of the simple forms is very frequent:

Qui est-ce qui chante?	*for*	Qui chante?
Qui est-ce que vous demandez?	"	Qui demandez-vous?
À qui est-ce que vous parliez?	"	À qui parliez-vous?
Qu'est-ce que cela prouve?	"	Que prouve cela?
Qu'est-ce que c'est?	"	Qu'est-ce?
Qu'est-ce que c'est que cela?	"	Qu'est-ce que cela?
De quoi est-ce qu'il parle?	"	De quoi parle-t-il?
Qu'est-ce qui vous a frappé?	(See §470, 2).	

The Relative Pronoun.

472. **Relative Pronouns.**

qui, *who, which, that; whom* (after a prep.).
que, *whom, which, that.*
dont, *whose, of whom, of which, etc.*
où, *in which, into which, at which, to which, etc.*
lequel, m. s.   lesquels, m. pl. ⎫
laquelle, f. s. lesquelles, f. pl. ⎬ *who, whom, which, that.*
quoi, *what, which.*

Obs.: For **qu'**, see §73.

473. Agreement. A relative pronoun, whether variable or invariable in form, is of the *gender, number* and *person* of its antecedent:

Moi qui étais (vous qui étiez) là.	I who was (you who were) there.
Les lettres que j'ai apportées.	The letters which I have brought.
Moi qui suis son ami(e).	I who am his friend (m. *or* f.).
Dieux (vous) qui m'exaucez!	(Ye) gods who hear me!
C'est nous qui l'avons dit.	It is we who have said it.
Je suis celui qui l'a dit.	I am the one who has said it.

a. When the antecedent is a predicate noun (or adj. as such), the relat. may agree in *person* either with this noun or with the subject of the sentence:

Nous sommes deux moines qui voyageons (voyagent).	We are two monks who are travelling.
Je suis le seul qui l'aie (ait) dit.	I am the only one who has said it.

b. The relative after **un + a** *plur.* is either sing. or plur. (usually according to the sense):

C'est un de mes (des) procès qui m'a (m'ont) ruiné.	It is one of my (of the) law-suits which has (have) ruined me.

But: L'astronomie est **une** des sciences qui **fait** (*or* **font**) le plus d'honneur à l'esprit humain.

474. Qui, Que. Both **qui** and **que** refer to antecedents (of either gender or number) denoting persons or things; their uses in detail are:—

1. **Qui** = 'who,' 'which,' 'that,' serves as *subject*; **qui** = 'whom' (of persons only, or things personified) may also be used after a prep.:

THE RELATIVE PRONOUN.

La dame qui a chanté.	The lady who (that) has sung.
Les amis qui sont arrivés.	The friends who (that) have come.
La vache qui beugle.	The cow which (that) lows.
Les livres qui ont été perdus.	The books which have been lost.
Les oiseaux qui volent.	The birds which (that) fly.
Ce qui m'amuse.	What (that which) amuses me.
Rien qui est beau.	Nothing that is beautiful.
La tante chez qui je demeure.	The aunt with whom I live.
Les amis à (de) qui je parlais.	The friends to (of) whom I spoke.
Rochers à qui je me plains.	Rocks to whom I complain.

a. **Qui**, without antecedent, sometimes = **celui qui** (**ceux qui**, etc.), or, when repeated, = **les uns ... les autres** :

Aimez qui vous aime.	Love him (the one) who loves you.
Jouera qui voudra.	Let those who will play.
Pour qui connait.	For any one who knows.
Qui d'un côté, qui de l'autre.	Some on one side, some on the other.

b. Similarly, in a few phrases (mostly exclamatory or parenthetical), **qui = ce qui** :

Voilà qui est étrange !	That is strange !
Qui pis est (*or* ce qui est pis).	What is worse.

2. **Que** = 'whom,' 'which,' 'that,' serves regularly as *direct object:*

Les ami(e)s que j'aime.	The friends whom (that) I love.
Le livre (cheval) que j'ai.	The book (horse) which I have.
Les plumes que j'ai achetées.	The pens which I have bought.
Ce que vous dites.	That which you say.
Rien que vous dites.	Nothing that you say.

a. **Que** stands also as *predicate nominative* (cf. §374, 1), and as *logical subject* of an impersonal verb :

Malheureuse que je suis !	Unhappy woman that I am !
Qu'est-ce qu'elle est devenue ?	What has become of her ?
À l'heure qu'il est.	At the present hour.
L'homme qu'il vous faut.	The man that you need.
Prenez ce qu'il vous faut.	Take what you need.

NOTES.—1. The **que** of emphatic inversions (§402, *a*, n.) is best explained as predicative **que**: 'C'est une belle ville **que** Paris' = 'C'est une belle ville **que** Paris (est)' *or* 'C'est une belle ville (ce) **que** (c'est) Paris'; 'Erreur **que** tout cela' = '(C'est) erreur **que** tout cela (est)' *or* '(C'est) erreur (ce) **que** (c'est) tout cela.' 2. The form **que** is often a *relative adverb*, not to be confounded in function with the relative proper: 'Dans le temps **que** cela arrivait'; 'C'est à vous **que** je parle' (*or* 'C'est vous à qui je parle').

475. Dont. The form **dont** = 'whose,' 'of whom,' 'of which,' etc., has the value of **de**+*a relat.*; it refers to antecedents (of either gender or number) denoting persons or things:

L'homme dont le fils est mort.	The man whose son is dead.
Les gens dont je parle.	The people of whom I speak.
Les plumes dont je me sers.	The pens which I make use of.
La gloire dont il est avide.	The fame for which he is eager.
Ce dont je me plains.	That of which I complain.

a. A noun after **dont**='whose' does not omit the art. as in Eng., and must follow its governing verb (cf. §477, 3):

Le monsieur dont j'ai trouvé la bourse.	The gentleman whose purse I found.

b. As compared with **d'où** (§476, *a*), dont has figurative force in expressions referring to extraction, lineage, etc.:

La maison dont il sort.	The family from which he comes.

c. Dont was originally an *adverb* (L. *de*+*unde*), and is often best construed as such:

Le pays dont il est venu.	The country whence he came.

476. Où. The adv. **où** (= 'where') is also used as a relative with the value of **dans** (à, sur, vers, etc.)+*a relat.*; if preceded by a prep., **où** = 'which,' 'where':

La maison où je loge.	The house in which I lodge.
Le siècle où nous vivons.	The age in which we live.
Le but où il tend.	The end towards which he tends.
Les villes par où je suis venu.	The cities through which I came.
L'endroit d'où il vient.	The place from which he comes.
D'où venez-vous?	Where do you come from?

a. **D'où**='from which,' 'whence,' is usually literal in force:

Le maison d'où il sort.	The house out of which he comes.

477. Lequel. The form **lequel** (**laquelle**, etc.) = 'who,' 'whom,' 'which,' 'that,' refers to persons or things, and varies in form to agree with its antecedent; it is chiefly used where **qui**, **que**, etc., may not be employed:—

1. **Lequel**, being inflected, stands where **qui**, **que**, from want of inflection, would be ambiguous, or it serves,

owing to its stress, to denote the more remote of two possible antecedents :

La sœur de mon ami laquelle vient d'arriver.	The sister of my friend who has just come.
Le fils du rédacteur lequel je viens de voir.	The son of the editor whom (*i.e.*, 'the son') I have just seen.

2. After a prep., **lequel** *may* be used of persons (cf. §474, 1), but *must* be used of things :

L'ami de qui (duquel, dont) je parle.	The friend of whom I speak.
Les chiens desquels (dont) je parle.	The dogs of which I speak.
La maison dans laquelle (où) je loge.	The house in which I lodge.

a. Lequel may not be used of persons after **en**, and it must be used of persons after **parmi, entre** :

Un homme en qui je crois.	A man in whom I believe.
Les amis parmi (entre) lesquels.	The friends among whom.

3. When depending on a noun governed by a prep., 'whose' must be turned by **duquel**, etc. (*not* 'dont'), which must *follow* the noun (cf. §475, *a*) :

La dame au fils de laquelle (*or* de qui) je donne des leçons.	The lady to whose son I give lessons.

NOTE.—Lequel is used exceptionally as an *adjective :* 'J'espère partir demain, auquel cas, etc.'; 'Je viens de toucher mille francs, de laquelle somme je payerai mes dettes.'

478. Quoi. The form **quoi** = 'what,' 'which,' is used without definite antecedent, and stands after a prep. (rarely otherwise) :

Voilà de quoi je parlais.	That is what I was speaking of.
Sur quoi il est parti.	Whereupon he went away.
C'est à quoi je pensais.	That is what I was thinking of.
Il m'a payé, ce à quoi je ne m'attendais guère.	He paid me, which I hardly expected.

a. De quoi + *infin.* (expressed or implied) denotes the *means* or *cause* of the action of the infinitive :

Il a de quoi vivre.	He has enough to live on.
Il a de quoi (*sc.* vivre, etc.).	He has means (is well off).
Donnez-moi de quoi écrire.	Give me something to write with.
Il n'y a pas de quoi.	There is no occasion (don't mention it, etc.).

b. **Quoi** stands without a prep. in a few expressions:

Quoi faisant, etc.	(By) doing **which**, etc.
Un je ne sais quoi de cruel.	A certain indefinable cruelty (lit. 'a I know not what of cruel.')

2. '**What**' (= 'that which') is **ce** + *a relat.* (cf. §462):

Je vois ce qui se passe.	I see **what** is going on.
Je sais ce que je sais.	I know **what** I know.
Ce dont je me plains.	That of **which** I complain.
Ce à quoi je me fiais.	What I was trusting **to**.
Il est sourd, ce qui est bien dommage.	He is deaf, **which** is a great pity.

479. Remarks. 1. The relative pronoun, often omitted in English, is never omitted in French:

Le tableau que j'ai vu là.	The picture (**which**) I saw there.
Le livre dont je parle est à moi.	The book (**which**) I speak of is mine.

2. Relative and antecedent should stand as near together as possible:

Il y a de ce livre une **édition qui** se vend, etc.	There is **an edition** of that book **which is sold**, etc.

Not: Une édition de ce livre qui, etc.

3. A prep. never ends the relative sentence, as sometimes in English:

Ce à quoi je me fiais.	What I was trusting to.

4. For Eng. forms in -ing = relative clause, see §366, 3.

EXERCISE LXXVI.

1. Whom did you see yesterday? 2. I saw him who was with you the day before yesterday. 3. I told you already what my reasons are. 4. What sort of weather is it this morning? 5. I think it will be fine. 6. I do not know to which of those men we were speaking. 7. What fine weather! I hope it will continue until we leave. 8. Who is that? 9. It is the man I sold my house to. 10. What was the matter this morning; I heard a great noise in the street? 11. What were you speaking of to that man you met? 12. I was speaking to him of what we were discussing yesterday. 13. Scoundrel that you are, if I catch you, I'll give you what you deserve. 14. What I complain of is that you make no progress in your studies. 15. I do not understand you; will you explain to me clearly what you mean? 16. What has become

of that young gentleman with whom I saw you? 17. I don't know what has become of him; I have not seen him lately. 18. Which of those ladies did you see? 19. I saw the one that was here yesterday. 20. What are you thinking of? 21. I am thinking of what we are going to do to-morrow. 22. What did your father tell you to do? 23. I have done what he told me to do. 24. The gentleman, whose son was visiting us last year, will come himself next year. 25. The lady, whose daughter has just been married, will spend some weeks with us next summer. 26. The people, of whom I speak, would never do such a thing. 27. I, who am your friend, tell you so, and you ought to believe it. 28. It was we who gave them their liberty, and yet to-day they are our enemies. 29. He has gone away, and what is worse, he has not paid his debts. 30. That is very strange! I sent him a letter, and yet he says he never received it. 31. To whom are you speaking, sir? 32. It is to you I am speaking, and I want you to pay attention to what I say. 33. The house they are coming out of belongs to my father. 34. The people of the village which he came from were very glad to be rid of him. 35. The gentleman, for whose house I offered such a high price, has bought another. 36. The cause, for which those soldiers fought, was the deliverance of their country. 37. The man, in whom I trust, will not deceive me. 38. That child is deaf and dumb, which is a great pity, for he seems very intelligent. 39. I thank you very much. 40. Don't mention it. 41. What I was expecting was that he would pay me. 42. That is not a poor man; he is well off. 43. Where is the pen I made use of yesterday? 44. Take what you need; there will be enough for all. 45. Which way did you come this morning? 46. I came the way you came yesterday. 47. There is, in that affair, something strange and mysterious.

THE INDEFINITE PRONOUN.

480.   **Indefinites.**

1. Adjectival forms :—

1. certain, *a certain;* pl. *certain.*
2. chaque, *each, every.*
3. différent(e)s, pl., *various, etc.*
4. divers, m. pl. } *various, etc.*
   diverses, f. pl.
5. maint, *many a.*
6. quelque, *some;* pl., *some (few).*

Obs.: Except for **divers**, the feminine and plural are formed like those of ordinary adjectives.

2. Pronominal forms:—

1. autrui, *others, other people, etc.*
2. chacun, m.　﹜ *each (one), every*
   chacune, f.　﹜ *(one).*
3. on (l'on), *one, people, etc.*
4. personne...ne, *nobody, etc.*
5. quelqu'un, m. s.　﹜ *somebody, etc.*
   quelqu'une, f. s.　﹜
   quelques-uns, m. pl.　﹜ *some (peo-*
   quelques-unes, f. pl.　﹜ *ple), etc.*
6. quelque chose, *something.*
7. rien...ne, *nothing.*

Obs.: 1. Unless otherwise indicated above, these forms are invariable. 2. On often becomes l'on after a vowel sound to avoid hiatus (especially after **et, on, où, que, lorsque**, etc., **qui, quoi, pourquoi, si, ainsi, aussi**), but not usually when a closely following word has initial **l**; **qu'on** almost always become **que l'on** when a closely following word has initial **k** sound. 3. For **quelqu'un(e)**, see §73. 4. Note the hyphen of the pl. of **quelqu'un**.

3. Adjectival *or* pronominal forms:

1. aucun...ne, *no; nobody, etc.*
2. autre, *other.*
3. même, *same, etc.*
4. nul...ne, m.　﹜ *no; nobody,*
   nulle...ne, f.　﹜ *etc.*
5. pas un...ne, *no; nobody, etc.*
6. plusieurs, m. *or* f. pl., *several.*
7. tel, m.　﹜ *such, etc.*
   telle, f.　﹜
8. tout, m. tous, m. pl.　﹜ *all, every,*
   toute, f. toutes, f. pl.　﹜ *etc.*
9. un, *a; one, etc.*

Obs.: The fem. and plur. are like those of adjs. of like ending, except the fem. of **nul** and the plur. of **tout**.

481. Use of Adjectival Forms. 1. **Certain** = '(a) certain,' pl. 'certain,' 'some', *precedes* its noun; the use of **un** in the sing. and of partitive **de** in the plur. is optional:

(Un) certain roi français.　　A certain French king.
(De) certaines gens.　　Certain (some) people.

a. **Certains** is exceptionally used as a pronoun:

Certains prétendent, etc.　　Some assert, etc.

NOTE.—**Certain**, placed *after* the noun, is an ordinary adj. = 'sure,' 'trustworthy,' 'positive,' etc. (cf. §430, 4).

2. **Chaque** = 'each,' 'every', is distributive and sing. only:

Chaque homme (femme).　　Each *or* every man (woman).

a. Distinguish **chaque** = 'every,' 'each,' which *individualizes* from **tout** = 'every,' 'all,' which *generalizes*:

Chaque homme a des passions.　　Every (each) man has passions.
Tout homme a une passion do-　　Every man has (all men have) a
　minante.　　　　　　　　　　　　　ruling passion.
Chaque année; tous les ans.　　Each year; every year.

3. **Différents, Divers** = 'various,' 'several,' 'sundry,' 'divers,' are indef. adjs. only when *plur.* and *before* nouns:

Différentes choses m'ont retenu. — Various things detained me.
On a essayé divers moyens. — Several methods have been tried.

NOTE.—With the sense of 'different,' 'diverse,' they are used as ordinary adjs.:

4. **Maint**, whether sing. or plur., = 'many a'; it is often repeated:

Maint(s) danger(s). — Many a danger.
Mainte(s) fois. — Many a time.
En mainte et mainte occasion. — On many an occasion.

5. **Quelque** = 'some'; when used of quantity or number, **quelque** = 'some (but not much or many),' 'a little,' 'a few,' and is of more limited force than the partitive some (§401):

Quelques amis sont pires que des ennemis. — Some friends are worse than enemies.
J'ai eu quelque difficulté. — I have had some (a little) difficulty.
Il a quelques amis ici. — He has some (a few) friends here.
Voici les quelques francs qui nous restent. — Here are the few francs we have left.

a. **Quelque** has *adverbial* force and is *invariable*:

(1) Before numerals (*not* nouns of number) = 'about,' 'some':

À quelque dix milles d'ici. — About (some) ten miles from here.
But: Quelques centaines de pas. — A few hundred paces.
À cent et quelques pas. — At a little more than 100 paces.

(2) Before adjs. or advs. = 'however' (cf. §351, 4, *a*):

Quelque riches qu'ils soient. — However rich they may be.
Quelque bien que vous parliez. — However well you may speak.

NOTE.—'However'+*adj.* is also expressed by **tout...que** (usually indic.), **si...(que)** (subj.), **pour...que** (subj.):

'Toutes bonnes qu'elles sont,' 'However good they are'; 'Si bonnes qu'elles soient', 'However good they are'; 'Si bonnes vos raisons soient-elles', 'However good your reasons are'; 'Pour bonnes qu'elles soient', 'However good they are.'

b. For the use of quelque(s)...que = 'whatever,' see §484.

482. Use of Pronominal Forms. 1. **Autrui** = 'others,' 'other people,' our neighbour (in general),' is rarely used except after a prep.:

Il ne faut pas convoiter les biens d'autrui.	We must not covet the goods of others.
La rigueur envers autrui.	Severity towards others.

NOTE.—'Others' is more usually **les autres, d'autres** (§483, 2, *b*); regularly so as subject or direct object.

2. Chacun = 'each,' 'each one,' 'every one' is the pron. corresponding to the adj. **chaque** (§481, 2):

Chacun d'eux a refusé.	Each (every) one of them refused.
Donnez à chacun(e) sa part.	Give to each his (her) share.
Des poires à deux sous chacune.	Pears at two cents each.

a. The possessive form to **chacun** is regularly **son**:

Mettez-les chacun(e) à sa place.	Put them each in **his** (her, its) place.

b. **Chacun** in apposition to **nous, vous**, takes, as its possessive, **notre, votre**:

Parlez chacun(e) à **votre** tour.	Speak each in **your** turn.

c. **Chacun**, in apposition to **ils, elles**, takes the possessive **leur** before the *direct obj.*; otherwise **son** *or* **leur**:

Elles récitent chacune **leur** verset (chacune à **son** *or* **leur** tour).	They each recite **their** verse (each in turn).

d. The reflexive to **chacun** = 'every one' is **se** (**soi**):

Chacun pour **soi**.	Every one for **himself**.

3. On = 'one,' 'some one,' 'we,' 'you,' 'they,' 'people,' etc., is used as *subject* of a verb in the 3rd sing. without specifying any person in particular:

On dit que la reine est malade.	They (people) say the queen is ill.
A-t-on allumé mon feu?	Has anyone lighted my fire?
On ne peut pas mêler l'huile avec l'eau.	One (we, you) cannot mix oil with water.

a. The **on** construction often corresponds to an Eng. *passive*, especially when the agent is not specified:

On a attrapé le larron.	The thief has been caught.
On croit que la guerre est finie.	It is thought the war is over.
On vous demande.	You are wanted.

b. **On** may not be replaced by a pers. pron. subject:

On est triste quand on est sans argent.	A man is sad when he is without money.

c. Since **on** is subject only, the corresponding direct and indirect object, when required, are borrowed from **vous**:

Lorsqu'**on** presse trop un poisson il **vous** échappe.	When **you** squeeze a fish too much it escapes **you**.

d. The reflexive to **on** is **se** (**soi**), and the possessive **son**, whatever be the Eng. equivalent:

On se demande.	People ask themselves.
On perdrait son temps.	You would lose your time.

e. Although **on** is invar., a fem. or plur. noun or adj. may relate to it, when the sense is clearly fem. or plur.:

On est plus jolie à présent.	She is prettier now.
On est si proches voisins.	We are such near neighbours.

f. **On** may replace a pers. pron., often with depreciatory force:

On y pensera.	I (we) shall see about it.
On se croit bien fin.	You (he, etc.) think yourself very cunning.

4. **Personne** and **rien** along with **ne** + *a verb*, or when *alone* (a verb understood) = 'nobody,' 'no one,' 'not anybody,' etc., and 'nothing,' 'not anything,' respectively:

Personne n'est venu.	Nobody (no one) has come.
Je n'ai parlé à personne.	I have spoken to nobody (not spoken to anybody).
Ne dites rien.	Say nothing (do not say a. t.).
Personne ici !—Personne.	No one here !—No one.
Qu'a-t-il dit ?—Rien.	What did he say ?—Nothing.

a. If the context contains or implies negation, **personne**, **rien**, assume affirmative force (= quelqu'un, quelque chose):

Il n'a rien dit à personne.	He said nothing to any one.
Personne n'a jamais rien dit.	Nobody has ever said anything.
Je vous défends de rien dire.	I forbid you to say anything.
Je crains de parler à personne.	I fear to speak to anybody.
Impossible de rien faire !	Impossible to do anything !
Il cessa de rien donner.	He ceased giving anything.
Où trouverai-je rien de pareil ?	Where shall I find anything like it ?
Sans parler à personne.	Without speaking to anybody.

b. The above rule does not apply to *pleonastic* **ne**, nor to *double negations*:

Je crains qu'il ne fasse mal à quelqu'un.	I fear he will hurt somebody.
Ne revenez pas sans voir quelqu'un.	Do not come back without seeing somebody.

NOTE.—The *pron.* **personne** is *masc.* (sometimes sylleptically fem. like **on**, 3, *e*, above); the *noun* **personne** is always *fem.* (cf. §380, 1, *c*).

5. Quelqu'un(e) = 'somebody,' 'someone,' 'anyone,' etc., with its plur. **quelques-un(e)s** = 'some,' 'some people,' 'any,' 'a few,' etc., is the pron. corresponding to the adj. **quelque** (§481, 5):

Il y a quelqu'un là.	There is **somebody** there.
Y a-t-il quelqu'un là ?	Is there **any one** there ?
A-t-il quelques-unes des fleurs ?	Has he **some (any)** of the flowers ?
Il en reste quelques-unes.	**A few** of them remain.
Quelqu'une des dames viendra.	**Some one** of the ladies will come.
Quelques-uns le croient.	**Some (people)** believe it.

6. Quelque chose = 'something,' 'anything,' and is *masc.*, though formed from the fem. noun **chose**:

Quelque chose est promis.	**Something** is promised.
A-t-il dit quelque chose ?	Did he say **anything** ?
A-t-il quelque chose de bon ?	Has he **anything** good ?

483. Use of Adjectival or Pronominal Forms.
1. **Aucun, nul, pas un**, along with **ne** + *a verb*, or when *alone* (a verb understood) = 'no,' 'not any,' 'not one' (as adj.) and 'none,' 'nobody,' 'no one,' 'not one' (as pron.):

Aucun ⎫	
Nul ⎬ écrivain ne le dit.	**No** writer says so.
Pas un ⎭	
Aucun ne le croit.	**No one** believes it.
Je n'en ai vu aucun(e).	I saw **none** of them.
Pas un de ses amis ne reste.	**Not one** of his friends remains.
A-t-il de l'espoir ?—Aucun.	Has he any hope ?—**None**.

a. **Aucun** (*not* 'nul' or 'pas un') becomes affirmative (= quelque or quelqu'un) with negative context (cf. §482, 4, *a.*):

Sans aucune cause.	Without **any** cause.
Rien pour aucun de nous.	Nothing for **any** of us.
Gardez-vous de faire aucune faute.	Take care not to make **any** mistake.

b. The plur. adj. **aucun(e)s** may be used (especially before nouns with no sing. or such as are preferably plur.); (**d')aucuns = quelques-uns**, is sometimes found in *naïf* or jocular style:

Il ne me rend aucuns soins. — He gives me no care.
(D')aucuns le croiraient. — Some would believe it.

2. **Autre** = 'other,' is usually preceded in the sing. by **un** or **l'**:

Une autre fois; d'autres livres. — Another time; other books.
En avez-vous un(e) autre? — Have you another?
Un autre dit le contraire. — Another says the contrary.
Les autres m'aideront. — The others will help me.
Entre autres choses. — Among other things.

a. Distinguish **un autre** = 'another (a different)' from **encore un** = 'another (an additional)':

Donnez-moi une autre plume }
　　〃　　〃 encore une 〃 } Give me another pen.

b. 'Others,' 'other people' = **les autres** *or* **d'autres**, sometimes **autrui** (cf. §482, 1):

Il se méfie toujours des autres. — He always suspects others.
D'autres pensent autrement. — Others think otherwise.
Bien d'autres. — Many others.

　Obs.: The **d'** of **d'autres** is partitive sign (cf. §403, 1, *b*).

c. **Autres** is often added familiarly to **nous, vous**:

Nous autres peintres. — We painters.
Vous autres Français parlez très vite. — You Frenchmen speak very fast.

d. Observe the following expressions with **autre**:

Autre part; de part et d'autre. — Elsewhere; reciprocally.
C'est (tout) un autre homme. — He is a very different man.
Parler de choses et d'autres. — To speak of this and that.
L'autre jour. — The other day.
Autre est promettre, autre est donner. — It is one thing to promise, and another to give.
Tout autre que lui. — Any one but him.
De temps à autre. — From time to time.
À d'autres (fam.). — Tell that to the marines (fam.).

e. For **l'un ... l'autre, les uns ... les autres**, see §483, 7, (2).
U

3. **Même** varies in meaning and form according to position and function:—

(1) *Preceding its noun* or as a *pronoun*, **même** = 'same,' and nearly always has the article:

La (les) même(s) chose(s).	The same thing(s).
Les miens sont les mêmes.	Mine are the same.
Donnez-moi des mêmes.	Give me some of the same.
Une même affaire.	One and the same business.
Des plantes de la même espèce.	Plants of the same species.

(2) *Following* the noun or pron. qualified, **même** = 'self,' 'very,' 'even,' and agrees, but has no article:

Dieu est la bonté même.	God is goodness itself.
Moi-même; elles-mêmes.	I myself; they themselves.
Cela même; celui-là même.	That itself; that man himself.
Les enfants mêmes.	The very (even the) children.

a. **Même** is also used as an *adverb* (invar.):

Il nous a même insultés.	He even insulted us.
Quand même il le dirait.	Even if he should say so.

b. **Même** forms a number of highly idiomatic locutions:

Cela revient au même.	That amounts to the same thing.
Êtes-vous à même de faire cela ?	Are you in a position to do that?
J'irai tout de même.	I shall go nevertheless.

4. **Plusieurs** = 'several'; it is sometimes used in the sense of **beaucoup** = 'many':

Plusieurs hommes (femmes).	Several men (women).
Apporte plusieurs des plumes.	Bring several of the pens.
J'en ai plusieurs.	I have several of them.
Plusieurs l'ont cru.	Many (people) believe it.

5. **Tel**, as adj., = 'such' (un tel = 'such a'), 'like'; tel, as pron., = 'many a one,' 'he', 'some', etc.:

Ne crois pas une telle histoire.	Do not believe such a story.
Tels sont mes malheurs.	Such are my misfortunes.
Il n'y a pas de tels animaux.	There are no such animals.
À telles et telles conditions.	On such and such conditions.
Telle qu'une tigresse.	Like (as) a tigress.
Tel qui rit vendredi dimanche pleurera (prov.).	Some (many a one, he) who laugh(s) on Friday will weep on Sunday.

a. Examples of more idiomatic uses are:

Tel père, tel fils.	Like father, like son.
Tel rit, tel pleure.	One laughs, another weeps.
Monsieur un tel (Mme une telle).	Mr. So-and-so (Mrs. So-and-so).
De la musique telle quelle.	Music such as it is.
Votre argent tel quel.	Your money intact.

NOTE.—'Such', as adv., is *si* or *tellement* (not 'tel'): 'Une si belle étoile'; 'Un homme tellement cruel.'

6. **Tout** (sing.) = 'all,' 'every,' 'any,' 'whole,' etc.; **tous** (plur.) = 'all':

Toute ma vie ; tous les hommes.	All my (my whole) life ; all (the) men.
Tout homme ; toute créature.	Every (any) man ; every creature.
Tous (toutes) sont venu(e)s.	All have come.
C'est tout ; de tous côtés.	That is all ; on all sides.
Tout m'effraie.	Everything frightens me.

a. Tout is often adverb = 'quite,' 'wholly,' 'very,' 'very much,' etc., and *agrees* like an adj., when immediately preceding a fem. adj. with *initial consonant* or h *aspirate*, but is *elsewhere invariable:*

Elles étaient toutes pâles et tout agitées.	They were quite pale and very much excited.

But: Ils étaient tout pâles et tout agités, etc.

NOTE.—So also, in the compound **tout-puissant**, *e.g.*, 'Elle est toute-puissante.'

b. Observe the following idiomatic expressions:

Tout le monde (cf. le monde entier).	Everybody (cf. the whole world).
Tous les mois ; pas du tout.	Every month ; not at all.
Tous les deux jours.	Every other (alternate) day.
Tous (les*) deux *or* les deux.	Both.
Tout à l'heure.	Presently (*or* a little ago).
Tout beau ; tout doux.	Gently (slowly) ; softly.
(Pour) tout de bon.	Seriously.

*Tous deux (trois, etc.)—without 'les'—usually denotes 'simultaneousness, (='both together,' etc.); les is obligatory above *ten*, and usual from *five* to *ten*.

c. For the distinction between **tout** and **chaque** see §481, 2, *a*; for tout…que = 'however,' see §481, 5, *a*, note.

7. Un is used either alone or as correlative to autre :—
(1) Un (as adj.) = 'a,' 'an,' (cf. § 398), 'one,' 'a certain'; un (as pron.) = 'one':

La maison est d'un côté.	The house is on one side.
Un monsieur A. l'a dit.	A (certain) Mr. A. said so.
Une des dames l'a dit.	One of the ladies said so.
Voici un crayon.—J'en ai un.	Here is a pencil.—I have one.
Les uns sont de cet avis, les autres n'en sont pas.	Some are of this opinion, (the) others are not.

a. Un as a pron. is often preceded by l', especially with a de clause:

L'un des consuls est arrivé.	One of the consuls has come.

(2) **L'un(e), l'autre (les un(e)s, les autres)** are combined into various correlative phrases, as follows:—

l'un l'autre = 'each other,' 'one another'; pl. ditto.
l'un et l'autre = 'both'; pl., 'both,' 'all.'
l'un ou l'autre = 'either'; pl., ditto.
ni l'un ni l'autre (... ne) = 'neither'; pl., 'neither,' 'none.'

Elles se flattent l'une l'autre.	They flatter each other.
Ils parlent les uns des autres.	They speak of one another.
Les uns pour les autres.	For one another.
L'une et l'autre occasion.	Both occasions.
Les uns et les autres parlent.	Both (all of them) speak.
Dites ceci aux uns et aux autres.	Say this to both (all).
Je prends l'un(e) ou l'autre.	I take either.
Parle à l'une ou à l'autre.	Speak to either.
Ni les un(e)s ni les autres ne sont pour vous.	Neither (none of them) are for you.
Ni pour l'un(e) ni pour l'autre.	For neither.

484. Indefinite Relatives.

1. Adjectival :—

Quelconque, *any (whatever, at all).*
Quel que (+subj. of être), *whatever.*
Quelque... que (+subj.), *whatever.*

2. Pronominal :—

Quiconque, *whoever.*
Qui que... (+subj. of être), *whoever.*
Quoi que... (+subj.), *whatever.*

Obs.: **Quelconque** takes s for the plur., and always follows its noun; **quiconque** is invariable; the other forms are made up from **quel, quelque, qui, quoi,** +**que**.

Un (deux) point(s) quelconque(s).	Any (two) point(s) whatever.
Des raisons quelconques.	Any reasons whatever (at all).
Quiconque parle sera puni(e).	Whoever speaks will be punished.
Quels que soient (puissent être) vos desseins.	Whatever be (may be) your designs.

Quelle que fût la loi.	Whatever the law might be.
Quelques efforts qu'il fasse.	Whatever efforts he makes.
Qui que tu sois (puisses être).	Whoever you be (may be).
Quoi que vous fassiez.	Whatever you do.

Obs.: For the use of the subjunctive, see §356, 4.

a. **Qui que** and **quoi que** are also used with **ce** before **soit**:

Qui que ce soit qui le dise.	Whosoever says it.
Quoi que ce soit qu'il dise.	Whatsoever he says.

EXERCISE LXXVII.

1. Certain people say the criminal has escaped. 2. Each day brings its labour. 3. We rise every morning at six o'clock. 4. I have seen him many a time. 5. I have no apples, but I have some pears and peaches. 6. However great and rich we may be, we must die. 7. Whatever your intentions were, your actions were not good. 8. However good your intentions were, you did not succeed in doing us good. 9. We should respect the rights of others. 10. Every one for himself is, happily, not a maxim which everybody practises. 11. If we do not love others, others will not love us. 12. Those children will receive, each one at his majority, their portion of their father's estate. 13. Mother, will you come down? You are wanted. 14. It is said that the robber has been caught. 15. It is not known whether the ship was wrecked or not. 16. When one is pretty, one is rarely ignorant of it. 17. People wonder why that young man associates with those scoundrels. 18. When one sees a noble action, it always gives one pleasure. 19. I have never seen any one who had so many noble qualities. 20. I am afraid to say anything about it to any one. 21. No one has ever done anything like that. 22. What a beautiful view! Did you ever see anything like it? 23. He went away without visiting anyone. 24. Did you find anything where you were looking yesterday? 25. I do not know anyone of his friends. 26. I doubt whether anyone of you will do so. 27. If I can do it without any expense, I shall do it willingly. 28. I do not like this book; give me another. 29. That little boy has had one apple, and now he wants another. 30. Frenchmen often laugh at us Englishmen, because we are less gay than they. 31. This man I have seen elsewhere, but that one I never saw anywhere. 32. These are the same people that were here yesterday morning. 33. That lady is goodness itself. 34. Even if you were to say so, I should not believe it. 35. That is a young man in whom I have confidence; I shall put him in a position to make his fortune. 36. Were there any children at

the meeting? 37. Yes, there were several. 38. I shall never accept such conditions. 39. I never saw such a foolish man. 40. If he were to say such a thing to me, I should put him out of doors. 41. He spent his whole life in doing good. 42. Our neighbour's daughters have become quite tall. 43. He comes to town every other week. 44. Where are the children? Both were here a little ago. 45. I found two apples in the basket, but neither is good. 46. Any line being given, draw a straight line which shall be equal to it. 47. There is no reason whatever which can persuade me. 48. Whoever has stolen that poor woman's money ought to be punished. 49. Whoever he is who told you that, he is mistaken. 50. Whatever that man may do, he will never succeed. 51. Whatever the reason may be, he will never come to see us.

THE ADVERB.

485. Simple Adverbs. The following list contains the commoner simple adverbs:—

ailleurs, *elsewhere.*
ainsi, *thus, so.*
alors, *then.*
après, *afterwards.*
assez, *enough, rather.*
aujourd'hui, *to-day.*
auparavant, *before.*
aussi, *also, too, as.*
aussitôt, *directly.*
autant, *as much.*
autrefois, *formerly.*
beaucoup, *much.*
bien, *well, very, much.*
bientôt, *soon.*
cependant, *however.*
certes, *indeed.*
combien(?), *how much(?).*
comme, *as, like.*
comment (?), *how (?).*
davantage, *more.*
dedans, *inside.*
dehors, *outside.*
déjà, *already.*

demain, *to-morrow.*
derrière, *behind.*
désormais, *henceforth.*
dessous, *under.*
dessus, *above.*
devant, *before.*
dorénavant, *henceforth.*
encore, *still.*
enfin, *at last.*
ensemble, *together.*
ensuite, *then.*
environ, *about.*
exprès, *on purpose.*
fort, *very.*
hier, *yesterday.*
ici, *here.*
jadis, *formerly.*
jamais, *ever, never.*
là, *there.*
loin, *far (off), a long way.*
longtemps, *(a) long (while).*
lors, *then,*

maintenant, *now.*
mal, *badly.*
même, *even.*
mieux, *better.*
moins, *less.*
ne ..., *not.*
néanmoins, *nevertheless.*
non, *no.*
où (?), *where (?).*
oui, *yes.*
parfois, *sometimes.*
partout, *everywhere.*
pas, *not.*
peu, *little.*
pis, *worse.*
plus, *more.*
plutôt, *rather.*
point, *not.*
pourquoi (?), *why (?).*
pourtant, *however.*
près, *near (by).*
presque, *almost.*
proche, *near (by).*

puis, *then, thereupon.*	surtout, *especially.*	tout, *quite, entirely.*
quand (?), *when (?).*	tant, *so much.*	toutefois, *however.*
que !, *how (!).*	tantôt, *soon, recently.*	très, *very.*
quelquefois, *sometimes.*	tard, *late.*	trop, *too (much).*
si, *so ; yes.*	tôt, *soon.*	vite, *quickly.*
souvent, *often.*	toujours, *always, still.*	volontiers, *willingly.*

486. Adverbs from Adjectives. Most adjectives become adverbs by the addition of -ment to the fem. sing. :

ADJ.	ADV.	ADJ.	ADV.
pur,	purement, *purely.*	doux,	doucement, *sweetly.*
strict,	strictement, *strictly.*	fou,	follement, *madly.*
actif,	activement, *actively.*	facile,	facilement, *easily.*
sec,	sèchement, *dryly.*	autre,	autrement, *otherwise.*

a. Adjectives ending in a *vowel* (*not* -e) drop the -e of the fem. on adding -ment :

poli(e),	poliment, *politely.*	décidé (e),	décidément, *decidedly.*
absolu(e),	absolument, *absolutely.*	etc.	etc.

NOTE.—The omitted e is denoted by a circumflex in assidûment, continûment, crûment, (in)dûment, gaîment (better 'gaiement'), nûment.

b. The following adjs. in -e change e to é on adding -ment.

aveugle,	aveuglément.	immense,	immensément.
commode,	commodément.	incommode,	incommodément.
conforme,	conformément.	opiniâtre,	opiniâtrément.
énorme,	énormément.	uniforme,	uniformément.

c. The following adjs. change the added -e of the fem. to é :

commun(e),	communément.	obscur(e),	obscurément.
confus(e),	confusément.	opportun(e),	opportunément.
diffus(e),	diffusément.	précis(e),	précisément.
expresse(e),	expressément.	profond(e),	profondément.
importun(e),	importunément.	profus(e),	profusément.

d. Adjectives in -ant, -ent (except lent, présent, véhément) assimilate -nt to m and add -ment to the masc. form :

constant,	constamment, *constantly.*	prudent,	prudemment, *prudently.*
élégant,	élégamment, *elegantly.*	etc.	etc.

But : Lentement, *slowly ;* présentement, *presently ;* véhémentement, *vehemently.*

e. Gentil gives gentiment, *nicely ;* the adv. to bref is brièvement (from a parallel form), *briefly ;* the adv. to impuni is impunément, (probably from L. *impune,* cf. *b.* above), *with impunity.*

f. The adverbs corresponding to bon, *good,* and mauvais, *bad,* are bien, *well,* and mal, *badly.* (From bon comes regularly bonnement = ' simply.')

487. Adjectives as Adverbs. Adjectival forms are not uncommonly used as adverbs, and, as such, are regularly *invariable* :—

1. A number of adjs. serve as advs. in certain fixed expressions :

Cette sottise lui coûte cher.   That folly is costing him **dear**.
Elles parlent **bas** (**haut**).   They speak **low** (**loud**).

Such expressions are :

coûter **bon**, *cost dear.*
sentir " *smell good.*
tenir " *stand firm.*
acheter **cher**, *buy dear.*
coûter " *cost* "
vendre " *sell* "
voir **clair**, *see clearly.*
prouver " *prove* "

arrêter **court**, *stop short.*
filer **doux**, *sing small.*
aller **droit**, *go straight.*
viser " *aim* "
chanter **faux**, *sing out of tune.*
frapper **ferme**, *strike hard.*
parler " *speak firmly.*

coûter **gros**, *cost dear.*
viser **haut**, *aim high.*
chanter **juste**, *sing in tune.*
frapper " *strike straight.*
sentir **mauvais**, *smell bad.*
écrire **serré**, *write small.*
(à) **vrai** dire, *speak truly.*
etc. etc.

So also, parler français (anglaise, etc.), cf. §399, *a*.

2. An adj. sometimes modifies another adj. :

Des dames **haut** placées.   Ladies of high rank.
Un **véritable** grand homme.   A truly great man.

3. Besides the above (1, 2), a few adjectival forms serve also as adverbs :

Je l'ai dit **exprès**.   I said it purposely.
Soudain nous vîmes l'ennemi.   Suddenly we saw the enemy.

Such forms are :

bref, *in short.*
exprès, *purposely.*
fort, *very, hard, loud, etc.*
juste, *exactly, etc.*

même, *even.*
proche, *near (by).*
soudain, *suddenly.*
*tout, *quite, very, etc.*

tout beau, *not so fast.*
tout doux, *gently.*
†vite, *quickly.*

*For the inflection of **tout** as adverb, see §483, 6, *a*.
†The adv. **vitement**='quickly' is familiar.

488. Adverbial Locutions. Phrases with adverbial function are numerous :

Je viendrai tout à l'heure.   I shall come presently.
Venez de bonne heure.   Come early.

Further examples are :

à bon marché, *cheap.*
à côté, *near, near by.*
à droite, *to the right.*
à jamais, *forever.*

à la fois, *at once.*
à l'avenir, *in future.*
à peine, *hardly.*
à peu près, *nearly.*

au juste, *exactly.*
au moins, *at least.*
çà et là, *here and there.*
d'abord, *at first.*

d'ailleurs, *besides*.	en effet, *in fact*.	tôt ou tard, *sooner or later*.
dès lors, *since*.	en haut, *above, up stairs*.	tour à tour, *in turn*.
d'ordinaire, *usually*.	là-bas, *yonder*.	tout à coup, *suddenly*.
d'où (?), *whence (?)*.	là-dessus, *thereupon*	tout de suite, *at once*.
du moins, *at least*.	plus tôt, *sooner*.	tout d'un coup, *all at once*.
en avant, *forward*.	sans doute, *doubtless*.	etc., etc.
en bas, *below, down stairs*.	tant mieux, *so much the better*.	

489. Comparison of Adverbs. 1. Adverbs are regularly compared like adjectives (§423) by the use of **plus, moins, aussi; que** = 'than', 'as':

Plus, moins, (aussi) facilement que Jean.	More, less, (as) easily than (as) John.

a. Further examples, illustrating §423, *a, b, c, d*, as applied to adverbs:

Il ne marche pas aussi (si) vite.	He does not walk as (so) fast.
Vite comme un éclair.	As quick as lightning.
Il marche plus vite que je ne pensais.	He walks faster than I thought.
De plus en plus vite.	Faster and faster.
Plus je le connais (et) moins je l'estime.	The more I know him the less I esteem him.

b. 'More than,' 'less than,' as adverbs of *quantity* = plus de, moins de, respectively; they must be carefully distinguished from plus (moins) que = 'more (less) than' in an elliptical sentence:

J'ai plus (moins) de dix francs.	I have more (less) than ten francs.
En moins d'une demi-heure.	In less than half an hour.
But: Un éléphant mange plus que six chevaux (ne mangent).	An elephant eats more than six horses (eat).

2. The following are *irregularly* compared

bien, *well*.	mieux, *better*.	beaucoup, *much*.	plus, *more*.
mal, *badly, ill*.	{ pis, *worse*. plus mal, *worse*.	peu, *little*.	moins, *less*.

a. Beaucoup = 'much (many)' or 'very much (many)' and is never modified by another adv. (except **pas**).

3. The superlative is formed by placing **le** (invar.) before the comparative of inequality:

Le plus souvent (moins souvent).	(The) most frequently (least f.).
Elle parle le plus (mieux, moins).	She speaks (the) most (best, least).

490. Position. 1. An adverb regularly stands immediately *after* its verb (rarely between subject and verb):

Charles porte souvent ma canne.	Charles often carries my cane.
On devrait lire lentement.	One should read slowly.
Se levant tard, se couchant tôt.	Rising early, going to bed late:
Ils l'ont bien reçu.	They have received him well.

Obs.: Hence the adv. comes between the aux. and the participle in comp. tenses.

  a. The adverbs **aujourd'hui, hier, demain, autrefois, tôt, tard, ici, là, ailleurs, partout**, never come between aux. and participle.

Il est parti hier.	He went away yesterday.
Je l'ai cherché partout.	I looked for it everywhere.

  b. Long adverbs in -ment not uncommonly stand after the past part. :

Il a parlé éloquemment.	He has spoken eloquently.

  c. Most adverbs of quantity (**peu, beaucoup, trop**, etc.), and a few short advs. like **bien, mal, mieux**, etc., as also advs. of negation, regularly *precede* the *infinitive*:

Tu ne devrais pas trop lire.	You should not read too much.
Il ne saurait mieux faire.	He cannot do better.
Il parle de ne pas aller.	He speaks of not going.

  d. Interrogative advs. head the phrase, as in Eng.; other advs. are not uncommonly placed first for emphasis (cf. §317, 3).

Quand allez-vous revenir?	When are you going to come back?
Aujourd'hui je vais me reposer.	To-day I am going to rest.
Malheureusement tout est perdu.	Unfortunately all is lost.

2. Adverbs usually precede the nouns, adjs., advs. and phrases modified by them :

Assez de livres, et assez chers.	Books enough, and dear enough.
Bien mal à propos.	Very unseasonably.

  a. For **combien !, comme !, que !, tant !**, and **plus (moins) ... plus (... moins)** with adjs. or advs., cf. §428, *a*.

3. Adverbial phrases follow the same rules as advs., except that only the shorter ones may usually come between aux. and verb :

Nous étions à peine partis.	Hardly had we gone.

NEGATION.

491. Negation without Verb. Non = 'no,' 'not, apart from a verb; it is often emphasized by **pas, point**:

L'avez-vous dit?—Non.	Did you say it?—No.
Vous viendrez?—Non pas (point).	You will come?—Certainly not.
Non, non, je n'irai pas.	No, no, I shall not go.
Non content de dire cela.	Not satisfied with saying that.
Riche ou non, il ne l'aura pas.	Rich or **not**, he shall not have it.
A-t-il, oui ou non, du talent?	Has he talent, yes or no?
Des idées non moins vastes.	Ideas not less vast.
Une maison non meublée (adj.).	A house not furnished.
Non seulement... mais encore.	Not only... but also.

a. For the use of que non, see §497, 1, *a*.

Negation with verb:—

492. Negative Forms. 1. Along with a verb, a negation consists regularly of two parts, **ne** (n', see §73) together with some other word or words; the principal correlative expressions of this kind are:

ne... pas, *not*.   ne... aucunement ⎫ *not at*   ne... rien, *nothing*.
ne... point, *not*.   ne... nullement   ⎭ *all*.   ne... ni(... ni) *neither..*
ne... guère, *hardly*.   ne... aucun   ⎫   *nor*.
ne... jamais, *never*.   ne... nul   ⎬ *no, none*.
ne... plus, *no more*.   ne... pas un ⎭
ne... que, *only*.   ne... personne, *nobody*.

NOTES.—1. **Point** is usually *more emphatic* than **pas**, and is *less common* in ordinary language. 2. Negation is often denoted by **pas** (without ne) in the language of the vulgar or ignorant: 'Ai-je pas dit cela? (=N'ai-je pas dit cela?).'

2. Other forms of less frequent use are:

a. Ne... quelconque='no... whatsoever (at all),' ne... qui que ce soit='nobody whatsoever (at all),' ne... quoi que ce soit='nothing whatsoever (at all).'

Je n'ai dit quoi que ce soit.	I said nothing at all.

b. Ne... brin (lit. 'mote'), or mie (lit. 'crumb'); or goutte (lit. 'drop'), or mot (lit. 'word')=ne... rien, in certain phrases:

Il n'y en a brin.	There is nothing of it.
Je n'y entends goutte.	I understand nothing of it.

c. **Ne... âme vivante,** or **homme qui vive,** or **âme qui vive,** etc. = **ne ... personne :**

Il n'y avait **âme vivante** dans la maison. — There was not a living soul in the house.

d. **Ne ... de** + *time, e.g.* la (ma) vie, de huit jours, etc. :

Je ne l'oublierai de ma vie. — I shall not forget it while I live.

493. Position. Ne always *precedes* the verb (and its conjunctive objects, if any); **pas, point** and other adverbs immediately *follow* the verb (and its conjunctive pronouns, if any); indefinites have their usual place. (For exceptions, see *a, b*):

Je ne le leur ai **pas** (**point**) dit.	I did not tell them it.
Je n'en ai **guère.**	I have hardly any of it.
Ne les a-t-il **jamais** vus ?	Did he never see them ?
Je n'y resterai **plus.**	I shall stay there no longer.
Il ne le veut **nullement.**	He does not wish it at all.
Il ne prend **aucun** soin.	He takes no care.
Personne ne peut le dire.	Nobody can say (it).
Il n'a mal **quelconque.**	He has no pain at all.
Je ne l'ai dit à **qui que ce soit.**	I have told it to nobody at all.

a. **Pas, point,** usually, and **plus,** often, precede the *simple infin.* (and its conjunctive objects); they may precede or follow **avoir, être,** either when alone or in a comp. infin. :

Il parle de ne **pas** vous voir.	He speaks of not seeing you.
Être ou ne **pas** être (n'être **pas**).	To be or not to be.
J'étais fâché de ne vous avoir **pas** vu (*or* de ne **pas** vous avoir vu, *or* de ne vous **pas** avoir vu).	I was sorry not to have seen you.

b. **Rien** (indef.) as object is treated as an adv. ; it may also precede an infin. like an adv. :

Il promet de ne **rien** dire. — He promises to say nothing.

c. The **que** of **ne ... que** must immediately precede the word which it modifies :

Je n'en ai vu **que** trois. — I saw only three of them.

d. To denote 'neither ... nor,' **ni** is placed before each co-ordinate (if not a finite verb) and **ne** stands before the finite verb (if any); when finite verbs are co-ordinated, **ne** stands before each of them, while **ni** also must stand with the last, but may not stand with the first, and is optional with others :

NEGATION.

Qui le sait?—Ni lui ni moi.	Who knows it?—Neither he nor I.
Il n'a ni parents ni amis.	He has neither relatives nor friends.
Je ne l'ai ni vu ni entendu.	I neither saw nor heard it.
Il ne sait ni lire ni écrire.	He can neither read nor write.
Je ne veux ni qu'il lise ni qu'il écrive.	I neither wish him to read nor to write.
Il ne le blâme ni ne le loue.	He neither blames nor praises it.
Je ne pouvais, (ni) ne devais, ni ne voulais céder.	I neither could, nor should, nor would yield.

494. Ellipsis of the Verb. If the verb be omitted (but understood), ne is also omitted, and the correlative itself denotes negation:

Est-il venu?—Pas encore (= Il n'est pas encore venu).	Has he come?—Not yet (= He has not yet come).
Qui est là?—Personne.	Who is there?—Nobody.
Plus de larmes; plus de soucis.	No more tears; no more cares.

a. **Pas**, when so used, *may not stand alone:*

Non (pas); pas encore; pas lui; pas du tout; pas ce soir, etc.	No; not yet; not he (him); not at all; not this evening, etc.

495. *Ne* alone as Negative. Negation with verbs is expressed by ne alone in certain cases, as follows:—

1. After **que = pourquoi?**, and usually after **que, qui** in rhetorical question or exclamation:

Que ne le disiez-vous plus tôt?	Why did you not say so sooner?
Que ne ferais-je pour lui?	What would I not do for him?
Qui ne voit cela?	Who does not see that?

2. After condition expressed by inversion:

N'eût été la pluie.	Had it not been for the rain.

a. Sometimes also in conditions regularly expressed with **si**:

Si je ne me trompe.	If I am not mistaken.
Qui, si ce n'est vous?	Who, if not you?

3. In dependent sentences after *negation* (either fully expressed or implied):

Je n'ai pas (j'ai peu) d'amis qui ne soient les vôtres.	I have no (I have few) friends who are not yours.
Il n'y a rien qu'il ne sache.	There is nothing he does not know.
Non que je ne le craigne.	Not that I do not fear him.
Impossible qu'il ne vienne!	Impossible that he will not come!
Ai-je un ami qui ne soit fidèle?—Non.	Have I one friend who is not faithful?—No.

a. More obscure cases of implied negation are **prendre garde que** = 'take care that not,' etc., and such expressions as **il tient** = 'it depends on' (used interrogatively):

Prenez garde qu'il ne tombe.	Take care he does not fall.
Gardez qu'il ne sorte.	Take care he does not go out.
À quoi tient-il qu'on ne fasse cela ?	What is the cause of that not being done ?

4. For the most part optionally, with **savoir, bouger**, and with **pouvoir, oser, cesser** + *infin.* (expressed or implied):

Je ne sais (pas).	I do not know.
Ne bougez (pas) de là.	Do not stir from there.
Je ne puis (pas) répondre.	I cannot answer.
Je ne puis (sc. infin.)	I cannot.
Il n'oserait (pas) le dire.	He would not dare to say so.
Elle ne cesse (pas) de pleurer.	She does not cease weeping.

a. Always **ne** *alone* in **je ne saurais** = 'I cannot':

Je ne saurais vous le dire.	I cannot tell you.
Ne sauriez-vous m'aider ?	Can you not help me ?

5. In a few set expressions, such as:

N'importe ; n'avoir garde.	It does not matter ; not to care.
Ne vous en déplaise.	By your leave.
N'avoir que faire de.	To have no use (whatever) for.
Il n'est pire eau que l'eau qui dort (prov.).	Still waters run deep.

496. Pleonastic *ne*. In a **que** clause ne is often pleonastic, as compared with English; thus, **ne** stands :—

1. After **empêcher** = 'prevent,' **éviter** = 'avoid,' **à moins que** = 'unless,' (or **que** so used):

Empêchez qu'il ne sorte.	Prevent him from going out.
J'évite qu'on ne me voie.	I avoid being seen.
À moins que je ne sois retenu.	Unless I be detained.

a. This **ne** is often omitted after **empêcher** and **éviter** (after empêcher mostly when negative or interrogative):

b. Ne may stand also after **avant que**:

Avant qu'il (ne) parte.	Before he goes away.

2. After expressions of *fearing* (**craindre, redouter**, etc., **avoir peur**, etc.), when *not negative* (or when nega-

tion is not implied by interrogation expecting negative answer, or by condition):

Je crains qu'il **ne** vienne. I fear he will come.
Craignez-vous qu'il **ne** vienne? Do you fear he will come?
But: Je ne crains pas qu'il vienne; sans craindre qu'il vienne; craignez-vous qu'il vienne?—Non; si je craignais qu'il vînt.

b. What it is (or is not) feared *will not happen* has the full negation **ne... pas** in the que clause:

Je crains qu'il **ne** vienne **pas**. I fear he will **not** come.
Je ne crains pas qu'il ne vienne pas. I do not fear he will **not** come.

a. Interrogation (condition) and negation neutralize each other, and **ne** stands:

Ne craignez-vous pas qu'il ne vienne? Do you not fear he will come?
Si je ne craignais qu'il **ne** vînt. If I did not fear he would come.
Quand même je ne craindrais pas qu'il ne vînt. Even though I did not fear he would come.

3. With a finite verb in the second member of a comparison of inequality, when the first member is *not negative* (or does not imply negation as above):

Il est (est-il) plus riche qu'il **ne** l'était (?). He is (is he) richer than he was (?).
Il gagne moins qu'il n'espérait. He earns less than he hoped.
But: Il n'est pas plus riche qu'il l'était; est-il plus riche qu'il était?—Non.

a. A negative interrogation implies affirmation, and **ne** stands:
N'est-il pas plus riche qu'il **ne** l'était? Is he not richer than he was?

NOTE.—**Autre, autrement, plutôt, plus tôt,** similarly take **ne**: 'Il est tout autre que je **ne** pensais.'

4. Usually after expressions of *doubt, denial* (**douter, nier, disconvenir,** etc., often **désespérer**), when *negative* (or when negation is implied as above):

Je ne doute pas qu'il **ne** vienne. I do not doubt that he will come.
Doutez-vous qu'il **ne** vienne?— Do you doubt whether he will come?—No.
Non.
But: Je doute qu'il vienne; doutez-vous qu'il vienne? (—question for information).

5. After **il s'en faut** *negatively, interrogatively,* or with **peu (guère,** etc.):

Il ne s'en fallut pas (de) beaucoup qu'il ne fût tué.	He came very near being killed.
Combien s'en faut-il que la somme n'y soit?	How much is lacking of the sum total?
Peu s'en est fallu que je ne vinsse.	I came very near coming.

6. With compound tenses after il y a (voilà), depuis:

Il y a (voilà) trois jours que je ne l'ai vu.	It is three days since I saw him (I have not seen him for, etc.).
Il avait grandi depuis que je ne l'avais vu.	He had grown since I saw him.
Depuis que je ne vous ai vu.	Since I saw you.

a. In a simple tense (§§337, 2, 338, 4) negatively, ne...pas, etc., must be used:

Voilà un an qu'il ne buvait plus.	He had drunk no more for a year.

USE OF CERTAIN ADVERBS.

497. Distinctions. The following are especially liable to be confounded in use:

1. **Oui, Si.** 'Yes' in *affirmation* or *assent* is **oui**; 'yes' is usually **si** in *contradiction*, in *correction*, in *dissent*:

L'avez-vous dit?—Oui, monsieur.	Did you say it?—Yes, sir.
Venez.—Oui, oui, j'irai.	Come.—Yes, yes, I shall go.
Il ne va pas.—Si, monsieur, il va.	He is not going.—Yes, (sir), he is (going).
Il ne va pas?—Mais si.	He is not going?—Yes, certainly.
Je n'irai pas.—Si, si, venez.	I shall not go.—Yes, yes, come.

NOTE.—The use of **si** (as also of the intensive **si fait**, etc.), though very common, is classed as *familiar* by the *Académie*; it is often avoided by **pardon**, etc., or other expressions: 'Il ne va pas.—**Pardon**, monsieur, (il va).'

a. **Oui, si,** and **non,** are often preceded by **que** (really with ellipsis of a whole **que** clause), and are then variously translated by 'yes,' 'so,' 'no,' 'not,' etc., or by a clause:

Je dis que oui (non).	I say yes (no).
Je crois que oui (non).	I think so (not).
Vous ne l'avez pas?—Oh! que si.	You haven't it?—Oh yes!
Le fera-t-il?—Je crois que oui.	Will he do it?—I think he will (do it).
Je dis que non.	I say it is not so.
Peut-être que non.	Perhaps not.

2. **Autant, Tant.** 'As much (many)'=autant; 'so much (many)'= tant:

Je gagne autant que vous.	I earn as much as you.
Il but tant qu'il en mourut.	He drank so much that he died from it.
J'ai tant d'amis; j'en ai autant que vous.	I have so many friends; I have as many as you.

3. **Plus, Davantage.** Plus is used in all senses of 'more' ('most,' see below); davantage (strengthened sometimes by bien='much,' encore='still')='more,' is regularly used only *absolutely**, and usually stands at the end of its clause:

N'en parle pas davantage. N'en parle plus.	Say no more about it.
Ne restez pas davantage. Ne restez plus.	Do not remain any longer.
Cela me plaît encore davantage (plus).	That pleases me still more.
Je suis riche; il l'est bien davantage (plus).	I am rich; he is much more so.

But only: J'en ai plus que lui; il est plus habile; plus de dix francs; c'est ce qui le flatte le plus, etc.

*Davantage is occasionally followed by que in archaic style.

4. **Ne...que, Seulement.** Seulement must be used, (1) when no verb is present, (2) when 'only' refers to the subject, (3) or to the verb, (4) or to a que clause, and (5) it may be used to strengthen a ne...que; otherwise 'only'=ne...que or seulement:

Seulement les braves.	Only the brave.
Seulement mon frère le sait.	Only my brother knows it.
Écoutez seulement.	Only listen.
Il dit seulement qu'il irait.	He only said he would go.
Il n'a seulement qu'à venir.	He has only to come.

But: Nous ne serons que trois (*or* trois s.); je ne veux que voir son père (*or* je veux seulement voir son père), etc.

a. 'Only,' referring to the subject, may be turned also by il n'y a que, ce n'est que; 'only,' referring to the verb, may be turned by the help of faire:

Il n'y a que les morts qui ne reviennent pas.	The dead only do not come back.
Elle ne fait que pleurer.	She does nothing but weep.

v

EXERCISE LXXVIII.

1. I will not sell it, cheap or dear. 2. You did it on purpose, did you not? 3. Not at all, it was quite accidental. 4. A christian ought to love not only his friends but even his enemies. 5. Those poor people had scarcely any bread to eat, when we found them. 6. We have said nothing at all about it. 7. That is a very complicated affair; I can understand nothing of it. 8. We did not see a living soul in the street, when we rose that morning. 9. Whom did you see? I saw nobody at all. 10. I shall be silent, so as not to hinder you from working. 11. He told me to do nothing until he returned. 12. I did not do it so as not to be punished. 13. What is the matter with that little boy? 14. I do not know, sir; I neither did nor said anything to him. 15. Would you not be glad to see our old friend? 16. No, I neither wish to see him nor speak to him. 17. I have a headache this evening; I can neither sing nor play. 18. Neither he nor his father were there. 19. I saw neither him nor his brother. 20. I have neither friend nor money, but I have strong arms and courage. 21. No more regrets; take courage, and forget the past. 22. Why did he not tell me so before leading me into this peril? 23. There is nobody here he does not know. 24. Take care that you are not deceived. 25. There is nothing which does not please me better than that. 26. Not one of those we invited has come. 27. Do you know where Dr. B. lives? 28. I cannot tell you. 29. If you have no use for this book, lend it to me. 30. Unless you do what you said, I shall not pay you. 31. Do you not fear he will go away? 32. I do not fear he will go away. 33. I am afraid our friends will not be there. 34. If I were afraid he would do it, I should do something to hinder him (from it). 35. If I were not afraid he would hurt himself with it, I should let him have it. 36. That man writes better than he speaks. 37. We do not wish more money than we have now. 38. I do not doubt that that is true. .39. Not much is lacking for the number to be complete. 40. We have not seen each other for three years. 41. It is more than three years since we were there. 42. I cannot go with you; I have no time. 43. Yes, you have, you are not so busy. 44. You have stolen my apples. 45. I tell you I have not. 46. But I say yes, for I saw you. 47. He has as much money as you have, but he has not as much as I have. 48. Let us say no more about it. 49. We are in a hurry; let us not stay any longer. 50. I have more than fifty francs, but he has more than I, and his brother has still more.

THE NUMERAL.

498. Cardinals. The cardinal numerals denote 'how many':

1. un(e).	4. quatre.	7. sept.	10. dix.
2. deux.	5. cinq.	8. huit.	11. onze.
3. trois.	6. six.	9. neuf.	etc.

See also §208, for remarks on formation and pronunciation.

a. **Un** (f. **une**) is the only cardinal which varies for *gender:*

Une (deux, trois, etc.) plume(s).	One (two, three, etc.) pen(s).
Vingt et une vaches.	Twenty-one cows.

b. Cardinals are invar. for *number*, except that s is added to quatre-vingt and the multiples of cent, but only when *immediately preceding a noun* (or *adj. + noun*), or when they themselves serve as *nouns of number:*

Quatre-vingts francs.	Eighty francs.
Trois cents (bonnes) plumes.	Three hundred (good) pens.
Deux cents millions.	Two hundred millions.
Trois cents de pommes.	Three hundred apples.
Les cinq cents.	The five hundreds.

But: Trois cent un francs; les cent hommes engagés; quatre-vingt-une plumes; deux cent mille; trois mille milles, etc.

N.B.—They are *not nouns of number in dates* (c. below) or when used *as ordinals* (§504): 'L'an quatre cent'; 'page deux cent'; 'page quatre-vingt.'

c. The form **mil** (*not* 'mille') is used in *dates* of the christian era from 1001 to 1999:

En mil huit cent quatre-vingt-onze.	In eighteen hundred and ninety-one.
(En) l'an mil six.	(In) the year 1006.

But: L'an mille (sometimes mil); l'an deux mille trois cent; l'an mille cent du monde, etc.

d. From 1100 to 1900 numbers are often expressed by *hundreds*, as so frequently in English:

Onze cent(s); treize cent(s).	Eleven hundred; thirteen hundred.
Quinze cent cinquante.	Fifteen hundred and fifty.

e. 'A (*or* one) hundred'=**cent**; 'a (*or* one) thousand'=**mille**:

Mille soldats.	A (one) thousand soldiers.

NOTE.—**Septante**=70, **octante**=80, **nonante**=90, **six-vingt(s)**=120, and **quinze-vingt(s)**=300, are now obsolete in the literary language.

499. Ordinals. The ordinal numerals denote order or place in a series relatively to the first; they are formed, from 3rd up, by adding **-ième** to the last consonant of the corresponding cardinal (**cinq** adding **u**, and **f** of **neuf** becoming **v** before **-ième**):

1st. premier. 3rd. troisième. 9th. neuvième. 101st. cent unième.
2nd. {second. 4th. quatrième. 21st. vingt et unième. etc., etc.
{deuxième. 5th. cinquième. 22nd. vingt-deuxième.

NOTES.—1. Besides the ordinary forms, **tiers** (f. **tierce**)='third,' **quart(e)** = 'fourth,' are used in a few expressions and in fractions: '**Le tiers** état,' 'The commoners'; '**En maison tierce**,' 'In the house of a third party'; '**Une fièvre quarte**', '**A quartan** ague.' 2. **Quint** = 'fifth' is used only in '**Charles-Quint**,' Charles V. (the Emperor)'; '**Sixte-Quint**,' '**Sixtus** V. (the Pope).'

a. Ordinals are like ordinary adjectives in inflection and agreement, and regularly precede the noun:

La (les) **première(s)** maison(s). The first house(s).
Nous sommes arrivés les **premiers**. We arrived first.

b. **Deuxième** instead of **second** is more usually employed in a series of more than two, and always in compounds:

Le **second** volume. The second volume (of two).
Le **deuxième** volume. The second volume (of three, etc.).
La cent **deuxième** fois. The hundred and second time.

500. Collectives. The following nouns are used with collective force:—

un(e) couple, *a couple (two).*
une paire, *a pair.*
une huitaine, *about eight.*
une douzaine, *a dozen.*
une quinzaine, *about fifteen.*
une vingtaine, *about twenty.*
une trentaine, *about thirty.*
une quarantaine, *about forty.*
une cinquantaine, *about fifty.*

une soixantaine, *about sixty.*
une centaine, *about a hundred.*
un cent, *a hundred.*
un millier, *(about) a thousand.*
un million, *a million.*
un milliard, } *a billion.*
un billion,
etc.

a. They take **-s** in the plur., and have the construction of ordinary nouns:

Il y a une centaine d'élèves. There are about 100 pupils.
Il y en a deux cents. There are two hundred of them.
Des milliers de gens. Thousands of people.
Deux millions de francs. Two million(s of) francs.

501. Fractions. The numerator is regularly denoted by a cardinal and the denominator by an ordinal; 'half' = **moitié**, f. (as noun) and **demi** (as adj. or noun):

$\frac{1}{2}$	{ un demi. { une moitié.	$\frac{1}{4}$	un quart.	$\frac{3}{16}$	trois seizièmes.
$\frac{2}{5}$	deux demis.	$\frac{3}{4}$	trois quarts.	$\frac{7}{100}$	sept centièmes.
$\frac{1}{3}$	un tiers.	$\frac{1}{5}$	un cinquième.	$\frac{10}{101}$	dix cent unièmes.
$\frac{2}{3}$	deux tiers.	$\frac{1}{7}$	un septième.	$\frac{11}{1000}$	onze millièmes.
		$\frac{1}{11}$	un onzième.		etc.

a. **Demi**, before its noun, is invar. and joined by a hyphen, but agrees elsewhere; as a *noun*, demi is hardly used, except in arithmetical calculations:

Une demi-heure; une heure et demie. — Half an hour; an hour and a half.

Quatre demis = deux. — Four halves = two.

La moitié de la somme. — Half the sum.

b. The *def. art.* is required before fractions followed by de + *a noun*, when the noun is determined by a def. art., a possessive, or a demonstrative, and similarly for pronominal substitutes for such constructions:

La moitié du temps. — Half the time.

Les trois quarts de ces (ses) biens. — Three-fourths of those (his) goods.

J'en prends les cinq sixièmes. — I take five-sixths of them.

502. Multiplicatives. 1. The following are used as adjs. or (absolutely) as nouns:

double, *double.*
triple, *triple.*
quadruple, *quadruple.*
quintuple, *fivefold.*
sextuple, *sixfold.*
septuple, *sevenfold.*
octuple, *eightfold.*
nonuple, *ninefold.*
décuple, *tenfold.*
centuple, *hundredfold.*

As *nouns*, le double, *the double,* etc.

La triple alliance. — The triple alliance.

Payer le double. — To pay twice as much.

a. Double is sometimes *adverb:*

Il voit double. — He sees double.

2. 'Once,' 'twice,' 'three times,' etc. = **une fois, deux fois, trois fois,** etc.:

Dix fois dix font cent. — Ten times ten make a hundred.

J'ai payé deux fois autant. — I paid twice as much.

503. Numeral Adverbs. They are formed from the ordinals by -ment, according to rule (§486):

premièrement, *first, firstly.*
secondement
deuxièmement } *secondly.*
troisièmement, *thirdly.*
etc.   etc.

a. Substitutes for them, of very frequent use, are: d'abord = 'at first,' 'puis, = 'then,' 'after that,' ensuite = 'then,' 'next', en premier lieu = 'in the first place,' en second lieu, etc. = 'in the second place,' etc.; or the Lat. adv. forms primo, secundo, tertio, etc. (abbreviated: 1°, 2°, 3°, etc.), are used.

Remarks on the Use of Numerals.

504. Cardinals and Ordinals. 1. Premier = 'first' is the only ordinal used to denote the day of the month or the numerical title of a ruler; otherwise, cardinals are employed:

Le premier (deux, dix) mai.   The first (second, tenth) of May.
Le onze de ce mois.   The eleventh of this month.
Napoléon (Grégoire) premier.   Napoleon (Gregory) the First.
Henri (Catherine) deux.   Henry (Catherine) the Second.

a. For other date idioms, see §219.

2. Other numerical titles (book, chapter, scene, page, etc.), are expressed as in Eng., ordinals being used before nouns and either cardinals or ordinals after nouns:

Tome troisième (trois).   Volume third (three).
La dixième scène du second acte.   The tenth scene of the second act.

a. The first of two ordinals joined by et ou, is not uncommonly replaced by a cardinal:

La quatre ou cinquième page.   The fourth or sixth page.

b. Cardinals must *precede* ordinals:

Les deux premières scènes.   The first two scenes.

505. Dimension. The various methods of indicating dimension may be seen from the following:—

(1) Une table longue de dix pieds.   A table ten feet long.
(2) Une table de 10 p. de longueur.   ″ ″ ″ ″ ″
(3) Une table de 10 p. de long.   ″ ″ ″ ″ ″
(4) Une table d'une longueur de 10 p.   ″ ″ ″ ″ ″

505–507.] REMARKS ON THE USE OF NUMERALS.

(5) La table est longue de 10 p.   The table is ten feet long.
(6) La table a 10 p. de longueur   ″ ″ ″ ″ ″ ″
(7) La table a 10 p. de long.   ″ ″ ″ ″ ″ ″
(8) La table a une longueur de 10 p. ″ ″ ″ ″ ″ ″

Obs.: 1. Dimension after an adj. is denoted by **de**, cf. (1), (5). 2. Substitutes for the adjectival construction of (1) are seen in (2), (3), (4). 3. The verb 'to be' is **être**, as in (5), or **avoir**, as in (6), (7), (8). 4. **Haut, large, long** (but *not* 'épais', 'profond') may be used as nouns, instead of **hauteur, largeur, longueur**, cf. (3), (7).

a. 'By,' of relative dimension, =**sur**; 'by,' after a comparative, =**de**:

Cette table a dix pieds de longueur   This table is ten feet long by three
 sur trois de largeur.   wide.
Plus (moins) grand de deux pouces.   Taller (shorter) by two inches.

506. Time of Day. The method of indicating the time of day may be seen from the following:—

Quelle heure est-il?	What time (o'clock) is it?
Il est une (deux) heure(s).	It is one (two) o'clock.
Il est trois heures et demie.	It is half-past three.
Trois heures (et) un quart.	A quarter past three.
Quatre heures moins un quart.	A quarter to four.
Trois heures dix (minutes).	Ten minutes past three.
Six heures moins cinq (minutes).	Five minutes to six.
Il est midi et demi.	It is half-past twelve (noon).
Il est minuit (et) un quart.	It is a quarter past twelve (night).
À huit heures du soir.	At eight o'clock in the evening.
À quelle heure?	At what o'clock?
À trois heures précises.	At three o'clock precisely.
Vers les trois heures.	Towards (at about) three o'clock.

Obs.: 1. 'It is (was, etc.)'=**il est (était,** etc.). 2. **Heure(s)** is never omitted. 3. **Et** is essential only at the half hour. 4. **Demi(e)** agrees with **heure** (f.) or with **midi** (m.), **minuit** (m.). 5. **Minutes** is often omitted. 6. 'A quarter to,' 'minutes to' is **moins** before the following hour. 7. 'Twelve o'clock' is *never* **douze heures**.

507. Age. Idiomatic expressions denoting age are:—

Quel âge avez-vous?	How old are you?
J'ai vingt ans.	I am twenty (years old).
Je suis âgé de vingt ans.	″ ″ ″ ″ ″
Une fille âgée de six ans.	A girl six years old (of age).
Plus âgé de deux ans.	Older by two years.

Obs.: 1. The construction with **avoir** is the more common. 2. **An(s)** may not be omitted in specifying age. 3. 'By'=**de**, after a comparison.

EXERCISE LXXIX.

Il a une vingtaine d'années.   ·   He is about twenty (years old).
Il a une trentaine de mille francs. He has about thirty thousand francs.

1. Columbus discovered America in the year 1492. 2. The French national *fête* is on the fourteenth of July, because [on] that day the Bastille was destroyed in the year 1789. 3. My father left England on the first of May, 1824. 4. Napoleon the First was a greater man than Napoleon the Third. 5. Charles the First of England and Louis the Sixteenth of France were both put to death. 6. The first train leaves at a quarter to five in the morning, and the second at twenty minutes past two in the afternoon. 7. We went to bed last night at half-past twelve. 8. The first two houses in the street belong to us. 9. We have only the last two chapters in the book to read. 10. The carriage arrived at half-past one in the morning. 11. The father gave his son a fifth of his property, when the son was twenty-one. 12. How old do you think that man is? 13. I should think he was about forty. 14. It is twenty years since I saw him. 15. That man is well off; he has an income of about twenty thousand francs a year. 16. The first volume of his works contains poetry, and the fourth novels. 17. This house cost three times as much as that one. 18. Ten times ten make a hundred. 19. We paid a hundred and twenty dollars for that horse. 20. That carriage cost one thousand one hundred dollars. 21. That old man is eighty-five years old. 22. [On] what day of the month did that happen? 23. It happened on the twelfth. 24. That table is two metres long by one metre wide. 25. We are going to have a house built sixty feet long by twenty-four wide. 26. What o'clock is it? 27. It is just noon. 28. A boy ten years old was killed last evening by a carriage in Queen street. 29. That girl is older than her brother by two years. 30. I am taller than my brother by two inches. 31. Will you come at two o'clock or at three? 32. I shall be there precisely at three. 33. Is that boy ten years old or eleven? 34. He is eleven.

THE PREPOSITION.

508. Simple Prepositions. The following list contains the commoner simple prepositions:

à, *to, at, in, on, etc.*
après, *after, next to.*
avant, *before.*
avec, *with.*
chez, *with, at—'s.*
contre, *against.*
dans, *in(to).*
de, *of, from, with, etc.*
depuis, *since, from.*
derrière, *behind.*
dès, *from, since.*
devant, *before.*

durant, *during.*
en, *in, to.*
entre, *between, among.*
envers, *towards.*
hormis, *except.*
jusque, *till, until.*
malgré, *in spite of.*
moyennant, *by means of.*
nonobstant, *notwithstanding.*
outre, *besides.*
par, *by, through.*

parmi, *among.*
pendant, *during.*
pour, *for.*
sans, *without.*
sauf, *save, except.*
selon, *according to.*
sous, *under.*
suivant, *according to.*
sur, *on, upon.*
vers, *towards.*
voici, *here is (are).*
voilà, *there is (are).*

509. Prepositional Locutions. Phrases with prepositional function (mostly ending in **de** or **à**) are numerous:

À côté de l'église.
Jusqu'à la semaine prochaine.
À travers la forêt.

Beside the church.
Until next week.
Through the forest.

Such locutions are:

à cause de, *on account of.*
à côté de, *by the side of.*
à force de, *by dint of.*
à l'égard de, *with regard to.*
à l'exception de, *except.*
à l'insu de, *unknown to.*
à travers, *across, through.*
au delà de, *beyond.*
au-dessous de, *under.*
au-dessus de, *above.*

au lieu de, *instead of.*
autour de, *around.*
au moyen de, *by means of.*
auprès de, *near by.*
au travers de, *across, through.*
d'après, *according to.*
en deçà de, *on this side (of).*
en dépit de, *in spite of.*
faute de, *for want of.*

jusqu'à, *as far as, until.*
par delà, *beyond.*
par-dessous, *under.*
par-dessus, *over.*
près de, *near.*
quant à, *as for.*
vis-à-vis de, *opposite.*
etc., etc.

510. Position. Prepositions regularly *precede* the governed word, as in English:

Je parle de Jean (de lui).   I speak of John (of him).

a. Conjunctive pers. prons. governed by **voici, voilà,** *precede:*

Me voici; les voilà.   Here I am; there they are.
En voici quelques-uns.   Here are some of them.

b. **Durant** is sometimes placed after its noun :

Durant sa vie (*or* sa vie durant). During his life.

511. Repetition. The preps. **à, de, en**, are regularly *repeated* before each governed substantive ; the repetition of other preps. is regular in *contrasts*, but is elsewhere optional, as in Eng.:

Il aime à lire et à écrire.	He likes to read and write.
Le père de Jean et de Marie.	The father of John and Mary.
En France ou en Italie.	In France or Italy.
Sur terre et sur mer.	By land and sea.
Par la persuasion ou par la force.	By persuasion or force.

But : **Pour lui et (pour) son frère,** etc.

Idiomatic Distinctions.

512. Prepositions vary greatly as to idiomatic force in different languages. In the following sections are given some of the various French equivalents of the commoner English prepositions.

513. About.

1. In the sense of 'around '=**autour de** :

Regardez autour de vous.	Look about you.
Autour de la place.	About the square.

2. In the sense of 'concerning,' 'of'=**de, à**:

De quoi parlez-vous ?	What are you talking about ?
À quoi pensez-vous ?	What are you thinking about ?

3. In the sense of 'with,' 'about (the person)'=**sur** :

Avez-vous de l'argent sur vous ?   Have you any money about you ?

4. Denoting *approximation*=**environ, près de, à peu près, vers** :

Environ (près de, à peu près) deux mille francs ; **vers (sur les) dix heures ; vers 1830.**   About two thousand francs ; about ten o'clock ; about 1830.

514. After.

1. Denoting *time, rank, order, position*=**après** :

Après dîner ; le premier après le roi ; on met l'adjectif après le nom ; courez après lui.   After dinner ; the first after the king ; the adjective is placed after the noun ; run after him.

2. In the sense of 'at the end of'= au bout de :

Au bout de trois siècles. — After three centuries.

3. Unclassified :

De jour en jour ; dessiné d'après Raphaël ; le lendemain de son retour ; il tient de sa mère. — Day after day ; drawn after Raphael ; the day after his return ; he takes after his mother.

515. Among.

1. In the sense of 'in the midst of,' 'surrounded by'= parmi (sometimes entre) :

Une brebis parmi les loups. — A sheep among wolves.
Il fut trouvé entre les morts. — He was found among the dead.

2. 'Among (distributively or reciprocally)'= entre :

Il le partagea entre ses amis. — He divided it among his friends.
Ils parlaient entre eux. — They spoke among themselves.

3. Unclassified :

C'était ainsi chez les Grecs. — It was so among the Greeks.

516. At.

1. Denoting *place, time,* = à (sometimes en) :

À l'école ; à Douvres ; à table ; à cinq heures ; à l'âge de ; en tête de ; en (au) même temps ; à la fin (enfin). — At school ; at Dover ; at table ; at five o'clock ; at the age of ; at the head of ; at the same time ; at last.

2. In the sense of 'at the house, etc., of,' 'at —'s'= chez :

J'ai été chez vous ; il est chez Monsieur Ribot. — I was at your house ; he is at Mr. Ribot's.

3. Unclassified :

À mes dépens ; à tout prix ; d'abord ; sous la main ; entrer par la fenêtre ; en haut (bas) ; au moins ; sur mer ; en guerre. — At my expense ; at any price ; at first ; at hand ; come (go) in at the window ; at the top (bottom) ; at least ; at sea ; at war.

517. Before.

1. Denoting *place*, in the sense of 'in front of,' 'in the presence of'= devant :

Mettez cela devant le feu; le jardin est devant la maison; il prêcha devant le roi. — Put that before the fire; the garden is before the house; he preached before the king.

2. Denoting *time, order* = avant:

Avant midi; je l'ai vu avant vous; mettez l'article avant le nom. — Before noon; I saw it before you; put the article before the noun.

3. Unclassified:

Sous mes yeux; la veille de la bataille; comparaître par-devant le juge. — Before my eyes; the day before the battle; to appear before the judge.

518. By.

1. Denoting the *agent* (after the passive) = par, de (cf. §320):

Elle fut saisie par le voleur; ils sont aimés de tous. — She was seized by the robber; they are loved by all.

2. Denoting *means, way*, etc. = par (usually):

Par la poste; par chemin de fer; par ce moyen; par un ami. — By post; by railway; by this means; by a friend.

3. Denoting *measure* = de; *relative dimension* = sur:

Plus grand de la tête; plus âgé de dix ans (de beaucoup); plus lourd d'une livre; moindre de la moitié; dix pieds sur six. — Taller by a head; older by ten years (by far); heavier by a pound; less by half; ten feet by six.

4. Unclassified:

De jour (nuit); à l'année; goutte à goutte; il est midi à ma montre; connaître de vue; de vive voix; un tailleur de son état; vendre au poids; fait à la main. — By day (night); by the year; drop by drop; it is noon by my watch; to know by sight; by word of mouth; a tailor by trade; to sell by weight; made by hand.

519. For

1. In the sense of 'for the sake of,' 'instead of,' '(in exchange) for' = pour.

Mourir pour la patrie; j'irai pour vous; donnez-moi ceci pour cela. — To die for one's country; I shall go for you; give me this for that.

2. Denoting *destination*:

Je pars pour la France ; une lettre pour vous. — I leave **for** France ; a letter **for** you.

3. Denoting a *period of time* (future) = pour :

Je resterai (pour) huit jours ; j'en ai pour dix ans. — I shall stay (**for**) a week ; I have enough of it **for** ten years.

NOTE.—'For' of *time not future* is variously rendered : 'J'étais huit jours absent *or* J'étais absent pendant huit jours,' 'I was absent **for** a week'; 'Il y a (voici, voilà) deux heures que je lis *or* Je lis depuis deux heures,' I have been reading **for** two hours.'

4. Unclassified :

Mot à mot ; un remède contre (pour) ; trembler de crainte ; par exemple ; quant à moi ; vendre dix francs *or* laisser (donner) pour dix francs ; remercier (punir) de ; changer pour (contre) ; c'est à vous de dire ; malgré tout cela. — Word **for** word ; a remedy **for** ; to tremble **for** fear ; **for** example ; as **for** me ; to sell **for** ten francs *or* to give **for** ten francs ; to thank (punish) **for**; to change **for** ; it is **for** you to say ; **for** all that.

520.   From.

1. Usually = de :

Il vient de Paris ; de trois à quatre heures ; je l'ai appris de lui. — He comes **from** Paris ; **from** three to four o'clock ; I heard it **from** him.

2. In the sense of 'because of,' 'out of,' 'through' = par :

Cela arriva par négligence ; par expérience (amitié). — That happened **from** carelessness ; **from** experience (friendship).

3. In the sense of 'dating from' = dès, depuis, à partir de :

Dès (depuis, à partir de) ce jour ; à partir de 1820. — **From** that day ; **from** 1820 (on).

4. Unclassified :

D'aujourd'hui en huit ; dessiné d'après nature ; boire dans un verre ; ôtez cela à l'enfant. — A week **from** to-day ; drawn **from** nature ; to drink **from** a glass ; take that **from** the child.

521.   In (into).

1. Denoting *place or time specifically*, *i. e.*, in the sense of 'within,' 'inside of,' 'in(to) the interior of' = dans (cf. §411, 2, 3):

Dans ce paquet (champ) ; dans la maison ; dans l'Afrique australe ; dans toute la ville ; dans la même année.

In this parcel (field) ; in(to) the house ; in South Africa ; in the whole city ; in the same year.

NOTE.—The governed noun usually has the *def. art.*

2. Denoting *place or time generally* = en, à (cf. §411, 2, 3) :

En Afrique ; à la maison ; aux champs ; au Canada ; à Berlin ; à la campagne (ville) ; en hiver ; au printemps ; en paix.

In Africa ; in the house (at home) ; in the fields ; in Canada ; in Berlin ; in the country (city) ; in winter ; in spring ; in peace.

NOTE.—The governed word after en has but *rarely the def. art.* (mostly in fixed expressions before initial vowel sound) : 'En l'air' ; 'En l'honneur de,' etc.

3. In the sense of 'at the end of (time)' = dans ; 'in the course of (time)' = en :

Le train part dans une heure ; on peut aller à L. en une heure.

The train leaves in an hour ; one can go to L. in an hour.

4. Denoting *place, after a superlative* = de :

La plus grande ville du monde.

The largest city in the world.

5. Unclassified :

Par la pluie ; le matin ; de nos jours ; par le passé ; à l'avenir ; d'avance ; entre les mains de ; à mon avis ; sous le règne de ; sous presse ; de cette manière ; un sur dix.

In the rain ; in the morning ; in our days ; in the past ; in the future ; in advance ; in the hands of ; in my opinion ; in the reign of ; in press ; in this way ; one in ten.

522. Of.

1. Usually = de :

Le toit de la maison ; la ville de Paris ; un homme d'influence ; une livre de thé ; digne d'honneur ; il parle d'aller.

The roof of the house ; the city of Paris ; a man of influence ; a pound of tea ; worthy of honour ; he speaks of going.

2. Denoting *material* = en :

Un pont en bois (fer) ; les pièces de dix francs sont en or.

A bridge of wood (iron) ; ten franc pieces are of gold.

3. Unclassified :

C'est aimable à vous ; sur 100 personnes 50 sont échappées ; docteur en médecine ; un des mes amis ; majeur.

It is kind of you ; of 100 persons 50 escaped ; doctor of medicine ; one of my friends ; of age.

523. On (upon).

1. Usually = **sur**:

Le livre est (je mets le livre) **sur** la table. — The book is (I put the book) on the table.

2. Is *omitted* in dates before specified days:

Le dix mai; je viendrai mardi; il arriva le lendemain. — On the tenth of May; I shall come on Tuesday; he arrived on the morrow.

3. Unclassified:

Par une belle journée d'été; mettre **au** feu; pendre **contre** le mur; **dans** la rue; **dans** l'île; **dans** l'escalier; **en** (**dans** un) voyage; **en** visite (congé); **en** chemin (route); **d'**un côté; tomber **par** terre; **aux** genoux; **dans** cette occasion; **à** cheval (pied); **à** droite (gauche); **à** son arrivée; **au** contraire; **pour** affaires. — On a fine summer day; to put on the fire; to hang on the wall; on the street; on the island; on the stairs; on a journey; on a visit (a holiday); on the way (the road); on one side; to fall on the ground; on one's knees; on that occasion; on horseback (foot); on the right (the left); on his arrival; on the contrary; on business.

524. Out of.

1. Unclassified:

Boire **dans** un verre; copier **dans** un livre; regarder **par** la fenêtre. — To drink out of a glass; to copy out of a book; to look out of the window.

525. Over.

1. In the sense of 'above' = **au-dessus de**:

Au-dessus de la porte étaient écrits ces mots; les nombres **au-dessus** de mille. — Over the door were written these words; the numbers over one thousand.

2. Denoting *motion above* = **sur, par, par-dessus**:

Passez la main **sur** ce drap; **par** monts et **par** vaux; il sauta **par-dessus** la haie. — Pass your hand over this cloth; over hill and dale; he leaped over the hedge.

3. Unclassified:

Au delà de la rivière; l'emporter **sur** (triompher **de**); se réjouir **de**; veiller **sur**. — Over the river; to triumph over; to rejoice over; to watch over.

526. Through.

1. Denoting *motion across* = à travers (au travers de), par :

Je passai à travers (au travers de) la forêt ; passer par Berlin.
I passed through the forest ; to pass through Berlin.

2. In the sense of 'because of,' 'owing to' = par :

Par négligence.
Through carelessness.

527. Till (until).

1. Unclassified :

Jusqu'à demain ; pas avant l'année prochaine ; jusqu'ici ; du matin au soir.
Till to-morrow ; not till next year ; till now ; from morning till night.

528. To.

1. Denoting the *indirect object* = à (cf. §440, 2) :

Je l'ai donné à un ami.
I gave it to a friend.

2. Denoting *motion to* = à, en (cf. §411, 2, 3) ; in the sense of 'to the house, etc., of,' 'to —'s ' = chez :

Il va à Paris (à l'école ; au Japon ; à un bal ; en France ; en Portugal ; chez eux ; chez mon ami).
He goes to Paris (to school ; to Japan ; to a ball ; to France ; to Portugal ; to their house, etc. ; to my friend's).

3. In the sense of 'towards' = vers (physical tendency), envers (moral tendency) :

Levez les yeux vers le ciel ; il est juste envers tous.
Raise your eyes to heaven ; he is just to all.

4. In the sense of 'as far as' = jusqu'à :

Venez jusqu'au bout de la rue.
Come to the end of the street.

5. Unclassified :

Le voyage (train) de Montréal ; écrire sous dictée ; dans ce but.
The journey (train) to Montreal ; to write to dictation ; to this end.

529. Towards.

See §528, 3.

530. Under (underneath).

1. Usually = sous :

Sous la table ; sous la loi ; sous peine de mort.
Under the table ; under the law ; under pain of death.

IDIOMATIC DISTINCTIONS.

2. Denoting *lower than, less than* = au-dessous de :

Au-dessous du coude ; vendre une chose au-dessous de sa valeur. — Under the elbow ; to sell a thing under its value.

3. Unclassified :

Fouler aux pieds ; à cette condition ; dans les circonstances ; dans la nécessité de ; mineur. — To tread under foot ; under this condition ; under the circumstances ; under the necessity of ; under age.

531. With.

1. In the sense of 'along with,' 'in company with' = avec :

Dinez avec moi à l'hôtel ; un officier avec des soldats. — Dine with me at the hotel ; an officer with some soldiers.

2. In the sense of 'at the house, etc.; of' = chez :

Il demeure chez nous. — He lives with us.

3. Denoting *instrument, manner* = avec (usually) :

Frapper avec un marteau ; écrire avec une plume ; avec courage (force). — To strike with a hammer ; to write with a pen ; with courage (force).

4. Denoting *a characteristic* = à :

Un homme à la barbe noire. — A man with a black beard.

5. 'With' of *accessory circumstance* is usually turned by an *absolute construction* :

Il parla les yeux baissés. — He spoke with downcast eyes.

6. In the sense of 'from,' 'on account of,' and after many *verbs* and *adjs.* = de :

Elle pleura de colère ; couvrir de ; content de. — She wept with anger ; to cover with ; satisfied with.

7. Unclassified :

À l'exception de ; à haute voix ; à bras ouverts ; de bon appétit ; à l'œil nu ; de tout mon cœur. — With the exception of ; with a loud voice ; with open arms ; with a good appetite ; with the naked eye ; with all my heart.

EXERCISE LXXX.

1. I was thinking of what you were talking about this morning.
2. He paid about twenty francs for that hat. 3. He will be here about

six o'clock in the evening. 4. The day after our arrival we went to see the museum. 5. That child has black eyes; he takes after his father. 6. The money was divided amongst the children. 7. Amongst all those people there is not one sensible person. 8. Art arrived at great perfection among the Greeks. 9. He was at my house, when I was at his. 10. They all laughed at my expense. 11. We all laughed at him. 12. The thief will have to appear before the court. 13. He will be here before a quarter past three. 14. That is greater by half than what we expected. 15. That box is six feet long by two wide. 16. It is a quarter to four by my watch. 17. I know that man by sight only. 18. He will leave for France in a week. 19. We lived in that city for twenty years. 20. I have been here for two years. 21. I traded my black horse for this white one. 22. I thanked him for his kindness. 23. From the fifteenth of May I shall live in that house. 24. They drank their wine from golden cups. 25. That picture is painted from nature. 26. In spring the weather is warm and the flowers open. 27. There is not so much misery in Canada as in Russia. 28. Let us live in peace with everybody. 29. There are several nations in North America. 30. Not one in a hundred was good. 31. Is your house (in) brick or stone. 32. It was kind of you to aid me in my misfortune. 33. In rainy weather we stay at home. 34. We shall go away on Saturday. 35. He is now on the road for England. 36. Our house is on this side of the street, and his is on that side. 37. When you come to the next street, turn to the right. 38. Instead of studying he is always looking out of the window. 39. His gun was hanging above the chimney. 40. The dog jumped over the fence. 41. He watched over my interests. 42. In passing through the forest we saw many rare plants. 43. We work from morning till night. 44. We are going to our friends' house. 45. The train for Paris will be here immediately. 46. They sold those goods under their value. 47. Wicked men tread God's laws under foot. 48. If you will live with us, we shall treat you well. 49. Do you remember the man with the big nose whom we saw yesterday? 50. She told us her story with tears in her eyes.

THE CONJUNCTION.

532. Conjunctions and Conjunctive Locutions.

†à (la) condition que³, *on condition that.*

*afin que², *in order that, so that.*

ainsi, *therefore, hence.*

ainsi que, *as well as, as.*

alors que, *when.*

à mesure que, *as, just as.*
*à moins que... ne³, *unless.*
après que, *after.*
à proportion que, *in proportion as.*
attendu que, *considering that.*
†au cas où³, *in case (that).*
*au cas que³, *in case (that).*
aussi, *hence, therefore.*
aussitôt que, *as soon as.*
*avant que¹, *before.*
*bien que⁴, *though, although.*
car, *for.*
*ce n'est pas que⁵, *not that.*
cependant, *however, yet.*
comme, *as.*
†dans le cas où³, *in case (that).*
*de crainte que... ne², *for fear that.*
†de façon que², *so that.*
†de manière que², *so that.*
de même que, *as well as.*
*de peur que... ne², *for fear that.*
depuis que, *since.*
†de (telle) sorte que², *so that.*
dès que, *as soon as, when, since.*
donc, *now, then, therefore.*
*en attendant que¹, *until.*
*en cas que³, *in case (that).*
encore, *yet, still.*
*encore que⁴, *though, although.*
†en sorte que², *so that.*
*en supposant que³, *supposing that.*
et, *and.*
et... et, *both... and.*
†jusqu' à ce que¹, *until.*
*loin que⁵, *far from.*
lorsque, *when.*
mais, *but.*
*malgré que⁴, *though, although.*
néanmoins, *nevertheless.*

ni, *nor.*
ni... ni (... ne), *neither... nor.*
*nonobstant que⁴, *notwithstanding that.*
*non (pas) que⁵, *not that.*
non seulement... mais encore, *not only... but also.*
or, *now.*
ou, *or.*
ou... ou, *either... or.*
outre que, *besides that.*
parce que, *because.*
partant, *therefore, hence.*
pendant que, *while, whilst.*
*pour peu que⁴, *if ever so little.*
*pour que², *in order that.*
pourtant, *yet, however.*
*pourvu que³, *provided that.*
puisque, *since.*
quand, *when.*
†quand même⁴, *though, even if.*
†que⁶, *that, than, as.*
*quoique⁴, *though, although.*
*sans que⁵, *without.*
selon que, *according as.*
†si³, *if (§351, 3, a).*
†si bien que², *so that.*
†si peu que⁴, *however little.*
sinon, *if not, or else.*
sitôt que, *as soon as.*
soit... soit, *whether... or.*
soit... ou, *whether... or.*
*soit que... soit que⁴, *whether... or.*
*soit que... ou que⁴, *whether... or.*
suivant que, *according as.*
*supposé que³, *suppose that.*
tandis que, *whilst, whereas.*
tant... que, *both... and.*
tant que, *as long as.*
†tellement... que², *so... that.*

toutefois, *yet, nevertheless.*   vu que, *seeing that.*
une fois que, *as soon as.*

* Followed by the *subjunctive.*
† Followed by the *indicative or subjunctive.*

N.B.—Conjunctions without * or † in the table are followed by the indicative.

1 See §351, 1 (time before which or up to which).
2 See §351, 2 (purpose or result).
3 See §351, 3 (condition).
4 See §351, 4 (concession).
5 See §351, 5 (negation).
6 See §349, §351, 6, and §535 (below).

Use of Certain Conjunctions.

533. Et. 1. When repeated, *et* usually denotes 'both ... and'; otherwise it stands with the last only of two or more clauses:

Et vous et lui (vous) savez mieux.   Both you and he know better.
Les femmes pleuraient, criaient   The women wept (and) screamed
    et gesticulaient.   and gesticulated.

2. 'And' after a verb of motion is usually untranslated:
Allez leur parler.   Go and speak to them.

534. Ni. 1. A finite verb with **ni**(... **ni**) must be preceded by **ne**:

Il n'a ni or ni argent.   He has neither gold nor silver.
Il ne mange ni ne boit.   He neither eats nor drinks.

     a. For the position of ni ... ni ... ne, see §493, *d.*

2. In sentences of negative force, 'and,' 'or,' are rendered by **ni**:

Honneurs ni richesses ne font le   Honours and wealth do not con-
    bonheur.   stitute happiness.

3. Observe the following equivalents of 'neither,' 'not either,' 'nor either,' 'nor,' when *not correlative.*

Je n'irai pas.—Ni moi non plus.   I shall not go.—Nor I either (*or*
                                    Neither shall I).
Il n'ira pas non plus.   He will not go either.
Il n'est pas allé, et il n'ira pas.   He has not gone, nor will he (go).

535. Que. 1. Que = 'that' is followed by the indicative or subjunctive according to the context:

Je dis que vous avez raison.   I say that you are right.
Je suis fâché que vous ayez raison.   I am sorry that you are right.

2. **Que** often replaces another conjunction; when so used, it takes the same construction as the conjunction for which it stands, except that **que** instead of **si** = 'if' always requires the subjunctive:

Quand vous aurez fini, et que vous aurez le temps.	When you have finished, and (when you) have time.
Venez que (= 'afin que,' 'pour que') je vous voie.	Come that I may see you.
Si vous venez demain, et que vous ayez le temps.	If you come to-morrow, and (if you) have time.

3. **Que** may not be omitted before a finite verb, as 'that' often is in English:

Je crois qu'il viendra et qu'il restera.	I think (that) he will come and (that he will) stay.

536. Distinctions. The following conjunctions are especially liable to be confounded in use:

1. **Quand, Lorsque.** They are equivalents in the sense of 'when,' but **quand** (*not* 'lorsque') serves also as an interrogative adverb in direct or indirect questions:

Quand est-il arrivé?	When did he come?
Dis-moi quand il est arrivé.	Tell me when he came.
Quand (*or* lorsque) je l'ai vu.	When I saw him.
Nous partirons lorsque (*or* quand) la lettre arrivera.	We shall leave when the letter comes.

2. **Pendant que, Tandis que.** Pendant que = 'while,' 'whilst,' 'during the time that'; tandis que = 'while,' 'whilst,' 'during the time that,' and also, 'whilst,' 'on the contrary,' 'whereas':

Lisez le journal pendant que j'écris ce billet.	Read the newspaper while I write this note.
Tandis que vous êtes ici.	Whilst you are here.
Le père travaille, tandis que le fils ne fait rien.	The father works, while the son does nothing.

3. **Depuis que, Puisque.** Depuis que denotes *time*; puisque denotes *cause assigned*:

Je suis solitaire depuis que mon frère est parti.	I am lonely since my brother went away.
Il me faut rester, puisqu'il n'y a pas de train ce soir.	I must remain, since there is no train this evening.

EXERCISE LXXXI.

1. For fear it should rain we shall not go away to-day. 2. He did his work so that all were pleased with him. 3. Unless you come to-morrow, we shall not wait for you. 4. Both he and his brother were there. 5. Go and get us some bread. 6. She neither laughs nor cries. 7. Those poor people are without bread or meat. 8. He does not believe what you say; nor I either. 9. We shall not be there; nor he either. 10. We have not gone away, nor shall we. 11. As soon as you are there and have the time, will you go and visit my brother? 12. If he is there and we see him, we shall tell him what you say. 13. When bread is dear and the weather is cold, the poor suffer. 14. I think we shall go away the day after to-morrow. 15. If your friend comes to the meeting and I am there, I shall speak to him. 16. Since you went away I have been writing letters. 17. Since you cannot do it, you must let me try. 18. Since you went away yesterday he has done nothing but play. 19. Since every action brings its recompense with it, we must pay attention to what we do. 20. While I was doing my exercise, she was writing her letters. 21. The good shall be rewarded, whilst the bad shall be punished. 22. When I saw him, he was busy working in his field. 23. As long as the world lasts, justice shall prevail over injustice. 24. He did his work, so that he was praised by all. 25. He was kind to the poor, so that he might be praised by all.

THE INTERJECTION.

537. Interjections. The commoner interjections and expressions used as such are:

1. Joy, admiration, approval:

Ah! *(ah!)*; ha, ha! or hi, hi! *(laughter)*; bon! *(good!)*; bien! *(good!)*; à merveille! *(capital!)*; à la bonne heure! *(well done!, that's right!)*; bis! *(encore!)*; bravo! or bravissimo! *(well done!, bravo!)*; hourra! or vivat! *(hurrah!).*

2. Disgust, disapproval, indifference:

Fi! *(fie!)*; fi donc! *(for shame!)*; fie de! *(fie on!)*; foin de! *(a plague upon!)*; pouah! *(disgusting!, faugh!)*; oh! *(oh!)*; bah! or ah! bah! *(nonsense!, pooh-pooh!)*; baste! *(enough!, pooh!, nonsense!)*; par exemple! *(dear me!)*; zest! *(pshaw!).*

3. Grief, fear, pain:

Ah! *(ah!)*; oh! *(oh)*; hélas! *(alas!)*; aïe! *(oh!, oh dear!)*; miséricorde! *(mercy!)*; ouf! *(suffocation, or relief and exhaustion).*

4. Surprise :

Ah ! *(ah !)*; oh ! *(oh !)*; eh ! *(ah !)*; ha ! *(ha!)*; comment ! *(what !)*; quoi ! *(what !)*; vraiment ! *(indeed !)*; tiens ! *(indeed !)*; par exemple ! *(you don't say so !)*; miséricorde ! *(mercy !)*.

5. Encouragement :

Allons ! *(come !)*; courage ! *(cheer up !)*; voyons ! *(come now !)*; çà ! or or çà ! or sus ! or or sus ! *(now then !)*; en avant ! *(forward !)*; ferme ! *(steady !)*; preste ! *(quick !)*.

6. Warning :

Gare ! *(look out !, take care !)*; holà *(stop !, stop !)*.

7. Calling :

hé ! or ohé ! or holà ! *(ho !, hoy !, halloo !)*; hem ! *(ahem !)*; st ! *(hi there !)*; qui vive ! *(who goes there !)*.

8. Calling for aid :

à moi ! or au secours ! *(help !)*; à l'assassin or au meurtre *(murder !)*; au voleur ! *(stop thief !)*; au feu ! *(fire !)*.

6. Silencing, stopping :

chut ! or st ! *(hush !)*; silence ! *(silence !)*; motus ! *(not a word !)*; tout doux or tout beau ! *(gently !, not so fast !)*; halte-là ! *(stop there !)*.

NOTE.—Akin to interjections are imitations of sounds : Cric crac ! *(breaking)*; drelin, drelin ! or drelin, din, din ! *(ringing)*; pan pan ! *(bang)*; pif paf ! *(gunshots)*; boum ! *(cannonading)*; rataplan ! *(drum)*; dare dare ! *(quick movement)*; cahin-caha *(jogging along)*; clopin-clopant *(hobbling)*; tic tac *(ticking)*, etc.

ABBREVIATIONS.

538. French Abbreviations. The following are the commoner abbreviations used in French :—

c.-à-d. = *c'est-à-dire*, that is.
Cie or C^o = *compagnie*, company.
etc. = *et cætera*.
fr. or f. = *francs*, francs.
h. = *heure*, hour.
in-f^o = *in-folio*, folio.
J.-C. = *Jésus-Christ*, Jesus Christ.
M. = *Monsieur*, Mr

MM. = *Messieurs*, Messrs.
M. R. or M. R ... = *Monsieur R.* or *Monsieur R Trois-Étoiles*, Mr. R. or Mr. R—.
M^d = *marchand*, merchant.
M^o (pl. M^{es}) = *maître*, master.
Mgr (pl. NNSS.) = *monseigneur*, my lord.
Mlle (pl. Mlles) = *Mademoiselle*, Miss.

Mme (pl. M^{es}) = *Madame*, Mrs.
M^n = *maison*, house, firm.
ms. (pl. mss.) = *manuscrit*, manuscript.
N.-D. = *Notre-Dame*, Our Lady.
N.S. = *Notre Seigneur*, Our Lord.
n° = *numéro*, number.
S.A.R. = *Son Altesse Royale*, His Royal Highness.

s.-ent. = *sous-entendu*, understood.
S. Exc. = *Son Excellence*, His Excellency.
S. M. (pl. LL. MM.) = *Sa Majesté*, His (Her) Majesty.
S.S. = *Sa Sainteté*, His Holiness.
s. v. p. = *s il vous plaît*, if you please.
V^e = *veuve*, widow.

Ier (in titles) = *premier*, the First.
II (in titles) = *deux*, the Second.
Le XVe siècle, etc. = *le quinzième siècle*, the 15th century.

1er (fem. 1ere) = *premier*, first.
2e = *deuxième*, second.
1° = *primo*, firstly.
7bre = *septembre*, September etc., etc.

PART IV.

EXERCISES IN TRANSLATION.

1.

The largest clock in[1] the world will be the one[2] which soon[3] will adorn the city-hall of Philadelphia. The dial of this colossal clock will be[4] ten metres in diameter, and will be placed and illuminated so as to be visible night and day everywhere in the city. The hands will be, one[5] four metres and the other three metres long; the bell of the striking part will weigh forty-six thousand pounds, and in order to wind the clock a steam-engine placed in the tower will be used daily (=one will use daily a steam-engine, etc.).

1 §144, 5.   3 §490.   4 §505, obs. 3.   5 §483, 7, (1), a.
2 §459.

2.

Horses[1], birds[1] and animals[1] of all (the) sorts speak a language as well as men[1]. We cannot understand all (=all that which) they say, but we understand enough of it to[2] know that they have thoughts[3] and feelings[3]. They are sad when they lose a companion, or when they are driven away[4] from home. They are pleased, when they are well treated[4], and angry when they are ill treated[4]. They have, so to speak, a conscience: they feel ashamed, when they do what displeases us, and are very glad, when they merit our approbation. Kindness[1] on our part towards them is as reasonable as love[1] and kindness[1] between brothers[3] of the same family.

1 §399.   2 §361, 2.   3 §400.   4 §321, 2, a.

3.

A rich[1] man, it is said[2], once[3] asked[4] a learned man what was[5] the reason that scientific men were[5] so often[3] seen at the doors of the rich, while[4] the rich were[6] very rarely seen[2] at the doors of the learned. "It is," replied[4] the scholar, "because the man of science knows[7] the value of riches[8], but the rich man does not always know the value of sciences."

1 §429.   3 §490.   5 §338, 5.   7 §204.
2 §321, 2, a.   4 §340.   6 §338, 1.   8 §399.

4.

Molière, the great French[1] author, was born[2] in Paris in the year one thousand six hundred and twenty-two[3]. His father was the king's upholsterer and was probably a rather rich[4] man. The son received[5] a good education, but not much is known[6] of his youth. When he was about twenty years old[7], he organized[5] a company of actors, which was[5] called *L'Illustre Théâtre*. But in this enterprise he did not succeed[5] very well. He soon[8] lost[5] all his money, and with his *troupe* was[5] forced to[9] leave Paris and (to) make a tour in [the] province[s]. This tour lasted[5] from sixteen hundred and forty-six to sixteen hundred and fifty-eight. During these years he travelled[5] over nearly the whole of France, and played[5] in many of the large cities. After his return to Paris he became[5] the king's favourite, and produced[5] the masterpieces which have rendered him so celebrated. At last, after fifteen years of great prosperity, he died[5] in sixteen hundred and seventy-three at the age of fifty-one.

1 §430, 1, (2).   4 §429.   6 §321, 2, *a*.   8 §490.
2 Past Def.   5 §340.   7 §507.   9 §359, 6.
3 §498, *c*.

5.

Speaking of the small world in which even the greatest live[1], Lord Beaconsfield used to tell[2] that Napoleon I., a year after he became Emperor, determined to[3] find out if there was[4] anybody in the world who had never heard of him. Within a fortnight the police of Paris had[5] discovered a wood-chopper at Montmartre, in Paris itself, who had never heard of the Revolution, nor of the death of Louis XVI., nor of the Emperor Napoleon.

1 §317, 6.   3 §359, 6.   4 §338, 5.   5 §312, 1.
2 §338, 2.

6.

Napoleon, the greatest general of modern times[1], was born[2] at Ajaccio on the 15th August, 1769. At the age of ten[3] he was sent to the military[4] school at Brienne, where he remained more than[5] five years. Then entering the French[4] army, he was, in 1796, appointed general of the army of Italy[6], and soon succeeded in conquering[7] that country. He used so well the opportunities which were offered him by the weakness of the Republic that in less than ten years he was elected Emperor. The ten years' struggle, in which he engaged with the purpose of subduing[8] Europe[9], ended with the battle of Waterloo in

1815. Banished to *(en)* St. Helena he died[10] there on the 5th of May, 1821. Twenty years after his death his remains were brought back to *(en)* France, and interred in the *Hôtel des Invalides*.

1 §309.   4 §430, 1, (2).   7 §353, 2.   9 §411, 1.
2 §Past Def.   5 §489, 1, *b*.   8 §359, 2.   10 §*mourut* or
3 §507, obs. 2.   6 §411, 2, note.   *est mort*.

7.

Great Britain[1] and Ireland[1] are two large islands in the west of Europe[1]. Great Britain is the larger of the two and comprises England[1], Scotland[1] and Wales[1]. The monarch of the United Kingdom of Great Britain[2] and Ireland[2] is Queen[3] Victoria who was born[4] on the 24th of May, 1819. She is the daughter of the Duke of Kent, son of George III. She ascended the throne on (*à*) the death of William IV. in 1837. She has to *(pour)* assist her in the government of the country a parliament which meets once a year at Westminster. When she appeared before *(le)* parliament for the first time, Queen Victoria declared that she would place her trust in the wisdom of her parliament and the love of her people, and she has not failed to keep this promise. Having thus early won the hearts of all her subjects, she has retained their affection during a long reign of more than[5] fifty years. Queen Victoria is a[6] widow; her husband, Prince[3] Albert of Saxe-Coburg-Gotha, whom she married in 1840, died in 1861, much regretted by the Queen and the people.

1 §411, 1.   3 §405.   5 §489, 1, *b*.   6 §408, 3.
2 §411, 2.   4 §*est née*.

8.

There was[1], in the City of Macon, a parrot which had learned to[2] say continually: "Who is there? Who is there?" This parrot escaped one day from its cage in the garden, and soon[3] flew into a wood near by, where a peasant saw it, and began to[2] chase it. The peasant had never seen a parrot in *(de)* all his life. He approached[4] the tree where the bird was, and was going to[5] kill the poor bird with his gun. At that moment the parrot began to[2] repeat the usual question: "Who is there? Who is there?" The peasant, terrified at these words, let his gun fall[6] from his hands. Then taking his[7] hat off, he said, with great respect: "My dear sir, I pray you to[8] excuse me, I thought that it was a bird."

1 §330.   4 §375, 1.   6 §310, 6, *a* and 7.   8 §359, 6.
2 §353, 7.   5 §357, 6.   7 §454, 1.
3 §490.

9.

The unknown[1] author of "Beowulf" was not a[2] native of England, and so the first of the long line of English[3] poets is really Cædmon. Bæda tells us a pretty story of the way in which[4] Cædmon became a[2] poet. He was already almost an[2] old man before he knew anything[5] of the art of poetry. At the feasts, in those days, everybody used to sing[6] in turn to[7] amuse the company, but Cædmon used to leave[6] the table before the harp was given[8] to him. One evening, when he had done thus, he went to the stable and lay down, after having[9] cared for the cattle, because, you must know, he was only a farm-servant in the monastery at Whitby. As he slept[10], some one appeared to him, and said, "Cædmon, sing a song to me." "I cannot[11] sing," he replied, "and that is why I left the feast." "Nevertheless," was the answer, "you must sing to me." "Well, then," asked Cædmon, "what shall I sing?" The other replied, "sing the beginning of created things[12]." Thereupon he made some verses, which he still remembered when he awoke. The Abbess Hilda, hearing of his dream, believed (that) the grace of God had been given him, and made him a[2] monk.

1 §430, 1, (3). 4 §475. 7 §361, 2. 10 §338, 1.
2 §408, 3. 5 §482, 4, *a*. 8 §321, 2, *a*. 11 §310, 4.
3 §430, 1, (2). 6 §338, 2. 9 §361, 4. 12 §399.

10.

A miser went[1] one day to market[2], and bought[1] some[3] fine apples. He carried[1] them home, arranged[1] them carefully in his cupboard, and used to go[4] and look at them almost every day, but would[5] not eat any until they began to spoil. Every time he did eat one he regretted it. But he had a son, a young school-boy, who liked apples; and one day, with a school-fellow, he found the miser's treasure. I do not know how he found the key of the cupboard; but he did[6], and you may imagine how many apples they ate. When they had[7] finished the apples, the old father came, and caught them. How angry[8] he was! How he shouted at them! "Wretches! where are my beautiful apples? You shall both be hanged! You have eaten them all!" His son replied: "Do not be angry, father[9]! You only eat the bad apples; we have not touched those; we have eaten the good ones, and left you yours."

1 §340. 4 §338, 2. 6 §336. 8 §423, *a*.
2 §409, ex. 4. 5 §345, 1, *b*. 7 §342, 3. 9 §454, 4.
3 §402, 1.

11.

A hungry[1] fox was one day looking for[2] a poultry-yard. It was late in the afternoon, and, as he was passing[3] a farmhouse, he saw[4] a cock and some hens which had[5] gone up into a tree for the night. He drew near[4], and invited[4] them to[6] come down and[7] rejoice with him on account of a new treaty of peace which had been formed between the animals. The cock said he was[8] very glad of it, but that he did not intend[8] to[9] come down before the next morning. "But," said he, "I see two dogs coming[10]; I have no doubt they will be[11] glad to[12] celebrate the peace with you." Just then the fox remembered that he had business[13] elsewhere, and, bidding the cock good-bye, began[4] to run. "Why do you run?" said the cock, "if the animals have made a peace, the dogs won't hurt you. I know them, they are good, loyal[14] dogs, and would not harm any one." "Ah," said the fox, "I am afraid they have[15] not yet heard the news."

[1] §430, 1, (3).   [5] §§309; 342, 2.   [9] §359, 2, a.   [13] §401.
[2] §§338, 1; 375, 3.   [6] §358, 7.   [10] §306, 3.   [14] §430, 3.
[3] §338, 1.   [7] §533, 2.   [11] §349, 5.   [15] §349, 4, a.
[4] §340.   [8] §338, 5.   [12] §434.

12.

A woodman, who was cutting[1] wood on the bank of a river, let[2] his axe fall[3] into the water. He at once[4] began[2] to[5] pray [to] the gods to[6] find it for him. Mercury appeared[2] and asked[2] him what was[7] the matter. "I have lost my axe," said[2] he. Having heard this, Mercury dived[2] into the water, and brought[2] up a golden axe. "Is this[8] yours?" "No," said the man. Next time Mercury brought up a silver one. "Is this one yours?" "No," said[2] the chopper again. The third time Mercury brought up an iron one, which the man said was his, as soon as he saw[2] it. "It is yours," said the god, "and for your honesty I shall give you the other two also."

[1] §338, 1.   [3] §310, 6, a, and 7.   [5] §358, 7.   [7] §338, 5.
[2] §340.   [4] §490.   [6] §359, 6.   [8] §316, 2.

13.

Two men were travelling[1] together, when they saw[2] a bear coming out[3] of the forest. The one climbed into a tree, and tried to[4] conceal himself in the branches. The other, when he saw that the bear would =was going to) attack him, threw himself upon the ground, and, when the bear came up he ceased to[4] breathe, for it is said[5] that a bear will not touch[6] a dead[7] body. When the bear had[8] gone, his companion came down, and asked: "What was it that the bear was saying to you?" His friend replied: "He advised me not[9] to travel with a friend who runs away at the approach of danger[10]."

1 §338, 1.   4 §359, 6.   7 §430, 1, (3).   9 §403, a.
2 §340.   5 §321, 2, a. 8 §342, 3.   10 §390.
3 §360, 3.   6 §375, 5.

14.

A well-known[1] English[2] actor, travelling to Birmingham by the Great Western[3] railway the other day, on approaching[4] Banbury, began to feel hungry, and determined to have one of the buns for which the town is famous.

The train having stopped, he called a boy, gave him sixpence, and asked him to get "two Banburys," promising him one of the two for his trouble.

Just as the train was about to start, the boy rushed up to the carriage in which the impatient actor was seated, and offering him threepence, exclaimed :—

"Here's your change, sir."

"Bother the change; where's the bun?" roared the hungry actor.

"There was only one left," replied the boy, "and I'm eating that!"

1 §430, 1, (3).   2 §430, 1, (2).   3 §408, 4, c, note.   4 §375, 1.

15.

Under a magnificent walnut-tree near the village, two little boys found a walnut. "It belongs to me," said the one, "for it was[1] I[2] who was the first to see it (= who have seen it the first)." "No, it belongs to me," exclaimed the other, "for it was[1] I[2] who picked it up." Thereupon there[3] arose between them a violent quarrel. "I am going to make peace[4] between you," said to them a third boy, who was passing at that moment. The latter placed himself between the two claimants, opened the walnut, and pronounced this sentence: "One of the shells belongs to him[5] who was the first to see the walnut; the other to him[5] who picked it up; as to the kernel, I keep it for the costs of the court." "This," added he, laughing, "is generally the end of lawsuits[4]."

1 §337, 3, b.   3 §332, 2.   4 §399.   5 §459.
2 §450, 3.

16.

Many years ago[1] there[2] lived in the city of Paris a celebrated[3] physician who was very fond of animals. One day a friend of his[4] brought to his house a favourite[3] dog, whose leg had been broken, and asked him if he could do anything for the poor creature. The kind doctor examined the wounded[5] animal, and, prescribing a treatment for him, soon[6] cured him, and received the warm thanks of his friend, who set a very high value upon his dog. Not very long afterwards, the doctor was in his room busy studying[7]. He thought[8] he heard a noise at the door, as if some animal was scratching in order to be let[9] in. For some time he paid no attention to the noise, but continued studying[10]. At last, however, he rose up and opened the door. To his great astonishment he saw enter the dog which he had cured, and with him another dog. The latter also had a broken[5] leg, and was able to move only with great difficulty. The dog which the surgeon had cured had brought his friend to his benefactor, in order that he, too, might be[11] healed; and, as well as he could, he made the doctor[12] understand that this was what he wanted.

1 §330, 4.
2 §332, 2.
3 §429.
4 §455, 3.
5 §430, 1, (3).
6 §490.
7 §358, 2.
8 §535, 3.
9 §321, 2, *a*.
10 §358, 7.
11 §351, 2.
12 §310, 6, *b*.

17.

There was once a cat who was a[1] great enemy of the rats. He had eaten a great many[2], and they were much afraid of him. So the chiefs of the rats called a meeting to[3] discuss what they should do to[3] rid themselves of him. A great many plans were proposed, but after a little discussion they were all abandoned. At last a young rat, who thought himself very clever, rose and said: "Do not despair my friends, I have not yet proposed a plan. A splendid idea occurs to me; I know what we can do. We can, if we are economical, soon save enough money to[3] buy a little bell. This we can attach to the neck of our old enemy, and, if he approaches, we can[4] flee to a place of safety."

The young rats all applauded the idea, but one of the old [ones], who up to this time had said nothing, gravely[5] asked the one who had made the speech if he would promise to put the bell on the cat. The young rat blushed, and said he would think of it[6].

The meeting rose shortly after, and the rats dispersed without doing anything[7].

1 §408, 3.
2 §445, 2, (1).
3 §361, 2.
4 §343, 2.
5 §490.
6 §446.
7 §482, 4, *a*.

18.

Long ago[1] the frogs, tired of having[2] a republic, resolved to[3] ask Jupiter to send them a king. Jupiter did not receive their petition with much favour, but as they seemed really to[4] desire one, he thought (that) it would be better to please[5] them. So, one fine day, when they were all expecting[6] their king, a great log fell from the sky into the pond, where they were [6]. They were very much afraid of the noise[7] it made, and they took refuge in holes and in the mud at the bottom of the pond. Little by little, however, they approached[8] their king to[9] get a good look at him, and seeing that he was so quiet, they became more bold, and finally leaped on him, and treated him with great familiarity. Then they complained again to Jupiter saying that the king he had sent was not worthy of their respect, and that they desired another, who would show[10] more vigour. In order to please them Jupiter sent them this time a stork, who immediately began to devour them with much avidity. They complained again, but Jupiter told them that, since[11] they had desired a king, they would be forced to quietly submit to the one[12] he had sent.

[1] §330, 4.   [4] §357, 6.   [7] §479, 1.   [10] §350, 1.
[2] §359, 2. – [5] §375, 2.   [8] §375, 1.   [11] §536, 3.
[3] §359, 6.   [6] §338, 1.   [9] §361, 2.   [12] §§459; 479, 1.

19.

The two youngest of my children were already in bed and asleep, the third had[1] gone out, but at my return I found him sitting beside my gate, weeping[2] very sore. I asked him the reason. "Father[3]," said he, "I took this morning from[4] my mother, without her knowing[5] it, one of those three apples you brought her, and I kept[6] it a long while; but, as I was playing some time ago[7] with my little brother in the street, a slave that went[8] by snatched it out of my hands, and carried it off; I ran after him asking for it, and besides, told him that it belonged to my mother, who was ill, and that you had taken a fortnight's journey to fetch it; but all in vain, he would[9] not give it back. And because I still followed him, crying out, he stopped and beat me, and then ran away as fast as he could, from one street to another, till at length I lost sight of him. I have since that been walking outside the town, expecting your return, to pray you, dear father, not to tell my mother [of] it, lest it should make her worse." And when he had[10] said these words, he began weeping again more bitterly than ever.

[1] §309.   [4] §375, 4.   [7] §330, 4.   [9] §345, 1, b.
[2] §305, 2.   [5] §351, 5.   [8] §338, 1.   [10] §342, 3.
[3] §454, 4.   [6] §339, 2.

20.

A celebrated Italian[1] painter had told his pupils to[2] ask the name of any *(tout)* person who might come[3] to his house during his absence in the city. One day three gentlemen came to[4] see the painter, and the latter was not at home. One of the pupils whose name was John opened the door for them[5], said that his master was not in, and let them depart without asking their names. When the master returned and[6] heard of the three gentlemen, he asked[7] John who they were. John could say nothing but, "I do not know, sir." The painter got angry, but John, with a few strokes of his pencil drew *(faire)* the portrait of the three, and gave it to his master, who immediately[8] recognized them. The artist admired the skill of the young man so much that he took the drawing, and kept it afterwards among his most precious possessions. It is needless to[9] add that he pardoned the pupil.

1 §430, 1, (2). 4 §357, 6. 6 §535, 2. 8 §490.
2 §359, 6. 5 §440, 2. 7 §375, 2. 9 §461, 2, (1), *a*.
3 §350, 1.

21.

A man *(celui)* who would[1] have friends must show himself friendly. A man was passing the night at an inn. He had just left a town, where he had spent several years. The landlord asked[2] him why he had left the place. He replied, "because my neighbors were so disagreeable and disobliging that one could not live with them." The landlord replied, "you will find exactly the same sort of neighbors where you are going." The following day another traveller came from the same place. He told the landlord that he was obliged to leave the place where he was living, and that it cost him great pain to part with his neighbors, who had been so kind and obliging. The landlord encouraged him by telling[3] him that he would find exactly the same sort of neighbors where he was going.

1 §310, 1. 2 §375, 4. 3 §365, 3.

22.

When I was[1] at school, I was[1] often very idle. Even in [the] class I used to play[1] with boys as idle as myself. We used to try[1] to hide this from[2] our master, but one day he caught[3] us cleverly.

"You must not be idle," said he. "You must not raise your[4] eyes from your books. You do not know what you lose by idleness[5]. Study while you are young; you will not be able to study when you are[6] old. If any one sees another boy, who is not studying, let him tell me[7].

"Now," said I to myself, "there is Fred Smith, I do not like him. If I see that he is not studying, I shall tell[7]."

Soon after, I saw Fred Smith looking out[8] of the window, and I told the master what I had seen. "Indeed!" said he, "how do you know he was idle?" "If you please, sir," said I, "I saw[9] him." "O you saw[9] him, and where were your eyes when you saw[9] him?"

I saw the other boys laugh[8], and I was[10] ashamed, for the master smiled, and said it was a good lesson for me.

1 §338. 4 §406.   7 §413.   9 §339, 2.
2 §375, 4. 5 §399.   8 §366, 3.   10 §338, 1.
3 §340. 6 §343, 2.

23.

When Lord Nelson was[1] quite a small child he left[2] one day his grandmother's house in company with a cowboy. The dinner hour passed[2], he was[1] absent, and could[1] not be[3] found, and the alarm of the family became very great, for they feared that he might have been[4] carried off by gypsies. At length, after search had been made[3] for him in various directions, he was[3] discovered alone, sitting composedly on the bank of a brook which he could not get over. "I wonder, child," said the old lady, when she saw[2] him, "that hunger and fear did not drive[5] you[6] home." "Fear[7]! grandmamma," replied the future hero, "I never saw fear!—what is it[8]?" Once, after the winter holidays, when he and his brother William had[9] started on horseback to return to school, they came back because a great deal of snow had[9] fallen, and William, who did not like to go away, said it was[10] too deep to advance. "If that be the case," said the father, "you certainly shall not go; but try it again, and I shall leave it to your honour. If the road is dangerous, you may return; but remember, boys[11], I leave it to your honour." The snow was deep enough to give them a reasonable excuse; but Horatio could not be[3] forced to go back. "We must go on," said he, "remember, brother[11], it was left to our honour!"

1 §338. 4 §349, 4, a.   7 §399.   10 §338, 5.
2 §340. 5 §349, 4.   8 §461.   11 §454, 4.
3 §321, 2, a. 6 §451, 1.   9 §309.

24.

The princes of Europe[1] have found out a manner of rewarding[2] their subjects who have behaved well, by presenting[3] them with about two yards of blue[4] ribbon, which is worn[5] on the shoulder. Those who are honoured with this mark of distinction are called knights, and the king himself is always at the head of the order. This is a cheap method of recompensing[2] the most important services; and it is very fortunate for kings[6] that their subjects are[7] satisfied with such[8] trifling rewards. Should[9] a nobleman lose his leg in a battle, the king presents him with two yards of ribbon, and he is paid for the loss of his leg. Should[9] an ambassador spend all his paternal fortune in[10] supporting the honour of his country abroad, the king presents him with two yards of ribbon, which is considered[5] the equivalent of his estate. In short, as long as a European king has a yard or two of blue or green ribbon, he need not fear he shall want[11] statesmen, generals and soldiers.

1 §411, 2. 4 §430, 1, (1). 7 §349, 4. 10 §358, 2.
2 §359, 2. 5 §321, 2. 8 §483, 5, a, note. 11 §349, 4, a.
3 §365, 3. 6 §309. 9 §355, p. 213.

25.

At a time when so much attention was being given[1] to ancient art[2] in Italy that modern art[2] was being neglected[1], Michael Angelo had resort to a stratagem in order to teach the critics the folly of judging such things according to fashion[2] or reputation[2]. He made a statue which represented[3] a beautiful girl asleep[4], and, breaking off an arm, buried the statue in a place, where excavations were being made[1]. It was soon found, and was lauded by critics[2] and by the public as a valuable relic of antiquity[2]. When Michael Angelo thought the time opportune, he produced the broken arm, and, to the great mortification of the critics, revealed himself as the sculptor.

1 §321, 2. 2 §399. 3 §338, 3. 4 §430, 1, (3).

26.

Had you seen us, Mr. Harley, when we were turned out of South-hill, I am sure you would have wept at the sight. You remember old Trusty, my dog; I shall never forget it while I live; the poor creature was blind with age, and could scarce crawl after us to the door; he went, however, as far as the gooseberry-bush, which you may remember stood on the left side of the yard; he was wont to bask in the sun there; when he had reached that spot, he stopped; we went on; I called him; he wagged his tail, but did not stir; I called again; he lay down; I whistled, and cried Trusty; he gave a short howl, and died! I could have lain down and died too; but God gave me strength to live for my children.

VOCABULARY.

FRENCH-ENGLISH.

A.

à, *prep.*, to, at, for, in.
abîmer, *v. r.*, to spoil.
absence, *n.f.*, absence.
absent, *adj.*, absent.
absolument, *adv.*, absolutely, quite.
accompagner, *v. r.*, to accompany.
acheter, *v ir.*(§241, 2), to buy.
affaire, *n.f.*, affair, business.
afin de, *prep.*, in order to.
afin que, *conj.*, that, in order that.
âge, *n. m.*, age; *quel âge a-t-il?*, how old is he?
agréable, *adj.*, agreeable, pleasant.
aimable, *adj.*, amiable, pleasant.
aimer, *v.r.*, to love, like; *aimer mieux*, to like better, prefer.
aîné, *adj.*, elder, eldest.
aller, *v.ir.*,(§242), to go; *comment allez-vous?*, *comment ça va-t-il?*, *comment ça va?*, how does it go?, how are you?
allumer, *v.r.*, to light, to kindle.
alors, *adv.*, then.
amener, *v.ir.*, (§241, 1), to lead to, bring.
ami, -e, *n.m.f.*, friend.
amusant, *adj.*, amusing.
amuser, *v. r.*, to amuse; *s'amuser*, to enjoy one's self.
an, *n. m.*, year.

ancien,-ne, *adj.*, old, former.
anglais, *n.* and *adj.*, English, Englishman.
Angleterre, *n.f.*, England.
animal, *n. m.*, animal.
année, *n.f.*, year.
août, *n. m.*, August.
apporter, *v. r.*, to carry to, bring.
apprendre, *v. ir.*, (§283), to learn.
après, *adv.*, *prep.*, after.
après que, *conj.*, after that, after.
après-demain, *adv.*, the day after to-morrow.
après-midi, *n.m.* or *f.*, afternoon.
arbre, *n. m.*, tree.
argent, *n. m.*, silver, money.
arrêter, *v.r.*, to stop; *s'arrêter*, to stop one's self, stop.
arrivée, *n. f.*, arrival.
arriver, *v.r.*, to arrive, come.
assassiner, *v. r.*, to assassinate, murder.
assemblée, *n.f.*, assembly, meeting.
assez, *adv.* and *n. m.*, enough.
attendre, *v. ir.*, (§291), to wait, wait for.
attraper, *v. r.*, to catch.
au, contraction for *à+le*.
au-dessous de, below, under.
au-dessus de, above, over.
aujourd'hui, *adv.*, to-day.
auparavant, *adv.*, before.
aussi, *adv.*, also, too, as.

aussitôt que, *conj.*, as soon as.
autre, *adj.* and *indef. pron.*, other.
avant, *prep.*, before.
avant que, *conj.*, before that, before.
avant-hier, *adv.*, the day before yesterday.
avec, *prep.*, with.
avoine, *n.f.*, oats.
avoir, *v. ir.*, (§238), to have; *qu'avez-vous?*, what is the matter with you?; *il y a*, there is, there are.
avril, *n. m.*, April.

B.

bal, *n. m.*, ball.
bateau, *n. m.*, boat; *bateau à vapeur*, steamboat.
bâtir, *v. r.*, to build.
bâton, *n. m.*, stick.
beau, bel, belle, *adj*, fine, beautiful, handsome; *il fait beau*, it is fine.
beaucoup, *adv.* and *n. m.*, much, many, very much.
beau-frère, *n. m.*, brother-in-law.
belle-mère, *n. f.*, mother-in-law.
belle-sœur, *n. f.*, sister-in-law.
besoin, *n.m.*, need; *avoir besoin de*, to need, to want.
beurre, *n. m.*, butter.
bien, *adv.* and *n. m.*, well; very; much, many; *eh bien!*, very well!

bien que, *conj.*, although.
bientôt, *adv.*, soon.
blanc, blanche, *adj.*, white.
blé, *n. m.*, wheat.
bois, *n. m.*, wood, forest.
boîte, *n. f.*, box.
bon, -ne, *adj.*, good, kind; *à la bonne heure*, all right.
bonheur, *n. m.*, happiness, good fortune.
bout, *n. m.*, end.
branche, *n. f.*, branch.

C.

ça, *dem. pron.*, contraction of *cela*, that.
Caïn, *n. m.*, Cain.
campagne, *n. f.*, country.
canadien, -ne, *adj.* and *n.*, Canadian.
canne, *n. f.*, cane.
capitale, *n. f.*, capital.
car, *conj.*, for.
carafe, *n. f.*, decanter, water-bottle.
ce, cet, cette, ces, *dem. adj.*, this, that, these, those; *ce...-ci*, this, *ce...-là*, that.
ce, *dem. pron.*, it, he, she, they; *ce qui, ce que*, what; *est-ce qu'il est?*, is he?; *n'est-ce pas?*, does he not?, etc., etc.
cela, *dem. pron.*, that.
celui, celle, *dem. pron.*, this, that, the one, he; *celui de mon frère*, my brother's; *celui-ci*, this one, the latter; *celui-là*, that one, the former.
chambre, *n. f.*, room.
champ, *n. f.*, field.
chanson, *n. f.*, song.
chant, *n. m.*, singing, song.
chanter, *v. r.*, to sing.
chapeau, *n. m.*, hat.
chapitre, *n. m.*, chapter.
charmant, *adj.*, charming.

charmer, *v. r.*, to charm, delight.
charpentier, *n. m.*, carpenter.
chasseur, *n. m.*, hunter.
chat, *n. m.*, cat.
chaud, *adj.* and *n. m.*, warm, heat; *il fait chaud*, it is warm; *il a chaud*, he is warm.
chemin, *n. m.*, road; *chemin de fer*, railway.
chêne, *n. m.*, oak.
cher, chère, *adj.*, dear; *moins cher*, cheaper.
cher, *adv.*, dear.
chercher, *v. r.*, to seek, look for, search; *aller chercher*, to go for, fetch, go and get; *envoyer chercher*, to send for.
cheval, *n. m.*, horse.
chez, *prep.*, at the house of, at the shop of, etc.; *chez moi*, etc., at home.
chien, *n. m.*, dog.
chose, *n. f.*, thing; *quelque chose*, *indef. pron. m.*, something.
cinq, *num. adj.*, five.
cinquième, *num. adj.*, fifth.
clou, *n. m.*, nail.
coin, *n. m.*, corner.
colline, *n. f.*, hill.
combien, *adv.* and *n. m.*, how much, how many; *combien de fois*, how often.
comme, *adv.*, how, as, like.
commencer, *v. ir.*, (§239), to commence, begin.
comment, *adv.*, how, what.
complet, -ète, *adj.*, complete.
connaître, *v. ir.*, (§269), to know.
conseil, *n. m.*, counsel, advice.
content, *adj.*, content, pleased, glad.

continuer, *v. r.*, to continue.
coquin, *n. m.*, rogue, scoundrel.
cordonnier, *n. m.*, shoemaker.
côté, *n. m.*, side; *à côté*, beside, next door.
coucher (se), *v. r.*, to lie down, go to bed.
couper, *v. r.*, to cut, cut down.
courage, *n. m.*, courage.
courir, *v. ir.*, (§246), to run.
cousin,-e, *n. m.* and *f.*, cousin.
couteau, *n. m.*, knife.
coûter, *v. r.*, to cost.
crayon, *n. m.*, pencil.
croire, *v. ir.*, (§272), to believe, think.
cueillir, *v. ir.*, (§247), to gather, pluck.
cuisine, *n. f.*, kitchen.

D.

dame, *n. f.*, lady.
dans, *prep.*, in, into.
de, *prep*, of, from, etc.
dé, *n. m.*, thimble.
décembre, *n. m.*, December.
déchirer, *v. r.*, to tear.
défaut, *n. m.*, defect, fault.
déjà, *adv.*, already.
déjeuner, *v. r.*, to breakfast.
déjeuner, *n. m.*, breakfast.
demain, *adv.*, to-morrow.
demander, *v. r.*, to ask, ask for.
demeurer, *v. r.*, to dwell, live.
demi, *adj.*, half; *à une heure et demie*, at half-past one.
dent, *n. f.*, tooth.
depuis, *prep.* and *adv.*, since.
depuis que, *conj.*, since.
dernièrement, *adv.*, lately.
derrière, *prep.*, behind.
dès que, *conj.*, as soon as.

descendre, *v. ir.*, (§291), to descend, go down, alight.

désirer, *v. r.*, to desire, wish, want ; *je désirerais*, I should like.

deux, *num. adj.*, two.

deuxième, *num. adj.*, second.

devant, *prep.*, before, in front of.

devoir, *v. ir.*, (§294), to owe ; *il doit le faire*, he is to do it ; *il devrait le faire*, he ought to do it ; *il a dû le faire*, he must have done it ; *il aurait dû le faire*, he ought to have done it.

Dieu, *n. m.*, God.

difficile, *adj.*, difficult.

dimanche, *n. m.*, Sunday.

dîner, *v. r.*, to dine.

dîner, *n. m.*, dinner.

dire, *v. ir.*, (§274), to say, tell.

dix, *num. adj.*, ten.

dix-huit, *num. adj.*, eighteen.

dix-neuf, *num. adj.*, nineteen.

dix-sept, *num. adj.*, seventeen.

domestique, *n. m. f.*, servant.

donner, *v. r.*, to give, give away.

dont, *rel. pron.*, of whom, of which, whose.

dormir, *v. ir.*, (§248), to sleep.

dos, *n. m.*, back.

doute, *n. m.*, doubt ; *sans doute*, no doubt.

douter, *v. r.*, to doubt ; *se douter*, to suspect.

douze, *num. adj.*, twelve.

E.

eau, *n. f.*, water.

école, *n. f.*, school.

écrire, *v. ir.*, (§275), to write.

écurie, *n. f.*, stable.

église, *n. f.*, church.

élevé, *adj.*, bred ; *bien élevé*, well-bred.

elle, elles, *pers. pron.*, she, her, it, they, them.

emmener, *v. ir.*, (§241, 1), to take away.

emporter, *v. r.*, to carry away, take off.

en, *pron.*, of him, of them, of it, some, any.

en, *prep.*, in, to.

encore, *adv.*, yet, still, again ; *pas encore*, not yet.

encre, *n. f.*, ink.

enfant, *n. m. f.*, child, boy, girl.

ennuyer, *v. ir.*, (§240), to annoy.

ensemble, *adv.*, together.

entrer, *v. r.*, to enter, go in, come in.

envie, *n. f.*, desire ; *avoir envie*, to have a desire, notion.

environ, *prep.* and *adv.*, about.

envoyer, *v. ir.*, (§243), to send.

épicier, *n. m.*, grocer.

espèce, *n. f.*, kind, sort.

et, *conj.*, and.

état, *n. m.*, state.

États-Unis, *n. m.*, United States.

étoffe, *n. f.*, cloth.

être, *v. ir.*, (§238), to be ; *être à*, to belong to.

étudier, *v. r.*, to study.

eux, *pers. pron.*, them, they.

exemplaire, *n. m.*, copy.

F.

fâché, *adj.*, sorry.

facile, *adj.*, easy.

facilement, *adv.*, easily.

faim, *n. f.*, hunger ; *avoir faim*, to be hungry.

faire, *v. ir.*, (§276), to do, make ; *faire faire*, to get done, have done ; *faire bâtir*, to have built ; *faire arriver (venir)*, to send for ; *cela ne fait rien*, that makes no difference, that doesn't matter ; *qu'est-ce que cela lui fait?*, what is that to him? ; *cela ne lui fait rien*, that is nothing to him ; *il fait beau*, it is fine.

falloir, *v. ir.*, (§298), to be necessary, have to ; *il faut que je* (with subj.), *il me faut* (with infin.), I must ; *que vous faut-il?*, what do you need?

famille, *n. f.*, family.

fat, *n. m.*, fop.

fatigué, *adj.*, tired.

femme, *n. f.*, woman, wife.

fenêtre, *n. f.*, window.

fer, *n. m.*, iron.

fermer, *v. r.*, to close, shut.

fête, *n. f.*, feast, birthday.

feu, *n. m.*, fire.

février, *n. m.*, February.

fièvre, *n. f.*, fever.

fille, *n. f.*, daughter, girl.

fils, *n. m.*, son, boy.

finir, *v. r.*, to finish.

foin, *n. m.*, hay.

fois, *n. f.*, time ; *une fois*, once ; *deux fois*, twice.

forêt, *n. f.*, forest.

fort, *adv.*, very, hard.

fou, fol, folle, *adj.*, mad, crazy.

frais, fraîche, *adj.*, fresh, cool.

franc, *n. m.*, franc (worth about 20 cents).

français, *adj.* and *n.*, French, Frenchman.

frapper, *v. r.*, to strike, knock.

VOCABULARY.

frère, *n. m.*, brother.
froid, *adj.* and *n. m.*, cold;
  il fait froid, it is cold;
  il a froid, he is cold.
fromage, *n. m.*, cheese.
fruit, *n. m.*, fruit.

G.

garçon, *n. m.*, boy.
garde, *n. f.*, guard; *prendre garde*, to take care.
gare, *n. f.*, railway-station.
gâter, *v. r.*, to spoil.
général, *n. m.*, general.
généreux, -se, *adj.*, generous, liberal.
gentil, -le, *adj.*, nice.
glissant, *adj.*, slippery; *il fait glissant*, it is slippery.
gouvernante, *n. f.*, governess.
grand, *adj.*, great, tall, large.
gros, -se, *adj.*, big, large.
guère, *adv.*; *ne ... guère*, hardly, scarcely.

H.

[h aspirate is indicated thus: '*h*].

'habit, *n. m.*, coat.
'Henri, *n. m.*, Henry.
heure, *n. f.*, hour; *à quatre heures*, at four o'clock; *quelle heure est-il?*, what o'clock is it?; *à quelle heure?*, at what o'clock?; *de bonne heure*, early; *à la bonne heure*, all right.
heureux, -se, *adj.*, happy.
hier, *adv.*, yesterday.
hirondelle, *n. f.*, swallow.
histoire, *n. f.*, story, history.
hiver, *n. m.*, winter.
homme, *n. m.*, man.
honnête, *adj.*, honest.
'honte, *n. f.*, shame; *avoir honte*, to be ashamed.
'huit, *num. adj.*, eight

I.

ici, *adv.*, here; *ici-bas*, here below.
il, ils, *pers. pron.*, he, it, they.
injure, *n. f.*, abusive language; *dire des injures*, to insult.
instruction, *n. f.*, education.
intelligent, *adj.*, intelligent.
intention, *n. f.*, intention; *avoir (l')intention*, to intend.

J.

jamais, *adv.*, ever; *ne ... jamais*, never.
janvier, *n. m.*, January.
jardin, *n. m.*, garden.
je, *pers. pron.*, I.
Jean, *n. m.*, John.
jeudi, *n. m.*, Thursday.
jeune, *adj.*, young.
joli, *adj.*, pretty.
jouer, *v. r.*, to play.
jour, *n. m.*, day; *bon jour*, good day, good morning; *tous les jours*, every day.
journée, *n. f.*, day; *toute la journée*, all day long.
juillet, *n. m.*, July.
juin, *n. m.*, June.
jusque, *adv.* and *prep.*, up to, as far as.
jusqu'à ce que, *conj.*, until.
juste, *adj.*, just.
justice, *n. f.*, justice.

L.

là, *adv.*, there; *là-bas*, yonder.
lac, *n. m.*, lake.
laisser, *v. r.*, to let, let ... have.
lait, *n. m.*, milk.
laitier, *n. m.*, milkman.
langue, *n. f.*, tongue, language.
le, la, l', les, *def. art.*, the.

le, la, l', les, *pers. pron.*, him, her, it, them.
leçon, *n. f.*, lesson.
lequel, laquelle, *rel.* and *inter. pron.*, who, which, which one, what one.
lettre, *n. f.*, letter.
leur, leurs, *poss. adj.*, their.
leur, *pers. pron.*, to them, them.
leur (le, la), *poss. pron.*, theirs.
lever, *v. ir.*, (§241), to raise; *se lever*, to rise.
libraire, *n. m.*, bookseller.
lieue, *n. f.*, league.
livre, *n. m.*, book.
livre, *n. f.*, pound.
Londres, *n. m.*, London.
long, -ue, *adj.*, long.
longtemps, *adv.*, long, a long time.
lorsque, *conj.*, when.
lui, *pers. pron.*, to him, to her; him, her; he.
lundi, *n. m.*, Monday.

M.

madame, *n. f.*, madam; contracted into *Mme*, Mrs.; *mesdames*, *plur.*, ladies;
mademoiselle, *n. f.*, Miss; contracted into *Mlle*; *mesdemoiselles*, *plur.*, young ladies.
mai, *n. m.*, May.
maintenant, *adv.*, now.
mais, *conj.*, but; *mais si*, yes indeed; *mais non*, not at all.
maison, *n. f.*, house.
mal, *n. m.*, evil, pain, ache; *avoir mal à*, to have a pain in, have ...-ache.
mal, *adv.*, ill, badly, not well.
malade, *adj.*, sick, ill.
malheur, *n. m.*, misfortune.
malle, *n. f.*, trunk.

maman, *n. f.*, mamma.
manger, *v. ir.*, (§239, 2), to eat.
marchand, *n.m.*, merchant.
marcher, *v. r.*, to walk, go.
mardi, *n. m.*, Tuesday.
Marie, *n. f.*, Mary.
mariée, *n. f.*, bride.
mars, *n. m.*, March.
matin, *n. m.*, morning; *le matin*, in the morning.
mauvais, *adj.*, bad, evil.
méchant, *adj.*, naughty, cross, bad.
médecin, *n. m.*, doctor, physician.
meilleur, *adj.*, better, best.
même, *adj.*, self, very.
mendiant, -e, *n. m. f.*, beggar.
merci, *n.m.*, I thank you, thanks.
mercredi, *n.m.*, Wednesday.
mère, *n. f.*, mother.
mètre, *n. m.*, metre, yard.
mettre, *v. ir.*, (§279), to put, put on; *mettre à la porte*, to put out of doors; *se mettre*, to dress; *il est bien mis*, he is well dressed; *se mettre à*, to begin; *se mettre à table*, to sit down to dinner, etc.
midi, *n. m.*, noon.
mien, -ne (le, la), *poss. pron.*, mine.
mieux, *adv.*, better, best.
minuit, *n. m.*, midnight.
moi, *pers. pron.*, to me, me; I.
moins, *adv.*, less; *à dix heures moins quinze*, at fifteen minutes to ten.
mois, *n. m.*, month.
moitié, *n.f.*, half.
mon, ma, mes, *poss. adj.*, my.
monde, *n. m.*, world; *tout le monde*, everybody.

monsieur, *n. m.*, sir, gentleman; contracted into *M.*, Mr.; *messieurs*, *plur.*, gentlemen.
montre, *n.f.*, watch.
morceau, *n. m.*, bit, piece.

N.

navire, *n. m.*, ship.
ne, *adv.*, no, not; *ne ... pas*, not; *ne ... jamais*, never.
nécessaire, *adj.*, necessary.
négligent, *adj.*, negligent, careless.
neuf, *num. adj.*, nine.
neuf, -ve, *adj.*, new.
ni, *conj.*, neither, nor; *ni ... ni*, neither ... nor.
noir, *adj.*, black.
non, *adv.*, no, not.
notre, nos, *poss. adj.*, our.
nôtre (le, la), *poss. pron.*, ours.
nous, *pers. pron.*, we, us.
nouveau, nouvel, nouvelle, new; *que dit-on de nouveau?*, *qu'y a-t-il de nouveau?*, what is the news?
novembre, *n.m.*, November.

O.

obéir, *v. r.*, to obey.
octobre, *n. m.*, October.
œuvre, *n. f. m.*, work.
offenser, *v. r.*, to offend.
oie, *n. f.*, goose.
oiseau, *n. m.*, bird.
on, *indef. pron.*, one, people, we.
oncle, *n. m.*, uncle.
onze, *num. adj.*, eleven.
or, *n. m.*, gold.
oser, *v. r.*, to dare.
ôter, *v. r.*, to take off.
ou, *conj.*, either, or.
où, *adv.*, where, whither, in which.
oui, *adv.*, yes.

ouvrage, *n. m.*, work.
ouvrier, *n. m.*, workman.

P.

pain, *n. m.*, bread.
panier, *n. m.*, basket.
papier, *n. m.*, paper.
par, *prep.*, by.
parce que, *conj.*, because.
pardon, *interj.*, I beg your pardon.
parent, -e, *n. m.f.*, relative, parent.
parler, *v. r.*, to speak.
partir, *v. ir.*, (§248), to depart, leave.
pas, *adv.*; *ne ... pas*, not; *je n'en ai pas*, I have none.
passé, *adj.*, past; *l'année passée*, last year.
passer, *v. r.*, to pass; *passer devant*, to go past.
passer chez, to call on.
pasteur, *n. m.*, pastor.
pâtisserie, *n.f.*, pastry.
pauvre, *adj.*, poor.
pays, *n. m.*, country.
paysan, -ne, *n. m. f.*, peasant.
pendant, *prep.*, during, for.
pendre, *v.ir.*, (§291), to hang.
pensée, *n. f.*, thought.
penser, *v. r.*, to think; *je pense à cela*, I think of that.
perdre, *v. ir.*, (§291), to lose.
perdrix, *n.f.*, partridge.
perdu, *adj.*, lost.
père, *n. m.*, father.
permission, *n. f.*, permission.
personne, *n. f.*, person; *plur.*, people.
personne, *pron. m.*, anybody, nobody; *ne ... personne*, nobody.
petit, *adj.*, little, small.
peu, *adv.* and *n. m.*, little, few.

VOCABULARY. 377

peur, *n. f.*, fear; *avoir peur*, to be afraid.
philosophie, *n. f.*, philosophy.
pierre, *n. f.*, stone.
pire, *adj.*, worse, worst.
plaire, *v. ir.*,(§282), to please; *s'il vous plaît*, if you please.
plaisir, *n. m.*, pleasure.
planche, *n.f.*, board, plank.
pleurer, *v. r.*, to weep, cry.
plume, *n. f.*, feather, pen.
plus, *adv.*, more; *ne... plus*, no more, no longer.
poche, *n. f.*, pocket.
poète, *n. m.*, poet.
poire, *n.f.*, pear.
poirier, *n. m.*, pear-tree.
poisson, *n. m.*, fish.
poliment, *adv.*, politely.
pomme, *n.f.*, apple.
pommier, *n. m*, apple-tree.
porte, *n.f.*, door.
porte-monnaie, *n.m.*, purse.
porter, *v. r.*, to carry, wear; *se porter*, to be, do.
poste, *n.f.*, post, post-office.
pour, *prep.*, for.
pour que, *conj.*, in order to.
pourquoi, *adv.*, why.
pouvoir, *v. ir.*, (§301), to be able; may, can; *cela se peut*, that may be.
précis, *adj.*, precise; *à trois heures précises*, at three o'clock precisely.
premier, -ère, *adj.*, first.
prendre, *v. ir.*, (§283), to take, get.
présent, *adj.*, present; *à présent*, at present, now.
presque, *adv.*, almost.
prêter, *v. r.*, to lend.
prier, *v. r.*, to pray, beg, ask.
printemps, *n. m.*, spring.
prochain, *adj.*, next; *l'année prochaine*, next year.

produit, *n. m.*, product.
professeur, *n. m.*, professor, teacher.
promener (se), *v. ir.*, (§241, 1), to take a walk, etc.
propriété, *n.f.*, property.
prospérité, *n.f.*, prosperity.
prune, *n.f.*, plum.
punir, *v. r.*, to punish.

Q.

quand, *adv.* and *conj.*, when, whenever; *depuis quand?*, how long?
quart, *n. m.*, quarter; *à six heures et quart*, at a quarter past six.
quatorze, *num. adj.*, fourteen.
quatre *num. adj.*, four.
que, *rel.* and *inter. pron.*, that, which, what.
que, *conj.*, that, than, as.
que, *adv.*, how; *ne... que*, only.
quel, -le, *adj.*, what, which.
quelque, *adj.*, some.
quelquefois, *adv.*, sometimes.
quelqu'un, -une, *indef. pron*, some one, any one.
qui, *rel.* and *inter. pron.*, who, that, whom; *à qui?*, whose?
quinze, *num. adj.*, fifteen; *quinze jours*, a fortnight.
quitter, *v. r.*, to leave.
quoi, *rel.* and *inter. pron.*, what.
quoique, *conj.*, although.

R.

raconter, *v. r.*, to relate, tell.
raison, *n. f.*, reason; *avoir raison*, to be in the right.
rappeler, *v. ir.*, (§241, 2), to recall.
réciter, *v. r.*, to recite.

récompense, *n. f.*, reward.
regarder, *v. r.*, to look at.
regretter, *v. r.*, to regret.
réjouir (se), *v.r.*, to rejoice.
rencontrer, *v. r.*, to meet.
rendre, *v. ir.*, (§291), to give back.
rentrer, *v. r.*, to return (home).
respecter, *v. r.*, to respect; *se respecter*, to respect one's self.
restaurant, *n. m.*, restaurant.
rester, *v. r.*, to stay.
retard, *n. m.*, delay; *en retard*, late.
retour, *n. m.*, return.
réunir (se), *v. r.*, to assemble, gather, meet.
réussir, *v. r.*, to succeed.
riche, *adj.*, rich.
rien, *indef. pron. m.*, anything, nothing; *ne.. rien*, nothing.
robe, *n.f.*, dress.
rouge, *adj.*, red.
rompre, *v. r.*, to break.
rue, *n.f.*, street.

S.

samedi, *n. m.*, Saturday.
sans, *prep.*, without.
sans que, *conj.*, without.
savoir, *v.ir.*, (§302), to know.
se, *ref. pron.*, one's self, for one's self; *cela se fait*, that is done; *cela se dit*, that is said.
seau, *n.m.*, pail.
seize, *num. adj.*, sixteen.
semaine, *n.f.*, week.
sept, *num. adj.*, seven.
septembre, *n. m.*, September.
si, *conj.*, if, whether.
si, *adv.*, so: yes; *mais si*, yes indeed.
sien, -ne (le, la), his, hers, its.

six, *num. adj.*, six.
sixième, *num. adj.*, sixth.
sœur, *n. f.*, sister.
soie, *n. f.*, silk.
soif, *n. f*, thirst; *avoir soif*, to be thirsty.
soir, *n. m.*, evening; *hier (au) soir*, yesterday evening; *le soir*, in the evening.
sommeil, *n. m.*, sleep; *avoir sommeil*, to be sleepy.
son, sa, ses, *poss. adj*, his, her, its.
sortir, *v. ir.*, (§248), to go out, come out.
sou, *n. m.*, halfpenny, cent.
souhaiter, *v. r.*, to wish.
soulier, *n. m.*, shoe.
sous, *prep.*, under.
souvenir, *n. m.*, remembrance.
souvent, *adv.*, often.
sucre, *n. m.*, sugar.
suite, *n. f.*, sequel; *et ainsi de suite*, and so on; *tout de suite*, immediately.
sur, *prep.*, on, upon; *sur vous*, with you, about you.
surtout, *n. m.*, overcoat.

T.

table, *n. f.*, table.
tableau, *n. m.*, picture.
tant, *adv.* and *n. m.*, so much, so many.
tant que, *conj.*, as long as.
tante, *n. f.*, aunt.
te, *pers. pron.*, thee, to thee; you, to you.
temps, *n. m.*, time, weather; *dans ce temps-là*, at that time; *de temps à autre*, now and then.
tête, *n. f.*, head.
thème, *n. m.*, exercise.
toi, *pers. pron.*, to thee, thee; to you, you.
tomber, *v. r.*, to fall.
tome, *n. m.*, volume.
ton, ta, tes, *poss. adj.*, thy, your.
tort, *n. m.*, wrong; *avoir tort*, to be in the wrong.
tôt, *adv.*, soon; *plus tôt*, sooner.
toujours, *adv.*, always, still.
tout, toute, tous, *adj.*, all, every.
train, *n. m.*, train.
travailler, *v. r.*, to work.
treize, *num. adj.*, thirteen.
trente, *num. adj.*, thirty.
très, *adv.*, very.
triste, *adj.*, sad.
trois, *num. adj.*, three.
tromper, *v. r.*, to deceive; *se tromper*, to be mistaken; *se tromper de chemin*, to take the wrong road.
trop, *adv.* and *n. m.*, too; too much, too many.
trouver, *v. r.*, to find; think; *aller trouver*, to go to; *vous trouvez ?*, do you think so ?; *se trouver*, to be.
tu, *pers. pron.*, thou, you.
tuer, *v. r.*, to kill.

U.

un, une, *num. adj.* and *indef. art.*, one, a, an.
utile, *adj.*, useful.

V.

vapeur, *n. f.*, steam.
vendre, *v. ir.*, (§291), to sell; *se vendre*, to sell.
vendredi, *n. m*, Friday.
venir, *v. ir.* (§259), to come; *venez me voir*, come and see me; *il vient de partir*, he has just gone.
vent, *n. m.*, wind.
vers, *prep.*, towards, about.
vertu, *n. f.*, virtue.
viande, *n. f.*, meat.
vieux, vieil, vieille, *adj.*, old; *mon vieux*, old fellow.
village, *n. m.*, village.
ville, *n. f.*, town, city.
vingt, *num. adj.*, twenty.
visiter, *v. r.*, to visit.
vite, *adv.*, quickly, fast.
voici, *prep.*, here is, here are, see here.
voilà, *prep.*, there is, there are, see there.
voir, *v. ir.*, (§304), to see.
voisin, -e, *adj.* and *n. m. f.*, neighbour.
voiture, *n. f.*, carriage.
voler, *v. r.*, to steal.
volume, *n. m.*, volume.
votre, vos, *poss. adj.*, your.
vôtre (le, la), *poss. pron.*, yours.
vouloir, *v. ir.*, (§305), to wish, will; *voulez-vous bien le faire ?*, will you kindly do it ?; *vous voudriez le faire*, you would like to do it.
vous, *pers. pron.*, you.

Y.

y, *pron.*, there, in it, to it.

ENGLISH-FRENCH.

[*h* aspirate is indicated thus: '*h*.]

A.

a, *un*.
abandon, *abandonner*.
abbess, *abbesse*.
ability, *capacité*, f., *talent*, m.
able; be —, *pouvoir* (§301).
about, *de*, *sur*, *environ*;
 — three o'clock, *vers les trois heures*; — it, *en*; bo —, *s'agir de*, *être sur le point de*, *aller* (§242).
above, *au-dessus de*.
abroad, *à l'étranger*.
absence, *absence*, f.
absent, *absent*.
absolutely, *absolument*.
abundant, *abondant*.
accept, *accepter*.
accidental, *accidentel*.
according to, *selon*.
account; on — of, *à cause de*.
ache; have head —, *avoir mal à la tête*.
acquaintance, *connaissance*, f.
acquire, *acquérir* (§244).
act, *agir*.
action, *action*, f.
actor, *acteur*, *comédien*.
add, *ajouter*.
address, *adresser*.
adjective, *adjectif*, m.
admire, *admirer*.
admit, *admettre* (§279).
adorn, *faire* (§276) *l'ornement de*.
advance, *avancer* (§239, 1).
advice, *avis*, m., *conseil*, m.
advise, *conseiller*.
affair, *affaire*, f.

affection, *affection*, f.
afraid; be —, *avoir peur*, *craindre* (§271); be much —, *avoir grand'peur*, *avoir bien peur*.
Africa, *Afrique*, f.
after, prep. and adv., *après*.
after, conj., *après que*.
afternoon, *après-midi*, m. f.
afterwards, *après*.
again, *encore*, *encore une fois*, *de nouveau*.
age, *âge*, m.
ago, *il y a*.
agreeable, *agréable*.
aid, *aider*.
alarm, *alarme*, f.
alight, *descendre* (§291).
all, *tout*; not at —, *pas du tout*.
allow, *permettre* (§279).
almost, *presque*.
alone, *seul*.
already, *déjà*.
Alsace, *Alsace*, f.
also, *aussi*.
although, *quoique*, *bien que*.
always, *toujours*.
ambassador, *ambassadeur*.
America, *Amérique*, f.
American, *américain*.
amiable, *aimable*.
among, amongst, *parmi*, *entre*, *chez*.
amuse, *amuser*.
an, *un*.
ancestors, *ancêtres*, *aïeux*.
ancient, *ancien*.
and, *et*.
angry at (with), *fâché de (contre)*; be (get) —, *se fâcher*.
animal, *animal*, m.

annoy, *ennuyer* (§240).
another, *un autre*, *encore un*.
answer, n., *réponse*, f.
answer, v., *répondre* (§291).
antiquity, *antiquité*, f.
anxious; be —, *tenir à* (§259).
any, *de*, *du*, *en*, *aucun*, *quelconque*, *tout*; don't give him —, *ne lui en donnez pas*; have you —?, *en avez-vous?*.
anybody, any one, *quelqu'un*; not ...— , *ne*....*personne*.
anything, *quelque chose*, m; not ....—, *ne* ....*rien*; — good, *quelque chose de bon*; not ....— good, *ne* .... *rien de bon*.
anywhere; not .... —, *ne* .... *nulle part*.
apiece, *chacun*, *la pièce*.
appear, *paraître* (§269), *sembler*, *comparaître* (§209).
appetite, *appétit*, m.
applaud, *applaudir*.
apple, *pomme*, f.
apple-tree, *pommier*, m.
appoint, *nommer*.
approach, n., *approche*, f.
approach, v., *s'approcher de*.
approbation, *approbation*, f.
approve, *trouver bon*.
argument, *argument*, m.
Ariosto, *Arioste*.
arise, *s'élever* (§241), *naître* (§281).
arithmetic, *arithmétique*, f.
arm, *bras*, m.
army, *armée*, f.
around, *autour de*.
arrange, *arranger* (§239).

arrival, *arrivée*, f.
arrive, *arriver*.
art, *art*, m.
article, *article*, m.
artist, *artiste*.
as, *aussi, si, comme, pendant que, en;* as ... —,
aussi ... que; not (—) so
... —, *pas (aussi) si* ...
que; — long —, *tant que;*
— soon —, *aussitôt que;*
— if, *comme si*.
ascend, *monter (sur)*.
ashamed ; be (feel) —, *avoir honte*.
ask, *demander, prier;* —
for, *demander;* — him
for it, *le lui demander*.
asleep, *endormi;* be —, *être endormi, dormir* (§248);
fall —, *s'endormir* (§245).
assail, *assaillir*(§247).
assemble, *se réunir*.
assist, *aider*.
associate, *s'associer*.
assure, *assurer*.
astonish, *étonner*.
astonishment, *étonnement*, m.
at, *à, chez, de;* — my father's, *chez mon père;* —
my house, *chez moi*.
attach, *attacher*.
attack, *attaquer*.
attention, *attention*, f. ; pay
(give) —, *faire* (§276) attention.
auburn, *châtain*.
audience, *assistants*, m. plur.
August, *août*, m.
Augustus, *Auguste*.
aunt, *tante*.
author, *auteur*.
autumn, *automne*, m.
avidity, *avidité*, f.
avoid, *éviter*.
await, *attendre* (§291).
awake, *se réveiller*.

axe, *'hache*, f.

B.

back, n., *dos*, m.; be —, *être de retour*.
bad, *mauvais, méchant*.
badly, *mal;* hurt (very) —,
faire beaucoup de mal à.
ball, *bal*, m.
banish, *bannir*.
bank, *bord*, m. ; on the —,
au bord.
barefoot, *nu-pieds, les pieds nus*.
bargain, *marché*, m.
bask, *se chauffer*.
basket, *panier*, m.
Bastille, *Bastille*, f.
battle, *bataille*, f.
be, *être, y avoir;* — (of
health), *se porter, aller*
(§242); — about to, *aller,
devoir* (§294) ; — (of
weather), *faire* (§276) ; —
(of age), *avoir;* — (of
time), *y avoir;* is he finishing?, *finit-il?;* are they
not?, *n'est-ce pas?;* how
are you?, *comment vous
portez-vous?, comment
allez-vous?, comment ça
va-t-il?, comment ça va?;*
I am well, *je me porte
bien, ça va bien;* it is fine,
il fait beau; I am to do
it, *je dois le faire;* is it?,
vraiment?.
bear, *ours*, m.
beard, *barbe*, f.
beast, *animal*, m.
beat, *battre* (§261).
beautiful, *beau*.
beauty, *beauté*, f.
because, *parce que*.
become, (suit) *seoir* (§295),
devenir (§259); *se faire*
(§276) ; what has — of
her?, *qu'est-elle devenue?*.

bed, *lit*, m. ; be in —, *être au
lit;* go to —, *se coucher*.
bed-room, *chambre à coucher*.
before, prep., *devant* (of
place); *avant* (of time).
before, conj., *avant que*.
before, adv., *auparavant*.
beg, *mendier*.
beggar, *mendiant*.
begin, *commencer* (§239, 1),
se mettre à (§279).
beginning, *commencement*, m.
behave, *se comporter*.
behead, *décapiter*.
behind, *derrière*.
believe, *croire* (§272) ; it is
believed, *on croit*.
bell, *cloche*, f.; little bell,
grelot, m.
belong, *être à, appartenir*
(§259).
benefactor, *bienfaiteur*.
beside, *à côté de*.
besides, *d'ailleurs*.
best, adj., *le meilleur*.
best, adv., *le mieux*.
better, adj., *meilleur*.
better, adv., *mieux;* be —,
valoir (§303) *mieux*.
between, *entre*.
beware, *prendre*(§283)*garde*.
bid good-bye, *dire* (§274) *adieu à*.
big, *grand, gros*.
bird, *oiseau*, m.
birthday, *fête*, f.
bite, *mordre* (§291).
bitterly, *amèrement*.
black, *noir*.
blind, *aveugle*.
blond, *blond*.
blue, *bleu*.
blush, *rougir*.
board, *planche*, f.
body, *corps*, m.
boil, *bouillir* (§248).
bold, *'hardi*.

VOCABULARY. 381

book, *livre*, m.
bookseller, *libraire*.
born ; be —, *naître* (§281).
both, *tous (les) deux, l'un et l'autre;* both.... and, *et....et.*
bother !, *peste de !*
bottom, *fond*, m.
box, *boîte*, f.
boy, *garçon, enfant.*
branch, *branche*, f.
brave, *brave.*
bread, *pain*, m.
break, *rompre, casser;* — one's arm, *se casser le bras;* — off, *casser, ôter.*
breakfast, n., *déjeuner*, m.
breakfast, v., *déjeuner.*
breathe, *respirer.*
brick, *brique*, f. ; — house, *maison en briques.*
bride, *mariée.*
bring, (carry) *apporter*, (lead) *amener* (§241, 1) ; — back, *ramener* (§241, 1) ; — down, *descendre* (§201) ; — up, *ramener à la surface.*
brook, *ruisseau*, m.
brother, *frère.*
brother-in-law, *beau-frère.*
build, *bâtir.*
building, *édifice*, m.
bun, *brioche*, f.
burn, *brûler.*
bury, *enterrer.*
business, *commerce*, m., *affaires*, f. plur.; on —, *pour affaires.*
busy, *occupé (de);* be — at, *être à.*
but, *mais;* nothing —, *ne....rien....que.*
butter, *beurre*, m.
buy, *acheter* (§241, 2).
by, *par, de, sur, à;* — what he says, *à ce qu'il dit.*

C.

cage, *cage*, f.
Cain, *Caïn.*
call, *appeler* (§241, 2); — on, *passer chez, visiter.*
can, *pouvoir* (§301), *savoir* (§302); what — he have done?, *qu'a-t-il pu faire?;* I could have, *j'aurais pu.*
Canada, *Canada*, m.
Canadian, *canadien.*
cane, *canne*, f.
cannon-shot, *coup* (m.) *de canon*, m.
capital, adj., *capital.*
capital, n., *capitale*, f.
card, *carte*, f.
care ; — for, *soigner* ; take —, *prendre* (§283) *garde.*
carefully, *soigneusement.*
careless, *négligent.*
carnival, *carnaval*, m.
carpenter, *charpentier.*
carriage, *voiture*, f.
carry, *porter* ; — off, *emporter* ; — the day, *l'emporter.*
case, *cas*, m.; in — (that), *au cas que;* if that be the —, *dans ce cas.*
cat, *chat*, m.
catch, *attraper.*
catholic, *catholique.*
cattle, *bétail*, m. s.
cause, *cause*, f.
cavalry, *cavalerie*, f.
cease, *cesser.*
ceasing ; without —, *sans cesse.*
celebrate, *célébrer* (§241).
celebrated, *célèbre.*
celebration, *fête*, f.
cent, *sou*, m.
centime, *centime*, m.
century, *siècle*, m.
certain, *certain.*
certainly, *certainement.*
change, *monnaie*, f.
chapter, *chapitre*, m.
charge, *charge*, f.
charitable, *charitable.*

charm, *charmer.*
charming, *charmant.*
charmingly, *à ravir.*
chase, *chasser.*
cheap, (à) *bon marché; peu coûteux;* cheaper, *à meilleur marché, moins cher.*
cheese, *fromage*, m
cherry, *cerise*, f.
chief, *chef.*
child, *enfant*, m. f.
chimney, *cheminée*, f.
China, *Chine*, f.
chopper, *bûcheron.*
christian, *chrétien.*
Christopher, *Christophe.*
church, *église*, f. ; at (to) —, *à l'église.*
city, *ville*, f. ; in the —, *à la ville.*
city-hall, *hôtel* (m.) *de ville.*
claimant, *prétendant.*
class, *classe*, f.
clean, *nettoyer* (§240).
clearly, *clairement.*
clever, *habile, fort.*
cleverly, *habilement.*
climb, *grimper.*
clock, *horloge*, f.
close, *fermer, clore* (§204).
cloth, *étoffe*, f.
clothe, *vêtir* (§200).
clothes, *habits*, m. plur.
clumsy fellow, *maladroit.*
coat, *habit*, m.
cock, *coq.*
cold, *froid;* be — (of living beings), *avoir froid;* be — (of weather), *faire* (§270) *froid;* I have — hands, *j'ai froid aux mains;* catch a —, *s'enrhumer.*
college, *collège*, m.
colossal, *colossal.*
Columbus, *Colomb.*
come, *venir* (§259), *arriver;* — back, — home, *revenir* (§259); — to see, — and see, *venir voir;* — down,

descendre (§291); — up, monter, arriver; — in, entrer; — out, sortir (§248); come !, voyons !, allons !.
comfortable; be —, faire (§276) bon.
command, commander.
commandment, commandement, m.
commence, commencer (§239).
commit, commettre (§279).
companion, compagnon, m.
company, compagnie, f.; in — with, en compagnie de.
complain, se plaindre (§271).
complete, complet.
complicated, compliqué.
compliment, compliment, m.
composedly, tranquillement.
comprise, comprendre (§283).
conceal, cacher.
concert, concert, m.
conclude, conclure (§265).
condemn, condamner.
condition, condition, f.
confess, avouer.
confidence, confiance, f.
confound, confondre (§291).
conquer, conquérir (§244), vaincre (§290).
conscience, conscience, f.
consecrate, bénir (§245).
consent, consentir (§248).
consider, considérer (§241).
construct, construire (§266).
contain, contenir (§259).
continually, sans cesse.
continue, continuer.
contract, contrat, m.
convenient, commode.
cool, frais.
copy, exemplaire, m., copie, f.
coral, corail, m.
corkscrew, tire-bouchon, m.

corner, coin, m.
costs, frais, m. plur.
cost, coûter.
country, pays, m.; — (as opposed to town), campagne, f.; (native) —, patrie, f.; in the —, à la campagne.
county-town, chef-lieu, m.
couple, couple, m. f.
courage, courage, m.; take —, prendre (§283) courage.
court, cour, f.
cousin, cousin, m., cousine, f.
cover, couvrir (§258).
cow, vache.
cowboy, vacher.
crawl, se traîner.
create, créer.
creature, créature, f.
crime, crime, m.
criminal, criminel.
critic, critique, m.
Croesus, Crésus.
crops, récolte, f.
cross, méchant.
crowd, foule, f.
crown, couronne, f.
cry, pleurer, crier; — out, crier.
cup, coupe, f.
cupboard, armoire, f.
cure, guérir.
curse, maudire (§274).
cut, couper.

D.

daily, tous les jours.
dance, danser.
danger, danger, m.
dangerous, dangereux.
dare, oser.
dark, noir; be —, faire (§276) noir (obscur).
daughter, fille.
day, jour, m., journée, f.; the — after, le lendemain

(de); the — after to-morrow, après-demain; the —before yesterday, avant-hier; all — (long), toute la journée; from — to —, de jour en jour; be — (daylight), faire (§276) jour.
dead, mort.
deaf-mute, deaf and dumb, sourd-muet.
deal; a great —, beaucoup.
dear, cher; not so —, pas si cher, moins cher.
death, mort, f.
debt, dette, f.
decanter, carafe, f.
deceive, tromper.
declare, déclarer.
decline, déchoir (§236).
deep, profond.
defect, défaut, m.
dejection, abattement, m.
delay, différer (§241).
delight in, se plaire à (§252).
delightful, charmant.
deliverance, délivrance, f.
deny, nier.
depart, partir (§248).
depend on, dépendre de (§291).
describe, décrire (§275).
deserve, mériter.
desire, n., envie, f.; I have no —, je n'ai pas envie.
desire, v., désirer, vouloir (§305).
despair, désespérer (§241).
destroy, détruire (§266).
determine, déterminer, résoudre (§284).
devour, dévorer.
dial, cadran, m.
diameter, diamètre, m.
die, mourir (§256); — away, se mourir.
difference, différence, f.; that makes no —, cela ne fait rien.
difficult, difficile.

VOCABULARY. 383

difficulty, *difficulté*, f.
diminish, *diminuer*.
dine, *dîner*.
dinner, *dîner*, m. ; the —
  hour, *l'heure du dîner*.
direct, *droit*.
direction, *direction*, f.
disagreeable, *désagréable*.
disappear, *disparaître*
  (§269).
discover, *découvrir* (§258).
discuss, *discuter*.
discussion, *discussion*, f.
dishes, *vaisselle*, f.
disobliging, *désobligeant*.
disperse, *se disperser*.
displease, *déplaire* (§282).
dispute, *se disputer*.
distinction, *distinction*, f.
distinguished, *distingué*.
distract, *distraire* (§289).
dive, *plonger* (§239).
divide, *partager* (§239).
do *faire* (§276) ; — (of
  health), *se porter* ; — you
  finish ?, *finissez-vous ?*; he
  does not speak, *il ne parle
  pas* ; does he not ?, *n'est-
  ce pas ?* ; don't speak, *ne
  parlez pas*.
doctor, *docteur, médecin*.
doctrine, *doctrine*, f.
dog, *chien*, m.
dollar, *dollar*, m., *piastre*,
  f.
door, *porte*, f.
doubt, n., *doute*, m. ; no
  —, *sans doute*.
doubt, v., *douter*.
dramatic, *dramatique*.
draw, *tracer* (§239); — near,
  s'approcher.
drawing, *dessin*, m.
dream, *rêve*, m., *songe*, m.
dress, n., *robe*, f.
dress, v., *se mettre* (§279),
  s'habiller ; be dressed,
  être mis.
drink, *boire* (§262).

drive, *conduire* (§266), *mener* (§241, 1), *mouvoir*
  (§299), *chasser* ; go for a
  —, be out for a —, *se
  promener* (§241) *en voiture* ; — away, *chasser*.
drown, *se noyer* (§210).
dry, *sec*.
duke, *duc*.
dupe, *dupe*, f.
during, *pendant*.
duty, *devoir*, m.

E.

each, *chaque, tout*.
each one, *chacun*.
each other, *se, l'un (à) l'autre*.
ear-ache, *mal aux oreilles*.
early, *de bonne heure*.
earn, *gagner*.
earth, *terre*, f.
easily, *facilement*.
easy, *facile*.
eat, *manger* (§239, 2) ; — (=
  graze), *paître* (§269).
economical, *économe*.
educated, *instruit*.
education, *éducation*, f.
eight, *huit*.
eighteen, *dix-huit*.
eighty, *quatre-vingt(s)*.
either, *ou* ; nor ... —, *ni
  ... non plus*.
eldest, *aîné*.
elect, *élire* (§278).
elephant, *éléphant*, m.
eleven, *onze*.
else, *autre* ; not .... anything —, nothing —, *ne
  .... rien autre*.
elsewhere, *autre part, ailleurs*.
emperor, *empereur*.
enclose, *clore* (§264).
enclosed, *ci-inclus*.
encourage, *encourager*
  (§239).
end, n., *fin*, f.

end, v., *finir, se terminer* ;
  come to a bad —, *finir mal*.
enemy, *ennemi*.
engage, *s'engager* (§239).
England, *Angleterre*, f.
English, *anglais* ; Englishman, *Anglais*.
engraver, *graveur*.
enjoy, *jouir de* ; — one's
  self, *s'amuser*.
enough, *assez* ; not —, *pas
  assez*.
enter, *entrer (dans)*.
enterprise, *entreprise*, f.
equal ; be — (to), *égaler*.
equivalent, *équivalent*, m.
error, *erreur*, f.
escape, *éviter, échapper*.
estate, *biens*, m. plur.
Europe, *Europe*, f.
European, *européen*, f.
even, *même* ; — if, —
  though, *quand même*.
evening, *soir*, m., *soirée*, f. ;
  in the —, *le soir* ; last —,
  hier (au) soir.
ever, *jamais*.
every, *tout, chaque* ; — Sunday, *tous les dimanches* ;
  — other day, *tous les
  deux jours*.
everybody, *tout le monde*.
everyone, *chacun*.
everywhere, *partout*.
evil, *mal*, m.
exactly, *exactement, pré-
  cisément*.
examine, *examiner*.
excavation, *excavation*, f.
exclaim, *s'écrier*.
excuse, n., *excuse*, f.
excuse, v., *excuser*.
exercise, *thème*, m.
exhibit, *exposer*.
expect, *attendre, s'attendre*
  (§291), *compter, espérer*
  (§241).
expense, *dépense*, f., *dépens*,
  m. plur.

explain, *expliquer.*
eye, *œil,* m., plur. *yeux.*

F.

face, *figure,* f., *visage,* m.;
shut the door in one's —,
*fermer la porte au nez à
qqun.*
fact, *fait,* m.
fail, *faillir* (§249); — in
(to), *manquer à.*
fairy, *fée,* f.; —story, *conte
de fée.*
faithful, *fidèle.*
fall *tomber*; —due, *échoir*
(§297); —out *se brouiller.*
familiarity, *familiarité,* f.
family, *famille,* f.
famous, *fameux.*
far, *loin*; be —, *s'en falloir*
(§298) *de beaucoup;* —
from, *loin que, loin de;*
— away, *loin, loin d'ici,
loin de vous, loin d'elle,
etc.*; as — as, *jusqu'à.*
farmer, *fermier, cultivateur.*
farmhouse, *ferme.*
farm-servant, *valet de ferme.*
fashion, *mode,* f.
fast, *vite.*
fastidious *difficile.*
fate, *destin,* m.
father, *père.*
fault, *défaut,* m.
favour, *faveur,* f.
favourable, *favorable.*
favourite, *favori.*
fear, n., *crainte,* f., *peur,* f.;
for — that, *de crainte que;*
for — of, *de crainte de.*
fear, v., *craindre* (§271),
avoir peur.
feast, *festin,* m., *banquet,* m.
feel, *sentir* (§248).
feeling, *sentiment,* m.
fell, *abattre* (§261).
fellow, *garçon*; the brave
little —, *le petit bonhomme.*

fence, *clôture,* f.
fetch, *aller* (§242) *chercher.*
fever, *fièvre,* f.
few, *peu, quelques*; but —,
*ne....guère, ne....que
peu.*
field, *champ,* m.
fifteen, *quinze.*
fifth, *cinquième.*
fifty, *cinquante.*
fight, *combattre* (§261).
finally... do, *finir par.*
find, *trouver*; be found, *se
trouver;* —out, *découvrir*
(§258).
fine, *beau*; be—(of weather),
faire beau (temps).
fine-looking, *beau, élégant.*
finger, *doigt,* m.
finish, *finir.*
fire, *feu,* m.
first, *premier;* make.. at
—, *commencer* (§239) *par.*
fish, n., *poisson,* m.
fish, v., *pêcher.*
fishing, *pêche,* f.
fit, *aller* (à) (§242).
fitting, *convenable.*
five, *cinq.*
flattering, *flatteur.*
flee, *fuir, s'enfuir* (§252).
fleet, *flotte,* f.
Florida, *Floride,* f.
flower, *fleur,* f.
fly, *voler.*
foggy; be —, *faire* (§276)
du brouillard.
folded, *croisé.*
follow, *suivre* (§287).
following, *suivant.*
folly, *folie,* f.
fond; be — of, *aimer.*
foolish, *fou.*
foot, *pied,* m.; on —, *à
pied.*
top, *fat.*
for, prep., *pour, pendant,
de, contre, par:* I am sorry
— it, *j'en suis fâché*; I

have been here — a week,
*je suis ici depuis une
semaine.*
for, conj., *car.*
forbid, *défendre* (§291).
force, n., *force,* f.
force, v., *forcer* (§239).
foreign, *étranger.*
forest, *forêt,* f.
forget, *oublier.*
form *former.*
former (the), *celui-là.*
fortnight, *quinzaine,* f.,
quinze jours, m.
fortunate, *heureux.*
fortune, *fortune,* f.; good
—, *bonheur,* m.
forty, *quarante.*
four, *quatre.*
fourteen, *quatorze.*
fourth, *quatrième.*
fox, *renard,* m.
franc, *franc,* m.
France, *France,* f.
free, *libre.*
freeze, *geler* (§241, 2).
French, *français;* Frenchman, *Français.*
fresh, *frais.*
Friday, *vendredi,* m.
friend, *ami,* m., *amie,* f.
friendly, *aimable.*
friendship, *amitié,* f.
frog, *grenouille,* f.
from, *de, à, à partir de,
dans, d'après, depuis.*
front; in — of, *devant.*
fruit, *fruit,* m.
frying-pan, *poêle,* f.
fulfil, *accomplir.*
full, *plein.*
future, *futur.*

G.

garden, *jardin,* m.
gate, *porte,* f.
gather, *cueillir* (§247).
gathering, *assemblée,* f.
gay, *gai.*

general, *général*.
generally, *en général, généralement*.
generous, *généreux*.
gentleman, *monsieur*
German, *allemand*.
get, *prendre* (§283), *aller* (§242) *chercher; devenir* (§259); — made, *faire faire*(§276);—there, *y arriver;* — up, *se lever* (§241); — over, *passer, traverser*.
ghost, *revenant*, m.
gird on, *ceindre* (§371).
girl, *fille*.
give, — away, *donner;* — back, *rendre* (§291).
glad (at, of), *content (de), charmé (de)*.
glory, *gloire*, f.
glove, *gant*, m.
go, *aller* (§242), *marcher*
— away, *s'en aller, partir* (§248); — for, — after, and get, *aller chercher;* — back (again), *retourner;*—to bed, *se coucher;* —down, *descendre* (§291); — down town, *aller en ville;* — home, *aller chez soi, rentrer;* — in (to), *entrer (dans);* — for a drive, *se promener* (§241) *en voiture;* — for a row, (sail), *se promener en bateau;* — (out) for a walk, *aller se promener (à pied), aller faire une promenade (à pied);* — on, *avancer* (§239); — out, *sortir* (§248); — past, — by, *passer;* —and see, — to see, *aller voir;* —to, *aller trouver;* — up, — upstairs, *monter*.
God, *Dieu*.
gold, *or*, m.
golden, *d'or*.

good, adj., *bon, brave;* be so — as to, be — enough to, *veuillez*.
good, n., *bien*, m.
good-bye, *adieu, au revoir*.
goodness, *bonté*, f.
goods, *marchandises*, f. plur.
gooseberry-bush, *groseillier*, m.
governess, *gouvernante*.
government, *gouvernement*, m.
grace, *grâce*, f.
grammar, *grammaire*, f.
grandfather, *grand-père, aïeul*.
grandmamma, grandmother, *grand'mère*.
grass, *herbe*, f.
gravely, *gravement*.
great, *grand, gros*.
Great Britain, *Grande-Bretagne*, f.
Greek, *grec*.
green, *vert*.
grind, *moudre* (§280).
grocer, *épicier*.
ground, *terre*, f.; upon the —, *à terre*.
grow, *croître* (§273).
grudge; have a — against, *en vouloir à* (§305).
guard, *garde*, m
gun, *fusil*, m.
gypsy, *bohémien*.

II.

hair, *cheveux*, m. plur.
half, *moitié*, f.
half-past two, *deux heures et demie*.
hand, *main*, f.; — (of a clock), *aiguille*, f.
handsome, *beau*.
hang, *pendre* (§291).
happen, *arriver, venir à* (§259).
happily, *heureusement*.
happiness, *bonheur*, m.

happy, *heureux, content*.
hard, adv., *fort*.
hardly, *à peine*.
harm, *faire* (§276) *mal à*.
harp, *'harpe*, f.
hasten, *se hâter, se dépêcher*.
hat, *chapeau*, m.
hate, *'haïr* (§254).
hatred, *'haine*, f.
have, *avoir* (§238); I.— to be there, *il faut que j'y sois;*—built, *faire* (§276) *bâtir;*—hair cut, *se faire couper les cheveux;* — to do with, *avoir affaire à*.
Havre, *le Hâvre*.
hay, *foin*, m.
he, *il, lui, ce, ça;* than —, *que lui;*—who, *celui qui*.
head, *tête*, f.
headache; have —, *avoir mal à la tête*.
heal, *guérir*.
health, *santé*, f.
hear, *entendre* (§291); — from, *recevoir* (§204) *des nouvelles de;* — of, *entendre parler de*.
heart, *cœur*, m.
heat, *chaleur*, f.
help, *aider*.
hen, *poule*, f.
hence, *aussi, donc*.
Henry, *'Henri*.
her, poss. adj., *son, sa, ses; lui ... la (à elle)*.
her, pers. pron., *la, elle;* to —, *lui, à elle*.
here, *ici;* — below, *ici-bas;* — is, — are, *voici*.
hero, *'héros*.
hers, her own, *le sien, à elle*.
herself, *se, elle-même*.
hide, *cacher*.
high, *'haut*.
hill, *colline*, f.
him, *le, lui, celui;* to —, *lui*.
himself, *se, soi, lui, lui-même*.

hinder, *empêcher.*
his, poss. adj., *son, sa, ses; lui... le (à lui).*
his, poss. pron., *le sien, à lui;* — own, *le sien.*
history, *histoire,* f.
hold, *tenir* (§259).
hole, *trou,* m.
holidays, *vacances,* f. plur.
holy, *bénit.*
home; (at) —, *chez soi, à la maison.*
honest, *honnête, loyal, probe.*
honesty, *loyauté,* f., *probité,* f.
honour, n., *honneur,* m.
honour, v., *honorer.*
hope, *espérer* (§241).
horse, *cheval,* m.
horseback; on —, *à cheval.*
hotel, *hôtel,* m.
hour, *heure,* f.
house, *maison,* f.; at (to) my —, *chez moi.*
how, *comment, comme, combien;* — far ?, *combien y a-t-il ?;* — many, — much, *combien, que;* — long have you been here ?, *depuis quand êtes-vous ici ?;* — happy she is !, *qu' elle est heureuse !.*
however, *cependant;* — good, *quelque bon que;* — that may be, *quoi qu'il en soit.*
howl, *cri,* m.
hundred (a, one), *cent.*
hungry, *affamé;* be (feel) —, *avoir faim.*
hunger, *faim,* f.
hunt, *chasser.*
hunter, *chasseur.*
hunting, *chasse,* f.
hurrah for !, *vive (nt) !.*
hurry; be in a —, *être pressé.*
hurt, *faire* (§276) *mal à;* — one's self, *se faire mal.*
husband, *mari, époux.*

I.

I, *je, moi.*
idea, *idée,* f.
idle, *paresseux.*
idleness, *paresse,* f.
if, *si.*
ignorant, *ignorant;* be — of, *ignorer.*
ill, adj., *malade.*
ill, adv. and n., *mal,* m.
ill-fortune, *malheur,* m.
ill treat, *maltraiter.*
illuminate, *illuminer.*
image, *image,* f.
imagine, *s'imaginer.*
immediately, *tout de suite.*
impatient, *impatient.*
important, *important.*
impossible, *impossible.*
in, *dans, en, à, de, sur;* be —, *y être, être chez soi.*
inch, *pouce,* m.
income, *revenu,* m.
increase, *augmenter.*
incur, *courir* (§246).
indeed !, *vraiment !.*
influence, n., *influence,* f.
influence, v., *influencer* (§239).
injustice, *injustice,* f.
ink, *encre,* f.
inn, *auberge,* f.
innkeeper, *aubergiste.*
instead of, *au lieu de.*
institution, *institution,* f.
insult, *dire* (§274) *des injures à, insulter.*
intelligent, *intelligent.*
intend, *avoir (l') intention de.*
intention, *intention,* f.
inter, *enterrer.*
interest, n., *intérêt,* m.; take — in, *prendre* (§283) *intérêt à, s'occuper de.*
interest, v., *intéresser.*
interesting, *intéressant.*
interview (private), *tête-à-tête,* m.

intimate, *intime.*
into, *dans, en;* — it, *y, là-dedans.*
introduce, *présenter.*
invention, *invention,* f.
invite, *inviter.*
Ireland, *Irlande,* f.
iron, *fer,* m.
island, *île,* f.
it, *il, elle, ce; le, la;* of —, *en;* — is you, *c'est vous;* — is they, *ce sont eux.*
Italian, *italien.*
Italy, *Italie,* f.
its, *son, sa, ses; en...le.*
itself, *lui-même; même.*

J.

Japan, *Japon,* m.
John, *Jean.*
joke, *plaisanter.*
journey, *voyage,* m.
judge, n.; be a good —, *se connaître (à, en)* (§269).
judge, *juger* (§239).
July, *juillet,* m.
jump, *sauter.*
June, *juin,* m.
just, *juste, précis;* have —, *venir* (§259) *de, ne faire* (§276) *que de;* — then, *à ce moment;* — as, *au moment où.*
justice, *justice,* f.

K.

keep, *garder, tenir* (§259).
kernel, *amande,* f.
key, *clef,* f.
kick out, *mettre* (§270) *à la porte.*
kill, *tuer, faire* (§276) *mourir.*
kind, n., *sorte,* f.
kind, adj., *bon (pour);* be so — as, be — enough to, *vouloir* (§305) *bien;* it is — of him to, *c'est bon à lui de.*

kindle, *allumer.*
kindly, *bien.*
kindness, *bonté,* f. ; have the — to, *vouloir* (§305) *bien, avoir la bonté de.*
king, *roi.*
kingdom, *royaume,* m. ; United—, *Royaume-Uni.*
kiss, *embrasser, baiser.*
kitchen, *cuisine,* f.
knee, *genou,* m.
knife, *couteau,* m.
knight, *chevalier.*
knock, *frapper.*
know, *savoir* (§302), *connaître* (§269) ; — how, *savoir* (§302).
knowledge, *connaissances,* f. plur.

L.

labour, *labeur,* m.
lack, *manquer ;* much is lacking, *il s'en faut de beaucoup.*
lady, *dame ;* young —, *demoiselle, jeune dame ;* young ladies (in address), *mesdemoiselles.*
lake, *lac,* m.
lamp, *lampe,* f.
lamp-shade, *abat-jour,* m.
landlord, *aubergiste.*
language, *langue,* f. ; — (of animals, etc.), *langage,* m.
large, *grand.*
last, *dernier, passé ;* — year, *l'année dernière, l'année passée ;* — evening, *hier (au) soir ;* — night, *cette nuit ;* at —, *à la fin, enfin.*
last, v., *durer.*
late, *tard, en retard ;* he is —, *il est en retard ;* it is —, *il est tard ;* it is getting —, *il se fait tard.*
lately, *dernièrement.*

Latin, *latin.*
latter (the), *celui-ci.*
laud, *louer.*
laugh (at), *rire (de)* (§285), *se moquer de.*
law, *loi,* f.
lawsuit, *procès,* m.
lazy, *paresseux.*
lead, *mener* (§241, 1), *conduire* (§266).
league, *lieue,* f.
leap, *sauter.*
learn, *apprendre* (§283), *savoir* (§302).
learned, — man, *savant.*
leave, v. tr., *quitter, laisser.*
leave, v. intr., *partir* (§218).
left, *gauche ;* be —, *rester ;* I have none —, *je n'en ai plus.*
leg, *jambe,* f.
lend, *prêter.*
length ; at —, *à la fin.*
less, *moins.*
lesson, *leçon,* f.
lest, *que ... ne, de peur que ... ne.*
let, *laisser, permettre* (§279) ;
— us give, *donnons ;* — him give, *qu'il donne ;* — have, *laisser ;* — in, *laisser entrer.*
letter, *lettre,* f.
liberal, *libéral.*
liberty, *liberté,* f.
library, *bibliothèque,* f.
lie (speak falsely), *mentir* (§248) ; —, *gésir* (§253) ; —
down, *se coucher.*
life, *vie,* f.
light, n., *lumière,* f.
light auburn hair, *cheveux châtain clair.*
like, v., *aimer, trouver, vouloir* (§305) ; I should (very much)—, *j'aimerais (bien), je voudrais (bien) ;* I should — you to do it, *je voudrais que vous le*

fassiez (fissiez) ; — it in, *se plaire à* (§282) ; —better, *aimer mieux.*
like, prep., *comme ;* anything — that (it), *quelque chose (rien) de pareil.*
line, *ligne,* f.
listen (to), *écouter.*
little, adj., *petit ;* —, adv., *peu ;* but —, *ne ... guère, ne ... que peu ;* however —, *pour peu que ;* a — ago, *il y a quelques moments ;* — by —, *peu à peu.*
live, *demeurer, vivre* (§292) ;
long — !, *vive(nt) !.*
living, *vivant ;* — is dear, *il fait cher vivre.*
log, *bûche,* f.
London, *Londres.*
long ; I —, *il me tarde de ;* be — in, *tarder à.*
long, *long, longtemps ;* have you been — here?, *y a-t-il longtemps que vous êtes ici ? ;* as — as, *tant que ;* I have not seen them for a — time, *il y a longtemps que je ne les ai vus.*
longer ; no —, *ne ... plus.*
look, *avoir l'air ;* — at, *regarder ;* — for, *chercher ;* — out of, *regarder par ;* get a good — at, *bien voir* (§304).
look out, *prendre* (§283) *garde.*
lose, *perdre* (§291).
loss, *perte,* f.
loud, *haut.*
love, n., *amour,* m. f., *affection,* f. ; my first —, *mes premières amours.*
love, v., *aimer.*
loyal, *loyal.*

M.

machine, *machine,* f.

mad, *fou.*
madam, *madame,* plur., *mesdames.*
magnificent, *magnifique.*
maid of all work, *bonne à tout faire.*
majority, *majorité,* f.
make, *faire* (§276), *rendre* (§291).
mamma, *maman.*
man, *homme;* the —, that —, *celui;* young men, *jeunes gens.*
manner, *manière,* f.
many, very —, a great —, *beaucoup;* — a, *maint.*
March, *mars,* m.
march, *marcher.*
mark, *marque,* f.
market, *marché,* m.; to (at) —, *au marché.*
marry (=give in marriage), *marier;* — (=take in marriage), *épouser, se marier (à, avec).*
Marseilles, *Marseille,* f.
Mary, *Marie.*
master, *maître.*
masterpiece, *chef-d'œuvre,* m.
matter; what is the — with him?, *qu'a-t-il?;* what is the —?, *qu'y a-t-il?, de quoi s'agit-il?;* no —, that does not —, *n'importe.*
maxim, *maxime,* f.
May, *mai,* m.
may, *pouvoir* (§301); — he do it, *qu'il le fasse;* that — be, *cela se peut;* I might have, *j'aurais pu.*
me, to me, *me, moi*
mean, *vouloir* (§305), *dire.*
meat, *viande,* f.
medicine, *médecine,* f
meet, *rencontrer, se réunir.*
meeting, *assemblée,* f.

memorandum, *mémoire,* m.
memory, *mémoire,* f.
mention; don't — it, *il n'y a pas de quoi.*
merchant, *marchand.*
Mercury, *Mercure.*
mere, *simple.*
merely, *seulement.*
merit, *mériter.*
method, *méthode,* f.
metre, *mètre,* m.
Michael Angelo, *Michel-Ange.*
Michaelmas, *la Saint-Michel.*
midst, *milieu;* into the —, *au milieu.*
mild; be —, *faire* (§276) *doux.*
mile, *mille,* m.
military, *militaire.*
milk, n., *lait,* m.
milk, v., *traire* (§289).
mill, *moulin,* m.
miller, *meunier.*
mine, my own, *le mien, à moi.*
minister, *ministre.*
minute, *minute,* f.; five —s to, *moins cinq (minutes).*
miser, *avare.*
misery, *misère,* f.
misfortune, *malheur,* m.
miss, *manquer.*
mistake; make a —, *se tromper.*
mistaken; be —, *se tromper.*
modern, *moderne.*
moment, *moment,* m.; this —, *à l'instant.*
monarch, *monarque,* m.
monastery, *monastère,* m.
money, *argent,* m.
monk, *moine.*
month, *mois,* m.
Montreal, *Montréal.*
more, *plus, encore, davantage;* have you any — money?, *avez-vous encore*

de l'argent?; I have no —, I have not any —, *je n'en ai plus;* — money than, *plus d'argent que;* I have some —, *j'en ai encore;* no —, *ne . . . plus.*
morning, *matin,* m.; in the —, *le matin;* good —, *bonjour;* it is a cold —, *il fait froid ce matin.*
mortification, *mortification,* f.
most, *très, bien, fort;* it is — beautiful, *c'est tout ce qu'il y a de plus beau;* the — *le plus;* — people, *la plupart des gens.*
mother, *mère.*
mouth, *bouche,* f.
move, *mouvoir, émouvoir* (§299), *se remuer.*
Mr., *M.*
Mrs., *Mme.*
much, *beaucoup, grand'chose, bien, très;* very —, *beaucoup;* as —, *autant;* so —, *tant, tellement.*
mud, *vase,* f.
museum, *musée,* m.
music, *musique* f.
must, *falloir* (§298); you —, *il vous faut* (with infin.), *il faut que vous* (with subj.); he — have done it, *il a dû le faire.*
my, *mon, le; me . . . . le;* — father's, *celui de mon père.*
myself, *me, moi, moi-même.*
mysterious, *mystérieux.*

N.

nail, *clou,* m.
name, *nom,* m.; be named, *s'appeler* (§241); what is his —?, *comment s'appelle-t-il?.*
nap, *somme,* m.
Napoleon, *Napoléon.*

VOCABULARY.

narrow; have a — escape, *l'échapper belle.*
nation, *nation,* f.
national, *national.*
native, *natif.*
natural, *naturel.*
nature, *nature,* f.
naughty, *méchant.*
near, *près de ;* — by, *tout près ;* be —, *penser.*
nearly, *près de, presque.*
necessary, *nécessaire ;* be —, *être nécessaire, falloir* (§298).
neck, *cou,* m.
need, n., *besoin,* m.
need, v., *avoir besoin, falloir* (§298); what does he —?, *que lui faut-il ?, de quoi a-t-il besoin ?*
needless, *inutile.*
neglect, *négliger* (§239).
negro, *nègre,* m.
neighbour, *voisin,* m., *voisine,* f.
neither, *ni l' un ni l' autre ... ne.*
neither... nor, *(ne...)ni... ni.*
never, *ne... jamais.*
nevertheless, *cependant.*
new, *neuf, nouveau.*
New Orleans, *la Nouvelle-Orléans.*
news, *nouvelle(s),* f.; what is the —?, *qu'y a-t-il de nouveau ?*
newly married couple, *nouveaux mariés.*
newspaper, *journal,* m.
next, *prochain, premier ;*
 —year, *l'année prochaine ;*
 — door, *à côté ;* the — one, *celui à côté ;* —morning, *le lendemain matin.*
nice, *joli, gentil.*
night, *nuit,* f.; all —, *(de) toute la nuit.*
nine, *neuf.*

nineteen, *dix-neuf.*
ninety, *quatre-vingt-dix.*
ninety-two, *quatre-vingt-douze.*
no, *non ;* — longer, — more, *ne... plus ;* —money, *(ne...) pas d'argent ;* —one, *(ne...) personne, aucun.*
noble, *noble.*
nobleman, *noble, gentilhomme.*
nobody, *(ne...) personne ;*
 — at all, *ne... qui que ce soit.*
noise, *bruit,* m.
none; we have —, *nous n'en avons pas ;* there are —, *il n'y en a pas ;* to have — left, *n'en avoir plus.*
nonsense !, *allons donc !.*
noon, *midi,* m.
nor, *ni, et ne... pas ;* — ... either, *ni... non plus.*
Normandy, *Normandie,* f.
north, *nord,* m.
North America, *Amérique (f.) du Nord.*
nose, *nez,* m.
not, *ne... pas (point), non ;*
 — that, *non pas que ;* — one, *(ne...) pas un.*
nothing, *(ne...) rien ;* that is — to him, *cela ne lui fait rien ;* —good, *(ne...) rien de bon ;* — at all, *(ne...) rien du tout, ne ... quoi que ce soit ;* do — but, *ne faire que.*
notice, *s'apercevoir (de)* (§204).
novel, *roman,* m.
now, *maintenant, à présent ; tiens !;* not to have —, *n'avoir plus ;* —and then, *de temps en temps*
number, *nombre,* m., *numéro,* m.
numerous, *nombreux.*

O.

oak, *chêne,* m.
oats, *avoine,* f.
obey, *obéir (à).*
oblige, *obliger* (§239).
obliging, *obligeant.*
occasion, *occasion,* f.
occasionally, *de temps en temps.*
occupied, *occupé.*
occur (of ideas), *venir* (§259) *à qqun. à l'esprit.*
o'clock, *heure,* f.; at four —, *à quatre heures.*
of, *de ;* — it, — them, *en, y.*
offend, *offenser, déplaire (à)* (§282).
offer, *offrir* (§258).
often, *souvent ;* how —, *combien de fois.*
oh, *oh.*
old, *vieux, âgé, ancien ;* — boy, — fellow, *mon vieux ;* how — are you ?, *quel âge avez-vous ?;* I am ten years—, *j'ai dix ans ;* — man, *vieillard.*
on, *sur, à, en, de.*
once, *une fois ;* at —, *tout de suite.*
one, adj., *un.*
one, indef. pron., *on ;* an iron —, *un en fer ;* a small —, *un petit ;* the — who, *celui qui ;* that — *celui-là.*
one's, *son ;* le.
one's self, *se, soi.*
only, *seulement, ne... que ;*
 — (one), *seul.*
open, v. tr., *ouvrir* (§258).
open, v.intr., *s'ouvrir* (§258), *éclore* (§204).
open, adj., *ouvert ;* wide—, *grand(e) ouvert(e).*
opium, *opium,* m.
opportune, *opportun.*
opportunity, *opportunité,* f.

or, *ou, ni* (after *sans*).
orator, *orateur.*
order, n., *ordre,* m.; in — to, *afin de;* in — that, *afin que.*
order, v., give —s, *ordonner;* — (=send for), *faire* (§276) *venir.*
organize, *organiser.*
other, *autre;* many —s, *bien d'autres.*
ought, *devoir* (§294); he — to do it, *il devrait le faire;* — to have done it, *il aurait dû le faire.*
our, *notre.*
ours, *le nôtre.*
ourselves, *nous, nous-mêmes.*
out; be —, *être sorti* (§248).
outside, *hors de.*
over, *sur;* be all — with, *en être fait de.*
overcoat, *surtout,* m., *pardessus,* m.
owe, *devoir* (§294).
own, *propre;* my —, *le mien;* of his —, *à lui.*

P.

pail, *seau,* m.
pain, *peine,* f.
paint, *peindre* (§271).
painter, *peintre.*
papa, *papa, mon père.*
paper, *papier,* m.
pardon, n., *pardon,* m.
pardon, v., *pardonner qqch. à qqun.*
parent, *parent,* m.
Parisian, *parisien.*
parliament, *parlement,* m.
parlour, *salon,* m.
parrot, *perroquet,* m.
part, n., *partie,* f., *part,* f.; play a —, *jouer un rôle;* on our —, *de notre part.*
part, v.; — with (from), *se séparer de.*
participle, *participe,* m.

partridge, *perdrix,* f.
pass, *passer* (*devant*).
passion, *passion,* f.
past, *passé,* m.
paternal, *paternel.*
patience, *patience,* f.
patient, *malade,* m. f.
pay, pay for, *payer* (§240); — attention, *faire* (§276) *attention.*
payment, *paiement,* m.
peace, *paix,* f.
peach, *pêche,* f.
pear, *poire,* f.
pear-tree, *poirier,* m.
peasant, *paysan.*
pebble, *caillou,* m.
peel, *peler* (§241, 2).
pen, *plume,* f.
pencil, *crayon,* m.
penny, *deux sous.*
people, on, *peuple,* m., *gens,* m. f. plur.; few —, *peu de gens;* most —, *la plupart des gens.*
perceive, *s'apercevoir (de)* (§294).
perfection, *perfection,* f.
perhaps, *peut-être.*
peril, *péril,* m.
permission, *permission,* f.
permit, *permettre* (§279); we are permitted to, *il nous est permis de.*
persist, *persister.*
person, *personne,* f.
persuade, *persuader.*
petition, *pétition,* f.
Philadelphia, *Philadelphie.*
philosophy, *philosophie,* f.
phrase, *phrase,* f.
physician, *médecin.*
pick up, *ramasser.*
picnic, *pique-nique,* m.
picture, *tableau,* m.
piece, *morceau,* m.
pitifully, *à faire pitié.*
pity; it is a —, *c'est dommage;* which is a great —, (*ce*) *qui est bien dommage.*
pity, v., *plaindre* (§271).
place, n., *lieu,* m., *endroit,* m., *place,* f.; it is my — to, *c'est à moi de.*
place, v., *mettre* (§279), *placer* (§239).
plain, *plaine,* f.
plainly, *franchement.*
plan, *plan,* m.
plant, n., *plante,* f.
plant, v., *planter.*
play, *jouer;* — at (games), *jouer à;* — on (instruments), *jouer de.*
pleasant, *aimable.*
please, *plaire (à)* (§282); if you —, *s'il vous plaît;* as we —, *comme il nous plaira.*
pleased, *content.*
pleasure, *plaisir,* m.
plum, *prune,* f.
pocket, *poche,* f.
poem, *poème,* m.
poet, *poète.*
poetry, *poésie,* f.
Poland, *Pologne,* f.
Pole, *polonais.*
police, *police,* f.
polite, *poli.*
political, *politique.*
pond, *étang,* m.
poor, *pauvre, mauvais.*
population, *population,* f.
portion, *part,* f.
portrait, *portrait,* m.
position; put in a — to, *mettre* (§279) *à même de.*
possession, *possession,* f.
possible, *possible.*
post, post-office, *poste,* f.; put in the —, *mettre* (§279) *à la poste.*
postage stamp, *timbre-poste,* m.
poultry-yard, *basse-cour,* f.
pound, *livre,* f.

powerful, *puissant*.
practise, *mettre* (§279) *en pratique*.
praise, *louer*.
pray, *prier*.
precious, *précieux*.
precisely (of hours), *précis;* at three o'clock —, *à trois heures précises*.
prefer, *aimer mieux, préférer* (§241).
prescribe, *prescrire* (§275).
present, adj., *présent;* at —, *à présent*.
present, n., *cadeau*, m.
present (with), *présenter*.
preserve, *confire* (§268).
president, *monsieur le président*.
pretend, *faire* (§276) *semblant de*.
pretended, *prétendu*.
pretty, adj., *joli*.
pretty, adv., *assez*.
prevail over, *l'emporter sur*.
prevent, *empêcher*.
price, *prix*, m.; at what —, *à quel prix*, (à) *combien*.
priest, *prêtre*.
prince, *prince*.
principle, *principe*, m.
probable, *probable*.
probably, *probablement*.
procession, *cortège*, m.
produce, *produire* (§260).
product, *produit*, m.
progress, *progrès*, m. plur.
promise, n., *promesse*, f.
promise, v., *promettre* (§279).
pronounce, *prononcer* (§239).
property, *propriété*, f., *biens*, m. plur.
prophet, *prophète*.
propose, *proposer*.
prosperity, *prospérité*, f.
prosperous, *florissant* (§251).
prove, *montrer*.
provide with, *fournir*.

province, *province*, f.
prudence, *prudence*, f.
public, *public;* — works, *les travaux publics;* the —, *le public*.
punish, *punir*.
pupil, *élève*, m. f.
purpose: on —, *exprès;* with the —, *dans le but*.
purse, *porte-monnaie*, m.
pursue, *poursuivre* (§287).
put, *mettre, attacher;* — on (clothing), *mettre* (§279); —out (fire, etc.), *éteindre* (§271); — out (of doors), *mettre à la porte;* — to death, *mettre à mort*.

Q.

quality, *qualité*, f.
quantity, *quantité*, f.
quarrel, *dispute*, f.
quarter, *quart*, m.; a — past one, *une heure* (et) *un quart*.
queen, *reine*.
question, *question*, f.
quiet, *tranquille*.
quietly, *tranquillement*.
quite, *tout*.

R.

railroad, railway, *chemin* (m.) *de fer*.
rain, n., *pluie*, f.
rain, v., *pleuvoir* (§300).
rainy; in — weather, *quand il pleut, quand le temps est à la pluie*.
raise, *lever* (§241).
rare, *rare*.
rarely, *rarement*.
rascal, *coquin*.
rat, *rat*, m.
rather, *assez*.
reach, *arriver à*.
read, *lire* (§278).
reading, *lecture*, f.
ready, *prêt*.
really, *réellement, vraiment*.

re-appear, *reparaître* (§269).
reason, *raison*, f.
reasonable, *raisonnable*.
receive, *recevoir* (§294).
recite, *réciter*.
recognize, *reconnaître* (§269).
recompense, n., *récompense*, f.
recompense, v., *récompenser*.
red, *rouge*.
refuge; take —, *se réfugier*.
regret, n., *regret*, m.
regret, v., *regretter*.
regular, *vrai*.
reign, n., *règne*, m.
reign, v., *régner* (§241, 1).
rejoice, *se réjouir*.
rejoin, *rejoindre* (§271).
relative, *parent*, m.
relic, *relique*, f.
religion, *religion*, f.
remain, *rester*.
remains, *restes*, m. plur.
remarkable, *remarquable*.
remember, *se souvenir* (§259), *se rappeler* (§241), *retenir* (§259); — me to them, *rappelez-moi à leur bon souvenir*.
render, *rendre* (§291).
repeat, *répéter* (§241).
reply, make a —, *répondre* (§291).
repose, *repos*, m.
represent, *représenter*.
republic, *république*, f.
reputation, *renommée*, f.
resemble, *ressembler à*.
resolve, *résoudre* (§284).
resort, have —, *avoir recours*.
respect, n., *respect*, m.
respect, v., *respecter*.
respectable, *respectable*.
rest (the), *les autres*.
rest, v. tr., *reposer*.
retain, *garder*.

return, n., *retour*, m.; on my —, *à mon retour*.
return, v., *revenir* (§259), *retourner*; — home, *rentrer*.
reveal, *révéler* (§241).
revolution, *révolution*, f.
reward, n., *récompense*, f.
reward, v., *récompenser*.
ribbon, *ruban*, m.
rich, *riche*.
riches, *richesse*, f.
rid; be — of, get — of, *se débarrasser de*.
ride; go for a —, be out for a —, *se promener* (§241) *à cheval*.
right, adj., *droit*; to the —, *à la droite*.
right, n., *droit*, m.; be (in the) —, *avoir raison*; all — !, *à la bonne heure !*.
rise (up), *se lever* (§241).
rival, *rival*.
river, *fleuve*, m., *rivière*, f.
road, *chemin*, m.; on the —, *en route*.
roar, *rugir*.
robber, *voleur*.
room, *chambre*, f.
round, *rond*.
row; go for a —, *se promener* (§241) *en bateau*.
rumour, *on dit*, m.
run, *courir* (§246); — away, *se sauver*; — over, *parcourir* (§246).
rush, *s'élancer* (§239); — up, *accourir* (§246).
Russia, *Russie*, f.
Russian, *russe*.
rustle, *bruire* (§263).

S.

sad, *triste*.
saddle, *seller*.
safety, *sûreté*, f.
sail; go for a —, *se promener* (§241) *en bateau*.
sale; for —, *à vendre*.
same, *même*.
satisfied, *satisfait, content*.
Saturday, *samedi*, m.
save, *sauver*; — (of money), *épargner*.
Saxon, *saxon*.
say, *dire* (§274); it is said, on *dit*; — no, *dire que non*; — yes, *dire que oui (si)*.
say again, *redire* (§274).
scarce, scarcely, *à peine*; — any, *très peu de*.
scholar, *savant*.
school, *école*, f.; at (to) —, *à l'école*.
school-boy, *écolier*.
school-fellow, *camarade d'école*.
science, *science*, f., man of —, *savant*.
scientific man, *savant*.
Scotland, *Écosse*, f.
scoundrel, *coquin, scélérat*.
scratch, *gratter*.
sculptor, *sculpteur*.
seaport, *port* (m.) *de mer*.
search; make a —, *chercher*.
seated, *assis*.
second, *second, deuxième*.
see, *voir* (§304); — again, *revoir* (§304).
seed, *graine*, f.
seek, *chercher*.
seem, *sembler*.
selfish, *égoïste*.
sell, v. tr., *vendre* (§291).
sell, v. intr., *se vendre* (§291).
send, *envoyer* (§240); — for, *envoyer chercher*, *faire* (§276) *venir*.
send up(-stairs), *faire* (§276) *monter*.
sense, *sens*, m.
sensible, *sensé, raisonnable*.
sentence, *sentence*, f.
seriously, *sérieusement*.
servant, *domestique*, m. f., *servante*, f.
service, *service*, m.
set, *mettre* (§279); — a high value upon, *attacher une grande valeur à*; — about, *se mettre à*.
seven, *sept*.
seventy, *soixante et dix*.
several, *plusieurs*.
severe, *sévère*.
sew, *coudre* (§270).
sewing-machine, *machine à coudre*, f.
shake hands, *se serrer la main, se donner la main*.
shame; it is a —, *c'est honteux*.
she, *elle, ce*.
shell, *coquille*, f.
ship, *navire*, m., *vaisseau*, m.
short, *petit*; in —, *bref*; be — of, *manquer de*.
shortly, *bientôt*.
should (=ought), *devoir* (§294).
shoulder, *épaule*, f.
shout (at), *crier (à)*.
show, *montrer, faire* (§276) *voir*; — in, *faire entrer*; — up (-stairs), *faire monter*.
shut, *fermer*.
side, *côté*, m.
sight, *spectacle*, m., *vue*, f.; lose — of, *perdre* (§291) *de vue*.
sign, *signer*.
silent; be (become) —, *se taire* (§252).
silk, *soie*, f.
silver, *argent*, m.
sin, *péché*, m.
since, prep., *depuis*.
since, conj., *depuis que, puisque*.
sing, *chanter*.
single, *seul*.

VOCABULARY. 393

sir, *monsieur.*
sister, *sœur.*
sister-in-law, *belle-sœur.*
sit down, *s'asseoir* (§295);
 — to dinner, *se mettre* (§279) *à table.*
sitting, *assis.*
six, *six.*
sixteen, *seize.*
sixty, *soixante.*
skill, *habileté,* f.
skin, *peau,* f.
sky, *ciel,* m.
slander, *médire (de)* (§274).
slave, *esclave.*
sleep, *dormir* (§248); go to —, *s'endormir* (§248).
slippery; be —, *faire* (§276) *glissant.*
slow, *lent.*
small, *petit.*
smell, *sentir* (§248).
smile, *sourire* (§285).
smoke, *fumée,* f.
snatch from (out of), *arracher à.*
snow, n., *neige,* f.
snow, v., *neiger* (§239).
so, *si,* *ainsi, tellement, aussi, c'est pourquoi;* not — ... as, *ne ... pas si ... que;* I think —, *je le crois;* I am —, *je le suis;* — as to, *afin de, de manière à;* — many, *tant;* — much, *tant, tellement;* — that, *afin que, de sorte que;* — well, *si bien, tant.*
so-called, *soi-disant, prétendu.*
soldier, *soldat.*
solve, *résoudre* (§284).
some, *de, du, quelque(s);* en; I have —, *j'en ai.*
somebody, some one, *quelqu'un.*
something, *quelque chose,* m.; — good, *quelque*

chose *de bon;* — strange and mysterious, *je ne sais quoi de mystérieux.*
sometimes, *quelquefois.*
son, *fils.*
song, *chanson,* f., *chant,* m.
soon, *bientôt;* as — as, *aussitôt que;* sooner, *plus tôt.*
sore, adv., *fort.*
sore; have a —, *avoir mal à.*
sorrow, *chagrin,* m.
sorry (for), *fâché (de).*
sort, *sorte,* f. ; what — of weather ?, *quel temps ?.*
soul, *âme,* f.
South America, *Amérique* (f.) *du Sud.*
southern, *méridional.*
sow, *semer* (§241, 1).
speak, *parler;* — French, *parler français;* so to —, *pour ainsi dire.*
speech, *discours,* m.
spend, *dépenser ;*—(of time), *passer.*
splendid, *magnifique*
spoil, *gâter.*
sport; make — of, *se moquer de.*
spot, *endroit,* m.
spring, n., *printemps,* m.; in —, *au printemps.*
spring, v., *sourdre* (§286).
stable, *écurie,* f., *étable,* m.
stake; be at —, *y aller de* (§242).
stand, *se tenir* (§259), *se trouver.*
start (with fear, etc.), *tressaillir*(§247), *partir*(§248).
statesman, *homme d' état.*
station; railway —, *gare,* f.
statue, *statue,* f.
stay, *rester, s' arrêter;* — in, *rester à la maison, rester chez soi.*
steal, *voler, dérober.*
steam, *vapeur,* f.

steam-boat, steamer, *bateau à vapeur,* m.
steam-engine, *machine à vapeur,* f.
step, *marcher.*
sterling, *sterling* (invar.).
St. Helena, *Sainte-Hélène,* f.
stick, *bâton,* m.
still, *encore, toujours.*
stir, *bouger*(§239), *se remuer.*
stone, *pierre,* f.
stop, *s'arrêter.*
stork, *cigogne,* f.
storm, *orage,* m.
story, *histoire,* f., *conte,* m.
stove, *poêle,* m.
straight, *droit.*
strange, *étrange.*
stratagem, *stratagème,* m.
street, *rue,* f.; from one — to another, *de rue en rue.*
strength, *force,* f.
striking part, *sonnerie,* f.
stroke, *coup,* m.
strong, *fort.*
struggle, n., *lutte,* f.
struggle, v., *lutter.*
study, n., *étude,* f.
study, v., *étudier.*
style; in (the) French —, *à la française.*
subdue, *subjuguer.*
subject, *sujet,* m.
submit, *se soumettre* (§279).
succeed, *réussir.*
such, *tel;* — a, *un tel.*
suffer, *souffrir* (§258), *subir.*
suffice, *suffire* (§268).
sufficient; be —, *suffire* (§268).
sugar, *sucre,* m.
suit, *convenir* (§259).
sum, *somme,* f.
summer, *été,* m.
sun, *soleil,* m.; the — is shining, *il fait du soleil.*
Sunday, *dimanche,* m.
superfluous, *de trop.*
support, *soutenir* (§259).

sure, *sûr*.
surgeon, *médecin*.
surprise, *surprendre* (§283).
suspect, *se douter, soupçonner*.
swallow, *hirondelle*, f.
swear, *jurer*.
Swedish, *suédois*.
sweet, *doux;* smell —, *sentir* (§248) *bon*.
swim, *nager* (§239).
sword, *épée*, f.

T.

table, *table*, f.
tail, *queue*, f.
tailor, *tailleur*.
take, *prendre* (§283), *porter, emporter, mener* (§241), *emmener* (241); — after, *tenir de* (§259); — away, *ôter, emporter;* — care, *prendre garde;* — a journey, *faire* (§276) *un voyage;* — off, *ôter;* — up, *monter*.
talk, *parler*.
tall, *grand*.
Tasso, *Tasse*.
tea, *thé*, m.
teach, *enseigner, apprendre* (§283).
teacher, *professeur*.
tear, *larme*, f.
tear, *déchirer*.
tell, *dire* (§274), *raconter;* tell (= understand), *comprendre* (§283), *savoir* (§302).
ten, *dix*.
terrify, *épouvanter*.
than, *que, de* (before numerals).
thanks, *remerciment(s)*, m.
thank, *remercier* (no) thanks, (no) I — you, *merci, je vous remercie*.
that, demonstr. adj., *ce;* — man, *cet homme-là*.

that, demonstr. pron., *ce, cela, celui-là;* — one, *celui-là;* all —, *tout ce qui;* — is *voilà, voilà qui, c'est, celui-là est*.
that, rel. pron., *qui, que lequel*.
that, conj., *que*.
the, *le;* — richer one is, *plus on est riche;* — less one has of them, *moins on en a*.
their, poss. adj., *leur*.
their, poss. pron., *le leur*.
them, *les, leur, eux, elles;* to —, *leur*.
themselves, *se, eux, eux-mêmes*.
then, *alors, lors*.
there, *là, y*.
there is, there are, *voilà, il y a;* — happen(s), *il arrive;* if — ever was one, *s'il en fut jamais;* — he comes !, *le voilà qui vient !*.
thereupon, *là-dessus*.
they, *ils, eux, elles, ce;* it is —, *ce sont eux*.
thief, *voleur*.
thimble, *dé*, m.
thine, *le tien*.
thing, *chose*, f.; this good —, *cela de bon*.
think, *penser, croire* (§272), *trouver;* what are you thinking of (about)?, *à quoi pensez-vous ?;* one would —, *on croirait;* what I — of him, *son fait*.
third, *troisième*.
thirsty; be —, *avoir soif*.
thirteen, *treize*.
thirty, *trente*.
this, demonstr. adj., *ce;* — man, *cet homme-ci*.
this, demonstr. pron., *ce, ceci, celui-ci;* — one,

celui-ci; — .... of mine, *mon ... que voici*.
thou, *tu, toi*.
though, *quoique, bien que*.
thought, *pensée*, f.
thoughtless, *étourdi*.
thousand; a —, *mille, mil*.
three, *trois*.
throne, *trône*, m.
through, *à travers, au travers de*.
throw, *jeter* (§241, 2).
Thursday, *jeudi*, m.
thus, *ainsi*.
thy, *ton*.
till, prep., *jusqu'à*.
till, conj., *jusqu'à ce que, que*.
time, *temps*, m., *époque*, f., *moment*, m., *fois*, f.; at that —, *dans ce temps-là;* a long —, *longtemps;* next —, *la prochaine fois;* four —s, *quatre fois;* what — is it ?, *quelle heure est-il ?;* have — to, *avoir le temps de;* be — to, *être temps de (que);* most of the —, *la plupart du temps;* at a — when, *à une époque où;* have a good —, *s'amuser bien*.
tire; be (get) tired (of being), *s'ennuyer* (§240).
tired, *fatigué, ennuyé*.
tiresome, *ennuyeux*.
to, *à, de, pour, envers, jusqu'à;* at a quarter – five, *à cinq heures moins (un) quart*.
to-day, *aujourd'hui*.
toe; step on one's —, *vous marcher sur le pied*.
together, *ensemble*.
to-morrow, *demain*.
too, *aussi, trop;* — many, — much, *trop*.
tooth, *dent*, f.; have the — ache, *avoir mal aux dents*.

VOCABULARY.

tooth-pick, *cure-dent*, m.
touch, *toucher* (à).
tour, *tour*, m.
towards, *envers*.
tower, *tour*, f.
town, *ville*, f.; in —, down —, *en ville*; to —, *à la ville*.
trace, *tracer* (§239, 1).
trade, *changer* (§239).
train, *train*, m.
translate, *traduire* (§266).
travel, n., *voyage*, m.
travel, v., *voyager* (§239); — over, *parcourir* (§240).
traveller, *voyageur*.
tread under foot, *fouler aux pieds*.
treasure, *trésor*, m.
treat, *traiter*.
treatment, *traitement*, m.
treaty, *traité*, m.
tree, *arbre*, m.
trifling, *insignifiant*.
troops, *troupes*, f., plur.
trouble, *peine*, f.
troupe, *troupe*, f.
true, *vrai*, *fidèle*.
trunk, *malle*, f.
trust, n., *confiance*, f.
trust, v., *avoir confiance en*, *se fier à*.
truth, *vérité*, f.
try, *tâcher*.
Tuesday, *mardi*, m.
turn, n., *tour*, m.; in —, *tour à tour*.
turn, v., *tourner*; — out of, *chasser de*; — out of doors, *mettre* (§279) *à la porte*.
twelve, *douze*; — o'clock, *midi*, m., *minuit*, m.
twenty, *vingt*.
two, *deux*.

U.

uncle, *oncle*.
under, *sous*, *au-dessous de*.
undergo, *subir*.
understand, *comprendre* (§283).
undertake, *entreprendre* (§283).
unfortunate, *malheureux*.
unhappy, *malheureux*.
United Kingdom, *Royaume-Uni*, m.
United States, *États-Unis*, m.
unknown, *inconnu*.
unless, *à moins que* ... *ne*.
until, *jusqu'à ce que*.
up to, *jusqu'à*.
upholsterer, *tapissier*.
us, *nous*.
use; have — for, *avoir besoin de*; make — of, *se servir de* (§248), *employer* (§240).
used, *accoutumé*; be — to, *avoir coutume de*; '— to' is often expressed by the Imperfect Indicative.
useful, *utile*.
useless; be —, *ne valoir* (§303) *rien*; it is — for you to say so, *vous avez beau dire*.
usual, *usuel*, *accoutumé*, *ordinaire*.

V.

vain; in —, *en vain*.
valuable, *précieux*.
value, *valeur*, f.
value; be of —, *valoir* (§303).
various, *plusieurs*.
vast, *vaste*.
verbal, *verbal*.
verse, *vers*, m.
very, *très*, *bien*, *fort*, *beaucoup*.
vice, *vice*, m.
victory, *victoire*, f.
view, *vue*, f.
vigour, *vigueur*, f.
village, *village*, m.
violent, *violent*.
violin, *violon*, m.
virtue, *vertu*, f.
virtuous, *vertueux*.
visible, *visible*.
visit, *visiter*.
volley, *volée*, f.
volume, *volume*, m., *tome*, m.

W.

wag, *remuer*.
wait (for), *attendre* (§291).
wake, *éveiller*.
Wales, *le pays de Galles*.
walk, *marcher*, *se promener* (§241); take a —, go (out) for a —, *faire* (§276) *une promenade*; — in, *entrer*.
walking; be good.—, *faire* (§276) *bon marcher*.
walnut, *noix*, f.
walnut-tree, *noyer*, m.
want, *avoir besoin*, *vouloir* (§305), *désirer*, *demander*, *manquer* (de).
warm, adj., *chaud*, *chaleureux*; be — (of living beings), *avoir chaud*; be — (of weather), *faire* (§276) *chaud*.
warm, v., *chauffer*.
wash, *laver*.
watch, n., *montre*, f.
watch, v., *veiller*.
water, *eau*, f.; make his mouth —, *lui faire* (§276) *venir l'eau à la bouche*.
way, *manière*, f., *moyen*, m.; in that —, *de cette manière-là*; in such a —, *de telle sorte que*; have one's —, *faire* (§276) *à sa tête*; which —, the —, *par où*.
we, *nous*, *on*.
weak, *faible*.
weakness, *faiblesse*, f.
wear, *porter*.

weather, *temps*, m.; the — is warm, *il fait chaud.*
Wednesday, *mercredi*, m.
week, *semaine*, f., *huit jours*; from — to —, *de semaine en semaine.*
weep, *pleurer.*
weigh, *peser* (§241).
welcome, *accueillir* (§247); be —, *être le bienvenu.*
well, *bien, eh bien;* very —, *très bien, eh bien;* be — off, *avoir de quoi vivre.*
well-bred, *bien élevé.*
well-known, *bien connu.*
west, *ouest*, m.
what, adj., *quel;* — o'clock is it?, *quelle heure est-il?.*
what, interrog. pron., *que, quoi;* — is that to him?, *qu'est-ce que cela lui fait?.*
what, rel. pron., *ce qui, ce que, ce dont, ce de quoi, ce à quoi;* not know — to do, *ne savoir que faire.*
whatever, *quoi que, quel que, qui que, quelconque.*
wheat, *blé*, m.
when, *quand, lorsque, que, à quelle heure;* hardly ... —, *à peine ... que.*
whenever, *quand.*
where, *où;* — ... from, *d'où.*
whether, *si, que, soit que;* — ... or, *(soit) que ... ou (que).*
which, interrog. adj., *quel.*
which, interrog. pron., *lequel.*
which, rel. pron., *qui, que, lequel;* in —, *dans lequel, où, dont;* of —, from —, *dont, duquel.*
while; a long —, *longtemps.*
while, prep., *en.*
while, whilst, conj., *pendant que, tandis que, tant que.*

whistle, *siffler.*
white, *blanc.*
who, interrog. pron., *qui.*
who, rel. prou., *qui, lequel.*
whoever, *qui que, quiconque, qui que ce soit.*
whole, *tout;* the — year, *toute l'année.*
whom, interrog. pron., *qui.*
whom, rel. pron., *qui, que, lequel;* of —, *dont, de qui, duquel.*
whose, *à qui, de qui, dont, duquel.*
why, *pourquoi.*
wicked, *méchant.*
wide, *large.*
wide open, *grand(e) ouvert(e).*
widow, *veuve.*
wife, *femme, épouse.*
will, *vouloir* (§305); — you kindly?, *voulez-vous bien?.*
William, *Guillaume.*
willing; he —, *vouloir* (§305).
willingly, *volontiers.*
win, *remporter, gagner.*
wind, n., *vent*, m.
wind, v., *remonter.*
window, *fenêtre*, f.
windy; be —, *faire* (§276) *du vent.*
wine, *vin*, m.
wing, *aile*, f.
winter, *hiver*, m.
wipe, *essuyer* (§240).
wisdom, *sagesse*, f.
wise, *sage.*
wish, *désirer, vouloir* (§305); as you —, *comme vous voudrez;* when (ever) you —, *quand vous voudrez;* if you —, *si vous voulez.*
with, *avec, de, chez, à, par;* — it, — them, *en.*
within, *dans, au bout de.*
without, prep., *sans;* — ... and (or), *sans ... ni.*
without, conj., *sans que.*

without; do —, *se passer de.*
woman, *femme.*
wonder, *s'étonner, se demander.*
wont; be —, *avoir coutume de.*
wood, woods, *bois*, m.
wood-chopper, woodman, *bûcheron.*
word, *mot*, m., *parole*, f.; send —, *faire* (§276) *savoir.*
work, n., *travail*, m., *ouvrage*, m., *œuvre*, f. m.
work, v., *travailler.*
workman, *ouvrier.*
world, *monde*, m.
worse, *plus mauvais, pire, pis, plus malade.*
worth; be —, *valoir* (§303).
worthy, *digne, brave.*
would, expressed often by Impf. Indic., or Condl.; — to God !, *plût à Dieu !;* I — as soon ... as, *j'aimerais autant ... que de.*
would-be, *soi-disant, prétendu.*
wound, *blesser.*
wrecked; be —, *faire* (§276) *naufrage.*
wretch, *misérable.*
write, *écrire* (§275).
wrong, *mal*, m.; be in (the) —, *avoir tort;* take the — road, *se tromper de chemin.*
wrong-doing, *malfaire.*

Y.

yard, *mètre*, m.; *cour*, f.
year, *an*, m., *année*, f.; last —, *l'année dernière, l'année passée.*
yes, *oui, si;* — you have, *si, si.*
yesterday, *hier.*
yet, *encore, cependant;* not —, *pas encore.*

yield, *céder* (§241, 1).
yonder, *là-bas.*
you, *vous, tu, te, toi.*
young, *jeune.*

your, *votre, ton.*
yours, *le vôtre, le tien; à vous, à toi.*

yourself, *vous, vous-même, te, toi, toi-même.*
youth, *jeunesse,* f.

INDEX.

A.

a (*à, á*), prncn., §16; elision, §73.
à (prep.), of indir. obj., §81, 3, §440, 2, §528, 1; verb + *à* = Eng. tran., §375, 2; idiomatic with verbs, §375, 4; with names of countries, §411, 3, obs.; denoting possession after *être*, §455, 1; in prepositional phrases, §509; repetition, §511; = 'concerning', 'of', §513, 2; of 'place', 'time', §516, 1, §521, 2; of 'motion towards', §528, 2; = 'with' (characteristic), §531, 4.
abbaye, prncn., §23, 2, exc.
abbreviations, §538.
'about', §513.
accent, accent marks, §2, 1, 2, 3; stress, §66, §67.
acute accent, §2, 1.
Achille, prncn., §42, 2, exc. 1, §51, 2, exc. 1.
adjective, §§414-436, see also possessive adj., demonstr. adj., interrog. adj., indef. adj., numeral; fem., §§414-415; plur. §§416-417; agreement, §§418-422; as adv., §487, §421; nouns as adjs., §422; comparison, §§423-427; position, §§428-431; with *à*, §433; with *de*, §434; with *en*, §435; with *en rers*, §436.
adverb, §§485-497; list, §485; in -*ment* from adjs., §486; adjs. as advs., §487; adverbial locutions, §488; comparison, §489; position, §490; negatives, §§491-496; distinctions in use, §497; numeral advs., §503.
afin que, +subj., §532, §351, 2.
'after', §514.
agir, impers., §332, 1, obs.
ai (at), prncn., §22.
aïeul, plur., §387.
aiguë, prncn., §45, exc. 2.
aiguille, prncn., §45, exc. 1.
ail, plur., §387.
aim, prncn., §35.
aimer, +*à*, +*de*, without prep., §360, 1.
ain, prncn., §35.
Aix, prncn., §62, exc. 3.
album, prncn., §37, exc.
Alfred, prncn., §43, exc.
aller,+infin., §310, 8; impers., §332, 1, obs.; *s'en aller*, §327.
allez, special force, §347, b.
allons, special force, §347, b.
almanach, prncn., §42, exc. 2.
alphabet, §1; names of letters and gender, §1, n. 3; prncn., §§16-63.
alphabetical equivalents, §76.
am, prncn., §34.
-*am*, prncn., §34, exc., 2.
âme qui vive, with *ne*, §492, 2, c.
âme vivante, with *ne*, §492, 2, c.
à moins que, with *ne*., §496, 1.
'among', §515.
amour, gender, §383, 3, *b*.
an, prncn., §34.
'and,' untranslated, §533, 2; =*ni*, §531, 2.
août, prncn., §16, 2, exc.
apostrophe, §2, 6.
apposition, use of art., §408, 4.
approuvé, §368, *a*.
après, §514.
après,+infin., §361, 4.
après-midi, gender, §383, 3, *a*.
aquatic, prncn., §55, exc.
archevêque, prncn., §42, 2, exc. 1.
archiduc, prncn., §42, 2, exc. 1.
arriver, impers., §332, 1, obs.
article, §§393-413, see also def. art. and indef. art.; agreement and repetition, §396; use with nouns, §§397-413; omission, §408; in appositions, §409, 4; unclassified examples, §409; with proper names, §§410-413.
'at', §516.
attendant; en — que, + subj., §532, §351, 1.
attendu, §368, *a*.
au, prncn., §24.
au, =*à*+*le*, §395.
aucun(s), §480, 3; use, §483, 1; with *ne*, §492.
aucunement, with *ne*, §492.
au-dessus de, §525, 1.
au-dessous de, §530, 2.
aussi, in comparison (adj.), §423; (adv.) §489.
autant, §497, 2,

INDEX. 399

autel, prncn., §24, exc.
automne, prncn., §52, exc. 1; gend., §383, 3, a.
autour de, §513, 1.
autre, §480, 3; use, §483, 2, 7, (2); with ne, §496, 3, n.
autrement, with ne, §496, 3, n.
autrui, §480, 2; use, §482, 1.
aux, =à+les, §395.
auxiliary verbs, use §§307-309; modal auxs., §310, 5, n.
avant, §517, 2.
avant que, with ne, §496, 1, b; avant que,+subj., §532, §351, 1.
avec, §531, 1, 3.
avoir, conjugn., §238; used to form comp. tenses, §307, §309; y avoir, §330; il y a and voilà, §330, 3; avoir besoin, etc.(without art.), §408, 1; avoir l'air, agreement of adj. with, §421, 4, c; denoting dimension, §505, obs. 3; denoting age, §507.
ay, prncn., §23.

B.

b, prncn., §40.
baptême, prncn., §54, exc. 2.
baptiser, prncn., §54, exc. 1.
Bayard, prncn., §23, 2, exc.
Bayonne, prncn., §23, 2, exc.
beaucoup, +de, agreement of verb, §312, 2, a, b; with partitive, §403, 1, d; replaced by plusieurs, §483, 4; comparison §489, 2; not modified, §489, 2, a.
'before', §517.
brl, §415. 1, (3).
bestiaux, §386, 4, n.
bétail, plur., §386, 4, n.
bien, prncn., §34, exc. 3.
bien, with partitive, §403, 1, b; irreg. comparison, §489, 2.
bien que,+subj., §532, §351, 4.
bis, prncn., §57, 2, exc. 1.
bœufs, prncn., §44, exc.
bon, comparison, §424; +à or pour, §433, §433, a, §436, a.
bouger, with ne alone, §495, 4.
bout; au — de, §514, 2.
brin, with ne, §492, 2, b.
Bruxelles, prncn.,§62, exc.3.
but, prncn., §60, 2, exc. 2.
'by', §518; of 'dimension', §505, a.

C.

c, prncn., §41; final, §39, 2.
ç, §41, 2, n.
ç', §456, 2, obs.
ça, for cela, §465, e, f; distinguished from çà and çà !, §465, f. n.
çà, çà !, distinguished from ça, §465, f. n.
Caen, prncn., §17, 4, exc.
capitals, use, §75.
cardinals, §498, §208; prncn., §208; in dates, etc., §504; for ordinals, §504, 2, a.
cas; au — où, +indic. or subj., §532, §351, 3; au — que, +subj., §532, §351, 3; dans le — où, +indic. or subj., §532, §351, 3; en — que, +subj., §532, §351, 3.
case relations, of nouns, §391; of conjunctive pers. prons., §440.
ce (adj.), §456, 1; use, §458.
ce (pron.), §456, 2; agreement of verb with, §312, 3; use §§461-464; +être, §461; c'est and il est, §461, 2, (1), a and notes; + a relat., §402; in phrases, §463; ce semble, §463, a;

pleonastic, §464; ce n'est pas que + subj., §532, §351, 5.
ceci, §456, 2; use,§465.
cedilla, §2, 4.
cela, §456, 2; use, §465; replaced by là, §465, d.
celui, §456, 2; use, §459.
celui-ci, §456, 2; use, §460.
celui-là, §456, 2; use, §460; replacing celui, 459, b.
cent(s), §408, b, c, d, c.
-cer, verbs in, §239.
cerise, prncn., §17, 4, exc.
certain, §480, 1; use, §481, 1.
certifié, §368, a.
cesser, with ne alone, §495, 4.
cet, for ce, §456, 1, obs.
ch, prncn., §42.
chacun, §480, 2; use, 482, 2.
chaque, §480, 1; use, §481, 2.
chef-d'œuvre, prncn., §44, exc.
chenil, prncn., §50, exc. 1.
chérubin, prncn., §42, exc. 1.
chez, §516, 2, §523, 2, §531, 2.
chimère, prncn., §42, 2 exc. 1.
Christ (Jésus-), prncn., §60, 2, exc. 1.
-ci, §458.
Cid (le), prncn., §43, exc.
ciel, plur., §387.
ci-inclus, §368, b.
ci-joint, §368, b.
Cinna, prncn., §53, exc. 2.
circumflex accent, §2, 3.
civil,+à l'égard de, §436, a.
ck, prncn., §49.
clef, prncn., §44, exc.
club, prncn., §40, exc. 2.
Coblentz, prncn., §63, exc. 2.
collationné, §368, a.
collectives, §500.
Colomb, prncn., §40, exc. 2.
combien, agreement, §312, 2, b.
comme, for que in comparison, §423, b.

comparison, of adjs., §§423-427; of advs., §489; irreg. (adj.), §424; irreg. (adv.), §489, 2; remarks, §427; followed by *ne*, §496, 3.
comparative, see comparison.
complement, predicative, §374; prepositional, §375; composite, §377.
compound adjs. plur., §421, 2.
compound nouns, plur., §389.
compound tenses, formation, §§307-309; sequence of subj., §353, 3; in condl. sent., §355, *a*, p. 213.
compris (*y*), *non*—, §368, *a*.
compte, prncn., §54, exc. 2.
'concerning', §513, 2.
condition; à la — que, +indic. or subj., §532, §351, 3.
conditional sentences, §354, §355; use of mood and tense in, §355.
conditional, tense §345, in condl. sent., §355, p. 213.
conditional anterior, tense, §346; replaced by plupf. subj., §352, 3; replaced by impf. indic. in 'result' clause, §355, *c*, p. 214.
conjunction, §§532-536; list, §532; with indic., subj., indic. or subj., see list, §532; use of certain, §§533-536; distinctions, §536.
conjunctive, pron., §437 and n.; use, §§440-449.
consonants, prncn., §§39-63; final, prncn., §39, 1, 2; double, §39, 3.
consonant sounds, §15.
Cortez, prncn., §63, exc. 1.
couple, gender, §333, 3, *e*.
craindre, with *ne*, §496, 2.
crainte; de — que . . . ne, + subj., §532, §351, 2.

creuse, prncn., §26, exc. 2.
croc, prncn., §41, 1, exc. 1.
cul-de-sac, prncn., §50, exc. 1.
curaçoa prncn., §16, 2, exc.

D.

d, prncn., §43; in 'liaison', §71.
d'abord, §503, *a*.
damner, prncn., §52, exc. 1.
dans, §521, 1, 3; with names of countries, §411, 3, obs.
dates, §504, §219.
dative, of pers. pron., §440, 2; ethical, §440, n.
davantage, §497, 3.
David, prncn., §43, exc.
de, as partitive sign, §§401-403; agent after passive, §320, §434, §518, 1; verb + *de* = Eng. transitive, §375, 1; idiomatic with verbs, §375, 4; with names of countries, §411, 2; *de* = 'in', after superl., §425, 2; denoting 'by how much', after superl., §427, 2; pleonastic after interrog., §468, n.; of 'dimension', §503, obs. 1, §507, obs. 3; in prepositional phrases, §509; repetition, §511; *de* = 'by' (measure), §518, 3; *de* = 'from', §520, 1; of 'place' (after supcrl.), §521, 4; *de* = 'of', §522, 1; *de* = 'with', §531, 6; = 'concerning', 'of', §513, 2.
de ee que, constr., §349, 4, *b*.
décider, + *à*, + *de*, §360, 2.
défier, + *à* + *de*, §360, 3.
definite article, forms, §394; contractions, §395; agreement and repetition, §396, §425, *a*; with general noun, §399; with partitive noun, §401; in titles, §405; for possessive adj.,

§406; distributively, §407; omission, §408, §411, 4; unclassified examples, §409; with names of persons, §410; with names of countries, §411; with names of cities, etc., §412; with names of mountains and rivers, §413; in superlative, §§425-427; replacing demonstr. adj., §458, *b*; in fractions, §501, *b*.
délice, gender, §383, *c*.
demi, agreement, §421, 4, *a*; in compounds, §389, 2, *a*, §421, 4, *a*; in fractions, §501, *a*.
demonstrative adjective, forms, §456, 1; agreement §457; repetition, §457, *a*; use, §458; replaced by def. art., §458, *b*.
demonstrative pronoun, forms, §456, 2; agreement, §457; use, §§459-465.
demonstratives, see demonstr. adj. and demonstr. pron.
depuis, §520, 3; with *ne*, §496, 6; —*que*, distinguished from *puisque*, §536, 3.
dernier, + subj., §350, 7; +*à*+infin. §558, 3, *a*.
des, = *de*+*les*, §395.
dès, §520, 3.
Descartes, prncn., §37, exc. 2.
descendre, +*à*, + dir. infin., §360, 4.
désobéir, passive use, §321, 1.
determinatives, position, §431.
déterminer, +*à*, +*de*, §360, 5.
deuxième, for *second*, §499, *b*.
devant, §517, 1.
devoir, +infin., §310, 2; +*de* +infin., §357, 6, *a*.
devrais, §9, 6.

INDEX. 401

différents, §480, 1 ; use, §481, 3.
diphthongization, absent in French, §3, 4 and n.
dire, +*de*, +dir. infin., §360, 6.
direct obj., §372.
disjunctive pron., §437 and n. ; use, §450 ; avoided, §450, 6, n.
divers, §480, 1 ; use, §481, 3.
dompter, prncn., §54, exc. 2.
donc, prncn., §41, 1, exc. 1.
donner, conjugation, §237.
dont, §472 ; use, §475.
dot, prncn., §60, 2, exc. 1.
double, as adv., §502, *a*.
du, =*de*+*le*, §395.
dû, agreement, §371, 4, *b*.
Dufresne, prncn., §57, exc. 2.
dur, +*pour*, §436, *a*.
durant, position, §510, *b*.

E.

e (*é*, *è*, *ê*), prncn., §17 ; *e* 'sourd', §17, 3, n. and obs. ; *e* 'muet', §17, 4 and §17, 3, n. and obs. ; to soften *g*, §45, 2, n. 2 ; elision, §73 ; stem-vowel *e* (*é*), §241 ; change of *e* to *é*, §516, 1, *b*.
eau, prncn., §24.
échecs, prncn., §41, 1, exc. 1.
-*ège*, (-*ége*), prncn., §17, 1, exc.
ei, prncn., §25.
ein, prncn., §35.
ein, prncn., §35.
'either', 'nor —', 'not —', §534, 3.
-*eler*, verbs in, §241, 2.
elision, §73.
elliptical tense forms, §336.
em, prncn., §34.
-*em*, prncn., §34, exc. 2.
émeute, prncn., §26, 2, exc. 2.

emm-, prncn., §34, exc. 1.
-*emment*, prncn., §17, 5.
empêcher, with *ne*, §496, 1.
empresser(s'), +*à*, +*de*, §360, 7.
en, prncn., §34.
-*en*, prncn., §34, exc. 2, 3.
en (pron. adv.), §438 ; use, §445, §450, 6, n.; position, §447, 3, (2).
en (prep.), in gerunds, §365, 3 ; agreement of past part., §371, 3, *a*; with names of countries (no art.), §411, 2 ; repetition, §511 ; of 'place', 'time', §516, 1, §521, 2, 3 ; of 'material', §522, 2 ; of 'motion towards', §528, 2.
encore que, + subj., §532, §351, 4.
encore un, §483, 2, *a*.
enivrer, prncn., §34, exc. 1.
ennoblir, prncn., §34, exc. 1.
ennui, prncn., §34, exc. 1.
en premier lieu, §503, *a*.
ensuite, §503, *a*.
entendre, + infin., constr. of obj., §372, 2, *b*.
entendu, §368, *a*, §371, 4, *a*.
entre, §515, 1, 2.
d'entre, after superl., §425, 2.
envers, §528, 3.
environ, §513, 4.
équateur, prncn., §55, exc. 2.
équestre, prncn., §55, exc. 3.
ès, =*en les*, §395, n. 2.
-*esse*, fem. ending, §384, 2.
est-ce que, use of, §316, 4.
estomac, prncn., §41, 1, exc. 1.
et (conj.), use of, §533 ; prncn. in 'liaision', §72, 4, obs.
été, invar., §319, obs.
-*eter*, verbs in, §241, 2.
ethical dative, §440, n.
être, §238 ; forming comp. tenses, §308, §309 ; form-

ing passive, §319 ; forming reflexive comp. tenses, §322, 2 ; as impers. verb, §330, 2 ; +*à*+infin., §358, 7, *b* ; +*à*, +*à* .... *de*, +*à* .... *d*, §360, 8.
eu (*eû*), prncn., §26 ; prncn. of *eu* of *avoir*, §26, 2, exc. 1.
eu, past part., agreement, §371, 4, *d*.
eun, prncn., §37.
-*eur*, fem. of, §415, 2, (2).
européen, prncn., §34, exc. 3.
évènement, prncn., §17, 1, exc.
éviter, with *ne*, §496, 1.
examen, prncn., §34, exc. 3.
excepté, §368, *a*.
ey, prncn., §27.

F.

f, prncn., §44 ; final, §39, 2 ; in 'liaison', §71.
fâché, +*contre*, §434, *a*.
façon ; *de* — *que*, +indic. or subj., §532, §351, 2.
faire, +infin., §310, 6 ; +*de* +infin., §357, 6, *b* ; of weather, etc., §329, 2 ; +infin., constr. of obj., §372, *a* ; passive force of trans. infin. after, §321, 3.
faisant, (*faisons*, etc.), prncn., §22, 2, exc.
fait (noun), prncn., §60, 2, exc. 2.
fait (past part.), agreement, §371, 4, *c*.
falloir, §331.
faon, prncn., §19, 2, exc.
fat, prncn., §60, 2, exc. 1.
fatiguer(se), +*à*, +*de*, §360, 0.
feminine, see gender.
femme, prncn., §17, 5.
feu, §421, 4, *b*.
fils, prncn., §50, exc. 2, §57, 2, exc. 1.

Z

finir, conjugation, §237; +à, +de, §360, 10.
fois (une fois, etc.), §502, 2.
fol, §415, 1, (3).
'for', §519.
force, agreement, §312, 2, a.
fort, +sur, §435, a.
foudre, gender, §383, 3, h.
fractions, §501.
franc de port, §421, 4, a.
'from', §520.
fusil, prncn., §50, exc. 1.
future, §343; in condl. sentence, §355; replaced by pres., §337, 4, 5; replaced by condl., §345, 3.
future anterior, §344; replaced by past indef., §339, 3.

G.

g, prncn., §45; in 'liaison', §71.
Gambetta, prncn., §60, exc. 3.
garde-, in compounds, §389, 5, a.
gaz, prncn., §63, exc. 1.
ge+a, o, u, §45, 2, n. 2.
gender, of nouns, §§379-384; by meaning, §380; by endings, §381; by derivation, §382; double, §383; formation of fem., §384, §414, §415; of adjs., §414, §415.
general noun, §399; and partitive, §404.
gens, gender, §383, 3, j.
gent, plur., §386, 5.
gentil, prncn., §51, 2, exc. 2.
geôle, prncn., §17, exc. 4.
Georges, prncn., §17, exc. 4.
gerund, §365, 3; English, §366, 2.
gésir, prncn., §57, 2, exc. 4.
Gil Blas, prncn., §57, 2, exc. 1.
gn, prncn., §46.

Goth, prncn., §60, exc. 4.
goutte, with ne, §492, 2, b.
grave accent, §2, 2.
grésil, prncn., §50, ex. 2.
gu, prncn., §45, 2, n. 1 and exc.
guère, with ne, §492.
Guide(le), prncn., §45, exc. 1.
Guise, prncn., §45, exc. 1.
guttural, prncn., §60, exc. 3.

H.

h, prncn., §47.
haïr, +de+infin., §358, 7, c.
haut, for hauteur, §506, obs. 4.
hélas!, prncn., §57, 2, exc. 1.
homme qui vive, with ne, §492, 2, c.
'however', §481, 5, a, (2) and n.
Humbert, prncn., §37, exc.
hymen, prncn., §34, exc. 2.
hymne, gender, §383, 3, d.
hyphen, use, §2, 7.

I.

i (î), prncn., §18; elision, §73.
ignorant, +sur, §435, a.
ignorer, +negative, constr. after, §349, 5, c.
il (impers.), agreement, §312, 4, §439, d; as subject of impers. verb, §328, §332, 2, §333; il y a, §330, 3; il est, §330, 2, §461, 1, (1), b; il faut, §331; il s'en faut, §331, 5; distinguished from ce, §461, 2, (1), a; il est vrai, §461, 2, (1), a; il semble, §463, a; il s'en faut, with ne, §496, 5; il y a, with ne, §496, 6.
ill-, prncn., §50, exc. 3.
im, prncn., §35.
imm-, prncn., §52, exc. 2.
imperative, §347; in condl.

sentence, §355, p. 213; replaced by fut., §343, 4.
imperfect, (indic.), §338; in narrative, examples of, §341; in condl. sentence, §355, p. 213; replacing plupf. or condl. ant. in condl. sentence, §355, c, p. 214; (subj.), §353, 2 and 4, e; for perf. subj., §353, 4, a.
impersonal verbs, §§328-333; verbs used impersonally, §332; de+infin. as logical subj. of, §359, 1.
importe (qu'), §312, 4, a.
in, prncn., §35.
'in', §521.
inn-, prncn., §53, exc. 2.
indefinite article, forms, §393; agreement and repetition, §396; use, §398; omission, §403; unclassified examples, §409; with names of persons, §410, 3.
indefinite adj., forms, §480, 1, 3, §484, 1; use, §481, §483, §484; position in negation, §493.
indefinite pron., forms, §480, 2, 3, §484, 2; use, §482, §483, §484; position in negation, §493, §493, b.
indefinites, see indef. adj. and pron.
indicative mood, §334, see also the various tenses; in conditions, §355, obs., p. 213.
indirect discourse, mood of, §334, n. 1; tense of, §338, 5;
indirect obj., §372, 2, §373, §440, 2, §528, 1.
indulgent, +pour or à, §436, a.
-ine, fem. ending, §384, 3.
infinitive mood, §355-364; without prep., §357, reference list, §357, 6; with

à, §358, reference list, §358, 7 ; with *de*, §359, reference list, §359, 6 ; historical, §359, 4 ; distinctions, §360 ; with other preps., §361 ; for subordinate clause, §362 ; with passive force, §363 ; for Eng. -ing, §364, §366, 3.
interjection, §537.
interrogation, word order, §316 ; indirect, §318.
interrogative adj., forms, §466, 1 ; agreement, §467 ; use, §468, §469, 1, *b*, 2.
interrogative locutions, §471.
interrogative pron., forms, §466, 2 ; agreement, §467 ; use, §§463-470.
interrogatives, see interrog. adj. and pron.
'into', §521.
intransitive verbs, §373.
inversions, rhetorical, §317.
irr-, prncn., §56, exc. 3.
irregular verbs, §§239-306 ; list of, §306 ; in *-er*, §§239-243 ; in *-cer*, *-ger*, §239 ; in *-yer*, §240 ; with stem-vowel *e* (ê), §241 ; in *-eler*, *-eter*, §241 ; in *-ir*, §§244-260 ; in *-re*, §§261-292 ; in *-oir*, §§293-305 ; in *-andre*, *-endre*, *-erdre*, *-ondre*, *-ordre*, §201.
-issime, superl. ending, §426, *a*.

J.

j, prncn., §48.
jadis, prncn., §57, 2, exc. 1.
jamais, with *ne*, §492.
Jean, prncn., §17, 4, exc.
Jeanne, prncn., §17, 4, exc.
Jérusalem, prncn., §34, exc. 2.
je soussigné, §450, 2, n.
jeûne, prncn., §26, 2, exc. 2.
Job, prncn., §40, exc. 2.

jumelle, §415, 1, (3).
jurer, +*de*, +dir. infin., §360, 11.
jusqu'à, §528, 4 ; *jusqu'à ce que*, +indic. or subj., §532, §351, 1.

K.

k, §1, n. 1 ; prncn., §49.

L.

l, prncn., §50 ; *l* mouillée, §51 ; final *l*, §39, 2.
-là, §458.
laissé, §371, 4, *a*.
laisser, +infin., §310, 7 ; +*de*+infin., §357, 6, *c* ; +*à*, +*de*, +dir. infin,. §36), 12 ; constr. of obj., §372, *b*.
large, for *largeur*, §505, obs. 4.
lasser (se), +*à*, +*de*, §360, 13.
Laure, prncn., §24, exc.
le (la, les), see def. art. and pers. pron. ; predicative, §442 ; pleonastic, §443 ; = 'one', 'so', §443, *b*.
Lefebvre, prncn., §40, exc. 1.
length, see quantity.
lequel?, §466, 2 ; use, §468.
lequel, §472 ; use, §477.
'less' ; 'less and less', §423, *d* ; 'the less', §423, *d* ; 'less than' (adv. of quantity), §489, *b*.
liaison, §§69-72.
Lille, prncn., §51, exc. 1.
linking, see *liaison*.
lip-rounding, §3, 2.
lis, prncn., §57, 2, exc. 4.
loin que, +subj., §532, §351, 5.
long, for *longueur*, §505, 4.
loquace, prncn., §55, exc 2.
lorsque, distinguished from *quand*, §536, 1.
l'un, §483, 7, (1), *a*.
l'un l'autre, §483, 7, (2).

M.

m, prncn., §52.
mm, prncn., §52, exc. 2.
Madrid, prncn., §43, exc.
maint, §480, 1 ; use, §481, 4.
Maistre, prncn., §57, 2, exc. 2.
mal, irreg. comparison, §489, 2.
Malesherbes, prncn., §57, exc. 2.
malgré que, +subj., §532, §351, 4.
ma mie, §452, n.
m'amour, §452, n.
manière, de — que, +indic. or subj., §532, §351, 2.
manquer, +*à*, +*de*, §360, 14.
mars, prncn., §57, 2, exc. 1.
masculine, see gender.
mauvais, prncn., §24, exc. ; irreg. comparison, §424.
meilleur, §424.
même, §480, 3 ; use, §483, 3.
Metz, prncn., §63, exc. 2.
meule, prncn., §26, exc. 2.
Michel, prncn., §42, 2, exc. 1.
mie, with *ne*, §492, 2, *b*.
mien, etc., for *le mien*, §455, 2.
mieux, §489, 2.
mil, in dates, §498, *c*.
mil, (= 'millet'), prncn., §51, 2, ex.
mille, prncn., §51, 2, exc. 1., §499, *e*.
million, prncn., §51, 2, exc. 1.
'mine', etc., translated, §455, 1.
moelle, prncn., §17, 2, exc.
mœurs, prncn., §57, 2, exc. 4.
moi, for *me*, §447, 3, (3), obs. 1.

moindre, §424.
moins, §189, 2; in comparison (adj.), §423, (adv.), §189; *moins de*, 489, §1, *b*; *à moins que... ne*, + subj., §532, §351, 3, — + *de deux*, agreement of, §312, 2, *c*.
mol, §415, 1, (3).
mon, for *ma*, §452, 1, obs. 1; in address, §454, 4.
monarchie, prncn., §42, exc. 1.
monsieur, prncn., §36, exc.
Montesquieu, prncn., §57, 2, exc. 2.
mood, see the various moods; of subordinate clause, §334, n. 2.
'more'; 'more and more', §423, *d*, §489; 'the more', §423, *d*, §489; 'more than', (adv. of quantity), §489, *b*.
mot, with *ne*, §492, 2, *b*.
multiplicatives, §502.

N.

n, prncn., §53; in 'liaison,' §71.
nabab, prncn., §40, exc. 2.
narrow, of sounds, §3, 1.
nasal vowels, prncn., §§33-33; in 'liaison,' §71.
nasal vowel sounds, §12, §13.
n'avoir garde, §495, 5.
ne (*n'*), §§492-496; with *pas*, *point*, etc., §492; position, §493; omission, §494; alone as negative, §495; pleonastic, §496; *ne...que*, position, §493, *c*; *ne...ni*, position, §493, *d*; *ne...que* and *seulement*, §497, 4.
negation, §§491-496; see also *ne*, *non*, *pas*, etc.

'neither...nor', translated, §493, *d*, §534, 3.
nenni, prncn., §17, 5.
nerfs, prncn., §44, exc.
net, prncn, §60, 2, exc 1.
neuf, prncn., §44, exc.
ni, use, §313, *b*, §534, 1; with *ne*, §492; *ni...ne*, position, §493, *d*.
n'importe, §435, 5.
nombre, + *de*, agreement with verb, §312, 2, *a*.
non (*pas*, *point*), §421; *que non*, §497, 1, *a*.
nonante, §499, *n*.
nonobstant, *que*, + subj., §532, §351, 4.
non (*pas*) *que*,+subj., §532, §351, 5.
'nor'; — 'either', §534, 3.
'not'; — 'either', §534, 3.
noun, §§379-392; gender, §§379-384, §§414-415; number, §§385-390; case relation, §391; agreement, §392; as adjs., §421, 3, §422, §430, 2, (3).
nous, for *je*, §439, *a*; pleonastic, §450, 5, *a*, *nous autres*, §453, 2, *c*.
nouvel, §415, 1, (3).
nu, agreement, §421, 4, *a*.
nul, §430, 3, §415, 1, (2), *b*; use, §483, 1; with *nc*, §492.
nullement, with *ne*, §492.
number, of nouns, §§385-390; general rule, §385; exceptions, §386; double plurs., §387; foreign nouns, §388; comp. nouns, §389; plur. of proper nouns, §390; of adjs., §§416-417.
numeral, §208, §§498-507; cardinals, §498; ordinals, §499; collectives, §500; fractions, §501; multipli-

catives, §502; adverb, §503; remarks on use, §§504-507; in dates, titles, etc., §504; for dimension, §505; for time of day, §506; for age, §507.

O.

o (*ô*), prncn., 19.
obéir, in passive, §321, 1.
object, dir. and indir., §372; position, §376.
obliger, +*à*, +*de*, §360, 15.
occuper(*s'*), +*à*, +*de*, §360, 16.
octante, §498, *n*.
oe, prncn., §28.
œil, plur. of, §387.
œu, prncn., §26.
œufs, prncn., §44, exc.
œuvre, gender, §383, 3, *i*.
'of', §522; 'a friend of mine', etc., §455, 3.
oi (*oî*), prncn., §28.
oignon, prncn., §28, 2, exc.
oin, prncn., §38.
om, prncn., §30.
omnibus, prncn., §57, 2, exc. 1.
on, prncn., §30.
on (*l'on*). §480, 2; use, §482, 3; replacing passive, §321, 2, *a*.
'on', §523.
'once' ('twice', etc.) §502, 2.
'one', =*le*, §443, *b*.
'only', translated, §497, 4.
'or', =*ni*, §534, 2.
ordinals, §499.
orge, gender, §383, 3, *g*.
os, prncn., §57, 2 exc. 4.
osé, agreement, §371, 4, *b*.
oser+infin., §310, 5; with *ne* alone, §495, 4.
'others', §§482-483, 2, *b*.
ou (*oû*, *où*), prncn., 29.
où (rel. pron.), §472; use, §476, §475, *b*.

INDEX.

oui, §497, 1 ; *que oui*, §497, 1, *a*.
oui, §368, *a*.
ouïn, prncn., §38.
ouïr, +infin., constr. of obj., §372, *b*.
ours, prncn., §57, 2, exc. 1.
'out of', §524.
outil, prncn., §50, exc. 1.
'over', §525.
'own', translated, §454, 3, §455, 4.
Oxford, prncn., §43, exc.
oy, prncn., §30.

P.

p, prncn., §54.
pal, plur., §387.
paon, prncn., §19, 2, exc.
pâque(s), gender, §383, 3, *f*.
par, §518, 1, 2, §520, 2, §525, 2, §526, 1, 2 ; agent after passive, §320 ; +infin., §361, 1 ; of price, §407, *a*.
par-dessus, §525, 2.
paraître, il paraît, constr. after, §349, 5, *a*.
pardonner, in passive, §321, 1.
parler français, etc., §487, 1, §399, *a*.
parmi, §515, 1.
participles, §§365-371 ; pres., §365 ; Eng. forms in -ing, §366 ; past, §§367-371 ; as adjs., position, §430, 1, (3).
partir ; à partir de, §520, 3.
partitive noun, §§400-404 ; partitive and general noun, §404.
pas, with *ne*, §492 ; position, §493 ; without verb, §494, *a* ; without *ne* (vulg.), §492, n. 2.
passé, §368, *a*.
passive voice, formation, §319 ; agreement of past part., §319 and obs. ; agent after, §320 ; limitations and substitutes, §321 ; replaced by *on*, etc, §482, 3, *a*.
past anterior, §342.
past definite, §340 ; in narrative, examples, §341 ; replaced by impf., §338, 8 ; in 'if' clauses, §355, *f*., p. 214.
past indefinite, §339 ; in narrative, examples, §341 ; subjunctive sequence after, §353, 4, *a*.
past participle, agreement in passive, §319 and obs. ; without aux., §368 ; as prep., §368, *a* ; with *être*, §369, §324, §370, 2 ; with *avoir*, §370 ; invar. after impers. *être*, §369, *a* ; remarks, §371.
pas un, §430, 3 ; use, §483, 1 ; with *ne*, §492.
Paul, prncn., §24, exc.
payé, §368, *a*.
pays (paysan, etc.), prncn., §23, 2, exc.
pendant que, distinguished from *tandis que*, §536, 2.
penser, +à, +dir. infin., §360, 17.
perfect subj., §353, 3 ; for plupf., §353, 4, *c* ; replaced by impf. subj., §353, 4, *b*.
periphrastic forms, in conjugation, §335, §366, 1.
Perrault, prncn., §50, exc. 2.
personal pronouns, §§437-451 ; forms, §437 ; agreement, §439 ; case relations and use of conjunctives, §440 ; reflexives, §444 ; position of subject, §§315-318 ; position of objects, §447 ; omission of obj., §449 ; disjunctives, use of, §450 ; in address, §451.

personne, §480, 2 ; use of, §482, 4 ; with *ne*, §492 ; gender, §482, 4, n.
petit, irreg. comparison, §424.
peu, irreg. comparison, §489, 2.
peu, +*de*, §312, 2, *a*, *b* ; with partitive, §403, 1, *d*.
peur ; de — que ... ne, + subj., §532, §351, 2.
peut-être que, constr., §349, 5, n. ; no inversion, §317, 3.
phonetic transcription, examples of, §77.
pire, §424.
pis, §489, 2.
plein, when invar., §421, 4, *a*.
plupart, agreement of verb, §312, 2, *a*, *b* ; with partitive, §403, 1, *c*.
pluperfect (indic.), §342 ; replaced by plupf. subj., §352, 3 ; replaced by impf. indic., §355, *c*, p. 214 ; (subj.), §353, §352 ; replaced by perf. subj., §353, 4, *c* ; replacing plupf. indic. or condl. ant., §352, 3 ; sequence, §353, 3, 4, *a* ; replacing plupf. indic. in 'if' clause or 'result' clause, §355, *b*, p. 214.
plural, see number.
plus, §489, 2 ; in comparison (adj.), §423, (adv.), §489 ; —*de*, §489, 1, *b* ; with *ne*, §492 ; *plus* and *davantage*, §497, 3 ; — *d'un*, agreement, §312, 2, *c*.
plusieurs, §480, 3 ; use, §483, 4.
plus tôt, with *ne*, §496, 3, n.
plutôt, with *ne*, §496, 3, n.
point, with *ne*, §492, and n. 1 ; position, §493.

possessive, adj., forms, §452, 1; agreement, §453; repetition, §453, *a*; use, §454; def. art. for, §406, §454, 1; *en*,+def. art. for, §445, 2, (2), §454, 2.
possessive pron., forms, §452, 2; agreement, §453; use, §455.
possessives, see poss. adj. and poss. pron.
pour, §519, 1, 2, 3; +infin., §361, 2;—*que*+subj.,§532, §351, 2;—*peu que*+subj., §532, §351, 4; —... *que*, constr., §481, 5, (2), n.
pourvu que, + subj., §532, §351, 3.
pouvoir, + infin., §310, 3; impers., §332, 1, obs.; with *ne* alone, §405, 4.
predicate noun, omission of art., §408, 3.
predicative complement, §374, §408, 3.
premier, in dates, etc., §504, §408, 4, *a*; +subj., §350, 3; +*à*+infin., §358, 3, *a*.
prendre garde, +*à*, +*de*, §360, 18.
preposition, §§505-531; list of simple, §508; position, §510; locutions, §509; repetition, §511; idiomatic distinctions,§§512-531.
prepositional complement, §375.
près;—*de*, §513, 4; *à peu—*, §513, 4.
present, indic., §337; as historical past, examples, §341; replaced by impf., §338, 5; in condl. sentences, §355, p. 213.
present participle, 365.
present subj., §353, 1.
Priam, prncn., §34, exc. 2.
prétendre, +*à*, +*dir.* infin., §360, 19.

prier, +*à*, +*de*, §360, 20.
primary tenses, see principal parts.
primo (*secundo*, etc.), §503, *a*.
principal parts, formation of tenses from, §174.
prompte, prncn., §54, exc.
pronominal advs., §438.
pronoun, §§437-484, see also personal, possessive, etc.
pronunciation, §§3-63; of vowels, §§16-21; of vowel combinations, §§22-32; of nasals,§§33-38; of consonants, §§39-63.
proper nouns, plur., §390; use of art. with, §§410-413.
propre, §454, 3.
pu, agreement, §371, 4, *b*.
puis, §503, *a*.
puisque, distinguished from *depuis que*, §536, 3.
punch, prncn., §37, exc., §42, exc. 1.
punctuation, §74.

Q.

q, prncn., §55.
qu, prncn., §55.
quadrupède, prncn., §55, exc. 2.
qualifier de, §403, 3, *c*.
quand, distinguished from *lorsque*, §536, 1.
quand (*même*), condl. after, §345, 6, §355, *e*, p. 214; sometimes takes subj., §351, 4, *b*, §352, 3; +indic. or subj., §532, §351, 4.
quantité,+*de*, agreement of verb, §312, 2, *a*.
quantity, of vowels, §68.
quart, §499, n. 2.
quatre-vingt(*s*), §498, *a*, *b*.
que ?, §466, 2; use, §470.
que !, §470, 1, *b*.

que(relat.), §472; use, §474; in inversions (emphatic), §474, 2, n., §462, *a*, n.; past part. invar. after, §371, 5.
que (conj.), condl. after, §345, 6; replacing other conjs., §351, 6, §535, 2; ='than', 'as', in comparison, §423, §489; with *ne*, §492; for *à moins que*, §496, 1; +indic. or subj., §532, §349, §351, 6, §535; not omitted, §535, 3.
quel ? §466, 1; use, §468, §469, 2.
quel !, §463, *a*.
quelconque, §484; with *ne*, §492, 2, *a*.
quel que, +subj. of *être*, §484.
quelque, §480, 1; use, §481, 5; as adv., §481, 5, *a*.
quelque chose, §480, 2; use, §482, 6.
quelque .... que, + subj., §481.
quelqu'un, §480, 2; use, §482, 5.
qu'est-ce qui ?, §470, 2.
question, direct, §316; indirect, §318.
qui ?, §466, 2; use, §469; replaced by *quel*, §469, *b*, §469, *b*.
qui, §472; use, §474; replacing *celui qui*, *les uns ... les autres*, *ce qui*, §474, 1, *a*, *b*; *qui que*,+subj. of *être*, §484; *qui que ce soit*, §484; *qui que ce soit* +*ne*, §492, 2, *a*.
quiconque, §484.
quint, §499, n. 2.
quintuple, prncn., §55, exc. 3.
quinze-vingt(*s*), §498, n.
Quirinal, prncn., §55, exc. 3

quoi?, §466, 2 ; use, §478.
quoi, §472 ; use, §478 ; *quoi que* . . . +subj., §484 ; *quoi que ce soit*, §484 ; with *ne*, §492, 2, *a*.
quoique, +subj., §532, §351, 4.

R.

r, prncn., §56 ; final, §39, 2.
rr, prncn., §56, exc. 2.
reciprocal verbs, §323.
reflexive pers. prons., §444.
reflexive verb, formation of comp. tenses, §322, 2 ; with reciprocal force, §323; agreement of past part., §324 ; omission of reflex. obj., §325 ; comparison with Eng., §326 ; replacing passive, §321, 2, *b*.
refuser, +*à*, +*de*, §360, 21.
Regnard, prncn., §46, exc. 2.
relative pron., forms, §472; agreement, §473 ; use, §§474-479 ; remarks, §479 ; not omitted, §479, 1; relative clause for Eng. -ing, §366, 3 ; indef. relat., §484.
résoudre, +*à*, +*de*, §360, 22.
restaurant, prncn., §24, exc.
Retz, prncn., §63, exc. 2.
rien, §480, 2 ; use, §482, 4 ; with *ne*, §492.
Robespierre, prncn., §57, exc. 2.
rompre, conjugation, §237.
Rochefoucauld (La), prncn., §50, exc. 2.
rounding (lip-), §3, 2 ; Passy's diagram, §7.

S.

s, prncn., §57 ; in 'liaison', §71.
sache, irreg. use, §352, 2.

sans, +infin., §361, 3 ; — *doute que*, constr., §349, 5, n. ; — *que*, +subj., §532, §351, 5.
Saône, prncn., §16, 2, exc.
savoir +infin., §310, 4 ; with *ne* alone, §495, 4.
se, prncn., §58.
sch, prncn., §59.
schéma, prncn., §59, exc.
sculpter, prncn., §54, exc. 2.
se, reflex. pron., §444, 1.
second, prncn., §41, 1, exc. 3.
sembler ; il semble, constr. after, §349, 5, *a*, 6, *c*.
semi-vowel sounds, §14.
s'en aller, conjugation, §327.
s'en falloir, §331, 5.
seoir, prncn., §17, exc. 4.
sept, prncn., §54, exc. 2.
septante, §493, n.
septième, prncn., §54, exc. 2.
sequence, of subj. tenses, §353.
serein, prncn., §17, exc. 4.
seul, +subj., §350, 3 ; +*à* +infin., §358, 3, *a*.
seulement, §497, 4.
sévère, +*à l'égard de*, §436, *a*.
'should', distinctions, §345, 1, *b*.
si, elision of *i*, §73 ; subjunctive after, §355, *b*, p. 214; replaced by *que*+subj., §351, 6 ; in conditional sentence, §354; omission, §355, *d*, p. 214 ; *si* (='whether') +fut. or condl., §355, *g*, p.214; for *aussi*, §423, *a*, §489, *a ;* +indic. or subj., §532, §351, 3, *a ;* — *bien que*, +indic. or subj., §532, §351, 4 ; —*peu que*, +indic. or subj., §532, §351, 4 ; *si* . . . *(que)*, constr., §481, 5, (2), n.

si (='yes'), *si fait*, §497, 1 ; *que si*, §497, 1, *a*.
six-vingt(s), §498, n.
' so ', = *le*, §413, *b*.
soi, reflex. pron., §444, 2.
soi-disant, §365, 2, n. 2.
soit que . . . *soit que (ou que)*, +subj., §532, §351, 4.
solennel, prncn., §17, 5.
son, for *sa*, §452, 1, obs. 1 ; for indef., §453, *b*.
sorte ; de (telle) — *que*, + indic. or subj., §532, §351, 2 ; *en* — *que*, +indic. or subj., §532, §351, 2.
sot, prncn., §60, 2, exc. 2.
soûl, prncn., §50, exc. 1.
sounds of French, description of, §3-15 ; symbols, table of, §5.
sourcil, prncn., §50, exc. 1.
sous, §530, 1.
St. Bernard, prncn., §43, exc.
stress, §66, §67.
subjunctive, §§348-353 ; in subordinate clause, §§348-334, n. 2 ; in noun clause, §349 ; in adjectival clause, §350 ; in adverbial clause, §351 ; in principal clause, §352 ; as imperative, §352, 1, *a ;* tense sequence §353.
'such', §483, 5 and n.
Suez, prncn., §63, exc. 1.
suffire, +*pour*+infin., §358, 7, *a*.
superlative, (adjs.), §§425-427, (advs.), §489, 3 ; relative, §425 ; absolute, §426 ; remarks, §427.
supposant ; en — *que*, + subj., §532, §351, 3.
supposé, §268, *a ; —que*, + subj., §532, §351, 3.
sur, = 'with', 'about (the person)', §513, 3 ; ='by' (relative dimension), §518,

3; ='on', 'upon', §523; of 'motion above', §525, 2.
syllabication, §64-65.

T.

t, prncn., §60.
-t-, inserted in interrog., §316, 1, a.
tabac, prncn., §41, 1, exc. 1.
taon, prncn., §16, 2, exc.
tandis que, distinguished from *pendant que*, §536, 2.
tant, §497, 2.
tellement ... que, +indic. or subj., §532, §351, 2.
tel, §480, 3; use, §483, 5.
témoin, §422, a.
tenses, formation of comp., §§307-309; formation from principal parts, §174; of indic., §§335-346; periphrastic Eng., §335; elliptical Eng., §336; in narration,§§338-341; tense sequence of subj., §353.
-teur, fem. of, §415, 2, (3).
'through', §526.
tiers, §499, n. 1.
'till', §527.
time, how expressed, §329, 1, §506.
'to', §528.
toi, for te, §447, 3, (3), obs. 1.
ton, for ta, §452, 1, obs. 1.
tous, prncn., §57, 2, exc. 4.
tous (les) deux, §483, 6, b.
tout, §480, 3; use, §483, 6; as adv. (variable), §483, 6, a; with gens, §383, 3, j.
tout ... que, constr., §481, 5, (2), a.
tout-puissant, §483, 6, a, n.
'towards', §529.
traiter de, §408, 3, c.
transitive verbs., §372, §373, n.; in Fr.=Eng. verb + prep., §375, 3.

travail, plur., §387.
travers; à—, au—de, §526, 1.
trembler, +à, +de, §360, 23.
trop, prncn., §19, 1, exc.
tu, ='you', 'thou', in address, §451, 1, 2.

U.

u (û, ù), prncn, §20; silent in qu, §45, 2, n. 1; q+u, §55.
ue, prncn., §31.
um, prncn., §37.
un, prncn., §37.
un, see indef. art.
un, (adj. pron.), §480, 3; use of, §483, 7.
un (num.), §498, a.
'under', §530.
'underneath', §530.
unique, +subj., §350, 3.
'until,'§527.
'upon', §523.
uy, prncn., §32.

V.

v, prncn., §61.
va, special force, §347, b.
valoir, impers., §332, 1, obs.
venir de+infin., §310, 9; + à, +de, +dir. infin., §361, 24.
verb, §§237-378; regular conjugations, §237; auxiliaries,§238; use of auxs., §§307-309; irreg. verbs, §§239-306; formation of comp. tenses, §§307-309; phrases, §310; agreement with subject, §§311-314; position of subject, §§315-318; passive voice, §§319-321; reflexives, §§322-327; impersonals, §§328-333; moods and tenses, §§334-371; indicative, §§334-346; imperative, §347;

subjunctive, §§348-353; infinitive, §§355-364 (p.216); participles, §§365-371; government, §§372-378.
vers, §513, 4, §528, 3.
vieil, §415, 1, (3).
viendrai, prncn., §34, exc. 3.
Vietor's diagram, §6.
villa, prncn., §51, exc. 1.
village, prncn., §51, exc. 1.
ville, prncn., §51, exc. 1.
vive, in qui vive, §352, 2, n.
voice(d), definition of, §3, 3, n.
voiceless, definition of, §3, 3, n.
voici, position of pers. pron. obj., §447, 2, n. 2, §510, a.
voilà, distinguished from il y a, §330, 3; position of pers. pron. obj., §447, 2, n. 2, §510, a; with ne, §496, 6.
voir, +infin., constr. of obj., §372, 2, b.
Vosges, prncn., §57, exc. 2.
votre (vos), for politeness, §454, 5.
vouloir, +infin., §310, 1.
voulu, agreement, §371, 4, b.
vous, agreement, §439, b, §319, obs. 2, §324, 2, n 2, §418, b; replacing on, §482, 3, c; vous autres, §483, 2, c; pleonastic, §450, 5, a; in address, §451.
vowels, prncn., §§16-21; vowel combinations, prncn., §§22-32.
vowel sounds, §§8-13; nasals. §§12-13; semi-vowels, §14.
voyons, special force, §347, b.
vu, §§363, a, §371, 4 a.

W.

w, §1, n. 1; prncn., §61.

'what?', as subject, §4 0, 2
'what' (= 'that which'), §478, 2.
'whatever', §484.
'whose?', §469, 2.
wide, definition of, §3, 1.
'will', distinctions, §343, 1, a.
'with', §531.

'would', distinctions, §345, 1, b.

X.

x, prnen., §62; in 'liaison', §71.

Y.

y, prnen., §21, §23, §27, §30, §32.
y, + avoir, §330.

y (pron. adv.), §438; use, §446, §450, 6, n.; position, §447, 3, (2).
-yer, verbs in, §240.
ym, prnen., §35.
yn, prnen., §35.

Z.

z, prnen., §63.
zinc, prnen., §41, 1. exc. 1.

www.ingramcontent.com/pod-product-compliance
Lightning Source LLC
Chambersburg PA
CBHW030558300426
44111CB00009B/1023